John Willis

Theatre World

1996-1997 SEASON

VOLUME 53

APPLAUSE

NEW YORK • LONDON

THEATRE BOOK PUBLISHERS

211 WEST 71ST STREET • NEW YORK NY • 10023

COPYRIGHT © 1999 BY JOHN WILLIS. ALL RIGHTS RESERVED. MANUFACTURED IN THE U.S.A.

LIBRARY OF CONGRESS CATALOG CARD NO. 73-82953

ISBN 1-55783-343-5 (cloth)

ISBN 1-55783-344-3 (paper)

Patricia Elliott (Theatre World Awards Board) and Maia M. Walter
(Theatre World Awards Attorney)

TO

MAIA M. WALTER, Esq.

Whose generosity, patience, and exceptional talent through her work with Volunteer Lawyers for the Arts, has enabled the "Theatre World Awards" to achieve Not-for-Profit Incorporation ensuring the continuing legacy of honoring outstanding new talent.

Chicago
photograph © Dan Chavkin

CONTENTS

EDITOR: JOHN WILLIS
ASSISTANT EDITOR: TOM LYNCH

Assistants: Stine Elbirk Cabrera, Alexander Dawson, Herbert Hayward, Jr., Barry Monush,
Christopher Morelock, Eric Ort, John Sala, John Stachniewicz
Staff Photographers: Gerry Goodstein, Michael Riordan, Michael Viade, Van Williams
Production: John Alston, Daniel Genis, Paul Sugarman, Bob Ward

BROADWAY PRODUCTIONS

(June 1, 1996-May 31, 1997)

Judd Hirsch, Marin Hinkle
Below: Jim Fyfe, Judd Hirsch, Dov Tiefenbach, Marin Hinkle

A THOUSAND CLOWNS

By Herb Gardner; Director, Scott Ellis; Sets, Henry Dunn, Ben Edwards; Costumes, Jennifer von Mayrhauser; Lighting, Rui Rita; Sound, Richard Dunning; Stage Manager, Jay Adler; Presented by Roundabout Theatre Company (Todd Haimes, Artistic Director; Ellen Richard, General Manager; Gene Feist, Founding Director); Press, Chris Boneau~Adrian Bryan-Brown/Erin Dunn, Stephen Pitalo; Previewed from Wednesday, June 12; Opened in the Criterion Center Stage Right on Sunday July 14, 1996*

CAST

Nick Burns..Dov Tiefenbach
Murray Burns ....Judd Hirsch
Albert Amundson ....Jim Fyfe
Sandra Markowitz ....Marin Hinkle
Arnold Burns...David Margulies
Leo Herman ....John Procaccino
UNDERSTUDIES: John Procaccino (Murray), Jackie Apodaca (Sandra), Jason Huber (Albert), Peter Van Wagner (Arnold/Leo), Tre Roy (Nick)

A new production of a 1962 comedy in three acts. The action takes place in Manhattan, 1962. During initial rehearsals, Murray was played by Robert Klein, Sandra by Jane Adams, and the director was Gene Saks. For original Broadway production with Jason Robards, Barry Gordon and Sandy Dennis, see *Theatre World* Vol.18.

Times (Ben Brantley): ...a listless, strangely elegiac interpretation of what is fondly remembered as a buoyant, madcap comedy." *News* (Howard Kissel): "The play could still charm but not with such a glum Burns." *Post* (Clive Barnes): "...an extraordinarily funny play with some brilliantly offbeat lines." Variety (Greg Evans): "...a credible, if uninspired, revival of Herb Gardner's 1962 warhorse."

*Closed August 10, 1996 after 32 performances and 38 previews.
Marc Bryan-Brown Photos

HUGHIE

By Eugene O'Neill; Director, Al Pacino; Sets, David Gallo; Costumes, Candice Donnelly; Lighting, Donald Holder; Company Manager, Don Roe; Stage Manager, Jack Gianino; Presented by Circle in the Square (Theodore Mann, Josephine R. Abady, Co-Artistic Directors; Press, Jeffrey Richards/Roger Bean, Irene Gandy; Previewed from Thursday, July 25; Opened in the Circle in the Square Uptown on Thursday, August 22, 1996*

CAST

Night Clerk ....Paul Benedict
Erie Smith...Al Pacino

A one-act drama performed without intermission. The action takes place in a small hotel on a West Side street in midtown New York during the summer of 1928.

Variety tallied 9 favorable, 4 mixed and 1 negative review. *Times* (Vincent Canby): "It's now apparent that Mr. Pacino knew what he was doing. However long he took to do it, he got it right," *News* (Kissel): "...slighter than much of O'Neill...would work better in a proscenium setting..." *Post* (Barnes): "Unlike most star actors, Pacino is incredibly adept at supressing the star image without losing either power or focus." *Variety* (Evans): The director also finds the play's considerable humor, sometimes in surprising places..."

*Closed November 2, 1996 after 56 performances and 28 previews.
T. Charles Erickson Photo

Left: Al Pacino
Below Left: Al Pacino
Below Right: Paul Benedict

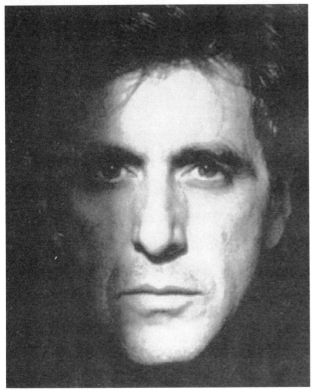

SUMMER AND SMOKE

By Tennessee Williams; Director, David Warren; Sets, Derek McLane; Costumes, Martin Pakledinaz; Lighting, Brian MacDevitt; Music/Sound, John Gromada; Stage Manager, Roy Harris; Presented by Roundabout Theatre Company (Todd Haimes, Artistic Director; Ellen Richard, General Manager, General Manager; Gene Feist, Founding Director); Press, Chris Boneau~Adrian Bryan-Brown/Erin Dunn, Stephen Pitalo; Previewed from Friday, August 16; Opened in the Criterion Center Stage Right on Thursday, September 5*

CAST

Young Alma	Nathalie Paulding
Young John	Chad Aaron
Reverend Winemiller	Ken Jenkins
Mrs. Winemiller	Roberta Maxwell
John Buchanan Jr.	Harry Hamlin
Pearl/Rosemary	Elisabeth Zambetti
Dusty/Vernon/Archie Kramer	Todd Weeks
Dr. Buchanan	James Pritchett
Alma Winemiller	Mary McDonnell
Rosa Gonzales	Lisa Leguillou
Nellie Ewell	Hayley Sparks
Mrs. Bassett	Celia Weeks
Roger Doremus	Adam LeFevre
Papa Gonzales	Emilio Del Pozo
Citizens of Glorious Hill	Carlo D'Amore, Geoffrey Dawe, Todd Lawson, Will McCormack, David Reilly

UNDERSTUDIES: Bernie McInerney (Reverend/Dr. Buchanan/Papa), Rebecca Finnegan (Alma), Geoffrey Dawe (John Jr/Roger), Todd Lawson (Dusty/Vernon/Archie), Jessica Ferrarone (Pearl/Rosa/Nellie/Rosemary), Karina LaGravinese (Young Alma), Jesse Eisenberg (Young John)

A new production of a 1948 drama in two acts. The action takes place in Glorious Hill, Mississippi, from the turn of the century through 1916. For original Broadway production see *Theatre World* Vol.5. For 1952 Off-Bdwy production with Geraldine Page see *Theatre World* Vol.8.

Variety tallied 4 favorable, 4 mixed and 6 negative reviews. *Times* (Brantley): "A musical sense of tempo is crucial to playing anything by Williams; here, nearly everyone seems to be following a different orchestral baton." (Canby): "...has one of the most complex and persuasive heroines in the entire literature of the American theatre." *News* (Kissel): "...everything thwarts the playwright's intentions." *Post* (Barnes): "...dominated, as it should be, by Mary McDonnell's Alma." *Variety* (Evans): "...the production has a vaguely impressionistic feeling."

*Closed August 20, 1996 after 53 performances and 22 previews.
Joan Marcus Photos

Top: Harry Hamlin, Mary McDonnell

SKYLIGHT

By David Hare; Director, Richard Eyre; Sets/Costumes, John Gunter; Lighting, Paul Gallo, Michael Lincoln; Sound, Freya Edwards; General Manager, Stuart Thompson; Stage Managers, Susie Cordon, Thom Widman; Presented by Robert Fox, Roger Berlind, Joan Cullman, Scott Rudin, The Shubert Organization, Capital Cities/ABC and Royal National Theatre; Press, Chris Boneau~Adrian Bryan-Brown/Bob Fennell, Stephen Pitalo; Previewed from Monday, September 9; Opened in the Royale Theatre on Sunday, September 19, 1996*

CAST

Kyra Hollis ....Lia Williams
Edward Sergeant ....Christian Camargo
Tom Sergeant..Michael Gambon

UNDERSTUDIES: Sarah Knowlton (Kyra), Michael Hall (Edward)

A drama in two acts. The action takes place in a flat in Northwest London.

Variety tallied 10 favorable, 6 mixed and 1 negative review. *Times* (Brantley): "...glows with a bewildered but invigorating respect for life as it is. To see that feeling rendered with such emotional eloquence by a team of first-rate artists is in itself a reason to hope." (Canby) "Michael Gambon is big not only in size, substance and voice, but also in his singular kind of destabalizing stage presence. News (Kissel) "...an absorbing, civilized piece of writing...Gambon and Williams make it an extremely pleasurable evening of theatre." *Post* (Barnes): "It is, deeply and truly, about people." *Variety* (Evans) "A play of uncommon richness, insight and humanity-and a production that boasts two of the finest performances to hit New York in recent years..."

*Closed December 29, 1996 after 116 performances and 12 previews.
Joan Marcus Photos

Michael Gambon, Lia Williams
Top: Michael Gambon

Sigourney Weaver

SEX AND LONGING

By Christopher Durang; Director, Garland Wright; Sets, John Arnone; Costumes, Susan Hilferty; Lighting, Brian MacDevitt; Sound, John Gromada; Company Manager, Rheba Flegelman; Stage Manager, Dianne Trulock; Presented by Lincoln Center Theater (Andre Bishop, Bernard Gersten, Directors); Press, Philip Rinaldi/Miller Wright, Brian Rubin; Previewed from Thursday, September 12; Opened in the Cort Theatre on Thursday, October 10, 1996*

CAST

Lulu ....Sigourney Weaver
Justin ....Jay Goede
Senator Harry McCrea..Guy Boyd
Bridget McCrea ....Dana Ivey
Reverend Davidson ....Peter Michael Goetz
Policeman/ Jack/ Special Witness..Eric Thal
UNDERSTUDIES: Felicity LaFortune (Lulu), Bill Dawnes (Justin/Police/Jack/Witness), Michael Arkin (Senator/Reverend), Cynthia Darlow (Bridget)

A comedy in three acts. The action takes place in and around Lulu's apartment, and in and around the Seanate.

Variety tallied 13 negative and 1 mixed review. *Times* (Brantley): "One questions the judiciousness of even producing Sex and Longing. But if it paves the way for fresher and more fluid works from Mr. Durang, it will actually have been worth it." *News* (Kissel): "I am trying to explain why anything so amateurish was produced...Dana Ivey stands out..." *Post* (Barnes): "...the whole plays slides inelegantly down the toilet." *Variety* (Evans) "...surrenders two of the playwright's most lethal weapons-sophistication and nuance-in the service of righteous indignation."

*Closed November 17, 1996 after 45 performances and 31 previews.
Joan Marcus Photos

Guy Boyd, Eric Thal, Sigourney Weaver, Dana Ivey, Jay Goede, Peter Michael Goetz

Dana Ivey

TAKING SIDES

By Ronald Harwood; Director, David Jones; Sets, David Jenkins; Costumes, Theoni V. Aldredge; Lighting, Howell Binkley; Sound, Peter Fitzgerald; General Manager, Marvin A. Krauss; Company Manager, Carl Pasbjerg; Stage Managers, Bob Borod, David Sugarman; Co-Producer, Hildy Parks; Presented by Alexander H. Cohen, Max Cooper, Duncan C. Weldon; Press, David Rothenberg/David J. Gersten; Previewed from Friday, October 4; Opened in the Brooks Atkinson Theatre on Thursday, October 17, 1996*

CAST

Major Steve Arnold	Ed Harris
Emmi Straube	Elizabeth Marvel
Lieutenant David Wills	Michael Stuhlbarg
Helmuth Rode	Norbert Weisser
Tamara Sachs	Ann Dowd
Wilhelm Furtwangler	Daniel Massey

UNDERSTUDIES/STANDBYS: Richard Clarke (Wilhelm), Mark La Mura (Arnold/Rode), Vera Farmiga (Emmi/Tamara), Tony Gillan (David)

A drama in two acts. The action takes place in Major Arnold's office in the American Zone of occupied Berlin, 1946.

Times (Brantley): "...singular accomplishment of Mr. Massey's brave, extravagant and, yes, trully brilliant performance." *News* (Kissel): "Sensitively directed by David Jones, evocatively designed and lit, thrillingly acted, Taking Sides, whatever its flaws, is a triumph." *Post* (Barnes): "...a knock-down, knockout exhibition of virtuoso, no-holds-barred acting from an admirable Ed Harris matched against the great English actor Daniel Massey."

*Closed December 29, 1996 after 85 performances and 14 previews.
Joan Marcus Photos

Left and Top: Ed Harris, Daniel Massey

MOSCOW THEATER SOVREMENNIK

Producers, Marina and Rina Kovalyov; English Translations, Erika Warmbrunn; Stage Managers, Joe Valentino, Olga Sultanova; Press, Denise Robert/Raisa Chernia, Arthur Cantor

THREE SISTERS

By Anton Chekohov; Director, Galina Volchek; Set, Pyotr Kirillov, Vyacheslav; Costumes, Vyacheslav Zaitsev; Music, Moisey Vainberg; Opened in the Lunt-Fontanne Theatre on Thursday, November 7, 1996*

CAST

Prozorov ....Boris Ovcharenko
Natalia Ivanova...Yelena Yakovleva
Olga ....Galina Petrova
Masha ....Marina Neyolova, Olga Drozdova
Irina ....Ekaterina Semyonova
Kulygin ....Gennady Frolov
Vershinin ....Valentin Gaft
Tuzenbach...Valery Shalnykh
Solyony ....Mikhail Zhigalov
Chebutykin...Igor Kvasha
Fedotik ....Avangard Leontiev
Rode ....Alexei Kutuzov
Ferapont...Rogwold Sukhoverko
Anfisa ....Galina Sokolova

INTO THE WHIRLWIND

By Eugenia Ginzburg; Director, Vladimir Poglazov; Set, Mikhail Frenkel; Opened in the Lunt-Fontanne Theatre on Friday, November 15, 1996*

CAST

Eugenia Ginzburg ....Marina Neyolova, Yelena Yakoveleva
Derkovskaya ....Galina Sokolova
Lidia ....Tatyana Biziaeva
Zina ....Liya Akhedzhakova
COMPANY: Lyudmilia Krylova, Galina Petrova, Inna Timofeeva, Tatyana Ryasnyaskava, Gennady Frolov, Maria Sitko, Olga Drozdova, Liliya Tolmacheva, Marina Khazova, Tamara Degtyariova, Marina Feoktistova, Natalia Katasheva, Tatyana Koretskaya, Alla Pokrovskaya, Elena Kozelhova, Nina Doroshina, Elena Millioti, Paulina Myasnikova, Ekaterina Semenova, Alexy Kutuzov, Gennady Frolov, Mikhail Zhigalov, Alexander Kakhun, Vasiliy Mishchenko, Vladimir Zemlyanikin, Vladislav Fedchenko, Alexander Berda, Maxim Razuvaev, Viktor Tulchinsky, Sergei Garmash, Ruslan Kovalevsky

Two dramas performed in Russian, with simultaneous English translation available in headphones.

Times (Marks): "...don't be put off by a shabby-looking production." (Canby): "many of the people in the audience..were clearly Russian speaking and adored what they saw." *News* (Kissel): "...restraint is no longer part of the actors' vocabulary." *Post* (Barnes): "It is sometimes horribly clear that there is their Chekhov, and there is our Chekhov." *Variety* (Evans): "Founded 40 years ago in artistic opposition to the repressive Soviet regime, the Sovremennik (Contemporary) Theater has made a welcome first visit to Broadway."

*Closed November 16 after 8 performances in repertory.

IT'S A SLIPPERY SLOPE

Written/Performed by Spalding Gray; General Manager, Steven C. Callahan; Production Manager, Jeff Hamlin; Presented by Lincoln Center Theater (Andre Bishop, Bernard Gersten, Directors); Press, Philip Rinaldi; Previewed from Sunday, November 3; Opened in the Vivian Beaumont Theater on Sunday, November 10, 1996*

A monologue about life after 50 and regaining one's equilibrium through the joys and terror of learning to ski.

Right: Spalding Gray

BRIGADOON

Sean Donnellan, Judy Kaye, Brent Barrett, Rebecca Luker

Music, Frederick Loewe; Lyrics/Book, Alan Jay Lerner; Conductor, John McGlinn; Stage Director, Christian Smith; Orchestrations, Ted Royal; Choreography, Gemze de Lappe based on original dances by Agnes de Mille; Sets/Costumes, Desmond Heeley; Lighting, Duane Schuler; Sound, Abe Jacob; Presented by New York City Opera; Press, Susan Woelzl; Opened in the New York State Theatre on Wednesday, November 13, 1996*

CAST

Tommy Albright	Brent Barrett
Jeff Douglass	Sean Donnellan
Maggie Anderson	Leslie Browne
Archie Beaton	William Ledbetter
Angus MacGuffie	James Bobick
Meg Brockie	Judy Kaye
Stuart Dalrymple	Joel Sorensen
Sandy Dean	Ron Hilley
Harry Beaton	Robert La Fosse
Andrew MacLaren	Don Yule
Fiona MacLaren	Rebecca Luker
Jean MacLaren	Elizabeth Ferrell
Charlie Dalrymple	George Dyer
Mr. Lundie	George Hall
Sword Dancers	Philipp Verges, William Ward
Bagpiper	Stephen Fox
Frank	Jon Brent Curry
Jane Ashton	Stacy Lee Tilton

Return of the City Opera version of the 1947 Broadway musical. For original Broadway production see *Theatre World* Vol.3.
Carol Rosegg Photos

Right: Elizabeth Ferrell, Robert La Fosse

CHICAGO

Music, John Kander; Lyrics, Fred Ebb; Book, Mr. Ebb, Bob Fosse; Script Adaptation, David Thompson; Based on the play by Maurine Dallas Watkins; Original Production Directed and Choreographed by Bob Fosse; Director, Walter Bobbie; Choreography, Ann Reinking in the style of Bob Fosse; Music Director, Rob Fisher; Orchestrations, Ralph Burns; Set, John Lee Beatty; Costumes, William Ivey Long; Lighting, Ken Billington; Sound, Scott Lehrer; Dance Arrangements, Peter Howard; Cast Recording, RCA; General Manager, Darwell Associates and Maria Di Dia; Company Manager, Scott A. Moore; Stage Managers, Clifford Schwartz, Terrence J. Witter; Presented by Barry & Fran Weissler in association with Kardana Productions; Press, Pete Sanders/Helen Davis, Clint Bond Jr., Glenna Freedman, Bridget Klapinski; Previewed from Wednesday, October 23; Opened in the Richard Rodgers Theatre on Thursday, November 14, 1996*

CAST

Velma Kelly	Bebe Neuwirth
Roxie Hart	Ann Reinking
Fred Casely	Michael Berresse
Sergeant Fogarty	Michael Kubala
Amos Hart	Joel Grey
Liz	Denise Faye
Annie	Mamie Duncan-Gibbs
June	Mary Ann Lamb
Hunyak	Tina Paul
Mona	Caitlin Carter
Matron "Mama" Morton	Marcia Lewis
Billy Flynn	James Naughton
Mary Sunshine	D. Sabella
Go-To-Hell-Kitty	Leigh Zimmerman
Harry	Rocker Varastique
Aaron	David Warren-Gibson
Judge	Jim Borstelmann
Martin Harrison	Bruce Anthony Davis
Court Clerk	John Mineo

Ann Reinking, Bebe Neuwirth

UNDERSTUDIES/STANDBYS: Nancy Hess (Velma/Roxie), John Mineo (Amos), Mamie Duncan-Gibbs (Mama/Velma), Michael Berresse (Billy), J. Loeffelholz (Mary), Mindy Cooper, Luis Perez, Michelle M. Robinson
MUSICAL NUMBERS: All That Jazz, Funny Honey, Cell Block Tango, When You're Good to Mama, Tap Dance, All I Care About, A Little Bit of Good, We Both Reached for the Gun, Roxie, I Can't Do It Alone, My Own Best Friend, Entr'acte, I Know a Girl, Me and My Baby, Mister Cellophane, When Velma Takes the Stand, Razzle Dazzle, Class, Nowadays, Hot Honey Rag, Finale

A new production of the 1975 musical in two acts. This production is based on the staged concert presented by City Center Encores last season. The action takes place in Chicago, late 1920s. Winner 0f 1997 "Tony" Awards for Revival of a Musical, Leading Actor in a Musical (James Naughton), Leading Actress in a Musical (Bebe Neuwirth), Direction of a Musical, Choreography, and Lighting. For original Broadway production with Gwen Verdon, Chita Rivera and Jerry Orbach see *Theatre World* Vol.32.

Variety tallied 18 favorable, 2 mixed and 1 negative review. *Times* (Brantley): "...about the joy of seducing an audience that goes to the theatre, above all, to be seduced." (Canby) " The triumph of *Chicago* is in its use of music and dance to evoke that era when jazz babies rouged their knees, gin was the knock-out punch of choice and get-rich-quick schemes were dime a dozen." *News* (Kissel) "AnnReinking has recreated Bob Fosse's choreography and, if I'm not mistaken, softened it a bit." *Post* (Barnes): "...stripped-down-to-basics approach..works sensationally well..performances are terrific." *Variety* (Evans) "...one can't help but be overwhelmed by the rare synthesis of talent past and present..."

*Still playing May 31, 1997. Moved to the Shubert Theatre on February 12, 1997.

+Succeeded by: 1. Nancy Hess during vacation 2. Nancy Hess during illness, Marilu Henner

Dan Chavkin Photos

Joel Grey, Ann Reinking

Bebe Neuwirth and Company

PRESENT LAUGHTER

By Noel Coward; Director, Scott Elliott; Sets, Derek McLane; Costumes, Ann Roth; Lighting, Brian MacDevitt; Sound, Raymond Schilke; General Manager, Albert Poland; Company Manager, Nick Kaledin; Stage Managers, Barnaby Harris, John Harmon; Presented by David Richenthal, Anita Waxman in association with Jujamcyn Theatres; Press, Jeffrey Richards/Irene Gandy, Mark Cannistraro, Roger Bean; Previewed from Friday, October 25; Opened in the Walter Kerr Theatre on Monday, November 18, 1996*

CAST

Daphne Stillington...Kellie Overbey
Miss Erikson..Margaret Sophie Stein
Fred...Steve Ross
Monica Reed..Lisa Emery
Garry Essendine...Frank Langella
Liz Essendine...Allison Janney
Roland Maule ....Tim Hopper
Henry Lyppiatt..Jeff Weiss
Morris Dixon...David Cale
Joanna Lyppiatt...Caroline Seymour +1
Lady Saltburn...Judith Roberts
UNDERSTUDIES: David Cale (Garry), John Wojda (Garry/Henry/Morris/Roland/Fred), Gayton Scott (Liz/Daphne/Joanna/Miss Erikson/Saltburn), Orlagh Cassidy (Liz/Monica/Daphne/Joanna), Susan Pellegrino (Monica/Miss Erikson/Saltburn), K.L. Marks (Henry/Roland/Morris/Fred)

A new production of a 1939 comedy in three acts. The action takes place in London, 1939.

Variety tallied 7 favorable, 3 mixed and 5 negative reviews. *Times* (Brantley): ...gutsy, often funny but exhaustingly overeager revival..offers more than a flash of full-frontal nudity..This is provocative stuff, all right..." (Canby): "...the hints about garry Essendine's bisexuality are in the text, the character is obviously more attracted to himself than to anybody else of either sex. This is what makes the character and Mr. Langella's performance so funny." *News* (Kissel): "I will, however, file a class-action suit on behalf of Noel Coward's admirers for the travesty..." *Post* (Barnes): "...performances are calculated, clever and devastatingly comic. Elliott has developed the sub-text..." *Variety* (Evans) "...full-frontal nudity and overt sexuality, gay or straight, pretty much shatters the delicate veneer of restraint and suggestion that gave the playwright his voice."

*Closed April 20, 1997 after 175 performances and 28 previews.
+Succeeded by: 1. Orlagh Cassidy

Carol Rosegg Photos

**Top: Jeff Weiss Frank Langella
Center: Frank Langella, Kellie Overbey
Right: Frank Langella, Tim Hopper**

JULIA SWEENEY'S GOD SAID HA!

Written/Performed by Julia Sweeney; Director, Beth Milles; Set, Michael McGarty; Lighting, Russell H. Champa; Costumes, Connie Martin; Sound, John Shivers; General Manager, Fremont Associates; Stage Manager, Franklin Keysar; Co-Producers, Pachyderm Entertainment, On the Fly Entertainment; Presented by James B. Freydburg & Jon Steingart, Gavin Polone, Georgia Frontiere, E.O.J. Prouctions, Caralyn Fuld, and Lifetime Television; Press, Chris Boneau~Adrian Bryan-Brown/Jackie Green, Michael Hartman, Stephen Pitalo, Janet George; Previewed from Thursday, November 7; Opened in the Lyceum Theatre on Tuesday, November 19, 1996*

A one-woman play performed without intermission.

Variety tallied 5 favorable, 5 mixed and 3 negative reviews. *Times* (Peter Marks): "Ms. Sweeney wants to share the powerful emotional current that has carried her through the terror. What she learns, we learn, and not just about death and disease, but about family." *News* (Kissel): "It needs to be more." *Post* (Barnes) "It must take a very special kind of arrogance to think that your own story is worth someone else's time...I imagine that Julia Sweeney..is a very nice person." *Variety* (Evans): "A more congenial stage presence than Julia Sweeney would be hard to imagine..a smaller, more intimate Off Broadway house would have better suited the unassuming charms..."

*Closed December 8, 1996 after 22 performances and 12 previews.
Joan Marcus, Claudia Kunin Photos

Right and Top: Julia Sweeney

THE REHEARSAL

By Jean Anouilh; Translation, Jeremy Sams; Director, Nicholas Martin; Sets, Robert Brill; Costumes, Michael Krass; Lighting, Kenneth Posner; Sound, Aural Fixation; Stage Managers, Jay Adler, Julie Baldauff; Presented by Roundabout Theatre Company (Todd Haimes, Artistic Director; Ellen Richard, General Manager; Gene Feist, Founding Director); Press, Chris Boneau~Adrian Bryan-Brown/Erin Dunn, Paula Mallino; Previewed from Thursday, October 31; Opened in the Criterion Center Stage Right on Thursday, November 21, 1996*

CAST

The Countess ....Frances Conroy
Damiens..Nicholas Kepros
The Count ....David Threlfall
Hortensia ....Kathryn Meisle
Hero ....Roger Rees
Villebosse ....Frederick Weller
Lucile ....Anna Gunn
Valets......................................Jeffrey Cox, Clay Hopper, Douglas Mercer
UNDERSTUDIES: Nance Williamson (Countess/Hortensia), Terry Layman (Hero/Damiens/Count), Tom Bloom (Count), Mary Frances Miller (Lucile), Jeffrey Cox (Villebosse)

A 1950 comedy of style in two acts. The action takes place in a French chateau over three days in 1950. For 1963 Broadway production with Coral Browne and Keith Michell see *Theatre World* Vol.20.

Variety tallied 5 favorable, 2 mixed and 8 negative notices. *Times* (Brantley): "...largely an unformed shadow of what it needs to be." (Canby) "...has beauty, style, humor and the most cohesive acting ensemble to appear at the Roundabout in some time." *News* (Kissel): "This is pretty ugly, and, on the basis of this production, I'm afraid we Anglo-Saxons just aren't up to it." *Post* (Barnes): "The new translation..seems a tone or two darker than before..." *Variety* (Evans): "...company of actors slowly peeling way the characters' masks of urbane sophistication to reveal the monsters underneath."

*Closed January 10, 1997 after 56 performances and and 25 previews.
Joan Marcus Photos

Top: Frances Conroy, Roger Rees
Left: David Threlfall, Roger Rees

JUAN DARIEN

A CARNIVAL MASS

By Julie Taymor and Elliot Goldenthal; Director/Puppets/Masks, Ms. Taymor; Sets/Costumes, G.W. Mercier, Ms. Taymor; Lighting, Donald Holder; Sound, Tony Meola; Musical Director, Richard Cordova; General Manager, Steven C. Callahan; Production Manager, Jeff Hamlin; Company Manager, Edward J. Nelson; Stage Manager, Jeff Lee; Presented by Lincoln Center Theater (Andre Bishop, Bernard Gersten, Directors) in association with Music-Theatre Group; Press, Philip Rinaldi/Miller Wright, Brian Rubin; Previewed from Thursday, October 31; Opened in the Vivian Beaumont Theater on Sunday, November 24, 1996*

CAST

Plague Victims/Schoolchildren/Tigers..... ....The Company
Mother (Dancer)/Old Woman ....Ariel Ashwell
Mother (Violinist)...Andrea Frierson Toney
Hunter..Kristofer Batho
Mr. Bones/Schoolteacher..... ....Bruce Turk
Shadows...Stephen Kaplin & Company
Juan (Puppet).....................Kristofer Batho, Andrea Kane, Barbara Pollitt
Juan (Boy)...Daniel Hodd
Drunken Couple..... ....Kristofer Batho, Andrea Kane
Senor Toledo..Martin Santangelo
Circus Barker/Street Singer..... ....David Toney
Green Dwarf..... ....Andrea Kane, Sophia Salguero
Marie Posa..... ....Sophia Salguero
Ballad of Return Soloist...Irma-Estel LaGuerre
UNDERSTUDIES: Khalid Rivera (Juan), Andrea Kane (Old Woman/Marie), Irma Estel LaGuerre (Vocalist), Tom Flynn (Hunter/Bones/Teacher/Barker/Street Singer), Kristofer Batho (Toledo)

A music theatre performed without intermission. The action takes place in the South American jungle.

Variety tallied 6 favorable and 5 mixed reviews. *Times* (Brantley): "...there are times when you may feel exhilaratingly like Alice falling down Wonderland's rabbit hole." *News* (Kissel): "This is a dark story, and Taymor tells it using a phantasmagoric array of puppets, masks and live actors..." *Post* (Barnes): ...magic in rich and joyous abundance positively suffuses evry moment..." *Variety* (Evans): "...one rather quickly becomes accustomed to the visual feast, and a more emotional, visceral connection is wanting."

*Closed January 5, 1997 after 49 performances and 20 previews.
Joan Marcus, Kenneth Van Sickle Photos

**Top: Martin Santangelo, Daniel Hodd, Bruce Turk
Center: "Mr. Bones"
Left: Andrea Frierson Toney, Daniel Hodd**

GYPSY OF THE YEAR

Co-Directors, Sam Ellis and Michael Lichtefeld; Stage Managers, Kenneth Hanson, Debora F. Porazzi, Charlene Speyerer; Presented by Michael Graziano, Tom Viola, Maria Di Dia; Presented in the Virgina Theatre on Monday, December 2 and Tuesday, November 3, 1996.

CAST INCLUDES

Nathan Lane (Host) ....Ernie Sabella (Host)
Whoopi Goldberg, Lou Diamond Phillips, Donna Murphy, Joel Grey, Marcia Lewis, Elaine Paige, Anthony Rapp, Adam Pascal, Wilson Jermaine Heredia, Jimmy Tate, Brenda Braxton, Florence Lacey, Linda Gabler Romoff, Billy Hipkins, and cast members from *A Funny Thing Happened...*, *Cats* (La Vie in Cats), *Chicago*, *Show Boat*, *Beauty and the Beast*, *Tony 'n Tina's Wedding*, *Sunset Boulevard* (The Paige Brigade), *The King and I*, *Victor Victoria* (Balloon Act), *The New Bozena*, *Cowgirls* (La Vie Bovine), *Miss Saigon*, *Grease*, *Rent* (I Still Haven't Found What I'm Looking For), *When Pigs Fly*, *Bring in 'da Noise Bring in 'da Funk*, *Smokey Joe's Cafe*, *Les Miserables*
GYPSY OF THE YEAR GYPSIES: Ty Taylor, Roxanne Barlow, Jean Marie, Angie L. Schworer, Aimee Turner, Julian Brightman, Timothy Albrecht, Silvia Aruj, Frank Berry, Jane Brockman, Carolyn M. Campbell, Victoria Lecta Cave, Kate Coffman, Tina Collari, Roosevelt A. Credit, Peter C. Ermides, Jamey Garner, Howard Kaye, Bryan Landrine, Nancy LeMenager, Sarah Litzinger, Cyndi Neal, Gregory Tapscott, Laurie Walton, Christopher Zelno

The eighth annual competition for Broadway Cares/Equity Fights AIDS raised $1,262,633.

Eric Silverman, Kenneth W. Hanson Photos

Top: *When Pigs Fly* **Company**
Left: Nathan Lane, Whoopi Goldberg

David Copperfield in *Dreams & Nightmares*

Wesley Fine in *Dreams & Nightmares*

DREAMS & NIGHTMARES

Adapted by David Ives; Visual Artistic Director, Eiko Ishioka; Additional Lighting, Robert Wierzel; Creative Advisor, Francis Ford Coppola; General Manager, 101 Productions; Stage Manager, J. Stan Jakubiec Jr.; Presented by Magicworks Entertainment, Pace Theatrical Group; Press, Richard Kornberg/Rick Miramontez, Don Summa, Billy Finnegan, Paula Wenger; Previewed from Tuesday, November 26; Opened in the Martin Beck Theatre on Thursday, December 5, 1996*

CAST
DAVID COPPERFIELD

An evening of grand illusion performed without intermission.

Variety tallied 10 favorable, 1 mixed and 1 negative review. *Times* (Brantley): "He's the skinny, kind of goofy boy down the block who performed card tricks at your daughter's birthday party and who never shed a certain self-concious awkwardness..." *Variety* (Evans): "...a crowd-pleasing (at some points a crowd-stunning) show that's already breaking box office records...more than a few skeptics will be transformed into believers."

*Closed December 29, 1996 after 54 performances and 20 previews.

Joan Marcus/Carol Rosegg Photos

ONCE UPON A MATTRESS

Music, Mary Rodgers; Lyrics, Marshall Barer; Director, Gerald Gutierrez; Choreography, Liza Gennaro; Musical Director/Vocal Arrangements, Eric Stern; Orchestrations, Bruce Coughlin; Sets, John Lee Beatty; Costumes, Jane Greenwood; Lighting, Pat Collins; Sound, Tom Morse; Dance Arrangements, Tom Fay; Cast Recording, RCA; Wigs/Hairstylist, Paul Huntley; General Manager, David Strong Warner; Production Supervisor, Steven Beckler; Production Manager, Peter Fulbright; Company Manager, Marcia Goldberg; Stage Manager, Brian Meister; Presented by Dodger Productions, Joop Van Den Ende; Press, Chris Boneau~Adrian Bryan-Brown/Susanne Tighe, Amy Jacobs; Previewed from Monday, November 18; Opened in the Broadhurst Theatre on Thursday, December 19, 1996*

CAST

King Sextimus	Heath Lamberts
Queen Aggravain	Mary Lou Rosato
Prince Dauntless	David Aaron Baker
Winnifred	Sarah Jessica Parker
Sir Harry	Lewis Cleale
Lady Larken	Jane Krakowski
Jester	David Hibbard+1
Master Merton	Tom Alan Robbins
Nightingale of Samarkand	Ann Brown
Royal Cellist	Laura Bontrager
Royal Ballet	Arte Phillips, Pascale Faye
Minstrel	Lawrence Clayton
Player Queen	David Jennings
Player Prince	David Elder
Player Princess	Bob Walton
Players	Arte Phillips, Nick Cokas, Stephen Reed
Knights/Lords/Ladies	Mr. Cokas, Mr. Elder, Mr. Jennings, Sebastian LaCause, Jason Opsahl, Mr. Phillips, Mr. Reed, Mr. Walton, Ms. Brown, Maria Calabrese, Thursday Farrar, Ms. Faye, Janet Metz, Tina Ou, Aixa M. Rosario Medina, Jennifer Smith, Thom Christopher Warren

UNDERSTUDIES/STANDBYS: Janet Metz (Winnifred), Tom Alan Robbins (Sextimus), Jennifer Smith (Queen), Bob Walton (Dauntless/Jester), David Elder (Harry), Ann Brown (Larken), Stephen Reed (Merton), Jason Opsahl (Minstrel) SWINGS: Pamela Gold, Thomas Titone

MUSICAL NUMBERS: Overture, Many Moons Ago, Opening for a Princess, In a Little While, Shy, The Minstrel The Jester and I, Sensitivity, Swamps of Home, Normandy, Spanish Panic, Song of Love, Entre'act, Quiet, Goodnight Sweet Princess, Happily Ever After, Man to Man Talk, Very Soft Shoes, Yesterday I Loved You, Lullaby, Finale

A new production of a 1959 musical in two acts. The action takes place in and about the castle, Spring, 1428. For original production with Carol Burnett, Jane White and Jack Gilford, see *Theatre World* Vol.15.

Variety tallied 1 favorable, 3 mixed and 12 negative reviews. *Times* (Brantley): "...an unhappy surprise..a sense of uneasy resignation emanates from the stage, as if no one was very happy to be there." (Canby): "Sara Jessica Parker has many gifts." *News* (Kissel): "...as fresh, inventive and funny as ever." *Post* (Barnes): "No show starring the ever lively and ever enchanting Sarah Jessica Parker can be quite dead. But it was deader than it ought to be." *Variety* (Evans): "...oddly constricted here. Much of the action is confined to one-third of the stage, the comedy doesn't always generate the laughs it should, and little is made of the secondary characters..."

*Closed May 31, 1997 after 187 performances and 33 previews.
Succeeded by: 1. Thom Chirstopher Warren.

Joan Marcus, Carol Rosegg Photos

Top: Sarah Jessica Parker
Left: Jane Krakowski, Lewis Cleale

Top: Sarah Jessica Parker and *Mattress* Ensemble
Left: David Aaron Baker in *Once Upon a Mattress*

MEN ARE FROM MARS, WOMEN ARE FROM VENUS

By John Gray; Based on his book; Set, Denise Stansfield; Lighting, Eric Todd; Sound, Joseph Light; Production Supervisor, Marty Hom; Presented by Skylar Communications; Press, Susan Blond; Opened in the Gershwin Theatre on Monday, January 27, 1997*

CAST

JOHN GRAY

A seminar in two acts. The opening night performance included a panel with guests Cindy and Joey Adams, Linda Dano, Frank Attardi, and Q-Tip.

Times (Marks): "...surprisingly inept and frequently embarrassing..." *Variety* (Evans): "...couldn't have chosen a less appropriate venue for his feel-good shtick..."

*Closed February 1, 1997.

THREE SISTERS

By Anton Chekhov; Translation, Lanford Wilson; Director, Scott Elliott; Sets, Derek McLane; Costumes, Theoni V. Aldredge; Lighting, Peter Kaczorowski; Sound, Raymond D. Schilke; Hairstylist/Wigs, Paul Huntley; Company Manager, Denys Baker; Stage Manager, Lori M. Doyle, Alex Lyu Volckhausen; Presented by Roundabout Theatre Company (Todd Haimes, Artistic Director; Ellen Richard, General Manager; Gene Feist, Founding Director); Press, Chris Boneau~Adrian Bryan-Brown/Erin Dunn, Paula Mallino; Previewed from Wednesday, January 22; Opened in the Criterion Center Stage Right on Thursday, February 13, 1997*

CAST

Andrei Prozorov..Paul Giamatti +1
Olga..Amy Irving
Masha ....Jeanne Tripplehorn
Irina ....Lili Taylor
Natalya Ivanovna ....Calista Flockhart
Kulygin...David Marshall Grant
Vershinin ....David Strathairn
Baron Tuzenbach...Eric Stoltz
Solyony...Billy Crudup
Chebutykin...Jerry Stiller
Fedotik ....Robert Bogue
Rodez..Justin Theroux
Ferapont ....Ben Hammer
Anfisa...Betty Miller
Maid..Keira Naughton
Soldiers...Matthew Lawler, Saxton Palmer
Musician...Gennady Gutkin, Gab Hegedus
UNDERSTUDIES/STANDBYS: Matthew Lawler (Andrei/Kulygin), Keira Naughton (Natalya/Irina), Robert Bogue (Vershinin), Justin Theroux (Tuzenbach/Solyony), Mitchell McGuire (Chebutykin/Ferapont), Jane Cronin (Anfisa), Saxon Palmer (Fedotik/Rodez), Jeroen Kuiper (Servants)

The 1901 four-act drama performed with two intermissions. The action takes place in a Russian provincial town at the turn of the century.

Variety tallied 4 favorable, 1 mixed and 12 negative reviews.

Times (Brantley): "...one is left with only a handful of fully integrated performances in a play that needs a meticulously balanced ensemble..Mr. Crudup, who turns his leading-man handsomeness into the frightening mask of an emotional cripple, is riveting..Ms. Flockhart, better known for her wistful ingenue roles..is smashing..." *News* (Kissel): "...muddies the play to the point it can no longer serve as a mirror..." *Post* (Barnes): "...one of drama's most terrifyingly truthful documents. It's a tragi-comedy echoing the long littleness of life, but here there seems to be an element of facile soap-opera melodrama..." *Variety* (Evans): "...the varied acting approaches seem the result of the director's ill-defined vision for the play."

*Closed April 6, 1997 after 61 performances and 26 previews.
+Succeeded by: 1. Mark Nelson

Carol Rosegg Photos

Top: Amy Irving, Jeanne Tripplehorn, Lili Taylor
Center: Eric Stoltz
Right: Amy Irving, David Strathairn

STANLEY

By Pam Gems; Director, John Caird; Sets/Costumes, Tim Hatley; Lighting, Peter Mumford; Sound, Freya Edwards; Music, Ilona Sekacz; Production Supervisor, Gene O'Donovan; Stage Managers, R. Wade Jackson, Deirdre McCrane; Presented by Circle in the Square (Gregory Mosher, Producing Director; M. Edgar Rosenblum, Executive Producer) and The Royal National Theatre; Press, Bill Evans/Michael S. Borowski, Jim Randolph, Terry M. Lilly; Previewed from Tuesday, February 4; Opened in the Circle in the Square Uptown on Thursday, February 20, 1997*

CAST

Hilda	Deborah Findlay
Stanley	Antony Sher
Henry	Barton Tinapp
Gwen	Barbara Garrick
Patricia	Anna Chancellor
Augustus John	Ken Kliban
Dorothy	Selina Cadell
Dudley	Peter Maloney
Elsie	Alison Larkin
Mrs. Carline	Victoria Boothby
Brian	Jase Blankfort
Tim	Chad Aaron

A drama in two acts. The action takes place in the village of Cookham in Berkshire and at Hampstead in London, 1920-59.

Variety tallied 6 favorable, 5 mixed and 3 negative reviews. *Times* (Brantley): "Mr. Sher undeniably soars. Riding on his back is one of this season's greater pleasures." *News* (Kissel): "...I hope this will bring Sher to the attention of the right casting agents. He certainly deserves better than this." *Post* (Barnes): "...Gems' play still tells us less about Spencer's painting tahn do the fugitive glimpses of it..." *Variety* (Evans): "...more interesting than likable...difficulty balancing its appealing artistry with a tiresome self-indulgence."

*Closed April 27, 1997 after 74 performances and 18 previews. Due to financial difficulties, Circle in the Square Theatre closed after this production.

Joan Marcus Photos

Top: Anna Chancellor, Antony Sher
Right: Antony Sher

25

Celia Weston, Dana Ivey

THE LAST NIGHT OF BALLYHOO

By Alfred Uhry; Director, Ron Lagomarsino; Sets, John Lee Beatty; Costumes, Jane Greenwood; Lighting, Kenneth Posner; Sound, Tony Meola; Music, Robert Waldman; General Manager, Albert Poland; Company Manager, Peter Bogyo; Stage Managers, Franklin Keysar, Bob E. Gasper; Associate Producer, Valentina Fratti; Presented by Jane Harmon, Nina Keneally, Liz Oliver; Press, Chris Boneau~Adrian Bryan-Brown/Andy Shearer, Patrick Paris, Janet George; Previewed from Friday, February 7; Opened in the Helen Hayes Theatre on Thursday, February 27, 1997*

CAST

Lala Levy ....Jessica Hecht +1
Reba Freitag..Celia Weston
Boo Levy...Dana Ivey +2
Adolph Freitag...Terry Beaver
Joe Farkas..Paul Rudd
Sunny Freitag ....Arija Bareikis +3
Peachy Weil...Stephen Largay
STANDBYS: Mandy Fox (Lala/Sunny), Robert Gomes (Joe/Peachy), Philip LeStrange (Adolph), Peggity Price (Reba/Boo)

A comic drama in two acts. The action takes place in Atlanta, Georgia, in December, 1939. Winner of 1997 "Tony" Award for Best Play.

Variety tallied 9 favorable, 5 mixed and 3 negative reviews. *Times* (Brantley): "...a sincere, good-hearted work, but it almost never feels spontaneous..." *News* (Kissel): "...Ivey conveys Boo's rigidity, and ultimately her desperation, consummately..the bedrock of reality makes Uhry's wise comedy even funnier." *Post* (Barnes): "This gorgeously acted play, stronger on dialogue than story, is extraordinarily funny." *Variety* (Evans): "With its wonderfully crafted script, equally fine direction and and ensemble so good it holds its own in the towering presence of star Dana Ivey, *Ballyhoo* looks a shoo-in..."

*Closed June 28, 1998 after 557 performances and 23 previews.
+Succeeded by: 1. Cynthia Nixon 2. Carole Shelley 3. Kimberly Williams

T. Charles Erickson, Carol Rosegg Photos

Terry Beaver, Carole Shelley

Stephen Largay, Jessica Hecht

Kimberly Williams, Paul Rudd

Terry Beaver, Jessica Hecht, Celia Weston, Dana Ivey

MANDY PATINKIN IN CONCERT

Musical Director, Paul Ford (piano); Director, Eric Cornwell; Sound, Otts Munderloh, Mary McGregor; Presented by Dodger Endemol Theatricals; Press, Chris Boneau~Adrian Bryan-Brown/Susanne Tighe, Amy Jacobs, Laura Matalon; Opened in the Lyceum Theatre on March 1, 1997*

CAST

MANDY PATINKIN

A concert performed with intermission to benefit charities: Association to Benefit Children, Chron's and Colitis Foundation, National Dance Institute, Peace Now, and Physicians for Human Rights.

Variety (Evans): "...he wraps all the songs in an emotionally charged melodrama that works because of his undeniable vocal talent and an unspoken link to a showbiz tradition that is all but absent from today's stage..."

*Closed March 23, 1997 after limited run of 15 performances.

(center) Cheryl Freeman, Carl Anderson

Yvette Cason, Lawrence Hamilton, Larry Marshall, Andre De Shields

Mandy Patinkin

PLAY ON!

Songs, Duke Ellington; Book, Cheryl L. West; Based on Twelfth Night by William Shakespeare; Conception/Direction, Sheldon Epps; Orchestrations/Musical Supervision, Luther Henderson; Choreography, Mercedes Ellington; Musical Director, J. Leonard Oxley; Sets, James Leonard Joy; Costumes, Marianna Elliott; Lighting, Jeff Davis; Sound, Jeff Ladman; Creative Consultant, Louis Johnson; Creative Historic Consultant, Frankie Manning; Musical Coordinator, William Meade; Cast Recording, Varese Sarabande; General Manager, Charlotte W. Wilcox; Company Manager, Susan Sampliner; Stage Managers, Robert Mark Kalfin, Lurie Horns Pfeffer, Jimmie Lee Smith, Matthew Aaron Stern; Presented by Mitchell Maxwell, Eric Nederlander, Thomas Hall, Hal Luftig, Bruce Lucker, Mike Skipper, and Victoria Maxwell in association with Kery Davis, Alan J. Schuster; Press, Richard Kornberg/Jim Byk, Rick Miramontz, Don Summa; Previewed from Friday, March 7; Opened in the Brooks Atkinson Theatre on Thursday, March 20, 1997*

CAST

Vy	Cheryl Freeman
Jester	Andre De Shields
Sweets	Larry Marshall
Miss Mary	Yvette Cason
CC	Crystal Allen
Duke	Carl Anderson
Rev	Lawrence Hamilton
Lady Liv	Tonya Pinkins

Denizens of Harlem.... ....Ronald "Cadet Bastine, Jacquelyn Bird Wendee Lee Curtis, Byron Easley, Alan H. Green, Frantz G. Hall, Gil P., Lacy Darryl Phillips, Lisa Scialabba, Erika Vaughn, Karen Callaway Williams
UNDERSTUDIES: Angela Robinson (Liv), Stacie Precia, Angela Robinson (Vy/Mary), Alan H. Green (Duke/Rev/Sweets), William Wesley (Duke), Frantz G. Hall (Rev), Gil P. (Sweets), Bryan S. Haynes (Jester), Lacy Darryl Phillips (Jester), Wendee Lee Curtis (CC)

MUSICAL NUMBERS: Take the A Train, Drop Me Off in Harlem, I've Got to Be a Rug Cutter, I Let a Song Go Out of My Heart, C Jam Blues, Mood Ingido, Don't Get Around Much Anymore, Don't You Know I Care, It Don't Mean a Thing, I Got It Bad and That Ain't Good, Hit Me witha Hot Note and Watch Me Bounce, I'm Just a Lucky So and So, Everything But You, Solitude, Black Butterfly, I Ain't Got Nothin' But the Blues, I'm Beginning to See the Light, I Didn't Know About You, Rocks in My Bed, Something to Live For, Love You Madly, Prelude to a Kiss, In a Mellow Tone

A musical comedy in two acts. The action takes place in the Magical Kingdom of Harlem during the Swingin' 40s.

Variety tallied 6 favorable, 6 mixed and 5 negative reviews. *Times* (Brantley): "...squanders its impressive assets by consistently overselling them..elegance is almost always sacrificed to steam-roller eagerness." *News* (Kissel): "I would have been content to skip the story and just listen to the talented cast perform Ellington's irresistible songs." *Post* (Barnes): "...the missing energy is essentially in the book and concept..good with reservations." *Variety* (Evans): "A musical has to work pretty hard to let such an inspired idea slip through the floorboards..."

*Closed May 11, 1997 after 61 performances and 19 previews.
Carol Rosegg Photos

BARRYMORE

By William Luce; Director, Gene Saks; Sets/Costumes, Santo Loquasto; Lighting, Natasha Katz; Hairstylist, Michael Kriston; General Manager, Frank P. Scardino; Company Manager, David Turner; Stage Managers, Susan Konynenburg, Jim Semmelman; Presented by Livent (U.S.); Press, Mary Bryant; Previewed from Friday, March 14; Opened in the Music Box Theatre on Tuesday, March 25, 1997*

CAST

John Barrymore ....Christopher Plummer
Frank ....Michael Mastro
UNDERSTUDIES: Jim Semmelman (Frank)

A drama in two acts. The action takes place one month before John Barrymore's death in 1942. Winner of 1997 "Tony" Award for Leading Actor in a Play (Christopher Plummer).

Variety tallied 8 favorable, 2 mixed and 2 negative reviews. *Times* (Brantley): "...provided Christopher Plummer with the chance to create a portrait of riveting complexity and paradox that defies easy psychology." *News* (Kissel): "...you keep wishing Plummer, who captures every color of this Barrymore brilliantly, had a greater palette to work with." *Post* (Barnes) "...a must-be-seen, must-be-savored Christopher Plummer..." *Variety* (Evans): "Luce's writing, never less than amusing, and always efficient..."

*Closed November 2, 1997 after 204 performances and 12 previews.
Cylla Von Tiedmann Photos

ANNIE

Music, Charles Strouse; Lyrics, Martin Charnin; Book, Thomas Meehan; Director, Martin Charnin; Choreography, Peter Gennaro; Orchestrations (orig.), Philip J. Lang; Musical Director/Supervisor, Keith Levenson; Sets, Kenneth Foy; Costumes, Theoni V. Aldredge; Lighting, Ken Billington; Sound, T. Richard Fitzgerald; General Manager, Marvin A. Krauss; Company Manager, Kim Sellon; Stage Managers, Bryan Young, Jeffrey M. Markowitz; Presented by Timothy Childs and Rodger Hess, Jujamcyn Theatres, in association with Terri B. Childs, Al Nocciolino; Press, Peter Cromarty/Alice C. Herrick; Previewed from Friday, March 14; Opened in the Martin Beck Theatre on Wednesday, March 26, 1997*

CAST

Annie ....Brittny Kissinger
Molly ....Christiana Anbri +1
Pepper ....Cassidy Ladden
Duffy ....Mekenzie Rosen-Stone +2
July ....Casey Tuma
Tessie ....Lyndsey Watkins +3
Kate ....Melissa O'Malley +4
Miss Hannigan ....Nell Carter +5
Bundles McCloskey/Sgt Thayer/Guard............................Michael E. Gold
Apple Seller/Fred McCracken/Ickes..........................Brad Wills
Dog Catchers................................Tom Treadwell, Sutton Foster
Sandy..Cindy Lou
Lt. Ward/Hull/Justice Brandeis ....Drew Taylor
Sophie, the Kettle/Mrs. Pugh/Perkins ....Barbara Tirrell
Fred/Jimmy Johnson/Howe ....Tom Treadwell
Grace Farrell ....Colleen Dunn
Drake/Bert Healy/Morganthau ....MichaelJohn McCann
Cecille/Star to Be/Ronnie Boylan ....Sutton Foster
Mrs. Greer/Bonnie Boylan ....Elizabeth Richmond
Annette/Connie Boylan ....Kelley Swaim
Oliver Warbucks..Conrad John Schuck
Rooster Hannigan..Jim Ryan
Lily..Karen Byers-Blackwell
Oxydent Hour of Smiles Producer............................Jennifer L. Neuland
H.V. Kaltenborn's Voice..Bryan Young
F.D.R. ....Raymond Thorne

Nell Carter

Casey Tuma, Cassidy Ladden. Melissa O'Malley, Lyndsey Watkins, Mekenzie Rosen-Stone, (front), Christiana Anbri, Brittny Kissinger

Brittny Kissinger, Conrad John Schuck, Raymond Thorne

UNDERSTUDIES: Alexandra Kiesman (Annie), Drew Taylor (Warbucks), Kelley Swaim (Grace), Christy Tarr (Grace/Lily), Barbara Tirrell (Miss Hannigan), Tom Treadwell (FDR), Michael E. Gold (Rooster), Jennifer L. Neuland (Lily), Mekenzie Rosen-Stone (Molly), Casey Tuma (Kate), Alexandra Kiesman (Tessie/Pepper/Duffy/July), Zappa (Sandy)

MUSICAL NUMBERS: Maybe, It's the Hard-Knock Life, Tomorrow, We'd Like to Thank You, Little Girls, I Think I'm Gonna Like It Here, NYC, You Make Me Happy (not in original), Easy Street, You Won't Be an Orphan for Long, You're Never Fully Dressed Without a Smile, Something Was Missing, I Don't Need Anything But You, Annie, New Deal for Christmas

A new production of the 1977 musical in two acts. The action takes place in New York City and Washington D.C., 1933. During the run, the producers shortened the show, including cutting "We'd Like to Thank You". For the original Broadway production with Andrea McArdle and Dorothy Loudon, see *Theatre World* Vol.33.

Variety tallied 5 favorable, 6 mixed and 8 negative reviews. *Times* (Marks): "Annie , the musical, is set in the Depression. The revival that opened last night at the Martin Beck Theatre may send you into one..so lacking in vitality that it wouldn't be a surprise to learn it had actually been running for the last 20 years." *News* (Kissel): "...efficient, but only fitfully capturing the power and spirit of the material." *Post* (Barnes): "...might do best with unaccompanied coach-parties of children from out of town." *Variety* (Evans): "...enjoyable, professional re-mounting..new song written especially for this production, "You Make Me Happy"takes full advantage of Carter's belting vocal style..."

*Closed October 19, 1997 after 238 performances and 14 previews.
+Succeeded by: 1. Kristen Alderson 2. Bianca Collins 3. Courtney Leigh 4. Jemini Quintos 5. Barbara Tirrell during illness

Joan Marcus/Carol Rosegg Photos

THE YOUNG MAN FROM ATLANTA

By Horton Foote; Director, Robert Falls; Sets, Thomas Lynch; Costumes, David C. Woolard; Lighting, James F. Ingalls; Music/Sound, Richard Woodbury; General Manager, Robert Cole; Company Manager, Steven Chaikelson; Stage Managers, Susie Cordon, John Handy; Presented by David Richenthal, Anita Waxman, Jujamcyn Theaters in association with The Goodman Theatre and Robert Cole; Press, Jeffrey Richards/Irene Gandy, Roger Bean, Mark Cannistraro, Timothy Haskell; Previewed from Thusday, March 13; Opened in the Longacre Theatre on Thursday, March 27, 1997*

CAST

Will Kidder..Rip Torn
Tom Jackson...Marcus Giamatti
Miss Lacey...Pat Nesbit
Ted Cleveland Jr..Stephen Trovillion
Lily Dale Kidder...Shirley Knight
Pete Davenport ....William Biff McGuire
Clara...Jacqueline Williams
Carson..Kevin Breznahan
Etta Doris Meneffree ....Beatrice Winde
UNDERSTUDIES: Edward Seamon (Will), Nada Rowand (Lily/Miss Lacey), William Cain (Pete), Tim Williams (Tom/Ted/Carson), Phyllis Bash (Etta/Clara) SWINGS: J.B. Adams, Christy Tarr

A drama in two acts. The action takes place in Houston, Texas, 1950.

Variety tallied 5 favorable, 5 mixed and 5 negative reviews. *Times* (Brantley): "...not a single performance here that can be faulted..The splendid Miss Knight, who doesn't waste a single fluttery gesture, brings an Ibsenesque weight..Mr. Torn has an imposing quality of emotional largeness that brings mythic dimensions..." *News* (Kissel): "...beautiful, moving..In this production, it is far easier to see why it won a Pulitzer." *Post* (Barnes): "This is that rare thing, a living play about living-and it brings luster to Broadway." *Variety* (Evans): "...its affecting portrait of shattered illusions (and the first-rate casts that presents it) won't soon be forgotten."

*Closed June 8, 1997 after 88 performances and 17 previews.
Liz Lauren Photos

Marcus Giamatti, Rip Torn
Below: Shirley Knight

A DOLL'S HOUSE

By Henrik Ibsen; Adaptation/Translation, Frank McGuinness from a literal translation by Charlotte Barslund; Director, Anthony Page; Design, Deirdre Clancy; Lighting, Peter Mumford; Music, Jason Carr; Sound, Scott Myers, John Owens; Production Supervisor, Gene O'Donovan; General Manager, Stuart Thompson; Stage Managers, Sally J. Jacobs, Tom Santopietro; Presented by Bill Kenwright in association with Thelma Holt; Press, Philip Rinaldi/Barbara Carroll; Previewed from Tuesday, March 25; Opened in the Belasco Theatre on Wednesday, April 2, 1997*

CAST

Nora Helmer	Janet McTeer
Torvald Helmer	Owen Teale
Kristine Linde	Jan Maxwell
Nils Krogstad	Peter Gowen
Dr. Rank	John Carlisle
Anne-Marie (Nanny)	Robin Howard
Helene (Maid)	Rose Stockton
Messenger	John Ottavino
Bobby, Ivan	Liam Aiken, Paul Tiesler

UNDERSTUDIES: Rose Stockton (Nora/Kristine), John Ottavino (Torvald/Nils), Kent Broadhurst (Rank/Messenger)

A new adaptation of the 1879 drama in three acts. The action takes place in a small Norwegian town, 1879. Winner of 1997 "Tony" Awards for Revival of a Play, Leading Actress in a Play (Janet McTeer), Featured Actor in a Play (Owen Teale), and Direction of a Play.

Variety tallied 14 favorable, 1 mixed and 3 negative reviews. *Times* (Brantley): "...you sit there, open-mouthed, grateful, admiring and shaken, and think "This is why I love the theater"..so completely and richly realized that you find yourself truly living through the character..somehow the sense that ordinary life has been heightened to the bursting point." *News* (Kissel): "McTeer makes Nora sexier than usual, but I'm not sure this is helpful." *Post* (Barnes): "Page's direction makes the whole play fascinating and, above all, coherent. He has been vastly helped by McGuiness' adaptation, which while not diverging from previous literal translations, is extremely supple and lifelike..." *Variety* (Evans): "...McTeer triumphs in showing how deep Nora's pain and fear go. In one flawlessly directed scene she dances the tarantella to distract her husband from the ominous letter that reveals her secret, the dance building in tension and pace as Nora's hysteria mounts."

*Closed August 31, 1997 after 150 performances and 8 previews.
Alistair Muir Photos

Owen Teale, Janet McTeer

Janet McTeer

Owen Teale

Lesley Ann Warren, Margaret Whiting, John Pizzarelli

Darcie Roberts, Jonathan Dokuchitz

Susan Misner and Men

DREAM

Lyrics, Johnny Mercer; Music, Harold Arlen, Rube Bloom, Hoagy Carmichael, Walter Donaldson, Duke Ellington, Ziggy Elman, Bernie Hanighen, Jerome Kern, Matt Malneck, Henry Mancini, Johnny Mercer, David Raskin, Victor Schertzinger, Billy Strayhorn, James Van Heusen, Harry Warren, Richard Whiting; Conceived by Louise Westergaard, Jack Wrangler; Director/Choreography, Wayne Cilento; Orchestrations, Dick Lieb; Musical Supervision, Donald Pippin; Musical Director/Vocal Arrangements, Bryan Louiselle; Dance Arrangements, Jeanine Tesori; Sets, David Mitchell; Costumes, Ann Hould-Ward; Lighting, Ken Billington; Sound, Peter Fitzgerald; Mercer Visualization, Jack Wrangler; General Manager, Ralph Roseman; Production Supervisor, Roy Sears; Production Coordinator, Tripp Phillips; Stage Manager, Diane DiVita; Company Manager, Joka Kops; Presented by Louise Westergaard, Mark Schwartz, Bob Cuillo, Roger Dean, Obie Bailey, Stephen O'Neil, Abraham Salaman; Press, Susan L. Schulman; Previewed from Tuesday, March 11; Opened in the Royale Theatre on Thursday, April 3, 1997*

CAST

Lesley Ann Warren	John Pizzarelli
Margaret Whiting	Brooks Ashmanskas
Jonathan Dokuchitz	Charles McGowan
Jessica Molaskey	Darcie Roberts
Todd Bailey	Angelo Fraboni.
Amy Heggins	Jennifer Lamberts
Nancy Lemenager	Susan Misner
Kevyn Morrow	Timothy Edward Smith
Ray Kennedy	Martin Pizzarelli
Jeffry Denman	Jody Ripplinger
Bill Szobody	Deborah Yates

STANDBYS/UNDERSTUDIES: Jane Summerhays (for Ms. Warren), Denise Lor (For Ms. Whiting), Jeffrey Denman, Jody Ripplinger, Bill Szobody, Deborah Yates

MUSICAL NUMBERS: Dream, Lazybones, On Behalf of the Traveling Salesmen, Pardon My Southern Accent, You Must Have Been a Beautiful Baby, Have You Got Any Castles Baby?, Goody Goody, Skylark, Dixieland Band, I Had Myself a True Love/I Wonder What Became of Me, Jamboree Jones Jive, Fools Rush In, Come Rain or Come Shine, Out of This World, I Remember You, Blues in the Night, One for My Baby, You Were Never Lovelier, Satin Doll, I'm Old Fashioned, Dearly Beloved, This Time the Dream's on Me, Something's Gotta Give, Too Marvelous for Words, I Thought About You, And the Angels Sing, The Fleet's In, G.I. Jive, I'm Doin' It for Defense, Tangerine, Day In Day Out, Jeepers Creepers, That Old Black Magic, Laura, You Go Your Way, My Shining Hour, Hooray for Hollywood, Accentuate the Positive, In the Cool Cool Cool of the Evening, Charade/Days of Wine and Roses, Moon River, On the Atchison Topeka and the Santa Fe

A two-act musical revue inspired by the lyrics of Johnny Mercer. The program segments are: Savannah, Magnificent Obsession-The Age of Decadence, Rainbow Room, Hollywood Canteen, and Academy Awards.

Variety tallied 1 favorable, 3 mixed and 8 negative reviews. *Times* (Marks): "Mercer, a brilliantly adaptive wordsmith..occupies a place of honor in the pantheon of pop lyricists. But how important his lyrics are is never really explored..Lesley Ann Warren..looks great..Ms. Whiting is authentic, and each time she enters, the show becomes significant." *News* (Kissel): "...has the quality of a '50s TV special..John Pizzarelli has a naturalness and charm that make his singing extremely engaging." *Post* (Barnes): ""If only they had dropped the stars and encouraged Cilento..to have staged a Mercer-oriented dancical..." *Variety* (Evans): "...does little to honor the great Mercer..giant Academy Award-like statues would be too kitschy even for an Oscar telecast, and a steam-blowing, cardboard-cutout train arrives straight from community theater."

*Closed July 6, 1997 after 109 performances and 24 previews.
Carol Rosegg Photos

EASTER BONNET COMPETITION

Director, Sam Ellis; Associate Director, Drew Geraci; Musical Supervisor, Seth Rudetsky; Choreography (opening), David Marques; Stage Managers, Jim Harker, John Atherlay, M.A. Howard; Producers, Michael Graziano and Tom Viola; Press, Chris Boneau~Adrian Bryan-Brown/Miguel Tuason; Presented in the Palace Theatre on Monday, April 7 and Tuesday, April 8, 1997*

CAST INCLUDES

Dana Ivey and Gary Beach, Tom O'Leary and Joan Almedilla, Ann Dusquesnay and Ken Prymus, Michael Chiklis and Greg Jbara, Ernie Sabella and David Sabella, Hal Holbrook and Bebe Neuwirth, Nell Carter, Whoopi Goldberg, Chita Rivera, Jeffrey Wright, Anne Runolfsson, Howard McGillin, The voice of Thom Christopher, and cast members from *Beauty and the Beast, Once Upon a Mattress, Annie* (Easter at the Warbucks Mansion), Metropolitan Opera (Hommage to Carmen), *Cats* (Now and Forever), *Stanley* (Stanley of Liberty), *Phantom of the Opera, Rent, Miss Saigon* (No Menus Please), *Tony 'n Tina's Wedding, Bring in 'Da Noise Bring in 'Da Funk, Smokey Joe's Cafe, Grandma Sylvia's Funeral, King and I* (Nightmares), *When Pigs Fly, Last Night of Ballyhoo, Present Laughter, Forbidden Bdwy Strikes Back* (Good Will), Dancers Responding to AIDS, *A Funny Thing Happened..* and *Chicago.*

BONNET SINGERS/DANCERS: Joyce Chittick, Holly Cruikshank, Joseph Favalora, Jeffrey Hankinson, Sebastian La Cause, Deborah Leamy, Tina Ou, Rommy Sandhu, Scott Spahr "Scooter", Kristi Sperling, Leslie Stevens, Branch Woodman, Frank Barr, Marion Beckenstein, Neil Cohen, Peter Coulianos, Margery Daley, Dan Egan, Katie Geissinger, Margo Gribb, Ray Harrell, Beverly Myers, David Ronis, Peter Stewart, Julie Tedoff, Cliff Townsend, Molly Wasserman, Stephanie Weems

The eleventh annual Broadway Cares/Equity Fights AIDS Easter fundraiser raised $1,474,272. *Phantom of the Opera* won the "Most Fabulous Bonnet Award" and "*A Funny Thing Happened on the Way to the Forum*" won the fundraising award.

Eric Silverman, Arturo E. Porazzi Photos

Top: The Finale
Center: Jason Samuels

Peter Reigert, Kate Nelligan in *An American Daughter*

Lynne Thigpen, Kate Nelligan

AN AMERICAN DAUGHTER

By Wendy Wasserstein; Director, Dan Sullivan; Sets, John Lee Beatty; Costumes, Jane Greenwood; Lighting, Pat Collins; Sound, Scott Lehrer, Donna Riley; General Manager, Steven C. Callahan; Production Manager, Jeff Hamlin; Company Manager, Mala Yee; Stage Manager, Roy Harris; Presented by Lincoln Center Theater (Andre Bishop and Bernard Gersten, Directors); Press, Philip Rinaldi/Miller Wright, Brian Rubin; Previewed from Thursday, March 20; Opened in the Cort Theatre on Sunday, April 13, 1997*

CAST

Lyssa Dent Hughes ....Kate Nelligan +1
Quincy Quince ....Elizabeth Marvel +2
Judith B. Kaufman ....Lynne Thigpen
Walter Abrahmson ....Peter Riegert +3
Morrow McCarthy..Bruce Norris
Timber Tucker ....Cotter Smith
Senator Alan Hughes ....Hal Holbrook +4
Charlotte "Chubby" Hughes...Penny Fuller
Jimmy ....Andrew Dolan +5
Billy Robbins ....Peter Benson
Television Crew ....Drew Barr, Denise Burse
                                            Ron Parady, Alison Tatlock
Boys (Voices) ....Erich Bergen
UNEDRSTUDIES: Lee Bryant (Lyssa; Chubby), Alison Tatlock (Quincy), Denise Burse (Judith), Andrew Dolan, Geoffrey Wade (Walter/Timber), Drew Barr (Morrow/Billy/Jimmy), Ron Parady (Senator)

A play in two acts. The action takes place in a Georgetown living room, Washington, D.C. Winner of 1997 "Tony" Award for Featured Actress in a Play (Lynne Thigpen).

Variety tallied 3 favorable, 3 mixed and 4 negative reviews. *Times* (Brantley): "...a play undone by the admirable desire to achieve too much." *News* (Kissel): "Kate Nelligan infuses great vitality and passion..Lynne Thigpen is smashing as her black, Jewish friend..the gay friend, played drolly by Bruce Norris..." *Post* (Barnes): "...a distict and often amusing attempt to expose that soft underbelly of American political life..it is a play that is at least provocative..." *Variety* (Evans): "...Wendy Wasserstein gets angry. Or rather the anger that's always slept beneath her humor wakes up and announces itself, sometimes too baldly, more often too predictably, but always with the playwright's commitment and compassion..her most ambitious work..."

*Closed June 29, 1997 after 88 performances and 27 previews.
+Succeeded by: 1. Kate Burton 2. Kate Jennings Grant 3. John Procaccino 4. Ralph Waite 5. Geoffrey Wade

Joan Marcus Photos

Hal Holbrook

Bruce Norris

THE GIN GAME

By D.L. Coburn; Director, Charles Nelson Reilly; Sets, James Noone; Costumes, Noel Taylor; Lighting, Kirk Bookman; Sound, Richard Fitzgerald; General Manager, Niko Associates; Managing Director, Fred Walker; Company Manager, Rick Shulman; Stage Managers, Mitchell Erickson, Anita Ross; Executive Producer, Manny Kladitis; Presented by National Actors Theatre (Tony Randall, Founder/Artistic Director); Press, Gary Springer~Susan Chicoine/Candi Adams, Ann Guzzi, Charlie Siedenburg, Tiina Piirsoo; Previewed from Friday, April 4; Opened in the Lyceum Theatre on Sunday, April 20, 1997*

CAST

Fonsia Dorsey ....Julie Harris
Weller Martin ....Charles Durning
STANDBYS: Natalie Norwick (Fonsia), Tom Troupe (Weller)

A new production of the 1977 play in two acts. The action takes place in a home for the elderly. For the original Pulitzer Prize-winning Broadway production with Jessica Tandy and Hune Cronyn, see *Theatre World* Vol.34.

Variety tallied 11 favorable and 2 mixed reviews. *Times* (Marks): "...a pair of silver-haired veterans of the stage are having at each other with an abandon enabled by a lifetime of actors' calluses and a radiant love of craft." *News* (Kissel): "When the play was first done..it was more austere than it is here..Durning has never been more winning. As for Harris..as poignant as she is funny." *Post* (Barnes): "...a demonstration that slightness can have a weight all of its own." *Variety* (Evans) "...a shaky production of a play that was formulaic even before spawning numerous imitations..."

*Closed August 31, 1997 after 144 performances and 20 previews.
Carol Rosegg Photos

Right and Below: Julie Harris, Charles Durning

Scenes from *Titanic* (Joan Marcus Photos)

TITANIC

Music/Lyrics, Maury Yeston; Book/Story, Peter Stone; Director, Richard Jones; Choreography, Lynne Taylor-Corbett; Orchestrations, Jonathan Tunick; Musical Supervision/Direction, Kevin Stites; Sets/Costumes, Stewart Laing; Lighting, Paul Gallo; Sound, Steve Canyon Kennedy; Action Coordinator, Rick Sordelet; Cast Recording, RCA; General Manager, Dodger Management Group; Company Manager, Steven H. David; Stage Managers, Susan Green, Richard Hester; Presented by Dodger Endemol Theatricals, Richard S. Pechter, John F. Kennedy Center for the Performing Arts; Press, Chris Boneau~Adrian Bryan-Brown/Susanne Tighe, Amy Jacobs; Previewed from Saturday, March 29; Opened in the Lunt-Fontanne Theatre on Wednesday, April 23, 1997*

CAST

Officers & Crew of R.M.S. Titanic

Capt. E.J. Smith...	John Cunningham
1st Officer William Murdoch...	David Costabile
2nd Officer Charles Lightoller...	John Bolton
3rd Officer Herbert J. Pitman	Matthew Bennett
Frederick Barrett, Stoker...	Brian d'Arcy James
Harold Bride, Radioman	Martin Moran
Henry Etches, 1st Class Steward...	Allan Corduner
Frederick Fleet, Lookout...	David Elder
Quartermaster Robert Hichens/Bricoux	Adam Alexi-Malle
4th Officer Joseph Boxhall/Taylor	Andy Taylor
Chief Engineer Joseph Bell/Wallace Hartley...	Ted Sperling
Stewardess Robinson	Michele Ragusa
Stewardess Hutchinson...	Stephanie Park
Bellboy	Mara Stephens

Passengers aboard R.M.S. Titanic

J. Bruce Ismay	David Garrison
Thomas Andrews	Michael Cerveris
Isidor Straus	Larry Keith
Ida Strauss	Alma Cuervo
J.J. Astor	William Youmans
Madeline Astor	Lisa Datz
Benjamin Guggenheim	Joseph Kolinski
Mme. Aubert	Kimberly Hester
John B. Thayer	Michael Mulheren
Marion Thayer	Robin Irwin
George Widener	Henry Stram
Eleanor Widener	Jody Gelb
Charlotte Cardoza	Becky Ann Baker
J.H. Rogers	Andy Taylor
The Major	Matthew Bennett
Edith Corse Evans	Mindy Cooper
Charles Clarke	Don Stephenson
Caroline Neville	Judith Blazer
Edgar Beane	Bill Buell
Alice Beane	Victoria Clark
Kate McGowen	Jennifer Piech
Kate Murphey	Theresa McCarthy
Kate Mullins	Erin Hill
Jim Farrell	Clarke Thorell
Frank Carlson	Henry Stram
Other Passengers	Charles McAteer

UNDERSTUDIES: Drew McVety (Barrett/Bride/Hichens/Boxhall/Rogers/Farrell), Andy Taylor (Barrett/Lightoller/Clarke), John Bolton (Bride/Murdoch), Jonathan Brody (Fleet/Bell/Hartley/Lightoller/Hichens/Farrell/Thayer/Guggenheim), Peter Kapetan (Bell/Hartley/Murdoch/Ismay/Beane/Astor/Guggenheim/Thayer/Guggenheim), John Jellison (Boxhall/Rogers/Pitman/Major/Capt. Smith/Beane/Astor/Straus/Thayer/Guggenheim), Joseph Kolinski (Smith/Andrews), Matthew Bennett (Ismay/Andrews), David Costabile (Ismay/Etches), Henry Stram (Etches), Lisa Datz (Kate McGowen/Caroline Clarke), Theresa McCarthy (Kate McGowen/Caroline Clarke), Melissa Bell (Kate Mullins/Kate Murphey/Aubert/Mrs. Astor), Kay Walbye (Mrs. Widener/Mrs. Thayer/Mrs. Beane/Mrs. Straus/Mrs. Cardoza), Jody Gelb (Mrs. Beane/Mrs. Straus)

SWINGS: Melissa Bell, Kay Walbye, Jonathan Brody, John Jellison, Drew McVety

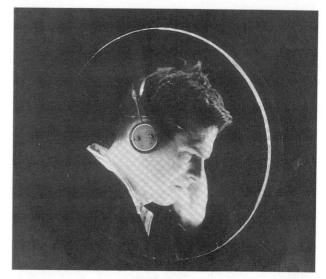

Martin Moran

Theresa McCarthy, Jennifer Piech, Erin Hill

David Garrison, Michael Cerveris, John Cunningham

The Company

MUSICAL NUMBERS: In Every Age, The Launching: How Did They Build Titanic?, There She Is, Loading Inventory, Largest Moving Object, I Must Get on That Ship, 1st Class Roster, Godspeed Titanic; Barrett's Song, What a Remarkable Age This Is, To Be a Captain, Lady's Maid, The Proposal, The Night was Alive, Hymn, Doing the Latest Rag, I Have Danced, No Moon, Autumn, Wake Up Wake Up!, Dressed in Your Pyjamas in the Grand Salon, The Staircase, The Blame, To the Lifeboats: Getting in the Lifeboat, Canons, We'll Meet Tomorrow; Still, Mr. Andrews' Vision, Finale DURING PREVIEWS: I Give You My Hand, Behind Every Fortune

A musical in two acts. The action takes place at Southampton, England and on board the Titanic, between April 10-15, 1912. Winner of 1997 "Tony" Awards for Best Musical, Score, Book of a Musical, Orchestration and Scenic Design.

Variety tallied 1 favorable, 5 mixed and 9 negative reviews. *Times* (Brantley): "Theater disaster cultists will have to wait..a perversely cool work. cerebral without being particularly imaginative..There is evidence of intelligence and variety in the music..." *News* (Kissel): "the score is solid, the book gives the story focus...resuly never achieves what you feel the show is constantly striving for..Among the standouts are Michael Cerveris..Brian d'Arcy James sings thrillingly..strong solos by Martin Moran as the radio operator and David Elder as the lookout." *Post* (Barnes): "This is, shall we say, a downer, at best." *Variety* (Evans): "A $10 million spectacle musical without spectacle. The songs stand out because they are most clearly songs, distinct from the operatic medleys and ensemble numbers that make up much of *Titanic's* big-throated, heroic-scale score."

Still playing May 31, 1997
Joan Marcus Photos

Alma Cuervo, Larry Keith

Jim Newman, Kristin Chenoweth, Casey Nicholaw

Marathon Dancers

Jim Newman, Debra Monk

STEEL PIER

Music, John Kander; Lyrics, Fred Ebb; Book, David Thompson; Conceived by Scott Ellis, Susan Stroman and Mr. Thompson; Director, Mr. Ellis; Choreography, Ms. Stroman; Orchestrations, Michael Gibson; Musical Director/Vocal Arrangements, David Loud; Sets, Tony Walton; Costumes, William Ivey Long; Lighting, Peter Kaczorowski; Sound, Tony Meola; Dance Arrangements, Glen Kelly; Projections, Wendall K. Harrington; Cast Recording, RCA; General Manager, Marvin A. Krauss; Company Manager, Carl Pasbjerg; Stage Managers, Beverly Randolph, Frank Lombardi; Presented by Roger Berlind; Press, Chris Boneau~Adrian Bryan-Brown/Michael Hartman, Jackie Green, Ellen Levene, Stephen Pitalo, Janet George; Previewed from Thursday, March 27; Opened in the Richard Rodgers Theatre on Thursday, April 24, 1997*

CAST

Bill Kelly ....Daniel McDonald
Rita Racine ....Karen Ziemba
Shelby Stevens...Debra Monk
Mick Hamilton...Gregory Harrison
Mr. Walker...Ronn Carroll
Buddy Becker ....Joel Blum
Bette Becker..Valerie Wright
Johnny Adel..Timothy Warmen
Dora Foster ....Alison Bevan
Happy McGuire ....Jim Newman
Precious McGuire ....Kristin Chenoweth
Luke Adams ....John C. Havens
Mick's Picks.........................Mary Illes, Rosa Curry, Sarah Solie Shannon
Corky...Casey Nicholaw
Dr. Johnson ....John MacInnis
Sonny..Gregory Mitchell
Preacher...Adam Pelty
Flying Dunlaps... .....Leigh-Anne Wencker, Jack Hayes, JoAnn M. Hunter, Robert Fowler, John MacInnis
Other Marathon Dancers/Ensemble... ....Julio Agustin, Leslie Bell, Andy Blankenbuehler, Brad Bradley, Ida Gilliams, Angelique Ilo, Dana Lynn Mauro,Elizabeth Mills, Scott Taylor
STANDBYS/UNDERSTUDIES: Brian Sutherland (Mick/Bill), Cady Huffman (Rita/Shelby), Timothy Warmen (Mick), Jim Newman (Bill), Brad Bradley (Buddy/Walker), Adam Pelty (Buddy/Luke), Julio Agustin (Johnny), Gregory Mitchell (Johnny), Casey Nicholaw (Luke/Walker), John MacInnis (Happy), Scott Taylor (Happy), Valerie Wright (Rita), Alison Bevan (Shelby), Mary Illes (Precious), Sarah Solie Shannon (Precious), Angelique Ilo (Dora), Leigh-Ann Wencker (Dora), Leslie Bell (Bette), JoAnn M. Hunter (Bette) SWINGS: Mr. Agustin, Ms. Bell, Ms. Ilo, Mr. Taylor

MUSICAL NUMBERS: Prelude, Willing to Ride, Everybody Dance, Second Chance, Montages: The Shag/Harmonica Specialty/The SprintsTwo Step, A Powerful Thing, Dance with Me/The Last Girl, Everybody's Girl, Wet, Lovebird, Leave the World Behind, Somebody Older, Running in Place, Two Little Words, First You Dream, Steel Pier, Final Dance DURING PREVIEWS: In Here, Winning, Looking for Love

A musical in two acts. The action takes place on Atlantic City's Steel Pier, August, 1933.

Variety tallied 5 favorable, 8 mixed and 6 negative reviews. *Times* (Brantley): "The overall dreamlike effect is hypnotic in the wrong ways; there's no center of energy to grab onto." *News* (Kissel): "There are some beautiful songs..Stroman's choreography has verve and style. The dancers execute her often intricate steps with enormous flair." *Post* (Barnes): "...has built-in book trouble-it is a theme rather than a story..a good idea gone mediocre." *Variety* (Evans): "...choreography from Susan Stroman that cannily blends period steps with her trademark innovations and some of Kander and Ebb's strongest writing in years..Monk's crowd-pleasing turn takes nothing away from the winning performances by the leads, McDonald and Ziemba."

*Closed June 28, 1997 after 76 performances and 33 previews.
Joan Marcus/Carol Rosegg Photos

Daniel McDonald

Karen Ziemba

Debra Monk

Gregory Harrison

Felicia Finley, Chuck Cooper

The Ladies

THE LIFE

Music, Cy Coleman; Lyrics, Ira Gasman; Book, David Newman, Mr. Gasman, Mr. Coleman; Director, Michael Blakemore; Choreography, Joey McKneely; Orchestrations, Don Sebesky, Harold Wheeler; Dance/Vocal Arrangements, Mr. Coleman, Doug Katsaros; Musical Director, Gordon Lowry Harrell; Sets, Robin Wagner; Costumes, Martin Pakledinaz; Lighting, Richard Pilbrow; Sound, Peter Fitzgerald; Cast Recording, Sony; Fights, B.H. Barry; Hairstylist, Bobby H. Grayson; General Manager, Marvin A. Krauss; Production Supervisor, Steven Zweigbaum; Company Managers, David Richards, Barbara Crompton; Stage Manager, Ara Marx; Presented by Roger Berlind, Martin Richards, Cy Coleman and Sam Crothers; Press, Judy Jacksina/Elisa Wolthausen, Laura Williams, Darrell Shipley, Kevin Blanchette; Previewed from Tuesday, April 8; Opened in the Ethel Barrymore Theatre on Saturday, April 26, 1997*

CAST

Jojo ....Sam Harris
Carmen ....Lynn Sterling
Chichi ....Sharon Wilkins
Frenchie ....Katy Grenfell
Tracy ....Judine Richard
Bobby/Cop ....Mark Bove
Oddjob/Shoeshine ....Michael Gregory Gong
Silky/Enrique ....Rudy Roberson
Slick/Shatellia ....Mark Anthony Taylor
Memphis ....Chuck Cooper
April ....Felicia Finley
Snickers ....Gordon Joseph Weiss
Lacy ....Vernel Bagneris
Queen ....Pamela Isaacs
Sonja ....Lillias White
Fleetwood ....Kevin Ramsey
Mary ....Bellamy Young
Doll House Dancer ....Stephanie Michels
Street Evangelists...................Judine Richard, Rudy Roberson,
                                                            Mark Anthony Taylor
Lou ....Rich Hebert
Other Ensemble ....Chris Ghelfi

Lillias White, Pamela Isaacs

UNDERSTUDIES: Kimberly Hawthorne (Queen), Tracy Nicole Chapman (Queen), Sharon Wilkins (Sonja), James Stovall (Fleetwood/Memphis/Silky), Michael Brian (Jojo/Lou/Snickers), Rudy Roberson (Lacy), Felicia Finley (Mary), Stephanie Michels (Mary) SWING: Tracy Nicole Chapman

MUSICAL NUMBERS: Check It Out!, Use What You Got, A Lovely Day to Be Out of Jail, A Piece of the Action, The Oldest Profession, Don't Take Much, Go Home, You Can't Get to Heaven, My Body, Why Don't They Leave Us Alone, Easy Money, He's No Good, I'm Leaving You, Hooker's Ball, Step Right Up, Mr. Greed, My Way or the Highway, People Magazine, We Had a Dream, Someday Is for Suckers, My Friend, We Gotta Go, Finale DURING PREVIEWS: Was That a Smile

A musical in two acts. The action takes place around 42nd St. The time is "Then" (late 1970s-early 1980s). Winner of 1997 "Tony" Awards for Featured Actress in a Musical (Lillias White), and Featured Actor in a Musical (Chuck Cooper).

Variety tallied 4 favorable, 6 mixed and 7 negative reviews. *Times* (Brantley): "...at least is alive. And it actually has some songs, and at least two performances, that linger in the memory." (Canby): "...by far the most entertaining new musical..more fresh, fully realized talent and go-for-broke pizazz than can be found anywhere else on Broadway..Mr. Coleman has composed not only his most driving, big-beat score since *Sweet Charity* but also his most varied and melodic work since *On the Twentieth Century*..." *News* (Kissel): "Is anyone, by the way, nostalgic for 42nd St. when it was a human sewer?" *Post* (Barnes): "...gritty and raucous new musical..whole cast moves like a smooth ensemble..in even the smallest, carefully, almost lovingly characterized roles..strong theatre with a vivid beat..." *Variety* (Evans): "What saves *The Life* from its morality-tale melodrama (everyone pays for their sins) is the collection of songs..The big performance comes from Lillias White..."

*Closed June 7, 1998 after 466 performances and 20 previews.
Carol Rosegg Photos

Bellamy Young, Sam Harris

Stockard Channing

THE LITTLE FOXES

By Lillian Hellman; Director, Jack O'Brien; Sets, John Lee Beatty; Costumes, Jane Greenwood; Lighting, Kenneth Posner; Sound, Aural Fixation; Score, Bob James; General Manager, Steven C. Callahan; Production Manager, Jeff Hamlin; Company Manager, Nina Skriloff; Stage Manager, Jeff Lee; Presented by Lincoln Center Theater (Andre Bishop, Artistic Director; Bernard Gersten, Executive Producer); Press, Philip Rinaldi/Miller Wright, Brian Rubin; Previewed from Thursday, April 3; Opened in the Vivian Beaumont Theater on Sunday, April 27, 1997*

CAST

Addie	Ethel Ayler
Cal	Charles Turner
Birdie Hubbard	Frances Conroy
Oscar Hubbard	Brian Kerwin
Leo Hubbard	Frederick Weller
Regina Giddens	Stockard Channing
William Marshall	Richard E. Council
Benjamin Hubbard	Brian Murray
Alexandra Giddens	Jennifer Dundas
Horace Giddens	Kenneth Welsh

UNDERSTUDIES: Aaron Harpold (Leo), Marjorie Johnson (Addie), Allie Woods Jr. (Cal), Jennifer Harmon (Birdie/Regina), Daniel Ahearn (Oscar/Horace), Jack Davidson (William/Benjamin), Stina Nielsen (Alexandra)

A 1939 drama in three acts. The action takes place in the Giddens home in a small Alabama town, 1900. The original 1939 production starred Tallulah Bankhead. For most recent Broadway revival with Elizabeth Taylor and Maureen Stapleton (1981), see *Theatre World* Vol.37.

Variety tallied 8 favorable, 3 mixed and 4 negative reviews. *Times* (Brantley): "...so wildly miscast and so haplessly misconceived that it is hard to figure out exactly what its creators had in mind." *News* (Kissel): "...lacks that theatricality..." *Post* (Barnes)" "...melodrama and nothing more..." *Variety* (Evans): "...so refreshing, so cunning..furthers the reputations of all involved, none more so than the playwright herself..flawless performances..In more ways than one, the play has never looked better."

*Closed June 15, 1997 after 57 performances and 27 previews.
Joan Marcus Photos

Richard E. Council, Frederick Weller, Stockard Channing, Brian Kerwin, Brian Murray

Robert Cuccioli as *Jekyll & Hyde* (Cylla Von Tiedmann Photo)

JEKYLL & HYDE

Music, Frank Wildhorn; Lyrics/Book, Leslie Bricusse; Conceived for the stage by Steve Cuden and Mr. Wildhorn; Based on the 1886 novella *The Strange Case of Dr. Jekyll and Mr. Hyde* by Robert Louis Stevenson; Director, Robin Phillips; Orchestrations, Kim Scharnberg; Musical Director, Jason Howland; Musical Supervisor, Jeremy Roberts; Sets, Mr. Phillips, James Noone; Costumes, Ann Curtis; Lighting, Beverly Emmons; Choreography, Joey Pizzi; Sound, Karl Richardson, Scott Stauffer; Vocal Arrangements, Mr. Howland, Ron Melrose; Special Effects, Gregory Meeh; Wigs, Paul Huntley; Fights, J. Allen Suddeth; Cast Recording, Atlantic; General Manager, Niko Associates; Company Manager, Bruce Klinger; Stage Managers, Maureen F. Gibson, David Hyslop; Presented by PACE Theatrical Group and FOX Theatricals, in association with Jerry Frankel, Magicworks Entertainment and The Landmark Entertainment Group; Press, Richard Kornberg/Rick Miramontez, Don Summa, Jim Byk; Previewed from Friday, March 21; Opened in the Plymouth Theatre on Monday, April 28, 1997*

CAST

John Utterson	George Merritt
Sir Danvers Carew	Barrie Ingram
Dr. Henry Jekyll/Edward Hyde	Robert Cuccioli
	Robert Evan (matinee)
Davie/Old Man/Manservant/Mr. Biset/Priest	David Chaney
Doctor/Lord G/Poole	Donald Grody
Kate	Leah Hocking
Alice/Maid/Whore/Bridemaid	Emily Scott Skinner
Molly	Molly Scott Pesce
Bet/Maid/Young Girl/Bridemaid	Jodi Stevens
Polly/Whore	Bonnie Schon
Mike/Groom	John Treacy Egan
Albert/Gent/Priest	Frank Mastrone
Ned/Patient/Tough	David Koch
Bill/Patient/Groom/Tough/*News*boy	Bill E. Dietrich
Jack/Footman/Tough/Doorman/Curate	Charles E. Wallace
Simon Stride	Raymond Jaramillo McLeod
Rupert/Sir Douglas/Police	Michael Ingram
Right Honorable Archibald Proops/Gent/Sir Peter	Brad Oscar
Lord Savage/The Spider	Martin Van Treuren
Lady Beaconsfield/Guinevere	Emily Zacharias
Gen. Lord Glossop/Siegfried/Police	Geoffrey Blaisdell
Emma Carew	Christiane Noll
Lucy/Boy Soprano at Wedding	Linda Eder

UNDERSTUDIES: Frank Mastrone (Jekyll/Hyde/Savage/Spider), Bill E. Dietrich (Jekyll/Hyde/Proops), Leah Hocking (Lucy/Emma), Emily Skinner (Lucy/Emma), Jodi Stevens (Lucy/Emma), Geoffrey Blaisdell (Utterson/Poole), Martin Van Treuren (Danvers), Donald Grody (Danvers), Bonnie Schon (Lady Beaconsfield/Guinevere), Brad Oscar (Poole), John Treacy Egan (Glossop/Bishop), David Koch (Stride) SWINGS: Paul Hadobas, Rebecca Spencer

Top: Christiane Noll, Robert Cuccioli

MUSICAL NUMBERS: Lost in the Darkness, Facade, Jekyll's Plea, Emma's Reasons, Take Me As I Am, Letting Go, No One Knows Who I Am, Good 'N' Evil, This Is the Moment, Alive, His Work and Nothing More, Someone Like You, Murder Murder, Once Upon a Dream, Obsession, In His Eyes, Dangerous Game, The Way Back, A New Life, Sympathy Tenderness, Confrontation, Dear Lord and Father of Mankind PRE-BROADWAY: Board of Governors, Bring on the Men, Girls of the Night

A musical in two acts. The action takes place in London.

Variety tallied 4 favorable, 4 mixed and 6 negative reviews. *Times* (Brantley): "...leaden, solemnly campy musical..it keeps saying the same things, with the slightest variation, over and over again." *News* (Kissel): "...restore 19th-century melodrama to a theatre that imagined it had outgrown such things. The audience, though, never outgrew them. It never cottoned to the cerebralization of the American musical..." *Post* (Barnes): "...splendidly virtuostic performance by Robert Cuccioli..a spirited and sexy Linda Eder..." *Variety* (Evans) "...dour, humorless..Eder fills the theater with her voice and the stage with her presence..."

Still playing May 31, 1997
Cylla Von Tiedemann Photos

46

Linda Eder, Robert Cuccioli

Robert Cuccioli

CANDIDE

Music, Leonard Bernstein; Lyrics, Richard Wilbur, Stephen Sondheim, John Latouche; Book, Hugh Wheeler; Based on the 1759 novel by Voltaire; Director, Harold Prince; Orchestrations, Mr. Bernstein, Hershy Kay; Musical Director, Eric Stern; Music Continuity/Additional Orchestrations, John Mauceri; Choreography, Patricia Birch; Sets, Clarke Dunham; Costumes, Judith Dolan; Sound, Jonathan Deans; Lighting, Ken Billington; Hairstylist, Bobby H. Grayson; Cast Recording, RCA; Production Supervisor, Clayton Phillips; Company Manager, Jim Brandenberry; Stage Manager, Bonnie Panson; Presented by Livent (U.S.); Press, Mary Bryant/Wayne Wolfe; Previewed from Saturday, April 19; Opened in the Gershwin Theatre on Tuesday, April 29, 1997*

CAST

Voltaire/Dr. Pangloss/Governor/Businessman/Police Chief.........Jim Dale
Old Lady ....Andrea Martin
Cunegonde... ....Harolyn Blackwell
Glenda Balkan
Candide ....Jason Danieley
Maximilian ....Brent Barrett
Paquette ....Stacey Logan
Baron/GrandInquisitor/Columbo/Pasha-Perfect...............Mal Z. Lawrence
Hugo/Radu/Don Issachar/Judge Gomez/
Fr. Bernard/Turhan Bey..... ....Arte Johnson +1
Sheep...D'vorah Bailey, Nanne Puritz
Heresy Agent..David Girolmo
Bulgarian Soldier ....Paul Harman
Governor's Aide ....Allen Hidalgo
Baroness ....Julie Johnson +2
Lion..Seth Malkin
Other Ensemble... ....Mary Kate Boulware, Diana Brownstone,
    Alvin Crawford, Christopher F. Davis, Sherrita Duran,Deanna Dys,
    Joy Hermalyn, Wendy Hilliard, Elizabeth Jimenez, Ken Krugman, Chad
    Larget, Shannon Lewis, Andrew Pacho, Owen Taylor, Eric Van Hoven
UNDERSTUDIES: Mal Z. Lawrence (Jim Dale roles), Paul Harman (Jim Dale roles), John Lankston (Jim Dale standby), Chad Larget, Eric van Hoven (Candide), Nanne Puritz (Cunegonde/Paquette), Mary Kate Boulware (Cunegonde/Sheep), Julie Johnson, (Old Lady), Joy Hermalyn (Old Lady/Baroness), Shannon Lewis (Paquette), Ken Krugman, Seth Malkin (Maximilian), Paul Harman, David Girolmo (Mal Z. Lawrence & Arte Johnson roles), Rachel Coloff (Baroness/Sheep), Alvin Crawford, Joseph McDonnell (Lion), Diana Brownstone (Sheep), Matthew Aibel (Bulgarian/Heresy Agent) SWINGS: Mr. Aibel, Ms. Coloff, Joseph P. McDonnell, Starla Pace

Jason Danieley, Jim Dale, Harolyn Blackwell

MUSICAL NUMBERS: Overture, Life Is Happiness Indeed, Best of All Possible Worlds, Oh Happy We, It Must Be So, Westphalian Chorale, Glitter and Be Gay, Auto-da-fe, Candide's lament, You Were Dead You Know, I Am Easily Assimilated, Quartet, Ballad of the New World, My Love, Alleluia, Sheep Song, Bon Voyage, Quiet, What's the Use, Make Our Garden Grow

A new production of a 1956 musical in two acts. Winner of 1997 "Tony" Award for Costume Design. For original Broadway production with Barbara Cook and Robert Rounseville, see *Theatre World* Vol.13. For Harold Prince's 1974 Broadway revival see *Theatre World* Vol.30.

Variety tallied 4 favorable, 1 mixed and 5 negative reviews. *Times* (Brantley): "The score of Candide remains absolutely delectable and the orchestra performs it beautifully..not only has in Ms. Blackwell a Cunegonde who happily scales the dangerous peaks of her songs, but an enchanting, honey-voiced Candide in Jason Danieley..Yet the show..seems desperately busy and over-packaged." *News* (Kissel): "...it is clear that whatever of Voltaire's spirit or wit the musical first captured in Bernstein's music and the original lyrics..are ill-served by the Wheeler book." *Post* (Barnes): "..a joyous experience, an operetta to savor musically..The amazing Martin, with her smokey voice and piquant manner, brings her own distinctive sorcery..Dale delivers the kind of Broadway top-banana pizzazz the show hasn't had before." *Variety* (Evans): "...returns one of Broadway's most beloved scores to the theatre..elaborately illustrated wooden cutouts, carnival midway banners, party lights and circus wagons turn the stage into a traveling freak show of 18th-century vintage, with flashes of medieval street fairs.."

*Closed July 27, 1997 after 103 performances and 11 previews.
+Succeeded by: 1. Avery Saltzman 2. Melissa Hart

Catherine Ashmore Photos

Stacey Logan, Jason Danieley, Andrea Martin

LONDON ASSURANCE

By Dion L. Boucicault; Director, Joe Dowling; Sets, Derek McLane; Costumes, Catherine Zuber; Lighting, Blake Burba; Sound, Mark Bennett; Hairstylist/Wigs, Paul Huntley; Company Manager, Denys Baker; Stage Managers, Jay Adler, Charles Kindl; Presented by Roundabout Theatre Company (Todd Haimes, Artistic Director; Ellen Richard, General Manager; Gene Feist, Founding Director); Press, Chris Boneau~Adrian Bryan-Brown/Erin Dunn; Previewed from Wednesday, April 16; Opened in the Criterion Center Stage Right on Wednesday, April 30, 1997*

CAST

Cool	John Horton
Martin	Robert Neill
Charles Courtly	Rainn Wilson
Richard Dazzle	Christopher Evan Welch
Sir Harcourt Courtly	Brian Bedford
Max Harkaway	David Schramm
Mr. Solomon Isaacs	Andrew Weems
Grace Harkaway	Kathryn Meisle
Pert	Rita Pietropinto
Mark Meddle	John Christopher Jones
James	Matthew Schneck
Lady Gay Spanker	Helen Carey
Mr. Adolphus Spanker	Ken Jennings

UNDERSTUDIES: Andrew Weems (Spanker/Dazzle/Meddle), Robert Neill (Courtly), Matthew Schneck (Martin/Isaacs), Victoria Beavan (Grace/Pert)

A new production of a 1841 five-act comedy, performed with one intermission. The action takes place in London and Gloucestershire, 1841.

Variety tallied 9 favorable, 2 mixed and 2 negative reviews. *Times* (Marks): "...the comic performance of the season..by that master thespian, Brian Bedford, who plays the preening, lascivious, utterly adorable Sir Harcourt Courtly.." *News* (Kissel): "...has prospered for a century and a half not because of its literary merits..or its social commentary..but because it provides delicious roles." *Post* (Barnes): "What a deliriously happy if rickety English classic.." *Variety* (Evans): "..a comic performance of the most assured kind."

*Closed June 22, 1997 after 88 performances and 16 previews.

Carol Rosegg Photos

Brian Bedford

Brian Bedford, Helen Carey

THE WIZARD OF OZ

Music, Harold Arlen; Lyrics, E.Y. Harburg; Book, John Kane; Adapted from the 1939 MGM film screenplay; Based on the novel by L. Frank Baum; Director/Adaptation, Robert Johanson; Orchestrations, Larry Wilcox; Choreography, Larry Wilcox; Music Director, Jeff Rizzo; Sets, Michael Anania; Costumes, Gregg Barnes; Lighting, Tim Hunter; Sound, David R. Paterson; General Manager, Geoffrey Merrill Cohen; Production Supervisor, Bob Murphy; Stage Manager, Lori K. Powell; Producer, Tim Hawkins; Presented by Madison Square Garden Productions; Press, Cathy Del Priore/Beth Hergenhan; Previewed from Wednesday, May 7; Opened in The Theater at Madison Square Garden on Thursday, May 15, 1997*

CAST

Dorothy Gale ....Jessica Grove
Toto ....Plenty
Aunt Em/Glinda...Judith McCauley
Uncle Henry/Winkie General ....Roger Preston Smith
ScarecrowHunk ....Lara Teeter
Tinman/Hickory ....Michael Gruber
Cowardly Lion/Zeke...Ken Page
Wicked Witch of the West/Almira Gulch...................................Roseanne
Prof. Marvel/Wizard..Gerry Vichi
Mayor of Munchkinland ....Louis Carry
Barristers..Wendy Coates, Jonas Moscartolo
Coroner...Derrick McGinty
Nikko ....Martin Klebba
Munchkins/Citizen of Oz/Flying Monkees.................Vivian V. Bayubay,
    Maggie Keenan Bolger, Patrick Boyd, Kai Braithwaite, Lindsy
    Canuel, Casey Colgan, Christine DeVito, Chantele M. Doucette,
    Peter William Dunn, Danielle Lee Greaves, Gail Cook Howell,
    Heidi Karol Johnson, Martin Klebba, Benjamin E. Lear, Don
    Mayo, M. Kathryn Quinlan, Gemini Quintos, D.J. Salisbury, Dana
    Scarborough, Samantha Sensale, Evan Silverberg, Andrea Szucs,
        Christopher Trousdale, Wendy Watts
SWINGS: ....Lenny Daniel, Jamie Waggoner
Children's Choirs...............Oceanside Oaks School #3, Brooklyn P.S.312,
        Queens P.S. 95, Scotch Plains NJ Terrill Middle School
UNDERSTUDIES: Patrick Boyd (Hickory/Tinman), Casey Colgan (Hunk/Scarecrow), Lenny Daniel (Henry/Winkie), Danielle Lee Greaves (Witch/Gulch), Gail Cook Howell (Em/Glinda), Don Mayo (Zeke/Lion/Marvel/Wizard), M. Kathryn Quinlan (Dorothy), Roger Preston Smith (Marvel/Wizard)

MUSICAL NUMBERS: Over the Rainbow, Cyclone, Come Out Come Out, Ding Dong the Witch is Dead, Follow the Yellow Brick Road, If I Only Had a Brian/Heart/the Nerve, We're Off to See the Wizard, Lions Tigers and Bears, Poppies/Optimistic Voices, Merry Old Land of Oz, King of the Forest, March of the Winkies, Finale

A stage adaptation of the 1939 film musical performed without intermission.

Times (Marks): "...wan facsimile is such a disservice to the original.."
News (Kissel): "...merchandise is likely to be the most tangible thing people take away from this production.." *Post* (Barnes): "And Roseanne? Well, unaccustomed as she is to stage appearances, she did very well, indeed." *Variety* (Evans): "...surprisingly chintzy..Rushed, truncated.."

*Closed June 8, 1997 after 45 performances and 15 previews.

+Succeeded by: 1. Danielle Lee Greaves during illness.
Joan Marcus, George Kalinsky Photos

Roseanne

Munchkins meet Dorothy

Lara Teeter, Jessica Grove, Michael Gruber, Ken Page, Roseanne

Stephen Bogardus, Alice Ripley, Peter Samuel, Marcus Lovett, Roger Bart, Judy Kuhn, Martin Vidnovic

KING DAVID

Music, Alan Menken; Lyrics/Book, Tim Rice; Director, Mike Ockrent; Orchestrations, Douglas Besterman; Musical Director/Vocal Arrangements, Michael Kosarin; Set, Tony Walton; Costumes, William Ivey Long; Lighting, David Agress; Sound, Jonathan Deans; Cast Recording, Buena Vista; Company Manager, Ken Silverman; Stage Managers, Alan Hall, Jim Woolley, Karen Potosnak; Co-Producer, Ritza B. Barath; Presented by Walt Disney Theatrical Productions and Andre Djaoui; Press, Chris Boneau~Adrian Bryan-Brown/Miguel Tuason, Patrick Paris, Patty Onagan; Previewed from Thursday, May 15; Opened in the New Amsterdam Theatre on Sunday, May 18, 1997*

CAST

David	Marcus Lovett
Bathsheba	Alice Ripley
Young Solomon	Daniel James Hodd
Joab	Stephen Bogardus
Samuel	Peter Samuel
Saul	Martin Vidnovic
Agag	Timothy Robert Blevins
Jesse	Michael Goz
Abner	Timothy Shew
Jonathan	Roger Bart
Michal	Judy Kuhn
Goliath	Bill Nolte
Young Absalom	Dylan Lovett
Absalom	Anthony Galde
Uriah	Peter C. Ermides
Abishag	Kimberly JaJuan

ENSEMBLE: Mark Agnes, Joan Barber, Stephanie Bast, Robin Baxter, Kristen Behrendt, Timothy Robert Blevins, Benjamin Breecher, Timothy Breese, Kristi Carnahan, Nick Cavarra, Philip A. Chaffin, Michael DeVries, Peter C. Ermides, Hunter Foster, Ray Friedeck, Anthony Galde, Michael Goz, Ellen Hoffman, Kimberly JaJuan, James Javore, Keith Byron Kirk, Ann Kittredge, David Lowenstein, Barbara Marineau, Donna Lee Marshall, Michael X. Martin, Karen Murphy, Bill Nolte, Ilysia Pierce, Ron Sharpe, Timothy Shew, Rachel Ulanet, Andrew Varela, Melanie Vaughn, Sally Wilfert, Laurie Williamson

UNDERSTUDIES: Peter C. Ermides (David), Kristen Behrendt (Bathsheba), Dominick Carbone (Young Solomon/Young Absalom), Michael DeVries (Joab/Samuel), Michael X. Martin (Saul), Hunter Foster (Jonathan/Absalom), Rachel Ulanet (Michal), Michael Goz (Goliath), Timothy Robert Blevins (Absalom)

MUSICAL NUMBERS: Prologue, Israel and Saul, Samuel Confronts Saul, Samuel Anoints David, The Enemy Within, There Is a View, Psalm 8, Genius from Bethlehem, Valley of Elah, Goliath of Gath, Sheer Perfection, Saul Has Slain His Thousands, You Have It All, Psalm 23, You Have It All/Sheer, Perfection, Hunted Partridge on the Hill, Death of Saul, How Are the Mighty Fallen, This New Jerusalem, David & Michal, The Ark Brought to Jerusalem, Never Again, How Wonderful the Peace, Off Limits, Warm Spring Night, When in Love, Uriah's Fate Sealed, Atonement, Caravan Moves On, Death of Absalom, Absalom My Absalom, Solomon, David's Final Hours, The Long Long Day, Finale

A two-act concert musical telling the story of the shepard boy who became King of Israel. This production re-opened the magnificent New Amsterdam Theatre, built in 1903 and now restored to its original splendor., The last legitimate production to play the main auditorium was Othello (1937) and the palace spent many years as a movie theatre before closing in 1982.

Times (Brantley): "...could actually do with a little more cheese..sober, respectful, packed with enough information for a month of Bible-study classes..." *News* (Kissel): "...earnest and ambitious but unexciting." *Post* (Barnes): "Marcus Lovett plays David with a furtive charm and stronggish voice, and even better singing comes from Martin Vidnovic..and an impassive Peter Samuel..big-time emoting comes from Judy Kuhn..." *Variety* (Evans): "Perhaps reverence is best left at the alter..showcases Menken's first-rate abilities as a pop craftsman..."

*Closed May 23, 1997 after limited run of 6 performances and 3 previews.

Joan Marcus Photos

ENCORES!: GREAT AMERICAN MUSICALS IN CONCERT

Fourth Season

Artistic Director, Kathleen Marshall; Musical Director, Rob Fisher;
Orchestra, The Cofee Club Orchestra; Sets, John Lee Beatty; Sound,
Bruce Cameron; Casting, Jay Binder; Producer, Judith E. Daykin

SWEET ADELINE

Music, Jerome Kern; Lyrics/Book, Oscar Hammerstein II; Adaptation,
Norman Allen; Director, Eric D. Schaeffer; Orchestrations, Robert Russell
Bennett; Lighting, Howell Binkley; Costumes, Gregg Barnes; Choreography, John DeLuca; Stage Manager, Clayton Phillips; Press, Philip Rinaldi;
Presented in City Center Thursday, February 13-16, 1997 (5 performances)

CAST

Dot ....Kristi Lynes
Emil Schmidt ....MacIntyre Dixon
Addie ....Patti Cohenour
Nellie ....Jacquelyn Piro
Lulu Ward ....Dorothy Loudon
Dan Ward...Gary Beach
Tom Martin...Hugh Panaro
Ruppert Day ....Patrick Breen
James Day ....Stephen Bogardus
Sid Barnett ....Steven Goldstein
Sultan ....Timothy Robert Blevins
Eddie ....Timothy Breese
Hester Van Doren Day..Myra Carter
Willie Day..Tony Randall
Dancers... ....Shannon Lewis, Alexandre Proia
ENSEMBLE... ......Anne Allgood, Vanessa Ayers, Jamie Baer, Christopher
Eaton Bailey, Kira Burke, Philip Chaffin, Lisa Ericksen, Peter Flynn,
John Halmi, Marc Heller, Damon Kirschenmann, Robert Osborne, Alet
Oury, Frank Ream, Margaret Shaffer, Eric van Hoven
MUSICAL NUMBERS: Overture Fin de Siecle, Play Us a Polka Dot,
"Twas Not So Long Ago, My Husband's First Wife, Her Am I, First Mate
Martin, Spring Is Here, Out of the Blue, Naughty Boy, Oriental Moon,
Mollie O'Donahue, Why Was I Born?, I've Got a New Idea, The Sun
About to Rise, Pretty Jennie Lee, Some Girl Is on Your Mind, Don't Ever
Leave Me, Indestructible Kate, Finaletto, Finale

A staged concert of a 1929 musical in two acts. The action takes place
in Hoboken, NJ, San Juan Hill, Cuba and New York City, 1898.

Stephen Bogardus, Patti Cohenour in Sweet Adeline

Dorothy Loudon

PROMISES, PROMISES

Music, Burt Bacharach; Lyrics, Hal David; Book/Adaptation, Neil Simon; Based on Billy Wilder's 1960 film The Apartment; Director/Choreography, Rob Marshall; Orchestrations, Jonathan Tunick; Lighting, Peggy Eisenhauer; Costumes, William Ivey Long; Stage Manager, Peter Hanson; Presented in City Center Thursday, March 20-23, 1997 (5 performances)

CAST

Chuck Baxter ....Martin Short
J.D. Sheldrake ....Terrence Mann
Fran Kubelik..Kerry O'Malley
Bartender Eddie ....Sean Martin Hingston
Mr. Dobitch...Eugene Levy
Sylvia Gilhooley...Mary Ann Lamb
Mr. Kirkeby ....Samuel E. Wright
Ginger Wong ....Cynthia Onrubia
Mr. Eichelberger ....Joe Grifasi
Vivien Della Hoya ....Carol Lee Meadows
Dr. Dreyfuss...Dick Latessa
Mr. Vanderhof ....Ralph Byers
Dentist's Nurse ....Kimberly Lyon
Company Nurse...Jill Matson
Company Doctor...Lloyd Culbreath
Peggy Olson...Jenifer Lewis
Lum Ding Hostess ....Tara Nicole
Waiter..Harrison Beal
Madison Square Garden Attendant............................Vince Pesce
Bartender Eugene..Sergio Trujillo
Marge MacDougall...Christine Baranski
Kark Kubelik...Mike O'Malley
Employee/Bar Patron ....Raymond Radriguez
Orchestra Voices... ....La Tanya Hall, Amy Jane London,
....Monica Pege, Kimberlee Wertz
MUSICAL NUMBERS: Overture, Half as Big as Life, Grapes of Roth, Upstairs, You'll Think of Someone, Our Little Secret, She Likes Basketball, Knowing When to Leave, Where Can You Take a Girl?, Wanting Things, You've Got It All Wrong, Turkey Lurkey Time, Entr'acte, A Fact Can Be a Beautiful Thing, Whoever You Are, Christmas Day, A Young Pretty Girl Like You, I'll Never Fall in Love Again, Promises Promises

A staged concert of a 1968 musical in two acts. The action takes place in New York City, 1968. For original Broadway production with Jerry Orbach, see *Theatre World* Vol.25.

Sarah Uriarte Berry, Rebecca Luker, Debbie Gravitte in *Boys from Syracuse*

Martin Short, Christine Baranski in *Promises Promises*

THE BOYS FROM SYRACUSE

Music, Richard Rodgers; Lyrics, Lorenz Hart; Book, George Abbott; Adaptation, David Ives; Based on *The Comedy of Errors* by William Shakespeare; Director, Susan H. Schulman; Orchestration, Hans Spialek; Choreography, Kathleen Marshall; Lighting, Peter Kaczorowski; Costumes, Toni-Leslie James; Cast Recording, DRG; Stage Manager, Peter Hanson; Presented in City Center Thursday, May 1-4, 1997 (5 performances)

CAST

Police Sergeant...Patrick Quinn
Duke of Ephesus ....Allen Fitzpatrick
Corporal...John Wilkerson
Dromio of Ephesus ....Michael McGrath
Antipholus of Ephesus ....Malcolm Gets
Tailor/Merchant of Ephesus................................Danny Burstein
Antipholus of Syracuse ....David Gaines
Dromio of Syracuse ....Mario Cantone
Merchant of Syracuse/Sorceror ....Kevin Ligon
Luce ....Debbie Gravitte
Adriana..Rebecca Luker
Luciana ....Sarah Uriarte Berry
Courtesan..Julie Halston
Fatima, Secretary to Courtesan ....Rachel Jones
Angelo the Goldsmith...Mel Johnson Jr.
Seeress...Marian Seldes
Aegeon..Tom Aldredge
Ladies of the Ensemble.... ....Rebecca Eichenberger, Susan Emerson,
....Rachel Jones, Sheryl McCallum, Alet Oury
Dancers... ....Sean Grant, Sean Martin Hingston, Darren Lee,
....Lisa Mayer, Carol Lee Meadows, Amiee Turner
MUSICAL NUMBERS: Overture, I Had Twins, Dear Old Syracuse, What Can You Do with a Man, Falling in Love with Love, Shortest Day of the Year, This Can't Be Love, Let Antipholus In, Entr'acte, Ladies of the Evening, He and She, You Have Cast Your Shadow on the Sea, Come with Me, Big Brother, Twins Ballet, Sing for Your Supper, Oh Diogenes, Finale

A staged concert of a 1938 musical comedy in two acts. The action takes place in Ancient Greece.

Gerry Goodstein Photos

BROADWAY PRODUCTIONS FROM PAST SEASONS THAT PLAYED THROUGH THIS SEASON

BEAUTY AND THE BEAST

Music, Alan Menken; Lyrics, Howard Ashman, Tim Rice; Book, Linda Woolverton; Director, Robert Jess Roth; Orchestrations, Danny Troob; Musical Supervision/Vocal Arrangements, David Friedman; Musical Director/Incidental Arrangements, Michael Kosarin; Choreography, Matt West; Sets, Stan Meyer; Costumes, Ann Hould-Ward; Lighting, Natasha Katz; Sound, T. Richard Fitzgerald; Hairstylist, David H. Lawrence; Illusions, Jim Steinmeyer, John Gaughan; Prosthetics, John Dods; Fights, Rick Sordelet; Cast Recording, Walt Disney Records; General Manager, Dodger Productions; Production Supervisor, Jeremiah J. Harris; Company Manager, Kim Sellon; Stage Managers, James Harker, John M. Atherlay, Pat Sosnow, Kim Vernace; Presented by Walt Disney Productions; Press, Chris Boneau/Adrian Bryan-Brown, Patty Onagan, Brian Moore, Michael Tuason; Previewed from Wednesday, March 9, 1994; Opened in the Palace Theatre on Monday, April 18, 1994*

CAST

Enchantress ....Wendy Oliver
Young Prince...Tom Pardoe
Beast...Jeff McCarthy +1
Belle ....Kerry Butler
Lefou...Harrison Deal
Gaston...Marc Kudisch
Three Silly Girls ....Lauren Goler-Kosarin, Pam Klinger,
                                                                       Linda Talcott Lee
Maurice ....Tim Jerome
Cogsworth...Gibby Brand
Lumiere ....Gary Beach
Babette..Pamela Winslow
Mrs. Potts ....Beth Fowler
Chip ....Andrew Keenen-Bolger, Joseph DiConcetto
Madame de la Grande Bouche.......................................Eleanor Glockner
Monsieur D'Arque ....Gordon Stanley
Townspeople/Enchanted Objects ....Anna Maria Andricain, Steven Ted
  Beckler, Kevin Berdini, Andrea Burns, Christophe Caballero, Sally Mae
  Dunn, Barbara Folts, Teri Furr, Gregory Garrison, Elmore James, Alisa
  Klein, Lauren Goler-Kosarin, Ellen Hoffman, Pam Klinger, Ken Mc-
  Mullen, Anna McNeely, Beth McVey, Bill Nabel, Wendy Oliver, Tom
  Pardoe, Raymond Sage, Joseph Savant, Sarah Solie Shannon, Matthew
  Shepard, Steven Sofia, Gordon Stanley, Linda Talcott Lee, David A.
                                                                       Wood, Wysandria Woolsey
Prologue Narrator ....David Ogden Stiers

MUSICAL NUMBERS: Overture, Prologue (Enchantress), Belle, No Matter What, Me, Home, Gaston, How Long Must This Go On?, Be Our Guest, If I Can't Love Her, Entr'acte/Wolf Chase, Something There, Human Again, Maison des Lunes, Beauty and the Beast, Mob Song, The Battle, Transformation, Finale

A musical in two acts. An expanded, live action version of the 1991 animated film musical with additional songs. Winner of 1994 "Tony" for Best Costume Design.

*Still playing May 31, 1997.

+Succeeded by: 1. Chuck Wagner, James Barbour

(Joan Marcus/Marc Bryan-Brown/Walt Disney Theatrical Photos)

James Barbour

The Company

BRING IN 'DA NOISE
BRING IN 'DA FUNK

Conceived/Directed by George C. Wolfe; Choreography, Savion Glover; Based on an idea by Mr. Glover and Mr. Wolfe; Music, Daryl Waters, Zane Mark, Ann Duquesnay; Book, Reg E. Gaines; Sets, Riccardo Hernandez; Costumes, Paul Tazewell; Lighting, Jules Fisher, Peggy Eisenhauer; Musical Supervision/Orchestration, Daryl Waters; Musical Director, Zane Mark; Vocal Arrangements, Ann Duquesnay; Cast Recording, RCA; Production Manager, Bonnie Metzgar; Stage Manager, Bonnie Panson; Presented by the Joseph Papp Public Theatre/New York Shakespeare Festival (George C. Wolfe, Producer); Press, Carol Fineman, Thomas Naro, Bill Coyle; Previewed from Tuesday, April 9, 1996; Opened in the Ambassador Theatre on Thursday, April 25, 1996*

CAST

Savion Glover	Baakari Wilder	Jimmy Tate
Vincent Bingham +1	Jeffrey Wright	Ann Duquesnay
Jared Crawford	Raymond King	Dule Hill

UNDERSTUDIES/STANDBYS: Baakari Wilder (for Mr. Glover), Lynette G. DuPre (For Ms. Duquesnay), Mark Gerald Douglas (For Mr. Wright), Dule Hill (for Mr. Wilder), Omar A. Edwards, Derick K. Grant, Joseph Monroe Webb (For Mr. Bingham, Mr. Hill, Mr. Tate, Mr. Wilder), David Peter Chapman (for Mr. Crawford, Mr. King)

PROGRAM: IN 'DA BEGINNING: Bring in 'da Noise Bring in 'da Funk, Door to Isle Goree, Slave Ships, SOM'THIN' FROM NUTHIN': Som'thin' from Nuthin'/Circle Stomp, Pan Handlers, URBANIZATION: Lynching Blues, Chicago Bound, Shifting Sounds, Industrialization, Chicago Riot Rag, I Got the Beat/Dark Tower, Whirligig Stomp, WHERE'S THE BEAT?: Now That's Tap, Uncle Huck-a-buck Song, Kid Go!, Lost Beat Swing, Green Chaney Buster Slyde, STREET CORNER SYMPHONY: 1956-Them Conkheads, 1967-Hot Fun, 1977-Blackout, 1987-Gospel/Hip Hop Rant, NOISE/FUNK: Drummin', Taxi, Conversations, Hittin', Finale

A dance musical in two acts telling the story, through tap, of black history from slavery to the present. Winner of 1996 "Tony" Awards for Direction of a Musical, Best Choreography, Featured Actress in a Musical (Ann Duquesnay) and Best Lighting Design.

Closed January 10, 1999 after 1,130 performances and 18 previews.

+Succeeded by:1. Omar A. Edwards

Michal Daniel Photos

Top: Raymond King, Jared Crawford

Center: (Back) Jared Crawford, Savion Glover

Right: Jimmy Tate, Savion Glover, Baakari Wilder, Vincent Bingham

Nadine Isenegger

CATS

Music, Andrew Lloyd Webber; Based on *Old Possum's Book Of Practical Cats* by T.S. Eliot; Orchestrations, David Cullen, Lloyd Webber; Prod. Musical Director, David Caddick; Musical Directors, Edward G. Robinson, Patrick Vaccariello; Sound, Martin Levan; Lighting, David Hersey; Design, John Napier; Choreography/Associate Director, Gillian Lynne; Director, Trevor Nunn; Cast Recording, Polydor; Casting, Johnson-Liff Associates; Company Manager, James G. Mennen; Stage Managers, Peggy Peterson, Tom Taylor, Suzanne Viverito; Executive Producers, R. Tyler Gatchell, Jr., Peter Neufeld; Presented by Cameron Mackintosh, The Really Useful Co., David Geffen, and The Shubert Organization; Press, Fred Nathan/Michael Borowski; Opened in the Winter Garden Theatre on Thursday, October 7, 1982*

CAST

Alonzo	Hans Kriefall
Bustopher/Asparagus/Growltiger	Richard Poole
Bombalurina	Marlene Danielle
Cassandra	Ida Gilliams +1
Coricopat	Steve Ochoa +2
Demeter	Emily Hsu
Grizabella	Liz Callaway
Jellylorum/Griddlebone	Nina Hennessey
Jennanydots	Carol Dilley
Mistoffelees	Jacob Brent
Mungojerrie	Roger Kachel
Munkustrap	Michael Gruber +3
Old Deuteronomy	Ken Prymus
Plato/Macivity/Rumpus Cat	Jaymes Hodges +4
Pouncival	Christopher Gattelli
Rum Tum Tiger	Ron DeVito +5
Rumpleteazer	Maria Jo Ralabate
Sillabub	Alaine Kashian
Skimbleshanks	Eric Scott Kincaid
Tantomile	Jill Nicklaus
Tumblebrutus	Randy Bettis
Victoria	Nadine Isenegger
Cat Chorus	Joel Briel, Susan Powers, Peter Samuel, Heidi Stallings

STANDBYS/UNDERSTUDIES: Jon Paul Christensen, Michael Ehlers, Matthew J. Vargo, Joel Briel, Peter Samuel, Angel Caban, Ida Gilliams, Lynn Sterling, Amy Splitt, Rusty Mowery, Jonathan Taylor, Jill Nicklaus, Heidi Stallings, Sally Ann Swarm, Carol Dilley, Susan Powers, Suzanne Viverito, Christopher Gattelli, Roger Kachel, Steve Ochoa, Hans Kriefall, Alaine Kashian

MUSICAL NUMBERS: Jellicle Songs for Jellicle Cats, Naming of Cats, Invitation to the Jellicle Ball, Old Gumbie Cat, Rum Tum Tugger,Grizabella the Glamour Cat, Bustopher Jones, Mungojerrie and Rumpleteazer, Old Deuteronomy, Aweful Battle of the Pekes and Pollicles, Jellicle Ball, Memory, Moments of Happiness, Gus the Theatre Cat, Growltiger's Last Stand, Skimbleshanks, Macavity, Mr. Mistoffolees, Journey to the Heavyside Layer, Ad-dressing of Cats

A musical in two acts with 20 scenes.

*Still playing May 31, 1997. The production clebrated its fourteenth birthday during the season and has now played more than 6000 performances. Winner of 1983 "Tonys" for Best Musical, Score, Book, Direction, Costumes, Lighting, and Featured Actress in a Musical (Betty Buckley as Grizabella). For original 1982 production see *Theatre World* Vol.39.
  +Succeeded by: 1. Meg Gillentine 2. Billy Johnson 3. Matt Farnsworth 4.Karl Wahl, Philip Michael Baskerville 5. Abe Sylvia

Carol Rosegg Photos

Above and Center: The Company

The Company

A CHRISTMAS CAROL

Music, Alan Menken; Lyrics, Lynn Ahrens; Book, Mike Ockrent, Lynn Ahrens; Based on the story by Charles Dickens; Director, Mike Ockrent; Choreography, Susan Stroman; Orchestrations, Michael Starobin; Musical Director, Paul Gemignani; Sets, Tony Walton; Costumes, William Ivey Long; Lighting, Jules Fisher, Peggy Eisenhauer; Sound, Tony Meola; Projections, Wendall K. Harrington; Flying by Foy; Dance Arrangements, Glen Kelly; Cast Recording, Columbia; Production Supervisor, Gene O'Donovan; Company Manager, Steven H. David; Stage Managers, Steven Zweigbaum, Clifford Schwartz; Producers, Dodger Productions/ Michael David, Edward Strong, Sherman Warner; Presented by American Express and Madison Square Garden; Press, Cathy Del Priore; Original Production opened in the Paramount Theatre on Thursday, December 1, 1994; Seasonal re-opening in the Paramount Theatre on Friday, November 22, 1996*

CAST

Scrooge	Tony Randall
Ghost of Christmas Present	Ben Vereen
Bob Cratchit	Nick Corley
Ghost of Christmas Past	Ken Jennings
Ghost of Jacob Marley	Paul Kandel
Mr. Smythe	James Judy
Mrs. Cratchit	Robin Baxter
Fred	Greg Zerkle
Fezziwig	Ray Friedeck
Mrs. Fezziwig	Joy Hermalyn
Scrooge's Mother/Blind Hag	Joan Barber
Scrooge's Father/Undertaker	Michael X. Martin
Mrs. Mops	Corinne Melancon
Emily	Emily Skinner
Scrooge at 18	Michael Moore
Ghost of Christmas Future	Valentina Kozlova
Young Marley	Ken Barnett
Sally	Whitney Webster

Scrooge at 12	Matthew Hoffman, Christopher Mark Petrizzo
Scrooge at 8	Zachary Stefan Petkanas, Evan Silverberg
Fan at 6/Want	Gemini Quintos, Diana Mary Rice
Fan at 10	Eliza Atkins Clark, Elizabeth Lundberg
Jonathon	Jason Fuchs, Evan J. Newman
Grace Smythe	Jennifer Blain, Cara Horner
Judge	Michael H. Ingram
Tiny Tim	Matthew Ballinger, Pierce Cravens
Old Joe/Hawkins	Don Mayo
Fiddler	Brad Bradley
Charity Men	Michael H. Ingram, Keith Byron Kirk, Seth Malkin
Urchins	Matthew Hoffman, Christopher Mark Petrizzo, Zachary Stefan Petkanas, Gemini Quintos, Diana Mary Rice, Evan Silverberg
Ensemble	Matthew Baker, Joan Barber, Ken Barnett, Robin Baxter, Leslie Bell, Carol Bentley, Brad Bradley, Betsy Chang, Eliza Atkins Clark, Candy Cook, Rosa Curry, Christopher F. Davis, Ray Friedeck, Peter Gregus, Jeffrey Hankinson, Joy Hermalyn, Michael H. Ingram, James Judy, Louisa Kendrick, Carrie Kenneally, Keith Byron Kirk, David Lowenstein, Elizabeth Lundberg, Jason Ma, Seth Malkin, Donna Lee Marshall, Michael X. Martin, Donna Lynn Mauro, Don Mayo, Elizabeth Mills, Corinnr Melancon, Michael Moore, Sean Thomas Morrissey, Adam Pelty, Gail Pennington, Christopher Mark Petrizzo, Angela Picinni, Pamela Remler, Samuel Reni, David Rosales, Emily Skinner, Whitney Webster, Greg Zerkle

MUSICAL NUMBERS: A Jolly Good Time, Nothing to Do With Me, You Mean More to Me, Street Song, Link By Link, Lights of Long Ago, God Bless Us Everyone, A Place Called Home, Mr. Fezziwig's Annual Christmas Ball, Abundance and Charity, Christmas Together, Dancing on Your Grave, Yesterday Tomorrow and Today, London Town Carol, Final Medley

A musical performed without intermission. The action takes place in London, 1880.

*Closed January 5, 1997 after seasonal run of 90 performances.
George Kalinsky Photos

Michael Chiklis

DEFENDING THE CAVEMAN

By Rob Becker; Music, R.B. & Michael Barrow; Company Manager, Todd Grove; Stage Manager, Jason Lindhorst; Presented by Contemporary Productions; Press, Merle Frimark and Marc Thibodeau/Erin Dunn, Colleen Brown; Previewed from Wednesday, March 1, 1995; Opened in the Helen Hayes Theatre on Sunday, March 26, 1995*, Transferred to the Booth Theatre Wednesday, January 29, 1997

CAST

ROB BECKER succeeded by MICHAEL CHIKLIS

A one-man comedy performed without intermission.

*Closed June 21, 1997 after 645 performances and 26 previews. Show was on hiatus between Jan.5-28, 1997.
Joan Marcus Photos

Rob Becker

A FUNNY THING HAPPENED ON THE WAY TO THE FORUM

Music/Lyrics, Stephen Sondheim; Book, Burt Shevelove and Larry Gelbart; Director, Jerry Zaks; Choreography, Rob Marshall; Orchestrations, Jonathan Tunick; Musical Supervision, Edward Strauss; Set/Costumes, Tony Walton; Dance Arrangements, David Chase; Hairstylist, David H. Lawrence; Cast Recording, Broadway Angel; Production Manager, Peter Fulbright; General Management, Dodger Productions; Company Manager, Marcia Goldberg; Stage Managers, Arthur Gaffin, Michael Pule; Presented by Jujamcyn Theatres, Scott Rudin/Paramount Pictures, Viertel-Baruch-Frankel Group, Roger Berlind, and Dodger Productions; Press, Chris Boneau~Adrian Bryan-Brown/Jackie Green, Susanne Tighe, Amy Jacobs, Stephen Pitalo, Stefanie Kastel; Previewed from Monday, March 18,1996; Opened in the St. James Theatre on Thursday, April 18, 1996*

CAST

Prologus(an actor)/Pseudolus	Nathan Lane +1
Proteans	Brad Aspel, Cory English, Ray Roderick
Hero	Jim Stanek
Philia	Jessica Boevers
Senex	Lewis J. Stadlen +2
Domina	Mary Testa
Hysterium	Mark Linn-Baker +3
Lycus	Ernie Sabella +4
Tintinabula	Pamela Everett
Panacea	Leigh Zimmerman +5
The Geminae	Susan Misner +6, Lori Werner
Vibrata	Mary Ann Lamb +7
Gymnasia	Stephenie Pope +8
Erronius	William Duell
Miles Gloriosus	Cris Groenendaal

UNDERSTUDIES: Bob Amaral (Psedolus/Hysterium/Lycus), Cory English, Kevin Kraft (Hero), Jennifer Rosin (Philia), Macintyre Dixon (Senex/Erronius), Kenneth Kantor (Senex/Miles/Lycus/Pseudolus), Ruth Gottschall (Domina), Patrick Garner (Hysterium/Lycus/Erronius),Kristin Willits (Vibrata), Holly Cruikshank, Leigh Zimmerman (Gymnasia), David Rogers (Senex) SWINGS: Michael Arnold, Shannon Hammons, Kevin Kraft, George Smyros, Aimee Turner, Kristin Willits

MUSICAL NUMBERS: Comedy Tonight, Love I Hear, Free, House of Marcus Lycus, Lovely, Everybody Ought to have a Maid, I'm Calm, Impossible, Bring Me My Bride, That Dirty Old Man, That'll Show Him, Funeral Sequence, Finale NOTE: Production omits Pretty Little Picture.

A new production of the 1962 musical in two acts. The action takes place on a street in Rome, 200 years before the Christian era. Winner of 1996 "Tony" Award for Leading Actor in a Musical (Nathan Lane). For original Bdwy production with Zero Mostel see *Theatre World* Vol.18. For 1972 revival with Phil Silvers see *Theatre World* Vol.28.

*Closed January 4, 1998 after 715 performances and 35 previews,

+Succeeded by: 1.Whoopi Goldberg, David Alan Grier 2. Dick Latessa, Robert Fitch 3. Ross Lehman 4. Bob Amaral 5. Holly Cruikshank 6. Tara Nicole 7. Pascale Faye, Carol Lee Mreadows 8. Kena Tangi Dorsey

Joan Marcus Photos

Whoopi Goldberg

David Alan Grier, Ross Lehman, Ernie Sabella, Dick Latessa

Joley Fisher

Susan Moniz, Jon Secada

GREASE

Music/Lyrics/Book by Jim Jacobs and Warren Casey; Director /Choreography, Jeff Calhoun; Orchestrations, Steve Margoshes; Musical Director/Vocal and Dance Arrangements, John McDaniel; Musical Coordinator, John Monaco; Sets, John Arnone; Costumes, Willa Kim; Lighting, Howell Binkley; Hairstylist, Patrik D. Moreton; Sound, Tom Morse; Associate Choreographer, Jerry Mitchell; Cast Recordings, RCA; General Manager, Charlotte W. Wilcox; Casting, Stuart Howard, Amy Schecter; Company Manager, Barbara Darwall; Stage Managers, Craig Jacobs, David Hyslop; Presented in associated with PACE Theatrical Group, TV Asahi; The Tommy Tune Production presented by Barry & Fran Weissler, Jujamcyn Theatres; Press, Pete Sanders/Ian Rand, Bruce Laurienzo, Meredith Oritt; Previewed from Saturday, April 23, 1994; Opened in the Eugene O'Neill Theatre on Wednesday, May 11, 1994*

CAST

Vince Fontaine	Joe Piscopo +1
Miss Lynch	Sally Struthers +2
Sonny Latierri	Carlos Lopez
Kenickie	Steve Geyer
Frenchy	Alisa Klein
Doody	Ric Ryder
Danny Zuko	Jon Secada +3
Marty	Deirdre O'Neill
Roger	Hunter Foster
Jan	Marissa Janet Winokur
Betty Rizzo	Joley Fisher +4
Sandy Dumbrowski	Susan Moniz +5
Patti Simcox	Dominique Dawes
Eugene Florczyk	Paul Castree
Straight A's	Clay Adkins, Brad Aspel, Paul Castree, Denny Tarver
Dream Mooners	Brad Aspel, Katy Grenfell
Heartbeats	Katy Grenfell, Janice Lorraine Holt, Lorna Shane
Cha-Cha Degregorio	Jennifer Cody
Teen Angel	Chubby Checker +6
Ensemble	Clay Adkins, Brad Aspel,

Gregory Cunneen, Jeff Edgerton, Katy Grenfell, Janice Lorraine Holt, Allison Metcalf, Connie Ogden, Lorna Shane, Denny Tarver

A new production of the 1972 musical in two acts with 13 scenes. The action takes place in and around Rydell High, 1950s. For original Broadway production see *Theatre World* Vol. 29. Over Thanksgiving Weekend (Nov.29-Dec.1, 1996), the national touring company headed by Peter Scolari and Jasmine Guy played 5 performances at City Center while the Bdwy company continued at the O'Neill Theatre.

*Closed January 25, 1998 after 1,503 performances and 20 previews.

+Succeeded by: 1. Brian Bradley, Nick Santa Maria, Dave Konig, Jeff Conaway 2. Mimi Hines, Marilyn Cooper 3. Jeff Trachta, Joseph Barbara, Vincent Tumeo, Sean McDermott 4. Tia Riebling, Susan Moniz, Jody Watley, Debbie Boone, Sheena Easton, Mackenzie Phillips, Tracy Nelson, Jasmine Guy, Angela Pupello 5. Lacy Hornkohl, Kelli Severson, Melissa Dye 6. Kevin-Anthony, Lee Truesdale, Darlene Love

Carol Rosegg, Craig Schwartz Photos

Lou Diamond Phillips, Faith Prince

THE KING AND I

Music, Richard Rodgers; Lyrics/Book, Oscar Hammerstein II; Director, Christopher Renshaw; Original Choreography, Jerome Robbins; Musical Staging, Lar Lubovitch; Musical Director, Michael Rafter; Musical Supervision, Eric Stern; Orchestrations, (original) Robert Russell Bennett, (new) Bruce Coughlin; Sets, Brian Thomson; Costumes, Roger Kirk; Lighting, Nigel Levings; Sound, Tony Meola, Lewis Mead; Hairstylist, David H. Lawrence; General Manager, David Strong Warner; Company Manager, Sandra Carlson; Stage Managers, Frank Hartenstein, Karen Armstrong; Presented by Dodger Productions, John F. Kennedy Center for the Performing Arts, James M. Nederlander, Perseus Productions with John Frost and the Adelaide Festival Centre in association with The Rodgers and Hammerstein Organization; Press, Chris Boneau~Adrian Bryan-Brown/Susanne Tighe, Cindy Valk; Previewed from Tuesday, March 19, 1996; Opened in the Neil Simon Theatre on Thursday, April 11, 1996*

CAST

Capt. Orton ....John Curless
Louis Leonowens..Ryan Hopkins +1
Anna Leonowens...Donna Murphy +2
Interpreter..Alan Muraoka
The Kralahome ....Randall Duk Kim
King of Siam ....Lou Diamond Phillips
Lun Tha ....Jose Llana
Tuptim...Joohee Choi +3
Lady Thiang ....Taewon Kim
Prince Chulalongkorn ....John Chang +4
Fan Dancer...Kelly Jordan Bit
Princess Yaowlak...Lexine Bondoc
Sir Edward Ramsey...Guy Paul
Royal Wives/Slaves/Guards/Guests.................Tito Abeleda, John Bantay,
Kristine Bendul, Camille M. Brown, Benjamin Bryant,
Meng-Chen Chang, Kam Cheng, Vivien Eng, Lydia Gaston,
Margaret Ann Gates, C. Sean Kim, Shawn Ku, Michael Lomeka,
Doan Mackenzie, Mary McGuiness, Paolo Montalban, Alan Muraoka,
Paul Nakauchi, Tina Ou, Andrew Pacho, Rommel V. Pacson,
Mami Saito, Lainie Sakakura, Khamla Somphanh, Carol To,
Yolanda Tolentino, Tran T. Thuc Hanh, Christine Yasunaga, Yan Ying,
Kayoko Yoshioka, Greg Zane, Zhang Zhenjun
Royal Children...............Kelly Jordan Bit, Lexine Bondoc, Kailip Boonrai,
Travis Feretic, Stephanie La, Jacqueline Te Lem, Erik Lin-Greenberg,
Cristina Matoto, Kenji Miyata, Brandon Marshall Ngai, Amy Y. Tai,
Jenna Noelle Ushkowitz, Shelby Rebecca Wong, Jeff G. Yalun

Small House of Uncle Thomas Ballet:
Eliza ....Yan YIng
Simon of Legree ....Tito Abeleda
Angel George...Meng-Chen Chang
Little Eva ....Tran T. Thuc Hanh
Topsy ....Tina Ou, Christine Yasunaga
Uncle Thomas...Mami Saito
Dogs ....Doan Mackenzie, Greg Zane, Zhang Zhenjun
Guards.......................Michael Lomeka, C. Sean Kim, Rommel V. Pacson
Propmen...................Benjamin Bryant, Paolo Montalban, Alan Muraoka,
Paul Nakuuchi
Archers... ....Kristine Bendul, Camille M. Brown, Vivien Eng,
Khamla Somphanh
Singers... .....Kam Cheng, Mary McGuinness, Carol To, Yolanda Tolentino
STANDBYS/UNDERSTUDIES: Raul Aranas, Paul Nakauchi (King), Barbara McCulloh, Kay McClelland, (Anna), Paul Nakauchi (King/Kralahome), Benjamin Bryant, Paolo Montalban (Lun Tha), Alan Muraoka (Kralahome), John Curless (Ramsey), Kam Chneg, Carol To (Tuptim), Jonathan Giordano (Louis), Guy Paul (Orton), Lydia Gaston, Yolanda Tolentino (Lady Thiang) SWINGS: Mr. Giordano, Devanand N. Janki, Susan Kikuchi, Joan Tsao

MUSICAL NUMBERS: Overture (shortened), I Whistle a Happy Tune, Royal Dance Before the King, My Lord and Master, Hello Young Lovers, March of the Siamese Children, A Puzzlement, Getting to Know You, We Kiss in a Shadow, Shall I Tell You What I Think of You?, Something Wonderful, I Have Dreamed, Small House of Uncle Thomas, Song of the King, Shall We Dance, Procession of the White Elephant, Finale, NOTE: Western People Funny cut during previews; Production also omits the Price/Louis "Puzzlement" duet.

A new production of the 1951 musical in two acts. The action takes place at the Royal Palace in Bangkok, 1860s. Winner of 1996 "Tony" Awards for Revival of a Musical, Leading Actress in a Musical (Donna Murphy), Best Scenic Design and Best Costume Design. For original Bdwy production with You Brynner and Gertrude Lawrence see *Theatre World* Vol.7.

*Closed February 22, 1998 after 807 performances and 27 previews.

+Succeeded by: 1. Matthew Ballinger 2. Faith Prince 3. Cornilla Luna, Johee Choi 4. R.J. Remo

Joan Marcus Photos

LES MISERABLES

By Alain Boublil and Claude-Michel Schonberg; Based on the novel by Victor Hugo; Music, Mr. Schonberg; Lyrics, Herbert Kretzmer; Original French Text, Mr. Boublil and Jean-Marc Natel; Additional Material, James Fenton; Direction/Adaptation, Trevor Nunn and John Caird; Orchestral Score, John Cameron; Musical Supervisor/Director, Dale Rieling; Design, John Napier; Lighting, David Hersey; Costumes, Andreane Neofitou; Casting, Johnson-Liff & Zerman; Cast Recording, Geffen; General Manager, Alan Wasser; Company Manager, Robert Nolan; Stage Managers, Marybeth Abel, Greg N. Kirsopp, Bryan Landrine; Executive Producer, Martin McCallum; Presented by Cameron Mackintosh; Press, Marc Thibodeau/Merle Frimark; Previewed from Saturday, February 28, 1987; Opened in the Broadway Theatre on Thursday, March 12, 1987* and moved to the Imperial Theatre on October 16, 1990.

CAST

PROLOGUE: Robert Evan +1(Jean Valjean), David Masenheimer +2 (Javert), Gary Moss, Robert Gallagher, Tom Zemon, Adam Hunter, Scott Hunt, John Capes, Stephen R. Buntrock, Peter Lockyer, Nick Wyman (Chain Gang), John Capes (Farmer), Kurt Kovalenko (Labourer), Ann Arvia (Innkeeper's Wife), Jeffrey Scott Watkins (Innkeeper), David McDonald (Bishop), Kipp Marcus, Peter Gunter (Constables)

MONTREUIL-SUR-MER 1823: Florence Lacey +3 (Fantine), Robert Gallagher (Foreman), Jeffry Scott Watkins, Scott Hunt (Workers), Dana Meller, Erika MacLeod, Gina Lamparella, Alexandra Foucard, Megan Lawrence (Women Workers), Alicia Irving (Factory Girl), Adam Hunter, Gary Moss, Scott Hunt (Sailors), Ann Arvia, Erika MacLeod, Alexandra Foucard, Megan Lawrence, Dana Meller, Alicia Irving, Sarah Uriarte Berry, Christeena Michelle Riggs (Whores), Madeleine Doherty (Old Woman), Gina Lamparella (Crone), Peter Gunther (Pimp), Tom Zemon (Bamatabois), Jeffrey Scott Watkins (Fauchelevent), Gary Moss (Champmathieu)

MONTFERMEIL 1823: Alexis Kalehoff, Alicia Morton, Kimberly Hannon, Hana Kitasei (Young Cosette/Young Eponine), Tregoney Shepherd +4 (Mme. Thenardier), Drew Eshelman +5 (Thenardier), Mr. Watkins (Drinker), Mr. Hunter, Ms. Foucard (Young Couple), Kipp Marcus (Drunk), David McDonald, Ms. MacLeod (Diners), Mr. Capes, Mr. Gunther, Mr. Zemon (Drinkers), Mr. Moss (Young Man), Ms. Meller, Ms. Lamprella (Young Girls), Ms. Lawrence, Mr. Hunt (Old Couple), Mr. Gallagher, Mr. Kovalenko (Travelers)

PARIS 1832: Christopher Trousdale, Alex Strange, Jordan Siwek, Evan Jay Newman (Gavroche), Ms. Doherty (Beggar Woman), Ms. Meller (Young Prostitute), Mr. Gallagher (Pimp), Christina Michelle Riggs +6 (Eponine), Mr. McDonald (Montparnasse), Mr. Kovalenko (Babet), Mr. Moss (Brujon), Mr. Capes (Claquesous), Gary Mauer +7 (Enjolras), Ricky Martin +8 (Marius), Tamra Hayden +9 (Cosette), Mr. Gallagher (Combeferre), Mr. Hunter (Feuilly), Mr. Watkins (Courfeyrac), Mr. Hunt (Joly), Mr. Zemon (Grantaire), Mr. Gunther (Lesgles), Mr. Marcus (Jean Prouvaire)

UNDERSTUDIES: Gary Moss, Ivan Rutherford (Valjean), Robert Gallagher, Tom Zemon (Javert), Gregory Brandt, Dave Hugo, Jeffrey Scott Watkins (Bishop), Alexandra Foucard, Alicia Irving, Erika MacLeod (Fantine), John Capes, David McDonald (Thenardier), Ann Ariva, Madeleine Doherty (Mme. Thenardier), Megan Lawrence, Dana Meller, Gina Lamparella (Eponine/Cosette), Scott Hunt, Kipp Marcus (Marius), Peter Gunther, Kurt Kovalenko (Enjolras) SWINGS: Greggory Brandt, Angel DeCicco, Dave Hugo, Cathy Nichols

Florence Lacey

MUSICAL NUMBERS: Prologue, Soliloquy, At the End of the Day, I Dreamed a Dream, Lovely Ladies, Who Am I?, Come to Me, Castle on a Cloud, Master of the House, Thenardier Waltz, Look Down, Stars, Red and Black, Do You Hear the People Sing?, In My Life, A Heart Full of Love, One Day More, On My Own, A Little Fall of Rain, Drink with Me to Days Gone By, Bring Him Home, Dog Eats Dog, Soliloquy, Turning, Empty Chairs at Empty Tables, Wedding Chorale, Beggars at the Feast, Finale

A dramatic musical in two acts with four scenes and prologue.

*Still playing May 31, 1997. A tenth anniversary company began performances March 6, 1997. Winner of 1987 "Tonys" for Best Musical, Best Score, Best Book, Best Featured Actor and Actress in a Musical (Michael Maguire, Frances Ruffelle), Direction of a Musical, Scenic Design and Lighting.
+ Succeeded by: 1. Ivan Rutherford, Robert Marien 2. Christopher Innvar 3. Juliet Lambert 4. Ann Arvia, Fuschia Walker 5. Nick Wyman 6. Sarah Uriarte Berry 7. Paul Avedisian, Stephen R. Buntrock 8. Tom Donoghue, Peter Lockyer 9. Jennifer Lee Andrews, Christeena Michelle Riggs

Joan Marcus Photos

Left: Ricky Martin

MASTER CLASS

By Terrence McNally; Director, Leonard Foglia; Set, Michael McGarty; Costumes, Jane Greenwood; Lighting, Brian MacDevitt; Sound, Jon Gottlieb; Musical Supervisor, David Loud; General Manager, Stuart Thompson; Company Manager, Bruce Klinger; Stage Managers, Dianne Trulock, Linda Barnes; Presented by Robert Whitehead & Lewis Allen and Spring Sirkin; Press, Bill Evans/Jim Randolph, Terry M. Lilly, Tom D'Ambrosio; Previewed from Tuesday, October 26; Opened in the Golden Theatre on Sunday, November 5, 1995*

CAST

Manny ....Gary Green +1
Maria Callas ....Patti LuPone +2
Sophie ....Theodora Fried
Stagehand ....Michael Friel +3
Sharon ....Helen Goldsby +4
Tony ....Jay Hunter Morris +5
UNDERSTUDIES: Lorraine Goodman (Sophie/Sharon), David Loud, Darren Motise (Manny), Matthew Walley (Stagehand/Tony).

A drama in two acts. The setting is a master class as soprano Maria Callas teaches young aspiring opera singers. Winner of the 1996 "Tony" Awards for Best Play, Leading Actress in a Play (Zoe Caldwell) and Featured Actress in a Play (Audra McDonald).

*Closed June 28, 1997 after 601 performances and 12 previews.

+Succeeded by: 1. David Loud, Gerald Steichen 2. Dixie Carter 3. Wally Dunn 4. Alaine Rodin-Lo 5. Matthew Walley

Joan Marcus Photos

Dixie Carter

Patti LuPone

MISS SAIGON

Music, Claude-Michel Schonberg; Lyrics, Richard Maltby, Jr., Alain Boublil; Adapted from Boublil's French Lyrics; Book, Mr. Boublil, Mr. Schonberg; Additional Material, Mr. Maltby, Jr.; Director, Nicholas Hytner; Musical Staging, Bob Avian; Orchestrations, William D. Brohn; Musical Supervisors, David Caddick, Robert Billig; Associate Director, Mitchell Lemsky; Design, John Napier; Lighting, David Hersey; Costumes, Andreane Neofitou, Suzy Benzinger; Sound, Andrew Bruce; Conductor, Edward G. Robinson; Stage Managers, Tom Capps, Sherry Cohen, Beerly Jenkins; Cast Recording (London), Geffen; Presented by Cameron Mackintosh; Press, Publicity Office/Marc Thibodeau/Merle Frimark~Dennis Crowley, Colleen Hughes; Previewed from Saturday, March 23, 1991; Opened in the Broadway Theatre on Thursday, April 11, 1991*

CAST

SAIGON - 1975
The Engineer..Joseph Anthony Foronda +1
Kim ....Joan Almedilla, Roxanne Taga, Elizabeth Paw
Gigi...Emily Hsu
Mimi...Zoie Lam
Yvette..Ai Goeku
Yvonne..Johanna Tacadena
Bar Girls ....Sekiya Billman, Frances Calma, Michelle Nigalan, Elizabeth Paw, Lisa Yuen
Chris...Tyley Ross +2
John ....Norm Lewis
Marines ......Donnell Aarone, Frank Baiocchi, Ronald Cadet Bastine, Erik Bates, Tony Capone, Andrew Driscoll, Steve Geary, Norman Wendall Kauahi, Jeff Reid, Roger Seyer, Stephen Tewksbury, Robert Weber, Frank Wright II
Barmen ....Alan Ariano, Eric Chang, Ming Lee
Vietnamese Customers ....Darrell Autor, Francis J. Cruz, Thomas C. Kouo, Juan P. Pineda, Glenn Sabalza, Ray Santos
Army Nurse..Andrea Rivette
Thuy ....Michael K. Lee
Embassy Workers, Vendors, etc..Company

HO CHI MINH CITY (Formerly Saigon)-April 1978
Ellen...Anastasia Barzee
Tam...................................Ambrose Eng, Thi Kim Thu Nguyen
Guards ....Mr. Cruz, Mr. Pineda
Dragon Acrobats ....Mr. Autor, Mr. Geary, Mr. Weber
Asst. Commissar ....Mr. Chan
Soldiers ....Mr. Ariano, Mr. Kauahi, Mr. Kouo, Mr. Sabalza, Mr. Santos
Citizens, Refugees ....Company

USA - September 1978
Conference Delegates ....Company

BANGKOK - October 1978
Hustlers ....Mr. Chan, Mr. Kauahi, Mr. Kouo, Mr. Sabalza, Mr. Santos
Moulin Rouge Owner ....Mr. Cruz
Inhabitants, Bar Girls, Vendors, Tourists.....................................Company

Luoyong Wang

Joan Almedilla, Tyley Ross

SAIGON - April 1975
Shultz ....Stephen Tewksbury
Doc ....Erik Bates
Reeves ....Tony Capone
Gibbons ....Ronald Cadet Bastine
Troy ....Frank Wright II
Nolen...Donnell Aarone
Huston..Andrew Driscoll
Frye..Frank Baiocchi
Marines, Vietnamese...Company

BANGKOK - October 1978
Inhabitants, Moulin Rouge Customers ....Company

UNDERSTUDIES: Norman Wendall Kauahi, Ming Lee, Ray Santos (Engineer), Michelle Nigalan, Elizabeth Paw (Kim), Frank Baiocchi, Erik Bates, Tony Capone (Chris), Donnell Aarone, Frank Wright II (John), Ai Goeku, Andrea Rivette (Ellen), Thomas C. Kouo, Juan P. Pineda (Thuy)

SWINGS: Karl Christian, Sylvia Dohi, Samuel T. Gerongco, Tina Horil, Leonard Joseph, Howard Kaye, Jason Ma, Marc Oka, Blake Riley, Todd Zamarripa

MUSICAL NUMBERS: The Heat is on in Saigon, Movie in My Mind, The Transaction, Why God Why?, Sun and Moon, The Telephone, The Ceremony, Last Night of the World, Morning of the Dragon, I Still Believe, Back in Town, You Will Not Touch Him, If You Want to Die in Bed, I'd Give My Life for You, Bui-Doi, What a Waste, Please, Guilt Inside Your Head, Room 317, Now That I've Seen Her, Confrontation, The American Dream, Little God of My Heart

A musical in two acts. The action takes place in Saigon, Bangkok, and the USA between 1975-79. *Still playing May 31, 1997. Winner of 1991 "Tonys" for Leading Actor in a Musical (Jonathan Pryce), Leading Actress in a Musical (Lea Salonga) and Featured Actor in a Musical (Hinton Battle).

+ Succeeded by: 1. Luoyong Wang 2. Matt Bogart

Joan Marcus Photos

64

THE PHANTOM OF THE OPERA

Music, Andrew Lloyd Webber; Lyrics, Charles Hart; Additional Lyrics, Richard Stilgoe; Book, Mr. Stilgoe, Mr. Lloyd Webber; Director, Harold Prince; Musical Staging/Choreography, Gillian Lynne; Orchestrations, David Cullen, Mr. Lloyd Webber; Based on the novel by Gaston Leroux; Design, Maria Bjornson; Lighting, Andrew Bridge; Sound, Martin Levan; Musical Direction/Supervision, David Caddick; Conductor, Jack Gaughan; Cast Recording (London), Polygram/Polydor; Casting, Johnson-Liff & Zerman; General Manager, Alan Wasser; Company Manager, Michael Gill; Stage Managers, Steve McCorkle, Bethe Ward, Richard Hester, Barbara-Mae Phillips; Presented by Cameron Mackintosh and The Really Useful Theatre Co.; Press, Merle Frimark, Marc Thibodeau; Previewed from Saturday, January 9, 1988; Opened in the Majestic Theatre on Tuesday, January 26, 1988*

CAST

The Phantom of the Opera ....Davis Gaines +1
Christine Daae..Tracy Shayne
          Laurie Gayle Stephenson, Teri Bibb (alternates)
Raoul, Vicomte de Chagny ....Brad Little +2
Carlotta Giudicelli ....Elena Jeanne Batman
Monsieur Andre..Jeff Keller
Monsieur Firmin...George Lee Andrews
Madame Giry ....Leila Martin
Ubaldo Piangi ....Frederic Heringes
Meg Giry ....Tener Brown
M. Rever ....Thomas James O'Leary
Auctioneer..Richard Warren Pugh
Porter/Marksman..Gary Lindemann
M. Lefevre...Kenneth Waller
Joseph Buquet...Philip Steele
Don Attilio/Passarino ....Peter Atherton
Slave Master/Solo Dancer ....Thomas Terry
Flunky/Stagehand..Jack Hayes
Policeman..Thomas Sandri
Page..Patrice Pickering
Porter/Fireman ....Maurizio Corbino
Spanish Lady..............................Marci DeGonge-Manfredi
Wardrobe Mistress/Confidante ....Mary Leigh Stahl
Princess...Raissa Katona
Madame Firmin ....Melody Johnson
Innkeeper's Wife ....Teresa Eldh
Ballet Chorus of the Opera Populaire ....Harriet M. Clark,
    Alina Hernandez, Cherylyn Jones, Lori MacPherson,
    Tania Philip, Kate Solmssen, Christine Spizzo
UNDERSTUDIES: Jeff Keller (Phantom), Raissa Katona, Laurie Gayle Stephenson (Christine), Gary Lindemann, James Romick (Raoul), Peter Atherton, Paul Laureano (Firmin), Richard Warren Pugh (Firmin/Piangi), George Lee Andrews, James Thomas O' Leary,Mr. Romick (Andre), Marcy DeGonge-Manfredi, Teresa Eldh, Melody Johnson (Carlotta), Patrice Pickering, Mary Leigh Stahl (Giry), Maurizio Corbino (Piangi), Cherilyn Jones, Kate Solmssen, Lori MacPherson (Meg), Thomas Terry (Master) Paul B. Sadler, Jr. (Dancer)

Right: Thomas James O'Leary

MUSICAL NUMBERS: Think of Me, Angel of Music, Little Lotte/The Mirror, Phantom of the Opera, Music of the Night, I Remember/Stranger Than You Dreamt It, Magical Lasso, Notes/Prima Donna, Poor Fool He Makes Me Laugh, Why Have You Brought Me Here?/ Raoul I've Been There, All I Ask of You, Masquerade/Why So Silent?, Twisted Every Way, Wishing You Were Somehow Here Again, Wandering Child/Bravo Bravo, Point of No Return, Down Once More/Track Down This Murderer, Finale

    A musical in two acts with nineteen scenes and a prologue. The action takes place in and around the Paris Opera house, 1881-1911.

* Still playing May 31, 1997. This production celebrated its ninth anniversary (3,777 performances) during this season. Winner of 1988 "Tonys" for Best Musical, Leading Actor in a Musical (Michael Crawford), Featured Actress in a Musical (Judy Kaye), Direction of a Musical, Scenic Design and Lighting. The title role has been played by Michael Crawford, Timothy Nolen, Cris Groendaal, Steve Barton, Jeff Keller, Kevin Gray, Marc Jacoby, Marcus Lovett, Davis Gaines and Thomas J. O'Leary.
+Succeeded by: 1. Thomas James O'Leary 2. Gary Mauer

Joan Marcus/Clive Barda Photos

RENT

Music/Lyrics/Book by Jonathan Larson; Director, Michael Greif; Arrangements, Steve Skinner; Muiscal Supervision/Additional Arrangements, Tim Weill; Choreography, Marlies Yearby; Original Concept/Additional Lyrics, Billy Aronson; Set, Paul Clay; Costumes, Angela Wendt; Lighting, Blake Burba; Sound, Kurt Fischer; Cast Recording, Dreamworks; General Management, Emanuel Azenberg, John Corker; Stage Managers, John Vivian, Crystal Huntington; Presented by Jeffrey Seller, Kevin McCollum, Allan S. Gordon, and New York Theatre Workshop; Press, Richard Kornberg/Don Summa, Ian Rand; Previewed from Tuesday, April 16, 1996; Opened in the Nederlander Theatre on Monday, April 29, 1996*

CAST

Mark Cohen	Anthony Rapp
Roger Davis	Adam Pascal
Tom Collins	Jesse L. Martin
Benjamin Coffin III	Taye Diggs
Joanne Jefferson	Fredi Walker
Angel Schunard	Wilson Jermaine Heredia
Mimi Marquez	Daphne Rubin-Vega +1
Maureen Johnson	Idina Menzel
Mark's Mom/Alison/Others	Kristen Lee Kelly
Christmas Caroler/Mr. Jefferson/Pastor/ Others	Byron Utley
Mrs. Jefferson/Woman with Bags/Others	Gwen Stewart
Gordon/The Man/Mr. Grey/Others	Timothy Britten Parker
Man with Squeegee/Waiter/Others	Gilles Chiasson
Paul/Cop/Others	Rodney Hicks
Alexi Darling/Roger's Mom/Others	Aiko Nakasone

UNDERSTUDIES: Gilles Chiasson, David Driver (Roger/Mark), Darius de Haas (Tom/Benjamin/Angel), Byron Utley (Tom), Rodney Hicks (Benjamin), Shelly Dickinson (Joanne), Simone (Joanne/Mimi), Mark Setlock (Angel), Yassmin Alers (Mimi/Maureen), Kristen Lee Kelly (Maureen) SWINGS: Ms. Allers, Mr. de Haas, Ms. Dickinson, Mr. Driver, Mr. Setlock, Simone

MUSICAL NUMBERS: Tune Up, Voice Mail (#1-#5), Rent, You Okay Honey?, One Song Glory, Light My Candle, Today 4 U, You'll See, Tango: Maureen, Life Support, Out Tonight, Another Day, Will I?, On the Street, Santa Fe, We're Okay, I'll Cover You, Christmas Bells, Over the Moon, La Vie Boheme/I Should Tell You, Seasons of Love, Happy New Year, Take Me or Leave Me, Without You, Contact, Halloween, Goodbye Love, What You Own, Finale/Your Eyes

A musical in two acts. The action takes place in New York City's East Village. Winner of 1996 "Tony" Awards for Best Musical, Best Original Score, Best Book of a Musical and Featured Actor in a Musical (Wilson Jermaine Heredia). Tragedy occured when the 35 year old author, Jonathan Larson, died of an aortic aneurysm after watching the final dress rehearsal of his show January 24, 1996.

*Still playing May 31, 1997.

+Succeeded by: 1. Marcy Harriel

Joan Marcus/Carol Rosegg Photos

**Top: Adam Pascal, Daphne Rubin-Vega
Center: Wilson Jermaine Heredia, Jesse L. Martin, Anthony Rapp
Left: Fredi Walker, Wilson Jermaine Heredia, Idina Menzel, Jesse L. Martin**

Adrian Bailey, Ken Ard, Victor Trent Cook, Frederick B. Owens

SMOKEY JOE'S CAFE

Music/Lyrics, Jerry Leiber and Mike Stoller; Director, Jerry Zaks; Musical Staging, Joey McKneely; Orchestrations, Steve Margoshes; Conductor/Arranger, Louis St. Louis; Music Coordinator, John Miller; Sets, Heidi Landesman; Costumes, William Ivey Long; Lighting, Timothy Hunter; Sound, Tony Meola; Hair/Make-up, Randy Houston Mercer; Production Supervisor, Steven Beckler; Production Manager, Peter Fulbright; Original Concept, Stephen Helper, Jack Viertel; Cast Recording, Atlantic; General Management, Richard Frankel; Company Manager, Laura Green; Stage Managers, Kenneth Hanson, Maximo Torres; Presented by Richard Frankel, Thomas Viertel, Steven Baruch, Jujamcyn Theatres/Jack Viertel, Rick Steiner, Frederic H. Mayerson and Center Theatre Group/Ahmanson/Gordon Davidson; Press, Chris Boneau/Adrian Bryan-Brown, Jackie Green, Patty Onagan, Meredith Moore, Ari Cohn, Scott Walton; Previewed from Wednesday, February 8,1995; Opened in the Virginia Theatre on Thursday, March 2, 1995*

CAST

Ken Ard	Adrian Baile	Brenda Braxton
D'Atra Hicks +1	Pattie Darcy Jones	Robert Neary
Frederick B. Owens	Billy Porter	Natasha Rennalls +2

STANDBYS: David Bedella, Bobby Daye, Cee-Cee Harshaw, Stacy Francis, J. C. Montgomer, Felicia Finley

MUSICAL NUMBERS: Neighborhood, Young Blood, Falling, Ruby baby, Dance with Me, Keep on Rollin', Searchin', Kansas City, Trouble, Love Me/Don't, Fools Fall in Love, Poison Ivy, Don Juan, Shoppin' for Clothes, I Keep Forgettin', On Broadway, D.W. Washburn, Saved, That is Rock & Roll, Yakety Yak, Charlie Brown, Stay a While, Pearl's a Singer, Teach Me How to Shimmy, You're the Boss, Smokey Joe's Cafe, Loving You, Treat Me Nice, Hound Dog, Little Egypt, I'm a Woman, There Goes My Baby, Love Potion #9, Some Cats Know, Jailhouse Rock, Fools Fall in Love, Spanish Harlem, I Who Have Nothing, Stand By Me, Finale

A musical revue in two acts.

*Still playing May 31, 1997.
+Succeeded by: 1. B.J. Crosby 2. Paige Price, DeLee Lively, Natasha Rennalls

Joan Marcus Photos

Brenda Braxton, B.J. Crosby, DeLee Lively, Pattie Darcy Jones

SUNSET BLVD.

Music, Andrew Lloyd Webber; Lyrics/Book, Don Black and Christopher Hampton; Based on the 1950 Billy Wilder film; Director, Trevor Nunn; Musical Staging, Bob Avian; Orchestrations, David Cullen, Lloyd Webber; Musical Supervision, David Caddick; Musical Director, Paul Bogaev; Design, John Napier; Costumes, Anthony Powell; Lighting, Andrew Bridge; Sound, Martin Levan; Cast Recording, Polydor; Production Supervisor, Peter Lawrence; Technical, Peter Feller, Arthur Siccardi; General Manager, Nina Lannan; Company Manager, Abbie M. Strassler; Stage Managers, Peter Lawrence, John Brigleb, Jim Woolley, Lynda J. Fox; Presented by The Really Useful Company; Press, Chris Boneau/Adrian Bryan-Brown/John Barlow; Previewed from Tuesday, November 1, 1994; Opened in the Minskoff Theatre on Thursday, November 17, 1994*

CAST

Norma Desmond	Elaine Paige
Joe Gillis	Alan Campbell
Max von Mayerling	George Hearn
Betty Schaefer	Alice Ripley
Cecil B. DeMille	Rod Loomis
Artie Green	Jordan Leeds
Harem Girl/Beautician	Lada Boder
Young Writer/Salesman/DeMilles's Asst.	John Scherer +1
Heather/2nd Masseuse	Susan Dawn Carson +2
Cliff/Salesman/Young Guard	Jim Newman +3
Jean/Beautician/Hedy Lamarr	Angie L. Schworer +4
Morino/Salesman/Hog Eye	Steven Stein-Grainer
Lisa/Doctor	Jane Bodle +5
1st Financeman/Film Actor/Salesman	Rich Herbert +6
Katherine/Psychiatrist	Alicia Irving +7
Harem Girl/Beautician	Lada Boder
Mary/1st Masseuse	Jennifer West
Sheldrake/Police Chief	Sal Mistretta
John/Salesman/Victor Mature	Mark Morales
Myron/Manfred	Dale Hensley
Financeman/Salesman/Party Guest	Tom Alan Robbins +8
Jonesy/Sammy/Salesman	James Dybas
Choreographer/Salesman	Dan O'Grady
Joanna/Astrologer	Wendy Walter

Elaine Paige

Karen Mason

STANDBYS/UNDERSTUDIES: Karen Mason (Norma), Susan Dawn Carson, Maureen Moore, Alisa Endsley (Norma), John Scherer (Joe), Jim Newman (Joe/Artie), Bruce Alan Johnson, Jordan Leeds, Matthew Dickens (Joe), Jane Bodle, Jennifer West, Kristen Behrendt (Betty), Rich Herbert (Max), Steven Stein-Grainger(Max/DeMille), James Dybas (DeMille/Sheldrake), Darrin Baker (Artie), Peter Kapetan (Sheldrake/Manfred), John Hoshko (Male Roles), Jennifer Stetor, Colleen Sudduth, Darlene Wilson (Female Roles)

MUSICAL NUMBERS: Overture, Prologue, Let's Have Lunch, Surrender, With One Look, Salome, The Greatest Star of All, Every Movie's a Circus, Girl Meets Boy, New Ways to Dream, The Lady's Paying, The Perfect Year, This Time Next Year, Sunset Boulevard, As If We Never Said Goodbye, Eternal Youth Is Worth a Little Suffering, Too Much in Love to Care, Finale

A musical in two acts. The action takes place in Los Angeles, 1949-50.

*Closed March 22, 1997 after 977 performances and 17 previews.
Succeeded by: 1. Bruce Alan Johnson 2. Alisa Endsley 3. Matthew Dickens 4. Lisa Mandel 5. Kristen Behrendt 6. Larry Small 7. Danielle Lee Greaves 8. Stephen Breithaupt

Donald Cooper, Joan Marcus Photos

VICTOR/VICTORIA

Music, Henry Mancini, Frank Wildhorn; Lyrics, Leslie Bricusse; Book/Direction, Blake Edwards; Choreography, Rob Marshall; Orchestrations, Billy Byers; Musical Director/Vocal Arrangements, Ian Fraser; Sets, Robin Wagner; Costumes, Willa Kim; Lighting, Jules Fisher, Peggy Eisenhauer; Sound, Peter Fitzgerald; Dance/Incidental Music, David Krane; Fights, B.H. Barry; Hairstylist, Michaeljohn; Cast Recording, Philips; Production Supervisor, Arthur Siccardi; General Manager, Niko Associates; Company Manager, Erich Hamner; Stage Managers, Arturo E. Porazzi, Bonnie L. Becker; Presented by Blake Edwards, Tony Adams, John Scher, Endemol Theatre Productions and Polygram Broadway Ventures; Press, Peter Cromarty/Hugh Hayes, Bill Klemm; Previewed from Tuesday, October 3, 1995; Opened in the Marquis Theatre on Wednesday, October 25, 1995*

Julie Andrews

CAST

Carroll Todd	Tony Roberts
Les Boys	Bill Burns, Michael-Demby Cain, Angelo Fraboni, Darren Lee, Peter Lentz, Gregory Mitchell, Michael O'Donnell, Vince Pesce, Arte Phillips
Simone Kalisto	Leslie Stevens
Richard Di Nardo	Michael Cripe
Cosmetic President/Miss Selmer	Cynthia Sophiea
Deviant Husband/Sal Andretti	Ken Land
Henri Labisse	Adam Heller
Gregor/Juke	Mason Roberts
Madame Roget/Hillella the Balloon Buffoon	Linda Gabler Romoff
Victoria Grant	Julie Andrews +1
Choreographer	Neal Benari
Andre Cassell	Richard B. Shull
Jazz Singer	Todd Hunter
Jazz Hot Musicians	Michael-Demby Cain, Arte Phillips, Bill Burns, Gregory Mitchell
Norma Cassidy	Rachel York +2
King Marchan	Michael Nouri
Squash (Mr. Bernstein)	Gregory Jbara +3
Street Singer	Tara O'Brien +4
Norma's Girls	Roxanne Barlow, Christiane Farr-Wersinger, Kimberly Lyon, Cynthia Onrubia, Aixa M. Rosario Medina, Leslie Stevens, Susan Taylor
Clam	Tom Sardinia +5

UNDERSTUDIES/STANDBY: Anne Runolfsson, Tara O'Brien (Victoria), Ken Land (Todd), Neal Benari (King/Sal), Roxane Barlow, Kimberly Lyon (Norma), Tom Sardinia, George Dudley (Squash/Cassell), Mason Roberts (Henri), Angelo Fraboni, Michael O'Donnell (Richard), Michael-Demby Cain (Jazz Singer), Linda Gabler Romoff (Street Singer) SWINGS: Robert M. Armitage, Robert Ashford, Joanne Manning, Elizabeth Mozer

MUSICAL NUMBERS: Overture, Paris By Night, If I Were a Man (shortened during run), Trust Me, Le Jazz Hot, The Tango, Paris Makes Me Horny, Crazy World (Andrews only), Who Can I Tell? (Minnelli, Welch), Louis Says (cut during run), King's Dilemma, Apache, You & Me, Almost a Love Song, Chicago Illinois, Living in the Shadows, Victor Victoria DURING TRYOUT: This Is Not Going to Change My Life, The Victoria Variations (I've No Idea Where I'm Going), Someone Else, Attitude, I Guess It's Time, I Know Where I'm Going

A musical comedy in two acts. The action takes place in Paris and Chicago.

Liza Minnelli

+Succeeded by: 1. Anne Runolfsson during illness, Liza Minnelli, Raquel Welch 2. Tara O'Brien 3. Tom Sardinia 4. Sally Ann Tumas 5. George Dudley

*Closed July 27, 1997 after 734 performances and 25 previews .
Carol Rosegg, Joan Marcus Photos

Tony Roberts, Raquel Welch

THE FANTASTICKS

Music, Harvey Schmidt; Lyrics/Book, Tom Jones; Director, Word Baker; Original Musical Director/Arrangements, Julian Stein; Design, Ed Wittstein; Musical Director, Dorothy Martin; Stage Managers, Kim Moore, James Cook, Steven Michael Daly, Christopher Scott; Presented by Lore Noto; Associate Producers, Sheldon Baron, Dorothy Olim, Jules Field, Cast Recording, MGM/Polydor; Opened in the Sullivan Street Playhouse on Tuesday, May 3, 1960*

CAST

The Boy ....Eric Meyersfield
The Girl...Christine Long +1
The Girl's Father ....William Tost
The Boy's Father..Gordon G. Jones
Narrator/El Gallo ....John Savarese +2
Mute ....Paul Blankenship
Old Actor ....Bryan Hull
Man Who Dies...Joel Bernstein
MUSICAL NUMBERS: Overture, Try to Remember, Much More, Metaphor, Never Say No, It Depends on What You Pay, Soon It's Gonna Rain, Abduction Ballet, Happy Ending, This Plumb is Too Ripe, I Can See It, Plant a Radish, Round and Round, They Were You, Finale

A musical in two acts suggested by *Les Romanesques* by Edmond Rostand.

*Still playing May 31, 1997. The world's longest running musical marked its 15,000th performance during this season.
Succeeded by: 1. Sarah Schmidt 2. Christopher Councill

Chuck Pulin Photo

John Savarese, Eric Meyersfield, Christine Long

Right: A Recent Cast: Lisa Mayer, Josh Miller

FORBIDDEN BROADWAY
STRIKES BACK

Created/Written/Directed by Gerard Alessandrini; Costumes, Alvin Colt; Sets, Bradley Kaye; Wigs, Robert Fama; Musical Director, Matthew Ward; Choreography, Phillip George; Consultant, Pete Blue; General Manager, Jay Kingwell; Stage Manager, Alex Lyu Volckhausen; Presented by John Freedson, Harriet Yellin, Jon B. Platt; Press, Pete Sanders/Glenna Freedman, Michael Hartman; This edition previewed from Thursday, September 5; Opened in the Triad Theatre on Wednesday, October 16, 1996*

CAST

Bryan Batt   Donna English
David Hibbard   Christine Pedi
                    Matthew Ward
UNDERSTUDIES: Whitney Allen, Phillip George, William Selby

PROGRAM INCLUDES: Parodt Tonight, Slowboat, Cameron Mackintosh, Big, Once Upon an Actress, So Miscast, The King Is Her, Disney, Patti Class, Miss Saigon, Grease, Michael Crawford, Stop Cats, Ethel Merman & Alan Campbell, Chicago, Tommy Tune/Da Savion Glover, Kiss Me Again Kate, Julie Andrews: Le Julie Hot, Spoonful of Julie, Tony Committee, Crazy Girl, Rant: Ouch, Too Gay 4 U, Think Punk, Seasons of Hype, This Ain't Boheme, Death and Resurrection, Grand Finale/Something Wonderful, Ta Ta Folks

Performed in two acts. This season's edition of the parody revue whose first edition originated at this theatre (then called Palssons) January 15, 1982.

Carol Rosegg Photos

David Hibbard, Donna English

Bryan Batt, Donna English, Edward Staudenmayer

Donna English, Bryan Batt, David Hibbard, Christine Pedi

GRANDMA SYLVIA'S FUNERAL

Conceived by Glenn Wein and Amy Lord Blumsack; Created by Wein, Blumsack and the original company; Director, Mr. Wein; Design, Leon Munier; Lighting, David J. Lander; Costumes, Peter Janis; Choreography, Joanna Rush; Stage Manager, Margaret Bodriguian; Press, John and Gary Springer/Sharon Rothe; Opened at the Playhouse on Vandam on Sunday, October 2, 1994*

CAST

Dave Schildner ....Paul Eagle
Rabbi Michael Wolfe ....David Ellzey, Bill Kraus
Elise Duey ....Holgie Forrester
Jerry Grossman ....Ron Gilbert
Dori Grossman ....Karen Ginsburg
Marlena Weiss Grossman ....Mary Wilson
Helen Krantz ....Sondra Gorney
Ava Gerard ....Brooke Johnson
Mark Grossman ....Marc Kamhi
Vlad Helsenrott...Morgan Lavere
Dr. Rachel Rosenbaum ....Simone Lazer
Melinda Franklin ....Janice Mautner
Dr. Byron Franklin ....Brocton Pierce
Sky Boy/Stuart Grossman ....David Eric Rosenberg
Natalie Chasen ....Joanna Rush
Fredo Iannuzzi ....Tom Darpi
Harvey Grossman..Stanley Allan Sherman
Helga Helsenrott ....Helen Siff
Rita Iannuzzi ....Justine Slater
Gary Grossman...Glenn Wein
Todd Grossman..Barry Weinberger
Grandma Sylvia ....Gail Bell

A theatrical funeral in two acts. The action takes place at the Helsenrott Jewish Mortuary and includes a "mitzvah Meal."

Succeeding Cast Members: Jaid Barrymore, Carol Shaya

*Still Playing May 31, 1997.
Frank Capri, Beck Lee Photos

Gail Bell

Mary Wilson

MY COZY LITTLE CORNER IN THE RITZ

Conceived/Developed by Judy Brown and William Baldwin Young; Directed and Staged by Thommie Walsh; Music/Lyrics, Cole Porter; Presented by Primavera Productions/Sally Sears; Press, Judy Jacksina; Opened in Eighty Eights on January 11, 1996*

CAST

Judy Brown ....William Baldwin Young

A cabaret musical.

PERFECT CRIME

By Warren Manzi; Director, Jeffrey Hyatt; Set, Jay Stone; Costumes, Nancy Bush; Lighting, Jeff Fontaine; Sound, David Lawson; Stage Manager, Annette M. Smith; Presented by The Actors Collective in association with the Methuen Company; Press, Debenham Smythe/Michelle Vincents, Paul Lewis, Jeffrey Clarke; Opened in the Courtyard Playhouse on April 18, 1987* and later transferred to the Second Stage, 47th St. Playhouse, Intar, Harold Clurman Theatre, Theatre Four, and currently The Duffy Theatre.

CAST

Margaret Thorne Brent ....Catherine Russell
Inspector James Ascher ....James Farrell
W. Harrison Brent ....Richard P. Gang
Lionel McAuley ....David Butler
David Breuer ....Patrick Robustelli
UNDERSTUDIES: Lauren Lovett (Females), J. R. Robinson (Males)

A mystery in two acts. The action takes place in Windsor Locks, Connecticut.

*Still playing May 31, 1997.

Joe Bly Photos

Scenes from *Perfect Crime*
Top: James Farrell, Catherine Russell
Left: Catherine Russell

STOMP

Created/Directed by Luke Cresswell and Steve McNicholas; Lighting, Mr. McNicholas, Neil Tiplady; Production Manager, Pete Donno; General Management, Richard Frankel/Marc Routh; Presented by Columbia Artists Management, Harriet Newman Leve, James D. Stren, Morton Wolkowitz, Schuster/Maxwell, Galin/Sandler, and Markley/Manocherian; Press, Chris Boneau/Adrian Bryan-Brown, Jackie Green, Bob Fennell; Previewed from Friday, February 18, 1994; Opened in the Orpheum Theatre on Sunday, February 27, 1994*

CAST

Ahmed Best   Maria Breyer   Michael Bove   Anthony
Johnson   Keith Middleton   Jason Mills   Kamal Sin-
                                  clair   Anthony Sparks

An evening of percussive performance art. The ensemble uses everything but conventional percussion to make rhythm and dance.

*Still playing May 31, 1997.
Stuart Morris, Steve McNicholas Photos

Fiona Wilkes, Theseus Gerard from original cast

Fraser Morrison, Theseus Gerard, Luke Cresswell, Carl Smith from original cast

TONY N' TINA'S WEDDING

Patrick Buckley, Suzanna Keller, guest star Kenny Kramer

By Artificial Intelligence; Conception, Nancy Cassaro (Artistic Director); Director, Larry Pellegrini; Supervisory Director, Julie Cesari; Musical Director, Lynn Portas; Choreography, Hal Simons; Design/Decor, Randall Thropp; Costumes/Hairstyles/Makeup, Juan DeArmas; General Manager, Leonard A. Mulhern; Company Manager, James Hannah; Stage Managers, Bernadette McGay, W. Bart Ebbink; Presented by Joseph Corcoran & Daniel Cocoran; Press, David Rothenberg/Terence Womble; Opened in the Washington Square Church & Carmelita's on Saturday, February 6, 1988*

CAST

Valentia Lynne Nunzio, the bride ....Susanna Keller
Anthony Angelo Nunzio, the groom.............................. Patrick Buckley
Connie Mocogni, maid of honor ....Susan Laurenzi
Barry Wheeler, best man ....Timothy Monagan
Donna Marsala, bridesmaid ....Susan Campanero
Dominick Fabrizzi, usher ....Joseph Barbara
Marina Gulino, bridesmaid ....Cheryl Giuliano
Johnny Nunzio, usher/brother of groom.............................Nick Gambella
Josephine Vitale, mother of the bride ....Victoria Barone
Joseph Vitale, brother of the bride.................................Richard Falzone
Luigi Domenico, great uncle of the bride ....Stan Winston
Rose Domenico, aunt of the bride..Cayte Thorpe
Sister Albert Maria, cousin of bride ....Fran Gennuso
Anthony Angelo Nunzio, Sr., father of groom ....Mark Nassar
Madeline Monroe, Mr. Nunzio's girlfriend...........................Karen Cellini
Grandma Nunzio, grandmother to groom...........................Elaine Unnold
Michael Just, Tina's ex-boyfriend ....Anthony T. Lauria
Father Mark, parish priest ....Gary Schneider
Vinnie Black, caterer ....Tom Karlya
Loretta Black, wife of the caterer ....Victoria Constan
Mick Black, brother of the caterer ....Robert R. Oliver
Nikki Black, daughter of the caterer ....Jodi Grant
Mikie Black, son of the caterer...John Walter
Pat Black, sister of the caterer ....Maria Gentile
Rick Demarco, the video man ....Kerry Logan
Sal Antonucci, the photographer...Tony Patellis

An environmental theatre production. The action takes place at a wedding and reception.

*Still playing May 31, 1997 after moving to St. John's Church and Vinnie Black's Coliseum.

Blanche Mackey Photos

Patrick Buckley, Susanna Keller

TUBES

Created and Written by Matt Goldman, Phil Stanton, Chris Wink; Director, Marlene Swartz; Artistic Coordinator; Caryl Glaab; Sets, Kevin Joseph Roach; Lighting, Brian Aldous; Costumes, Lydia Tanji, Patricia Murphy; Sound, Raymond Schilke; Computer Graphics, Kurisu-Chan; Stage Manager, Kevin Cunningham; Press, David Rothenberg; Opened at the Astor Place Theatre on Thursday, November 7, 1991*

CAST

Blue Man Group (Matt Goldman, Phil Stanton, Chris Wink)

An evening with the performance group, performed without intermission.

*Still playing May 31, 1997.

Martha Swope Photo

Blue Man Group

PRODUCTIONS THAT CLOSED PRIOR TO SCHEDULED BROADWAY PREMIERE

WHISTLE DOWN THE WIND

Music, Andrew Lloyd Webber; Lyrics, Jim Steinman; Book, Patricia Knop; Based on the novel by Mary Hayley Bell and the 1961 film; Director, Harold Prince; Orchestrations, David Cullen, Lloyd Webber; Musical Supervisor, Michael Reed; Musical Director, Patrick Vaccariello; Sets, Andrew Jackness; Costumes, Florence Klotz; Lighting, Howard Binkley; Sound, Martin Levan; Choreography, Joey McKneely; Projections, Wendall K. Harrington; General Manager, Nina Lannan; Company Manager, Devin Km Keudell; Production Supervisor, Scott Faris; Stage Managers, Dale Kaufman, Valerie Lau-Kee Lai; Presented by The Really Useful Company; Press, Chris Boneau~Adrian Bryan-Brown/John Wimbs, Ken Werther; Previewed from Friday, December 6; Opened in Washington D.C.'s National Theatre on December 12, 1996*

Cameron Bowen, Davis Gaines, Abbi Hutcherson, Irene Molloy

CAST

Swallow ....Irene Molloy
Brat...Abbi Hutcherson
Poor Baby...Cameron Bowen
Aunt Dot ....Candy Buckley
Boone ....Timothy Nolen
Minister ....Allen Fitzpatrick
Edward ....Chuck Cooper
Earl...David Lloyd Watson
Rod..Timothy Shew
Sheriff Cookridge ....Mike Hartman
Candy ....Lacey Hornkohl
Amos ....Steve Scott Springer
The Man ....David Gaines
Preacher ....Ray Walker
Townspeople...........Adinah Alexander, Johnetta Alston, Dave Clemmons,
Chuck Cooper, Georgia Creighton, Allen Fitzpatrick, Emily Rabon Hall,
Mike Hartman, Melody Kay, Wayne W. Pretlow, John Sawyer,
Timothy Shew, Bob Stillman, Ray Walker, Laurie Williamson,
Wysandria Woolsey
The Children ....Sasha Allen, Alex Bowen,
Graham Bowenm, Gina DeStefano, Rori Godsey, Scott Irby-Ranniar,
Clarence Leggett, David Lloyd Watson, Julia McIlvaine
UNDERSTUDIES: Emily Rabon Hall (Swallow), Bob Stillman, Ray
Walker, Dave Clemmons (The Man), John Sawyer (Amos), Allen Fitzpatrick (Boone), Adinah Alexander (Dot), Melody Kay (Candy), Julia
McIlvaine (Brat), Alex Bowen (Baby) SWINGS: Kathryn Blake, Dave
Clemmons, Manoel Felciano, Wysandria Woolsey

Irene Molloy, Davis Gaines

MUSICAL NUMBERS: Vaults of Heaven, Spider, Grownups Kill Me, Whistle Down the Wind, The Vow, Safe Haven, Tire Tracks and Broken Hearts, If Only, Cold, When Children Rule the World, Annie Christmas, No Matter What, Act I Finale, A Kiss is a Terrible Thing to Waste, Wrestle with the Devil, Nature of the Beast, Finale

A musical in two acts. The action takes place in a small Louisiana town, just before a Christmas in the 1950s.

*Closed February 9, 1997 after 70 performances and 6 previews. The NYC opening was postponed, then cancelled.
Joan Marcus Photos

The Company

PRODUCTIONS FROM PAST SEASONS
THAT CLOSED DURING THIS SEASON

PRODUCTION	OPENED	CLOSED	PERFORMANCES
Big	4/28/96	10/13/96	193 & 23 previews
Buried Child	4/30/96	6/30/96	71 & 16 previews
Cowgirls	3/19/96	1/5/97	321 & 16 previews
Curtains	4/13/96	7/16/96	27 at Intar
			64 at Houseman
A Delicate Balance	4/21/96	9/29/96	186 & 27 previews
A Fair Country	2/1/96	6/30/96	153 & 21 previews
The Food Chain	8/7/95	6/9/96	352
How To Succeed...	3/23/95	7/14/96	548 & 16 previews
An Ideal Husband	5/1/96	1/26/97	309 & 7 previews
Love Thy Neighbor	3/24/96	1/5/97	236 & 5 previews
Moon Over Buffalo	10/1/95	6/30/96	308 & 20 previews
Papa	4/16/96	7/13/96	73 & 20 previews
Seven Guitars	3/28/96	9/8/96	187 & 11 previews
State Fair	3/27/96	6/30/96	118 & 8 previews
Sunset Blvd.	11/17/94	3/22/97	977 & 17 previews
Tartuffe: Born Again	5/30/96	6/23/96	29 & 26 previews

Joyce Van Patten, Matt McGrath in *A Fair Country* (Ken Howard)

Betty Buckley in *Sunset Blvd.* (Francesco Scavullo)

Madeleine Potter, Kim Hunter, Stephanie Beacham in *Ideal Husband* (Joan Marcus)

Daniel Jenkins, Crista Moore, Gene Weygandt in *Big* (Joan Marcus)

ATLANTIC THEATRE COMPANY

Twenty-third Season

Artistic Director, Neil Pepe; Managing Director, Hilary Hinkle; Company Manager, Bardo Ramirez; Press, Chris Boneau~Adrian Bryan-Brown/Andy Shearer, Amy Jacobs, Janet George

Tuesday, Sept.17-Oct.27, 1997 (28 performances and 14 previews)
EDMOND by David Mamet; Director, Clark Gregg; Sets, Kevin Rigdon; Costumes, Kaye Voyce; Lighting, Howard Werner; Fights, Tito Enriquez; Stage Manager, Matthew Silver   CAST: Leslie Silva (Fortune Teller/Whore/Shill), David Rasche (Edmond), Mary Anne Urbano (Wife/Subway Woman/Whorehouse Manager/Peepshow Girl), Mary McCann (Glenna/B-Girl), Rod McLachlan (Man in Bar/Prison Guard/Pawnshop Owner), Isiah Whitlock Jr. (Bartender/Leafleteer/Mission Preacher), Jordan Lage (Manager/Interrogator/Hotel Clerk), Neil Pepe (Shill/Police/Chaplain/Pawnshop Man), Kevin Thigpen (Card Sharp/Pimp/Customer)
    A dark urban fable.

Thursday, Oct.10-26, 1997 (11 performances)
ALL THINGS CONSIDERED; Written/Directed by David Pittu CAST: Christian Baskous, Heather Burns, Ron Butler, Johanna Day, Amy Mohn, Maggie Moore, David Pittu, Josh Stamberg, Cynthia Schlimmer, Rob Sedgwick
    A comedy inspired by 1950's Hollywood melodramas. Performed as a late night attraction.

Thursday, Jan.16-Mar.15, 1997 (47 performances and 14 previews)
MINUTES FROM THE BLUE ROUTE by Tom Donaghy; Director, David Warren; Sets, Derek Mclane; Costumes, Mark Wendland; Lighting, Donald Holder; Music/Sound, John Gromada; Stage Manager, Janet Takami   CAST: Matt McGrath (Oldest), Elizabeth Franz (Mother), Stephen Mendillo (Father), Catherine Kellner (Youngest)
    A drama in two acts. The action takes place in a suburban home over Labor Day weekend.

Wednesday, Mar.26-May 17, 1997 (41 performances and 13 previews)
THE JOY OF GOING SOMEWHERE DEFINITE by Quincy Long; Director, William H. Macy; Sets, Kyle Chepulis; Costumes, David Zinn; Lighting, Howard Werner; Music, Joshua Rosenblum; Stage Manager, Janet Takami CAST: Guy Boyd (Raymond), J.R. Horne (Merle), Jordan Lage (Junior), Neil Pepe (Stranger), Dale Soules (Patsy/Older Woman/Waitress), Felicity Huffman (Marie)
    A noir comedy in two acts. The action takes place in the Northwoods.

Wednesday, May 28-June 29, 1997 (22 performances and 13 previews)
CLEAN by Edwin Sanchez; Director, Neil Pepe; Sets, Todd Rosenthal; Costumes, David Zinn; Lighting, Howard Werner; Music/Sound, Fabian Obispo; Fights, Rick Sordelet; Stage Manager, Darcy Stephens CAST: Victor Anthony (Gustavito), Paula Pizzi (Mercy), Victor Argo (Kiko), Rod McLachlan (Father), Nelson Vasquez (Junior), Ron Butler (Norry)
    A drama in two acts.

Gerry Goodstein, Joe Bly, Alysa Wishingrad Photos

Top: Catherine Kellner, Matt McGrath in *Minutes from the Blue Route*
Below: Victor Anthony, Victor Argo, Ronnie Butler in *Clean*

BROOKLYN ACADEMY OF MUSIC

(Battery Park City) Tuesday, Sept.17-Nov.10, 1996 (41 performances)
CHIMÈRE; Created/Directed by Bartabas; Costumes, Marie-Laurence Schakmundes; Musical Director, Jean-Pierre Droulet CAST: Zingaro Troupe
 France's equestrian theatre group and their daredevil horsemanship.

The Beatification of Area Boy

(Majestic) Wednesday, Oct.9-13, 1997 (5 performances)
THE BEATIFICATION OF AREA BOY by Wole Soyinka; Director, Jude Kelly; Design, Niki Turner; Lighting, Mark Pritchard; Sound, Mic Pool, Roman Kung; Musical Directors, Tunji Oyelana, Juwon Ogungbe CAST: Femi Elufowoju Jr. (Sanda), Denise Orita (Mama Put), Janice Acquah (Miseyi), Marcia Hewitt (Mama Put's Daughter), Wale Ogunyemi (Barber), Ombo Gogo Ombo (Big Man Shopping/Military Governer), Makinde Adeniran (Boyko/Aide-de-Camp), Yomi A. Michaels (Judge/Military Officer), David Webber (Trader)
 The West Yorkshire playhouse presents a Nigerian drama.

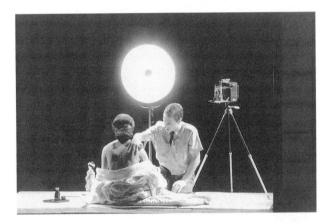

(Majestic) Sunday, Dec.1-14, 1997 (7 performances)
THE SEVEN STREAMS OF THE RIVER OTA; Written/Directed by Robert Lepage; Conceived by Eric Bernier, Normand Bissonnette, Rebecca Blankenship, Marie Brassard, Anne-Marie Cadieux, Normand Daneau, Richard Frechette, Marie Gignac, Patrick Goyette, Ghislaine Vincent, Macha Limonchik, Gerard Bibeau, Robert Lepage; Sets, Carl Fillion; Costumes/Wigs, Marie-Chantale Vaillancourt, Yvan Gaudin; Lighting, Sonoyo Nishikawa CAST: Patrick Goyette, Rebecca Blankenship, Marie Brassard, Norman Daneau, Richard Frechette, Marie Gignac, Anne-Marie Cadieux, Eric Bernier, Ghislaine Vincent
 An eight-hour epic based on the experiences of the Holocaust and the Hiroshima atomic bombing.

The Seven Streams of River Ota

(Majestic) Saturday, Jan.18-Feb.23, 1997 (32 performances)
THE STEWARD OF CHRISTENDOM by Sebastian Barry; Director, Max Stafford-Clark; Design, Julian McGowan; Lighting, Johanna Town; Music, Shaun Davey; Sound, Paul Arditti; Stage Manager, Rob Young CAST: Donal McCann (Thomas Dunne), Ali White (Maud), Tina Kellegher (Annie), Aislin McGuckin (Dolly), Carl Brennan (Willie), Rory Murray (Matt/Recruit), Maggie McCarthy (Mrs. O'Dea), Kieran Ahern (Smith)
 The Out of Joint Theatre company in a drama set in Ireland, 1932.

John Haynes, Simon Warner Daniel Rest Photos

Donal McCann, Tina Kellegher in *Steward of Christendom*

DRAMA DEPT.

Artistic, Douglas Carter Beane; Managing Director, Michael S. Rosenberg; Director of R&D, David Semonin; Press, Chris Boneau~Adrian Bryan Brown/Miguel Tuason, Clint Bond Jr.

(Greenwich House) Saturday, June 15-30, 1997 (15 performances)
KINGDOM OF EARTH by Tennessee Williams; Director, John Cameron Mitchell; Set, Brad Stokes; Lighting, Robert Perry; Costumes, Jonathan Bixby; Sound, Aural Fixation; Stage Manager, Robert Speck CAST: Tom Lacy (Reader), Scott Lawrence (Chicken), Cynthia Nixon (Myrtle), Peter Sarsgaard (Lot), Allen Durgin (Amanuensis 1), D. Scott Eads (Amanuensis 2)

A revision of the 1968 drama The Seven Descents of Myrtle in two acts. The action takes place in rural Mississippi in 1970, soon after Mr. Williams' release from the psychiatric division of Barnes Hospital in St. Louis.

Cynthia Nixon, Peter Sarsgaard in *Kingdom of Earth*

(Playwrights Horizons Studio) Monday, Nov.25, 1997 (1 performance)
THE SHAPER by John Steppling; Director, John Cameron Mitchell; Stage Manager, Lynn R. Camilo CAST: Kevin Corrigan (Felix), Cynthia Kaplan (Reesa), Wayne Maugans (Bud), Cynthia Nixon (Jill), Maryann Urbano (Sherry), John Ventimiglia (Del), Charles Tucker

(Ohio Theatre) Tuesday, Jan.7-Feb.1, 1997 (26 performances and 1 preview)
JUNE MOON by Ring Lardner and George S. Kaufman; Music/Lyrics, Mr. Lardner; Director, Mark Nelson; Sets, Bill Clarke; Lighting, Kirk Bookman; Costumes, Jonathan Bixby; Projections, Wendall K. Harrington; Sound, Kai Harada; Musical Director, Robert Lamont; Stage Managers, Andrew Bryant, Lynn R. Camilo CAST: Geoffrey Nauffts (Fred Stevens), Stacy Highsmith (Edna Baker), Robert Joy (Paul Sears), Becky Ann Baker (Lucille), Cynthia Nixon (Eileen), Albert Macklin (Maxie), Amy Hohn (Goldie/Miss Rixey), Robert Lamont (Window Cleaner), Peter Jacobson (Benny Fox), Robert Ari (Mr. Hart)

A 1929 three-act comedy, performed with one intermission. The action takes place in and around New York City.

Robert Joy, Cynthia Nixon in *June Moon*

Gerry Goodstein, Yoom Kim Photos

82

ENSEMBLE STUDIO THEATRE

Artistic Director, Curt Dempster; Executive Director, Evangeline Morphos; Executive Producer (Marathon), Jamie Richards; Associate producer (Marathon), John Forbes; Production Stage Manager, Gretchen Knowlton; Press, Jim Baldassare

Tuesday, May 6-18, 1997 (14 performances)
MARATHON '97: SERIES A; Lighting, Greg MacPherson; Sets, Bruce Goodrich; Costumes, Laura Churba; Sound, Geoffrey Sitter
Tennessee and Me by Will Scheffer; Director, Bob Balaban CAST: Joseph Siravo (Me)
Mafia on Prozac by Edward Allan Baker; Director, Ron Stetson CAST: Michael McCormick (Jay), Victor Slezak (Tee), Joe White (Matt)
Sisters by Cherie Vogelstein; Director, Kirsten Sanderson CAST: Judy Gold (Rita), Marla Sucharetza (Judy), Ted Neustadt (Man)
The Potato Creek Chair of Death by Robert Kerr; Director, Richard Caliban CAST: Gabriel Mann (Michael), Janet Zarish (Valerie), Chris Ceraso (Cedric), Alethea Allen (Deirdre), Kristin Griffith (Ellen/Linda/Voice/Guy)

Wednesday, May 21-June 1, 1997 (13 performances)
MARATHON '97: SERIES B; Lighting, Greg MacPherson; Sets, Mike Allen; Costumes, Amela Baksic; Sound, Geoffrey Sitter
Mistress by Michael Weller; Director, Susann Brinkley CAST: Roscoe Born (Sandler), Bob Balaban (Spode), Rob Sedgwick (Marshall)
A Backward Glance by Julie McKee; Director, Julie Boyd CAST: Sandra Shipley (Evelyn), Stephanie Roth (Cherry)
Patronage by Romulus Linney; Director, Tom Bullard CAST: Dan Ziskie (Husband), Dana Reeve (Wife), Chris North (Musician), Marc Romeo (Visitor)
Real Real Gone by Michael Louis Wells; Director, Jamie Richards CAST: Joseph Lyle Taylor (Carl), Thomas McHugh (Mitchell)

Wednesday, June 4-15, 1997 (13 performances)
MARATHON '97: SERIES C; Lighting, Alistair Wandesforde-Smith; Sets, Michael Allen; Costumes, Bruce Goodrich; Sound, Laura Grace Brown
Getting In by Frank D. Gilroy; Director, Chris Smith CAST: Thomas McHugh (Bill Duffy), Marc Romeo (Torelli), Paul Whitthorne (Whitley), Dan Dailey (Dean Strong/Carswell), Polly Adams (Secretary/Mrs. Duffy), Bill Cwikowski (Prof. Jenson/Dean Chamberlin), Melinda Page Hamilton (Emily/WAAC)
Sparrow by Vicki Mooney; Director, Curt Dempster CAST: Socorro Santiago (Merriweather Bear Den)
What I Meant Was by Craig Lucas; Director, Peg Denithorne CAST: Johnny Giacalone (Fritzie), Tom Bozell (J. Fred), Elaine Bromka (Helen), Scotty Bloch (Nana)
When It Comes Early by John Ford Noonan; Director, Daniel Selznick CAST: Kathleen Chalfant (Mickey Webring), Harris Yulin (J.C. Webring)

Craol Rosegg Photos

Alethea Allen, Chris Ceraso, Gabriel Mann in *Potato Creek Chair of Death*

Dana Reeve, Dan Ziskie, Chris North in *Patronage*

Tom Bozell, Johnny Giacalone in *What I Meant Was*

IRISH REPERTORY THEATRE

Artistic Director, Charlotte Moore; Producing Director, Ciaran O'Reilly; Development Director, Fran Reinhold; Press, James L.L. Morrison/Tom D'Ambrosio

Friday, July 12, 1996-Sept.8, 1997 (52 performances and 6 previews)
DA by Hugh Leonard; Set, Shelley Barclay; Lighting, Gregory Cohen; Costumes, David Toser; Stage Manager, Elizabeth Larson CAST: Ciaran O'Reilly (Charlie), Paul McGrane (Oliver), Brian Murray (Da), Aideen O'Kelly (Mother), Malcolm Adams (Young Charlie), John Leighton (Drumm), Julia Gibson (Mary Tate), Paddy Croft (Mrs. Prynn)
A drama in two acts. The action takes place in the kitchen and places remembered, 1968 and times remembered.

Friday, Oct.11-Dec.22, 1996 (61 performances and 13 previews)
THE IMPORTANCE OF BEING EARNEST by Oscar Wilde; Directed/Designed by Tony Walton; Lighting, Kirk Bookman; Sound, Randy Freed; Stage Manager, Elizabeth Larson CAST: Eric Stoltz (Algernon), Thomas Carson (Lane/Merriman), Daniel Gerroll (John Worthing), Nancy Marchand (Lady Bracknell), Melissa Errico (Gwendolen), Schuyler Grant (Cecily), Sloane Shelton (Miss Prism), John Fiedler (Rev. Chasuble)
A trivial comedy for serious people in three acts. The action takes place in London and Hertfordshire, England, 1895.

Friday, Jan.17-Mar.29, 1997 (67 performances and 6 previews)
MY ASTONISHING SELF by Michael Voysey; Lighting, Gregory Cohen; Stage Manager, John Brophy CAST: Donal Donnelly (George Bernard Shaw)
A one-man show from the writings of George Bernard Shaw.

(McLucas Studio) Thursday, Jan.30-Feb.16, 1997 (12 performances)
YEATS ON STAGE: THE PLAYS Members of the company preform staged readings of the full canon of William Butler Yeats.

John Leighton, Ciaran O'Reilly, Aideen O'Kelly, Malcolm Adams, Brian Murray in *Da*

Paul McGrane, Louise Favier in *Plough and the Stars*

Tuesday, Mar.25-May 11, 1997 (40 performances and 9 previews)
THE PLOUGH AND THE STARS by Sean O'Casey; Director, Charlotte Moore; Set, Akira Yoshimura; Lighting, A.C. Hickox; Costumes, Mirena Rada; Sound, George Zarr; Stage Manager, Kathe Mull CAST: Blythe Baten (Mollser), Dara Coleman (Capt. Brennan), Terry Donnelly (Mrs. Gogan), Louise Favier (Nora Clitheroe), Rosemary Fine (Rosie Redmond), Pauline Flanagan (Bessie Burgess), Con Horgan (Bartender/Sgt. Tinley), Des Keough (Fluther Good), John Keating (The Covey), John Leighton (Uncle Peter), Paul McGrane (Jack Clitheroe), Tim Smallwood (Lt. Langon/Corp. Stoddard)
A 1916 four-act drama performed with one intermission. The action takes place in Dublin, 1915-16.

(McLucas Studio) Saturday, Apr.5-May 11, 1997 (29 performances and 8 previews)
THE INVISIBLE MAN and **THE NIGHTINGALE AND NOT THE LARK** by Jennifer Johnston; Director, Ciaran O'Reilly; Sets, David Raphel; Lighting, Ken Davis; Costumes, Victor Whitehurst; Stage Manager, John Brophy CASTS: Invisible W.B. Brydon (Tony), Tony Coleman (Mack) Nightingale Paddy Croft (Mamie), Tony Coleman (Owen), Elizabeth Whyte (Janet)
Two one-act plays.

Wednesday, May 21, 1997 (1 performances)
ONLY ANGELS by Katharine Houghton; Director, Ciaran O'Reilly CAST: David Elliot, Ciaran O'Reilly, Schuyler Grant, Henry Polic II, Charlotte Moore, Hal Robinson

Carol Rosegg, Sheila Ferrini Photos

Nancy Marchand, Melissa Errico, Daniel Gerroll, Eric Stoltz in
Importance of Being Earnest

JEWISH REPERTORY THEATRE

Twenty-third Season

Artistic Director, Ran Avni; Managing Director, Michael Lichtenstein; Press, Shirley Herz/Wayne Wolfe, Sam Rudy, James Timk

(All performances at Playhouse 91) Tuesday, June 11-July 7, 1996 (22 performances and 10 previews)
THE SHAWL by Cynthia Ozick; Director, Sidney Lumet; Sets, Tony Walton; Costumes, Sharon Sprague; Lighting, Kirk Bookman; Sound, JR Conklin; Stage Manager, Jana Llynn CAST: Dianne Wiest (Rosa), Wendy Makkena (Stella), Patrick Brinker, Robert S. Lavelle (Police), Dina Spybey (Hortense), Salem Ludwig (Mr. Peterfreund), Boyd Gaines (Garner Globalis), Bob Dishy (Simon Persky)
   A drama in two acts. The action takes place in Queens, NYC and Miami Beach.

Dianne Wiest in *The Shawl*

Saturday, Oct.12-Nov.17, 1996 (29 performances and 8 previews)
431 OF MY CLOSEST FRIENDS by Miriam Kouzel Billington, Peter Goldman and David Presby; Director, Mr. Goldman; Sets/Costumes, Michael Bottari and Ronald Case; Lighting, Jeremy Kumin; Sound, Robert Campbell; Stage Manager, Julia Murphy CAST: Miriam Kouzel Billington (Myra Gutkin), David Presby (Everybody Else)
   A shonda in two acts.

Saturday, Jan.11-Feb.2, 1997 (15 performances and 9 previews)
CONCERT PIANIST; Written/Performed by Barry Neikrug; Director, Joe Cacaci; Set/Lighting, Richard Meyer; Stage Manager, Ken Jensen
   A one-man comedy performed without intermission.

Saturday, Apr.26-May 18, 1997 (15 performances and 8 previews)
THE DISPUTATION by Hyam Maccoby; Director, Robert Kalfin; Sets, Alexander Solodunko; Lighting, Rob Williams; Costumes, Austin Sanderson; Music, Jeff Lundon; Stage Manager, Ruth E. Kramer CAST: William Verderber (raymond de Penaforte), Suzanne Toren (Queen Yolande), Larry Pine (King James I), Joe Palmieri (Don Alconstantini), Lex Woutas (Attendant/King's Officer), David Edwards (Pablo Christiani), Brenda Thomas (Consuelo), Seana Kofoed (Judith), George Morfogen (Rabbi Moses Ben Nachman)
   A drama based on the Barcelona Disputation of 1263.

Carol Rosegg, Bunny Photos

Miriam Kouzel Billington, David Presby in *431 of My Closest Friends*

LA MAMA EXPERIMENTAL THEATER CLUB

Thirty-fifth Season

Founder/Artistic Director, Ellen Stewart; Press, Jonathan Slaff

Thursday, Jan.16-Mar.9, 1997
THREE SISTERS by Anton Chekhov; Translation, Michele Minnick; Director, Richard Schechner; Sets, Chris Muller; Costumes, Linette Del Monico; Lighting, Russell Champa CAST: Drew Barr (Andre), Shaula Chambliss (Irina), Sudipto Chatterjee (Rode), Maria Vail Guevarra (Masha), Lars Hanson (Kulygin), Ronobir Lahiri (Ferapont/Fedotik), David Letwein (Tusenbakh), Michele Minnick (Anfisa), Jeff Ricketts (Solyony), Rebecca Ortese (Olga), John Schmerling (Chebutykin), Robin Weigert (Natasha), Frank Wood (Vershinin)

Four acts in four styles. This version of Chekhov's drama moves through time. The first act takes place in 1901, the second in the early 1920s, the third in a 1950s Siberian slave camp and the last act here and now in the theatre.

Kanadehon *Hamlet*

Amy Sedaris, Penny Boyer in *Little Freida Mysteries*

Wednesday, Feb.6-Apr.19, 1997 (41 performances)
THE LITTLE FREIDA MYSTERIES by David and Amy Sedaris (The Talent Family); Director, Tom Aulino; Set, Hugh Hamrick; Lighting, Howard Thies CAST: Amy Sedaris (Elder Freida), Penny Bower (Freida), Chuck Coggins, David Rakoff

A comedy about an eccentric family living in Cape Seemore.

Tuesday, Feb.18-23, 1997 (7 performances)
KANADEHON HAMLET by Harue Tsutsumi; Director, Toshifumi Sueki; Sets/Costumes, Seiji Moriwaki; Choreography, Shozan Nebuya CAST: Kiyama Theatre Company of Japan, featuring Minoru Uchida, Takashi Fujiki, Akio Hayashi, Nagatoshi Sakamoto, Koichi Kubo

A backstage comedy in which a 19th century Kabuki troupe attemps Shakespeare.

Thursday, Feb.20-Mar.2, 1997 (10 performances)
THE QUADROON BALL; An American Tragedy by Damon Wright; Director, Terrell W. Robinson; Sets, Mark Tambella; Lighting, David Adams; Costumes, Jamie Smith CAST: Yvette Ganier (Jeanette), Charmaine Lord (Marie-Celine), Perri Gaffney (Edwina), Derek Jamison, Robert Steffen, C.P. Thornhill, Michael Connors, Stanley Earl Harrison

Thursday, Mar.6-16, 1997 (10 performances)
OUT OF THE SOUTH by Paul Green; Director, Barbara Montgomery; Sets, Jun Maeda; Lighting, Shirley Prendergast; Costumes, Jamie Smith
  Supper for the Dead CAST: Arthur French, Saraellen, Shirley Black Brown, Betty Neals, Charlotte, Charlotte Brathwaite
  Quare Medecine CAST: Howard Atlee, Joe Pichette, Mark Foley, Christine Mosere
  White Dresses CAST: Howard Atlee, Joyce Lee, Saraellen, James Stovall
  Three one-act plays.

Derek Jamison, Charmain Lord, Robert Steffen in *Quadroon Ball*

Saraellen, Howard Atlee in *Out of the South*

Thursday, April 17-27, 1997 (9 performances) transferred to Theatre Row Theatre, May 1-4, 1997 (5 performances)
  I COUNT THE HOURS by Stig Dalager; Director, Roger Hendricks Simon; Set/Costumes, John C. Scheffler; Lighting, Jeffrey Richardson; Music/Sound, David J. Simon CAST: Sybil Lines, Elizabeth Flynn-Jones, Nannette Deasy, Derek Lively, Abigail Haley Simon
  A drama set in Sarajevo.

Thursday, Apr.24-May 4, 1997 (10 performances)
AGAMEMNON by Aeschylus; Adapted/Directed by Alexander Harrington; Music, John Allman; Translation, Richard Lattimore; Set/Lighting, Tom Sturge; Costumes, Murell Horton CAST: Novella Nelson (Clytemnestra), Cullen Wheeler (Agamemnon), Robertson Carricart (Aegisthus), Lori Putnam (Cassandra), Jerry Ball, Chris Dylewski, Robert Ian Mackenzie, James McDaniel, Robert Molossi, Thom Rice, John Schmerling
  An adaptation featuring music and the text spoken in a pastiche of ancient and archaic Greek pronunciations.

Jonathan Slaff, Tom Brazil, Teruo Tsurta Photos

Amy Brenneman, John Benjamin Hickey

Ndehru Roberts, Kevin Carroll

LINCOLN CENTER THEATER

Twelfth Season

Artistic Director, Andre Bishop; Executive Producer, Bernard Gersten; General Manager, Steven C. Callahan; Production Manager, Jeff Hamlin; Development Director, Hattie K. Jutgir; Press, Philip Rinaldi/Miller Wright, Brian Rubin

Thursday, Mar.6-May 25, 1997 (57 performances and 37 previews) **GOD'S HEART** by Craig Lucas; Director, Joe Mantello; Sets, Robert Brill; Costumes, Toni-Leslie James; Lighting, Brian MacDevitt; Music/Sound, Dan Moses Schreier; Video/Projections, Batwin + Robin; Stage Manager, Thom Widmann CAST: Ndehru Robert (Carlin), Amy Brenneman (Janet), John Benjamin Hickey (David), Kia Joy Goodwin (Angela), Lisa Leguillou (Ana), Viola Davis (Eleanor), Julie Kavner (Barbara), Kevin Carroll (Cashmere/Dr. Farkas), Kisha Howard, Kim Yancey Moore, Akili Prince, Peter Rini, Pamela Stewart
A drama in two acts. The action takes place after dark in New York City.

For other Lincoln Center Theater productions: *Sex and Longing, Juan Darien, An American Daughter* and *The Little Foxes,* see BROADWAY CALENDAR.

T. Charles Erickson Photos

Viola Davis, Julie Kavner

Amy Brenneman, Ndehru Roberts

89

MCC THEATER
(MANHATTAN CLASS COMPANY)

Eleventh Season

Executive Directors, Robert LuPone and Bernard Telsey; Associate Director, W.D. Cantler; House Manager, Michael P. Connor; Press, Chris Boneau~Adrian Bryan-Brown/Erin Dunn, Paula Mallino

Monday, July 22-30, 1997 (6 performances)
PERFORMANCE LAB; Producers, Kent Adams, Jens Kohler; Stage Manager, Juliana Hannett

EVENING A: **Hey I've Got a Problem**; Created/Performed by Dale Goodson; Another Complex by Cara Buono; Director, Gus Reyes CAST: Dana Eskelson, Justin Theroux; **Tackling Kerouac**; Written/Performed by Robert Boulanger; Director, Liza O'Keeffe; **Food from Heaven** by Mary Sue Price; Director, Eva Saks CAST: Judith Hawking, Rica Martens; **Marina & Titiana** (an execerpt from Babes in the Woods) by Michael Huston and Cynthia Babak; Director, Joe Gilford CAST: M. Huston, C. Babak, Tim Parsons; **Simply Curious**; Written/Performed by Abigail Revasch; Director, Zak Berkman; Company K by John Woodson; From novel by William March; Director, Russ Jolly CAST: Michael Connor, Christopher Burns, Jose Dominguez, Michael Hall, Daniel Pearce, Steve Ramshur

EVENING B: **Black Candy**; Written/Performed by Nancy Giles; **An Empty Coffee Shop** by Annie Evans; Director, Christopher McCann CAST: Scott Rymer, Orlagh Cassidy; **The Ostrich** by James Rayfield CAST: Scott Hudson; **My World and Welcome to It!**; Written/Performed by Kathryn Rossetter; **Only Some Can Take the Strain** by Howard Barker; Director, Robert Emmett CAST: Robert Zukerman, Jeffrey Cox, Jan Maxwell; **Florence Gump**; Written/Performed by Kathryn Rossetter and Nancy Giles; **Jude Ciccolella-Some Original Songs** with Carver Blanchard; Checkout by Maureen McDuffee; Director, Brian Mertes CAST: Rebecca Boudig, Matt Faber; **A Long-Ago Bruise** by Julian Sheppard; Director, Brian Duguay; Music, Max Surla CAST: Jens Kohler; **Snow White X** by Russell Lees; Director, Stephen Willems CAST: Kent Adams, Cathy Schaffer, Jan Maxwell

EVENING C: **Joey's Jive** by Dan Moran; Director, H. Marsden Davis CAST: David M. Pincus, Honor Moor; **Sand**; Written/Directed by Michele Remsen CAST: Jennifer Albano, Nadia Dajani; **Negotiation** by Billy Aronson; Director, Evan Handler CAST: Matthew Lewis, Christopher McCann; **Joe and Stew's Theatre of Brotherly Love and Financial Success** by Jacquelyn Reingold; Director, Julie Boyd CAST: Murphy Davis, Bill McGuire, Chris McCann; **On the Road to AngelBear** by Meghan Cary; **At the Opera with Madam Frau Frau and Ammonia**; Created/Performed by Evelyn Tuths and Holly McCracken; **Tequila for Two** by Laura McCreary; Director, Donna Moreau-Cupp CAST: Carter Inskeep, Kathryn Rossetter; **A Part of the Story** by Neena Beber; Director, Maria Mileaf CAST: Daniel Blinkoff, Susan Cremin, Joey Golden, Pamela Gray, Felicity Jones, John McAdams

Friday, Oct.25-Nov.23, 1996 (18 performances and 9 previews)
THE GRAVITY OF MEANS by John Kolvenbach; Director, Russ Jolly; Sets, Russell Parkman; Costumes, Erik Bruce; Lighting, Karen Spahn; Music/Sound, David Van Tieghem; Stage Manager, Bernadette McGay CAST: Christopher Collet (Alan), Chris Eigeman (Peter), Susan Floyd (Judy), Lenny Venito (Marty)
   A comedy in two acts. The action takes place in Peter and Alan's apartment, a local bar, and a restaurant.

Wednesday, Feb.19-Apr.6, 1997 (35 performances and 13 previews)
GOOD AS NEW by Peter Hedges; Sets, Rob Odorisio; Costumes, Sharon Sprague; Lighting, Blake Burba; Music/Sound, David Van Tieghem; Stage Manager, David Sugarman CAST: Jennifer Dundas succeeded by Chelsea Altman (Maggie), John Spencer (Dennis), Laura Esterman (Jan)
   A brutal comedy in two acts.

Joan Marcus Photos

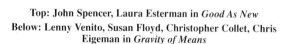

Top: **John Spencer, Laura Esterman** in *Good As New*
Below: **Lenny Venito, Susan Floyd, Christopher Collet, Chris Eigeman** in *Gravity of Means*

Chris Eigeman, Christopher Collet in *Gravity of Means*

Laura Esterman, Jennifer Dundas in *Good As New*

Sevanne Martin, Linda Emond, Kathleen Chalfant, Ellen Muth in *Nine Armenians*

MANHATTAN THEATRE CLUB

Twenty-fifth Season

Artistic Director, Lynne Meadow; Executive Producer, Barry Grove; General Manager, Victoria Bailey; Associate Artistic Director, Michael Bush; Play Development, Kate Loewald; Development Director, Mark Hough; Company Manager, James Triner; Musical Theatre Program, Clifford Lee Johnson III; Press, Chris Boneau~Adrian Bryan-Brown/Andy Shearer, Patrick Paris, Janet George

(Stage II) Friday, Oct.11-Nov.24, 1997 (25 and 28 previews)
THE BLUES ARE RUNNING by Michael Cristofer; Director, Melvin Bernhardt; Sets, James Youmans; Costumes, Jess Goldstein; Lighting, Kenneth Posner; Sound, Raymond D. Schilke; Stage Manager, Mark Cole CAST: Paul Giamatti (Pyle/Boo/Johnny), Marcus Giamatti (Stile/Mickey/JoJo)
A drama in two acts. The action takes place in Central Park, 2 A.M.

(Stage I) Tuesday, Oct.22, 1996-Jan.12, 1997 (72 performances and 24 previews)
NINE ARMENIANS by Leslie Ayvazian; Director, Lynne Meadow; Set, Santo Loquasto; Costumes, Tom Broecker; Lighting, Kenneth Posner; Sound, Aural Fixation; Music, George Mgrdichian; Choreography, Michele Assaf; Stage Manager, Diane DiVita CAST: Linda Emond (Armine/Mom), Michael Countryman (John/Dad), Ed Setrakian (Pop/Vartan), Kathleen Chalfant (Non/Marie), Ellen Muth (Virginia/Ginya), Cameron Boyd (Raffi), Sophie Hayden succeeded by Leslie Ayvazian during illness (Aunt Louise), Richard Council (Uncle Garo), Sevanne Martin (Ani), Ed Setrakian (Elderly Man)
A drama performed without intermission. The action takes place in an American suburb and Armenia.

Marcus Giamatti, Paul Giamatti in *The Blues Are Running*

92

(Stage II) Tuesday, Dec.10, 1996-Feb.9, 1997 (35 performances and 27 previews)
NEAT; Written/Performed by Charlayne Woodard; Director, Tazewell Thompson; Set, Donald Eastman; Costumes, Jane Greenwood; Lighting, Brian Nason; Music/Sound, Fabian Obispo; Stage Manager, Lisa Iacucci
A monodrama on coming-of-age in the 1960s performed in two acts.

(Stage I) Tuesday, Jan.28-Apr.20, 1997 (62 performances and 33 previews)
PSYCHOPATHIA SEXUALIS by John Patrick Shanley; Director, Daniel Sullivan; Sets, Derek McLane; Costumes, Jane Greenwood; Lighting, Pat Collins; Sound, John Kilgore; Stage Manager, Michael Brunner
CAST: Margaret Colin (Ellie), Daniel Gerroll (Howard), Andrew McCarthy (Arthur), Edward Herrmann (Dr. Block), Park Overall (Lucille)
A comedy in two acts. The action takes place in New York City.

(Variety Arts Theatre) Tuesday, Feb.25-May 4, 1997 (40 performances and 40 previews)
THE GREEN HEART; Music/Lyrics, Rusty Magee; Book, Charles Busch; Based on story by Jack Ritchie; Director, Kenneth Elliott; Musical Staging, Joey McKneely; Musical Director/Arrangements, Joe Baker; Orchestrations, Curtis McKonly; Sets, James Noone; Costumes, Robert Mackintosh; Lighting, Kirk Bookman; Sound, Tom Morse; Stage Manager, Pamela Edington CAST: John Ellison Conlee (McPherson), Jeff Edgerton (Harvey), Alison Fraser (Uta), Lovette George (Ruby), Don Goodspeed (Dallas), Julie J. Hafner (Molly/Clara), David Andrew Macdonald (William Graham), Karyn Quackenbush (Estelle), Jay Russell (Manager/Rutherford), Tim Salamandyk (Minister/Santiani), Karen Trott (Henrietta Lowell), Elizabeth Ward (Edith/Lydia), Ruth Williamson (Mrs. Tragger)
MUSICAL NUMBERS: Our Finest Customer, I'm Poor, Picture Me, Henrietta's Elegy, I Can't Recall, Til Death Do They Part, Tropical Island Breezes, The Easy Life, Get Used to It, Why Can't We Turn Back the Clock?, Horns of an Immoral Dilemma, I'm the Victim Here, The Green Heart, What's It Gonna Take (to Make It Clear Across the Lake), Finale
A musical comedy in two acts. The action takes place in NYC, Dutchess County and The Adirondacks. The same story was the basis for the 1971 film *A New Leaf*.

Joan Marcus, Susan Johann Photos

Charlayne Woodard in *Neat*

David Andrew Macdonald, Karen Trott in *Green Heart*

Daniel Gerroll, Margaret Colin, Edward Herrmann, Park Overall, Andrew McCarthy in *Psychopathia Sexualis*

(clockwise from top ctr) Byron Jennings, Sam Trammell, Richie Coster, Dan Futterman, Jamie Harris, Dermot Crowley in *Dealers Choice*

(Stage II) Tuesday, Mar.18-May 4, 1997 (32 performances and 24 previews)
DEALERS CHOICE by Patrick Marber; Director, John Tillinger; Set, David Gallo; Costumes, Laura Cunningham; Lighting, Kenneth Posner; Sound, Aural Fixation; Stage Manager, James Fitzsimmons CAST: Jamie Harris (Mugsy), Ritchie Coster (Sweeney), Dermot Crowley (Stephen), Dan Futterman (Frankie), Sam Trammell (Carl), Byron Jennings (Ash)
A suspenseful comedy in three acts, performed with one intermission. The action takes place in the kitchen, dining room and basement of a London restaurant.

(Stage II) Tuesday, May 20-July 6, 1997 (24 performances and 32 previews)
SEEKING THE GENESIS by Kia Corthron; Director, Kaia Calhoun; Set, Christine Jones; Costumes, Tom Broecker; Lighting, Scott Zielinski; Sound, Fabian Obispo; Fights, J. Allen Suddeth; Stage Manager, Laurie Goldfeder CAST: Kevin Rahsaan Grant (Kite), Donn Swaby (Justin), Sharon Washington (Teacher), Aunjanue Ellis (C Ana), Lindsay E. Finnie (Kandal), Soraya Butler (Cheryl/Customer), Lloyd Goodman (Mitch), Chris McKinney (Sac), Armand Schultz (Pizzaman/Professor)
A drama in two acts.

(Stage I) Wednesday, April 30-July 27, 1997 (80 performances and 23 previews)
COLLECTED STORIES by Donald Margulies; Director, Lisa Peterson; Sets, Thomas Lynch; Costumes, Jess Goldstein; Lighting, Kenneth Posner; Sound, Mark Bennett; Stage Manager, Jane E. Neufeld CAST: Maria Tucci (Ruth Steiner), Debra Messing (Lisa Morrison)
A drama in two acts. The action takes place in a Greenwich Village apartment.

Joan Marcus, Susan Johann Photos

Maria Tucci, Debra Messing in *Collected Stories*

94

THE NEW GROUP

Third Season

Artistic Director, Scott Elliott; Executive Producer, Claudia Catania; Literary Manager, Kevin Scott; Assistant Artistic Director, Marie Masters; Press, Chris Boneau~Adrian Bryan-Brown/Michael Hartman, Lisa Zaks

(Performances at INTAR Theatre) Saturday, Oct.26-Nov.24, 1996 (22 performances and 5 previews)
THIS IS OUR YOUTH by Kenneth Lonergan; Director, Mark Brokaw; Set, Allen Moyer; Costumes, Eric Becker; Lighting, Mark McCullough; Sound, Julie Tudor; Stage Manager, Brandy Rowell CAST: Josh Hamilton (Dennis), Mark Ruffalo (Warren), Missy Yager (Jessica)
 A drama in two acts. The action takes place in Dennis' apartment on the Upper West Side, March 1982.

Tuesday, Feb.4-Mar.2, 1997 (18 performances and 6 previews)
THE FLATTED FIFTH by Seth Zvi Rosenfeld; Director, Jo Bonney; Set, Kevin Joseph Roach; Costumes, Kaye Voyce; Lighting, Traci Klainer-McDonnell; Music, Oliver James; Fights, J. Allen Suddeth; Stage Manager, Judith M. Tucker CAST: Danny Hoch (Sonny), David Deblinger (Schlomo/Guide/Sam/Soldier), Nicole Ari Parker (Ninya), Rebecca Cohen Alpert (Security/Rifka), Jose Joaquin Garcia (Ray), Sarita Choudhury (Balu)
 A drama performed without intermission. The action takes place in New York City and Jerusalem, 1994-96.

Carol Rosegg Photos

Danny Hoch, Jose Garcia in *The Flatted Fifth*

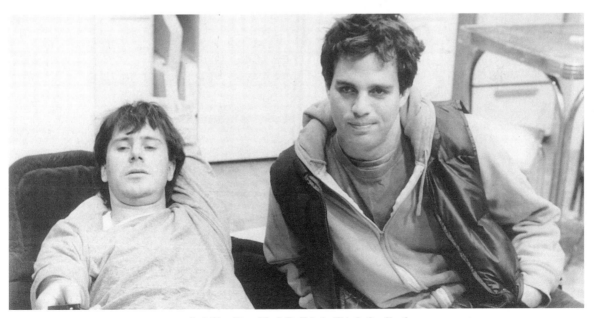

Josh Hamilton, Mark Ruffalo in *This Is Our Youth*

NEW YORK SHAKESPEARE FESTIVAL

JOSEPH PAPP PUBLIC THEATER

Forty-second Season

Producer, George C. Wolfe; Artistic Producer, Rosemarie Tichler; Managing Director, Mark Litvin; Associate Producer, Wiley Hausam; Artistic Associate, Brian Kulick; Development Director, Shelby Jiggetts; General Manager, Michael Hurst; Press, Carol R. Fineman/Thomas V. Naro, Bill Coyle, Liam O'Brien

(Delacorte/Central Park) Tuesday, June 18-July 14, 1996 (13 performances and 11 previews)
HENRY V by William Shakespeare; Director, Douglas Hughes; Sets, Neil Patel; Costumes, Paul Tazewell; Lighting, Brian MacDevitt; Music/Sound, David Van Tieghem; Fights, Rick Sordelet; Stage Manager, Buzz Cohen CAST: Louise J. Andrews (French Citizen), Teagle F. Bougere (Louis), Andre Braugher (King Henry V), Yusef Bulos (Sir Thomas Erpingham), Christian Camargo (Earl of Cambridge/Duke of Orleans), Torquil Campbell (Boy), Kathleen Chalfant (Isabel/Mistress Quickly), Jarlath Conroy (Lt. Bardolph), David Constabile (Bishop of Ely, M. Le Fer), Danyon Davis (Duke of Gloucester), William Robert Doyle (Alexander Court/Soldier), Benim Foster (Duke of Berri/Soldier), Michael Gaston (Capt. Gower), Michael C. Hall (Earl of Warwick), T.J. Kenneally (Soldier), Adam Soham Larmer (Soldier), Kenneth L. Marks (Capt. Fluellen), Elizabeth Marvel (Katharine), Jerry Meyer (Corp. Nym), George Morfogen (Charles VI), Michael Neeley (Soldier), Kristine Nielsen (Alice), Daniel Oreskes (Constable of France), Daniel Pearce (Soldier), Robert Ramirez (Soldier), Mary Randle (French Citizen), Lance Reddick (Lord Scroop of Masham/John Bates), Gus Rogerson (Sir Thomas Grey/Michael Williams), Douglas Stewart (Duke of York/Soldier), Henry Stram (Montjoy), Jeff Weiss (Archbishop of Canterbury/Ensign Pistol), John Woodson (Exeter)

Performed with one intermission. The action takes place in England and France. This marks the 31st production in the NYSF Shakespeare Marathon.

Andre Braugher in *Henry V*

Francis Jue, Robert Ramirez, Herb Foster, Boris McGiver, Michael Cumpsty, Henry Stram, Peter McRobbie in *Timon of Athens*

(Delacorte/Central Park) Tuesday, Aug.8-Sept.1, 1996 (13 performances and 11 previews)
TIMON OF ATHENS by William Shakespeare; Director, Brian Kulick; Sets/Costumes, Mark Wendland; Lighting, Mimi Jordan Sherin; Sound, Tom Morse; Music, Mark Bennett; Choreography, Naomi Goldberg; Stage Manager, James Latus CAST: Teagle F. Bougere (Poet/Senator), Yusef Bulos (Merchant), Michael Cumpsty (Timon), Mark H. Dold (Servilius), Herb Foster (Sempronius), Michael C. Hall (Caphis/Creditor/Servant/Soldier), Francis Jue (Ventidius/Creditor/Bandit), Adam Soham Larmer (Servant), Jerry Mayer (Old Athenian/Bandit), Boris McGiver (Lucullus), Peter McRobbie (Painter/Senator), Geoffrey Owens (Lucius), Susan Pilar (Timandra), Robert Ramirez (Senator/Creditor/Bandit/Servant), Matthew Saldivar (Jeweler/Creditor/Senator/Servant), Jack Stehlin (Alcibiades), Henry Stram (Flavius), Sean Patrick Thomas (Lucilius), Sam Tsoutsouvas (Apemantus)

Performed with one intermission. The action takes place in Athens and surrounding wilderness. This is the 32nd play in the NYSF Shakespeare Marathon.

(Public/Newman) Tuesday, Oct.29-Dec.8, 1996 (24 performances and 24 previews)
GOLDEN CHILD by David Henry Hwang; Director, James Lapine; Sets, Tony Straiges; Costumes, Martin Pakledinaz; Lighting, Richard Nelson, David J. Lander; Sound, Dan Moses Schreier; Projections, Wendall K. Harrington; Stage Manager, Buzz Cohen CAST: Stan Egi (Andrew Kwong/Eng Tieng-Bin), Julyana Soelist Yo (Eng Ahn), Tsai Chin (Eng Siu-Yong), Jodi Long (Eng Luan), Liana Pai (Eng Eling), John Christopher Jones (Rev. Baines)
A drama in two acts. The action takes place in a taxi travelling between Manhattan and Kennedy Airport, as well as Fukien, Southeast China, 1918-the present.

(Public/LuEsther) Tuesday, Nov.19-Dec.22, 1996 (15 performances and 25 previews)
INSURRECTION: HOLDING HISTORY; Written/Directed by Robert O'Hara; Sets, James Schuette; Costumes, Toni-Leslie James; Lighting, David Weiner; Sound, Red Ramona; Music, Zane Mark; Choreography, Ken Roberson; Stage Manager, Lisa Gavaletz CAST: Bruce Beatty (Nat Turner/Ova' Seea' Jones), Jeremiah W. Birkett (Hammet), Ellen Cleghorne (Gertha/Clerk Wife/Mistress Motel), Robert Barry Fleming (Ron), Nathan Hinton (TJ), T.J. Kenneally (Reporter/Cop/Clerk Husband/Buck Naked/Detective), Vickilyn Reynolds (Mutha Wit/Mutha), Heather Simms (Octavia/Katie Lynn), Sybyl Walker (Izzie Mae/Clerk Son)
A comedy performed without intermission. The action takes place Here and There, now (1990s) and then (1831).

(Public/Martinson) Tuesday, Nov.12-Jan.5, 1997 (52 performances)
HENRY VI by William Shakespeare; Director, Karin Coonrod; Sets, P.K. Wish; Costumes, Constance Hoffman; Lighting, Kevin Adams; Sound, Darron L. West; Music, Glen Moore; Stage Manager, Erica Schwartz CAST: Fanni Green (Warwick/Duchess of Gloucester), Jan Leslie Harding (Joan of Arc/Somerset/Lady Grey), Walker Jones (Winchester/Edward IV), Boris McGiver (Talbot/Jack Cade/George of Clarence), Patrick Morris (Humphrey of Gloucester/Prince Edward of Lancaster), Tom Nelis (Henry VI/Bastard of Orleans), Angie Phillips (Queen Margaret), Steven Skybell (Richard Plantagenet), Mark Kenneth Smaltz (Salisbury/Gloucester/Charles the Dauphin)
Three Shakespeare plays (*Henry VI Parts 1,2,3*) in a two-part adaptation performed in repertory: Part I: The Edged Sword (31 perf.) and Black Storm (21 perf.). These are #33 and #34 in the NYSF Shakespeare Marathon.

Jodi Long, Julyana Soelistyo in *Golden Child*

Bruce Beatty, Robert Barry Fleming, Ellen Cleghorne in *Insurrection: Holding History*

(Public/LuEsther) Wednesday, Feb.5-Apr.27, 1997 (66 performances and 7 previews)
A HUEY P. NEWTON STORY; Created/Performed by Roger Guenveur Smith; Sound, Marc Anthony Thompson; Set/Lighting, David Welle

A mondrama on the late co-founder of the Black Panther Party performed without intermission.

(Public/Anspacher) Tuesday, Feb.18-Apr.5, 1997 (28 performances and 26 previews)
ANTONY & CLEOPATRA by William Shakespeare; Director, Vanessa Redgrave; Sets, John Arnone; Costumes, Ann Hould-Ward; Lighting, Rui Rita; Sound, JR Conklin; Music, Mark Bennett; Musical Director, Christopher Drobny; Stage Manager, James Latus CAST: Teagle F. Bougere (Eros), Don Campbell (Veteran), George Causil (Alexas), Peter Francis James (Ventidius), Fanni Green (Charmian), David Harewood (Antony), Nancy Hower (Octavia), Jason Ma (Mardian), Boris McGiver (Sextus Pompeius/Decretus), Julio Monge (Maecenas), Alex Allen Morris (Enobarbus), Carrie Preston (Octavius Caesar), Ben Shenkman (Menas), Steven Skybell (Agrippa), Sam Tsoutsovas (Lepidus/Dolabella), Jennifer Wiltsie (Iras), Vanessa Redgrave (Cleopatra). Avery Glymph (Ensemble)

Performed with one intermission. The action takes place in Egypt, Rome, Parthia, Greece and Alexandria, 40 BC to 30 BC. This is production #35 in the NYSF Shakespeare Marathon.

Roger Guenveur Smith in *A Huey P. Newton Story*

Bill Camp, Mischa Barton, Dianne Wiest in *One Flea Spare*

(Public/Martinson) Tuesday, Feb.25-Mar.29, 1997 (24 performances and 15 previews)
ONE FLEA SPARE by Naomi Wallace; Director, Ron Daniels; Sets, Riccardo Hernandez; Costumes, Paul Tazewell; Lighting, Scott Zielinski; Sound, Stuart J. Allyn; Music, Michael Rasbury; Stage Manager, C.A. Clark CAST: Mischa Barton (Morse), Bill Camp (Bunce), John De Vries (Mr. William Snelgrave), Dianne Wiest (Mrs. Darcy Snelgrave), Paul Kandel (Kabe)

A drama in two acts. The action takes place during the 1665 London plague.

(Public/Martinson) Tuesday, Apr.15-May 18, 1997 (15 performances and 24 previews)
THE GYPSY & THE YELLOW CANARY; Adpated/Performed by Irene Worth; Based on a story by Prosper Merimee; Set, Myung Hee Cho; Lighting, Chad McArver

A one-woman drama.

Michal Daniel Photos

Don Campbell, Vanessa Redgrave, David Harewood in *Antony and Cleopatra*

NEW YORK THEATRE WORKSHOP

Seventeenth Season

Artistic Director, James C. Nicola; Managing Director, Nancy Kassack Diekmann; Associate Artistic Director, Linda S. Chapman; Production Managers, Susan R. White, N. Joseph Levy; General Manager, Christine Andreadis; Press, Richard Kornberg/Don Summa, Ric Maramontez, William Finnegan, Paula Wenger

Friday, Sept.13-Oct.20, 1996 (22 performances and 18 previews)
VIEW OF THE DOME by Theresa Rebeck; Director, Michael Mayer; Sets, Neil Patel; Costumes, Michael Krass; Lighting, Frances Aronson; Sound, Darron L. West; Stage Manager, Lisa Iacucci CAST: Jim Abele (Sen. Geoffrey Maddox), Patrick Breen (Tommy), Candy Buckley (Annabeth Gilkey), Tom Riis Farrell (E.T. Black), Julia Gibson (Emma), Dion Graham (David), Richard Poe (Arthur Woolf)
    A drama performed without intermission. The action takes place in Washington, D.C.

Thursday, Oct.31, 1996-Jan.5, 1997
O SOLO MIO FESTIVAL: So...It's Come to This and **EMMETT;** Written/Performed by Emmett Foster; Director, Kirk Jackson; Sets, Mark Wendland; Costumes, Paul Tazewell; Lighting, Matthew Frey; Sound, Red Ramona; Stage Manager, Charles Means
Monster; Written/Performed by Dael Orlandersmith; Director, Peter Askin
    Three solo performances playing in repertory.

Friday, Feb.7-Mar.30, 1997 (35 performances and 18 previews)
A QUESTION OF MERCY by David Rabe; Based on an essay by Richard Selzer; Director, Douglas Hughes; Sets, Neil Patel; Costumes, Jess Goldsmith; Lighting, Michael Chybowski; Music/Sound, David Van Tieghem; Stage Manager, Charles Means CAST: Zach Grenier (Dr. Robert Chapman), Stephen Spinella (Thomas), Juan Carlos Hernandez (Anthony), Michael Kell (Eddie-Doorman), Veanne Cox (Susanah), Christopher Burns (Cop)
    A two-act drama dealing with the issues of suicide.

Friday, May 2-June 8, 1997 (20 performances and 18 previews)
THE DEVILS by Elizabeth Egloff; Adapted from the novel by Fyodor Dostoyevsky; Director, Garland Wright; Sets, Douglas Stein; Lighting, James F. Ingalls; Costumes, Susan Hilferty; Sound, David Van Tieghem; Stage Manager, Charles Means CAST: Michael Arkin (Gov. Lembke), Bill Camp (Stavrogin), Lynn Cohen (Mrs. Stavrogin), James Colby (Kirilov), Randy Danson (Mrs. Lembke), Patrice Johnson (Marie), Patrick Kerr (Liputin), Christopher McCann (Shatov), Boris McGiver (Shigalyov), Denis O'Hare (Peter Verkhovensky), Daniel Oreskes (Blum), Nathalie Paulding (Matryosha), Frank Raiter (Stepan Verkhovensky), Kali Rocha (Dasha Shatov), Anthony Thomas (Virginsky)
    A drama in three acts.

Joan Marcus Photos

Julia Gibson, Patrick Breen in *View of the Dome*

Stephen Spinella, Julia Hernandez, Veanne Cox, Zach Grenier in
Question of Mercy

Bill Camp, Nathalie Paulding, Denis O'Hare in *The Devils*

PEARL THEATRE COMPANY

Thirteenth Season

Artistic Director, Shepard Sobel; Managing Director, Parris Relkin; Marketing/Development Director, Mona Z. Koppelman

Friday, Aug.30-Oct.12, 1996 (35 performances and 10 previews)
MISALLIANCE by Bernard Shaw; Director, Robert Williams; Set, Emily Beck; Costumes, Sarah Eckert; Lighting, Stephen Petrilli; Sound, Aural Fixation; Stage Manager, Martha Donaldson CAST:Jack Koenig (Johnny Tarleton), Bradford Cover (Bentley Summerhays), Kathleen Mc-Nenny (Hypatia Tarleton), Carol Schultz (Mrs. Tarleton), Robert Hock (Lord Summerhays), Robert Stattel (John Tarleton), Tom Dunlop (Joey Percival), Janet Zarish (Lina Szczepanowska), Greg McFadden (Gunner)
A 1910 social satire in two acts. The action takes place in Hindhead, England, 1909.

Friday, Oct.18-Nov.30, 1996 (32 performances and 13 previews)
CYMBELINE by William Shakespeare; Director, Shepard Sobel; Set, Robert Joel Schwartz; Lighting, Paul Armstrong; Costumes, Murell Horton; Music, Thomas Cabaniss; Stage Manager, Dale Smallwood CAST: Kathleen McNenny (Imogen), Brian G. Kurlander (Iachimo), Arnie Burton (Cloten), John Wylie (Pisanio), Bernard K. Addison, Konrad Aderer, Tara Blau, Nathan Hinton, Ryan Jensen, Jack Koenig, Peter Kybart, Carol Schultz, Edward Seamon
The action moves through the landscapes of Ancient Rome, Britain, Wales and Italy.

Friday, Dec.6, 1996-Jan.18, 1997 (35 performances and 10 previews)
THE BARBER OF SEVILLE by Beaumarchais; Translation, Michael Feingold; Director, John Rando; Set, Robert Joel Schwartz; Costumes, Murell Horton; Lighting, Stephen Petrilli; Music, Thomas Cabaniss; Choreography, Alice Teirstein; Sound, Aural Fixation; Stage Manager, Bill McComb CAST: Joseph Siravo (Count Almaviva), Arnie Burton (Figaro), Hope Chernov (Rosina), John Wylie (Bartolo), Ryan Jensen (Brighteyes/Alcade), Edward Seamon (Youngster/Notary), Helmar Augustus Cooper (Don Bazil), Konrad Aderer (Alguazil)
A new translation of a 1775 comedy in two acts. The action takes place in Seville.

Arnie Burton, Joseph Siravo, Hope Chernov in *Barber of Seville*

Friday, Jan.24-Mar.2, 1997 (28 performances and 10 previews)
VENICE PRESERV'D by Thomas Otway; Director, Rich Cole; Set, Robert Joel Schwartz; Costumes, Murell Horton; Lighting, Stephen Petrilli; Music/Sound, Robert Murphy; Stage Manager, Dale Smallwood CAST: John Wylie (Priuli), David Adkins (Jaffeir), Joey Collins (Pierre), Hope Chernov (Belvidera), Robin Leslie Brown (Aquilina), Bernard K. Addison (Renault/Friar), Lex Woutas (Spinosa/Executioner), Konrad Aderer (Eliot/Officer), Edward Seamon (Bedamore/Duke), Mark Giordano (Revellido), Christopher Moore (Mezzana), Tara Blau (Maid), Robert Hock (Antonio)
A 1682 five-act drama performed with one intermission. The action takes place in Venice, 1618.

Friday, Mar.14-Apr.26, 1997 (35 performances and 10 previews)
THE GUARDSMAN by Ferenc Molnar; Translation, Grace I. Colbron and Hans Bartsch; Acting Version, Philip Moeller; Director, Russell Treyz; Set, Robert Joel Schwartz; Costumes, Murell Horton; Lighting, Stephen Petrilli; Sound, Kai Harada; Stage Manager, Megan Schneid CAST: Ruby Holbrook (Mama), Petra Wright (Liesl), Tom Bloom (Actor), Joanne Camp (Actress), Helmar Augustus Cooper (Critic), Dane Knell (Creditor), Anna Minot (Usher)
A comedy in three acts. The action takes place in Vienna, 1911.

Friday, May 2-June 1, 1997 (24 performances and 10 previews)
THE CHAIRS by Eugene Ionesco; Translation, Donald M. Allen; Director, John Morrison; Set, Beowulf Borritt; Lighting, Stephen Petrilli; Costumes, Murell Horton; Sound, Robert Murphy; Stage Manager, Kay Foster CAST: Robert Hock (Old Man), Marylouise Burke (Old Woman), Christopher Graham (Orator)
A 1952 absurdist comedy.

Tom Bloom, Megan Schneid Photos

David Adkins in *Venice Preserv'd*

PLAYWRIGHTS HORIZONS

Twenty-sixth Season

Artistic Director, Tim Sanford; Managing Director, Leslie Marcus; General Manager, Lynn Landis; Literary Manager, Sonya Sobieski; Production Manager, Christopher Boll; Development Director, Jill Garland; Press, James L.L. Morrison/Tom D'Ambrosio

Friday, Sept.20-Nov.10, 1996 (25 performances and 27 previews)?
FIT TO BE TIED by Nicky Silver; Director, David Warren; Set, James Youmans; Costumes, Teresa Snider-Stein; Lighting, Donald Holder; Music/Sound, John Gromada; Stage Manager, C.A. Clark CAST: T. Scott Cunningham (Arloc), Jean Smart (Nessa), Dick Latessa (Carl), Matt Keeslar (Boyd)
A comedy in two acts. The action takes place in New York City between Thanksgiving week and the New Year.

(Studio) Wednesday, Oct.30-Nov.17, 1996 (17 performances and 6 previews)
DEMONOLOGY by Kelly Stuart; Directot, Jim Simpson; Sets, David Harwell; Costumes, Therese Bruck; Lighting, Anne M. Padien; Sound, Michael Clark CAST: Marisa Tomei (Gina), Rocco Sisto (DeMartini), Bray Poor (Collins), Kathleen Glaudini (Child)
A dark comedy about office politics and sexual obsession in two acts.

Thursday, Dec.12, 1996-Jan.19, 1997 (17 performances and 29 previews)
CLOUD TECTONICS by Jose Rivera; Director, Tina Landau; Set, Riccardo Hernandez; Costumes, Anita Yavich; Lighting, Frances Aronson; Music, Mark Bennett; Sound, Mr. Bennett, JR Conklin; Stage Manager, Martha Donaldson CAST: Camilia Sanes (Celestina del Sol), John Ortiz (Anibal de la Luna), Javi Mulero (Nelson de la Luna)
An urban fairytale performed without intermission. The action takes place in Los Angeles over forty years.

Joan Marcus Photos

Marisa Tomei, Rocco Sisto in *Demonology*

T. Scott Cunningham, Matt Keeslar in *Fit to Be Tied*

Michael Parks, Lauren Ward in *Violet*

Friday, Feb.14-Apr.6, 1997 (32 performances and 29 previews)
VIOLET; Music, Jeanine Tesori; Lyrics/Book, Brian Crawley; Based on *The Ugliest Pilgrim* by Doris Betts; Director, Susan H. Schulman; Choreography, Kathleen Marshall; Orchestrations, Joseph Joubert, Buryl Reid; Music Director, Michael Rafter; Sets, Derek McLane; Costumes, Catherine Zuber; Lighting, Peter Kaczorowski; Sound, Tony Meola; Fights, Luis Perez; Cast Recording, Resmirandaj; Stage Manager, Perry Cline CAST: Stephen Lee Anderson (Father), Kirk McDonald (Creepy Guy/Bus Driver 2/Radio Singer/Billy Dean/Virgil), Michael McElroy (Flick), Michael Medeiros (Leroy Evans/Waiter/Mechanic/Lead Radio Singer/Bus Driver 3/Earl), Cass Morgan (Old Lady/Hotel Singer/Old Lady 2), Paula Newsome (Woman with Fan/Music Hall Singer/Mabel), Michael Park (Monty), Amanda Posner (Young Vi), Roz Ryan (Knitting Woman/Landlady/Hotel Singer 2/Gospel Solo), Lauren Ward (Violet), Robert Westenberg (Bus Driver/Preacher /Rufus)

MUSICAL NUMBERS: Opening/Surprised, On My Way, Luck of the Draw, Question & Answer, All to Pieces, Let It Sing, Who'll Be the One (If Not Me), You're Different, Lonely Stranger, Anyone Would Do, Lay Down Your Head, Hard to Say Goodbye, Promise Me Violet, Raise Me Up, Down the Mountain, Look at Me, That's What I Could Do, Bring Me to Light

A musical drama in two acts. The action takes place in North Carolina, Tennessee, Arkansas and Oklahoma, during Sept. 1964.

(Studio) Wednesday, Apr.16-May 4, 1997 (9 performances and 14 previews)
THE YOUNG GIRL AND THE MONSOON by James Ryan; Director, William Carden; Sets, David Harwell; Lighting, Chris Dallos; Costumes, Therese Bruck; Sound, Bruce Ellman; Stage Manager, Judith Schoenfeld CAST: Michael O'Keefe (Hank), Shannon Burkett (Constance), Susan Floyd (Erin), Saundra Santiago (Giovanna), Todd Gearhart (Jack), Marilyn Chris (Faye)

A dramatic comedy in two acts.

Friday, May 16-June 22, 1997 (17 performances and 28 previews)
BABY ANGER by Peter Hedges; Director, Michael Mayer; Sets, Mark Wendland; Costumes, Jess Goldstein; Lighting, Frances Aronson; Music/Sound, David Van Tieghem; Stage Manager, William H. Lang CAST: John Pankow (Larry Paterson), Kristen Johnston (Mary Kay Paterson), Robert Ari (Man), Linda Emond (Woman), Ben Shenkman (Jeremy Dodge), Carl J. Matusovich (Shawn Paterson), Adam Rose (Eric)

A comedy in two acts. The action takes place in New York City and Orlando, Florida, in the not too distant future.

Joan Marcus Photos

Shannon Burkett, Michael O'Keefe in *Young Girl and the Monsoon*

**Ben Shenkman, Kristen Johnston, Carl J. Matusovich, John Pankow
in *Baby Anger***

PRIMARY STAGES

Twelfth Season

Artistic Director, Casey Childs; Associate Producer, Seth Gordon; General Manager, Margaret Chandler; Literary Manager, Andrew Leynse; Press, Tony Origlio/Kevin Rehac, Michael Cullen, Shelley Roberts

Wednesday, Oct.2-Nov.10, 1997 (26 performances and 14 previews)
MISSING/KISSING; Written/Directed by John Patrick Shanley; Sets, Brad Stokes; Costumes, Laura Cunningham; Lighting, Brian Nason; Music/Sound, David Van Tieghem; Stage Manager, Bridget Murray Edwards
    Missing Marisa CAST: Daniel Oreskes (Eli), Jake Weber (Terry)
    Kissing Christine CAST: Laura Hughes (Christine), Jake Weber (Larry), Reiko Aylesworth (Server)
    Two one-acts.

(Theatre 3) Saturday, Nov.16-Dec.1, 1996 (15 performances and 1 preview)
NIGHTMARE ALLEY; Music/Lyrics/Book/Orchestrations, Jonathan Brielle; Based on the novel by William Lindsay Gresham; Director/Choreography, Danny Herman; Design, Michael Hotopp; Costumes, Catherine Zuber; Lighting, Gene Lenehan; Sound, Bruce D. Cameron; Musical Director, Phil Reno; Stage Manager, Christine Catti CAST: Willy Falk (Stan), Vicki Fredrick (Zeena/Mrs. Peabody), Sarah E. Litzsinger (Molly Cahill), Nick Jolley (Clem), Ken Prymus (Pete), Evan Thompson (Ezra/Marshall), Silvia Aruj, Carolyn Campbell, Victoria Lecta Cave, Nancy Lemenager (Science Girls), Jonas Moscartolo (Major Mosquito)
MUSICAL NUMBERS: Opening/Ten In One, Someday Sometime, Tough Cookies, Questions, Kid, Molly Interlude, Shuffle the Cards, Whatever It Takes, Lucky Heart, Human Nature, This Is Not What I Had Planned, Science, The Code, Indecent Exposure, All Will Come To You, Cross That River, Caroline, Hit 'em Where It Hurts, Nobody Home, I Still Hear It All, Don't You Love to Watch What People Do, Unpredictable You, Get Her to Do It, Nightmare Alley, Song of the Road
    A musical drama in two acts. This co-production with The Directors Company, tells the story of the rise and fall of a 1930s con artist.

Jake Weber, Reiko Aylesworth, Laura Hughes in *Missing/Kissing*

Wednesday, Jan.8-Feb.9, 1997 (26 performances and 8 previews)
SECOND-HAND SMOKE by Mac Wellman; Director, Richard Caliban; Set, Kyle Chepulis; Costumes, Anita Yavich; Lighting, Brian Aldous; Music/Sound, Mike Nolan; Stage Manager, Christine Catti CAST: David Greenspan (Mr. Glitter/Mom), Matt Servitto (Mister Phelan), Frank Deal (Harry Custom), Kristine Nielsen (Sylvia), Joanna P. Adler (Dewey/Susannah), Kristin Di Spaltro (Susan), Vera Farmiga (Linda), David Patrick Kelly (William Hard)
    A drama performed without intermission.

Thursday, Feb.20-Mar.23, 1997 (20 performances and 13 previews)
NOT WAVING...by Gen LeRoy; Director, Chris Smith; Set, Tony Walton; Costumes, Sharon Sprague; Lighting, Michael Lincoln; Sound, Randy Freed; Stage Manager, Bridget Murray Edwards CAST: Sloane Shelton (Gabby), Kyra Sedgwick (Nicole), Nancy Jo Carpenter (Helen), Tim Michael (Mark)
    A drama in two acts. The action takes place in New York City.

Wednesday, Apr.2-May 4, 1997 (34 performances)
HATE MAIL by Bill Corbett and Kira Obolensky; Director, Seth Gordon; Set, Brian Whitehill; Lighting, Deborah Constantine; Music/Sound, David Van Tieghem CAST: Joanna Adler, Nathan Smith
    An alternative to *Love Letters*.

Wednesday, Apr.16-Aug.9, 1997 (97 performances and 20 previews) transferred to John Houseman Theatre on Wednesday, Aug.13, 1997
MERE MORTALS AND OTHERS by David Ives; Director, John Rando; Sets, Russell Metheny; Costumes, Anita Yavich; Lighting, Phil Monat; Sound, Aural Fixation; Stage Manager, Christine Catti CAST: Arnie Burton, Jessalyn Gilsig, Nancy Opel, Anne O'Sullivan, Willis Sparks, Danton Stone
PROGRAM: Foreplay or: The Art of the Fuge, Mere Mortals, Time Flies, Speed-the-Play, Dr. Fritz or: The Forces of Light, Degas C'est Moi
    Six short comedies.

James Leynse, Andrew Leynse Photos

Kyra Sedgwick, Sloane Shelton in *Not Waving*...

ROUNDABOUT THEATRE COMPANY

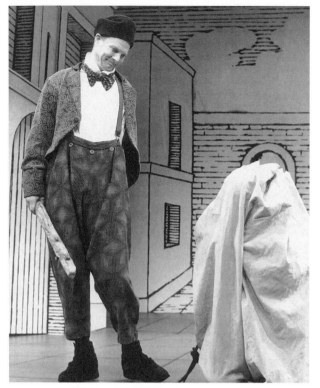

Bill Irwin

Artistic Director, Todd Haimes; General Manager, Ellen Richard; Founding Director, Gene Feist; Development/Public Affairs Director, Julia C. Levy; Marketing Director, David B. Steffen; Artistic Associate, Jim Carnahan; Press, Chris Boneau~Adrian Bryan-Brown/Erin Dunn, Paula Mallino

(Off-Bdwy Productions in Laura Pels Theatre) Wednesday, Dec.4, 1996-Mar.23, 1997 (85 performances and 41 previews)
SCAPIN by Moliere; Adaptation, Bill Irwin and Mark O'Donnell; Director, Mr. Irwin; Sets, Douglas Stein; Costumes, Victoria Petrovich; Lighting, Nancy Schertler; Sound, Tom Morse; Music, Bruce Hurlbut; Dance Historians, Richard Powers, Michelle Robinson; Stage Manager, Nancy Harrington CAST: Maduka Steady (Octave), Christopher Evan Welch (Sylvestre), Bill Irwin (Scapin), Hillel Meltzer, Sean Rector (Gendarme/Porter), Kristin Chenoweth succeeded by Fleur Phillips (Hyacinth), Count Stovall (Argante), Gerry Vichi (Geronte), Jonathan Wade (Leander), Marina Chapa (Zerbinette), Mary Bond Davis (Nerine), Bruce Hurlbut (Keyboard)

A new adaptation of the 17th-century comedy in two acts. The action takes place on the street before the houses of Argante and Geronte.

The *Scapin* company

Saturday, Mar.29-June 29, 1997 (65 performances and 31 previews) **ALL MY SONS** by Arthur Miller; Director, Barry Edelstein; Sets, Narelle Sissons; Costumes, Angela Wendt; Lighting, Donald Holder; Sound, Kurt B. Kellenberger; Stage Manager, Leila Knox CAST: John Cullum (Joe Keller), Linda Stephens (Kate Keller), Michael Hayden (Chris Keller), Angie Phillips (Ann Deever), Stephen Barker Turner (George Deever), Stephen Stout (Dr. Jim Bayliss), Anne Lange (Sue Bayliss), Jed Diamond (Frank Lubey), Keira Naughton (Lydia Lubey), Sean Fredricks (Bert)

A 1947 drama in two acts. The action takes place at the Keller home on the outskirts of an American town, 1946.

For other Roundabout Theatre productions: *A Thousand Clowns*, *Summer and Smoke*, *The Rehearsal* and *London Assurance* see BROADWAY CALENDAR.

Joan Marcus Photos

Top Left: Linda Stephens, Michael Hayden
Top Right: John Cullum
Right: John Cullum, Linda Stephens, Michael Hayden

SECOND STAGE THEATRE

Eighteenth Season

Artistic Director, Carole Rothman; Producing Director, Suzanne Schwartz Davidson; Associate Producer, Carol Fishman; Literary Manager/Dramaturg, Christopher Burney; Production Manager, Peter J. Davis; Press, Richard Kornberg/Don Summa, Rick Miramontez, William Finnegan, Paula Wenger

Wednesday, June 26-July 28, 1997 (14 performances and 25 previews)
ALIENS IN AMERICA; Written/Performed by Sandra Tsing Loh; Director, Steve Kaplan; Lighting, Traci Klainer-McDonnell; Sound, Aural Fixation; Set, Lauren Helpern; Stage Manager, Delicia Turner
A humorous monologue performed without intermission.

Friday, Nov.15, 1996-Jan.12, 1997 (24 performances and 45 previews)
TOOTH OF CRIME (SECOND DANCE); A co-production with Signature Theatre Company; See "Signature" for details.

Tuesday, Dec.10, 1996-Feb.2, 1997 (25 performances and 40 previews)
THE RED ADDRESS by David Ives; Director, Pamela Berlin; Set, Christine Jones; Costumes, David C. Woolard; Lighting, Donald Holder; Sound, John Kilgore; Stage Manager, Susan Whelan CAST: Kevin Anderson (E.G.), Ned Eisenberg (Dick), Welker White (Ann/Waitress/Prostitute), Jon DeVries (Driver), Cady McClain (Lady), Josh Hopkins (Soldier/Maitre d')
A psychological mystery performed without intermission.

Tuesday, Mar.18-May 18, 1997 (39 performances and 33 previews)
SYMPATHETIC MAGIC by Lanford Wilson; Director, Marshall W. Mason; Set, John Lee Beatty; Costumes, Laura Crow; Lighting, Dennis Parichy; Sound, Chuck London; Music, Peter Kater; Fights, B.H. Barry; Stage Manager, Denise Yaney CAST: David Bishins (Ian Anderson), Jeff McCarthy (Don Walker), Ellen Lancaster (Barbara De Biers), Herb Foster (Carl Conklin White), David Pittu (Pauly Scott), Dana Millican (Susan Olmsted), Tanya Berezin (Liz Barnard), Jordan Mott (Mickey Picco)
A drama in two acts. The action takes place in San Francisco and the Bay area.

Thursday, May 29-July 13, 1997 (25 performances and 29 previews)
SOMETHING BLUE; Written/Performed by Michaela Murphy; Director, Tim Blake Nelson; Set, Derek McLane; Costumes, Crystal Thompson; Lighting, Jan Kroeze
A comic monologue about a wedding, performed without intermission.

Susan Cook Photos

Cady McClain, Kevin Anderson in *The Red Address*

Jordon Mott, David Bishins in *Sympathetic Magic*

Michaela Murphy in *Something Blue*

SIGNATURE THEATRE COMPANY

Sixth Season

Founding Artistic Director, James Houghton; Managing Director, Thomas C. Proehl; Associate Director, Elliot Fox; Development Director, Ellen Barker; Playwright for this season, Sam Shepard; Press, James L.L. Morison/Tom D'Ambrosio

(In residence at Public/Stein Shiva Theater) Tuesday, Oct.22-Dec.15, 1996 (46 performances and 18 previews)
WHEN THE WORLD WAS GREEN (A CHEF'S FABLE) by Joseph Chaikin and Sam Shepard; Director, Mr. Chaikin; Sets, Christine Jones; Costumes, Mary Brecht; Lighting, Beverly Emmons; Stage Manager, Donald Fried CAST: Alvin Epstein (Old Man), Aime Quigley (Interviewer), Woody Regan (Pianist)
    and
CHICAGO by Sam Shepard; Sets, E. David Cosier; Costumes, Teresa Snider-Stein; Lighting, Beverly Emmons; Sound, Red Ramona; Stage Manager, Donald Fried CAST: Elie Chaib (Police), Wayne Maugans (Stu), Leslie Silva (Joy), Amie Quigley (Mira), Sean Partick Reilly (Joe), Lia Chang (Sally), Clark Middletown (Jim)
    Two one-acts.

(Lucille Lortel Theatre) Friday, Nov.15, 1996-Jan.12, 1997 (24 performances and 45 previews)
TOOTH OF CRIME (SECOND DANCE) by Sam Shepard; Music/Lyrics, T Bone Burnett; Director, Bill Hart; Sets, E. David Cosier; Costumes, Teresa Snider-Stein; Lighting, Anne Militello; Sound/Score, David Van Tieghem; Video, Kevin Cunningham, Wild Kind; Musical Director, Loren Toolajian; Stage Managers, Ruth Kreshka, James FitzSimmons CAST: Vincent D'Onofrio (Hoss), Rebecca Wisocky (Becky), Sturgis Warner (Meera), Jeffrey Anders Ware (Ruido Ran), Jesse Lenat (Chaser), Paul Butler (Doc), Kirk Acevedo (Crow), Michael Deep (Ref)
    A revised version of a 1972 drama with music. A co-production with Second Stage Theatre.

Leslie Silva, Wayne Maugans in *Chicago*

Vincent D'Onofrio, Kirk Acevedo in *Tooth of Crime*

Tuesday, Jan.28-Mar.23, 1997 (42 performances and 14 previews)
THE SAD LAMENT OF PECOS BILL ON THE EVE OF KILLING HIS WIFE, KILLER'S HEAD and **ACTION** by Sam Shepard; Director, Darrell Larson; Music (Pecos Bill), Loren Toolajian; Sets, E. David Cosier; Costumes, Teresa Snider-Stein; Lighting, Jeffrey S. Koger; Sound, Red Ramona; Stage Manager, Donald Fried
Pecos Bill CAST: Romain Fruge (Pecos Bill), Julie Christensen (Slue-Foot Sue)
Killer's Head CAST: Jamey Sheridan succeeded by Bill Pullman, Treat Williams, Scott Glenn, Dermot Mulroney, Arliss Howard, Stephen Lang, John Diehl, Ethan Hawke
Action CAST: Bruce MacVittie (Jeep), John Diehl (Shooter), Debbon Ayre (Liza), Tanya Gingerich (Lupe)
    Three one-acts.

Tuesday, Apr.15-May 31, 1997 (35 performances and 13 previews)
CURSE OF THE STARVING CLASS by Sam Shepard; Sets, E. David Cosier; Costumes, Teresa Snider-Stein; Lighting, Jeffrey S. Koger; Sound, Red Ramona; Stage Manager, Emily Taylor CAST: Paul Dawson (Wesley), Deborah Hedwall (Ella), Gretchen Cleevely (Emma), Darrell Larson (Taylor), Jude Ciccilella (Weston), Jack R. Marks (Ellis), Kevin Carrigan (Malcolm), Clark Middletown (Emerson), Joe Caruso (Slater)
    A 1978 dark comedy in three acts. The action takes place on a rundown farm.

Carol Rosegg, Joan Marcus Photos

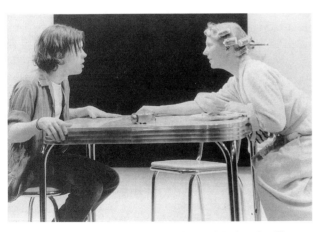

Paul Dawson, Deborah Hedwall in *Curse of the Starving Class*

VINEYARD THEATRE

Sixteenth Season

Artistic Director, Douglas Aibel; Executive Director, Barbara Zinn Krieger; Managing Director, Jon Nakagawa; Production Manager, Mark Lorenzen; Press, Shirley Herz/Sam Rudy

Wednesday, Oct.16-Nov.24, 1996 (21 performances and 20 previews)
THE WAITING ROOM by Lisa Loomer; Director, David Schweizer; Sets, G.W. Mercier; Costumes, Gail Brassard; Lighting, Peter Kaczorowski; Sound, Darron L. West; Music, Mitchell Greenhill; Stage Manager, Elizabeth M. Berther CAST: Veannee Cox (Victoria), June Kyoko Lu (Forgiveness from Heaven), Chloe Webb (Wanda), Byron Jennings (Douglas), Damian Young (Larry), Lou Liberatore (Ken), William Langan (Oliver), James Saito (Blessing from Heaven), Michele Shay (Brenda/Bridget/Jade Ornament/Cerise/Bruce), Dylan Grewan, Mike Toto (Orderlies)
   A comedy in two acts. The action takes place in NYC, England and China.

(Vineyard 26th St) Wednesday, Dec.23-23, 1996 (12 performances)
THE MERRY MULDOONS; Music, James Kurtz; Libretto, Barbara Zinn Krieger; Based on the novel *The Merry Muldoons and the Brighteyes Affair* by Brooks McNamara; Director/Choreography, Lisa Brailoff; Set/Costumes, David Brooks; Lighting, Scott Clyve CAST: Travis Greisler, Sara Zelle, Mark Peters, Anthony Emeric, Kate Haggarty, Ellen McQueeney, Andrew Boyer
   A family opera set in New York City during the 1890s.

(clockwise from Top L) Veanne Cox, Michele Shay, Chloe Webb, June Kyoko Lu in *Waiting Room*

Travis Greisler, Mark Peters, Sara Zelle in *Merry Muldoons*

Thursday, Feb.27-Apr.13, 1997 (29 performances and 18 previews) transferred to Century Theatre on Tuesday, May 6, 1997
HOW I LEARNED TO DRIVE by Paula Vogel; Director, Mark Brokaw; Set, Narelle Sissons; Costumes, Jess Goldstein; Lighting, Mark McCullough; Sound, David Van Tieghem; Stage Manager, Thea Bradshaw Gillies CAST: Mary-Louise Parker succeeded by Jayne Atkinson, Molly Ringwald (Li'l Bit), David Morse succeeded by Joel Colodner, Bruce Davison (Peck), Michael Showalter succeeded by Christopher Duva (Male Greek Chorus), Johanna Day (Female Greek Chorus), Kerry O'Malley (Teenage Greek Chorus)
   A drama performed without intermission.

Thursday, Apr.24-May 18, 1997 (25 performances)
MY MARRIAGE TO ERNEST BORGNINE by Nicky Silver; Director, David Warren CAST: J. Smith-Cameron, Mary McCormack, Mark Blum, Adam LeFevre, James Van Der Beek
   A developmental lab of a new comedy.

Carol Rosegg Photos

David Morse, Mary-Louise Parker in *How I Learned to Drive*

108

WPA THEATRE
(WORKSHOP OF THE PLAYERS ART)

Twentieth Season

Artistic Director, Kyle Renick; Managing Director, Lori Sherman; Production Manager, Hugh Walton; Literary Advisor, Constance Grappo; Press, Jeffrey Richards/Mark Cannistraro, Laramie Dennis, Irene Gandy, Roger Bean, Timothy Haskell

Monday, June 3-Aug.3, 1996 (47 performances and 16 previews) transferred to Lucille Lortel Theatre Tuesday, Aug.6-Oct.20, 1996 (80 performances)
THE BOYS IN THE BAND by Mart Crowley; Director, Kenneth Elliott; Set, James Noone; Lighting, Phil Monat; Costumes, Suzy Benzinger; Sound, John Kilgore; Stage Manager, Chris De Camillis CAST: David Drake (Michael), Jeff Woodman succeeded by Christopher Sieber (Donald), James Lecesne (Emory), David Bishins (Hank), Sean McDermott (Larry), William Christian (Bernard), Robert Bogue (Alan), Scott Decker (Cowboy), David Greenspan (Harold)
A revised version of the 1968 play in two acts. The action takes place in the East 50s, New York City, 1968.

Saturday, Oct.26-Dec.1, 1996 (20 performances and 18 previews)
THE RED DEVIL BATTERY SIGN by Tennessee Williams; Director, Michael Wilson; Sets, Jeff Cowie; Costumes, David C. Woolard; Lighting, Michael Lincoln; Sound/Music, John Gromada; Video, Batwin + Robin; Stage Manager, Lori Lundquist CAST: Stephen Mendillo (Griffin), Frederick Neumann (Judge Collister/Pharmacist), Elizabeth Ashley (Woman Downtown), Angelica Torn (Hooker/Wasteland Kid), Timothy Leigh Williams (Drunk/Wasteland Kid), William Devine (Charlie/Wolf), Timothy Warmen (Crewcut), James Victor (King Del Rey), Annette Cardona (Perla)
A 1975 drama in two acts. The action takes place in Dallas, Texas, 1963.

Thursday, Dec.12, 1996-Jan.26, 1997 (41 performances and 7 previews)
FLIPPING MY WIG; Written/Performed by Charles Busch; Director, Kenneth Elliott; Musical Director, Dick Gallagher; Set, B.T. Whitehill; Lighting, Michael Lincoln; Costumes, Robert Legere; Sound, John Kilgore; Stage Manager, Christina Massie
An autobiographical entertainment performed without intermission.

David Greensoan, Scott Decker in *Boys in the Band*

Elizabeth Ashley, James Victor in *Red Devil Battery Sign*

Tuesday, Mar.18-Apr.20, 1997 (20 performances and 15 previews)
ON HOUSE by Kevin Heelan; Director, Constance Grappo; Set, Anne C. Paterson; Lighting, Jack Mehler; Sound/Music, Robert C. Cotnoir; Stage Manager, Richard A. Hodge CAST: Ron Domingo (Veluz), Christopher Duva (Bonyer), Ken Garito (Kodti), Tristine Skyler (Woman), Trish McCall (Burken), Lance Reddick succeeded by Dion Graham (Housekeeper/Governor), Lewis Merkin (Mr. Pete)
A comedy in two acts. The action takes place in a Catholic hospital outside Baltimore.

Tuesday, May 20-June 21, 1997 (20 performances and 14 previews)
FAIRY TALES; Music/Lyrics, Eric Lane Barnes; Director, Mark Cannistraro; Musical Director, Daniel Harris; Orchestrations, Ernest Ebell; Choreography, Jackson McDorman; Set, Hugh Walton; Lighting, Jack Mehler; Costumes, Jennifer Kenyon; Stage Manager, Bethany Ford CAST: Keith Anderson, Valerie Hill, Stephen Hope, Rob Maitner, Stephanie McClaine
MUSICAL NUMBERS: Flying Dreams, Stonewall Serenade, Gay Guys, Illinois Fred, You're the Bottom, God Hates Fags, Grace, Heaven to Me, Love Don't Be a Stranger, When You Meet an Angel, Garbage, Muses, Parade, My Ambition, Letter Song, Ballad of Tammy Brown, Thanksgiving, Anniversary Five, Dear Dad, American Beauty, A Hummingbird, A Few Words about Matthew, Keepers of the Light
A musical revue in two acts. A previous version of this show played the Duplex cabaret earlier in the season.

Carol Rosegg, Carmen de Jesus Photos

Valerie Hill, Rob Maitner, Keith Anderson, Stephen Hope, Stephanie G. McClaine in *Fairy Tales*

YORK THEATRE COMPANY

Twenty-eighth Season

Producing Artistic Director, Janet Hayes Walker; Associate Artistic Director, James Morgan; Managing Director, Joseph V. De Michele; Press, Keith Sherman/Jim Byk, Kevin Rehac, Charlie Siedenberg

(All performances at St. Peter's Church) Friday, Sept.13-15, 1996 (4 performances)
HARRIGAN 'N HART; Music, Max Showalter; Lyrics, Peter Walker; Book, Michael Stewart; Director, William Westbrooks; Musical Director, David LaMarche
  Part of the Musicals in Mufti series.

Friday, Sept.20-22, 1996 (4 performances)
CARMELINA; Music, Burton Lane; Lyrics, Alan Jay Lerner; Additional Lyrics, Barry Harman; Book, Mr. Lerner, Joseph Stein; Director, Michael Leeds; Musical Director, Barry Levitt; Stage Manager, Alan Bluestone CAST: Nick Anselmo (Roberto), P.J. Benjamin (Vittorio), David Brummel (Mayor Manzoni/Priest), Nina Dova (Rosa), Allen Fitzpatrick (Carleton Smith), Tom Flagg (Bellini/Steve Karzinski), Terri Girvin (Narrator/Mildred Karzinski), Debbie Gravitte (Signora Carmelina Campbell), Rebecca Judd (Flo Braddock), Daniel Marcus (Walter Braddock), Gretchen Weiss (Gia)
MUSICAL NUMBERS: Prayer/Carmelina, Why Him?, Someone in April, Signora Campbell, You're a Woman, Love Me Tomorrow, One More Walk Around the Garden, All That I Dreamed He Would Be, It's Time for a Love Song, Image of Me, I Will Kill Her, Sorry As I Am, Image of You, Finale
  A revised version of a 1979 musical in two acts. The action takes place in Italy, 1961.

Friday, Sept.27-29, 1996 (4 performances)
OH CAPTAIN!; Music/Lyrics, Jay Livingston and Ray Evans; Book, Al Morgan and Jose Ferrer; Director, Robert Tolan; Musical Director, Kevin Wallace; Stage Manager, Alan Bluestone CAST: Shari Berkowitz (Neighbor), Stephen DeRosa (Crew/Spaniard), Susan Emerson (Lisa/Neighbor), SuEllen Estey (Mae), Robin Haynes (Capt. Henry St.James), Jay Aubrey Jones (Crew/Clerk), Tom Mardirosian (Enrico Manzoni), Chuck Muckle (Crew/Guide), Gayton Scott (Bobo), Karen Ziemba (Maud St.James)
MUSICAL NUMBERS: Very Proper Town, Life Does a Man a Favor, Very Proper Week, Capt. Henry St.James, Three Paradises, Surprise, Hey Madame, Femininity, It's Never Quite the Same, We're Not Children, Give It All You've Got, Keep It Simple, Morning Music of Montmarte, You Don't Know Him, I've Been There and I'm Back, Double Standard, All the Time, You're So Right for Me, Finale
A 1958 musical in two acts. The action takes place in Suburban London, on board the S.S. Paradise, and in Paris.

Wednesday, Dec.11, 1996-Feb.2, 1997 (44 performances and 14 previews)
NO WAY TO TREAT A LADY; Music/Lyrics/Book by Douglas J. Cohen; Based on the novel by William Goldman; Director, Scott Schwartz; Choreography, Daniel Stewart; Orchestrations, David Siegel; Musical Director, Wendy Bobbitt; Sets, James Morgan; Lighting, Mary Jo Dondlinger; Costumes, Yvonne De Moravia; Sound, Jim van Bergen; Cast Recording, Varese Sarabande; Stage Manager, Alan Bluestone CAST: Adam Grupper (Morris Brummell), Alix Korey (Flora/Alexandra/Carmela/Mrs. Sullivan/Sadie), Paul Schoeffler (Christopher "Kit" Gill), Marguerite MacIntyre (Sarah Stone)
MUSICAL NUMBERS: I Need a Life, Only a Heartbeat Away, So Far So Good, Safer in My Arms, I've Been a Bad Boy/What Shall I Sing?, First Move, I Hear Humming, Lunch with Sarah, You're Getting Warmer, Front Page News, So Much in Common, One of the Beautiful People, Still, I Have Noticed a Change/Morris Life, One More from the Top, Finale
  A musical comedy thriller in two acts. The action takes place in New York City.

Wednesday, Mar.26-May 4, 1997 (29 performances and 12 previews)
THE LAST SWEET DAYS; Music, Nancy Ford; Lyrics/Book, Gretchen Cryer; Director, Worth Gardner; Sets, James Morgan; Costumes, Jonathan C. Bixby; Lighting, Kirk Bookman; Sound, David Gotwald; Virtual Orchestra, Fred Bianchi, David Smith; Stage Manager, Barnett Feingold CAST: Willy Falk (Isaac/Michael), Ellen Foley (Ingrid), Roman Fruge (Arthur/Voice), Ellen Sowney (Wednesday)
MUSICAL NUMBERS: Last Sweet Days of Isaac, Transparent Crystal Moment, My Most Important Moments, Liebestod, Woman on the Run, Changing, It's Hard to Care, Mary Margaret's House in the Country, Sleep My Baby, I Bring Him Sea Shells, She's My Girl, Like a River, Goodbye Plastic Flowers, Finale
  A combination/revision of two prior musicals, 1970's *Last Sweet Days of Isaac* and 1973's *Shelter*. The new cast recording, titled *Shelter*, is on Original Cast.

Top: Marguerite MacIntyre, Adam Grupper, Alix Korey in *No Way to Treat a Lady*
Below: Willy Falk, Ellen Sowney in *Last Sweet Days*

Carol Rosegg Photos

(One Dream Theatre) Friday, June 7-30, 1996 (16 performances and 2 previews) The Barrow Group presents:
GOOD by C.P. Taylor; Director, Seth Barrish; Set/Costumes, Markas Henry; Lighting, Russell H. Champa; Sound, One Dream; Musical Director, Peter Eldridge; Stage Manager, Christine Lemme; Press, Shirley Herz/Wayne Wolfe CAST: Ava-Maria Carnevale (Helen), Larry Clarke (Hitler/Chorus), Vera Farmiga (Anne), Peter Giles (Bok/Dispatch), Aaron Goodwin (Halder), Larry Green (Freddie), Jen Jones (Mother), Reade Kelly (Bouller/2nd Doctor), Stephanie Meade (Elizabeth/Sister), Paul Rice (Doctor/Eichmann), Stephen Singer (Maurice)
A 1981 drama in two acts. The action takes place in Germany, 1930s.

(Ohio Theatre) Tuesday, June 11-23, 1996 (11 performances) The Magellan Project presents:
IVANOV by Anton Chekhov; Translation, Paul Schmidt; Director, Joumana Rizk; Set, Christine Jones, Shawn Lewis; Lighting, Christopher Landy; Costumes, Jonathan Green; Stage Manager, Bernadette McGay; Press, Tony Origlio CAST: Victor Slezak (Ivanov), Michael Pemberton (Borkin), Kati Kormendi (Anna), Lee Richardson (Count Shabelevsky), David Callahan (Lvov), Stephen Mendillo (Lebedev), Nancy Franklin (Zinaida), Camilla Enders (Sasha), Crystal Bock (Martha), Bill Quigley (Kosykh), Anne MacMillan (Avdotya), Leonid Vashenko (Gavrila), Bill Velin, Max Baker, James Gunn, Michael Swiskay, Emily DePew (Guests)
A new translation performed with one intermission.

Aaron Goodwin, Vera Farmiga in *Good* (Joan Marcus)

(Grove St. Playhouse) Wednesday, June 12-Sept.1, 1996 The Glines presents:
HEAVENLY DAYS by John Glines; Director/Set, Peter Pope; Lighting, David Jensen; Costumes, Jenny Lombard; Music/Sound, Thomas Hasselwander; Stage Manager, Richard Guido CAST:James F. Stanley (Hermes), Michael McLernon (Zeus/Brian), Martin Outzen succeeded by D. Matt Crabtree (Mark), George Hahn succeeded by Wade Gasque (Boots)
A comedy in two acts. The action takes place in Mykonos, Greece.

(Vineyard 26th St.) Wednesday, June 12-30, 1996 (16 performances and 2 previews) National Asian American Theatre Company presents:
THE GAOL GATE by Lady Gregory and **PURGATORY** by W.B. Yeats; Director, Tim Vasen; Sets/Costumes, Hyun-joo Kim; Lighting, Jeremy Stein; Music, Genji Ito; Stage Manager, Heather Cousens; Press, Shirley Herz/Sam Rudy, Adam Meza CASTS: Gaol Mia Katigbak (Mary Cahel), Midori Nakamura (Mary Cushin), Andy Pang (Gatekeeper) Purgatory Les J.N. Mau (Old Man), Andy Pang (Boy)
Two Irish one-acts.

(Billie Holiday Theatre) Thursday, June 13-July 28, 1996 (39 performances) Marjorie Moon presents:
IN MY FATHER'S HOUSE by Sam-Art Williams; Director, Walter Dallas; Set/Costumes, Felix E. Cochren; Lighting, William H. Grant III; Sound, Jim Coughlin; Stage Manager, Avan; Press, Howard and Barbara Atlee CAST: Peggy Alston (Brenda Ann), Maurice Carlton (Man 2/Sid), Caroline Stefanie Clay (Woman 1/Cheryl), Amani Gethers (B.T.), Marvin-Kazembe Jefferson (Man 3/Sylvester), Kim Sullivan (Larry Thurman), John Canada Terrell (Man 1/Tony), Charles Weldon (Joshua Thurman)
A drama in two acts. The action takes place in Los Angeles, 1992.

(29th St. Rep) Thursday, June 13-July 13, 1996 (17 performances and 5 previews) 29th St. Repertory Theater presents:
PICK UP AX by Anthony Clarvoe; Director, James Abar; Set, Andrea Bechert; Lighting, Rob Perry; Sound, Adam Adams; Costumes, Cathy Small; Stage Manager, Gregory A. Little; Press, Gary and John Springer/Candi Adams CAST: Thomas Wehrle (Brian Weiss), Neil Necastro (Keith Rienzi), David Mogentale (Mick Palomar)
A comedy in two acts. The setting is Silicon Valley, early 1980s.

Lee Richardson, Kati Kormendi, Victor Slezak in *Ivanov* (Carol Rosegg)

Andy Pang, Les J.N. Mau in *Purgatory* (Carol Rosegg)

(East River Park Amphitheater) Sunday, June 16-July 14, 1996 (13 performances and 11 previews) En Garde Arts presents:
THE TROJAN WOMEN A LOVE STORY by Charles L. Mee Jr.; Director, Tina Landau; Sets, James Schuette; Lighting, Blake Burba; Costumes, Anita Yavich; Sound, Christopher Todd; Stage Manager, Martha Doanaldson; Press, James L.L. Morrison CAST: Christina Chang (Sei), James Crawford (Bill), Sandra A. Daley (Eisa), Jason Danieley (Aeneas), Nancy Hume (Andromache), Marin Mazzie (Helen/Dido), Tom Nelis (Talthybius), Jane Nichols (Hecuba), Sharon Scruggs (Cassandra), Steven Skybell (Menelaus), Stephen Webber (Ray Bob), Veronica Cruz, Adrianna Dufay, David Fraiolo, Crispin Freeman, Andrew Garman, Heath Kelts, Erika Latta, Lee Lewis, Rebecca Lowman, Donnie Mather, Alexandra Perlof, Brian Quirk, Mark Rizzo, Kelli Ronci, Hope Salas, Tanya S.J. Selvaratnam, Pamela Shaddock, Beau VanDonkelaar, Anna Wilson

A modern re-telling of the Greek tragedy performed in the ruins of the East River Amphitheatre, the original home of the New York Shakespeare Festival.

(Tribeca Performing Arts Center) Tuesday, June 18-22, 1996 (7 performances) HAI presents:
TONY AND SON by Louis A. Delgado Jr.; Director, Max Daniels; Set, Miguel Lopez-Castillo; Lighting, Douglas Cox; Costumes, Gay Howard; Sound, Max Sargent; Press, David Rothenberg CAST: David Vayas (Tony), Mtume Gant, Stacie Linardos, AJ Lopez, Delilah Picart, Robert Rodriguez

A contemporary urban drama.

(top) Marin Mazzie, Heath Kelts, Stephen Webber, Andrew Garman, James Crawford, Tom Nelis in *Trojan Women*.. (William Rivelli)

(Beacon Theatre) Tuesday, June 18-30, 1996 (15 performances and 1 preview) Sal Michaels, Arthur Katz, and Anita MacShane present:
YOUR ARMS TOO SHORT TO BOX WITH GOD; Adapted/Directed by Vinnette Carroll; Music/Lyrics, Alex Bradford and Micki Grant; Arrangements, H.B. Barnum; Musical Director, Robert "Butch" Sam; Additional Music/Choral Director, Rev. Melvin C. Dawson; Sets/Costumes, William Schroder; Lighting/Stage Manager, Scott Clyve; Sound, Thunder Audio; Choreography, Talley Beatty, Phaze Farrington; Press, Judy Jacksina/Amy Groeschel CAST: Stephanie Mills, Teddy Pendergrass, Bebe Winans, Raquelle Chavis, Aubrey Lynch, Derrick Minter MUSICAL NUMBERS: Prologue, Truly Blessed, Beatitudes, We're Gonna Have a Good Time, Stranger in Town, Miracle Dance, We are the Priests and Elders, Something Is Wrong In Jerusalem, It Was Alone, I Know I Have to Leave Here, Be Careful Whom You Kiss, What Have You Done, The Trial, Judas Death, You Better Stop, Your Arms Too Short, Give Us Barrabas, Were You There?, See How They Done My Lord, Come on Down, Veil of the Temple, Funeral Oration, Can't No Grave Hold My Body Down, When I Think of the Goodness of Jesus, I Love You So Much Jesus, Because He Lives, Finale

A musical adaptation of the book of St. Matthew in two acts.

(HERE) Wednesday, June 19-July 31, 1996 (7 performances) HERE presents:
BRADLEY GLENN SUBURBAN POET; Written/Performed by Bradley Glenn; Additional Material, Mo Williams; Directors, Randolph Curtis Rand, Phippy Kaye; Sound, John Collins, Scott Mascena, John Collins; Stage Manager, Meredith Palin; Press, Barbara Busachino

The inside story of growing up white, midwestern and catholic on the mean streets of suburbia.

(Workhouse Theater) Wednesday, June 19-July 1, 1996 (12 performances) Seraphim Theatre Company presents:
WHITE MAN DANCING by Stephen Metcalfe; Director, Sarah Cusik CAST: Vincent Angell, Joseph Lyle Taylor, Christine Tucci

A romantic comedy.

Sharon Scruggs in *Trojan Women*... (William Rivelli)

Bradley Glenn *Suburban Poet*

(Carnegie/Weill Hall) Wednesday, June 19-23, 1996 (6 performances)
Carnegie Hall presents:
LOUISIANA PURCHASE; Music/Lyrics, Irving Berlin; Book, Morrie Ryskind; Based on a story by B.G. DeSylva; Music Director, Rob Fisher; Director, Scott Baron; Orchestrations, Robert Russell Bennett, N. Lang Van Cleve; Cast Recording, DRG CAST: Merwin Goldsmith (Sam Liebowitz/Dean Joseph T. Manning), John Wylie (Col. Davis Sr.), Michael Marotta (Col. Davis Jr.), Rick Crom (Capt. Whitfield), Michael McGrath (Jimmy Taylor), Debbie Gravitte (Beatrice), James Ludwig (Lee Davis), Alet Oury (Emmy-Lou), Judy Blazer (Marina Van Linden), Taina Eng (Mme. Yvonne Bordelaise), George S. Irving (Sen. Oliver P. Loganberry), Keith Byron Kirk (Alphonse), Peter Eldridge, Lauren Kinhan, Darmon Meader, Kim Nazarian (The Martins), Jamie Baer, Peter Flynn, Kim Lindsay
MUSICAL NUMBERS: Overture, Apologia, Sex Marches On, Louisiana Purchase, It's a Lovely Day Tomorrow, I'd Love to Be Shot From a Cannon with You, It'll Come to You, Outside of That I Love You, You're Lonely and I'm Lonely, Dance with Me (Tonight at the Mardi Gras), Wild about You, Latins Know How, What Chance Have I with Love?, The Lord Done Fixed Up My Soul, Fools Fall in Love/Old Man's Darling-Young Man's Slave, You Can't Brush Me Off, Finale
A 1940 musical in two acts. The action takes place in New Orleans during Mardi Gras, 1940.

(Miranda Theatre) Thursday, June 20-23, 1996 (6 performances) The Moonlight Series presents:
AN EVENING WITH JESSE JAMES by Jim Neu; Director, Joel Goldes CAST: Greg Baglia, Liz Davis, Henry Leyva, Jerry Mettner, Cheryl Rogers, Theresa Weber

George S. Irving, Taina Elg, Debbie Gravitte, Rob Fisher, Michael McGrath, Judy Blazer in *Louisiana Purchase* **(Steve J. Sherman)**

(Chicago City Limits) Wednesday, June 26, 1996- Gus Selmont presents:
CHICAGO CITY LIMITS' RIGHT TO LAUGH PARTY; Artistic Director, Paul Zuckerman; Press, Keith Sherman/Kevin Rehac CAST: Andrew Daly, Carl Kissin, Denny Siegel, John Cameron Telfer, Frank Spitznagel
Latest edition of the long-running improvisational comedy troupe. In April '97, the group started performing @*ChicagoCityLimits.comedy*.

(Fool's Space) Thursday, June 27-July 21, 1996 (13 performances and 3 previews) Phil Leach presents:
ONCE UPON A TIME IN THE BRONX by Michael McCarthy; Director, Joseph Giardina; Set, Scott Schreck; Lighting, Christopher Gorzelnick; Costumes, Patricia Shipman; Sound, J.J. Lask; Stage Manager, Cynthia Wise; Press, Peter Cromarty/Alice C. Herrick CAST: Joseph Riccobene (Frankie), Joshua Nelson (JoJo), Barbara Cassidy (Margaret), Carlos DePaula (Jimmy), Jonathan Hova (Sal), Richard S. Guerreiro (Mikey), Ron Riley (Jeri), Roisin Harden (Delia), John DiBenedetto (Bobby), Tim Barrett (Charlie), Denise LeDonne (Edie), Timothi-Jane Graham (Annie)
A drama exploring a Bronx neighborhood.

Carl Kissin, Andrew Daly, (front) John Cameron Telfer, Denny Siegel of Chicago City Limits (T. Charles Erickson)

(Synchronicity Space) Friday, June 28-July 20, 1996 (13 performances) Present Tense Productions presents:
BIPOLAR EXPEDITIONS; Sets, Robert Dew; Lighting, David Allen Comstock; Stage Manager, Bess Eckstein; Press, Gary and John Springer/Candi Adams **The Man with David's Face** by Susannah Nolan; Director, Peter Michael Marino CAST: Justin Kennedy (George), Mary Denmead (Roz), Sally Winters (Dahlia), Scott Cain (Bennett/David), Marie Trusits (Roberta), Michael Irwin (Roger), Peter Heffernan (Jack), Laura Fois (Mary)
A Month of Sundaes by Robert Remington Wood; Director, Jacques Levy CAST: Peggy Cowles (Regina), Mary Ann Volvonas (Mary), Mark Gorman (Phil)
Two one-acts.

Marie Trusits, Scott Cain in *Bipolar Expeditions* **(Chris De Lazzero)**

(Criterion/Laura Pels Theatre) Saturday, June 29-Nov.10, 1996 (117 performances and 17 previews) Edgar Lansbury, Everett King and Dennis J. Grimaldi present:
GRACE & GLORIE by Tom Ziegler; Director, Gloria Muzio; Sets, Edward Gianfrancesco; Costumes, Robert Mackintosh; Lighting, Brian Nason; Sound, John Gromada; Stage Manager, Alan Fox; Press, Jeffrey Richards/Mark Cannistraro, Rachel Peller CAST: Estelle Parsons (Grace Stiles), Lucie Arnaz succeeded by Bonnie Franklin (Gloria Whitmore)

A comedy in two acts. The action takes place in the Blue Ridge Mountains, Virginia.

(Theater for the New City) Tuesday, July 9-28, 1996 (39 performances and 12 previews) The Ridiculous Theatrical Company presents:
PHAEDRA; Adapted/Performed by Everett Quinton; Director, Bill Nobes; Sound, Michael Van Meter; Lighting, Cordelia Aitkin; Costumes, Larry McLeon; Wigs/Makeup, Zsamira Ronquillo; Set, Rue Catorz; Stage Manager, Flavine

Freely adapted from the Greek tragedy. The action takes place in 428 B.C.

(St. Peter's) Wednesday, July 10-Aug.11, 1996 (31 performances and 8 previews) New American Stage Company presents:
ACTS OF PROVIDENCE by Edward Allan Baker; Director, Ron Stetson; Sets, Edward Gianfrancesco; Lighting, Jeff Segal; Stage Manager, Eileen Myers; Press, Shirley Herz/Miller Wright **A Dead Man's Apartment** CAST: David McConeghey (Lonnie), Ilene Kristen (Nickie), Alexondra Lee (Valerie), Michael Cambden Richards (Al)
Dolores CAST: Ilene Kristen (Sandra), Fiona Gallagher (Dolores)
Two one-act plays.

(New Victory Theater) Thursday, July 11-31, 1996 Theatreworks USA presents:
THE COLOR OF JUSTICE by Cheryl L. Davis; Director, Ted Pappas; Music, Jeffrey Lunden; Sets, James Noone; Lighting, Frances Aronson; Costumes, Martha Bromelmeier; Stage Manager, Ruth E. Kramer CAST: Jonathan Bolt (Edwards/Davis), Gil Deeble (Oliver Brown/Teacher), Sheryl McCallum (Leola Brown/Jane), Selena Nelson (Linda), Jonathan Earl Peck (Thurgood Marshall), Ross Tatum (Jack Greenberg/Justice Warren), Ava Coffee, Steve Pudenz, Thomas Silcott

A drama performed without intermission.

(Westside Theatre/Upstairs) Monday, July 15, 1996-still playing May 31, 1997 James Hammerstein, Bernie Kukoff, Jonathan Pollard present:
I LOVE YOU, YOU'RE PERFECT, NOW CHANGE; Music/Arrangements, Jimmy Roberts; Lyrics/Book, Joe Dipietro; Director, Joel Bishoff; Musical Director, Tom Fay; Sets, Neil Peter Jampolis; Costumes, Candace Donnelly; Lighting, Mary Louise Geiger; Sound, Duncan Edwards; Cast Recording, Varese Sarabande; Production Supervisor, Matthew G. Marholin; Press, Bill Evans/Jim Randolph CAST: Jordan Leeds succeeded by Danny Burstein, Robert Roznowski, Jennifer Simard, Melissa Weil STANDBYS: Thomas Michael Allen, Jill Geddes, Kevin Pariseau, Cheryl Stern

MUSICAL NUMBERS: Cantata for a First Date, Stud and a Babe, Single Man Drought, Why Cause I'm a Guy, Tear Jerk, I Will Be Loved Tonight, Hey There Single Guy/Gal, He Called Me, Wedding Vows, Always a Bridesmaid, Baby Song, Marriage Tango, On the Highway of Love, Waiting Trio, Shouldn't I Be Less in Love with You, I Can Live with That, I Love You You're Perfect Now Change

A two-act musical revue for hopeful heterosexuals.

Lucie Arnaz, Estelle Parsons in *Grace & Glorie* (Carol Rosegg)

Jennifer Simard, Melissa Weil, Jordan Leeds, Robert Roznowski in *I Love You, You're Perfect, Now Change* (Carol Rosegg)

Peter Slutsker, Becky Watson, Robert Sapoff, Michael McGrath in
The Cocoanuts (Gerry Goodstein)

Lisa Fischer, Kellie D. Evans in *Born to Sing!* (Carol Rosegg)

(Bryant Park) Saturday, July 20-Aug.10, 1996 (4 performances) Some Other Shakespeare in the Park presents:
MUCH ADO ABOUT NOTHING by William Shakespeare; Director, Kathleen Powers; Choreography, Wendy Roberts; Music, Danton Bankay; Press, Monique Odom CAST: Danton Bankay (Balthasar), Frank Bradley (Borachio/Friar Francis), Maria Carreras (Ursula), Tim Cusick (Verges), Eric Hanson (Hugh Oatcake), Rob Harrison (Benedick), Jennifer Hill (Balthasar's Muse), Ted Hoffstetter (George Seacole), Timothy Jeffryes (Leonato), Christine Mascott (Dogberry), Lolly Mozersky (Beatrice), Danielle Rayne (Margaret), Christopher Rubin (Antonio), Erik Sherr (Don John), Brett Thacher (Conrade), Chris Todd (Don Pedro), Cory Walter (Claudio), Seana Lee Wyman (Hero)
Performed without intermission.

(American Place Theatre) Saturday, July 27, 1996-Jan.5, 1997 (165 performances and 22 previews) Raymond J. Greenwald and The American Jewish Theatre present:
THE COCOANUTS; Music/Lyrics, Irving Berlin; Book, George S. Kaufman; Adaptation/Director/Choreography, Richard Sabellico; Musical Director/Arrangements, C. Lynne Shankel; Set, Jeff Moderger; Costumes, Jonathan Bixby; Lighting, Brian Nason; Sound, Ivan Pokorny, David Lynd; Stage Manager, Jason Brouillard; Press, Jeffrey Richards/Mark Cannistraro, Scott Susong CAST: Michael Waldron (Jamison), Brad Bradley (Eddie the Bellboy), Alec Timerman (Robert Adams), Celia Tackaberry (Mrs. Potter), Laurie Gamache (Penelope Martyn), Becky Watson (Polly Potter), Michael Berresse (Harvey Yates), Michael McGrath succeeded by Frank Moran, Frank Ferrante (Henry W. Schlemmer-Groucho), Peter Slutsker (Willie the Shill-Chico), Robert Sapoff (Silent Sam-Harpo), Michael Mulheren (Hennessey)
MUSICAL NUMBERS; Florida by the Sea, A Little Bungalow, Pack Up Your Sins and Go to the Devil (not in orig.), We Should Care, Always (cut from orig.), Five O'Clock Tea, Tango Melody, When My Dreams Come True (from 1929 film version), Shaking the Blues Away (not in orig.), Tale of a Shirt, Finale
A revised version of a 1925 musical comedy in two acts. Tha action takes place at Florida's Cocoanut Hotel.

(One Dream Theatre) Thursday, July 25-Aug.18, 1996 (13 performances and 3 previews) Carol R. Fineman and Worth St. Theater present:
ORESTES: I MURDERED MY MOTHER; Adapted/Directed by Jeff Cohen; Sets/Lighting, Edward Pierce; Costumes, Moe Schell; Sound, Patrick Denny; Stage Manager, Heather Cousens; Press, Carol R. Fineman CAST: Peter Appel (Jerry Gulf/Menelaus/Dr. Strauss), Milo Bernstein (Holland Smith/Tyndareus/Apollo/Ken Skyler), Christine Cowin (Jenny Lake/Helen/Kris), John L. Damon (Pylades), Kathryn Hahn (Hermione/Carla Santiago/Karen Beck/Trailer Park Woman), Corrina Lyons (Elektra), Paul Whitthorne (Orestes)
A contemporary adaptation of the Euripides play performed without intermission.

(Union Square Theatre) Wednesday, July 31-Dec.1, 1996 (133 performances and 8 previews) Vy Higginsen & Ken Wydro, and Mitchell Maxwell & Alan J. Schuster in association with SuperVision Productions and Workin'Man Theatricals present:
BORN TO SING!; Music, W. Naylor; Lyrics/Book, Vy Higginsen and Ken Wydro; Director, Mr. Wydro; Sets, Mike Fish; Costumes, Carlos Falchi, Malissa Drayton; Lighting, Marshall Williams; Sound, DonJuan Holder; Stage Movement, Charles Stewart; Stage Manager, Leopold M. John; Press, Keith Sherman/Jim Byk, Kevin Rehac, Charlie Siedenburg CAST: Lisa Fischer (Doris Winter), Kellie D. Evans (Mama Winter), Tanya Blount (Dottie Winter), Stacy Francis (Samantha Summers), Charles Stewart (Minister of Music), Jessica Care Moore, Debora Rath, Shari Headley, Smanatha Davis (Narrator), Charles Perry (Auditioner), Anita Wells, Anissia Bunton, Kim Summerson (Harris Sisters), Pierre Cook, Tyrone Flower, Richard Hartley, Damon Horton, Ronnie McLeod (Four Guys), Dawn Green, Sheila Slappy, Robin Cunningham, Lorraine Moore, Anita Wells
MUSICAL NUMBERS: Lead Us On, Interpretations, Lord Keep Us Day By Day, Sweeping through the City, Blessed Assurance, Is My Living in Vain, Narration/Poem, Give the Child a Break, And the Winner Is, Your Time Will Come, Born to Sing, Harmony, Who Needs Who?, Take a Stand, Sky's the Limit, Who You Gonna Blame?, Center Peace, Attention Must Be Paid, Poem, Face to Face, Take the High Way, Finale
A musical in two acts.

(NYC/NJ Parks) Thursday, Aug.1-25, 1996 (17 performances and 6 previews) Puerto Rican Traveling Theatre presents:
BLACKOUT (EL APAGON) by Jose Luis Gonzalez; Adaptation/Direction, Rosalba Rolon; Set, Regina Garcia; Musical Director, Ricardo Pons; Stage Manager, Jay Quinones; Press, Max Eisen/Laurel Factor CAST: Tony Chiroldes Carbia, Jorge B. Merced

A comedy with music. The action takes place in New York City during a blackout.

(Douglas Fairbanks Theater) Thursday, Aug.1, 1996-still playing May 31, 1997 Gail Homer Seay, Peter Hauser, Jane M. Abernethy in association with Marc Howard Segan present:
Howard Crabtree's **WHEN PIGS FLY**; Conceived by Howard Crabtree and Mark Waldrop; Music, Dick Gallagher; Lyrics/Sketches/Direction, Mark Waldrop; Costumes, Howard Crabtree; Sets/Lighting, Peter Hauser; Cast Recording, RCA: Sound, Rob Gorton; Musical Director, Philip Fortenberry; Stage Manager, Glynn David Turner; Press, Tony Origlio/Michael Cullen CAST: Stanley Bojarski, Keith Cromwell, John Treacy Egan, David Pevsner, Jay Rogers, Michael West, Keith Cromwell (understudy) SUCCEEDING CAST: James Heatherly, Blake Hammond, John Wasiniak, Ray Friedeck
MUSICAL NUMBERS: When Pigs Fly, You've Got to Stay in the Game, Torch, Light in the Loafers, Coming Atttractions with Carol Ann, Not All Man, Patriotic Finale, Wear Your Vanity with Pride, Hawaiian Wedding Day, Shaft of Love, Sam & Me, Bigger Is Better, Laughing Matters, Over the Top, Finale

A gay musical revue in two acts. Mr. Crabtree died on June 28, 1996 just five days after finishing work on this production.

(NYC Parks) Saturday, Aug.3-Sept.15, 1996 (13 performances) Theater for the New City presents:
IT'S TOAST; Music, Christopher Cherney; Lyrics/Director, Crystal Field; Set, Anthony Angel; Design, Mary Blanchard; Set, Walter Gurbo; Sound, Paul Garrity; Masks, Pamela Mayo; Costumes, Seth Hanson; Press, Jonathan Slaff CAST: Johnson Anthony, Lucy Caban, Desteny Cruz, Israel Cruz, Joseph C. Davies, Andy DeLaRosa, Crystal Field, Cheryl Gadsden, Michael David Gordon, Bob Grimm, Inez Guzman, Jerry Jaffe, Terry Lee King, Sonia Kasarov, George Kodar, Mark Marcante, Craig Meade, Rob Miller, R.J. Maharaj, Julia Paskin, Jessy Ortiz, Denise Olivares, Primy Rivera, Jason Rodriguez, Liana Rosario, Monica Santana, Carol Sims

This NYC-set musical marks the 25th anniversary of Theater for the New City street theater productions.

Michael West, David Pevsner in *When Pigs Fly* (Gerry Goodstein)

David Pevsner, Jay Rogers, Stanley Bojarski, John Treacy Eagan in *When Pigs Fly* (Gerry Goodstein)

(Synchronicity Space) Monday, Aug.5-27, 1996 (8 performances) Bartalk Productions in association with Synchronicity Space presents: **SMASH THE TREADMILL** by Rick Mowat and Marty Grabstein; Director, Alan Braunstein; Costumes, Terry Graziano; Music, Lisa Dean; Press, Jonathan Slaff CAST: The Lab Rats (Rick Mowat, Marty Grabstein), David Fenton, Paula Ficara, The Cap'n.

A spoof on obedience.

(Circle in the Square Downtown) Wednesday, Aug.7-October, 1996 Delsener/Slater Enterprises and Theatre-A-Go-Go! present: **VALLEY OF THE DOLLS**; Adapted from the novel by Jacqueline Susann and the screenplay by Helen Deutsch and Dorothy Kingsley; Director, Tom Booker; Sets, Wade Thomas; Costumes, Heather Stanfield, The Cast; Lighting, Jim Jatho; Sound, Tree Fort Studios, Curt Anderson; Press, Ellen Zeisler/Eric Latzky, Ron Lasko CAST: Jackie Beat (Helen Lawson), Toom Booker (Mel Anderson), Melissa Christopher (Jennifer North), Eliza Coyle (Anne Wells), Joe Dietl (Mr. Bellamy/Stagehand), Kate Flannery (Nelly O'Hara), Jessica Hughes (Miriam Polar), Michael Irpino (Ted Casablanca/Chardot), Alex Leydenfrost (Kevin Gilmore), Ken Marino (Tony Polar), Jon Samuel (Lyon Burke), Nan Schmid (Miss Steinberg), Lisa Galipeau, Heather Stanfield (Ensemble)

A camp adaptation of the 1967 film.

(Harold Clurman Theatre) Friday, Aug.9-31, 1996 (20 performances and 1 preview) Love Creek Productions presents: **CUCUMBERS**; Written/Directed by Le Wilhelm; Set, Viola Bradford; Lighting, Richard Callahan; Stage Manager, Kirsten Walsh; Press, Francine L. Trevens CAST: Devin Quigley (Joyce), Diane Hoblit (Aunt Doll), Tracy Newirth (Linda), Cecila Frontero (Terry), Michelle McCall (Sissy), Cynthia Granville (Veda), Carol Halstead (Patsy), Vicki Weidman (Charlotte), Nancy McDoniel (Lavinia)

A comedy in two acts. The setting is the Ozark mountains.

(Interart Theatre) Monday, Aug.12-Sept.15, 1996 Interart Theatre presents: **O WHOLLY NIGHT AND OTHER JEWISH SOLECISMS**; Written/Performed by Deb Margolin; Director, Margot Lewitin; Press, Peter Cromarty

A young Jewish woman waits for the Messiah.

(Vineyard 26th St.) Monday, Aug.12-Sept.1, 1996 Peculiar Works Project presents: **FREIHEIT MAKES A STAND**; Written/Directed by Barry Rowell; Lighting, David Castaneda; Sets, Jacob Harlow; Music, David Lynch CAST: Ernest Abuba (Aufidius), Richard Sheinmel (Freiheit), Randy Lake, Jacki Goldhammer

Suggested by Shakespeare's Coriolanus.

(Synchronicity Space) Wednesday, Aug.14-31, 1996 (17 performances) Synchronicity Space and Fifth Business Productions present: **KEATS** by David Shepard; Director, Douglas Hall; Set, Mark Symczak; Lighting, David Alan Comstock; Press, John Amato CAST: Austin Pendleton (John Keats)

The action takes place in Rome, 1821.

(Nada) Thursday, Aug.15-25, 1996 (10 performances) Untitled Theater Company #61 presents: **MY HEAD WAS A SLEDGEHAMMER** by Richard Foreman; Director, Edward Einhorn CAST: Rufus Collins (Dr. Majextico), Julia Martin (Assistant)

Rick Mowat, Marty Grabstein in *Smash the Treadmill* (Jonathan Slaff)

Devon Quigley, Carol Halstead, Cecilia Frontero in *Cucumbers* (Bill Swartz)

Deb Margolin in *O Wholly Night...* (Carol Rosegg)

Justin Kirk, Hal Robinson in *Old Wicked Songs* (Carol Rosegg)

(Inner Space Theater) Thursday, Aug.15-25, 1996 (10 performances)
Black Box Productions in association with WINK Productions presents:
THE WIFE, THE BRIDE, THE NUN AND THE ACTRESS; Stage
Manager, Luiz Russo Cut by Gordon Osmond; Director, Geoffrey Tange-
man CAST: Beth Allen (Lucy), Steve Deighan (Scott), John Evans
(Waiter), Brad Thomas (Kirk)
An Ordinary Morning by Jeffery Scott Elwell; Director, Geoffrey Tange-
man CAST: Ross McKenzie (Anne), Thomas F. Walsh (Henry)
A Brooklyn Romance by Marcy Lovitch; Director, Louise Bylicki
CAST: Steve Sherling (Vinnie), Jospeh Tudisco (Nick), Joe Moretti
(Louie), Andrea DeVaynes (Gloria), Larry Bialock (Don Don), Alyson
Lawther (Donna Marie)
Night Class by James Serpento; Director, Louise Bylicki CAST: Sharon
Port (Sr. Mary Agnes), Camille Carida (Lucy), Carole Mansley (Beadle),
Tom Nolan (Grogg), Daniel Zen (Cooney), Steve Deighan (Dobbins)
   An evening of diva comedies.

(Promenade Theatre) Friday, Aug.16, 1996-Mar.9, 1997 (210 perfor-
mances and 23 previews) Daryl Roth & Jeffrey Ash in association with
The Barrow Group present:
OLD WICKED SONGS by Jon Marans; Director, Seth Barrish; Set/Cos-
tumes, Markas Henry; Lighting, Howard Werner; Sound, Red Ramona;
Stage Manager, D.C. Rosenberg; Press, Shirley Herz/Sam Rudy CAST:
Hal Robinson (Prof. Josef Mashkan), Justin Kirk (Stephen Hoffman)
   A drama in two acts. The action takes place in Vienna, Austria during
1986. Performed last season at the Jewish Repertory Theatre.

(Washington Sq. Park) Thursday, Aug.22-Sept.15, 1996 (13 perfor-
mances and 3 previews) Gorilla Repertory presents:
KING LEAR by William Shakespeare; Director, Christopher Sanderson;
Press, Peter Cromarty/Hugh Hayes, Andrew Schinder CAST: Copernicus
(King Lear), Tim McDonnell (Kent), Paul Barry (Gloucester), Scott Wood
(Edgar), Courtney Casaves (Edmund), Amo Gulinello (Fool), Christina
Cabot (Goneril), Carrie Murphy (Regan), Cerris Morgan-Moyer
(Cordelia)
   A performance using the elements of city and nature.

(Prospect Park) Thursday, Aug.22-Sept.1, 1996 (9 performances and 1
preview) Kings County Shakespeare Company in association with Cele-
brate Brooklyn presents:
TWO GENTLEMEN OF VERONA by William Shakespeare; Director,
Deborah Wright Houston; Press, Jonathan Slaff CAST INCLUDES: T.
Thomas Brown (Valentine), Michael Oberlander (Protheus), Jeff Ricketts
(Speed), Randy Aromando (Launce), Cate Smi (Julia), Heather Gillespie
(Silvia)

(Riant Theatre) Friday, Aug,.23-Sept.15, 1996 (24 performances) Riant
Theatre & B.E.T. Productions present:
THE LADY GENTIAN VIOLET by Ronald V. Micci; Director, Van
Dirk Fisher; Press, Bruce Lynn CAST: Joe Corey (Plantation Daddy), Eric
Nutter (Jefferson), Daniel Seth Lubiner, Eric Strongbow (Horace
Winthrop), Selena Lovecraft, Brini Maxwell/Ben Sander (Gentian Violet),
Eric Hunsley (Beauford Beauregard)
   A comedy in two acts. The action takes place in the Old South, after the
Civil War.

Copernicus in *King Lear* (Barrett W. Benton)

120

Elise Stone in *What the Butler Saw* **(Gerry Goodstein)**

Brooke Marie Procida, Marc Eliot, Robin Gray in *No In Between*
(Carol Rosegg)

Branch Woodman, Michael McElroy, Jamie MacKenzie in
Disappearing Act **(Carol Rosegg)**

(Bouwerie Lane Theatre) Friday, Aug.23-Dec.20, 1996 re-opened Thursday, May 29-June 15, 1997 Jean Cocteau Repertory presents:
WHAT THE BUTLER SAW by Joe Orton; Director, Scott Shattuck; Sets, Patrick Heydenburg; Costumes, Susan Soetaert; Lighting, Giles Hogya; Press, Jonathan Slaff CAST: Joseph J. Menino (Dr. Prentice), Molly Pietz (Geraldine Barclay), Elise Stone (Mrs. Prentice), Kennedy Brown succeeded by Neeraj Kochhar (Nicholas Beckett), Craig Smith (Rance), Christopher Black (Sgt. Match)
A comedy set in an asylum.

(Don't Tell Mama) Monday, Aug.26-Sept.5, 1996 (7 performances) ETB Productions presents:
NO IN BETWEEN; Original Songs, Elliot Weiss and Mike Champagne; Book, Mike Champagne; Director, Dan Held; Musical Director/Arrangements, Steve Steiner; Conductor, Ed Goldschneider; Stage Manager, David Bonilla; Press, Tony Origlio/Michael Cullen CAST: Marc Eliot, Robin Gray, Brooke Marie Procida
MUSICAL NUMBERS: No In Between, Alan's Song, Haven't We Met, What You Don't Know about Woman, I Don't Remember Christmas, You Can Always Count on Me, Side by Side by Side, I'm Gonna Live Forever, You are There, Life that Jack Built, Not a Day Goes By, Finale
A musical mindscape in one act.

(47th St. Theatre) Monday, Aug.26-Oct.6, 1996 (39 performances and 10 previews) Jeff Bannon, Phyllis Miriam in association with Bosco Ltd., Shawn Churchman, Normand Kurtz and Steven M. Levy present:
DISAPPEARING ACT; Music/Lyrics, Mike Oster; Director/Choreography/Vocal Arrangements, Mark Frawley; Musical Director/Arrangements, Ron Roy; Sets, Bill Clarke; Costumes, Greg Barnes; Lighting, Tim Hunter; Sound, Jim van Bergen; Stage Manager, Brian Rardin; Press, Pete Sanders/Michael Hartman CAST: Michael McElroy, Jamie MacKenzie, Branch Woodman
MUSICAL NUMBERS: Fear and Self-Loathing, They Say, Men Who Like Their Men, Gentrification, Just Go Shopping, I Had to Laugh, A Secret, Children Are a Blessing, Friendly Vacation, Let Me In, Something's Wrong with this Picture, Rants and Raves, I Slept with a Zombie, The Ride Home, Looks Like It Might Rain, Dance Floor, All Tied Up on the Line, In Here, Dear Diary, What Do Ya Know, Fruits of Domestic Bliss, Old Flame, In Our Community, Someone I Missed, Ounce of Prevention, An Ordinary Day, Trio for Three Buddies, Faded Levi Jacket, Disappearing Act
A gay musical revue in two acts.

(Lambs Theatre) Wednesday, Aug.28-Dec.1, 1996 (95 performances and 8 previews) Black Bags Three Productions in association with Edmund Gaynes and The Mathewson Foundation present:
MATTY: *An Evening with Christy Mathewson*; Written/Performed by Eddie Frierson; Director, Kerrigan Mahan; Costumes, Suzan Kay Frierson; Lighting, Lawrence Oberman; Set, Robert Smith; Stage Manager, Tiffany Yelton; Press, David Rothenberg
A one-man play on the life of the turn-of-the-century baseball star.

(Inner Space) Tuesday, Sept.3-15, 1996 (12 performances) Wink Productions and Straight from the Heart Productions present:
THE HOT L BALTIMORE by Lanford Wilson; Director, Thomas Cote CAST: Heather Ann Barclay, Lawrence Cioppa, Maddy De Leon, Yael Gani, James M. Gordon, Ruth Jaffe, Jason Raymond, James Sutton, Jane Lincoln Taylor, Joseph Tudisco, Wendell Ward, Desiree Warner, Sarah Sido Weinberger

(Rainbow & Stars) Tuesday, Sept.3-28, 1996 (40 perfromances) Music-Theatre Group presents:
3 OF HEARTS; Music, Mary Rodgers; Lyrics, Marshall Barer, Martin Charnin, John Forster, Richard Maltby Jr., Mary Rodgers, William Shakespeare, Stephen Sondheim, Mark Waldrop; Director, Mark Waldrop; Conception/Original Direction, Richard Maltby Jr.; Musical Director/Arrangements, Patrick S. Brady; Lighting, Matt Berman; Costumes, Angelina Avallone; Stage Manager, Jeni Mahoney; Press, David Lotz/David Gersten CAST: Faith Prince, Mark Waldrop, Jason Workman MUSICAL NUMBERS: I'm Looking for Someone, Something Known, Opening for a Princess, Happily Ever After, In a Little While, Normandy, Shy, Yesterday I Loved You, Don't Take My Word for It, Hey Love, Nebraska Show Me a..., At the Same Time, Like Love, Once I Had a Friend, The Boy from..., Oh Mistress Mine, Back Here at Square One, Double or Nothing, 3 of Hearts, In Every Bedtime Story, Love Is on Parade

A musical revue. Previously performed at Eighty-Eight's as *Hey Love*, also the title of the Varese Sarabande cast recording.

(Samuel Beckett Theatre) Tuesday, Sept.3-Oct.5, 1996 (29 performances) Flip Productions and Tennessee Project present:
THE ALL-NUDE COLLEGE-GIRL REVUE by Lisa Faith Phillips; Director/Set, Todd Stuart Phillips; Lighting, David Comstock; Costumes, Ms. Phillips, Annie Rainford, Pam Wilterdink; Sound, Flip Prod., Philip Goetz; Stage Manager, Barbara Kovsky CAST: Dory Binyon (Carlotta), Ingrid Rifler (Ginger), Guelmari Oppenheimer (Cat), Pam Wilterdink (Babydoll), Allison Hope (Suzy), Yvonne Lewis (Eve), Melissa McGovern (Rusty), Sara Knight (Annie)

A comedy in two acts. The action takes place in the Peek-A-Boo Club in Boston's Combat Zone, 1986.

Mark Waldrop, Mary Rodgers, Jason Workman, Faith Prince of
3 of Hearts **(Carol Rosegg)**

(Solo Arts Group) Wednesday, Sept.4-Oct.30, 1996 (24 performances) Solo Arts Group and Antitheatrical Theatrical presents:
4 EVER SOLO FESTIVAL; Press, Kevin Mark Mazuzan, Bobby Reed PROGRAMS: *Goddess*; Written/Performed by Abigail Gampel; Director, Jane Young; *Twelve Angry Women*; Written/Performed by Danny McWilliams; Director, Kristine Zbornik; *Jumping Off the Fridge*; Written/Performed by Ellen Hulkower; Director, Margarett Dykstra; *Just Another White Chick from Westchester*; Written/Performed by Fia Perera; Director, Carol Tiers

(Producer's Club) Wednesday, Sept.4-21, 1996 (10 performances and 2 previews) Sebastian Productions presents:
WHAT DOESN'T KISS US by Dan Remmes; Director, Renner Davis; Lighting/Sound, Beau Decker; Press, Gary and John Springer~Susan Chicoine/Candi Adams CAST: Victoria Noone (Joy), Chris Dolman (Byron), Robert Corddry (Waiter), Dan Remmes (Karl), Jennifer Perry (Psychiatrist)

A romantic comedy in two acts.

(Theatre Off Park) Wednesday, Sept.4-29, 1996 (19 performances and 4 previews) Rattlestick Productions presents:
VOLUNTEER MAN by Dan Clancy; Director, Tracy Brigden; Set, Van Santvoord; Lighting, Chad McArver; Costumes, Mirena Rada; Sound, Chad Collins; Stage Managers, Marienne Chapman, John Evans; Press, Peter Cromarty/Hugh Hayes CAST: Ray Anthony Thomas (Melvin), Reed Birney (Keith), Elizabeth Bove (Nurse)

A drama performed without intermission. The action takes place in NYC's Good Samaritan Hospital, 1995.

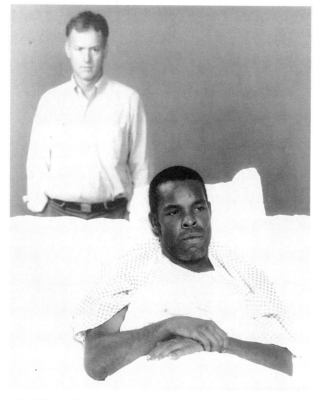

Reed Birney, Ray Anthony Davis in *Volunteer Man* **(Carol Rosegg)**

(Circle Rep Lab) Thursday, Sept.5-22, 1997 (8 performances and 10 previews) Circle Repertory Theater presents:
900 ONEONTA; Written/Directed by David Beaird; Set, Shawn Motley; Lighting, John Lewis; Costumes, Laurie Churba; Sound, Jason Fox; Stage Manager, Francys Olivia Burch; Press, Jeffrey Richards/Roger Bean CAST: Leland Crooke (D andy), Venida Evans (Carrie), Missi Pyle (Burning Jewel), Sam Groom (Morely), Jon Cryer (Gitlo), Barbara Eda-Young succeeded by Hallie Foote (Persia), Devon Abner (Woodrow), Barry McEvoy (Fr. Bourette), Mikel Sarah Lambert (Beauty), Garret Dillahunt (Tiger), Michelle Hurd (Palace)

A drama in two acts. The action takes place in Bastrop, Louisiana, 1980. Unfortunately, Circle Repertory closed due to financial difficulties after this production, not completing their 28th season.

(Chelsea Playhouse) Thursday, Sept.5-29, 1996 (16 performances) The Lark Theatre Company presents:
HEATING AND COOLING by Sara Plath; Director, Russ Jolly; Sets, Ann Keehbauch; Lighting, Marcus Abbott; Costumes, Carol Brys; Sound, Phil Lee; Stage Manager, Shelli Aderman; Press, Chris Boneau~Adrian Bryan-Brown/Meredith Towers CAST: Brian Russell (Brian Renquist), Laura E. Johnston (Lavender Featherbright), Bill Christ (Harry Rockoffski), Ivan Davila (Beano), Polly Humphrys (La Fontaine), Gene A. Morra (Krepski), Booster (Mary Purdy), James Wiggins (Sam)

A philosophical comedy about air-conditioning, performed without intermission.

Jon Cryer, Michelle Hurd, Garret Dillahunt, Missi Pyle in
900 Oneonta   (Scott Susong)

(Theatre 3) Thursday, Sept.5-28, 1996 (12 performances and 4 previews) Fallen Leaf and Cyndy Fujikawa present:
HELMUT SEES AMERICA by George Malko; Director, John Stewart; Set, Dawn Robyn Petrlik; Lighting, Debra Dumas; Sound, David Van Tieghem; Costumes, Carol Brys; Stage Manager, Anita Vatavuk; Press, Jim Baldassare CAST: Pamela Nyberg (Christina-Marie Klammer), Maduka Steady (Shawaun Johnson), Dan Daily (Mackenzie Carlson), Paul Meek (Hotel Staff/State Department), Chase Damon

A drama performed without intermission. The action takes place in a motel room in Wisconsin.

(Theatre Row Theatre) Thursday, Sept.5-29, 1996 (21 performances and 5 previews) Susann Brinkley & Ron J. Kastener present:
THE SLEEPING HIPPO; Written/Directed by Max Mayer; Set, Rob Odorisio; Lighting, Donald Holder; Costumes, Sheree Coluccelli; Sound, Aural Fixation; Stage Manager, David P. Smith CAST: Rebecca Creskoff (Mary), Bill Camp (Alif), Douglas Weston (Nate), Phyllis Sommerville (Carol/Freyda)

A drama in two acts. The action takes place in the East Village.

(Theater for the New City) Thursday, Sept.5-22, 1996 (9 performances and 3 previews) Theater for the New City presents:
BEATA, THE POPE'S DAUGHTER by Mario Fratti; Director, Vera Beren; Set, Mark Symczak; Lighting, Stewart Wagner; Stage Manager, Ci Herzog; Press, Peter Cromarty CAST: Dominic Chianese (Pope), Seana Kofoed (Beata), Gene Silvers (Gustav), Mary Carol Johnson (Teofila), Peter Johl (Piotr), James Kohli (Ahmet), Peter Lucas (Zeki)

A drama in two acts. The action takes place in Rome, 1981.

(Kaufman Theater) Friday, Sept.6-29, 1996 (19 performances and 6 previews) Lucille Lortel presents:
BACK ON THE BOULEVARD; Musical Director, Dick Gallagher; Set, Michael Anania; Lighting, F. Mitchell Dana; Stage Manager, Ed Baldi; Press, Gary & John Springer~Susan Chicoine/Candi Adams CAST: Liliane Montevecchi

A musical revue.

Makuda Steady, Pamela Nyberg in *Helmut Sees America*
(Sherry Camhy)

Bill Camp, Rebecca Creskoff, Douglas Weston in *Sleeping Hippo*
(Jessica White)

(Miranda Theatre) Friday, Sept.6-27, 1996 (16 performances) The Quaigh Theatre in association with The Miranda Theatre presents:
THE WILD GUYS by Andrew Wreggitt and Rebecca Shaw; Director, Peter Jensen; Set, CJ Howard; Lighting, Scott Clyve; Costumes, Vern Malone; Sound, David Zipperer; Stage Manager, Kaddy Feast; Press, Gail Parenteau CAST: Charles O'Hara (Stewart), Bill Bartlett (Andy), Derek Le Dain (Randall), David M. Pincus (Robin)
A comedy in two acts. The action takes place in Lone Pine, Alberta, Canada.

(Nada Theatre) Monday, Sept.9-Oct.2, 1996 (12 performances) Artaban Theatre Company presents:
DOM JUAN IN MANHATTAN; Adapted from Moliere; Translation, Ethan Gelber; Director, Robert Gourp CAST: Jean Brassard (Dom Juan), Robert Gourp (Sganarelle), Artaban Theatre
A funky adaptation of the classic.

(West Bank Downstairs) Wednesday, Sept.11-28, 1996 (12 performances) A.T.O.M.I.C. Theater Company presents:
WHITE MEN/NOIR WOMEN; Written/Performed by Michael P. Scasserra (White Men) and Toni Schlesinger (Noir Women) and **INSIGNIFICANT OTHERS** by Michael P. Scasserra, Toni Schlesinger and Cynthia Boorujy; Press, Kristina Stroh CAST: Charlene Bitzas, Michele Conte, Rick Hickman, Nancy Lee, Craig Williams
One-act plays.

(Ceative Place Theatre) Wednesday, Sept.11-28, 1996 (10 performances and 2 previews) re-opened Mar.5-29, 1997 (16 performances) Madeline Ann presents:
IT BEGINS WITH A KISS...; Written/Directed by Sammy Busby; Press, Shirley Herz/Wayne Wolfe, Adam Meza
Dying to Kiss You CAST: Katherine Keane, Tom Berdik
Dance for Me Sweetheart CAST: Jenna Kellard, Luke Sabis
Superior Smoke CAST: Elena Aaron, Sammy Busby
A love trilogy.

(Nuyorican Poet's Cafe) Thursday, Sept.12-Oct.6, 1996 (13 performances and 3 previews) Nuyorican Pet's Cafe and Theater Double present:
JASON AND MEDEA by Dennis Moritz; Conceived/Directed/Additional Material by Michael LeLand II; Design, Tim Kuhrtz; Choreography, Kip Martin; Music, Serena Berger, Elliot Levin; Press, Gary Springer~Susan Chicoine/Tiina Piirsoo, Ann Guzzi CAST: Shelita Birchett (Medea), Christopher Kendra (Jason), Jim Boyle (Ageus), Frances Mammana (Nurse), Redman Maxfield (Creon), Peter Patrikios (Tutor), Frank Serafin (Messenger), Anne Delano, Brett Halsey, Janice Hughes, Steven O'Brien, Erin Smith, Jacqueline Sydney, Marianne Ryan
A contemporary adaptation of the ancient myth.

(Center Stage) Thursday, Sept.12-29, 1996 (12 performances) Company of Angels presents:
EXTREMITIES by William Mastrosimone; Director, Paul Griffin; Lighting, George Polis; Sound, Nando Caraballo; Stage Manager, Lisa Preston CAST: Syl Farrell (Marjorie), Paul Griffin (Raul), Andrea Ashford (Terry), Kendall Pettygrove (Patricia)
A drama in two acts.

David M. Pincus, Derek Le Dain, Bill Bartlett, Charlie O'Hara in *Wild Guys* **(Beth Whitman)**

Sammy Busby, Elena Aaron in *It Begins with a Kiss* **(David L. Stevens)**

Shelita Birchett in *Jason and Medea* **(George Kandelaki)**

(American Jewish Theatre) Thursday, Sept.12–Nov.10, 1996 (54 performances and 7 previews) Pearl Productions in association with Edmund Gaynes present:

EINSTEIN: A STAGE PORTRAIT by Willard Simms; Directed/Performed by John Crowther; Set, Eric Warren, Robert L. Smith; Lighting, Lawrence Oberman; Costumes, Il Creativo Productions; Sound, Chuck Estes; Stage Manager, D. Mark Lyons; Press, David Rothernberg

The action takes place in Princeton, NJ, 1946.

(29th St. Rep. Theatre) Thursday, Sept.12–Oct.12, 1996 (15 performances and 5 previews) 29th St. Repertory & Weissberger Theater Group present:

PIG by Tammy Ryan; Director, Tim Corcoran; Set, Sal Perrotta; Lighting, Jeremy Kumini; Sound, Rick Beenders; Stage Manager, Gregory A. Little; Press, Gary Springer~Susan Chicoine/Candi Adams CAST: Leo Farley (Jack Robinson), Susan Wisdom (Irene Robinson), Moira MacDonald (Jeanann Robinson), Karen Phillips (Peggy Robinson), Ronda Music (Maureen Robinson), Paula Ewin (Bernice O'Conner), Robert Suttile (George O'Conner), Thomas Wehrle (Jason Robinson), Frank Rodriguez (Santos Rodriguez)

A drama in two acts. The action takes place in Queens, NYC, on Labor Day 1990.

Leo Farley, Thomas Wehrle in *Pig* (Greg Little)

(Lamb's Theatre) Saturday, Sept.14, 1996–July 13, 1997 (363 performances and 10 previews) Catco and Skyline Entertainment present:

MAGIC ON BROADWAY; Choreography, Tiger Martina; Lighting, Gregory Cohen; Sound, Robert Cotnoir; Press, Richard Rubenstein/Alan Locher CAST: Joseph Gabriel, Lucy Gabriel, Romano Frediani, Heather Rochelle Harmon, Melanie Doskocil, Kathleen Grimaldi, Karen Mascari, Victoria Whitten

A revue of magic acts and dancing.

Joseph Gabriel in *Magic on Broadway*

(Judith Anderson Theatre) Tuesday, Sept.17–Oct.6, 1996 (16 performances and 1 preview) Dorian Gray Productions presents:

DORIAN GRAY; Music, Gary David Levinson; Lyrics, Allan Rieser; Book, Mr. Rieser, Don Price; Based on the novella *The Picture of Dorian Gray* by Oscar Wilde; Director/Staging, Don Price; Musical Director/Arrangements, James Mironchik; Set, Sal Perrotta; Costumes, Mary Nemecek Peterson; Lighting, Kimo James; Sound, Rick Beenders; Stage Manager, Souglas Shearer; Press, Les Schecter CAST: Tom Rocco (Basil Hallward), Chris Weikel (Lord Henry Wotton), Brian Duguay (Dorian Gray), Laura Stanczyk (Sibyl Vane), Gerrianne Raphael (Mrs. Vane), Ronald K. Morehead (James Vane), Ari Zohar Klingman (Victor), Mary Setrakian (Gladys), Amy D. Forbes (Polly), Jim Straz (Alan Campbell), John Greenbaum (Host), Whitney Allen (Hetty)

MUSICAL NUMBERS: Beauty Past All Dreaming, Discover the Man You Are, I Would Give My Sould for That, Counterfeit Love, Marriage, Love that Lives Forever, Don't Throw Your Love Away, What Will Happen to Me Now?, Dorian Gray, Take Care of Your Heart, What Dark November Thoughts/Let Me Believe in You, The Prayer, Blue Gate Fields Hotel, As Long as There are Men, Stay, We are But Patters of Paint, I'll Call My Soul My Own

A musical in two acts. The action takes place in London, late 1880s.

**Right: Brian Duguay, Chris Weikel in
*Dorian Gray***

(John Houseman Theatre) Tuesday, Sept.17-Nov.3, 1996 (39 performances and 17 previews) Elliot Martin & Ron Shapiro in association with Lee Mimms & Amick Byram present:

RADIO GALS; Music/Lyrics/Book by Mike Craver and Mark Hardwick; Director/Choreography, Marcia Milgrom Dodge; Set, Narelle Sissons; Costumes, Michael Krass; Lighting, Joshua Starbuck; Sound, Tom Morse; Musical Supervisor, Christopher Drobny; Arrangements, Mr. Hardwick, Klea Blackhurst, Mr. Craver, Emily Mikesell; Stage Manager, Daniel Munson; Press, Jeffrey Richards/Irene Gandy, Roger Bean, Mark Cannistraro CAST: Carole Cook (Hazel C. Hunt), M. Rice (Miss Mabel Swindle), P.M. Craver (Miss Azilee Swindle), Emily Mikesell (America), Klea Blackhurst (Rennabelle), Rosemary Loar (Gladys Fritts), Matthew Bennett (O.B. Abbott)

MUSICAL NUMBERS: Wedding of the Flowers, Sunrise Melody, Aviatrix Love Song, Horehound Compound, If Stars Could Talk, When It's Sweetpea Time in Georgia, Dear Mr. Gershwin, Tranquil Boxwood, Faeries in My Mother's Flower Garden, A Fireside A Pipe & A Pet, Edna Jones the Elephant Girl, Paging the Ether, Royal Radio, Weather Song, Buster He's a Hot Dog Now, Why Did You Make Me Love You?, Kittens in the Snow, Old Gals, A Gal's Got to Do What a Gal's Got to Do, NBC Broadcast, Finale

A musical comedy in two acts. The action takes place in Cedar Ridge, Arkansas, late 1920s.

P.M. Rice, Emily Mikesell, Carole Cook, M. Craver, Klea Blackhurst in *Radio Gals* (Gerry Goodstein)

(Theatre East) Wednesday, Sept.18, 1996-Jan.26, 1997 (69 performances and 9 previews) Theatre East presents:

AMERICANA; Written and Musical Arranged by John A. Mezzano Jr.; Directors, Sharon Hillegas, Mishar Productions; Dramatic Supervisor/Stage Manager, Michael S. Hillegas; Choreography, Kris Foltz, Dawn Tynan; Costumes, Alice Kirkland; Sets, Curtis Smith; Press, Shirley Herz/Adam Meza CAST: David A. Baecker, Melanie Farrow, Diana Pappas, Nathan Smith, Suzi Teitelman, Wendy Weiss, Jeremiah Brooks

A revue highlighting 100 years of American music.

(American Theatre of Actors) Wednesday, Sept.18-28, 1996 (11 performances) A Household Name Theatre Company presents:

A MESSAGE FOR THE BROKEN HEARTED by Gregory Motton; Director/Set/Lighting, River Eirtree; Sound, Julene Mays, Candice Owens; Stage Manager, Ms. Owens CAST: Tracy Lee Bell (Linda), Kirk Marcoe (Mickey), Jenifer Sparks (Jenine), David Teschendorf (Stevenson)

A drama in two acts. The setting is North London.

(Tribeca Performing Arts Center) Thursday, Sept.19-Oct.27, 1996 (35 performances) Shadow Productions presents:

EVOLUTION by Steven Guyer; Choreography, Stacie Boord, Katy Psenicka; General Manager, Kathryn Frawley; Press, Ms. Boord

A cast of seventeen performs thirteen music theatre vignettes against a carnival backdrop.

Chris Lynch, Michelle Daniels, Rebecca Gentile in *Evolution* (Will Shively)

(McGinn/Cazale Theater) Tuesday, Sept.24-Nov.10, 1996 (35 performances and 14 previews) The Westside Theatre presents:

POLITICAL ANIMAL; Written/Performed by Douglas McGrath; Director, Peter Askin; Set, Rob Odorisio; Costumes, Candice Donnelly; Lighting, Phil Monat; Sound, Bruce Ellman; Video, Dennis Diamond; Stage Manager, Renee Lutz; Press, Chris Boneau~Adrian Bryan-Brown/Erin Dunn, Paula Mallino

A one-man comedy.

Douglas McGrath in *Political Animal* (Joan Marcus)

(Theatre Four) Tuesday, Sept.24-Oct.20, 1996 (22 performances and 10 previews) Valiant Theatre Company presents:
RHINOCEROS by Eugene Ionesco; Adaptation, Theresa Rebeck; Director, Michael Murray; Set, Karl Eigsti, Ted Simpson; Costumes, Amela Baksic; Lighting, Neil Peter Jampolis; Sound, Aural Fixation; Stage Manager, Allison Sommers; Press, Gary Springer~Susan Chicoine CAST: Heather Carnduff (Waitress), Burt Edwards (Old Gentleman), Michael Etheridge (Grocer/Fireman), David Green (Logician), Zach Grenier (John), J.R. Horne (Bofford), Peter Jacobson (Berenger), Debbie Lamedman (Grocer's Wife), Cortez Nance Jr. (Bar Owner/Fireman), Erin J. O'Brien (Daisy), Geoffrey Owens (Doddard), Elizabeth Van Dyke (Housewife/Mrs. Beef)
A new adaptation of the absurdist comedy in two acts. The action takes place in The Square, The Office, John's Bedroom and Berenger's Apartment.

(Westside Theatre/Downstairs) Tuesday, Sept.24, 1996-Aug.30, 1997 David Stone, Amy Nederlander-Case, Barry & Fran Weissler and Manhattan Theatre Club present:
FULL GALLOP by Mark Hampton and Mary Louise Wilson; Director, Nicholas Martin; Set, James Noone; Costumes, Michael Krass; Lighting, David F. Segal; Sound, Bruce Ellman; Stage Manager, Ira Mont; Press, Pete Sanders/Glenna Freedman CAST: Mary Louise Wilson succeeded during vacation by Carole Monferdini (Diana Vreeland), Jacqueline Chambord (Yvone)
A play in two acts. The action takes place in Diana Vreeland's Park Avenue apartment, 1971.

Mary Louise Wilson in *Full Gallop* (Carol Rosegg)

Ted Zurkowski, Karen Lynn Gorney in *Richard III* (Dave Cross)

(City Center) Wednesday, Sept.25-29, 1996 (6 performances) ICM Artists in association with Kritas Productions and The National Theater of Greece present:
ELEKTRA by Sophocles; Director, Lydia Koniordou; Sets/Costumes, Dionysis Fotopoulos; Translation, Yorgos Heimonas; Music, Takis Farazis; Choreography, Apostolla Papadamaki; Lighting, Alekos Yiannaros; Press, Jeffrey Richards/Roger Bean CAST: Alexandfros Mylonas (Tutor), Miltos Dimoulis (Orestes), Yorgos Karamichos (Pylades), Lydia Koniordou (Elektra), Tania Papadopoulou (Chrysothemis), Aspasia Papathanasiou (Clytemnestra), Stefanos Kyriakidis (Aegisthus)
Performed without intermission.

(78th St. Theatre Lab) Thursday, Sept.26-Oct.20, 1996 (13 performances and 3 previews) 78th St. Theatre Lab presents:
THE PACKWOOD PAPERS by Karen Houppert and Stephen Nunns; Director/Sound/Lighting, Eric Nightengale; Costumes, Nancy Brous; Stage Manager, Erika Gimbel; Press, Jim Baldassare CAST: Toby Wherry (Bob Packwood), Katherine Heasley (Elaine Franklin), Michael Puzzo (Charlie Shepard), John Marino (Senators), Kimberly Reiss (Kerry Whitney), Ruth Nightengale (Florence Graves/Jean McMahon)
A drama based on a recent Senate ethics investigation.

(West-Park Church) Thursday, Sept.26-Oct.20, 1996 (16 performances) Frog & Peach Theatre Company presents:
RICHARD III by William Shakespeare; Director, Lynnea Benson; Fights, Al Foote III; Costumes, Janet Thomas; Set, John Kelly; Choreography, Tom Knutson; Stage Manager, Josephine M. Gallarello; Press, Gary Springer~Susan Chicoine/Candi Adams CAST: Ted Zurkowski (Richard III), Aris Alvarado (Prince Edward), Angela Bonacasa (Lady Ratcliff), Bryant Fraser (Hastings), Karen Lynn Gorney (Queen Elizabeth), Mervyn Haines Jr. (Lord Cardinal), Leone Fogle Hechler (Lady Anne), Tom Knutson (King Edward/Clarence), Vivien Landau (Jane Tyrrel), Howard I. Laniado (Lord Derby/Schrivener), Eric Masters (Catesby), Midori Nakamura (Richmond), Jack Rewkowski (Dorset), Douglas Stone (Buckingham), Carolyn Sullivan-Zinn (Duchess of York), Terry Tocantins (Lord Rivers), Silvana Vienne (Mistress Shore)

Maripat Donovan in *Late Night Catechism*

Robert Jimenez, Paul Albe, Susanne Wasson in *Lady Strass*
(Jonathan Slaff)

Perri Gaffney, Clifford Mason in *Two Bourgeois Blacks*

(St. Luke's) Thursday, Sept.26, 1996-still playing May 31, 1997 Entertainment Events & Joe Cocoran Productions present:
LATE NITE CATECHISM by Vicki Quade and Maripat Donovan; Director, Patrick Trettenero; Design, Marc Silvia; Lighting, Tom Sturge; Stage Manager, Stephen Sweeney; Press, David Rothenberg/David Gersten CAST: Maripat Donovan (Sister), George Bass (Fr. Martinez)
An interactive comedy in two acts. The setting is an adult catechism class.

(Phil Bosakowski Theatre) Friday, Sept.27-Oct.13, 1996 (15 performances) Judith Shakespeare Company presents:
TABULA RASA by Molly Louise Shepard; Director, Philip Hernandez; Set, Jason Ardizzone; Lighting, Carolyn Sarkis; Costumes, Emily Ockenfels; Sound, Jeffrey Swan Jones; Stage Manager, Lillian K. Minnich; Press, Publicity Office/Colleen Hughes CAST: Marlene C. Chavis (Toxie), Joanne Zipay (Thadia), Eve Holbrook succeeded by Jennifer Chudy (Tad), Matthew David Barton (Paul), Linda Tvrdy (Mrs. Desmond), Jeffrey Shoemaker (Mr. Desmond), Godfrey L. Simmons Jr. (Samuel), Joyia D. Bradley (Jynx)
A drama in two acts. The action takes place in East Texas, late 1970s.

(Workhouse Theater) Friday, Sept.27-Oct.19 (13 performances and 2 previews) returned Wednesday, Dec.4-15, 1997 (6 performances and 4 previews) Seraphim presents:
A FAMILY MAN by Tom Szentgyorgyi; Director, Troy Hollar; Set, Michael Shweikardt; Costumes, Laurie Churba; Lighting, Jeff Croiter; Sound, Laura Brown; Stage Manager, Lisa Dent; Press, Gary Springer~Susan Chicoine/Candi Adams CAST: Harley Adams, Catherine Corpeny, Dawn Evans, Laura Kirk, John Korkes, Craig Mathers, Krisin Moreu, Marc Romeo, Joseph L. Taylor
A drama involving a young man on the run froma loan shark.

(Ubu Rep Theater) Tuesday, Oct.1-20, 1996 (20 performances and 1 preview) Ubu Repertory presents:
LADY STRAUSS by Eduardo Manet; Translation, Phyllis Zatlin; Director, Andre Ernotte; Set, Watoku Ueno; Lighting, Greg MacPherson; Music/Sound, Robert Gould; Costumes, Carol Ann Pelletier; Stage Manager, Robin C. Gillette; Press, Jonathan Slaff CAST: Susanne Wasson (Mrs. Eliane Parkington Simpson), Paul Albe (Bertrand Le Brun-Slick), Robert Jimenez (Manuel Sierra-Flash)
A drama set in a dilapidated mansion in Belize.

(Henry St. Settlement) Tuesday, Oct.1-27, 1996 (23 performances and 1 preview) Henry St. Settlement presents:
TWO BOURGEOIS BLACKS by Clifford Mason; Director, Arthur French; Lighting/Set, Christophe Pierre; Sound, Tim Schallenbaum; Costumes, Anne Moore-Skeete; Press, Max Eisen/Laurel Factor CAST:Perri Gaffney (Marie), Clifford Mason (Lester)
A comedy in two acts. The setting is a large Eastern city.

(Radio City Music Hall) Wednesday, Oct.2-20, 1996 (23 performances) Abhann Productions and Moya Doherty present:
RIVERDANCE; Music, Bill Whelan; Director, John McColgan; Musical Director, David Hayes; Sets, Robert Ballagh; Production Design, Chris Slingsby; Lighting, Rupert Murray; Costumes, Jen Kelly; Sound, Michael O'GormanPress, Merle Frimark/Joel W. Dein LEAD DANCERS: Jean Butler, Colin Dunne, Maria Pages
A return engagement of last season's Irish dance show.

Kricker James, Ginger Grace in *To Moscow*
(Gerry Goodstein)

Eve Ensler in *Vagina Monologues* (Carl Saytor)

Joseph McKenna, Chuck Montgomery in *Death in a Landslide*
(Sarah Hemphill)

(One Dream Theatre) Thursday, Oct.3-27, 1996 (13 performances and 3 previews) Chain Lightning Theatre presents:
TO MOSCOW by Karen Sunde; Director, Steve Deighan; Sets, Bill Kneissl; Costumes, Meganne George; Lighting, Scott Clyve; Sound, Randy Morrison; Stage Manager, David Bonilla; Press, Shirley Herz/Wayne Wolfe, Vanessa Melnick CAST: Carol Emshoff (Masha), Gregory Seel (Konstantin Stanislavsky), Blainie Logan (Lydia/Anya), Kricker james (Anton Chekhov), Brandee Graff (Lika), Ginger Grace (Olga), Steve Kelly (Moskvin), Dominique Kay Reino (Maria Lilina)
A two-drama about Chekhov and the Moscow Art Theatre. The action takes place in St. Petersburg and Moscow, 1896-1904.

(HERE) Thursday, Oct.3, 1996-Jan.5, 1997 (61 performances and 9 previews) HOME for Contemporary Theatre and Art and Stephen Pevner present:
THE VAGINA MONOLOGUES; Written/Performed by Eve Ensler; Set, Wendy Evans Joseph; Lighting, Heather Carson; Press, Richard Kornber/Don Summa
Performed without intermission.

(Gove St. Playhouse) Thursday, Oct.3-20, 1996 (11 performances and 3 previews) Skin & Bones Productions in association with Kathleen Glynn & Michael Moore present:
DEATH IN A LANDSLIDE by Jay Martel; Director, Kirk Jackson; Set, Jason Sturm; Lighting, Charlie Spickler; Costumes, Liz McGarrity; Sound, Gary Schreiner; Stage Manager, Amy Joan Lewis; Press, Jim Baldassare CAST: Roy Bokhour (Abel Troutman/Pundit 3), Linda Hill (Vivian Finn), Christopher Hunt (Pundit 2/Sen.Borden/Secret Service), Bruce Katzman (Pundit 1/Rev. Twist/Pres. Ed Thorton), Joseph McKenna (Death), Chuck Montgomery (Cuff Riley), Sue Scarlett (Nora Thorton)
A comedy in two acts. The action takes place in a political consultant's office in our nation's capital.

(Theatre Row Theatre) Friday, Oct.4-20, 1996 (17 performances) Abingdon Theatre Company presents:
CEDAR CREEK by Ed Steele; Director, Taylor Brooks; Sets, Joseph B. St.Germain; Lighting, David Castaneda; Costumes, Gweneth West; Press, Peter Michael Brouwer CAST: Linnea Dakin (Lois Marie Swann), Daphne Gaines (Wrenn Farmer), Christopher Havard Trapani (Junior), Kathryn Graybill (Lake Swan), Ray Atherton (Troy Springer), Pamela Paul (Jessie Springer), Chris Brady (Lou Phillips), E.Patric Coker (G.W. Farmer), William Shuman (Baird)
A drama in two acts. The action takes place in Virgina's Shenandoah Valley, 1942-43.

(Gene Frankel Theatre) Friday, Oct.4-13, 1996 (6 performances) A Place in the Sun Productions presents:
A FEW GOOD MEN by Aaron Sorkin; Director, Victoria Ward CAST: Kevin Sanders (Dawson), William Christopher Stevens (Downey), Angel Caban (Markinson), Roddy Gerard (Kendrick), Christopher Silber (Weinberg), Glenn Dandridge (Ross), Bill Hunter (Kaffee), Angie Kristic (Jo Galloway), Ken Sharp (Nathan Jessup), Kenneth Green (Howard), Victor Hearn (Judge), Joe Surette (Santiago), Colin O'Brien, Kelly O'Bryan, Joanne Newborn, Rolando P. Garcia, Gordon Holmes, John Nathaniel Smith, Demetriee Tyler Williams, Antonio Suarez, David P. Conley

(Theatre for the New City) Friday, Oct.4-26, 1996 (20 performances and 3 previews) Ma-Yi Theatre Ensemble presents:
FLIPZOIDS by Ralph Pena; Director/Design, Loy Arcenas; Lighting, Blake Burba; Music/Sound, Fabian Obispo; Stage Manager, Sue Jane Stoker; Press, Gary Springer~Susan Chicoine/Candi Adams CAST: Mia Katigbak, Ken Leung, Ching Valdes-Aran
    Filipino-Americans testing the "melting pot".

(Nada) Monday, Oct.7-27, 1996 (11 performances) the deep ellum ensemble presents:
LEONCE AND LENA by Georg Buchner; Translator/Director/Design, Matthew Earnest CAST: Routh Havis, Trae Hicks, Shawn Parr, Helena Prince, Susan Rae Skelton, William Cook, Marisa Diotalevi, Chris Johnson, Suzan Perry

(Raw Space) Wednesday, Oct.9-26, 1996 (14 performances and 2 previews) Annette Moskowitz/Alexander E. Racolin (Play Producers) and Bill Schwartz present:
A CHOICE OF WEAPONS by Arthur Schwartz; Director/Design, Matt Miller; Costumes, Everett Hoage; Press, Gary Springer~Susan Chicoine/Candi Adams   CAST: Richard Bourg (Gen. Tarkov), Max Faugno (Wolf Brodsky), Roslyne Hahn (Itka Schindel), Glen Heroy (Doctor/Bulhvney), Edward Nattenberg (Mayer Schindel), G.W. Reed (Cossack/Ivanov), Stephen Ringold (David Schindel), Conrad Wolfson (Rabbi), Stefanie Zadravec (Anna), Howard Feller (Reuben)
    A drama set in czarist Russia, late 19th century. Presented as tribute to the late Alexander E. Racolin, a prolific off-Broadway producer.

Edward Nattenberg, Richard Bourg in *Choice of Weapons*
(Steve Demas)

Leslie Beatty, Sheyvonne Wright in *When a Diva Dreams*
(Cindy Warwick)

(Miranda Theatre) Wednesday, Oct.9-27, 1996 (13 performances and 2 previews) Merlin Entertainment, Michel Wallerstein and the Garrison Group presents:
WHEN A DIVA DREAMS by Gary Garrison; Director, Michael Walling; Set/Lighting, Jack Mehler; Costumes, Jason Webber; Music, Sheyvonne, Ben Wright; Stage Manager, Anita Dwyer; Press, Francine L. Trevens CAST: Sheyvonne Wright (Miss Red), Blythe Baten (Dee-Dee), Kate Fitzgerald (Penny), Leslie Beatty (Crystal), David Buffam (Lipton), Laura Patrick (Marty), Gisele Richardson (Adelle/Jam)
    A drama in two acts. The action takes place in New Orleans.

(Clemente Soto Velez Cultral Center) Wednesday, Oct.9-26, 1996 (12 performances) Ground Floor Theatre Lab presents:
TOY PLANET by Daniel Trujillo; Director, Alfred Preisser; Press, Jocelyn Cramer CAST: Josh Stark, F.L. Dammann
    A comedy about a weird brother and a normal brother.

(Theatre Foray) Thursday, Oct.10-27, 1996 (12 performances) MikBeth Productions presents:
BLOOD DUES by Edward Musto; based on the book by Dotson Rader; Director, Richard Galgano; Lighting, Davin Pickell; Sound, Chagrin da Largo; Set, Allen Rooney; Stage Managers, Gary Adamsen, Jeannine A. Myers CAST: Zeke Rippy (Dotson Rader), Dannette Bock (Kristin Thorn/Germaine Greer), Mick Hilgers (Tennessee Williams), Craig Watkinson (Christopher/Andy Warhol), Frank Avoletta (Hank/Arkansas), Nomi Tichman (Barbara/The Woman), Sean Hagerty (Tom/Abbie Hoffman), Dana Watkins (Jann Eller)
    A drama in two acts. The action takes place in Berkeley, CA., NYC, Michigan, San Francisco, LA, New Orleans, Washington D.C. and Boston, 1958-72.

(Irish Arts Center) Friday, Oct.11-27, 1996 (10 performances and 6 previews) Reckless Theatre Company presents:
BASEBALL IN ZANZIBAR by Ty Adams; Director, Frank Pisco; Set/Lighting, Rob Kaplowitz; Costumes, Sara J. Southey; Stage Manager, L. Donovan; Press, Chris Boneau~Adrian Bryan-Brown/Miguel Tuason, Patrick Paris CAST: Colleen Davenport (Gable), Mark Bateman (Phyllis), Andrea Maulella (Alphie), Steven McCloskey (James), James Georgiades (Vallencourt), Jack Gwaltney (Hyatt)

A drama in two acts. The action takes place in a New Orleans mental health clinic.

(Samuel Beckett Theater) Saturday, Oct.12-27, 1996 (10 performances) New Directions Theater presents:
RED LIGHTS AND DRAGONS by Herman Raucher; Director, Charles Loffredo CAST: Sandra M. Bloom, Dori Kelly, Courtney Rohler, Kevin Shine, Judy Stone, Carl Sturmer, James Sutton, Lisa Tracy, Glen Williamson, Lisbeth Zelle

(St. Clemennt's Theatre) Tuesday, Oct.15-Nov.9, 1996 (24 performances and 4 previews) Pan Asian Repertory presents:
THE INNOCENCE OF GHOSTS by Rosanna Staffa; Director, Peter C. Brosius; Set, Myung Hee Cho; Costumes, San-Jin Lee; Lighting, Victor En Yu Tan; Music, Karl Frederik Lundeberg; Sound, Peter Griggs; Stage Manager, Lisa Ledwich CAST: Anney Giobbe (Sophie), Tina Chen (Dr. Gao), Mel Duane Gionson (Man), Emi Kikuchi (Chinese Woman)

A drama set in Hangzhou, People's Republic of China, 1988.

(Henry St. Settlement) Wednesday, Oct.16-Dec.1, 1996 (40 performances) New Federal Theatre presents:
JOE TURNER'S COME AND GONE by August Wilson; Director, Clinton Turner Davis; Set, Felix E. Cochren; Lighting, Shirley Prendergast; Costumes, Vassie Welbeck-Browne; Music, Todd Barton; Stage Manager, Malik; Press, Max Eisen/Laurel Factor CAST: Mike Hidge (Seth Holly), Peggy Alston (Bertha Holly), Arthur French (Bynum Walker), Ron Riley (Rutherford Selig), Chad L. Coleman (Jeremy Furlow), Jerome Preston Bates (Herald Loomis), Shakia Rashed (Zonia Loomis), Joyce Lee (Mattie Campbell), Aaron Beener (Reuben Mercer), Caroline Stefanie Clay (Molly Cunningham), Kim Yancey Moore (Martha Pentecost)

A drama in two acts. The action takes place in Pittsburg, 1911.

James Georgiades, Andrea Mauella in Baseball in *Zanzibar* (Yoon Kim)

Anney Giobbe, Tina Chen in *Innocence of Ghosts* (Carol Rosegg)

(Expanded Arts) Thursday, Oct.17-Nov.9, 1996 (12 performances and 3 previews) re-opened (Red Room Theatre) Wednesday, Apr.2-26, 1997 (16 performances) Cressid Theater Company presents:
EDWARD THE SECOND by Christopher Marlowe; Director, Will Nolan; Set/Lighting, Curt Beech; Costumes, Christina Perrin; Press, Tony Origlio/Kevin Rehac CAST: Spencer Aste succeeded by Brian Sloan (Warwick), Brian de Benedictus (Bishop of Canterbury), George Demas (Mortimer), Brett Glazer (Arundel), Alan T. Jackson (Earl of Lancaster), Michael Laurence (Edward), Eric McNaughton (Earl of Leicester/Bishop of Coventry), Bill Migliore (Spencer), Jason Novak (Gaveston), Edgar Oliver (Lightborn), Brian Osborne (Baldock), Marc Palmieri (Edmund/Earl of Kent), Monica Steuer (Queen Isabella)

An adaptation set in the world of sexual deviance, drugs, music and fashion of NYC's Lower East Side while remaining true to the original text.

(Creative Space Theatre) Thursday, Oct.17-Nov.2, 1996 (11 performances and 5 previews) In the Company of Actors presents:
MARIE AND BRUCE by Wallace Shawn; Director, Chuck Blasius; Stage Manager, Victoria Epstein CAST: George Ashiotis (Antoine/Tim/Waiter), Kate Blumberg (Enid/Jean), Alsion Brunell (Bettina/Ilsa), Ron Butler (Herb/Fred/Ed), John Alban Coughlan (Bruce), Patricia R. Floyd (Marie), Richard Stegman (Henry/Bert)

A drama peformed without intermission. The setting is New York City.

Jason Novak, Michael Laurence in *Edward the Second* (Will Nolan)

Michael Knight, Linda Lavin in *Cakewalk* **(Joan Marcus)**

(Village Gate 52nd St.) Thursday, Oct.17, 1996-Sept.7, 1997   Gene Wolsk, Rad Productions and Art D'Lugoff present:
A BRIEF HISTORY OF WHITE MUSIC; Conceived by DeeDee Thomas and David Tweedy; Production Supervision, Ken Bloom and Barry Kleinbort; Set, Felix E. Cochren; Lighting, Alan Keen; Costumes, Debra Stein; Sound, Stan Wallace; Musical Director, Alva Nelson; Arrangements, Nat Adderley Jr. Alva Nelson, Art Yelton; Press, Shirley Herz/Kevin McAnarney CAST: James Alexander, Wendy Edmead, Deborah Keeling, Glen Turner (during previews)
MUSICAL NUMBERS: Overture, Who Put the Bomp, Bei Mir Bist Du Schoen, I Got a Gal in Kalamazoo, That'll Be the Day, Teenager in Love, Where the Boys Are, Leader of the Pack, Walk Like a Man, Love Potion No.9, Blue Suede Shoes, Love Me Tender medley, Jailhouse Rock, California Dreaming, Monday Monday, Surfin' USA, I Got You Babe, Itsy Bitsy Teeny Weenie Yellow Polkadot Bikini, These Boots are Made for Walking, Do Wah Diddy Diddy, Son of a Preacher Man, To Sir with Love, Downtown, She Loves You, I Wanna' Hold You Hand, With a Little Help from My Friends, Sgt. Pepper's Lonely Hearts Club Band, Imagine, We Can Work It Out
A soulful look at white pop music.

(Currican Theatre) Thursday, Oct.17-Nov.17, 1996 Currican/Playful Productions presents:
RECREATION by Penn Jillette; Director, Mike Wills; Lighting, Mike Gottlieb; Sound, Andrew S. Keister; Set, Mark Symczak; Stage Manager, David A. Winitsky CAST: Dean Bradshaw (James Ewing), Kelly Mc-Shain (Amber/Kiki/Delivery Boy/Angel/Laurie), Andrew Totolos (Dee-Jay/Tim/Dr. Richard/Waiter/Exercise Enthusiast)
A drama performed without intermission.

(Phil Bosakowski Theatre) Thursday, Oct.17-Nov.3, 1996 (15 performances and 1 preview) JB Theatrical Productions presents:
THE SIXTH COMMANDMENT by Jeffrey Swan Jones; Director, Kathleen Brant; Set, John Peifer; Lighting, John Tissot; Costumes, Suzan Perry, Carolyn Sarkis; Sound, Rick Peeples; Press, Jonathan Slaff CAST: Kelly Au Coin (George), Mimi Dykes (Ruth), Greg Petroff (Webber), Ron Faber (Black)
A drama about a militant anti-abortionist based on real-life events.

(Variety Arts Theatre) Friday, Oct.18, 1996-Jan.5, 1997 (71 performances and 22 previews) Julian Schlossberg, Meyer Ackerman, Donna Knight present:
CAKEWALK by Peter Feibleman; Director, Marshall W. Mason; Music, Carly Simon, Teese Gohl; Set, Michael McGarty; Costumes, Laura Crow; Lighting, Tharon Musser; Sound, Randy Freed; Press, Chris Boneau~Adrian Bryan-Brown/Jackie Green, Janet George CAST: Linda Lavin (Lilly), Michael Knight (Cuff), Suzanne Groder (Women), Kirby Mitchell (Men), Erik Leeper (Interviewer/Intern), Deborah Jolly (Interviewer)
A drama about writer Lillian Hellman performed without intermission.

(Gramery Arts Theatre) Friday, Oct.18-Nov.16, 1996 Repertorio Espanol and Teatro Estudio present:
OBSCURE RUMORS; Written/Directed by Abelardo Estorino; Set/Costumes, Carlos Repilado; Lighting, Saskai Cruz; Music, Juan Pinera CAST: Alfredo Alonso (Milanes), Adria Santana (Women), Rene Losada (Men)
A Cuban drama performed without intermission.

(Folksbiene Theatre) Saturday, Oct.19-Jan.26, 1997 (57 performances) Folksbiene Yidddish Theatre affiliated with the Workmen's Circle presents:

THE MAIDEN OF LUDMIR; Music, John Clifton; Lyrics/Book, Mariam Hoffman; Director, Robert Kalfin; Musical Director, Herbert Kaplan; Sets, Alexander Solodukho; Costumes, Gail Cooper-Hecht; Ligthing, Robert Williams; Stage Manager, Kim Jones; Press, David Powell Smith CAST: Zypora Spaisman (Khashe-Bashe), Mina Bern (Woman with Rooster), Bernard Mendelovitch (Reb Motele), Rachel Botchan (Khan-Rukhele), Hy Wolfe (Reb Monish Verbermakher), Suzanne Toren (Sara)

A musical based on a true story. The action takes place in the Ukrainian town of Ludmir during the 19th century.

(Cherry Lane Theatre) Tuesday, Oct.22, 1996-Jan.5, 1997 (74 performances and 10 previews) Falstaff presents:

THE NEW BOZENA; Director, Rainn Wilson; Set, Chris Muller; Costumes, Melissa Toth; Lighting, Adam Silverman; Sound, Andrew S. Keister; Stage Manager, J. Philip Bassett; Press, Tony Origlio/Kevin Rehac CAST: David Costabile (Ramon), Michael Dahlen (Spiv Westenberg), Kevin Isola (Revhananvaan Sahaanahanadaan)

A slacker vaudeville performed without intermission. The post-modern clowns perform Winter is the Coldest Season.

(Town Hall) Tuesday, Oct.22-27, 1996 (7 performances) Ester Rachel Kaminska Jewis Theatre of Warsaw presents:

WANDERING STARS by Sholem Aleichem; Adaptation/Director, Szymon Szurmiej; Choreography, Thomasz Tworkowski; Musical Director, Teresa Wronska; Sets/Costumes, Marian Stanczak; Sound, Krzysztof Wojtysiak; Lighting, Mieczyslaw Korczynski; Press, Max Eisen/Laurel Factor CAST: Jerzy Walczak, Joanna Wojcik-Przybylowska, Juliusz Berger, Nenryk Rajfer, Golda Trncer, Seweryn Sem Dalecki, Wanda Siemaszko, Waldemar Gawlik, Szymon Szurmiej

A musical play in Yiddish.

(Mint Theatre) Wednesday, Oct.23-Nov.3, 1996 (10 performances and 2 previews) Six Figures Theatre Company presents:

THE ADDING MACHINE by Elmer L. Rice; Director, Linda Ames Key; Press, Gary Springer~Susan Chicoine/Candi Adams CAST: Nick Dantos, Julie Flanders, Andria Laurie, Dan Leventritt, Shane Mishler, Joseph O'Brien, Richard Simon, Kaadi Taylor, Susan P. Vaughn

(Sanford Meisner Theatre) Thursday, Oct.24-Nov.10, 1996 (12 performances) Perkasie Productions presents:

ABSENT FRIENDS by Alan Ayckbourn; Director, Steve Keim; Press, Gary Springer~Susan Chicoine/Candi Adams CAST: Janice Hoffmann (Diana), Holly Hawkins (Evelyn), Patrick Fitzpatrick (John), Kurt Elftmann (Paul), Mary Aufman (Marge), Tony Cormier (Colin)

A comedy about a group of friends.

(Musical Theatre Works) Thursday, Oct.24-Nov.16, 1996 (16 performances) Kingfisher Entertainment presents:

THE LAST WEDDING by Joan McHale; Director, Dan Metelitz; Press, Penny M. Landau CAST: Todd Anthony-Jackson, Chris Fischer, Susan Knott, Cam Kornman, Joe Viviani, Ina Withers

(Nada) Thursday, Oct.24-Nov.2, 1996 (9 performances)

THE MONEKY CHRONICLES; Written/Directed by Jefferson D. Arca CAST: Morrow Wilson, Edward O'Blenis, J.D. Carter, Joshua Feinstein, Kevin Hayes, Rachel Kramer, Kelly Lacy, Nicole Landers, David Lapkin, Nicole Weitz

A wild comedy set in the future.

David Costabile, Michael Dahlen, Kevin Isola in *New Bozena* (David S. Allee)

(Alpha & Omega Theatre) Thursdau, Oct.24-Nov.17, 1996 (16 performances) Alpha and Omega Theatre Company presents:
THE PLAYBOY OF THE WESTERN WORLD by J.M. Synge; Director, Peter Dobbins; Costumes/Set, Shane Klein   CAST: John Regis (Christy), Colleen Crawford (Pegeen Mike), Jennifer Piech (Widow Quinn), Drew Kelly (Shawn Keogh), Stan Tracy (Michael James)
   The 1907 Irish folk comedy.

(West End Theatre) Friday, Oct.25-Nov.18, 1996 (16 performances) West End Theatre presents:
FORTINBRAS by Lee Blessing; Director, Barbara Grecki; Set/Lighting, Kevin Ash; Costumes, Victoria Grecki   CAST: Michael D. Cleeff (Hamlet), Gary Trahan (Osric), Tim Farley (Horatio), Jack Cleary (Ambassador/Marcellus), Kevin Ash (Fortinbras), Jack Peteley (Barnardo/Captain), Samantha Pulak, Constance Witman (Maidens), George W. Reily (Polonius), Kathleen McInerney (Ophelia), John Canary (Claudius), Paula Hoza (Gertrude), Gordon Holmes (Laertes)

(Center Stage) Friday, Oct.25-Nov.3, 1996 (16 performances)
REGISTERED MALE; Director, Mark Harborth; Sets, Leon L. Munier; Lighting, Richard Schaefer; Costumes, Michael Bottari and Ronald Case; Press, Kevin P. McAnarney   CAST: Scott Carpenter, J Deyling, James Grattan, Dennis Keeley, Rodney Sexton, Ken Stewart, Andy Zeffer
   An evening of gay readings, scenes and monlogues.

(Theatre Row Theatre) Friday, Oct.25-Nov.17, 1996 (19 performances and 5 previews) Willow Cabin Theatre Company presents:
STREET SCENE by Elmer Rice; Director, Edward Berkeley; Set, John Kasarda; Costumes, Linann Easley; Lighting, Matthew McCarthy; Press, Jim Baldassare   CAST: Zachary Ansley, Cynthia Besteman, John Billeci, John Bolger, David Cheaney, Sophie Comet, Alvin Crawford, Mary Cushman, Kenneth Favre, Ken Forman, Makeda Harris, Ibi Janko, Herb Klinger, Tasha Lawrence, Verna Lowe, Angela Nevard, Barbara Pitts, Dede Pochos, Linda Powell, Jed Sexton, Joel Van Liew, Andre Ware
   A 1929 drama set in New York City.

Gordon Holmes, Kevin Ash, Kathleen McInerney, Tim Farley in *Fortinbras*

Tasha Lawrence, John Bolger in *Street Scene* **(Carol Rosegg)**

(Clemente Soto Velez Center) Tuesday, Oct.29-Nov.2, 1996 (14 performances) Faux-Real Theatre Company presents:
WILLIAM SHAKESPEARE'S HAUNTED HOUSE; Director, Mark Greenfield; Lighting, Sarah Sidman; Press, Jim Baldassare   CAST INCLUDES: Veronika Korvin, Christine Tracy, Eric Dean Scott, Mark Greenfield
   A house haunted by Shakespeare's characters.

(Pulse Ensemble Theatre) Wednesday, Oct.30-December, 1996 Pulse Ensemble Theatre presents:
TOP GIRLS by Caryl Churchill; Director, Alexa Kelly; Press, Judy Jacksina   CAST: Susan Barrett, Elizabeth Cloe, Sydney Davalos, Joyce DeGroot, Stephanie Fybel, Ivana Kane, Susan McGeary, Elizabeth Rothan, Claudia Traub, Inger Tudor
   A drama set in a London restaurant, the provinces and the Top Girls employment agency.

(from top) Veronika Korvin, Christine Tracy, Eric Dean Scott in *William Shakespeare's Haunted House* **(Barrett Benton)**

(Nada) Thursday, Oct.31-Nov.24, 1996 (22 performances)
WANT'S UNWISHED WORK or *A Birthday Play* by Kirk Wood Bromley; Director, Aaron Beall CAST: Spencer Aste, Tara Bahna-James, Jody Booth, Lisa Colbert, Tim Ellis, Dan Flamhaft, Al Foote, Suzanne Goldklang, Pietro Gonzalez, Douglas Gregory, Ginny Hack, Kate Hampton, Ian Hill, Sven Holmberg, Billie James, Laura Knight, Yuri Lowenthal, Rizwan Manji, Melanie Martinez, Christine Mascott, Alexander Stephano, P.J. Sosko, Hank Wagner, Adam Wald, Todd Woodard

A verse play based on Shakespeare's *Loves Labor's Lost* and Aristophane's *Lysistrata*. The action takes place in Athens, Georgia.

(Theatre on 3) Thursday, Oct.31-Nov.3, 1996 (6 performances) Naked Angels presents:
FLYOVERS by Jeffrey Sweet; Director, John McCormack; Set, George Xenos; Lighting, Greg MacPherson; Flyer Design, Robert Brook Allen CAST: Jace Alexander, Nicole Burdette, Jodie Markell, Geoffrey Nauffts

(Atlantic Theatre) Friday, Nov.1-Dec.29, 1996 (63 performances and 7 previews) David Stone and Amy Nederlander-Case present:
THE SANTALAND DIARIES by David Sedaris; Adapted/Directed by Joe Mantello; Costume, Isaac Mizrahi; Set, Ian Falconer; Lighting, Jan Kroeze; Sound, David Van Tieghem; Stage Manager, Pamela Edington; Press, Chris Boneau~Adrian Bryan-Brown/Jackie Green, Andy Shearer, Janet George CAST: Timothy Olyphant, Erika Slezak (voice)

A comedy performed without intermission. During previews, *Season's Greetings to Our Friends and Family* with Karen Valentine, was performed as a curtain-raiser.

Timothy Olyphant in *Santaland Diaries* (Joan Marcus)

(Greenwich House Theatre) Friday, Nov.1-Dec.8, 1996 (33 performances and 12 previews) Rowan Joseph, Shane P. Partlow and Eric N. Schwartz present:
THE QUEEN OF BINGO by Jeanne Michaels and Phyllis Murphy; Director, Rowan Joseph; Set, Robert P. Johnson; Costumes, Charlotte Deardorff; Lighting, F. Burris Jackes; Stage Manager, Steve Wildern; Press, Shirley Herz/Sam Rudy, Adam Meza CAST: Carmen Decker (Sis), Nancy-Elizabeth Kammer, Tracy Davis (Fr. Mack/Caller)

A comedy performed without intermission. The action takes place at a Battle Creek, Michigan church bingo soiree.

(Irish Arts Center) Friday, Nov.1, 1996-Feb.23, 1997 (109 performances and 6 previews) Robert M. Cavallo presents:
FAMILY VALUES by Carl Ritchie; Director, Norman Hall; Set, Daniel Ettinger; Lighting, Phil Hymes; Stage Manager, Sarah Jane Runser; Press, Gary Springer~Susan Chicoine/Candi Adams CAST: Ellen Evans (Barbara), Joel Fabiani (Ed), Patty Jamieson (Christine), James Hallett (Philip), Jeff P. Weiss (Lewis), Craig Adams (Mark)

A New York City-set comedy in two acts.

(Producer's Club) Friday, Nov.1-25, 1996 (14 performances and 2 previews) Mad Women present:
THE THEORY OF RELATIVES by Trude W. Martin; Suggested by Elayne Wilks; Director, Barbara B. Meyer; Set, Sterling B. Plenert; Costumes, Deanna Lynne Goede; Lighting, Beau Decker; Stage Manager, Christy K. Cole; Press, Francine L. Trevens CAST: Elayne Wilks (Gertrude Berg aka Molly Goldberg)

A drama performed without intermission. The action takes place in Berg's Park Ave. apartment.

Elayne Wilks in *Theory of Relatives* (Carol Rosegg)

(Raw Space) Friday, Nov.1-16, 1996 (12 performances and 5 previews)
The Beach Group presents:
ALONE AT THE BEACH by Richard Dresser; Director, Gary Walter;
Set, J.C. Svec; Lighting, Shaheed Muhammad; Press, Gary Springer~Susan Chicoine/Candi Adams CAST: Kelly Champion, Tony Freeman, Dee
Dee Friedman, Barbara Halas, Timothy Harris, Sean Havens, Atli Kendall
    A comedy set in the Hamptons.

(Dixon Place) Saturday, Nov.2-23, 1996 (10 performances and 1 preview) returned at Theatre 3 Wednesday, Feb19-22, 1997 (5 performances)
Dixon Place (Nov) and Naked Angels (Feb) present:
BLACK COMEDY: THE WACKY SIDE OF RACISM; Created/Performed by Nancy Giles; Director, Ellie Covan; Set, George Xenos; Lighting, Greg MacPherson; Sound, Dick Connette; Stage Manager, J.M.
Wilson

(Theatre 22) Monday, Nov.4-12, 1996 (4 performances) Plank and Passion Theatre Company presents:
TRIFLES & TOMFOOLERIES by George Bernard Shaw; Director,
Zoe Dodd; Set, Ed Askew; Lighting, Jason Marion CAST: Orlaith de
Burca, Chris Carrick, Mark J. Dempsey, Carl J. Frano, Ciaran Riley,
Veronica Watt
    Two one-acts: *Overruled* and *The Music Cure*.

(John Montgomery Theatre) Wednesday, Nov.6-23, 1996 (9 performances and 3 previews) John Montgomery Theatre Company presents:
ROSENCRANTZ & GUILDENSTERN ARE DEAD by Tom Stoppard;
Director, Colette Duvall; Set, Bob Celli; Costumes, Sidney Fortner; Lighting, Jessie; Press, Shirley Herz/Wayne Wolfe, Jason Deck CAST: Russ
Hamilton, Patrick Hillan, Tucker McCrady
    An absurdist chronicle of two characters from *Hamlet*.

**Russ Hamilton, Patrick Hillan in *Rosencrantz & Guidenstern are
Dead* (Scott Whnn)**

Martin Rudy in *Movers and Shakers* (Dylan Whitehand)

(Theater for the New City) Wednesday, Nov.6-24, 1996 (12 performances and 1 preview) Theater for the New City presents:
MOVERS AND SHAKERS; Written/Directed by Frank Biancamano;
Lighting, Ian Gordon; Costumes, Mary Marsicano; Stage Manager, Primy
Rivera; Press, Francine L. Trevens CAST: Antonia Stout (Lori Graham),
David Ige (John Artebello), T.D. White (Tamiel Kasdaye), Kathleen Gates
(Anita Cummings), Ari Tomais (Hotel Manager/Jeremy Jensen), Jerry
Jaffe (Lou Karamazov), Jess Hanks (Waiter)
    A comedy set in Los Angeles.

(Trilogy Theatre) Wednesday, Nov.6-24, 1996 (16 performances) Amiable Productions presents:
GOING ON! by Charles Dennis; Director/Design, Carol Bennett Gerber;
Stage Manager, Kimmarie Bowens; Press, Richard Biles CAST: Lane
Binkley (Lynn), Charles E. Gerber (Alfred), Holly Hawkins (Diva voice),
Bill Tatum (Neil voice), Kimmarie Bowens (Ernie voice), CB Gerber
(ASM voice)
    A comedy about understudies. The action takes place backstage at a
Broadway theatre, 1992.

(Kaufman Theatre) Wednesday, Nov.6, 1996-May 25, 1997 (155 performances and 16 previews) Abrams Gentile Entertainment presents:
BEAT: A Subway Cop's Comedy ; Written/Performed by John DiResta;
Developed/Directed by Donna Daley; Set, Thomas Baker; Costumes,
Anne-Marie Wright; Lighting/Sound, Matt Berman; Music, Albert Evans,
Ron Kaehler; Stage Manager, Bonnie Boulanger; Press, Pete
Sanders/Glenna Freedman, Clint Bond Jr.
    A one-man show performed without intermission.

John DiResta in *Beat* (Gerardo Somoza)

(CSC Theatre) Wednesday, Nov.6-Dec.8, 1996 (25 performances and 7 previews) Classic Stage Company presents:
THE ENTERTAINER by John Osborne; Director, David Esbjornson; Set, Hugh Landwehr; Costumes, Elizabeth Hope Clancy; Lighting, Frances Aronson; Sound, Mark Bennett; Musical Director, Christopher Drobny; Stage Manager, Jana Lynn; Press, Denise Robert CAST: Douglas Seale (Billy Rice), Kate Forbes (Jean Rice), Jean Stapleton (Phoebe Rice), Brian Murray (Archie Rice), Barry McEvoy (Frank Rice)
A 1957 drama in two acts. The action takes place in a British seaside town, 1957.

(Mint Theatre) Thursday, Nov.7-23, 1996 (15 performances) Linda Ames Key in association with Watermark Theater and Lynn Seippel presents:
THE SECRET OF LIFE by David Simpatico; Director, Roger Mrazek; Sets, Anthony Costa; Lighting, Matt Berman; Costumes, Shelley Norton; Stage Manager, Kaddy Feast; Press, Judy Jacksina CAST: Joanne Genelle (Carla), Bob Yarnall (Robert), William Flatley (Sterling), Anne Lilly (Cherry Bomb), Susan Korowski (Bess), Jane Young (Irene)
A drama performed without intermission.

(City Center) Thursday, Nov.7-17, 1996 (11 performances)
TANGO X 2; Created/choreographed/Performed by Miguel Angel Zotto and Milena Plebs; Press, Philip Rinaldi
A theatrical evening of dance from the *Tango Argentino* stars.

**Tony Meindl, Monika Kendall in *Cybele: A Love Story*
(Henry Grossman)**

(Judith Anderson Theatre) Thursday, Nov.7-17, 1996 (11 performances and 1 preview) PASSAJJ Productions presents:
CYBELE: A LOVE STORY; Music/Lyrics/Adaptation, Paul Dick; Based on book by Bernard Eschasseriaux; Director, Lisa Brailoff; Musical Director, Christopher McGovern; Set, Donald L. Brooks; Lighting, Matthew McCarthy; Costumes, Christine Darch; Stage Manager, Scott H. Schneider; Press, Gary Springer~Susan Chicoine/Candi Adams CAST: Monika Kenall (Francoise), Tony Meindl (Pierre), Karen Arneson (Sonia), Allison Baker (Sister Brigitte), Jack Fletcher (Carlos), Chris Goffredo (Antoine), Judith Jarosz (Sister Marie), Jesse Johnson (Christophe), Bruce Montgomery (Father), Stephanie Pakowitz (Helene), Christina Seymour (Isabelle), Denise Wilbanks (Madeleine)
MUSICAL NUMBERS: Stones from a Star, Another Night Another Moon Another Shore, I Had a Future, We Touch a Lot, No Greater Joy, Lonely Children, Ring That Bell, Be a Daffodil, And Now It's My Turn, I Knew He Wouldn't Be Coming Back to Begin With, A Kiss on My Brow, Each Sunday, Knife Into You, I'll Tell You My Name, Eighteen/Thirty Four, Meant to Be Married, Pierre, Come to the Fair, Pierre My Love, Sensitive So Sensitive, How Could You, My Best Christmas, Follow Forever, A Real Man, Happier with Her, Memory of a Dark Mind, Town Talk, Cybele
A musical in two acts. The action takes place in Vill D'Avray, a small suburb of Paris, 1956.

(Center Stage) Thursday, Nov.7-24, 1996 (14 performances) Triad Arts Ensemble presents:
THE COLLECTION by Harold Pinter, and **SEXUAL PERVERSITY IN CHICAGO** by David Mamet CASTS: Chris Lucey, Cate Smit, Mark Gorman, William Mitchell
Two one-acts.

**Chris Lucey, Cate Smith, Mark Gorman, William Mitchell
in *Sexual Peversity in Chicago***

(28th St. Theater) Friday, Nov.8-24, 1996 (9 performances and 3 previews) Africa Arts Theater Company presents:
PARADISE IS CLOSING DOWN by Pieter-Dirk Uys; Director, George Ferencz; Design, Bill Stabile; Costumes, Sally Lesser; Lighting, Jeff Tapper; Sound, Genji Ito; Stage Manager, Kevin G. Ewing III; Press, Patt Dale CAST: Margie Ryan (Molly), Louise Martin (Mouse), Jacqueline Pennington (Anna), Kevin Mambo (William).
A drama set against race riots in Capetown.

(47th St. Theatre) Thursday, Nov.7-Dec.15, 1996 (29 performances and 10 previews) Randall L. Wreghitt, Georgia Buchanan, Norma Langworthy, Richard & Peter Fitzgerald present:
THE SPRINGHILL SINGING DISASTER; Written/Performed by Karen Trott; Director, Lonny Price; Sets, Derek McLane; Costumes, Gail Brassard; Lighting, Phil Monat; Sound, Red Ramona; Stage Manager, Craig Palanker; Press, James L.L. Morrison/Tom D'Ambrosio
A comic solo play with music. Performed last season at Playwrights Horizons.

(Radio City Music Hall) Thursday, Nov.7, 1996-Jan.5, 1997 (195 performances) Radio City Music Hall presents:
RADIO CITY CHRISTMAS SPECTACULAR; Director/Choreography, Robert Longbottom; Sets, Michael Hotopp, Charles Lisanby; Costumes, Greg Barnes, Pete Menefee, Frank Spencer; Lighting, Ken Billington, Jason Kantrowitz; Choreography, Linda Haberman, Violet Holmes, Russell Markert, Scott Salmon, Marianne Selbert; Musical Director, David Chase; Stage Manager, John Bonanni CAST INCLUDES: Charles Edward Hall (Santa Claus), Deborah Bradshaw, Melanie Vaughn ((Mrs. Claus), Ann Brown, Melissa Hough (Clara), Laurie Welch, Randy Coyne, Maradith Meyer, Patrick Hancock (Skaters), Kyle Hershek, Reed Van Dyke, Michael J. Gilden (Tinker), Kristoffer Elinder (Thinker), Joanne Palenzuela (Tannenbaum), Ernie Lee (Bartholomew), Leslie Stump-Vanderpool (Thumbs), Steve Babiar, Marty Klebba
PROGRAM: Overture, Santa's Gonna Rock and Roll, Nutcracker, Parade of the Wooden Soldiers, Here Comes Santa Claus, Christmas in New York, Ice Skating in the Plaza, Santa & Mrs Claus in Concert, Carol of the Bells, Santa's Toy Fantasy, Living Nativity: One Solitary Life, Joy to the World
The annual holiday revue.

Kevin Mambo, Jacqueline Pennington in *Paradise Is Closing Down* (Jonathan Slaff)

Karen Trott in *Springhill Singing Disaster* (Joan Marcus)

Cederic Harris, Albert Hall, Wood Harris, Jonathan Earl Peck, Robb Leigh Davis, Geoffrey C. Ewing, Sean Squire, Danny Johnson, Keith Randolph Smith in *Soldier's Play* (Carol Rosegg)

(Theatre Four) Tuesday, Nov.12-Dec.8, 1996 (24 performances and 8 previews) Valiant Theatre Company presents:
A SOLDIER'S PLAY by Charles Fuller; Director, Clinton Turner Davis; Sets/Costumes, Felix E. Cochren; Lighting, Dennis Parichy; Sound, Aural Fixation; Stage Manager, Daniel L. Bello; Press, Gary Springer~Susan Chicoine/Candi Adams CAST: Albert Hall (Sgt. Vernon C. Walters), Jonathan Walker (Capt. Charles Taylor), Sean Squire (Corp. Bernard Cobb), Wood Harris (Pvt. Melvin Peterson), Robb Leigh Davis (Corp. Ellis), Jonathan Earl Peck (Pvt. Louis Henson), Keith Randolph Smith (Pvt. James Wilkie), Cedric Harris (Pvt. Tony Smalls), Geoffrey C. Ewing (Capt. Richard Davenport), Danny Johnson (Pvt. C.J. Memphis), P.J. Brown (Lt. Byrd), Barton Tinapp (Capt. Wilcox)
A 1982 drama in two acts. The action takes place at Ft. Neal, Louisiana, 1944.

(UBU Rep Theatre) Tuesday, Nov.12-Dec.1, 1996 (16 performances) Playwrights' Preview Productions presents:
SCAR by Murray Mednick; Director, Vivian Sorenson; Set, George Xenos; Lighting, Jason Boyd; Costumes, Marcia Canestrano; Sound, Michael Keck; Music, Joseph Campbell; Press, Keith Sherman/Anne Sussman CAST: Richard Cox (Stevie), Debbon Ayer (Molly), Darrell Larson (Matt)
A drama performed without intermission. The action takes place in autumn, 1985.

(Theatre for the New City) Wednesday, Nov.13-Dec.21, 1996 (20 performances and 4 previews) Irondale Ensemble Project presents:
ANDREW CARNEGIE PRESENTS THE JEW OF MALTA by Christopher Marlowe and the Irondale Ensemble; Director, Jim Niesen; Set, Ken Rothchild; Costumes, Hilarie Blumenthal; Lighting, A.C. Hickox; Press, Tony Origlio/Kevin Rehac CAST: Joe Fuer, Michael-David Gordon, Terry Greiss, Rana Kazkaz, Patrena Murray, John Silvers, Brigitte Viellieu-Davis, Patrice Wilson
A "textual colliding" of Marlowe's farce with company improvisation.

(Liberty Theatre) Thursday, Nov.14, 1996-Jan.5, 1997 (63 performances and 4 previews) Jedediah Wheeler and En Garde Arts presents:
THE WASTE LAND by T.S. Eliot; Director, Deborah Warner; Lighting, Jean Kalman; Stage Manager, Amy Richards; Press, James L.L. Morrison/Tom D'Ambrosio CAST:Fiona Shaw
A dramatic presentation of the 1922 poem performed without intermission. This marked the first legit production in 42nd St.'s Liberty Theatre since 1933.

(78th St. Theatre Lab) Thursday, Nov.14-Dec.1, 1996 (16 performances and 1 preview) ARTemis Productions in affiliation with the 78th St. Theatre Lab present:
REINCARNATION by Jessica Litwak; Director, Daniela Varon; Sets/Costumes, Meganne George; Lighting, Paul Ziemer; Sound, Eric Nightengale; Press, Lee Weinstein CAST: Andrea Haring (Madame Ceuili), Jessica Litwak (Rosie)
A psychic comedy performed without intermission. The action takes place in Manhattan, in the present and the great beyond.

(New Perspectives Theatre) Thursday, Nov.14-Dec.7, 1996 (13 performances and 2 previews) New Perspectives Theatre Company presents:
ANATOMY OF A LOVE AFFAIR by Deirdre Hollman; Director, Melody Brooks; Press, Chris Boneau~Adrian Bryan-Brown/Erin Dunn, Paula Mallino CAST: Collette Wilson, Don Draxler
A drama that takes place during the final hours of an eight year interracial relationship.

Terry Greiss, Joe Fuer, Patrena Murray, Michael-David Gordon in *Andrew Carnegie Presents The Jew of Malta* **(Gerry Goodstein)**

Fiona Shaw in *The Waste Land* **(Joan Marcus)**

Beyond Born to Rumba **cast**

(DUO Theatre) Friday, Nov.15, 1996- DUO Latin Theatre Collective presents:
BEYOND BORN TO RUMBA!; Music/Lyrics/Book/Direction by Michelangelo Alasa' CAST: Gabriel Colon, Cat Lippencott, Anthony Ruiz, Al D. Rodriguez
A musical sequel to 1991's Born to Rumba! .

(Phil Bosakowski Theatre) Friday, Nov.15-Dec.1, 1996 Playwrights/Actors Contemporary Theater presents:
THE GODDESS CURE by Adam Kraar; Director/Choreography, Shela Xoregos; Set, Shannon Corbin Rednour; Lighting, Clarence L. Taylor; Costumes, Katherine Hammond; Sound, Jeffrey Swann Jones; Stage Manager, Elizabeth Snow Wagoner CAST: Gary Bryan Budoff (Barry), Frank Enos (Stranger), Jacqueline Barsh (Bea), Patricia Randell (Dr. Shoshanna Ruebel), Kristine Watt (Elizabeth)
A two-act comedy set in New York City.

(Raymond J. Greenwald Theatre) Saturday, Nov.16-Dec.15, 1997
American Jewish Theatre presents:
ANNE FRANK AND ME; Written/Directed by Cherie Bennett; Set,
James Wolk; Costumes, Pamela Scofield; Lighting, Susan White; Sound,
Bruce Ellman; Stage Manager, Carol Dacey-Charles; Press, Jeffrey
Richards/Mark Cannistraro CAST: Richard H. Blake (Jack/Jacques),
Christopher Cook (Eddie/Edouard), Abigail Hardin (Little Bit/Liz-Beth),
Careena Melia (Mimi Baker/Mimi Poulin), Janan Raouf (Suzanne
Lee/Suzanne Lebeau), Karen Shallo (Rene Zooms/Renee Bernhardt),
Mandy Siegfried (Chrissy/Christina), John Simeon Sloan (David), Greta
Storace (Mary Burns/Anne Frank), Rachel Ulanet (Nicole), David Winton
(Urkin/Jean Bernhardt)
A drama performed without intermission. The action takes place in an
American suburb, 1996 and in Nazi-occupied Europe, 1942-44.

(UBU Rep Theatre) Sunday, Nov.17-30, 1996 (12 performances) re-
turned to (47th St. Theatre) Mar.11-July 13, 1997 Playwrights' Preview
Productions, Frances Hill & Associates with T.L. Reilly present:
MEN ON THE VERGE OF A HIS-PANIC BREAKDOWN by
Guillermo Reyes; Director, Joseph Megel; Lighting, Jason Boyd, Jeff Nel-
lis; Set, George Xenos; Costumes, Leonard Pollack, Ramona Ponce;
Sound, Matthew De Gumbia, Johnna Doty; Choreography, Annmaria
Mazzini; Stage Manager, Jen McGlashan; Press, Keith Sherman/Anne
Sussman CAST: Felix A. Pire
PROGRAM: The Gay Little Immigrant that Could, Goodbye to Senor
Daddy, Hispanically Correct, Federico Writes Again, Castro's Again, Cas-
tro's Queen, EFL: English as a Stressful Language, Drag Flamingo, Mar-
riage of Federico
A one-man play performed without intermission.

**Above and Top: Felix A. Pire in *Men on the Verge of a His-Panic
Breakdown* (Nigel Teare)**

(Victoria Theatre) Friday, Nov.22, 1996-still playing May 31, 1997
Ron Brown Productions in association with Jimmy Glover, Richard Haase
and Two Per Cent Solution Productions present:
GODSPELL; Music/Lyrics, Stephen Schwartz; Original
Conception/Book, John-Michael Tebelak; Director, Richard Haase;
Choreography, Gene Compson; Musical Director/Arrangements, Davina
Haase; Press, Bruce Lynn CAST: Michael L. James (Jesus), Ray Cham-
pion (Judas), N'Tombkhona (Peggy), Marla Neal, Dolli Grace, Adrienne
Unae, Natasha Yvette Williams, Warrick Harmon, Erik Dumesane, Bishop
Willie Gholson, Randi Harmon, Walter Coppage
An all-black version of the 1971 musical. This version is set in the
twenty-first century.

(Synchronicity Space) Friday, Nov.22-Dec.8, 1996 (11 performances
and 3 previews) Present Tense Productions presents:
MIND BODY AND SPIRIT by Timothy Nolan; Directors, Susan Jef-
fries, Vincent Marano, Steve Keim; Press, Gary Springer~Susan
Chicoine/Candi Adams CAST: Pandora Richardson, Angela Trento, J.D.
Wyatt, Sally Winters, Sheik Mahmud-Bey, Marlon Hargreaves, Lou Sones
PROGRAM: *What's in a Name, The Bull Ring, Pop's Closet*
Three one-act plays.

(Theatre Row Theatre) Saturday, Nov.23, 1996-Jan.5, 1997 (45 perfor-
mances) Anne Strickland Squadron and Eric Krebs present:
**WHAT'S A NICE COUNTRY LIKE YOU DOING IN A STATE
LIKE THIS?;** Music, Cary Hoffman; Lyrics/Book, Ira Gasman; Director,
Miriam Fond; Musical Director, Ken Lundie; Set, Joseph Miklojcik Jr.;
Lighting, Robert Bessoir; Costumes, Anne-Marie Wright; Stage Manager,
Michael J. Chudinski; Press, Tony Origlio/Kevin Rehac CAST: David Ed-
wards, Janine LaManna, Sean McCourt, Vontress Mitchell, Karen Quack-
enbush
MUSICAL NUMBERS: Opening, Liberal's Lament, Church & State, One
Night Stand, Be Frank, Farewell (First Amendment), Button A, Militia
Song, I'm in Love, M.C.P., Last One of the Boys, Coffee Bar Suite,
Honky, Coalition, Farrakhan, Fill 'er Up, Reality Check, Pee Wee, I'm Not
Myself, Watch Your Language, Homeless Suite, Rights of Bill, How Do I
Say I Love You?, New York Suite, Daisy, Finale
A new version of the 1973 satirical revue performed without intermis-
sion.

Lillian K. Munnich, Brian Kustrup, Don Garrity, Joyia D. Bradley, Sarah Thurmond, Philip Hernandez in *King John* (Paula Cort)

***A Midsummer Night's Dream* (Winnie Klotz)**

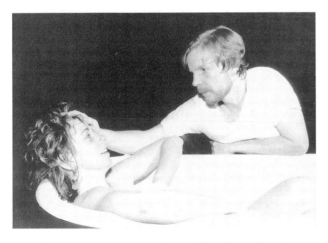

Paula Ewin, Leo Farley in *Night of Nave* (Steve Pirozzi)

(West End Theatre) Sunday, Nov.24-26. 1996 (3 performances) Judith Shakespeare Company presents:
KING JOHN by William Shakespeare; Director, Kathleen Brant; Stage Manager, Sharon Rum; Press, Publicity Office/Colleen Hughes CAST: Joyia D. Bradley, Kelli M. Cruz, Joy Dixon, Don Garrity, Alithea H. Hages, Philip Hernandez, Brian Kustrup, Jeffrey Shoemaker, Godfrey L. Simmons Jr., Sarah Thurmond, Lisa Walker, Joanne Zipay, Robin Flanagan, Lillian K. Minnich, Jacqueline Noguera, Dan O'Driscoll
 Part of the "Shakespeare Unplugged" series.

(Metropolitan Opera) Monday, Nov.25-Dec.21, 1996 (8 performances) The Metropolitan Opera presents:
A MIDSUMMER NIGHT'S DREAM; Music, Benjamin Britten; Libretto, Mr. Britten and Peter Pears; Based on the play by William Shakespeare; Director, Tim Albery; Conductor, David Atherton; Sets/Costumes, Anthony McDoanld; Lighting, Thomas Webster; Choreography, Phillippe Giraudeau; Press, Peter Clark/Charles Sheek, Melissa Labbe CAST: Nick Stahl (Puck), Derek Lee Ragin (Oberon), Sylvia McNair (Tytania), Jeffrey Wells (Theseus), Victoria Livengood (Hippolyta), Kurt Streit (Lysander), Rodney Gilfry (Demetrius), Jane Bunnell (Hermia), Nancy Gustavson (Helena), Peter Rose (Bottom), John Del Carlo (Quince), Barry Banks (Flute), James Courtney (Sung), Anthony Laciura (Snout), Bradley Garvin (Starveling), William Scot Murray (Cobweb), Nicholas Frisch (Peaseblossom), Benjamin Diskant (Mustardseed), Benjamin Unger (Moth)
 A three-act opera. The action takes place in the woods outside Athens.

(Sargent Theatre) Tuesday, Nov.26, 1996-Jan.19, 1997 (25 performances) American Theatre of Actors and Shining Star Productions present:
YOU SHOULDN'T HAVE TOLD by Anne L. Thompson-Scretching; Director, Marc Anthony Thomas; Set, Morten R. Salbu; Costumes, Tameko; Lighting/Sound, Vincent Feller; Stage Manager, Paris Denise Rhoad CAST: Cecelia "CeCe" Antoinette, Carol Johnson (Aunt Freda Tauber), Kenneth Atkins. Dwight Wigfall (Ray-Ray King), Monique Berkley (Tracy King), Femi Emiola, D'Ann Byrd (Carolyn King), Zacerous Jones, Allan Jackson (Jojo King), Jane Galvin-Lewis, Flora Gillard (Essie Ford), Kimberly "Q" Purnell, Cheryl Lane-Lewis (Marie King), Tyler Mason (Larry Drayson), Jewdyer Osborne, Ian Friday (Stanley Youngston), Andress Williams, Lisa Armstrong (Rosetta Greene), Gia Williams. Andrea Holder (Sara Dunkin)
 A drama in two acts.

(29th St. Rep) Friday, Nov.29-Dec.29, 1996 (15 performances and 6 previews) 29th St. Rep presents:
NIGHT OF NAVE by Bill Nave; Director/Sound, Vera Beren; Sets, Charles Kirby; Lighting, Stewart Wagner; Stage Manager, Patrice Ellison; Press, Gary Springer~Susan Chicoine/Candi Adams
PROGRAM: *Visiting Oliver* CAST:Paula Ewin (Ruth), Neil Necastro (Clement), David Mogentale (Oliver), Patrick John (Stan)
When People Still Smoked Cigarettes CAST: Elizabeth Elkins (May), Charles Willey (Jesse), Vincent Rotolo (Sonny)
With Spirit and with Fire CAST: Paula Ewin (Naomi), Leo Farley (John)

 Three one-acts.

(Chelsea Playhouse) Sunday, Dec.1-21, 1996 (20 performances and 1 preview) Housing Works presents:
EVERY BEAT FACE AIN'T BEAUTIFUL; Written/Performed by Ray Brockington (Hustler who Walks), Loreen Bryant (Hustler who Sews), Robert Fields (Hustler who Walks), Benito Garcia (Diva's Dresser), Anthony Grey (Everyman), Cookie Mejias (Hustler who Walks), Tracy Moran (Guy Running), Charles Shaw (Diva), Erik Smith (Hustler who Walks), Micah Gaugh (Interpreter); Director, Victoria McElwaine; Music/Lyrics, Elaine Sabal; Sets, Krista Landers; Costumes, Rick Gradone; Lighting, David Herrigel; Press, Gary Springer/Susan Chicoine/Candi Adams
MUSICAL NUMBERS: Welcome Visitors, Hustlin', Husband Material. Charles' Song, Duelin' Divas, The Walk, Love Me in the Daylight, One Night in Manhattan
    A musical wriiten and performed by homeless and formerly homeless people living with HIV/AIDS.

Cookie Mejias, Robert Fields in *Every Beat Face Ain't Beautiful*
(Philip-Lorca diCorcia)

(St. Clements Theater) Tuesday, Dec.3-22, 1996 (24 performances) Crystal Theater Productions presents:
WARP by Lenny Kleinfeld; Conception, Stuart Gordon; Director, Philip Baloun; Set, Cecile Bouchier; Costumes, Jose M. Rivera; Lighting, Peter L. Smith; Sound, Bernard Fox; Fights, Chris Harrison; Music/Sound, Richard Dysinger; Stage Manager, Rachel Stern; Press, Jeffrey Richards CAST: Todd Alan Johnson (Janitor/Faceless One/Prince Chaos), Kane Schirmer (David Carson/Lord Cumulus), Tanya Oesterling (Mrs. O'-Grady/Ego/Snurtle), Denise Thomas (Penny Smart/Sargon), Scott Thomson (Bank President/Dr. Victor Vivian Symax/Infinity/Faceless One), Darlene Mann (Mary Louise/Valerie/Snurtle), Kofi (Bank Employee/Yggthion/Xander), Ed Criscimanni (Psychiatric Director/Lugulbanda), Chris MacEwen (Faceless One/Snurtle/He Who Dreams)
    A revised version of a 1973 science-fiction adventure.

(John Montgomery Theatre) Wednesday, Dec.4-21, 1996 (9 performances and 3 previews) John Montgomery Theatre Company presents:
FAITH HEALER by Brian Friel; Director, Bruce A. Katlin; Lighting, Jessie; Set, Susan Tammany; Costumes, Laura Lee Ash; Stage Manager, Gwen Morreale; Press, Shirley Herz/Wayne Wolfe CAST: Patrick Hillan (Frank), Elisabeth S. Rodgers (Grace), Richard Fay (Teddy)
    A 1979 drama performed in two acts.

Todd Alan Johnson, Kofi, Kane Schirmer in *Warp*
(Patrick Mulcahy)

(Greenwich St. Theatre) Wednesday, Dec.4-15, 1996 (10 performances and 1 preview) Flock Theatre Company presents:
KICKING INSIDE by Jeannie Zusy; Director, Frits Zernike CAST: Irene Glezos, Tanya Greve, Hugh Hunter, Grace Miglio, Frits, Jeannie Zusy

(Mint Theater) Thursday, Dec.5-22, 1996 (13 performances) Mint Theater Company in association with Lu presents:
MR. PIM PASSES BY by A.A. Milne; Director, Jonathan Bank; Set/Lighting, Mark T. Simpson; Costumes, Eden S. Miller; Stage Manager, Jennifer Moody; Press, Mark-Leonard Simmons CAST: Lisa M. Bostnar (Olivia Marden), Ken Kliban (George Marden), Alice Cannon (Lady Marden), Bill Roulet (Carraway Pim), Cole Freeman (Dinah Marden), Jeffrey Roop (Brian Strange), Ahri Birnbaum (Anne)
    A 1920 comedy in two acts.

Ken Kliban, Bill Roulet, Lisa Bostnar in *Mr. Pim Passes By*
(Barry Burns)

(Philip Bosalowski Theatre) Thursday, Dec.5-22. 1996 (13 performances and 6 previews) Protean Theatre Company in association with Fanfare Theatre Ensemble presents:
THE LONDON CUCKOLDS by Edward Ravenscroft; Adaptation, John Byrne; Director, Owen Thompson; Sets, Sal Perrotta; Lighting, John McClure; Costumes, Hilary Oak; Stage Manager, Giacinta Pace; Press, Kevin P. McAnarney/David Gersten CAST: John Ahlin (Alderman Dashwell), Mark Alan Cajigao (2nd Sweep/2nd Watch), Michael Daly (Frank Townly), Caroline Ficksman (Engine), Lisa Ann Goldsmith (Jane), Alvaro J. Gonzalez (Alderman Doodle), John Grace (1st Sweep/1st Watch), Alex Grossman (Linkboy), Jeff Gurner (Ned Ramble), Tricia Paoluccio (Arabella), Elizabeth Richmond (Eugenia), Patrick Tarpey (Roger), Richard B. Watson (Valentine Loveday)
American premiere of a 1681 Restoration farce.

(Samuel Beckett Theatre) Friday, Dec.6-22, 1996 (21 performances) ArrowMaker Entertainment and PluralArts International present:
JULIUS CAESAR: THE FALL AND RISE OF A WALL STREET STAR by William Shakespeare; Adaptation/Director, Todd Jonathan Fletcher; Sets, Beowulf Borritt; Costumes, Maureen Fleming; Press, Maya/Penny M. Landau CAST: Zeb Hollins III (Julius Caesar), Alice M. Gatling (Antonia), Joe Paulson (Marcus Brutus), Adrian Witzke (Caius Cassius), Nina-Marie Gardner, Derek Lively, James Stanley
An modern adaptation.

(Judith Anderson Theater) Saturday, Dec.7-22, 1996 (12 performances and 2 previews) The Other Theater presents:
THREE BY BECKETT; Lighting, Rocky Greenberg; Sets, June Maeda; Costumes, Mary Brecht; Press, Zeller/Ron Lasko
Not I; Director, Luly Santagnelo CAST: Wendy vanden Heuvel (Mouth), Peter Nichols Davis (Auditor)
Quad 1 and 2; Director, Lulu Santangelo CAST: Peter Nichols Davis, Mary Forcade, Carolyn Lucas, Wendy vanden Heuvel
Nacht und Traume; Director, Joseph Chaikin CAST: Will Hare (Dreamer), Mark Isaac Epstein (His Dreamt Self), Peter Nichols Davis (Hands)

(Theatre Off Park) Wednesday, Dec.11, 1996-Feb.2, 1997 (43 performances and 4 previews) Rattlestick Productions presents:
MESSAGE TO MICHAEL by Tim Pinckney; Director, Michael Scheman; Set, Van Santvoord; Lighting, Ed McCarthy; Costumes, Susan Branch; Sound, Jeremy M. Posner; Stage Manager, Federica Lippi; Press, Peter Cromarty/Hugh Hayes CAST: David Beach (Michael), Michael Malone (Kenny), Kevin Cristaldi (Ron), Eric Paeper (Danny), Tony Meindl (Greg), Rick Hammerly (Robbie)
A comedy in two acts. The action takes place in New York City.

(Harold Clurman Theatre) Thursday, Dec.12-29, 1996 (13 performances and 6 previews) Willow Cabin Theatre Company presents:
A CHILD'S CHRISTMAS IN WALES by Dylan Thomas; Adaptation, Jeremy Brooks and Adrian Mitchell; Director, Edward Berkeley; Sets, John Kasarda; Costumes, Dede Pochos, Tasha Lawrence; Lighting, Matthew McCarthy; Musical Director, Christine Radman; Choreography, Nora Kasarda; Press, Jim Baldassare CAST: Zachary Ansley, Cynthia Besteman, John Billeci, Alvin Crawford, Fiona Davis, Kenneth Favre, Ken Foreman, Larry Gleason, Robert Harryman, Ryan S. Hull, Hugh Kelly, Jean-Christophe Labrunye, Verna Lowe, Angela Nevard, Dede Pochos, Christine Radman, Maria Radman, Lizzie Raetz, Jed Sexton, Joel Van Liew
A return engagement of last season's holiday show.

Mark Alan Cajigao, Elizabeth Richmond in *London Cuckolds* (J McClure)

David Beach, Michael Malone in *Message to Michael* (Carol Rosegg)

143

(Grove St. Playhouse) Sunday, Dec.15-17, 1996 (3 performances)
ALL ABOUT CHRISTMAS, EVE! by John Michel; Directors, Eddie Cobb, Mr. Michel; Music Director, Jeffrey Claflan CAST: Eddie Cobb, Greg Cobert, Michael Della Jacono, C.T. East, Thom Hansen, John Michel, Laura Natta, Philip Stohr, Albert Walsh

(Kaufman Theatre) Wednesday, Dec.18, 1996-Jan.12, 1997 (28 performances) Doo Gooder Productions present:
ON DEAF EARS by Robin Rothstein; Director, John Ruocco; Set, Bill Wood; Lighting, Chris Dallos; Costumes, Jeffrey Wallach; Sound, Vincent Apollo CAST: Chevi Colton (Sadie), Rosemary Prinz (Evelyn), Gil Rogers (Jimmy O'Hara), Susan Finch, Richard Sheinmel, Dana Smith, Mark Robert Gordon
  A drama set in Florida.

(John Houseman Theatre) Saturday, Dec.21, 1996-Jan.5, 1997 (15 performances and 1 preview) Eric Krebs presents:
FYVUSH FINKEL FROM SECOND AVENUE TO BROADWAY; Ligthing, Robert Bessoir; Musical Director, Ian Finkel; Press, David Rothenberg/David J. Gersten CAST: Fyvush Finkel, Ian Finke l
PROGRAM: Bie Mir Overture, Bumble Bee Freilach, Yiddish Theatre Klezmer Medley, Finkel & Son, Songs in My Mother Tounge and in English, As Long As I'm with You, Mambo Jambo, Gershwin Tribute, In the Barrel House, No on the Top, If I Were a Rich Man, I'm Glad I'm Not Young Anymore, L'Chaim to Life
  Comedy and music from a lifetime of entertaining.

(Samuel Beckett Theater) Thursday, Dec.26-30, 1996 (6 performances) New Directions Theater presents:
THE DELUSION OF ANGELS by Don Rifkin; Director, Eliza Beckwith CAST: Charles Loffredo, Courtney Rohler, James Sutton, Wendell Ward

Fyvush Finkel in *From Second Ave. to Broadway* (David Gersten)

(Synchronicity Space) Thursday, Dec.28, 1996-Feb.9, 1997 (28 performances and 6 previews) Jewish Theatre of New York presents:
LOVE LETTERS TO ADOLF HITLER; Director, Tuvia Tenenbom; Music, Philip Rubin; Set, Mark Symczak; Lighting, David Alan Comstock; Stage Manager, Genia Domico; Press, David Hirsh CAST: Susanna Schmitz (Ritschi), Mary F. Unser (Anna), Catherine Curtin (Anne-Marie), Dana White (Mia), Samme Johnston Spolan (Friedel), Ellen David (Maria)
  Letters found at the Reich Chancellery performed without intermission.

(Musical Theatre Works) Friday, Jan.3-25, 1997 (11 performances) Dr. Guffy Theatre Company presents:
A PIECE OF CAKE by Richard Valley; Director, Kevin G. Shinnick; Set/Lighting/Sound, Andy Eller, Paul Weissman, Ljubisha Milemkovic CAST: John Barba (Sir Charles Straightaway), Kerry J. Dolan (Cindy Dickler), John Stanisci (Barrie Farrington), Angela Jane Ford (Diana Farrington), Peter Anthony Timony (Bobby Kaufman), Craig Bachman (Casey Corker)
  A farce in two acts (and under two hours).

(Raymond J. Greenwald) Saturday, Jan.4-Feb.2, 1997 (14 performances and 19 previews) American Jewish Theatre presents:
VILNA'S GOT A GOLEM by Ernest Joselovitz; Director, Lou Jacob; Set, David P. Gordon; Costumes, Greco; Lighting, Thomas C. Hase; Musical Director, Jeff Warschauer; Stage Manager, Lee J. Kahrs; Press, Jeffrey Richards/Mark Cannistraro CAST: David Ingram (Zebi), Richard Topol (Zavel), Stan Lachow (Zeizel), Angela Pietropinto (Shulamis), Thomas Pasley (Enzo), Jason Kravits (Isaac), Scott Rabinowitz (Isador), Susan Blackwell (Basha)
  A drama in two acts. The action takes place in Vilna, a small town in Eastern Europe, 1899.

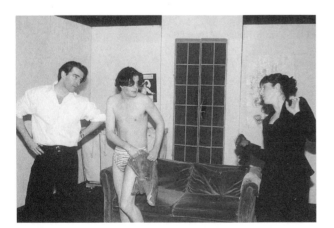

A Piece of Cake (Kevin Shinnick)

(Eighty-Eight's) Monday, Jan.6-Mar.1997
ERIK AND THE SNOW MAIDENS; Written/Directed by John-Richard Thompson; Musical Director/Arrangements, Bobby Peaco CAST: Elena Bennett (Erik), Gentry Leland Claussen (Heigel), Dezur Kenna (Anna Dorothea), Lizz Manners (Maia), Bobby Peaco (Mistress Karelia)
A musical fantasy.

(HERE) Tuesday, Jan.7-Feb.2, 1 997 (19 performances and 5 previews) Target Margin Theatre presents:
SOUTH by Julian Green; Director, David Herskovits; Set, Marsha Ginsberg; Lighting, Lenore Doxsee; Costumes, David Zinn, Audrey Fisher; Sound, Wayne Frost; Stage Manager, Allison C. Kyle; Press, Shirley Herz/Sam Rudy CAST: Will Badgett (Edward Broderick), Marissa Chibas (Regina), Tony Jackson (Colored Child/Barnabus), Billie James (Miss Priolleau/Colored Child), Rizwan Manji (Jimmy), Mary Neufeld (Mrs. Priolleau), Lenore Pemberton (Eliza), Maria Porter (Mrs. Strong), Thomas Jay Ryan (Jan Wicziewsky), Greig Sargeant (Uncle John), Yuri Skujins (Eric MacClure), Douglass Stewart (Jeremy), Maria Striar (Angelina), James Urbaniak (Mr. White)
A 1955 drama in two acts. The action takes place on a Carolina plantation on the eve of the Civil War.

(Grove St. Playhouse) Wednesday, Jan.8-Feb.16, 1997 (28 performances and 7 previews) G.R.E.A.T. Entertainment presents:
WHIPLASH: A TALE OF A TOMBOY; Written/Performed by Shelly Mars; Director, Janice Deaner
An autobiographical theatre piece.

(New Victory Theater) Wednesday, Jan.8-26, 1997 (21 performances) Theatre for a New Audience in association with The International Shakespeare Globe Centre presents:
THE TWO GENTLEMEN OF VERONA by William Shakespeare; Director, Jack Shepherd; Sets, Jenny Tiramani; Costumes, Susan Coates; Music, Calire van Kampen; Stage Manager, Mary Ellen Allison; Press, Gary Springer~Susan Chicoine/Charlie Siedenburg CAST: Matthew Scurfield (Duke), Lennie James (Valentine), Mark Rylance (Proteus), George Innes (Antonio), Ateven Alvey (Thurio), Graham Brown (Eglamour), Andrew Fielding (Host), Ben Walden (Speed), Jim Bywater (Launce), Stephanie Roth (Julia), Anastasia Hille (Silvia), Aicha Kossoko (Lucetta), Amanda Orton (Attendant)
Performed in two acts. The action takes place in Verona, Milan and a forest.

Marissa Chibas, Thomas Jay Ryan in _South_ (Jamey O'Quinn)

Mark Rylance in _Two Gentlemen of Verona_ (John Tramper)

(Soho Rep) Wednesday, Jan.8-Feb.7, 1997 (19 performances) Soho Rep presents:
A DEVIL INSIDE by David Lindsay Abaire; Director, Julian Webber; Set, Molly Hughes; Stage Manager, Gretchen Knowlton CAST: Larry Block, Mary Louise Burke, Bill Dawes, Heather Goldenhersh, John McAdams, Pamela Nyberg

(HERE) Thursday, Jan.9-Feb.1, 1997 (16 performances) Orange Thoughts Theater & Film presents:
CATER-WAITER by Eric Lane; Director, Martha Banta; Set, Kate Kennedy; Costumes, Susan J. Slack; Lighting, Matthew Frey; Sound, Paul Aston; Stage Manager, Gerald Cosgrove CAST: Tim Deak (Rob), Tyrone Mitchell Henderson (Gary), Jed Diamond (Eddie/Actor/Waiter), James Georgiades (Earl)
A comedy performed without intermission. The action takes place in New York City, 1987-94.

James Georgiades, Tim Deak in _Cater-Waiter_ (Barclay Hughes)

(Judith Anderson Theatre) Friday, Jan.10-Feb.9, 1997 (21 performances and 11 previews) Pure Orange Productions presents:
MARKING by Patrick Breen; Director, Elizabeth Gottlieb; Set, Henry Dunn; Lighting, Jeff Croiter; Costumes, Kaye Voyce; Music/Sound, Red Ramona; Stage Manager, Dana Williams; Press, Richard Kornberg/Don Summa, Rick Miramontez, William Finnegan, Paula Wenger CAST: Peter Dinklage (Peter), Seth Gilliam (Andre), Sarah Knowlton (Paula), Brian F. O'Byrne (Dag), Adina Porter (Colleen), Amy Ryan (Halley), Francie Swift (Rebecca), Maria Tucci (Jessica)
A black comedy in two acts.

(78th St. Theater Lab) Monday, Jan.13-Feb.2, 1997 (11 performances and 1 preview)
SLEEPING WITH MOM & DAD by Scott Manus; Director, Warren Etheredge; Set, Shaun Motley; Costumes, Neslihan Danisman; Lighting, Anne Duston Cheney; Press, Gail Parenteau CAST: Larry Bell, Samantha Brown, Bruce Meakem, Andy Meyer, Abagail Walker, Catherine Zambri, Dorothy Walker, (on video) Beth Littleford
A comedy in two acts.

(CSC Theatre) Wednesday, Jan.15-Feb.9, 1997 (22 performances and 6 previews) Foundry Theatre presents:
YOU SAY WHAT I MEAN BUT WHAT YOU MEAN IS NOT WHAT I SAID; Conceived/Composed by Grisha Coleman; Director, Talvin Wilks; Additional Music/Arrangements, Jonathan Stone; Set, Kevin Cunningham; Lighting, Kevin Adams; Costumes, Anita Yavich; Sound, Barry Wolifson; Stage Manager, Samuel Moses Jones; Press, James L.L. Morrison/Tom D'Ambrosio CAST: Hot Mouth: Grisha Coleman, Helga Davis, Ching Gonzalez, Ezra Knight, David Thomson
MUSICAL NUMBERS: Tell It Like It Is, Moment that I Saw It, Afrokode, Ain't Got a Gal, Watermellon, Nobody Knows..., Trocket, Country Lament, She Tore/Oya, Madame X, yousaywhatimeanbutwhatyoumeanisnotwhatisaid, O Little Child, One Born One Gone, Douvet Par Ici, Dinner
An a capella musical performed without intermission.

(Vineyard Theater) Wednesday, Jan.15-Feb.2, 1997 (14 performances and 4 previews) Onyx Theatre Company presents:
A NOT SO QUIET NOCTURNE; Written/Directed by Jaye Austin-Williams; Set, Cornell Riggs; Lighting, Ann Marie Duggan, Kristina Kloss; Costumes, Joanna Cummings; Cinematography, Ann Narie Bryan; Sound, Mio Morales; Press, Jonathan Slaff CAST: Michele Banks (Charlyn), Darren Boone, Ann Marie Bryan, Robin Cornett, Rodney Gilbert, Laura Johnston, Jomo Kalman, Jon Malmed, Lewis Merkin, Walker Richards, Nancy Rogers, Joan Valentina, Bernadine Vivani, Lisa Weems, Devernie Winston
Deaf and hearing actors perform this contemporary drama.

(Sylvia and Danny Kaye Playhouse) Wednesday, Jan.15-Feb.16, 1997 (25 performances and 4 previews) New Federal Theatre and Kaye Playhouse present:
DO LORD REMEMBER ME by James de Jongh; Director, Regge Life; Set, Kent Hoffman; Lighting, Shirley Prendergast; Costumes, Vassie Welbeck-Browne; Stage Manager, Jacqui Casto; Press, Max Eisen/Laurel Factor CAST: Barbara Montgomery, Glynn Turman, Roscoe Orman, Ebony Jo-Ann, Chuck Patterson
20th anniversary production of a play based on first-hand testimony of balck men and women born in slavery in ante-bellum America.

Adina Porter, Peter Dinklage in *Marking*

(clockwise from Top L) Catherine Zambri, Abagail Walker, Bruce Meakem, Samantha Brown, Andy Meyer, Larry Bell in *Sleeping with Mom and Dad* (Dan Howell)

Ching Gonzalez, Grisha Coleman, Ezra Knight, David Thompson, Helga Davis in *You Say What I Mean...* (Sasha Stollman)

146

(Harold Clurman Theater) Thursday, Jan.16-26, 1997 (9 performances) Blue Light Theatre Nightlife Series presents:
SPIN: A Comedy of Preposterous Political Positions by Christopher Piehler; Director, Alfredo Galvan; Press, Gary Springer~Susan Chicoine/Candi Adams CAST: Erika Iverson, Scott Nankivel, Jon Rothstein, Tom Staggs, James Stanley, Elizabeth Warner

(Theater for the New City) Thursday, Jan.16-Feb.9, 1997 (16 performances) Theater for the New City presents:
MOCK TRIAL; Written/Directed by Romulus Linney; Set, Mark Marcante; Lighting, Arjan Smook; Costumes, Allison Ronis; Stage Manager, Alisa Phillips; Press, Jonathan Slaff CAST: Heather Robinson (Judge), Christopher Cappiello (Prosecution), Nancy Joyce Simmons (Defense), John-Martin Green (Gen. Smith), Christopher Roberts (John Adam Jones), Dave Johnson (Former Gov. Bancroft), Anthony Pick (Col. Reardon)
A drama performed without intermission. The action takes place in an American law school in the near future.

(Theatre Row Theatre) Thursday, Jan.16-Feb.2, 1997 (9 performances and 3 previews) Darren Lee Cole in association with Dark Horse Productions presents:
THE LAST MANHATTAN by Doug Dunlop; Director, Darren Lee Cole; Press, Gary Springer/Susan Chicoine/Tiina Piirsoo CAST: Kelly Curtis, Herschel Sparber, Owen Hollander, Patrick Tull, Brett Lafield, Joan Porter Hollander
A drama that examines how Manhattan changed from the Native to the New Americans.

(P.S.19) Thursday, Jan.16-Feb.1, 1997 (8 performances and 1 preview) The Irish American Theatre Company in association with Rapid Deployment Productions and Thomas Henry presents:
SOME THINGS YOU NEED TO KNOW BEFORE THE WORLD ENDS: A Final Evening with the Illuminati by Larry Larson and Levi Lee; Director, Mark Lang; Sets, Jung H. Griffin; Lighting, Mike Appel; Costumes, Zita Davis; Sound, Mike Schmetterer; Press, Alma Malabanan CAST: Mark Lang (Rev. Eddie), Matthew Lai (Brother Lawrence)
A religious satire.

Elise Stone, Molly Pietz in *Mother Courage...* (Jonathan Slaff)

(Bouwerie Lane Theatre) Thursday, Jan.17-Apr.13, 1997 (34 performances and 2 previews) Jean Cocteau Repertory presents:
MOTHER COURAGE AND HER CHILDREN by Bertolt Brecht; Adaptation, Eric Bentley and Darius Milhaud; Director, Robert Hupp; Musical Director, Ellen Mandel; Set, Robert Klingelhoefer; Costumes, Margaret A. McKowen; Lighting, Brian Aldous; Press, Jonathan Slaff CAST INCLUDES: Elise Stone (Mother Courage), Harris Berlinsky, Will Leckie, Kennedy Brown, Molly Pietz
An adaptation featuring a folk song score.

(Samuel Beckett Theater) Wednesday, Jan.22-Mar.9, 1997 (22 performances and 28 previews) Six Two Nine Entertainment presents:
DREAMSTUFF; Music/Lyrics, Sal Lombarde; Book/Director, John Pantozzi; Musical Director/Orchestrations/Vocal Arrangements, Barry Levitt; Musical Staging, Pamela Sousa; Sets, Michael Schweikardt; Costumes, Muriel Stockdale; Lighting, John Lasiter; Sound, Scott O'Brien; Stage Manager, Colleen Marie Davis; Press, Tony Origlio/Michael Cullen CAST: Carol Woods (Vy), Joshua Tucker succeeded by Evan Ferrante (Aladdin), Aileen Quinn succeeded by Kathleen Riley (Princess), David Figlioli (Killam), Louise DuArt (Sylvia), Steven Minichiello (Chandler) MUSICAL NUMBERS: Cityscape, It's Magic if You Believe, I Have a Boy/I Need a Boy, Can't You Just See Me?, It was Only Yesterday, All My Life, Mom I'm Sorry, Lights and Music, I am Killam, Three Unique Things, Guilt & Pain, My Master, Get By, Flying, Job and a Drink, Time, Finale
A musical update of the Aladdin tale set in New York City. First performed in two acts, the production was altered during the run to be performed without intermission.

Aileen Quinn, Louise DuArt, Evan Ferrante in *Dreamstuff*
(Carol Rosegg)

Melanie Anastasia Brown, Magnolia Santibanez, Nashid Fareed in
Igloo Tales **(Patrice Argant)**

Richard Kline in *Boychik* **(Carol Rosegg)**

Heath C.A. Stanwhyck, Alberta Handelman in *Mrs. Cage*
(Carol Rosegg)

(Nada) Thursday, Jan.23-Feb.9, 1997 (10 performances and 4 previews) Faux-Real Theatre Company presents:
IGLOO TALES; Adapted/Directed by Mark Greenfield; Lighting, Micghael Casselli; Costumes, Mai Loan Tran; Stage Manager, Megan McDonnell; Press, Jim Baldassare CAST: Melanie Anastasia Brown, Don Downie, Nashid Fareed, David Gochfeld, Aiko Jirai, Veronika Korvin, Magnolia Santibanez, Patrick Selitrenny, Josh Stark, Christine Tracy
A collection of Inuit myths and folktales performed without intermission.

(Theater for the New City) Thursday, Jan.23-Feb.16, 1997 Theater for the New City presents:
HALF OFF by Harry Kondoleon; Director, Tom Gladwell; Set, Donald Brooks CAST: Crystal Field, Larry Fleischman, Melissa Hurst, Andy Reynolds, Stephen Sinclair, Laura Wickens

(Theatre Four) Tuesday, Jan.28-Mar.27, 1997 (45 performances and 10 previews) Michael Mann and Barrie & Lynn Wexler present:
BOYCHIK by Richard W. Krevolin; Director, Max Mayer; Design, Thomas Lynch; Lighting, Jeff Croiter; Sound, Guy Sherman, Aural Fixation; Costume, Tommy Hilfiger; Stage Manager, Laurie Ann Goldfeder; Press, Peter Cromarty/Kate Cambridge CAST: Richard Kline (Larry Levin)
A monodrama performed without intermission.

(Tribeca Performing Arts Center) Wednesday, Jan.29-Feb.2, 1997 (5 performances) Tribeca Performing Arts Center and National Black Touring Circut present:
BROTHER MALCOLM X by Frank G. Greenwood; Director, Ron Milner; Set/Lighting, Reid Downey; Sound, Bill Swayze, Dan Spahn; Costumes, Carmen Cavello; Stage Manager, Malik; Press, Max Eisen/Laurel Factor CAST: Duane Shepard
Reminiscences of a black revolutionary in two acts.

(Kaufman Theater) Thursday, Jan.30-Feb.23, 1997 (17 performances and 5 previews) Blooming Grove Theater Ensemble presents:
MRS. CAGE by Nancy Barr; Director, Alberta Handelman; Set, Bruce Goodrich; Lighting, Matthew J. Williams; Stage Manager, David LaRosa; Press, Jim Baldassare CAST: Alberta Handelman (Mrs. Martin Cage), Heath C.A. Stanwhyck (Lt. Ruben Angel)
A drama performed without intermission.

(New Victory Theater) Saturday, Feb.1-Mar.2, 1997 (20 performances) New 42nd St. and Mabou Mines present:
PETER AND WENDY; Adapted by Liza Lorwin from the novel by J.M. Barrie; Director, Lee Breuer; Puppetry Director, Jane Catherine Shaw, Basil Twist; Sets/Lighting/Puppet Design, Julie Archer; Music/Arrangements, Johnny Cunningham; Costumes, Sally Thomas; Fights, B.H. Barry; Sound, Edward Cosla; Stage Manager, Jody Kuh CAST: Karen Kandel (Narrator), Basil Twist, Jane Catherine Shaw, Sam Hack, Sarah Provost, Jessica Smith, Jenny Subjack, Lute Ramblin'
Bunraku puppets and a narrator present the tale of Peter Pan. This version is based on Barrie's 1911 novel rather than his 1904 play.

(John Houseman Studio) Tuesday, Feb.4-23, 1997 (18 performances and 3 previews) SKT presents:
LIKE IT IS; Written/Performed by Johnathan F. McClain; Director, Holly Derr; Lighting, Paul Jones; Press, Susan Harley
   A monodrama about characters in New York City.

(Cherry Lane Theatre) Tuesday, Feb.4-Mar.16, 1997 (31 performances and 16 previews) Evangeline Morphos, Judith Resnick, Joan and Richard Firestone, Frederick M. Zollo, Mara Gibbs present:
IN-BETWEENS by Bryan Goluboff; Director, Dante Albertie; Set/Costumes, Beowulf Boritt; Lighting, Ken Moreland; Sound, Hector Olivieri; Stage Manager, David A. Winitsky; Press, Richard Kornberg/Don Summa, Rick Miramontez, William Finnegan CAST: Tony Cucci (Eddie), Andrew Miller (Peanut), Mark Hutchinson (Ray), Carolyn Maeumler (Lolli)
   A drama in two acts. The action takes place in a third floor walk-up apartment in the Bronx.

(Altered Stages) Wednesday, Feb.5-22, 1997 Altered Stages presents:
SEEING THINGS by Michael Boodro; Director, John Norris CAST: John Himmel (Bunny), Robert Zaleski, Peter Calandra

Tony Cucci, Andrew Miller in *In-Betweens* **(Carol Rosegg)**

Capitol Steps **cast (Fredde Lieberman)**

(Theatre of Riverside Church) Wednesday, Feb.5-Mar.2, 1997 (23 performances and 2 previews) Melting Pot Theatre Compnay presents:
THE PORTABLE PIONEER AND PRAIRIE SHOW; Music, Mel Marvin; Lyrics, David Chambers, Mr. Marvin; Book, Mr. Chambers; Director, Lori Steinberg; Musical Director, Greg Pliska; Set, Ann Keehbauch; Costumes, Sue Gandy; Lighting, Deborah Dumas; Choreography, Cynthia Khoury; Stage Manager, Jennifer N. Rogers; Press, Gary Springer~Susan Chicoine/Candi Adams CAST: Leenya Rideout (Karin Andersson), Sean McCourt (Paul Andersson), David M. Lutken (Karl Andersson), Larry Cahn (Tyrone Pendergast), Susan Emerson (Cordelia Crosby), Samuel D. Cohen (Johnny Slade), Rebecca Rich (Redeye Annie)
   A musical in two acts. The action takes place in Minnesota, late 1800s.

(John Houseman Theater) Wednesday, Feb.5-still playing May 31, 1997 Eric Krebs and Anne Strickland Squadron in association with Capitol Steps present:
CAPITOL STEPS; Conceived/Written/Directed by Bill Strauss and Elaina Newport; Set, R.J. Matson; Lighting, Bob Bessoir; Costumes, Robyn Scott; Sound, Maryanne Mundy; Press, David Rothenberg/David J. Gersten CAST: Mike Carruthers, Janet Davidson Gordon, Ann Johnson, Mike Loomis, Tyjuana Morris, Elaina Newport, Bill Strauss, Mike Tilford, Brad Van Grack, Amy Felices Young, Jamie Zemarel
   Musical political satire in two acts. Each performance features five of the company members and a pianist.

(Tribeca Performing Arts Center) Wednesday, Feb.5-9, 1997 (5 performances) Tribeca Performing Arts Center and National Black Touring Circuit presents:
GOD'S TROMBONES; Adapted by Vinnette Carroll from the book by James Weldon Johnson; Director, Woodie King Jr.; Musical Director, Paul Vincent Hendricks; Choreography, Kathleen Sumler; Lighting, Antoinette Tynes; Costumes, Vassie Welbeck-Browne; Stage Manager, Malik; Press, Max Eisen/Laurel Factor CAST: Trazana Beverly (Rev. Sister Marion Alexander), Todd Davis (Rev. Ridgely Washington), Cliff Frazier (Rev. Ridgely Washington), Theresa Merritt (Rev. Sister Rena Pinkston), Joseph A. Walker (Rev. Bradford Parhan), Debbie Blackwell-Cook (Sister Odessa Jackson), Sabrynaah Pope, Don Corey Washington, Ernest Witherspoon
A gospel musical based on a book of poetic sermons, in two acts.

(American Place Theatre) Wednesday, Feb.5-June 15, 1997 (120 performances and 13 previews) American Place Theatre presents:
STONEWALL JACKSON'S HOUSE by Jonathan Reynolds; Director, Jamie Richards; Set, Henry S. Dunn; Lighting, Chad McArver; Costumes, Barbara A. Bell; Sound, Kurt B. Kellenberger; Stage Manager, Joe Witt; Press, Gary Springer~Susan Chicoine/Charlie Siedenburg CAST: Lisa Louise Langford (LaWanda), R.E. Rodgers (Junior), Katherine Leask (Mag), Ron Faber (Barney), Mimi Bensinger (Del)
An incendiary comedy in two acts. The action takes place in Stonewall Jackson's House, a historical restoration in Lexington, Virginia.

Katherine Leask, R.E. Rodgers, Lisa Louise Langford, Mimi Bensinger, Ron Faber in *Stonewall Jackson's Place* (Martha Holmes)

((Expanded Arts) Wednesday, Feb.5-Mar.1, 1997 (13 performances and 3 previews) Expanded Arts and Cressid Theatre Company presents:
BEIRUT by Alan Bowne; Director, Deloss Brown; Set/Lighting, Robert Spahr; Costumes, Melissa Bruning; Press, Shirley Herz/Kevin P. McAnarney CAST: Michael Laurence (Torch), Jenny Maguire (Blue), Jeremy Johnson (Guard)
A sexual passion drama.

(Next Stage) Thursday, Feb.6-23, 1997 (12 performances) The Next Stage presents:
TO THE HAND; Director, Gus Reyes; Sets, Jana and Steven Thompson; Lighting, David Castneda; Press, Kevin P. McAnarney
The Further Adventures of Gussie Mae in America; Written/Performed by Letitia Guillory; Music, Marvin Sewell; Choreography, Asma Feyijinmi
Whatever the Matter May Be; Written/Performed by Misi Lopez Lecube
Two solo plays by women of color.

(American Place Theatre) Friday, Feb.7-Mar.2, 1997 (9 performances and 20 previews) Scott Allyn & Richard L. Barovick present:
ROBBERS by Lyle Kessler; Director, Marshall W. Mason; Set, Loren S. Sherman; Costumes, Laura Crow; Lighting, Phil Monat; Sound, Jim Van Bergen; Music, Peter Kater; Stage Manager, Tamlyn Freund; Press, Peter Cromarty/Hugh Hayes CAST: Michael Rapaport (Ted), John Doman (Pop), Jonathan Hadary (Feathers/Owner), Reiko Aylesworth (Lucinda), Paul Ben-Victor (Vinnie), Elizabeth Rodriguez (Cleo)
A comedy in two acts. The action takes place in Brooklyn.

Michael Rapaport, Reiko Aylesworth in *Robbers* (Carol Rosegg)

(Ohio Theater) Saturday, Feb.8-Mar.1, 1997 (11 performances and 2 previews) The Rorschach Group presents:
KING GORDOGAN by Radovan Ivsic; Adaptation, Allan Graubard; Director, Andrew Frank; Set, Douglas Huszti; Lighting, Jeff Croiter; Costumes, Laurie Churba; Sound, Raymond Schilke; Press, Gary Springer~Susan Chicoine/Candi Adams CAST: Daniel Reinisch (Loony), Shea Whigham (Odan), John Gould Rubin (Fool), Neil Maffin (Gordogan), Alexander Stefano (Earsnipper), Jason Howard (Eyegouger), Krista Ruhe (Bird), Christy Baron (White), Mitchell Riggs (Knight), Jonathan Uffelman (Tinatine), Fiona Jones (Peasant), Patricia Litzen (Messenger), Caroline McGee (Teeleeka)

American premiere of 1943 black farce from Croatia.

(A Theatre) Tuesday, Feb.11-Mar.2, 1997 (19 performances) Seanachai Theater Company presents:
HYSTERICAL BLINDNESS by Laura Cahill; Director, Jared Harris; Set, Doug Huszti; Lighting, Jeff Croiter, Jim Vermulen; Sound, Kurt Kellenburger; Stage Manager, Christina Prestia; Press, Publicity Office/Bob Fennell CAST: Jill Larson (Virginia), Amy Ryan (Debby), Tim Williams (Bobby), Jenny Robertson (Beth), Bill Sage (Rick), William Wise (Nick)

A dramatic comedy performed without intermission. The action takes place in New Jersey, 1987.

Amy Ryan, Bill Sage in *Hysterical Blindness* (Shonna Valeska)

**Sango, Nambu, Gyuzo, Danna in *Tokyo Shock Boys*
(Particia Eichwalder)**

Neil Maffin, John Gould Rubin in *King Gordogan* (Joan Marcus)

(Minetta Lane Theatre) Tuesday, Feb.11-Apr.13, 1997 (63 performances and 9 previews) Arthur Cantor, Murray Pope, Shuji Shibata present:
THE TOKYO SHOCK BOYS; Devised by The Cast; Director, Murray Pope; Music, Satoshi Nishikata; Musical Director, Paul Jackson; Arrangements, Mr. Nishikata, Mr. Jackson; Production Manager, Justin C. Reiter; Press, James L.L. Morrison/Tom D'Ambrosio CAST: Tokyo Shock Boys (Dana, Gyuzo, Nambu, Sango)

Samurai vaudeville performed without intermission.

(Judith Anderson Theatre) Wednesday, Feb.12-16, 1997 (6 performances) Red Light District presents:
UNIDENTIFIED HUMAN REMAINS AND THE TRUE NATURE OF LOVE by Brad Fraser; Director, Marc Geller; Lighting, Frank Dendanto III; Music, Daniel T. Denver; Stage Manager, Jeremy Freiburger CAST: Marc Geller (David), Tracey Gilbert (Candy), Shawn Brentham (Robert), Robert J. Dyckman (Kane), Sally Frontman (Jerri), Tyler Pace (Bernie), Mary Beth Kowalski (Benita)

(Theatre Off Park) Wednesday, Feb.12-Mar.9, 1997 (12 performances and 4 previews) Rattlestick Productions presents:
HEART OF A MAN by Jennifer Christman; Director, Abby Epstein; Sets, Van Santvoord; Lighting, Chad McArver; Costumes, Dana Bauer; Press, Peter Cromarty/Hugh Hayes CAST: Elizabeth Hanly Rice (Jane), Jordan Lage (Alex), Kathryn Hahn (Edie)

A modern love triangle.

Austin Pendleton in *Richard III* (Barbara Rosenberg)

Michelle Merring, Shawn Sears, Stephanie Bishop, (front) Jason Hayes in *Space Trek* (Carol Rosegg)

Talmadge Lowe, Matthew Saldivar in *Two Gentlemen of Verona* (Scott Suchman)

(New Perspectives) Wednesday, Feb.12-Mar.8, 1997 (14 performances and 2 previews) New Perspectives Theater Company presents:
RICHARD III by William Shakespeare; Adapted/Directed by Carol Kastendieck; Design, Melissa Bruning; Lighting, Richard Tatum; Sound, Stephen Spoonamore; Music, Richard Bennett; Fights, David Dean Hastings, Angela Bonacasa; Stage Manager, Barbara Good; Press, Chris Boneau~Adrian Bryan-Brown/Erin Dunn, Paula Mallino CAST: Austin Pendleton (Richard), Karin Amano (Duke of York), Melody Brooks (Elizabeth), Al Choy (Derby), India Cooper (Margaret), Ron Domingo (Murderer2/Mayor), Mark Ehrlich (Richmond), Tim Farley (Ratcliffe/Lancaster), Albert Michael Goudy (Edward iv), Dawn A. Greenidge (Lady Anne), Sarah Kate (Grey/Prince of Wales), James Kohli (Rivers), Ken Leung (Buckingham), Milton Loayza (Murder/Clergy), Anthony O'Donoghue (Henry VI), Richard Omar (Hastings), Marion Pearce (Duchess of York), Jospeh W. Rodriguez (Clarence/Tyrrel), Karen B. Samuelsohn (Dorset/Mistress Shore), Anthony Zelig (Catesby)

An adaptation presented entirely from Richard's perspective.

(Theatre 22) Thursday, Feb.13-Mar.2, 1997 (12 performances) Untitles Theatre Company #61 presents:
THE STORY OF THE LIVING METHUSELAH; Written/Directed by Edward A. Einhorn; Sets, David Maxine; Choreography, Kim Anthony; Music, Brian Patton; Sound, John Hudak; Lighting, Thomas Pasquenza; Press, Howard and Barbara Atlee CAST: Jason Katz (Methuselah), Erin Kelley (Serah), Dan Leventritt (Doctor), Julia Martin, Mira Kingsley (Handmaidens)

A comedy about the oldest living man in history.

(Chelsea Playhouse) Thursday, Feb.13-Mar.9, 1997 (29 performances and 5 previews) Joyce M. Sarner in association with Spectrum Stage presents:
SPACE TREK, A MUSICAL PARODY; Music/Lyrics, Rick Crom; Book, Marc Lipitz; Director, Vincent Sassone; Choreography, Karen Molnar; Musical Director, John Bowen; Set, William F. Moses; Costumes, Carol Brys; Lighting, Jason Livingston; Sound, Kelly Dempsey; Stage Manager, Tracy Jackson; Press, Peter Cromarty/Robert Rave CAST: Stephanie Jean (Ensign Bambi), Billy Sharpe (Chief Engineer Sloshy), Adam Wald (Ensign Chicks-Love), Jason Hayes (Capt. Slim Qick), Shawn Sears (Mister Schlock), Michelle Merring (Lt. Yomama), Randy Lake (Dr. Moans), Hank Jacobs (Capt. Christian Spike)
MUSICAL NUMBERS: Opening Sequence, Captain of the Ship, Shoulda Been Coulda Been Mine, Ballad of Happy Planet, Hello Boys, Problem with Us, Ensign's Lament, Picnic on a Planet, Amour Time, To Be a Captain, Brain Drain, Spike's Turn, Got to Get a Life, Finale

A musical comedy performed without intermission. The setting is the Spaceship Merchandise.

(St. Peter's) Friday, Feb.14-Mar.16, 1997 (21 performances and 10 previews) Blue Light Theater Company presents:
THE TWO GENTLEMEN OF VERONA by William Shakespeare; Director, Dylan Baker; Set, Michael Vaughn Sims; Costumes, Susan Branch; Lighting, Mark Stanley; Sound, Raymond D. Schilke; Choreography, Debra Zalkind; Stage Manager, Christina Massie; Press, Gary Springer~Susan Chicoine/Candi Adams CAST: Talmadge Lowe (Valentine), Greg Naughton (Proteus), Larry Nathanson (Speed), Vivienne Benesch (Julia), Robert Brock (Ol'Lucius/Eglamour), Mark Shelton (Antonio/Outlaw), James Matthew Ryan (Panthino/Outlaw), Jow Grifasi (Launce), Fred Dog (Crab), Camilia Sanes (Silvia), Molly Regan (Duchess), Matthew Saldivar (Thurio), Jean Kanaley (Ursula/Outlaw), Matthew Semrick (Host)

Performed in two acts. This version is set in Texas, 1876.

(Thirteenth St. Rep Theatre) Friday, Feb.14-May 4, 1997 (36 performances) Thirteenth St. Repertory presents:
VOLLEY BOYS by Mark Dunn; Director/Design, Grace Riskin; Lighting, Gavin Smith; Stage Manager, Leticia Raines CAST: Paul Hiatt, Gavin Smith (Cooper), Kavin M. Coleman, Roberto A. Cabrera (Jefferies), Edward Kassar, Brad Coustan (Carter), Leo DiStefano, Joshua Lewis Berg (Venetti), Peter Furst, Robert Bruce (Turley), Paul Wells, Michael Calderon (Mallory)
A psychological drama performed without intermission. The action takes place in a basement/rec room somewhere in the northeast.

(The Salon) Saturday, Feb.15-Mar.1, 1997 (12 performances) INNO Productions by arrangement with Edgar Lansbury presents:
IN CIRCLES by Gertrude Stein and Al Carmines; Director, Randolph Curtis Rand; Musical Director, David Tice; Set, Rodney Cueller; Lighting, James Vermeulen; Costumes, Carol Brys; Stage Manager, Rick Hagg; Press, Keith Sherman/Jim Byk CAST: Danielle Ferland, Laurent Giroux, Sarah Knapp, Gary Leimkuhler, Robin Miles, Nicky Paraiso, Barbara Rosenblat, Anthony Santelmo Jr.
Settings of Stein's words to music.

(Upstairs at Rose's Turn) Sunday, Feb.16-Apr.27, 1997 (12 performances) B.O.N. Productions presents:
IMPALED ON A MAGNOLIA by Beth Glover and Randy Buck; Director, Mr. Buck; Press, Jim Baldassare CAST: Beth Glover
A one-woman comedy about the self-discovery of a young Southern woman.

**Gary Leimkuhler, Nicky Paraiso, Barbara Rosenblat in *In Circles*
(Nigel Teare)**

(St. Clement's) Monday, Feb.17-Mar.15, 1997 (15 performances and 14 previews) Theatre for a New Audience presents:
THE CHANGELING by Thomas Middleton and William Rowley; Director, Robert Woodruff; Set, Neil Patel, Miriam Gouretsky; Lighting, Don Holder, Felice Ross; Costumes, Kasia Walicka Maimone; Soundscape, Darron L. West; Choreography, Sa'as Magal; Stage Manager, Elizabeth Burgess; Press, Gary Springer~Susan Chicoine/Cgarlie Siedenburg CAST: Firdous Bamji (Antonio), Melissa Bowen (Isabella), Joel Carino (Pedro), Reg E. Cathey (Lollio), Thom Christopher (Vermandero), Glenn Fleshler), Marin Hinkle (Beatrice), Lee Lewis (Diaphanta), Christopher McCann (De Flores), Chris McKinney (Alsemero), Ntare Mwine (Tomazo), Frederick Neumann (Alibius), Trellis Stepter (Alonzo), Amy Lee, David Matiano, Beverley Prentice, Nadia Tarr, Jennifer Tarrazi-Scully (Inmates of the Asylum)
A drama in two acts. The action takes place in Alicant, Spain.

(John Houseman Studio) Wednesday, Feb.19-Mar.29, 1997 (16 performances and 4 previews) St. Bocephus Productions presents:
GUNNIN' FOR JESUS by James Oakes, Tammy Lany and Charlie Schulman; Director, Mr. Schulman; Musical Director, Mark McCarron; Lighting/Stage Manager, Jennifer Jonassen; Press, Jim Baldassare CAST: James Oakes (Fr. Sullivan), Tammy Lang (Tammy Faye Starlite)
A comedy with songs. The action takes place in Nashville.

(The Kitchen) Wednesday, Feb.19-Mar.2, 1997 (10 performances)
STAR 69; Written/Performed by Linda Hill
The personal odyssey of an actress threatened by a stalker.

(Angel Orensanz Foundation for the Arts) Thursday, Feb.20-Mar.9, 1997 (11 performances) Milagro presents:
THE EXTERMINATOR by Robert Alan Margolis; Director, Liza Williams; Set/Costumes, David R. Gammons CAST: Jim Christopher, Michelle Daimer, Tom Hughes, Roberta Pikser, D. Zhonzinsky
An absurdist tragedy.

**Ntare Mwine, Chris McKinney in *The Changeling*
(Gerry Goodstein)**

(West-Park Church) Thursday, Feb.20-Mar.16, 1997 (12 performances and 4 previews) Frog & Peach Theatre Company presents:
CYMBELINE by William Shakespeare; Director, Ted Zurkowski; Press, Gary Springer~Susan Chicoine/Candi Adams CAST: Lynnea Benson (Imogen), Mervyn Haines Jr. (Cymbeline), Aris Alvarado, Angela Bonacasa, Bryant Fraser, Leone Fogle Hechler, Vivien Landau, Howard I. Laniado, Eric Masters, Michael McFadden, Alicia Meer, Jack Rewkowski, Douglas Stone, Carolyn Sullivan-Zinn, Terry Tocantins

(Kraine Theater) Thursday, Feb.20-Mar.16, 1997 (12 performances and 4 previews) Peccadillo Theater Company in association with Steppin' Out Productions presents:
IN A GARDEN by Philip Barry; Director Wackerman; Set/Lighting, Kimo James; Costumes, Susan Soetaert; Stage Manager, Megan McDonnell; Press, Gary Springer~Susan Chicoine/Candi Adams CAST: Dale Carman (Roger Compton), Trudy Steibl (Miss Mabie), Jim Scholfield (Adrian Terry), Lillian Langforth (Lissa Terry), Howard Atlee (Frederick), Tom Biglin (Norrie Bliss)
A 1924 three-act comedy performed with one intermission. The action takes place at Adrian Terry's home on Sutton Place, 1925.

Tom Biglin, Lillian Langford in *In a Garden* (Jerry Banberger)

(Theatre for a New City) Thursday, Feb.20-Mar.9, 1997 (13 performances) Blue Heron Theatre and Yangtze Repertory Theatre present:
BETWEEN LIFE AND DEATH; Written/Directed by Gao Xingjian; Translation, Joanna Chan; Choreography, Bin-Jung Lee; Set/Costumes, Christopher Thomas; Lighting, Woohyung Lee; Press, Jonathan Slaff CAST: Eleonora Kihlberg (Woman), Mari Yeh (Dancer), Bin-Jung Lee (Mime), Young Yat-De
An avant-garde drama.

(Theatre Row Theatre) Friday, Feb.21-Apr.13, 1997 (43 performances and 11 previews) Theater Three Collaborative and Other Pictures present:
THE BEEKEEPER'S DAUGHTER by Karen Malpede; Directir, Ivica Boban; Set, Maxine Willi Klein; Lighting, Carol Mullins, Russell Hodgson; Music/Sound, David Van Tieghem; Costumes, Sally Ann Parsons; Projections, J. Mole; Stage Manager, Juliana Hannett; Press, Gary Springer~Susan Chicoine CAST: George Bartenieff (Robert), Christen Clifford (Admira), Myriam Cyr (Rachel), Beth Dixon (Sybil), Michael Louden (Jamie)
A drama performed without intermission. The action takes place on an island in the Adriatic Sea, 1993.

Mari Yeh, Eleonora in *Between Life and Death* (Jonathan Slaff)

(One Dream Theatre) Sunday, Feb.23-Mar.16, 1997 (14 performances and 2 previews) Chain Lightning Theatre presents:
THE GREAT GOD BROWN by Eugene O'Neill; Director, Kricker James; Sets, Bill Kneissl; Masks, Katerina Fiore; Costumes, Eden S. Miller; Lighting, Randall Glickman; Sound, Randy Morrison; Stage Manager, Jennifer Moody; Press, Shirley Herz/Wayne Wolfe, James Timko CAST: David Aston-Reese (Dion Anthony), Carol Emshoff (Dion's Mother), Brandee Graff (Margaret), George Henderson (Youngest Son), Cheryl Horne (Cybel), Dawn Jamieson (Billy's Mother), Devon Michaels (Second Son), Frank Natasi (Dion's Father), Billy Prahin (Eldest Son), Roland Sands (Billy's Father), Lyle Walford (Billy)
A 1926 psychological thriller in two acts.

(Theatre 3) Tuesday, Feb.25-Mar.2, 1997 (7 performances) Nakes Angels presents:
STRAY CATS by Warren Leight; Director, Jo Bonney; Sets, George Xenos; Lighting, Alistair Wandesforde-Smith; Costumes, Veronica Worts; Sound, Rob Gould; Stage Manager, Lisa Gavaletz CAST: Taro Alexander, Lewis Black, Nathan Hinton, Ean Sheehy
Performed without intermission.

Beth Dixon, Christen Clifford in *Beekeeper's Daughter* (Lisa Maizlich)

(Raw Space) Wednesday, Feb.26-Mar.23, 1997 (24 performances) The Actors Studio Free Theater at Raw Space under the management of Pure Orange productions presents:
MAJOR CRIMES by Jay Presson Allen; Based on the book Breaking and Entering by Connie Fletcher; Director, Arthur Penn; Set, Michael Mc-Carty; Sound, Otts Munderloh; Costumes, Azan Kung; Lighting, Jeff Croiter; Fights, Rick Sordelet; Stage Manager, Shelli Aderman; Press, Bill Evans/Jim Randolph CAST: Kelly Curtis (Annie), Margaret Whitton (Gilda), Pamela Wiggins (Julia), Rosalyn Coleman (Pat), Justin Reinsilber (T-Shirt/Cop/Bartender), Dominic Chianese (Geezer/Drew), Judette Jones (Inspector Kipplinger), Matt Mabe (Dave/Speeder/Bobby), Marissa Chibas (Luz), Deirdre Madigan (Jolene), William Christian (Battery Perp./Hartley), Paul Geier (Burt), Armand Schultz (Sid), Jim Quinn (Brian), Alice Yates (Brenda Denmark), Isiah Whitlock Jr. (Gary), Joseph Siravo (Mario), David Wolos-Fonteno (Lonny Yates), Robert Hogan (Cullum), Brian Keeler (Gordon), Michael Kelly (Croney)

A drama in two acts.

(Greenwich House Theatre) Thursday, Feb.27-May4, 1997 (49 performances and 3 previews) re-opened at (Minetta Lane Theatre) Tuesday, May20-still playing May 31, 1997 Tectonic Theater Project presents:
GROSS INDECENCY: *The Three Trials of Oscar Wilde*; Written/Directed by Moises Kaufman; Sets, Sarah Lambert; Lighting, Betsy Adams; Costumes, Kitty Leech; Sound, Wayne Frost; Stage Manager, Rachel Putnam; Press, Shirley Herz/Kevin P. McAnarney CAST: Michael Emerson (Oscar Wilde), William D. Dawes (Lord Alfred Douglas), Robert Blumenfeld (Queensbury/Gil/Lockwood), Trevor Anthony (Clarke), John McAdams (Carson/Narrator), Andy Paris (Narrator/Atkins/Judge), Greg Pierotti (Narrator/Wood/Shaw), Troy Sostillio (Narrator/Parker/Harris), Greg Steinbruner (Narrator/Mavor/Taylor)

A drama in two acts. The action takes place in England.

(Westbeth Theatre Center) Thursday, Feb.27-Mar.31, 1997 (17 performances and 10 previews) David Binder and Alize present:
HEDWIG AND THE ANGRY INCH; Written/Performed by John Cameron Mitchell; Music/Lyrics, Stephen Trask; Director, Peter Askin; Set/Projections, James Youmans; Lighting, Kevin Adams; Costumes, Fabio Toblini; Sound, Scott Stauffer; Wigs, Mike Potter; Press, Publicity Office/Bob Fennell CAST: John Cameron Mitchell (Hedwig/Tommy Gnosis), Miriam Shore (Yitzak), Cheater (The Angry Inch)

A rock 'n' roll drag biography. The action spans Berlin, a Kansas trailer park and the Madison Sq. Garden area TGIF restaurant.

(All Souls Players) Thursday, Feb.27-Mar.16, 1997 (9 performances and 6 previews) BroadHollow Players in association with All Souls Players present:
ON THE ROAD TO VICTORY; Adaptation/Staging/Additional Music & Lyrics, Michael Tester; Musical Supervision/Orchestrations/Vocal Arrangements, Steve Steiner; Musical Director, Christine Talbott; Set, Michael J. Hilger; Lighting, Brian A. Sciarra; Costumes, R. Cordaro; Sound, Gary Haglich; Stage Manager, Marge Gilcher; Press, Shirley Herz/Kevin P. McAnarney CAST: Kevin Fox, Mary Beth Griffith, Suzanne Mason, Emmett Murphy, Erin Pender, Mitch Poulos, Rusty Reynolds, Pegg Winter

A two-act boogie woogie musical revue.

(Miranda Theatre) Thursday, Feb.27-Mar.23, 1997 (12 performances and 4 previews) The Worth Street Theater presents:
WHOA-JACK; Wriiten/Directed by Jeff Cohen; Adapted from Buchner's *Woyzeck*; Set/Lighting, Edward Pierce; Costumes, Brian Mear; Choreography, Sarah Adriance; Press, Carol R. Fineman CAST: Douglass Stewart, T.J. Kenneally, John L. Damon, Michael Bennett, Cathy Clifford-Nicholson, Jack R. Marks, John Rosenfeld, Ethan Sandler, Phoenix Saunders, Susan Spain, David Stamper, Maya Thomas

The action takes place on a Southern army base, 1960.

Top: Michael Emmerson, Bill Dawes Front: Greg Steinbruner, Troy Sostillio, Andy Paris in *Gross Indecency* **(Jim McGrath)**

John Cameron Mitchell in *Hedwig & the Angry Inch* **(John Bruce)**

(Vineyard/26th St.) Friday, Feb.28-Mar.2, 1997 (6 performances) Watermark Theater Wordfire Festival presents:
THE MAN IN ROOM 304; Written/Performed by Craig Alan Edwards; Director, Cheryl Katz; Press, Richard Kornberg/Don Summa
A fictional account of the last night of Dr. Martin Luther King's life. The action takes place in Memphis, Tennessee, 1968.

(Judith Anderson Theatre) Friday, Feb.28-Mar.23, 1997 (18 performances and 4 previews) Willow Cabin Theatre Company presents:
DON JUAN COMES BACK FROM THE WAR by Odon von Horvath; Translation, Christopher Hampton; Director, Edward Berkley; Set, John Kasarda; Costumes, Linann Easley; Lighting, Matthew McCarthy; Press, Jim Baldassare CAST: Kenneth Favre (Don Juan), Jacqueline Brooks, Cynthia Besteman, Sarah Lively Clarke, Tasha Lawrence, Verna Lowe, Angela Nevard, Dede Pochos, Christine Radman, Maria Radman
A drama in which the anti-hero returns home from the front.

(Raymond J. Greenwald Theatre) Saturday, Mar.1-31, 1997 American Jewish Theatre presents:
NAMES; Written/Directed by Mark Kemble; Set, William Barclay; Costumes, Gail Cooper Hecht; Lighting, Phil Monat; Sound, Red Ramona; Stage Manager, Carol Dacey Charles; Press, Jeffrey Richards/Mark Cannistraro, Timothy Haskell
A drama in two acts. The action takes place in New York's Algonquin Hotel, 1952.

Mai Kretser, Tony Glazer in *Fassbinder in the Frying Pan*
(Melissa Kay Cohen)

(Pier 63) Monday, Mar3 -25, 1997 (6 performances and 2 previews) Tribeca Lab presents:
FASSBINDER IN THE FRYING PAN by Rainer Werner Fassbinder; Translations, Denis Calandra; Design/Lighting, Teddy Jefferson; Costumes, Diane Specioso, April Furr; Music, Prissteens; Stage Manager, Ilene Leventhal; Press, Tony Origlio/Kevin Rehac
The Bitter Tears of Petra von Kant; Director, Stuart Rudin CAST: Marilyn Alex (Valerie von Kant), Flo Cabre Andrews (Karin Thimm), Jacqueline Bowman (Marlene), Bo Corre (Petra von Kant), Cayenne Douglass (Gabriele von Kant), Tricia Parks (Sidonie)
Bremen Freedom; Director, Deborah Stoll CAST: Jacqueline Bowman (Luisa), Tony Glazer (Mittenberger), Andrew Hampsas (Rumpf), Maia Kretser (Geesche), Marc Krinsky (Bohm), Ernest Mingione (Timm), Harvey Perr (Zimmerman), Michael Solomon (Johann), David Steinberg (Gottfried), Andre Ware (Fr. Markus)
Two one-acts performed in a 1929 lightship, the Frying Pan, docked off Pier 63 in Chelsea.

(Ubu Rep Theater) Tuesday, Mar.4-23, 1997 (20 performances and 1 preview) Ubu Repertory Theater presents:
CROSSCURRENTS by Gerty Dambury; Translation, Richard Philcox; Director, Francoise Kourilsky; Set, Watoku Ueno; Lighting, Greg MacPherson; Costumes, Carol Ann Pelletier; Music/Sound, Genji Ito; Stage Manager, Robin C. Gillette; Press, Jonathan Slaff CAST: La Tonya Borsay (Fructuese), Aasif Mandvi (Paul), Bryan Hicks (Merchat), Kavitha Ramachandran (Marie), Bina Sharif (Mother), Jay Palit (Father)
A drama in two acts. The action takes place on an island in the Indian Ocean.

Aasif Mandvi, Lan Tonya Borsay, Bryan Hicks in *Crosscurrents*
(Jonathan Slaff)

156

(Century Theatre) Tuesday, Mar.4-Apr.13, 1997 (33 performances and 14 previews) Edwards/Adams Theatrical, Frances Hill & Associates, Sterling Productions in association with Endernol Theatre Productions, Metropolitan Entertainment Group, J.C. Compton and the Century Center, Playwrights Preview Productions present:
MINOR DEMONS by Bruce Graham; Director, Richard Harden; Set, Patrick Mann; Costumes, Alan Michael Smith; Lighting, Jeffrey McRoberts; Music/Sound, Matt Balitsaris; Stage Manager, Liz Reddick; Press, Peter Cromarty/Hugh Hayes, Kate Cambridge CAST: Reed Birney (Deke Winters), Amelia Marshall (Diane Gardner), Charlie Hofheimer (Kenny Simmonds), Susan Pellegrino (Carmella DelGatto), Steve Ryan (Vince DelGatto), Alexandra O'Karma (Mrs. Simmonds), David B. McConeghey (Mr. Simmonds), Robin Haynes (Mr. O'Brien)
   A drama in two acts. The action takes place in a small town outside of Pittsburgh during winter.

(CSC Theatre) Tuesday, Mar.4-Apr.6, 1997 (25 performances and 8 previews) Classic Stage Company presents:
ANOTHER PART OF THE HOUSE by Migdalia Cruz; Director, David Esbjornson; Sets, Chris Muller; Costumes, Michael Krass; Lighting, Ken Posner; Sound, John Kilgore; Press, Denise Robert CAST: Irma St. Paule (Maria Josefa), Patricia Triana (Bernarda), Sarah Erde (Adela), Doris Difarnecio, Kadina Halliday, Mercedes Herrero, Seth Kanor, Paula Pizzi, Adriana Sevan
   A drama inspired by Federico Garcia Lorca's *House of Bernada Alba*.

(Creative Place Theatre) Wednesday, Mar.5-29, 1997 (14 performances and 2 previews) Madeline Ann Theatre Company presents:
IT BEGINS WITH A KISS...; Written/Directed by Sammy Busby; Press, Shirley Herz CAST: Sammy Busby, Marilyn Torres
   A romantic comedy.

Reed Birney, Charlie Hofheimer in *Minor Demons* **(Carol Rosegg)**

(Union Square Theatre) Wednesday, Mar.5-Aug.24, 1997 (184 performances and 14 previews) Back Row Productions/Peter Holmes a Court, Columbia Artists Management in association with Richard Frankel, Marc Roth by arrangement with Dein Perry and Nigel Triffitt present:
TAP DOGS; Created/Choreographed by Dein Perry; Directed/Designed by Nigel Triffitt; Music, Andrew Wilkie; Lighting, David Murray; Sound, Darryl Lewis; Stage Manager, Arabella Powell; Press, Chris Boneau~Adrian Bryan-Brown/John Wimbs, Miguel Tuasaon CAST: Dein Perry, Darren Disney, Christopher Horsey, Drew Kaluski, Ben Read, Nathan Sheens, Billy Burke, Jeremy Keisman, Gil Stroming
   A dance-theatre piece performed without intermission.

(John Montgomery Theatre) Wednesday, Mar.5-22, 1997 (9 performances and 3 previews) John Montgomery Theatre Company presents:
OTHELLO by William Shakespeare; Director/Design, Thom Fudal; Costumes, Kate Haggerty; Press, Shirley Herz/Wayne Wolfe CAST: Geoffrey Owens (Othello), Patrick Hillian (Iago), Mary Alice McGuire (Aemilia), Judy Turkisher (Desdemona), Jay Veduccio, Robert Bowen Jr., John Kooi, Kenneth Cavett, Matthew Bray, Michelle Pirret

(Altered Stages) Thursday, Mar.6-22, 1997 (14 performances) Yankee Rep presents:
RICHARD CORY by A.R. Gurney; Director, Susan Conley CAST: Arthur Aulisi (Richard Cory), Tina Gilbertson, Jorji Knickrem, Gary Ray, Diane Vuletich, Jim Andralis, Celia Bressack, Jeanne Hime, Valerie Donaldson, Colin Dwyer, Delton Murphy, Herb Ouellette, Kate Pennell

Tap Dogs **(Joan Marcus)**

(Ohio Theater) Thursday, Mar.6-15, 1997 (11 performances) Sightlines Theater Company presents:
AMERICAN ROSE by Susan Hansell; Director, Eileen Phelan; Musical Director/Arranger, Kate Sullivan CAST: Leslie Beatty, Crystal Bock, Victoria Boomsma, Patricia Chilsen, Sandra Daley, Leslie Jones, Eunkyung Lee, Masha Obolensky, Jean Taylor, Yvonne Willrich-Teague, Kelly McCann, Kerry Lescinski, Kate Sullivan

A drama focusing on women during World War II.

(Irish Arts Center) Thursday, Mar.6-30, 1997 (18 performances and 2 previews) Three Pillows Theatre presents:
DUEL OF ANGELS by Jean Giraudoux; Translation, Christopher Fry; Director, Nissim Israel; Sets, Farshad Shahrohki, Bob Green, William Laux; Costumes, Lauren Cordes, Tonya Leonard; Lighting, Aaron Gallemore; Stage Manager, Vonder Gray; Press, Francine L. Trevens CAST: Michael Welden (Marcellus), Stephen Payne, Todd Fredericks (Joseph), Salem Ryan (Gilly), Diana Mari (Paola), Redman Maxfield (Armand), Margalit Kestin (Lucile), Melania Levitsky (Eugenie), Max Mankind (Mace-Bearer/Servant/Clerk), Maire Mansouri, Vonder Gray (Barbette), William Laux, Calvin Wynter (Customer)

A drama in three acts.

(Mint Theater) Friday, Mar.7-23, 1997 (14 performances) Min Theater Company in association with Shakespeare Mailing Service presents:
PERICLES PRINCE OF TYRE by William Shakespeare; Director, Jonathan Bank; Set, Kristen Maynard; Lighting, Mark T. Simpson; Costumes, Vickie B. Davis; Music, Peter Griggs; Movement, Rebecca Holderness; Stage Manager, Margarita G. Ruiz CAST: Robert Boardman, Lisa M. Bostar, Danny Campbell, Charlene Hunter, Cassandra Johnson, Michael J. Lerner, Stina Nielsen, Dennis Rees, Alem Brhan Sapp, Oliver Vaquer, Don E. Williams

(Lucille Lortel Theatre) Tuesday, Mar.11-May 25, 1997 (73 performances and 12 previews) Bernie Brillstein, James D. Stern, Harriet Newman Leve by special arrangement with Lucille Lortel present:
BUNNY BUNNY *Gilda Radner: A Sort of Romantic Comedy* by Alan Zweibel; Director, Christopher Ashley; Set, David Gallo; Costumes, David C. Woolard; Lighting, Michael Lincoln; Projections, Jan Hartley; Sound, Jim van Bergen; Stage Manager, Kate Broderick; Press, Merle Frimark/Joel W. Dein CAST: Bruno Kirby (Alan), Paula Cale (Gilda), Alan Tudyk (All Others)

A romantic comedy in two acts based on the relationship of a writer and the late comedienne. The action takes place in NYC and LA, 1975-89.

(Lamb's Little Theatre) Wednesday, Mar.12-May 4, 1997 (36 performances and 6 previews) Fellowship for the Performing Arts presents:
GENESIS; Adaptation, Buzz McLaughlin and Max McLean; Director, John Pietrowski; Sets, Ron Kadri; Lighting, Christopher Gorzelnik; Sound, Richard M. Rose; Stage Manager, Mary Godinho; General Manager, Arthur Cantor; Press, Denise Robert CAST: Max McLean

One-man performance of tales from the first 35 chapters of the Book of Genesis, first book of the Bible.

(Theatre 3) Thursday, Mar.13-May 11, 1997 (40 performances) Naked Angels presents:
EASTER by Will Scheffer; Director, Richard Caliban; Set, George Xenos; Lighting, Greg MacPherson; Costumes, Anita Yavich; Sound, Peter Hylenski; Stage Manager, Bryan Mason CAST: Ken Marks (Matthew), Jodie Markell (Wilma), Sean Runnette (Herman), Kenneth P. Strong (Zaddock)

A drama set in America's heartland.

(The Salon) Thursday, Mar.13-16, 1997 (4 performances) Sacred Space Theatre Compnay presents:
...AND OTHER FAIRY TALES by William Kernen; Director, Clyde Baldo; Set, Christina Fallon; Lighting, Andris Kasparovics; Costumes, Deanna Berg; Stage Manager, Herbert W. Miller CAST: Jerry Ferris (Brian), Elise James (Ann), Richard Kohn (Harry), Karina Krepp (Ann at 30), Krystal Muccioli (Ball), Laura Rose (Ann at 18), Emmy Rossum (Angelica), Ruth Sherman (Martha)

A three-act drama performed with one intermission.

(Currican Theater) Friday, Mar.14-23, 1997 (13 performances)
DURANG/DURANG by Christopher Durang; Director, Douglas S. hall; Set/Costumes, Daniel Korte; Music/Sound, Michael Walczak; Lighting, Jeff Nellis CAST: Tad Carter, Michael Edmund, Evan Giller, Margaret Inoue, Jane Jakimetz, Gayle Kelly Landers, Jack Levin, Sally Miller, Marilyn Rall, Kevin Scott, Lenore Somerstein, Matthew Wallis

Top: Bruno Kirby, Paula Cale in *Bunny Bunny*
Below: Max McLean in *Genesis* **(David Kent)**

(Bouwerie Lane Theatre) Friday, Mar.14-May 16, 1997 (20 performances and 2 previews) Jean Cocteau Repertory presents:
OTHELLO by Scott Shattuck; Costumes, Amela Baksic; Sets, Edward Haynes; Lighting, Jonathan Polgar; Composer/Sound, Ellen Mandel; Fights, Trent Dawson; Press, Jonathan Slaff CAST: Abner Genece (Othello), Joseph Menino (Iago), Molly Pietz (Desdemona), Patrick Hall (Cassio), Elise Stone (Emilia), Craig Smith, Christopher Black, Harris Berlinsky, Amy Fitts, Neeraj Kochhar, Will Leckie, Raplee Nobori, Matthew Edison, Matt Shale

(Harold Clurman Theatre) Friday, Mar.14-16, 1997 (5 performances) Love Creek Productions presents:
BOSTON PROPER by Edward L. Musto; Director, Vincent S. Randall; Set, Viola Bradford; Costumes, Rayell Noone; Lighting, Richard Callahan CAST: Mark W. French (Ted Daniels), Kim Russell (Michelle Thompson), Christian Georges (Brian Monroe), Devin Quigley (Candy McIntyre), Ernie Charles (Rusty Thompson)

(Players Theatre) Tuesday, Mar.18-Apr.20, 1997 (31 performances and 9 previews) Barter Theatre presents:
DOCTOR DOCTOR; Music/Lyrics, Peter Ekstrom; Additional Lyrics/Material, David DeBoy; Director, Richard Rose; Musical Director/Arrangements, Albert Ahronheim; Set, Crystal Tiala; Costumes, Amanda Aldridge; Lighting, David G. Silver-Friedl; Sound, Scott Koenig; Stage Manager, Bill McComb; Press, Jeffrey Richards/Mark Cannistraro, Timothy Haskell CAST: Buddy Crutchfield (Jay), Jill Geddes (Audrey), Nancy Johnston (Gloria), James Weatherstone (William), Albert Ahronheim (Receptionist)
MUSICAL NUMBERS: The Human Body, Oh Boy How I Love My Cigarettes!, The Consumate Picture, I'm a Well-Known Respected Practitioner, Tomorrow, World of My Own, And Yet I Lived On, Willie, The Right Hand Song, Please Dr. Fletcher, Take It Off Tammy, Its My Fat!, Nine Long Months Ago, Hymn, Medicine Man Blues, Private Practice, Nurse's Care, I'm Sure of It, I Loved My Father, Jesus Is My Doctor, Bing Bang Boom!, Eighty Thousand Orgasms, Good Ole Days of Sex, Do I Still Have You, I Hope I Never Get, Finale
A musical comedy revue in two acts.

James Weatherstone, Nancy Johnston in *Doctor Doctor* (Carol Rosegg)

Abner Genece, Joseph Menino in *Othello* (Jonathan Slaff)

(47th St. Theatre) Tuesday, Mar.18-May 18, 1997 (43 performances and 6 previews) Evangeline Morphos, Mara Gibbs, Gary Shaffer present:
MY ITALY STORY by Joseph Gallo; Director, Joe Brancato; Set, Jeff Cowie; Lighting, Jeff Nellis; Hairstylist, Terence McFarland; Sound, Johanna Doty; Stage Manager, Kathleen J. Dooner; Press, Richard Kornberg/Jim Byk CAST: Daniel Mastrogiorgio (Thomas DeGato)
A one man play performed without intermission.

(INTAR Theatre) Wednesday, Mar.19-Apr.13, 1997 (15 performances and 6 previews) INTAR Hispanic American Arts Center and The Women's Project & Productions present:
TERRA INCOGNITA; Music, Roberto Sierra; Libretto/Director, Maria Irene Fornes; Musical Director, Stephen Gosling; Sets, Van Santvoord; Costumes, Willa Kim; Lighting, Philip Widmer; Press, Patricia Fox; Press, Shirley Herz/Kevin P. McAnarney, Adam Meza, Wayne Wolfe CAST: Jennifer Alagna, Lawrence Craig, John Muriello, Candace Rogers O'Connor, Matthew Perri
An opera for the theatre. The action takes place in the Spanish town where Columbus first set sail for the New World.

Al Smith, Minerva Scelza, Tom Day in *Returner* (Kareem Black)

James Whalen in *Woyzeck*

Willem Dafoe in *The Hairy Ape* (Mary Gearhart)

(Fourth St. Theatre) Wednesday, Mar.19-Apr.6, 1997 (12 performances and 4 previews) Lost Tribe Theatre Company presents:
RETURNER; Written/Directed by Stephen F. Kelleher; Set, Jennifer Campbell; Music, Joey Kanner; Lighting, Philip D. Widmer; Video, David Furhur; Stage Manager, Jamie Salzano; Press, Gary Springer~Susan Chicoine/Charlie Siedenburg CAST: Tom Day (Jeeter Green), Deanna Deignan (Dori Engler), Carolyn DeMerice (Jordan Weiss), Michael Irby (Oscar Hidalgo), John Ryerson (Hoke), Minerva Scelza (Magda Rivera), Al Smith (Red), Larry Swanson (Tommy Flaherty)
A drama in two acts. The action takes place in New York City, 2007 A.D.

(Hamlet of Bank Street) Thursday, Mar.20-29, 1997 (13 performances) Esperance Theatre Company presents:
WOYZECK by Georg Buchner; Director, Myk Watford; Costumes, Sarah Carlson; Choreography, Taryn Smith; Fights, Howard Overshown; Sets, Kent Gasser; Lighting, Izzy Einsidler CAST: James Whalen (Woyzeck), Spencer Aste, Michael Behrens, Kent Gasser, Ruth Henry, Ron Matthews, Howard Overshown, Taryn Smith, Adria Woomer-Stewart, Gary Van Lieu, Wendy Wilde
This production is set on a small town American military base during the 1950s.

(Selwyn Theatre) Friday, Mar.21-May 25, 1997 (46 performances and 11 previews) Frederick Zollo, Ron Kastner, Hal Luftig, Nicholas Paleologos and The Wooster Group present:
THE HAIRY APE by Eugene O'Neill; Director, Elizabeth LeCompte; Set, Jim Clayburgh; Lighting, Jennifer Tipton; Music, John Lurie; Sound, James J.J. Johnson, John Collins; Video, Christopher Kondek, Philip Bussmann; Press, Pete Sanders/Helene Davis, Clint Bond Jr. CAST: Willen Dafoe (Robert Smith, "Yank"), Scott Renderer (Paddy), Dave Shelley (Long), Kate Valk (Mildred Douglas), Peyton Smith (Aunt), Ray Faudree (Prisoner on Video), Paul Lazar (I.W.W. Secretary)
A 1921 comedy of ancient and modern life in eight scenes, performed without intermission. This marks the first legit show in 42nd St.'s Selwyn Theatre since 1935.

(Altered Stages) Tuesday, Mar.25-June 28, 1997 (22 performances and 2 previews) Chrysler Theatre Company presents:
AIRBORNE FROM DEERBORN by Richard Krevolin; Directors, Stephen Stahl, Rhett Dennis; Choreography, Luigi; Press, Maya/Penny M. Landau CAST: Jenifer Shaw, Megan Hunt, Ruth Kulerman
The life and times of a Broadway gypsy.

(St. Clement's) Tuesday, Apr.1-13, 1997 (15 performances and 1 preview)
NIJINSKY-DEATH OF A FAUN by David Pownall; Director, Jennie Buckman; Choreography, Nicholas Johnson, Gillian Lynne; Lighting, Simon Bennison; Costumes, Brenda Hawkins; Press, Shirley Herz/Kevin P. McAnarney, Sam Rudy CAST: Nicholas Johnson
One-man play featuring excerpts from famous Nijinsky dance roles. The action takes place in Switzerland, August 1929.

Norman Siopis, Matthew Cassillo, Susan Stout in *Reality Daydreams*
(Karen Dolan)

Charlie Schroeder, Stephen Pell, Eureka, Lisa Herbold, Christa
Kirby, Everett Quinton in *Corn* **(Carol Rosegg)**

Allan Tibbetts, Sheryl Dold in *Censored* **(David Morgan)**

(Trilogy Theatre) Tuesday, Apr.1-26, 1997 (15 performances and 5 previews) Deborah K. Backus presents:
REALITY DAYDREAMS by Michael Racanelli; Directors, Jamie Foster, Norman Siopis; Costumes, Claire Davis; Set, John E. Cobbs Jr.; Lighting, The Universe; Press, Gary Springer~Susan Chicoine/Charlie Siedenburg CAST: Maezie Murphy, Tracy Appleton, Caroline Weglarz, Andrew R. Cooksey, Susan Stout, Chuck Bunting, Norman Siopis, Debbie D'Amore, Anthony Grasso, Bill Mullen, Martin Epstein
Four one-act plays: *Private Thoughts, Title Wave, Celestial Terminal and Galactic U-Turn.*

(Theatre Off Park) Wednesday, Apr.2-27, 1997 (16 performances and 4 previews) Rattlestick Productions presents:
WINNING by David Van Asselt; Director, Laura Josepher; Sets, Van Santvoord; Costumes, Chad McArver; Music, Michael Whalen; Press, Peter Cromarty/Hugh Hayes CAST: Maura Russo (Debra Nuldoon), Sam Guncler (James Foster), Jennifer Regan (Janice), William Severs, John Tormey
A drama examining the conflict between business ethics and personal integrity.

(Chelsea Playhouse) Wednesday, Apr.2-May 24, 1997 (40 performances and 8 previews) Ridiculous Theatrical Company presents:
CORN; Music/Lyrics, Virgil Young; Book, Charles Ludlam; Director, Everett Quinton; Additional Music/Lyrics, Lance Cruce and Mary Rodriguez; Music Director, Mr. Cruce; Sets, Garry Hayes; Lighting, Richard Currie; Costumes, Romona Ponce; Wigs/Makeup, Zsamira Ronquillo; Stage Manager, Cory Lippiello; Press, James L.L. Morrison/Tom D'Ambrosio CAST: Eureka (Maw McCoy), Lisa Herbold (Lola Lola), Christa Kirby (Rachel McCoy), Randy Lake (Ruben Hatfield), Stephen Pell (Aunt Priscilla), Everett Quinton (Paw Hatfield), Lenys Sama (Dude Greasman), Jimmy Szczepanek (Melanie McCoy), Charlie Schroeder (Moe Hatfield)
A 1972 musical in two acts.

(Ohio Theater) Thursday, Apr.3-21, 1997 (13 performances and 4 previews) Via Theater presents:
CENSORED; Written/Conceived/Directed by Brian Jucha; Choreography, The Company; Lighting, Roma Flowers; Sets, Bob Fagella; Orchestrations, Rod Hohl; Costumes, Kasia Walicka-Maimone; Sound, Darron L. West; Stage Manager, Robin Riddell; Press, Tony Origlio/Michael Cullen CAST: Melanie Cortier, Sheryl Dold, Gheidi Flanagan, Leah Gray, Will Keenan, Kristen Lee Kelly, Cheryl Lewis, Matthew R. Mohr, Johnnie Moore, Jennifer Pace, Megan Spooner, Allan Tibbetts, Adriene Thorne
A dance theatre piece set in a world of film noir mystery. The last performance took place at Lincoln Center's Alice Tully Hall.

(Judith Anderson Theatre) Friday, Apr.4-20, 1997 (12 performances and 5 previews) Abingdon Theatre Company presents:
THE MOST IMPORTANT AMERICAN PLAYWRIGHT SINCE TENNESSEE WILLIAMS by William Shuman; Director, Elaine Smith; Set, George Xenos; Lighting, David Castaneda; Costumes, Carol Brys; Sound, Tim Cramer; Stage Manager, C.C. Banks; Press, Gary Springer~Susan Chicoine/Candi Adams CAST: Nicholas Piper (Willy Kinderman), Ed Steele (A. Richard Cutter), Lee Steinhardt (Angela Montalbano)
A comedy about a playwright.

Renee Taylor, Joseph Bologna, Nanette Fabray in *Bermuda Avenue Triangle* (Joan Marcus)

(Third Eye Rep Theatre) Friday, Apr.4-28, 1997 Third Eye Repertory presents:

THE MARRIAGE OF BETTE AND BOO by Christopher Durang; Director, Sue Kim; Set/Lighting, Shawn Rozsa; Costumes, Meredith Charles CAST: Josh Gildrie (Boo), Meredith Charles (Bette), Josh Aaron McCabe (Narrator), Mike Cash, Spencer Leuenberger, Jessica Mandoki, Mark Peters, Elizabeth Martin, Milda De Voe

(Angel Orensanz Foundation) Friday, Apr.4-13, 1997 (10 performances) Lucky devil Theatre Company presents:

TRAGEDY: PROMETHEUS BOUND and **THE TROJAN WOMEN**; Director, Torquil Campbell; Translations, James Scully and John Harrington (Prometheus Bound), John Barton (Trojan); Sets, Jerry Sonnenberg; Lighting, Robert Williams; Costumes, Brendan Cooper; Music, Chris Seligman; Stage Manager, Ralo; Press, Sarah Olmsted CASTS: Claudia Besso, Marie Carlisle, Kevin Chalmers, Char Daigle, Danielle Duvall, Christine Gillespie, Jo Anne Glover, Marc Goodman, Makeda Harris, Heather Hubbard, Nick Keene, Jessica Lambert, Roya Maroufkhani, Sarah Olmsted, Paolo Pagliacolo, David Paluck, Connie Rafferty, Desmond Reilly, Joanna Reynolds

Two Greek tragedies.

(Promenade Theatre) Saturday, Apr.5-Oct.12, 1997 Starhearts Productions, Richard A. Rosen, Jerry Greenberg, Norman Pattiz, Nicholas Eliopoulos, Doc McGhee, Stephen Schnitzer present:

BERMUDA AVENUE TRIANGLE by Renee Taylor and Joe Bologna; Director, Danny Daniels; Sets, James Noone; Costumes, Gail Cooper-Hecht; Lighting, Tharon Musser; Sound, Jon Gottlieb; Stage Manager, Meredith J. Greenburg; Press, Bill Evans, Loving & Weintraub/Paul Alexander, Dennis Harmon CAST: Ronnie Farer (Angela), Priscilla Shanks (Rita), Nanette Fabray (Tess), Renee Taylor (Fannie), Manny Kleinmuntz (Rabbi Levine), Joe Bologna (Johnny) DURING PREVIEWS: Vince Viverito (Mugger)

A comedy in two acts. The action takes place in Las Vegas.

(Samuel Beckett Theatre) Saturday, Apr.5-18, 1997 (7 performances) Interborough Repertory Theater and Del-Sign Project present:

A MIDSUMMER NIGHT'S DREAM by William Shakespeare; Directors, Luane Davis, Cash Tilton; Set, Andris Krumkalns; Costumes, D.V. Thompson; Lighting/Visual Effects, John Adams Jr.; Music, Succor; Sound, David Bullard; Stage Manager, Mimi Craig; Press, MAYA/Penny M. Landau CAST: Alberto Acosta (Starveling Shadow/Titania fairy), Andy Brown (Demetrius Shadow/Oberon Fairy), Cynobia Demps (Philostrate/Puck Shadow), Roy Doliner (Peter Quince), James Fackler (Demetrius), Josh Frager (Lysander), Kate Anna Haggerty (Titania/Hippolyta Shadow), Vivian Hasbrouk (Hermia Shadow), Peaseblossom), Laurence Kaiser (Theseus/Oberon Shadow), Amanda Kaplan (Lysander Shadow/Mustardseed), Michael Dunn Litchfield (Snug Shadow/Oberon Fairy), Nicholas Little (Flute Shadow/Oberon Fairy), Barry Magnani (Bottom Shadow/Oberon Fairy), Maria Alaina Mason (Quince Shadow/Cobweb), Jenine Mayring (Helena), Grant McKeown (Starveling), Gregory Mikell (Egeus/Snout), Craig D. Pearlberg (Flute), Collette Porteous (Hermia), David Craig Rosenberg (Snug/Egeus Shadow), Rashmi Singh (Snout Shadow/Oberon Fairy), Gerald Small (Oberon/Theseus Shadow), Ed Smit (Bottom), Krista Sutton (Helena Shadow/Moth), Gameela Wright (Puck/Philostrate Shadow), Kimberly Wright (Hippolyta/Titania Shadow)

Performed in two acts. In this production, characters are followed by their subconcious mind.

(Ubu Rep Theatre) Saturday, Apr.5-27, 1997 (14 performances) Playwrights' Preview Productions presents:

CONFIRMING THE SEARCH: THAT GIRL'S STILL HERE SOMEWHERE; Written/Performed by Nadine Mozon; Director, Ben Harney; Press, Keith Sherman/Kevin Rehac

A one-woman poetry/performance piece.

(Samuel Beckett Theater) Sunday, Apr.6-20, 1997 (9 performances and 2 previews) New Directions Theater and Interborough Repertory Theater presents:
THE GODSEND by Richard Willett; Director, Charles Loffredo; Set, Andris Krumkalns; Lighting, John Adams Jr.; Costumes, Julia Van Vliet; Press, Shirley Herz/Sam Rudy CAST: Patricia R. Floyd (Gail), Judy Stone (Beverly), Jamie Heinlein (Susan), Glen Williamson (Jeff), Wendell Ward (Henry), James Sutton (Joe), Cindy Chesler (Angela)
    A comedy in two acts. The action takes place in an upstate New York summer house.

(Tribeca Performing Arts Center) Wednesday, Apr.9-May 11, 1997 (30 performances) Tribeca Performing Arts Center in association with New Federal Theatre presents:
THE LAST STREET PLAY by Richard Wesley; Director, Thomas Bullard; Set, Rob Odorisio; Lighting, Shirley Prendergast; Costumes, Edmond Felix; Sound, Tim Schellenbaum; Press, Max Eisen/Lisa Liu CAST: Ella Joyce (Rita), Gordon T. Skinner (Frankie), Arthur French (Zeke), Kenn Green (Tiny), Ramon Moses (Lucky), Brian K. Spivey (Eldridge), Chad L. Coleman (Braxton)
    A 1977 drama performed without intermission. The action takes place in Newark, NJ.

(Ubu Rep Theatre) Wednesday, Apr.9-26, 1997 (15 performances) Playwrights' Preview Productions presents:
FEAR ITSELF by Eugene Lee; Director, Joe Morton; Press, Keith Sherman/Kevin Rehac CAST: S. Epatha Merkerson, Eric LaRay Harvey, Count Stovall, Sharon Washington
    A drama about a young football star with a unique gift for poetry.

(Greenwich St. Theater) Wednesday, Apr.9-20, 1997 (13 performances) Flock Theater Company presents:
THE CROSSING by Irene Glezos; Director, Marlise Tronto; Design, Peter Nigrini CAST: Pat Dias, Irene Glezos, Gerry Goodstein, Juan Mora, Adam Roth, Ben Schiff, D.J. Sharp, David Weck, Jeannie Zusy

Patricia R. Floyd, Wendell Ward in *The Godsend* (Carl Sturmer)

Gordon Skinner, Chad Coleman in *Last Street Play*

(Theatre East) Thursday, Apr.10, 1997- Tom Lynch Productions presents:
KEROUAC; Music, Shelly Gartner; Lyrics, Benita Green, Reena Heenan; Book, Reena Heenan; Director, James B. Nicola CAST INCLUDES: Robert Maier (Jack Kerouac), Steve Curtis (Neal Cassady), Nomi Tichman (Mother), David Petrolle (Allen Ginsberg), Patrick G. Pettys (William Burroughs)
    A musical biography in two acts.

(Present Company) Thursday, Apr.10-27, 1997 (12 performances) The Present Company presents:
OFFENDING THE AUDIENCE by Peter Handke; Director, John Clancy; Stage Manager, Daniel P. Hope; Press, Elena K. Holy CAST: Laura Agudelo, Brian Dykstra, Patrick Frederic, Halle Markle
    A speak-in with four actors speaking directly to an audience.

(Theatre at Chelsea Arts) Friday, Apr.11-May 18, 1997 (26 performances and 2 previews) American Renaissance Theatre of Dramatic Arts presents:
LIONS AND FOXES; *The Life of Lucrezia Borgia* by Quiche Kemble; Director, Rich Stone; Costumes, Jeanette Anne Ryan; Lighting, Kimberly Patterson; Sets, Gang of Two; Press, Jonathan Slaff CAST: Rob Miller (Machiavelli), Quiche Kemble (Lucrezia Borgia), Dean Storm Bradshaw (Cesare Borgia), Chris Andersson (Vecellio), Trey Burvant (Alfonso), Kevin Keaveney (Duke D'este)
    A drama in two acts. The action takes place in Rome and Ferrara, 1497-1510.

Quiche Kemble in *Lions and Foxes* (Jonathan Slaff)

(Hamlet of Bank Street) Friday, Apr.11-20, 1997 (8 performances and 3 previews) Esperance Theatre Company presents:
MY ALICE; Written/Directed by Shay Gines; Press, Angel Hayes CAST: Kent Gasser, Christopher Borg, Susan Borg, Susan DiGuilio, Wendy Wilde
A haunted love story about Lewis Carroll and his "ideal child friend."

(28th St. Theatre) Wednesday, Apr.16-May 10, 1997 (13 performances and 3 previews) Lark Theatre Company presents:
ON MY KNEES by Elizabeth Logun; Director, John Clinton Eisner; Music, James Adler; Set, Larry M. Gruber; Lighting, James Michael Hultquist; Costumes, Carols Brys, William F. Moser; Sound, Jo Van Horn/Full House; Stage Managers, Jane Hogan, Margarita G. Ruiz; Press, Peggy Friedman~Jean Goetz CAST: Elizabeth Logan (Gwen), Barbara Andres (Mum), Donald Christopher (Dad)
A drama in two acts. A British postal worker finds herself on a mystical journey to New Mexico.

(Theatre Row Theatre) Wednesday, Apr.16-20, 1997 (6 performances) Red Light District presents:
EXIT THE KING by Eugene Ionesco; Director/Set/Costumes, Marc Geller; Lighting, Jennifer Mann; Stage Manager, Jeremy Freiburger CAST: Bill Roulet (Guard), Marilyn Duryea (Servant), Sally Frontman (First Queen), Tracey Gilbert (New Queen), Thomas F. Walsh (Doctor), Marc Geller (King)
A drama performed without intermission. The setting is the throne room of King Berenger I.

(28th St. Theatre) Saturday, Apr.19-May 10, 1997 (8 performances and 8 previews) Lark Theatre Company presents:
HEARTBREAK by Jack Heifner; Director, Steven Williford; Set, Larry M. Gruber; Lighting, James Michael Hultquist; Costumes, Carol Brys, William F. Moser; Sound, Jo Van Horn/Full House; Stage Managers, Jane Hogan, Margarita G. Ruiz; Press, Peggy Friedman~Jean Goetz CAST: Patti Whipple (Karen/Helen), Andrew Lincoln (Mark/Brad), Michael Edward Sabatino (Vincent/Paul), Beth Glover (Pamela Cynthia), Randall McNeal (Jason/Eric)
A drama about a group of friends who find themselves the subject of a dead friend's bestseller.

Kent Gasser, Susan DiGuilio in *My Alice*

(Creative Place Theatre) Thursday, Apr.17-26, 1997 (6 performances) Kathy Towson/Creative Voives presents:
TWIGS by George Furth; Director, Tom Smith CAST: Ellen Turkelson
A comedy about three sisters and their mother.

(Mint Space) Friday, Apr.18-May 4, 1997 (12 performances) Whispering Chimes Music presents:
CAPTIVE; Music/Musical Director, Robert Collister; Lyrics/Book, Leslie Collins; Director, Mark-Leonard Simmons; Set, Kristen Maynard; Lighting, Christopher Brown; Costumes, Christine Darch; Choreography, Ahri Birnbaum; Stage Manager, Jennifer Mello CAST: Christina Seymour (Mary Jemison), Joseph Melendez (Sheninjee), Jim Jacobson (Chief Hiokotoo), John Tedeschi (Eric Von Pelt), Adam Matalon (Jacques), Paul Malamphy (St.Pierre/Gen. Armstrong), Richard Bassin, Toni Condos, Michael Dicus, Catherine Lavalle, Jennifer Mello, Erin Lee Peck, Kalani Queypo, Gina Zavalis
A gothic musical based on the true story of a woman abducted by Seneca Indians. The action takes place in the Rochester area of New York, 1759.

(HERE) Saturday, Apr.19-May 24, 1997 (17 performances and 4 previews) Christina Monczrz & Sasha Duncan, IxChel Arts Group and Banshee Productions:
OURSELVES ALONE by Anne Devlin; Director, Veronica Young; Set, George Xenos; Costumes, Anna Chu; Lighting, Jeffrey McRoberts; Music, Black '47; Press, Shirley Herz/Kevin P. McAnarney CAST: Sasha Duncan, Jacqueline Kealy, Gilli Foss, James Hanlon, Edward Tully, Michael Reilly, Myles O'Connon, Tim Mitchell, Greg O'Donovan, Stephen Gabis, Eric Martin Brown, John Henry Cox
A drama set in Belfast, 1980s.

Barbara Andres, Elizabeth Logun in *On My Knees* (Joan Marcus)

164

(Classic Stage Company) Saturday, Apr.19-May 25, 1997 (29 performances and 9 previews) Blue Light Theater Company presents:
WAITING FOR LEFTY by Clifford Odets; Director, Joanne Woodward; Set, Michael Schweikardt; Costumes, Laurie Churba; Lighting, Deborah Constantine; Sound, Raymond D. Schilke; Stage Manager, Christina Massie; Press, Gary Springer~Susan Chicoine/Candi Adams CAST: Jerry Mayer (Fatt), PJ Brown (Joe), Marisa Tomei (Edna/Secretary), Greg Naughton (Miller), Lee Wilkof (Fayette/Dr. Barnes), Scott Whitehurst (Irv/Henchman), Lisa Renee Pitts (Florrie), Wood Harris (Sid), Bernie Sheredy (Clayton/Grady), Alex Draper (Actor), Peter Jacobson (Dr. Benjamin), Robert Hogan (Agate), Allen K. Bernstein, Kurt Elftmann, Gregory Vaughn Ward, Christopher Peterson (Union)
    A 1935 drama performed without intermission. The action takes place in a union hall.

(American Jewish Theatre) Saturday, Apr.19-May 25, 1997 American Jewish Theatre presents:
YIDDLE WITH A FIDDLE; Music, Abraham Ellstein; Lyrics/Book, Isiah Sheffer; Director, Lori Steinberg; Choreography, Naomi Goldberg; Musical Director, Lanny Meyers; Sets, Ann Keehbauch; Costumes, Jonathan Bixby; Lighting, Michael Lincoln; Press, Jeffrey Richards CAST: Aileen Quinn (Yiddle), Sean McCourt (Froym), Mark Lotito (Kalamutke), Philip Hoffman, Regina O'Malley
    A musical based on a1936 film. The action takes place in Poland, 1936.

(Promenade Theatre) Sunday, Apr.20-still playing May 31, 1997 Jeffery Ash, Ben Sprecher & Bill Miller present:
STAR BILLING; Written/Performed by Alexander H. Cohen
    A one-man retrospective with the famed Broadway producer reflecting on his 56 years in the business. Presented on Sun-Mon nights.

(8th St. Theatre Lab) Sunday, Apr.20-Aug.3, 1997 (12 performances and 2 previews) 78th St. Theatre Lab presents:
THE FROG PRINCE by David Mamet; Director, Eric Nightengale; Set, Rosana Rosa; Costumes, Sybil Kempson; Press, Jim Baldassare CAST: Ruth Nightengale (Witch), Vincent Sagona (Servingman), Toby Wherry (Prince), Karen Wright (Milkmaid)
    Adaptation of classic fairy tale.

Karen Wright, Toby Wherry in *The Frog Prince*
(Barrett W. Benton)

(St. Clement's Theatre) Tuesday, Apr.22-May 10, 1997 (22 performances and 5 previews) Pan Asian Repertory presents:
SHANGHAI LIL'S; Music, Louis Stewart; Lyrics/Book, Lilah Kan; Director/Choreography, Tisa Chang; Musical Director, Eric Johnston; Sets, Robert Klingelhoefer; Costumes, Terry Leong; Lighting, Stephen Petrilli; Stage Manager, Lisa Ledwich CAST: Steven Eng (Chase), Jeanne Sakata (Lil), Mimosa (Sara), Timothy Huang (Jerry), Emy Coligado (Hyacinth), Maria E. Aggabao (Peony), Susan Ancheta (Mei-Mei), Matt Hyland (Wally)
MUSICAL NUMBERS: Dream Time Hour, Uncertain Times, Growing Up Is So Exciting, It's Really a Home, Tango, Is It Really Possible, Sneezing Jingle, At Shanghai Lil's, Ballroom Waltz, It's Time to Dance, Jerry's Farewell, War Duet, Wally's Lament, I'm Confused By My feelings for Him, Tai Chi Ballet, Moon Song, Patriot's Salute, Finale
    A musical set in San Francisco's Chinatown during World War II.

(Theatre for the New City) Wednesday, Apr.23-May 24, 1997 (13 performances and 7 previews) Irondale Ensemble Project presents:
THE SEAGULL by Anton Chekhov; Director, Jim Niesen; Press, Tony Origlio/Shelley Roberts CAST:Yvonne Brechbuhler, Joe Fuer, Michael-David Gordon, Terry Greiss, Rana Kazkaz, Barbara Mackenzie-Wood, Patrena Murray, Nicole Potter, John Silvers, Brigitte Viellieu-Davis

(INTAR Theatre) Wednesday, Apr.23-May 18, 1997 (20 performances and 8 previews) INTAR Hispanic American Arts Ceneter and Women's Project & Productions present:
UNDER A WESTERN SKY by Amparo Garcia; Director, Loretta Greco; Set, Christine Jones; Lighting, Kevin Adams; Costumes, Kaye Voyce; Music/Sound, David Van Tiegham; Stage Manager, Jennifer Spring; Press, Shirley Herz/Kevin P. McAnarney CAST: Irma Bello, Gilbert Cruz, Sol Miranda, Felix Solis
    A drama set in a small Mexican American town in Texas.

(Synchronicity Space) Saturday, Apr.26-May 11, 1997 (9 performances and 3 previews) Past Tense Productions present:
THE BIG TREES by Robert Remington Wood; Director, Jacques Levy; Set, Deborah R. Rosen; Lighting, David Alan Comstock; Press, Gary Springer~Susan Chicoine/Candi Adams CAST: Sheik Mahmud-Bey, Charles Chessler, Mark Gorman, Michelle Persley, Alison Spada, Sally Winters
    A drama about interracial friendship.

Marisa Tomei, P J Brown in *Waiting for Lefty* (Scott Suchman)

(Producers Club) Thursday, May 1-18, 1997 (13 performances and 4 previews) Italian-American Repertory Company presents:
PAINTED LADIES by Michael Mararian; Director, Lissa Moira; Set, Sal Perrotta; Lighting, Jeremy Kumin; Sound, Beau Decker; Press, Tony Origlio/Michael Cullen CAST: Jennifer Cohn, Cory Einbinder, John Fedele, Thomas Pennacchini

A comedy set in Hell's Kitchen, New York City.

(28th St. Theatre East) Thursday, May 1-18, 1997 (14 performances) Mutt Rep presents:
WAITING WOMEN by Silvia Gonzalez S.; Director, Liz Ortiz-Mackes CAST: Judy Alvarez, Daniel Damiano, Elizabeth Flax, Eileen Galindo, Stacey Miller, Greg Mulpagano, Melanee Murray, Emma Palzere, Dan Remmes, Liza Sabater, Elena Soto-Raspa, Beth Ann Charles

(New Victory Theater) Friday, May 2-11, 1997 (8 performances) The New 42nd Street presents:
SALVADOR: THE MOUNTAIN, THE MANGO AND THE CHILD by Suzanne Lebeau; Translation, John Van Burek; Director, Gervais Gaudreault; Sets; Francine Martin; Costumes, Mireille Vachon; Lighting/Stage Manager, Dominique Gagnon; Press, Margi Briggs-Lofton/Lauren Daniluk CAST: Jean-Guy Viau (Salvador), Carole Chatel (Mother), Marcela Pizarro (Teresa/Ana/Bianca/Maria), Patrice Coquereau (Father/Enrique/Jose/Alvaro), Alejandro Venegas (Musician)

Montreal's Le Carrousel company performs this South American fable.

(Raw Space) Friday, May 2-11, 1997 (13 performances and 1 preview) Columbia University presents:
AMERICAN SILENTS; Conceived/Written/Directed by Anne Bogart; Musical Adaptation/Direction, Christopher Drobny; Sound, Kurt Kellenberger; Sets, Neil Patel; Lighting, Mimi Jordan Sherin; Costumes, Vicki R. Davis; Press, Chris Boneau~Adrian Bryan-Brown/Paula Wenger CAST INCLUDES: Scott Nankivel

16 graduate acting students from Columbia U. in a play about the personalities of early film.

Amy Hart Redford, Timothi Jane Graham in *Touch My Face* (Barnaby Hall)

(Sanford Meisner Theatre) Wednesday, May 7-12, 1997 (6 performances) Green Candle Theatre Company presents:
BALLROOM OF FORGIVENESS and CURBDRIVERS OF REDEMPTION; Written/Directed by Stephen J. Goldberg; Sets/Lighting, Chris Cwieka; Costumes, Will Geisler; Press, Jeffrey Richards/Timothy Haskell CASTS: John Alexander, Ben Ash, Rachel Bissex, Chris Cwieka, Nina Desormeux, Rachel Dreher, Tracey Girdich, Jordan Gullikson, Paul Schnable

Two plays in repertory.

(Fourth St. Theatre) Thursday, May 8-24, 1997 (10 performances and 6 previews) Rachel Colbert and Aerial Productions present:
TOUCH MY FACE; Written/Directed by Jan Jalenak; Set, George Xenos; Costumes, Nicole Miller; Lighting, Jeff Croiter; Sound, Aural Fixation; Stage Manager, Martha Donaldson; Press, Tony Origlio/Shelley Roberts CAST: Timothi-Jane Garaham (Melon), Charle Landry (Matthew), Deirdre Lewis (Melissa), Nancy McDoniel (Matty), Matthew Rauch (Jackson), Amy Hart Redford (Cara)

(29th St. Rep Theatre) Thursday, May 8-June 7, 1997 (15 performances and 6 previews) 29th Street Rep presents:
BUFFALO KILL by Rooster Mitchell; Sets, Kimo James; Lighting, Greg Dratva; Sound, Gerard Drazba; Fights, J. David Brimmer; Stage Manager, Patrice Ellison; Press, Gary Springer~Susan Chicoine/Candi Adams
The Killer and the Comic; Director, Tim Corcoran CAST: David Mogentale (Carl Dean Tucker), Paul Zegler (Barney Goldrose)
Never the Same Rhyme Twice; Director, Michael Hillyer CAST: Paula Ewin (Sam), Elizabeth Elkins (Jo), Ruby Hondros (Tommi), Susan Barrett (Charlie)

Two brutal comedies.

Paula Ewin, Elizabeth Elkins in *Buffalo Kill* (Gregory A. Little)

Amy Coleman, Grace Garland, Bob Stillman, Stephen Bienskie, Dean Bradshaw in *The Last Session* (Ned Rosen)

Julian Brightman in *Songbox*

**Carolyn Swift, Dan Moran, Cheryl Gaysunas, Jim Grollman in
Suburban Motel (Carol Rosegg)**

(Currican Theatre) Thursday, May 8-Aug.31, 1997 (111 performances) transferred to (47th St. Theatre) Friday, Oct.3, 1997 Currican/Playful Productions presents:
THE LAST SESSION; Music/Lyrics, Steve Schalchlin; Book, Jim Brochu; Director, Mike Wills; Musical Director/Arrangements, Michael D. Gaylord; Set, Eric Lowell Renschler; Lighting, Michael Gottlieb; Sound, Andrew S. Keister; Stage Manager, Andrew Totolos; Press, Keith Sherman/Kevin Rehac CAST: Bob Stillman (Gideon), Dean Bradshaw (Jim), Grace Garland (Tryshia), Amy Coleman (Vicki), Stephen Bienskie (Buddy)
MUSICAL NUMBERS:Save Me a Seat, Preacher and the Nurse, Somedody's Friend, The Group, Going It Alone, At Least I Know What's Killing Me, Friendly Fire, Connected, One More Song, When You Care
A musical in two acts. The action takes place in a recording studio.

(Raw Space) Thursday, May 8-June 1, 1997 (22 performances) The Actors Studio under the management of Pure Orange Productions presents:
TATJANA IN COLOR by Julia Jordan; Director, Elizabeth Gottlieb; Set, Henry Dunn; Costumes, Katherine Roth; Lighting, Jeff Croiter; Sound, Red Ramona CAST: Angela Bettis, Brian Dykstra, Justin Kirk, Christy Romano, Tatyana Yassukovich

(Don't Tell Mama) Monday, May 12-June 30, 1997 (7 performances)
SONGBOX; Written/Performed by Julian Brightman; Director, Scott Spahr; Musical Director, Christopher McGovern
A one-man musical journey.

(Theatre Off Park) Tuesday, May 13-June 29, 1997 (32 performances and 8 previews) Rattlestick Productions presents:
SUBURBAN MOTEL by George F. Walker; Director, Daniel De Raey; Sets, Van Santvoord; Lighting, Chad McArver; Costumes, Rachel Gruer; Sound, Laura Grace Brown; Stage Managers, Nicoletta Arlia, Genia Domico; Press, Peter Cromarty/Hugh Hayes
Problem Child CAST: Christopher Burns (RJ), Tasha Lawrence (Denise), Alan Benson, Mark Hammer (Phillie), Kathleen Goldpaugh (Helen)
Criminal Genius CAST: Dan Moran (Rolly), Jim Grollman (Stevie), Alan Benson, Mark Hammer (Phillie), Carolyn Swift (Shirley), Cheryl Gaysunas (Amanda)
The first two of a cycle of six dramas performed in repertory: *Problem Child, Criminal Genius, Risk Everything, Adult Enetertainment, Featuring Loretta* and *The End of Civilization*.

(Lamb's Theatre) Wednesday, May 14-June 22, 1997 (34 performances and 8 previews) Puerto Rican Traveling Theatre presents:
TO CATCH THE LIGHTNING by Carmen Rivera; Director, Mac Ferra; Translation, Raul Davila; Set, Van Santvoord; Lighting, Philip Widmer; Sound, Yolanda Wright; Costumes, Mirena Rada; Stage Manager, Sergio Cruz; Press, Max Eisen/Lisa Liu CAST: Doris Difarnecio (Cassandra), Chaz Menia (Antonio), Johnny Sanchez (Gideon), Marilyn Seri (Samanta)

A drama set somewhere in the near future.

(Mint Theater) Friday, May 16-June 1, 1997 (14 performances) Mint Theater Company presents:
THE SPIRIT OF MAN by Peter Barnes; Sets, Kristen Maynard; Lighting, Christopher Brown; Costumes, Sarah Beers; Music, Joshua Rosenblum; Stage Manager, Sara Jones; Press, Jonathan Bank
A Hand Witch of the Second Stage; Director, Mark-Leonard Simmons CAST: Ray Atherton (Fr. Nerval), Angela Roberts (Marie Blin), Richard Edward Long (Claude Delmas), Jack Luceno (Henri Mondor)
From Sleep and Shadow; Director, Linda Ames Key CAST: Erika Rolfsrud (Abegail), Tony Cormier (Rev. Guerdon), Harry Peerce (Israel Yates)
The Night of Simhat Torah; Director, Mark-Leonard Simmons CAST: david Rosenbaum (Seer), Jerome Koenig (Maggid), Bill Roulet (Rev. Mendel)

Three one-acts on man's relationship with his maker.

Johnny Sanchez, Marilyn Seri in *To Catch the Lightning*

Bill Roulet, David Rosenbaum, Jerome Koenig in *Spirit of Man* (Barry Burns)

(Axis Theatre) Wednesday, May 21-June 14, 1997 (12 performances and 2 previews) AXIS Company presents:
PLAY by Samuel Beckett; Director, Randy Sharp; Press, Ami Armstrong CAST: Michael Gump, Robert Ierardi, Wren Arthur

(Miller Theatre) Wednesday, May 21-June 7, 1997 (13 performances)
SARATOGA INTERNATIONAL THEATER INSTITUTE; Director, Anne Bogart; Sound, Darron L. West; Sets, Neil Patel; Lighting, Mimi Jordan Sherin; Stage Manager, Megan Wanlass; Press, Zeisler/Ron Lasko CAST: J. Ed Araiza, Akiko Aizawa, Will Bond, Leon Ingulsrud, Andrew Kranis, Ellen Lauren, Kelly Maurer, Jefferson Mays, Tom Nelis, Barney O'Hanlon, Karenjune Sanchez, Stephen Webber, Megan Wanlass, Darron L. West

Three plays written by the company in repertory: *Going Going Gone, The Medium* and *Small Lives/Big Dreams.*

(Judith Anderson Theatre) Thursday, May 22-June 15, 1997 (27 performances and 6 previews) The Working Theatre presents:
A DROP IN THE BUCKET by Edward Belling; Director, Mark Plesent; Set, Daphne Kaplan; Lighting, Tyler Micoleau; Costumes, Sarah Eckert; Sound, Johnna Doty; Press, Tony Origlio/Michael Cullen CAST: Dolores Stoon (Bea), Carol Morley (Doris), Bill Wise (Barry), Randy Frazier (Bus Driver/Casino Manager)

A dark comedy in two acts. The action takes place in Atlantic City and NYC.

(Synchronicity Space) Thursday, May 22-June 8, 1997 (10 performances and 4 previews) No-Pants Theatre Company presents:
EVERYTHING IN MIST; Written/Directed by Dominic Orlando; Press, Gary Springer~Susan Chicoine/Candi Adams CAST: Mo Bertran, Karin Bowersock, Hope Garland, Ben Hersey, Elizabeth Juviler, Kevin A. King, Jeffrey Edward Peters, Suzi Takahashi, Sean Weil
A futuristic adventure set in 2035.

(Greenwich St. Theatre) Thursday, May 22-June 1, 1997 (10 performances) Villar-Hauser Theatre Company & Works By Women in association with Marnee May present:
NELLIE; Book, Bernice Lee; Music, Jaz Dorsey; Lyrics, Dorsey and Lee; Director, Scott Pegg; Musical Director, James Mironchik; Choreography, Andrea Andresakis; Set/Lighting, Nadine Charlsen; Sound, Ian Smith; Costumes, Bill Lewk; Stage Manager, Susan D. Lange CAST: Jeanine Serralles (Nellie), Timothy Estin (Cockerill), Garrison Phillips (Pulitzer), Veronica Burke (Ms. Cochrane), John Quilty (Chester/Bobby/Inmate), John Sacco (Charles/Albert/Prisoner/Inmate), George Cambus (Reporter/Madden/Judge/Phelps), Lorca Peress (Anna Schuiltz/Nurse/Inmate), Jerry Rago (Cochrane/Reporter), Oliver Buckingham (Simon/Reporter), Jane Lowe (Mrs. Galbertson), Charlotte Parsons (Cleaning Woman/Nurse), Sara Jo (Newsboy/Nurse), Jessica Bowen (Newboy)
MUSICAL NUMBERS; Nellie Don't Go, Been There Done That, Alone, What Choices Are Left for Me?, Why Did Ya Go?, Come Luv, Papa's Song, Always Remember, Mexico, Check It Out, Gettin Ready for Love, Happy Am I, We Don't Waste Food, You Are There, Easy Breezy, Woman Who Acts Like a Man, Mother of the Bride, Away with Age, Could I?, Nellie Paves the Way, Still Be Me?, International Reporters Song, Look At Me!, And I Know
A two-act musical biography of Nellie Bly. The action takes place in New York City and Pittsburgh, 1890s.

Top: Lorca Peress, Jeanine Serralles, Jane Lowe; Front: Jessica Bowen, Kristen Peck in *Nellie* (Andrea Andrejakis)

(28th St. Theatre) Tuesday, May 27-June 14, 1997 (16 performances and 2 previews) Emerging Artists Theatre Company presents:
LEOPOLD & LOEB by George Singer; Director, Renee Philippi; Set, Steven Capone; Lighting, Brian Haynsworth; Costumes, Gizela Juric; Music/Sound, Lewis Flinn; Press, Chris Boneau~Adrian Bryan-Brown/Michael Hartman, Stephen Pitalo CAST: Brian Weiss (Nathan Leopold Jr.), Marc Palmieri (Richard Loeb)
A drama based on the famous murder case. The action takes place in Chicago, 1920s.

(Producer's Club) Tuesday, May 27-June 1, 1997 (7 performances) Sydney Davolos Productions presents:
HIDDEN IN THIS PICTURE by Aaron Sorkin; Director, Satch Huizenga; Press, Chris Boneau~Adrian Bryan-Brown/Erin Dunn CAST: John Loprieno (Robert), Bruce Katlin, Stephen Peabody, Michael Toolan-Roche
A revised version of this play, retitled *Making Movies*, played the Promenade Theatre in 1990.

(Studio Theatre) Wednesday, May 28-June 14, 1997 (14 performances) The Turnip Theatre Company presents:
DEEP DISH by Sean O'Donnell; Director, Frank Licato CAST: Joe Ambrose, Gino DiIorio, Alicia Harding, Tom Hitchcock, Stephanie Martini, Shawn McNesby, Lisa Stock
A film noir parody set in "Tinseltown", 1945.

Marc Palmieri, Brian Weiss in *Leopold & Loeb* (Jim McGrath)

(St. Clement's Theatre) Wednesday, May 28-June 4, 1997 (8 performances and 2 previews) The Acting Company presents:
AS YOU LIKE IT by William Shakespeare; Direction/Design, Liviu Ciulei; Costumes, Smaranda Branescu; Lighting, Dennis Parichy; Sound, Michael Creason; Music, Scott Killian; Fights, Felix Ivanov; Press, Chris Boneau~Adrian Bryan-Brown/John Barlow, Amy Jacobs CAST: Kevin James Kelly (Orlando), William Hulings (Charles), Heather Robison (Celia), Felicity Jones (Rosalind), Marc Damon Johnson (Touchstone), Kevin Orton (Jaques/Le Beau), Robert Alexander Owens (Duke Senior/Duke Frederick), Mary F. Randle (Audrey), Drew Richardson (Phebe)

(Hamlet of Bank Street) Wednesday, May 28-June 8, 1997 (11 performances and 2 previews) Esperance Theatre Company presents:
HOW TO FIT A WOMAN IN A BOTTLE By Maria Dahvana Headley; Director, Trevor Williams; Sets, Kent Gasser; Lighting, Ron Matthews; Costumes, Arieyla Wald-Cohain; Press, Bill Coyle CAST: Michael Behrens, Shay Gines, Jenna Jolley, Jason McCullough, Nurit Monacelli, Wendy Wilde
A dark comedy.

(John Montgomery Theatre) Wednesday, May 28-June 14, 1997 (9 performances and 3 previews) John Montgomery Theatre Company presents:
FINALE; Press, Shirley Herz/Wayne Wolfe
The Doll by Patricia Minskoff; Director, Jessie Ericson Onuf CAST: Alexandra Eitel, Jack Doulin
Seduction by Joe Borini; Director, Richard Kuranda CAST: Fran Gercke, Kristianne Kurner
Birthday by Suzanne Bachner; Director, Patricia Minskoff CAST: Colette Duvall, Felicia Scarangello
Three one-act plays.

(West End Theatre) Thursday, May 29-June 16, 1997 (15 performances) Centerfold Productions presents:
OTHELLO by William Shakespeare; Director, Steve Satta; Sets, Kevin Ash; Lighting, A.C. Hickox; Costumes, Jared B. Leese CAST: Austin Pendleton (Iago), Bernard K. Addison (Othello), Michael Brandt, Tercio Bretas, Chuck Brown, Matt Burnett, Libby Christophersen, Scott Galbraith, Kate Konigsor, Mark Lien, Kevin Reifel, Rik Walter, Donald Warfield, Emily Jo Weiner

(John Houseman Studio) Friday, May 30-June 28, 1997 (17 performances and 5 previews) The Barrow Group presents:
WOMEN OF MANHATTAN by John Patrick Shanley; Director, Paul Rice; Sets/Costumes, Markas Henry; Lighting, Robert Cangemi; Sound, Laura Grace Brown; Stage Manager, Joanna Schifter; Press, Shirley Herz CAST: Katie Davis (Billie), Fiona Gallagher (Rhonda Louise), Elizabeth Hanly Rice (Judy), Patrick F. Kline (Bob), Scott Lawrence (Duke)
A drama performed without intermission.

(Liederkranz Club) Friday, May 30, 1997 (1 performance) American Chamber Opera Company presents:
DORA by Melissa Shiflett; Libretto, Nancy Fales Garrett; Based on *Fragment of an Analysis of a Case of Hysteria* by Sigmund Freud; Director, Diane Schenker; Musical Director, Douglas Anderson CAST: Nancy Loesch (Dora), Bethany Reeves, Kathryn Wright, Pamelia Phillips, Mark Victor Smith, Keith Jamison, Kyle Pfortmiller
An opera where a teen-age girl visits the famous Dr. Freud.

Felicity Jones, Heather Robison in *As You Like It* **(T. Charles Erickson)**

Shay Gines, Jenna Jolley, Wendy Wilde in *How to Fit a Woman in a Bottle*

Katie Davis, Elizabeth Hanley Rice, Fiona Gallagher in *Women of Manhattan* **(Joan Marcus)**

PROFESSIONAL REGIONAL COMPANIES

ACTORS THEATRE OF LOUISVILLE

Louisville, Kentucky

Thirty-third Season

Producing Director, Jon Jory; Executive Director, Alexander Speer; Associate Director, Marilee Hebert Slater; General Manager, James Roemer; Sets, Paul Owen; Public Relations Director, James Seacat

SYLVIA by A.R. Gurney; Director, Nagle Jackson; Lighting, Brian Scott; Costumes, Kevin R. McLeod   CAST: Twyla Hafermann, Robert Sicular, Karen Grassle, Audrie Neena.

EAST OF EDEN **(Pillars of Fire/Breaking the Chain)** by John Steinbeck; Adapted by Alan Cook; Directors, Jon Jory, Frazier W. Marsh; Lighting, Greg Sullivan; Costumes, Marcia Dixcy Jory   CAST: Tom Stechschulte, Tommy Schrider, Richard Kuhlman, Cordis Heard, Craig Bockhorn, Bob Burrus, Jenna Ster, Justin Hagan, Robert Montano, Fred Major, Peggy Cowles, Anne Marie Nest, Rick Galiher, Jonathan Bolt, Sarah Burke, Donald Li, Briton Green, David Ray, Everette Ruby, James Edward Quinn, Jared Randolph, Missy Thomas, Clint Vaught, Martha Sorrentino.

A TUNA CHRISTMAS by Jaston Williams, Joe Sears, Ed Howard; Director, Ken Albers; Lighting, Brian Scott; Costumes, Delmar L. Rinehart CAST: V. Craig Heidenreich, William McNulty.

A CHRISTMAS CAROL by Charles Dickens; Adaptation, Jon Jory, Marcia Dixcy Jory; Director, Frazier W. Marsh; Sets, Virginia Dancy, Elmon Webb; Lighting, Karl E. Haas; Costumes, Lewis D. Rampino, Hollis Jenkins-Evans   CAST: Ted Bouton, Brian Keeler, Ann Hodapp, Brian Anthony Wilson, Peggity Price, Adale O'Brien, Fred Major, Mark Sawyer-Dailey, Raymond L. Chapman, Bob Burrus, Jared Randolph, Claire Anne Longest, Scot Anthony Robinson, Justin Hagan, Twyla Hafermann, Kathleen Early, Miriam Brown, Scott Parrish, Eric Keith, Bayne Gibby, Larry Barnett, Chris Bosen, Robert Michael, James Quinn, David Ray.

THE GIFT OF THE MAGI by O. Henry; Adaptation/Music/Lyrics, Peter Ekstrom; Director, Jennifer Hubbard; Music Director, Scott Kasbaum; Costumes, Hollis Jenkins-Evans; Lighting, Tony Penna CAST: Deanne Lorette, Jeff Talbott.

ONLY A BIRD IN A GILDED CAGE; Conceived/Written and Directed by Jon Jory, in collaboration with Karma Camp, Scott Kasbaum; Music/Arrangements, Scott Kasbaum; Choreographer, Karma Camp; Lighting, Ed McCarthy; Costumes, Delmar L. Rinehart   CAST: Twyla Hafermann, Claire Anne Longest, Scott Kasbaum, V. Craig Heidenreich, Fred Major, Adale O'Brien, Kathleen Early, William McNulty, Deanne Lorette, Bart Shatto, Bob Burrus.

Teyla Hafermann, Robert Montano, Donald Li, Tom Stechschulte in *East of Eden*

Deanne Lorette in *Only a Bird in a Gilded Cage*

HAVING OUR SAY; Adapted by Emily Mann from the book by Sarah L. Delany and A. Elizabeth Delany with Amy Hill Hearth; Director, Tazewell Thompson; Lighting, Ed McCarthy; Costumes, Marcia Dixcy Jory CAST: Crystal Laws Green, Shona Tucker.

PRIVATE EYES; Written and Directed by Steven Dietz; Lighting, Ed McCarthy; Costumes, David Zinn CAST: Lee Sellars, Kate Goehring, V Craig Heidenreich, Twyla Hafermann, Adale O'Brien.

LIGHTING UP THE TWO-YEAR OLD by Benjie Aerenson; Director, Laszlo Marton; Lighting, Ed McCarthy; Costumes, David Zinn CAST: Bob Burrus, Lou Sumrall, Allen Fitzpatrick, George Kisslinger.

ICARUS by Edwin Sanchez; Director, Melia Bensussen; Lighting, Greg Sullivan; Costumes, Marcia Dixcy Jory CAST: Denise Casano, Nelson Vasquez, Julie Halston, Ray Fry, Ross Gibby.

GUNSHY by Richard Dresser; Director, Gloria Muzio; Lighting, Ed McCarthy; Costumes, David Zinn CAST: Maryann Urbano, V Craig Heidenrieich, William McNulty, Twyla Hafermann, Lee Sellars.

IN HER SIGHT by Carol K. Mack; Director, Robert Scanlan; Lighting, Greg Sullivan; Costumes, Marcia Dixcy Jory CAST: Angela Reed, David Staller, Tommy Schrider, Fred Major, Allen Fitzpatrick, Toni Gorman, Dianne Archer, Brian Carter, Christine Carroll.

POLAROID STORIES by Naomi Iizuka; Director, Jon Jory; Lighting, Greg Sullian; Costumes, Marcia Dixcy Jory CAST: Scot Anthony Robinson, Monica Bueno, Kim Gainer, Denise Casano, Bruce McKenzie, Michael Ray Escamilla, Miriam Brown, Nelson Vasquez, Danny Seckel, Caitlin Miller.

HOT 'N' COLE; Music/Lyrics, Cole Porter; Devised by David Armstrong, Mark Waldrop, Bruce Coyle; Director/Choreographer, Karma Camp; Musical Director, Scott Kasbaum; Lighting, Ed McCarthy; Costumes, Delmar L. Rinehart CAST: Darrin Baker, Jerry Christakos, John Hoshko, Mylinda Hull, Becca Kaufman, Cynthia Thomas, Scott Kasbaum, Gayle King.

THE TRIUMPH OF LOVE by Pierre Carlet de Chamblain de Marivaux; Adaptation, Stephen Wadsworth; Director, Jon Jory; Sets, John Conklin; Lighting, Amy Appleyard; Costumes, Marcia Dixcy Jory CAST: Angela Reed, Twyla Hafermann, V Craig Heidenreich, Fred Major, Joseph Jah, Robyn Hunt, William McNulty.

ALWAYS... PATSY CLINE; Conceived by Ted Swindley; Director, Frazier T. Marsh; Musical Director, Gayle King; Lighting, Brian Scott; Costumes, Delmar L. Rinehart CAST: Molly Andrews, Adale O'Brien.

Richard Trigg Photos

V Craig Heidenreich, Kate Goehring in *Private Eyes*

Miriam Brown, Michael Ray Escamilla in *Polaroid Stories*

Twyla Hafermann, William McNulty in *Gunshy*

172

ALLEY THEATRE

Houston, Texas

Fiftieth Season

Artistic Director, Gregory Boyd; Managing Director, Paul R. Tetreault;

IN THE JUNGLE OF THE CITIES by Bertolt Brecht; Director, Gregory Boyd; Sets/Lighting, Kevin Rigdon; Costumes, Esther Marquis CAST: James Black, John Feltch, Charles Krohn, Annalee Jefferies, Shelley Williams, Sherri Parker Lee, Adrian Porter, Alex Allen Morris, Jeffrey Bean, Joe Kirkendall, Aaron Krohn, Tricia Cox, Shelley Calene.

INHERIT THE WIND by Jerome Lawrence and Robert E. Lee; Director, Gregory Boyd; Sets/Lighting/Costumes, Kevin Rigdon   CAST: Danielle Odom, Whitney Rogers, Matthew Peters, Andrew Zimmer, Shelley Williams, Rutherford Cravens, John Feltch, Paul Ficht, Gordon Fox, James Coate, Marjorie Carroll, Alex Allen Morris, Jeffrey Bean, Leon Jacobs, Neil David Seibel, Tom Lacy, Bettye Fitzpatrick, Paul Hope, James Black, Charles Krohn, Beach Vickers, Joe Kirkendall, Peter Murphy, Adrian Porter, Richard Collins, Michael Farrand, David Bell, Darwin Miller, Aaron Krohn, Jonathan McVay, Lee Pace, Tricia Cox, Ellen Suits, David Born, James Cowan, Robert Peeples.

SYLVIA by A.R. Gurney; Director, Joe Brancato; Sets, Jeff Cowie; Lighting, Rui Rita; Costumes, Tina Cantu Navarro   CAST: Melissa Bowen, Edmond Genest, Annalee Jefferies, Stewart Clarke.

A CHRISTMAS CAROL by Charles Dickens; Adaptation, Michael Wilson; Original Staging Recreated by Shelley Williams; Sets, Jay Jagim; Lighting, Howell Binkley; Costumes, Ainslie Bruneau   CAST: James Black, John Feltch, Gordon Fox, Paul Hope, Alex Allen Morris, Rutherford Cravens, Joseph Guerrero, Christopher Lange, Rob Farmer, Bettye Fitzpatrick, Heidi Cole Trenbath, Katrina Rebsch, Katy Lu Siciliano, Charles Krohn, Jeffrey Bean, Eileen Morris, Jonathan McVay, Ryan Evans, Russell Pruett, Marjorie Carroll, Jentry Brown, Jillian Riley, Alyssia Thomas, Aaron Krohn, Adrian Porter, Tricia Cox, Meghan Kane, Ashley Sutton, Ryan Perry, Kyle Swarts, Barry Busby, Matthew Peters, Rachel Garrett, Katie Hagan, Garrett Landers-Genzer, Jonathan Sims, Rebecca Skupin.

TAKING STEPS by Alan Ayckbourn; Director, Michael Bloom; Sets, Robert Schmidt; Lighting, Rui Rita; Costumes, Tina Cantu Navarro CAST: Liann Pattison, James Colby, Keith Reddin, Dan Daily, Rutherford Cravens, Chelsea Altman.

HAVING OUR SAY by Emily Mann; Adapted from the book by Sarah L. Delany and A. Elizabeth Delany, with Amy Hill Hearth; Director, Roberta Levitow; Sets, Edward E. Haynes, Jr.; Lighting, Dawn Chiang; Costumes, Alvin B. Perry CAST: Delores Mitchell, Vinie Burrows.

TWILIGHT: LOS ANGELES, 1992; Written and Performed by Anna Deavere Smith.

George Garga, (backround) James Black in *In the Jungle of Cities*

THE GREEKS (Part One: The War and the Murders/Part Two: The Gods); Adapted from works by Aeschylus, Euripides, Sophocles and Homer by John Barton and Kenneth Cavander; Music, John Gromada; Director, Gregory Boyd; Choreographer, Sara Rudner; Sets/Lighting, Kevin Rigdon; Costumes, Susan Tsu   CAST: Jean Arbeiter, Jennifer Arisco, Kevin Bapp, Jeffrey Bean, James Black, Gregory Boyd, Michael Bubrick, Erin Cornell, Rayme Lyn Cornell, Allison Easter, Debra Eisenstadt, John Feltch, Bettye Fitzpatrick, Elizabeth Heflin, H. Hy Hetherington, Julia C. Hughes, Jacqueline Knapp, Charles Krohn, Lauren Lovett, Jonathan McVay, Jodi Melnick, Sherri Parker Lee, Lee Pace, Brian Peterson, Corliss Preston, Linda Sastradipradja, Randy Sparks, Shelley Williams, Greg Wise, Rebecca Wortman.

LOVE! VALOUR! COMPASSION! by Terrence McNally; Director, Michael Wilson; Sets, Tony Straiges; Lighting, Rui Rita; Costumes, McKay Coble   CAST: James Alba, Paul Hope, William Westenberg, John Feltch, James Black, Jeffrey Cox, Roland Rodriguez.

PICASSO AT THE LAPIN AGILE by Steve Martin; Director, Gregory Boyd; Set/Lighting, Kevin Rigdon; Costumes, Esther Marquis   CAST: Rutherfod Cravens, Charles Krohn, Shelley Williams, Jeffrey Bean, Sherri Parker Lee, Noble Shropshire, Al Espinosa, Kevin Waldron, Curtis Billings.

Bruce Bennett Photos

173

AMERICAN CONVSERVATORY THEATER

San Francisco, California

Thirty-first Season

Artistic Director, Carey Perloff; Managing Director, Heather Kitchen; Lighting, Peter Maradudin, Mimi Jordan Sherin.

SCHLEMIEL THE FIRST; Based on the play by Isaac Bashevis Singer; Conceived and Adapted by Robert Brustein; Director/Choreographer, David Gordon; Music/Musical Director, Zalmen Mlotek; Lyrics, Arnold Weinstein; Sets, Robert Israel; Costumes, Catherine Zuber CAST: Maureen McVerry, Thomas Derrah, Marilyn Sokol, Remo Airaldi, Vontress Mitchell, Scott Ripley, Will LeBow, Charles Levin, Dawn-Elin Fraser, Johnny Moreno, Samantha Phillips, Ryan Rilette, Jonathan Sale, Michael Larsen.

THE ROSE TATTOO by Tennessee Williams; Director, Carey Perloff; Sets, Kate Edmunds; Costumes, Deborah Dryde CAST: Kathleen Widdoes, Tina Jones, Marco Barricelli, Michael DeGood, Sharon Lockwood, Michelle Morain, Wilma Bonet, Domenique Lozano, Zachary Barton, Lisa Peers, Luis Oropeza, Charla Cabot, Charles Dean, Roberta Callahan, Shirley Roecca, Steve W. Bailey, David Jacobs, Mischa Pincus-Karam, Andrew Kelsey, Galen Murphy-Hoffman, Norah Molina, Emmanuela Prigioni.

TRAVELS WITH MY AUNT by Graham Greene; Adapted and Directed by Giles Havergal; Sets/Costumes, Stewart Laing CAST: Ken Ruta, Charles Dean, Geoff Hoyle, Bryan Close.

MACHINAL by Sophie Treadwell; Director, Laird Williamson; Sets, Ralph Funicello; Costumes, Judith Anne Dolan CAST: Mark Booher, Michael DeGood, Shirley Roecca, Alice Rorvik, Matt DeCaro, Michelle Morain, Roberta Callahan, Peter Ackerman, Velina Brown, Shannon Malone, Baomi Butts-Bhanji, Michael Gene Sullivan, Amelia Rosenberg, Steven W. Bailey, Warren D. Keith, Mark Harelik.

THE ROYAL FAMILY by George S. Kaufman and Edna Ferber; Director, Albert Takazauckas; Sets, J.B. Wilson; Costumes, Beaver Bauer CAST: Linda Hoy, Hector Correa, Steven W. Bailey, Michael DeGood, Tom Blair, Sharon Lockwood, Elizabeth Eidenberg, Bryan Close, DeAnn Mears, Will Marchetti, Valerie Leonard, Aloysius Gigl, Rod Gnapp, James Carpenter, Shannon Malone, Derek Doran Wood.

SINGER'S BOY by Leslie Ayvazian; Director, Carey Perloff; Sets, Loy Arcenas; Costumes, Susan Hilferty CAST: Olympia Dukakis, Gerald Hiken, Anne Pitoniak, Stephen Caffrey, Michele Shay.

MRS. WARREN'S PROFESSION by George Bernard Shaw; Director, Richard Seyd; Sets, Kate Edmunds; Costumes, Walker Hicklin CAST: Maura Vincent, Charles Lanyer, Concetta Tomei, Raye Birk, Matthew Boston, William Paterson.

Ken Friedman Photos

DeAnn Mears, Valerie Leonard in *Royal Family*

Raye Birk, Concetta Tomei, Maura Vincent in *Mrs. Warren's Profession*

Anne Pitoniak, Stephen Caffrey, Olympia Dukakis in *Singer's Boy*

174

ARENA STAGE

Washington, D.C.

Forty-sixth Season

Artistic Director, Douglas C. Wager; Executive Director, Stephen Richard; Founding Director, Zelda Fichandler; Production Director, Dennis A. Blackledge; BLPress Director, Brook Butterworth

BLUES FOR AN ALABAMA SKY by Pearl Cleage; Director, Kenny Leon; Sets, Marjorie Bradley Kellogg; Costumes, Susan E. Mickey; Lighting, Ann G. Wrightson CAST: Phylicia Rashad, Mark Young, Hassan El-Amin, Deirdre N. Henry, Wendell Wright

THE MISER by Moliere; Translated/Adapted by John Strand; Director, Kyle Donnelly; Sets, Linda Buchanan; Costumes, Lindsay W. Davis; Lighting, Allen Lee Hughes CAST: Matthew Rauch, Holly Twyford, Henry Martin Leyva, J. Fred Shiffman, Sarah Marshall, Tana Hicken, Henry Strozier, Marty Lodge, Franchelle Stewart Dorn, Naomi Jacobson, Jennifer Abigail Lopez, Richard Bauer

IT AIN'T NOTHIN' BUT THE BLUES by Charles Bevel, Lita Gaithers, Randal Myler, Ron Taylor, Dan Wheetman; Director, Mr. Myler; Musical Director, Mr. Wheetman; Musical Staging, Donald McKayle; Sets, Andrew V. Yelusich; Costumes, Patricia A. Whitelock; Lighting, Don Darnutzer CAST: Mississippi Charles Bevel, Carter Calvert, Lita Gaithers, Eloise Laws, Chic Street Man, Ron Taylor, Dan Wheetman

ARCADIA by Tom Stoppard; Director, Douglas C. Wager; Sets, Zack Brown; Costumes, Paul Tazewell; Lighting, Kenneth Posner CAST: Wendy Hoopes, J. Paul Boehmer, Richard Bauer, David Marks, Wendell Wright, Tana Hicken, Ralph Cosham, Christina Haag, Holly Twyford, Terrence Caza, Alex Draper, Michael Barry

MOLLY SWEENEY by Brian Friel; Director, Kyle Donnelly; Sets, Linda Buchanan; Costumes, Nan Cibula-Jenkins; Lighting, James F. Ingals CAST: Jenny Bacon, T J Edwards, Richard Bauer

VOIR DIRE by Joe Sutton; Director, Gordon Edelstein; Sets, Andrew Wood Boughton; Costumes, Paul Tazewell; Lighting, Allen Lee Hughes CAST: Vanessa Aspillaga, Steve Cell, Robin Weigert, Tana Hicken, Phyllis Yvonne Stickney, Miranda Kent, Drew Kahl, Patrick Trainor

Top: Phyllis Yvonne Stickney, Steve Cell in *Voir Dire*

Below: Liz Larsen, Sal Viviano, Dana Krueger, Donna Migliaccio in
Sunday in the Park with George

SUNDAY IN THE PARK WITH GEORGE; Music/Lyrics, Stephen Sondheim; Book, James Lapine; Director, Eric D. Schaeffer; Music Director, Jon Kalbfleisch; Sets, Zack Brown; Costumes, Patricia Zipprodt; Lighting, Allen Lee Hughes CAST: Sal Viviano, Liz Larsen, Dana Krueger, Donna Migliaccio, Wallace Acton, Robert DuSold, SuEllen Estey, Lawrence Redmond, April Harr Blandin, Sherri L. Edelen, Netousha N. Harris, Roxanne Orkin, Carter Calvert, Daniel Patrick Felton, Christopher Monteleone, Andrew Ross Wynn

GHOSTS by Henrik Ibsen; Translation, Nicholas Rudall; Director/Design, Liviu Ciulei; Costumes, Paul Tazewell; Lighting, Nancy Schertler CAST: Patricia Ageheim, Wendell Wright, Henry Strozier, Tana Hicken, Charles Janasz

Joan Marcus, Stan Barouh Photos

ARIZONA THEATRE COMPANY

Tucson and Phoenix, Arizona

Thirtieth Season

Artistic Director, David Ira Goldstein; Managing Director, Jessica L. Andrews; Public Relations Director, Hope J. Towner

ACTORS: Sally Jo Bannow, Christopher Michael Bauer, Yolande Bavan, Kalimi A. Baxter, Suzanne Bouchard, Shana Bousard, Renee Morgan Brooks, Raymond L. Chapman, Sheffield Chastain, Jospeh P. Concannon, Patrick B. Concannon, Fiona Davis, David Downing, Apollo Dukakis, David Ellenstein, Nicolas Glaeser, Roberto Guajardo, Vincent Gutierrez, Erika L. Heard, Dan Hiatt, Geoff Hoyle, Francis Jue, Laurie Kennedy, Mike Lawler, James J. Lawless, Sabrini LeBeauf, Julia Lema, Benjamin Livingston, Joel David Maurice, Terri McMahon, Dawnnie Mercado, Michael Miranda, Karmin Murcelo, Robert Nadir, Marcus Naylor, Annabelle Nunez, Dwayne Palmer, Tonye Patano, Lucille Patton, Paige Price, Neal Racioppo, Richard Russell Ramos, Steve Ramshur, Linda Reid, Timm Rogers, Stacy Ross, Ken Ruta, Molly Shaffer, Matthew Shepard, Bob Sorenson, Charles St. Clair, Jeff Steitzer, Benjamin Stewart, Dennis Stowe, Kim Sullivan

DIRECTORS/CHOREOGRAPHERS: Benny Sato Ambush, David Ira Goldstein, Joe Joyce, Michael Leeds, Garry Q. Lewis, Abel Lopez, Kathleen Marshall, Lawrence Sacharow, Anthony Taccone

PRODUCTIONS: *Two Gentlemen of Verona, La Malinche, Three Tall Women, The Illusion, Swinging on a Star, Seven Guitars*

Tim Fuller, Carl Davis Photos

Lucille Patton, Laurie Kennedy in *Three Tall Women*

Benjamin Livingston, Sabrina LeBeauf in *Two Gentlemen of Verona*

Raymond L. Chapman, David Ellenstein in *The Illusion*

CENTER STAGE

Baltimore, Maryland

Artistic Director, Irene Lewis; Managing Director, Peter W. Culman; Production Manager, Katharyn Davies; Press, Becky Dodd, John Lanasa

GALILEO by Bertolt Brecht; English Version by Charles Laughton; Director, Irene Lewis; Sets, Tony Straiges; Costumes, Katherine Roth; Lighting, Richard Nelson; Choreographer, Ken Roberson. CAST: Robert Foxworth, Alex Scott, Glynis Bell, Michael Louden, Patrick Husted, TJ Edwards, Gerry Vichi, René Augesen, Michael Rudko, Maren E. Rosenberg, Chad Lawrence Walsh, Firdous Bamji, Wil Love, John Campion, Bo Foxworth, Daniel L. Robertson III, Mueen J. Ahmad, Dan Garrett, Nathan Garrison, Michael Lyons, Bruce R. Nelson.

TRIUMPH OF LOVE; Book, James Magruder; Music, Jeffrey Stock; Lyrics, Susan Birkenhead; Based on the play by Marivaux; Director, Michael Mayer; Choreographer, Doug Varone; Musical Director, Bradley Vieth; Sets, Heidi Landesman; Costumes, Catherine Zuber; Lighting, Brian MacDevitt. CAST: Susan Egan, Denny Dillon, Christopher Sieber, Robert LuPone, Mary Beth Peil, Kenny Raskin, Daniel Marcus.

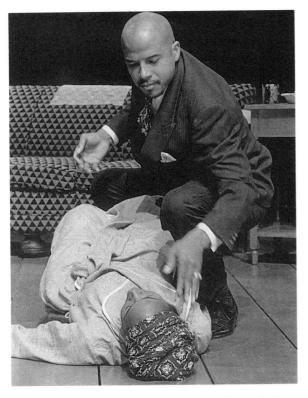

Lester Purry, Shawana Kemp in *Thunder Knocking on the Door*

Robert Sean Leonard in *The Glass Menagerie*

THUNDER KNOCKING ON THE DOOR: A BLUSICAL TALE OF RHYTHM AND THE BLUES by Keith Glover; Director, Marion McClinton; Musical, Olu Dara; Choreographer, Ken Roberson; Sets, Neil Patel; Costumes, Alvin Perry; Lighting, William H. Grant III CAST: Harriet D. Foy, Charles Weldon, Shawana Kemp, Victor Mack, Lester Purry.

ROMEO AND JULIET by William Shakespeare; Director, Irene Lewis; Sets, Michael Yeargan; Costumes, Candice Donnelly; Lighting, Mimi Jordan Sherin CAST: Robert Dorfman, Lewis Shaw, Dan Garrett, Kevin O'Donovan, Brian Mysliwy, Clayton LeBouef, Mark Zeisler, Wil Love, Mark Elliot Wilson, Caitlin O'Connell, Jonathan Earl Peck, Michael Hall, Scott Brasfield, Kali Rocha, Denis O'Hare, Lawrence O'Dwyer, Robb Bauer, Janel Bosies, James Brown, Ted Frankenhauser, Nathan Garrison, Mcihael Lyons, Dianne Signiski, Leigh Pilzer .

THE GLASS MENAGERIE by Tennesse Williams; Director, Tim Vasen; Sets, Tony Straiges; Costumes, Tom Broecker; Lighting, Jeremy Stein CAST: Robert Sean Leonard, Pamela Payton-Wright, Katie MacNichol, Jon Brent Curry.

SEVEN GUITARS by August Wilson; Director, Marion McClinton; Sets, Neil Patel; Costumes, Michael Alan Stein; Lighting, Pat Dignan CAST: Clayton LeBouef, Lisa Louise Langford, Harriet D. Foy, Russell Andrews, Keith Randolph Smith, LeLand Gantt, Linda Powell.

Richard Anderson Photos

CENTER THEATRE GROUP/AHMANSON THEATRE

Los Angeles, California

Thirtieth Season

Artistic Director/Producer, Gordon Davidson; Managing Director, Charles Dillingham; General Manager, Douglas Baker; Associate Producer, Madeline Puzo; Press, Director, Tony Sherwood

THE HEIRESS by Ruth and Augustus Goetz; Director, Gerald Gutierrez; Sets, John Lee Beatty; Costumes, Jane Greenwood; Lighting, Beverly Emmons CAST: Cherry Jones, Donald Moffat, Frances Sternhagen, Michael Cumpsty, Patricia Conolly, Kate Finneran, Jennifer Harmon, Karl Kenzler, Michelle O'Neil

SHOW BOAT; Music, Jerome Kern; Lyrics/Book, Oscar Hammerstein II; Based on the novel by Edna Ferber; Director, Harold Prince; Choreography, Susan Stroman; Design, Eugene Lee; Costumes, Florence Klotz; Lighting, Richard Pilbrow; Musical Director, Roger Cantrell CAST: Ned Beatty, Cloris Leachman, Teri Hansen, Kevin Gray, Valerie Pettiford, Michel Bell, Anita Berry, Keith Savage, Jacquey Maltby, Kip Wilborn, Tiffany Stoker, Wade Williams, George McFaniel, Lorraine Foreman, George Masswohl, F. Blossom DeWitt, Vince Metcalfe, Tim Howard, Marlaina Andre, Karen-Angela Bishop, Shane W. Bland, Susan Brady, Susan Burke, Kristin Carbone, Sabrina Carten, Marc Cedric, Esther Farrell, Keith Fortner, Luvenia Garner, Steve Girardi, Nathan Lee Graham, Topaz Hasfal, Tom Hildebrand, Melanie Johnson, Edward Knuckles, Kelly Marshall, William Clarence Marshall, Joy L. Matthews, Melony K. Matthews, Ross Neill, Barry Newell, Lyle Nicholson, D.J. O'Keefe, Tom Pickett, Rebecca Poff, Tanya Rich, Jimmy Rivers, Rachel Rockwell, Alex Sharp, Ron Small, Julie Stobbe, Dan Sutcliffe, Brandi Ward, ErnestWilliams Jr., Terrell Marcus Brooker, Amy Centner, Cleavon McClendon III, Larelle S. Rose, Bluejean Secrest

SWAN LAKE; Music, Tchaikovsky; Director/Choreography, Matthew Bourne; Design, Lez Brotherston; Lighting, Rick Fisher; Orchestration, Rowland Lee CAST: Scott Ambler, Jacqueline Anderson, Barry Atkinson, Teresa Barker, Sarah Barron, Stephen Berkeley-White, Lee Boggess, Matthew Bourne, Darren Ellis, Vicky Evans, Maxine Fone, Valentina Formenti, Heather Habens, Ben Hartley, Floyd Hendricks, Phill Hill, William Kemp, Michela Meazza, Jonathan Mitchell, Mark Mitchell, Isabel Mortimer, Eddie Nixon, Neil Penlington, Emily Piercy, Arthur Pita, Simon Reglar, Alex Rose, Colin Ross-Waterson, Tom Searle, Lynn Seymour, Kirsty Tapp, Andrew Walkinshaw, Ewan Wardrop, Ben Wright, William Yong

PROPOSALS by Neil Simon; Director, Joe Mantello; Sets, John Lee Beatty; Costumes, Jane Greenwood; Lighting, Brian MacDevitt CAST: Kelly Bishop, L. Scott Caldwell, Suzanne Cryer, Katie Finneran, Matt Letscher, Ron Rifkin, Peter Rini, Reg Rogers, Mel Winkler

Dee Conway, Craig Schwartz, T. Charles Erickson, Catherine Ashmore, Jay Thompson Photos

Donald Moffat, Michael Cumpsty, Cherry Jones in *The Heiress*

Adam Cooper, Scott Ambler in *Swan Lake*

Reg Rogers, L. Scott Caldwell in *Proposals*

180

CENTER THEATRE GROUP/MARK TAPER FORUM

Los Angeles, California

Thirtieth Season

Artistic Director, Gordon Davidson; Managing Director, Charles Dillingham; Producing Director, Robert Egan; General Manager, Douglas C. Baker; Associate Artistic Director, Corey Madden; Press Director, Nancy Hereford

CHANGES OF HEART by Pierre Carlet de Chamblain de Marivaux; Translation/Adaptation/Direction, Stephen Wadsworth; Sets, Thomas P. Lynch; Costumes, Martin Pakledinaz; Lighting, Michael Philippi CAST: Kathryne Dora Brown, Laurence O'Dwyer, Paul Anthony Stewart, Mary Lou Rosato, Maria Canals, John Michael Higgins, John Rafter Lee, Lira Angel, Ginta Rae, Gibson Frazier, Larry Paulsen

HAVING OUR SAY by Emily Mann; Adapted from the book by Sarah L. Delany and A. Elizabeth Delany with Amy Hill Hearth; Director, Walter Dallas; Sets, Edward E. Haynes Jr.; Costumes, Dana R. Woods; Lighting, D Martyn CAST: Frances Foster, Lynne Thigpen

MOLLY SWEENEY by Brian Friel; Director, Gwen Arner; Sets, Kate Edmunds; Costumes, Susan Hilferty; Lighting, Paulie Jenkins CAST: Jane Fleiss, Colin Lane, Alan Scarfe

ARCADIA by Tom Stoppard; Director, Robert Egan; Sets, David Jenkins; Costumes, Marianna Elliott; Lighting, Kevin Rigdon CAST: Angela Bettis, Douglas Weston, Jefry Alan Chandler, Mark Capri, Howard Shangraw, Kandis Chappell, David Manis, Kate Burton, Suzanne Cryer, John Vickery, Daniel Zelman, Christopher Masterson

Paul Anthony Stewart, Kathryne Dora Brown, John Michael Higgins in *Changes of Heart*

Frances Foster, Lynne Thigpen in *Having Our Say*

VALLEY SONG; Written/Directed by Athol Fugard; Set/Costumes, Susan Hilferty; Lighting, Dennis Parichy CAST: Athol Fugard, LisaGay Hamilton

DEMONOLOGY by Kelly Stuart; Director, David Schweizer; Sets, Christopher Barreca; Costumes, Maggie Morgan; Lighting, Geoff Korf CAST: Rocco Sisto, Lola Glaudini, Matthew Glave, Kathleen Glaudini

THE JOY OF GOING SOMEWHERE DEFINITE by Quincy Long; Other creative credits same as Demonology CAST: Wolfe Bowart, Gregg Henry, Frederick Coffin, Matthew Glave, Susan Tyrell, Rocco Sisto, Elizabeth Berridge, Peter Golub

THE STREET OF THE SUN by Jose Rivera; Director, David Esbjornson; Sets, Christopher Barreca; Costumes, Elizabeth Hope Clancy; Lighting, Geoff Korf CAST: Bertila Damas, Catherine Dent, Robert Dorfman, Dawnn Lewis, Vanessa Marquez, Jeanne Mori, Javi Mulero, John Ortiz, Victor Raider-Wexler, Herschel Sparber

MULES by Winsome Pinnock; Director, Lisa Peterson; Sets, Christopher Barreca; Costumes, Candice Cain; Lighting, Geoff Korf CAST: Gall Grate, Saundra Quaterman, Bahni Turpin

NINE ARMENIANS by Leslie Ayvazian; Director, Gordon Davidson; Sets, Ralph Funicello; Costumes, Mimi Maxmen; Lighting, Paulie Jenkins CAST: Leslie Ayvazian, Apollo Dukakis, Zak Gavin, Cheryl Giannini, Magda Harout, Sarah Koskoff, Tom Mardirosian, George Mgrdichian, Hal Robinson, Tiffany Ellen Solano

Jay Thompson Photos

Kate Burton, John Vickery in *Arcadia*

Tiffany Ellen Solano, Magda Harout, Zak Gavin in *Nine Armenians*

CINCINNATI PLAYHOUSE IN THE PARK

Cincinnati, Ohio

Thirty-seventh Season

Producing Artistic Director, Edward Stern; Executive Director, Buzz Ward; Press, Bruce E. Coyle

THE NOTEBOOK OF TRIGORIN by Tennessee Williams; Adapted from Ann Dunnigan's translation of *The Seagull* by Anton Chekov; Director, Stephen Hollis; Set, Mingo Cho Lee; Lighting, Brian Nason; Costumes, Candice Donnelly   CAST: Jack Cirillo, Natacha Roi, Timothy Altmeyer, Jed Davis, Donald Christopher, Jeff Woodman, Stina Nielsen, Sonja Lanzener, Philip Pleasants, Alan Mixon, Lynn Redgrave, John Sharp, Eleanor B. Shepherd, Poppi Kramer, Jack Marshall, Bruce Pilkenton.

SONGPLAY: THE SONGS AND MUSIC OF KURT WEILL; Conceived, Adapted and Directed by Jonathan Eaton; Arranger/Musical Director, David Seaman; Choreographer, Daniel Pelzig; Sets, Paul Shortt; Costumes, David Kay Mickelsen; Lighting, James Sale CAST: Michael Brian, Herb Downer, Kim Lindsay, Karen Murphy, Pedro Porro, Craig Priebe.

THE MOST HAPPY FELLA; Book/Music/Lyrics, Frank Loesser; Director, Victoria Bussert; Choreographer, Williamichael Badolato; Musical Director, Larry Pressgrove; Sets, John Ezell; Lighting, Peter E. Sargent; Costumes, James Scott CAST: Whit Reichert, Lovette George, Kirsti Carnahan, Julia Klein, Stephanie Lynge, Tara Tyrrell, Gina Carlette, Bill Bush, Eric Millegan, Monte Black, John Payonk, Alma Cuervo, Hunter Bell, Timothy Scott Bennett, Timothy Cole, Brian Sutherland, Tom Souhrada, Keith Lorcna Weirich, Scott Brush, Michael Etzwiler.

Pedro Porro, Kim Lindsay in *Songplay*

Lynn Redgrave, Stina Nielsen in *Notebook of Trigorin*

THE COMPLEAT WORKS OF WLLM SHKSPR (ABRIDGED) by Jess Borgeson, Adam Long, Daniel Singer; Director, Pamela Hunt; Sets, Thomas C. Umfrid; Lighting, Kirk Bookman; Costumes, John Carver Sullivan CAST: Kevin Henderson, Bill Kocis, Jamison Stern.

A CHRISTMAS CAROL by Charles Dickens; Adapted and Written by Howard Dallin; Director, Michael Haney; Sets, James Leonard Joy; Costumes, David Murin; Lighting, Kirk Bookman CAST: Alan Mixon, Mark Mochabee, David Haugen, Robert Elliott, Gordon Brode, Gregory Procaccino, Raye Lankford, Christopher Bissonnette, Emily Bissonnette, Michael Pemberton, Dale Hodges, Tom Dacey Carr, Jennifer Marshall, Bridget Renee Nurre, Kiera Davenport, Justin Nurre, Richard Jackson II, Regina Pugh, Shannon Doyle, Jack Marshall, Ellen Baker, Robert Bales, Bryan J. Young, Brad Seligmann, Susan Baker, Lisa Blankenship, Francie Huffstetler, John Sharp, Alan Jestice, Bruce Pilkenton, Poppi Kramer.

THE TURN OF THE SCREW by Jeffrey Hatcher; from the story by Henry James; Director, Melia Bensussen; Sets, Rob Odorisio; Costumes, Gordon DeVinney; Lighting, Mary Louise Geiger CAST: Tom Dunlop, Jurian Hughes

SYLVIA by A.R. Gurney; Director, John Going; Sets, James Leonard Joy; Costumes, Howard Tsvi Kaplan; Lighting, Kirk Bookman CAST: Raye Lankford, Geoffrey Wade, Pamela Burrell, Paul DeBoy

IN WALKS ED; Written/Directed by Keith Glover; Sets, David Gallo; Lighting, Kevin Adams; Costumes, Michael Alan Stein CAST: Joe Quintero, Anthony Chisholm, Keith Randolph Smith, Kim Brockington, Leland Gantt.

HAVING OUR SAY by Emily Mann.; Director, Loretta, Greco; Sets, Robert Brill; Lighting, Max DeVolder; Costumes, Clyde Ruffin CAST: Venida Evans, Emily Yancy.

VALLEY SONG by Athol Fugard; Director, Charles Towers; Sets, Ursula Belden; Lighting, Jackie Manassee; Costumes, Gordon DeVinney CAST: Nesbitt Blaisdell, Brienin Bryant.

PRIVATE LIVES by Noel Coward; Director, Edward Stern; Sets, Joseph P. Tilford; Lighting, Besty Adams; Costumes, Gordon DeVinney CAST: Peter Pamela Rose, J. Paul Boehmer, Anderson Matthews, Hope Chernov, Naomi Bailis.

Sandy Underwood Photos

DETROIT REPERTORY THEATRE

Detroit, Michigan

Thirty-ninth Season

Artistic/Managing Director, Bruce E. Millan; Press, Dee Andrus; Sets, Richard Smith & Bruce Millan; Lighting, Kenneth R. Hewitt, Jr.; Costumes, B.J. Essen.

THE STILLBORN LOVER by Timothy Findley; Director, Patricia Ansuini CAST: Council Cargle, Barbara Busby, Hollis Huston, Dorry Peltyn, Natalie A. Chillis, Ray Schultz, John Biedenbach.

CRUMBS FROM THE TABLE OF JOY by Lynn Nottage; Director, Janet Cleveland CAST: Sheila Alyce, Toya Brazell, Harold Hogan, Donna Biscoe, Teri L. Clark.

SOMEWHERE IN BETWEEN by Craig Pospisil; Director, Bruce E. Millan CAST: Michael Joseph, Natalie Chillis, J. Center, Maggie Patton, Harold Hogan, Cecilia Foreman.

AMAZING GRACE by Michael Cristofer; Director, Lonnie Fleischer CAST: Cynthia Blaise, Dee Andrus, Yvonne DeQue, J. Alve-Lyndon Jones, Leslie-Ann Williams, J. Center, Keegan-Michael Key, Lynch Travis, William Boswell.

Bruce E. Millan Photos

Harold Hogan, Tonya Brazell, Donna Biscoe in *Crumbs from the Table of Joy*

(front) Cynthia Blaise, (left) J. Alve-Lyndon Jones, Keegan-Michael Key, (right) Yvonne DuQue, William Boswell in *Amazing Grace*

Council Cargle, Barbara Busby in *Stillborn Lover*

EAST HEIGHTS PRODUCTIONS

Sherman Oaks, California

President, Ann Greyson; Vice President, Vivian Siminski

BLUEBEARD by Charles Ludlam; Director, Gregor Ogan; Sets, Marco Deleon; Design, Vivian Siminski; Lighting, Richard Taylor CAST: Mitch Rubman, Janet Delong, Richard Magram, Carolyn Chiodini, Marc Shrem, Natalie King, Kara Maria Miller

BLUE WINDOW by Craig Lucas; Director, Brian Lord; Sets, Justine Smith; Design, Vivian Siminski; Lighting, Elisabeth Flack CAST: Beth Stolarczyk, LeeAnn Matusek, Petro Nicholas, Lauren Bailey, Brian J. Wasiak, Caleb Sweazy, Lara Baird

Right: Lauren Bailey, Brian Masiak in *Blue Window*

Below: Marc Shrem, Kara Miller, Richard Magram, Natalie King, Carolyn Chiodini in *Bluebeard*

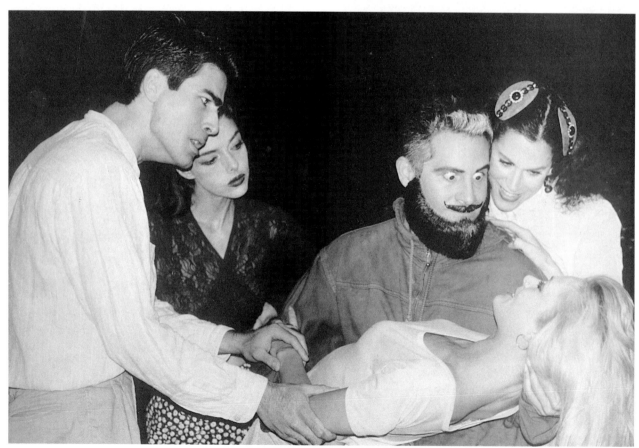

GEFFEN PLAYHOUSE

Los Angeles, California

First Season

Producing Director, Gilbert Cates; Managing Director, Lou Moore; Press Director, Gary W. Murphy

QUILLS by Doug Wright; Director, Adrian Hall; Sets, Barry Robinson; Costumes, Melina Root; Lighting, Peter Maradudin CAST: Robert Dorfman, Paul Anthony Stewart, Margo Skinner, Martin Rayner, Howard Hesseman, Robin Terry, David Permenter, Colette Kilroy, Javier Armijo, Robert Baker, Antonia Bath, Kirsten Beyer, Jeremy Lee, CB Smith

LOVE! VALOUR! COMPASSION! by Terrence McNally; Director, Joe Mantello; Sets, Loy Arcenas; Costumes, Jess Goldstein; Lighting, Brian MacDevitt CAST: William Bumiller, Richard Bekins, T. Scott Cunningham, Ian Ogilvy, Mario Cantone, Mitchell Anderson, Randy Becker, Ian Ogilvy

BY JEEVES; Music, Andrew Lloyd Webber; Lyrics/Book/Director, Alan Ayckbourn; Based on the Jeeves stories by P.G. Wodehouse; Choreography, Sheila Carter; Musical Director, Steven Smith; Sets, Roger Glossop; Costumes, Louise Belson; Lighting, Mick Hughes CAST: John Scherer, Edward Keith Baker, Donna Lynne Champlin, Randy Redd, Kevin Ligon, Merwin Goldsmith, Nancy Anderson, Emily Loesser, Ian Knauer, Jonathan Stewart, Steven Smith, Tom Ford, Molly Renfroe, Court Whisman

SHLEMIEL THE FIRST; Conceived/Adapted by Robert Brustein; Based on the play by Isaac Basevis Singer; Director/Choreography, David Gordon; Music/Orchestrations, Hankus Netsky; Lyrics, Arnold Weinstein; Additional Music/Musical Director, Zalmen Mlotek; Sets, Robert Israel; Costumes, Catherine Zuber; Lighting, Neil Peter Jampolis CAST: Alice Playten, Thomas Derrah, Maureen McVerry, Remo Airaldi, Vontress Tyrone, Benjamin Evett, Will LeBow, Charles Levin, Victor Buno, Wendell Goodrum, Al Nowicki, Arianna Ortiz, Michael Larsen

Craig Schwartz Photos

Top: Jonathan Stewart, Kevin Ligon, Ian Knauer, Randy Redd, Edward Keith Baker Middle: Merwyn Goldsmith, Donna Lynne Champlin, Alan Ayckbourn, John Scherer, Emily Loesser Front: Nancy Anderson in *By Jeeves*

Howard Hesseman, Robin Terry in *Quills*

Top: Ian Ogilvy, Randy Becker, Mitchell Anderson, T. Scott Cunningham, Richard Bekins Front: Mario Cantone, William Bumiller in *Love! Valour! Compassion!*

GEORGE STREET PLAYHOUSE

New Brunswick, NJ

Artistic Director, Gregory S. Hurst; Managing Director, Diane Claussen; Production Manager, Edson Womble; Press, Leslie Williams

AVOW by Bill C. Davis; Director, Gillian Lynne; Sets, Stephan Olson; Costumes, James Scott; Lighting, Donald Holder CAST: Peter Gantenbein, Michael Booth, Michael Rupert, Christina Haag, Suzanne Inman, Rosemary Prinz, Richard Russell Ramos.

THE GLASS MENAGERIE by Tennessee Williams; Director, Gregory S. Hurst; Sets, Hugh Landwehr; Costumes, Teresa Snider-Stein; Lighting, Dennis Parichy CAST: William Hulings, Leslie Hendrix, Heather Robison, Danny Swartz.

SING A CHRISTMAS SONG; Loosely Based on *A Christmas Carol* by Charles Dickens; Music, Garry Sherman; Lyrics/Libretto, Peter Udell; Director, Gregory S. Hurst; Choreographer, Deborah Roshe; Sets, Atkin Pace; Costumes, Kim Krumm Sorenson; Lighting, F. Mitchell Dana; Musical Directors, Garry Sherman, Andrew Wilder CAST: Philip Anthony, Clent Bowers, Jessica Dillan, Kim Hawthorne, Erich McMillian-McCall, Rudy Roberson, Sharon Wilkins.

LOST IN YONKERS by Neil Simon; Director, Susan Kerner; Sets, Ray Recht; Costumes, Deirdre Sturges Burke; Lighting, F. Mitchell Dana CAST: Darien Scott Shulman, Jason Marcus, Sam Guncler, Carolyn Swift, Anita Keal, David Kener, Elaine Bromka.

SYLVIA by A.R. Gurney; Director, Wendy Liscow; Set/Costumes, Anita Stewart; Lighting, Christopher Akerlind CAST: Katherine Heasley, Jonathan Bustle, Robin Groves, Billy Padgett.

Peter Gantenbein, Michael Booth, Michael Rupert in *Avow*

Kim Hawthorne, Erich MacMillan McCall, (kneeling) Clent Bowers, Sharon Wilkins, Rudy Roberson, Jessica Dillan, Philip Anthony in *Sing a Christmas Song*

ADVENTURES OF HUCKLEBERRY FINN by Mark Twain; Adapted by Randal Myler; Director, Gregory S. Hurst; Sets, Rob Odorisio; Costumes, Deirdre Sturges Burke; Lighting, Joshua Starbuck CAST: Stacey Todd Holt, Amelia White, Donna Davis, Michael A. Shepperd, Shannon Stocke, Debra Funkhouser, Tami Dixon, Joseph Abel, Tom Brennan, David S. Howard, Ed Sala, Chris Lowry, Reathel Bean, Len Duckman.

AND THEN THEY CAME FOR ME: REMEMBERING THE WORLD OF ANNE FRANK by James Still; Director, Susan Kerner; Sets, Robert Koharchick; Costumes, Barbara Forbes; Lighting, Brenda Veltre CAST: John Socas, Ron Scott, Karen Zippler, Michelle Spires.

Miguel Pagliere, Gerry Goodstein Photos

Michelle Spires, Karen Zippler in
And They Came for Me

GOLDEN APPLE DINNER THEATRE

Sarasota, Florida
Twenty-sixth Season

Executive Director, Robert Ennis Turoff; Press, Creative Ink.

WONDERFUL LIFE!: THE MUSICAL; Book, Doug E. Holmes; Lyrics, Walter Willison; Music, John Kroner; Director, Robert Ennis Turoff; Musical Director, Michael Sebastian; Choreographer, Brad Wages; Sets, Rick Cannon, Benjamin M. Turoff; Costumes, B.G. Fitzgerald CAST: Christopher Swan, Beth Duda, Bob Moak, Kyle Ennis Turoff, Jacquiline Rohrbacker, Michael Marcello, Jay Strauss, B.G. Fitzgerald, Annie Morrison, Chris Caswell, Roy Johns, Betty Lloyd, Michelle Atwell, Kathleen Gillett, Michael Bajjaly, Steve Diklich, Jeff Sargent, Blake Walton, Kendall Klepper, Cassie Abate, Huck Walton, Ben Caswell.

FUNNY MONEY by Ray Cooney; Director, Jon Merlyn; Sets, Jon Merlyn, Jan Van Wart; Costumes, B.G. Fitzgerald; Lighting, Ben Turoff CAST: Roberta MacDonald, Roy Sornensen, Blake Walton; Phillip Swender, Jenny Aldrich, Don Walker, Ashley Strand, Benjamin M. Turoff.

THE UNSINKABLE MOLLY BROWN; Music/Lyrics, Meredith Willson; Book, Richard Morris; Director, Robert Ennis Turoff; Michael Director, Michael Sebastian; Choreographer, Charlene Clark; Sets, Jan Van Wart; Costumes, B.G. Fitzgerald; Lighting, Ben Turoff CAST: Kyle Ennis Turoff, Brad Wages, Jeff Sargent, Cory Chenault, Phillip Swender, Benjamin M. Turoff, Kathleen Gillett, Sasha C. Hanna, Amanda Teates, Jeffrey Atherton, Jacquiline Rohrbacker, Bob Moak, Roy Johns, Heath Jorgenson, Charlene Clark, Mohair Saint Claire, Ashley Strand, Michael Bajjaly.

MOON OVER BUFFALO by Ken Ludwig; Director, Will Mackenzie; Sets/Lighting, Benjamin M. Turoff; Costumes, B.G. Fitzgerald CAST: Jane Connell, Kyle Ennis Turoff, Jeff Sargent, Robert Ennis Turoff, Roberta MacDonald, Jenny Martin, Brad Wages, Harold Dull.

Walter Willison, Marianne Carson Rhodes, Doug Holmes in *Greenwillow*

Brad Wages, Jeff Sargent, Kyle Ennis Turoff, Phillip Swender, Cory Chenault in *Unsinkable Molly Brown*

Huck Walton, Cassie Abate, Tracey Williams, Kendall Klepper, Christopher Swan, Ben Caswell in *Wonderful Life!*

GREENWILLOW; Music/Lyrics, Frank Loesser; Book, Douglas Holmes, Walter Willison, Frank Loesser; Based on a novel by B.J. Chute; Director, Walter Willison; Musical Director, Michael Sebastian; Choreographer, Brad Wages; Sets, Benjamin M. Turoff; Costumes, B.G. Fitzgerald CAST: Jeffrey Atherton, Richard Bigelow, Helon Blount, Andrew Driscoll, Cynthia Heininger, Douglas Holmes, Roy Johns, Chrystal Lee, James Pritchett, Sam Reni, Marianne Carson Rhodes, Jacqueiline Rohrbacker, Lorraine M. Sheeler, Maggi Taylor, Walter Willison, Maxine Wood.

HEART AND SOUL: THE LIFE AND TIMES OF FRANK LOESSER IN HIS OWN WORDS; Book, Frank Loesser, Susan Loesser, Emily Loesser; Conceived by Richard Sabellico, Don Stephenson; Director, Robert Ennis Turoff; Sets, Benjamin M. Turoff; Musical Director, Michael Sebastian; Costumes, B.G. Fitzgerald CAST: Marianne Carson, Roy Johns, Laura Kenyon, John D. Smitherman, Kyle Ennis Turoff.

Donna Des Isles Photos

187

GOODMAN THEATRE

Chicago, Illinois

Artistic Director, Robert Falls; Executive Director, Roche Schulfer

Randy Newman's **FAUST**; Music/Lyrics, Randy Newman; Book, Mr. Newman, David Mamet; Director, Michael Greif; Choreography, Lynne Taylor-Corbett; Orchestrations, Michael Roth; Musical Director, Joseph Church; Sets, Thomas Lynch; Costumes, Mark Wendland; Lighting, Christopher Akerlind CAST: Kurt Deutsch, David Garrison, Robert Fitch, Ken Page, Steve Boles, Craig Bennett, Benjamin LeVert, Zaks Lubin, Aisha deHaas, Marites Cumba, Anthony Wayne Johnson, Erin E. Smith, Kent Zimmerman, Raun Ruffin, Tina Gluschenko, Joseph Church, Susan Kokot, Cheridah Best, Sala Iwamatsu, Erin Hill, Seth Hoff, Ron Wilson, Bellamy Young, Sheri Scott, Stanley Wayne Mathis

THE YOUNG MAN FROM ATLANTA by Horton Foote; Director, Robert Falls; Sets, Thomas Lynch; Costumes, David C. Woolard; Lighting, James F. Ingalls CAST: Rip Torn, Shirley Knight, Marcus Giamatti, Pat Nesbit, Stephen Trovillion, William Biff McGuire, Jacqueline Williams, Kevin Breznahan, Beatrice Winde

LIGHT UP THE SKY by Moss Hart; Director, David Petraca; Sets, Michael Yeargan; Costumes, Jess Goldstein; Lighting, Duane Schuler CAST: Jeff Dumas, Scott Lowell, Jennifer Erin Roberts, Tim Monsion, Mary Beth Fisher, William Brown, Bobo Lewis, Tom Kiefuss, Steve Pickering, Julie Boyd, Marc Vann, Thomas Carroll

ALL THE RAGE by Keith Reddin; Director, Michael Maggio; Set, Linda Buchanan; Costumes, Nan Cibula-Jenkins; Lighting, Pat Collins CAST: Steve Pickering, Leslie Lyles, Robert Breuler, Tim Edward Rhoze, Darryl Alan Reed, Marc Vann, Andrew White, Del Close, Lara Phillips, Ian Barford, John Montana

MA RAINEY'S BLACK BOTTOM by August Wilson; Director, Chuck Smith; Sets, Scott Bradley; Costumes, Paul Tazewell; Lighting, Robert Christen CAST: Gary Houston, Paul Ratliff, Ernest Perry Jr., Tim Edward Rhoze, Percy Littleton, Harry J. Lennix, Felicia P. Fields, Paul Amandes, Lori Holton Nash, Dwain A. Perry

SEEKING THE GENESIS by Kia Corthron; Director, Walter Dallas; Sets, Robert C. Martin; Costumes, Karin Kopischke; Lighting, Kathy A. Perkins CAST: Raphael Vargas Chestang, Demetrius D. Thornton, Kava Stewartson, Ora Jones, Rachel Robinson, Kim Leigh Smith, Christopher Brown, Tim Edward Rhoze, Rick Sandoval

TRANSFORMATIONS; Conception, Regina Taylor; Sets, Todd Rosenthal; Costumes, Loren Coco Mayer; Lighting, Joseph Appelt CAST: Cheryl Lynn Bruce, Tab Baker, Henry Godinez, Darryl Alan Reed, Ora Jones, Raun Ruffin

PROGRAM: *Prophecy* by Peter Handke; Director, Marianne Kim; *The Owl Answers* by Adrienne Kennedy; Director, Susan V. Booth; *Dr. Kheal* by Maria Irene Fornes; Director, Regina Taylor; *Red Cross* by Sam Shepard; Director, Henry Godinez; *The One* by Oliver Pitcher; Director, Cheryl Lynn Bruce

Liz Lauren Photos

Rip Torn, Stephen Trovillion in *Young Man from Atlanta*

Kurt Deutsch, David Garrison in *Faust*

Andrew White, Ian Barford in *All the Rage*

188

GOODSPEED OPERA HOUSE

East Haddam, Connecticut

Thirty-third Season

Artistic Director, Michael Price; Associate Producer, Sue Frost; Resident Musical Director, Michael O'Flaherty; Press, Jennifer Wislocki, (NYC) Max Eisen

(1996 Productions)

SWEENEY TODD: THE DEMON BARBER OF FLEET STREET; Music/Lyrics, Stephen Sondheim; Book, Hugh Wheeler, from an adaptation by Christopher Bond; Sets, Charles E. McCarry; Costumes, Pamela Scofield; Lighting, Phil Monat; Musical Director, Michael O'Flaherty CAST: Nancy Anderson, Abigal Bailey, Michael Brian, Jesse Bush, Alleen Fitzpatrick, Andy Gale, James Holdridge, Angela C. Howell, Julie James, Rebecca Judd, Christopher Kauffmann, Seth Malkin, Barbara Marineau, Michael McCoy, Timothy Nolen, Bill Nolte, David Pursley, Harry Sokol, Tina Stafford, Susan Tilson, Price Waldman, Paul G. Woodson.

PAPER MOON; Book, Martin Casella; Music, Larry Grossman; Lyrics, Ellen Fitzhugh; Based on the novel *Addie Pray* by Joe David Brown and the Paramount Pictures Film *Paper Moon*; Director, Matt Caslla; Choreographer, John Carrafa; Musical Director, Michael O'Flaherty; Sets, James Youmans; Costumes, David C. Woolard; Lighting, Kenneth Posner CAST: J.B. Adams, Larry Alexander, Natalie Blalock, Brett Cramp, Lindsay Cummings, Lynn Eldredge, Catherine Fries, Ariel harris, Julie Johnson, Roy Leake Jr., Joanna Pacitti, Sandy Rosenberg, Blair Ross, Ken Triwush, Schele Williams, Craig Zehms, Mark Zimmerman.

ANNIE; Book, Thomas Meehan; Music, Charles Stouse; Lyrics/Director, Martin Charnin; Sets, Peter Harrison; Costumes, Theoni V. Aldredge; Lighting, Phil Monat; Choreographer, Michele Assaf; Musical Director, Michael O'Flaherty CAST: Kaitlyn Ashley, Christy Baron, Nora Blackall, Douglas Carabe, Bobby Clark, Evin Diaz-Hennessey, Samantha Diaz-Hennessey, Julie Dobrow, Ron Holgate, Shawnda James, Cassandra Kubinski, Courtney Leigh, Craig Mason, Lynn McNutt, Marc Mouchet, Tiffany Provencher, Alene Robertson, Jodi Stevens, Carl Tarpley, Billy Vitelli, Judith Marie Walton, Brad Willis, Ron Wisniski, Sparky.

Lindsay Cummings, Mark Zimmerman in *Paper Moon*

The orphans of *Annie*

NORMA TERRIS THEATRE

BATTLE CRY OF FREEDOM; Conceived and Dramatized by Jack Kyrieleison; Sets, Peter Harrison, Costumes, Jan Finnell; Lighting, Donald Holder; Musical Director, Jay Atwood; Director, Ron Holgate CAST: Donna Lynne Champlin, David Eric, Gary Marachek, Sherl McCallum, Michael Moore, James Stovall.

MIRETTE; Book, Elizabeth Diggs; Music, Harvey Schmidt; Lyrics, Tom Jones; Based on the book *Mirette on the High Wire* by Emily Arnold McCully; Sets, James Morgan; Costumes, Suzy Benzingre; Lighting, Phil Monta; Choreographer, Janet Watson; Director, Drew Scott Harris CAST: Marshall Bagwell, Steve Barton, David Duffield, Kelly Mady, Michaeljohn McGann, Carol Schuberg, Tony Sicuso, Kelley Swaim, Barbara Tirrell, Gerry Vichi.

BY JEEVES; Music, Andrew Lloyd Webber; Lyrics/Book/Direction, Alan Ayckbourn; Based on the *Jeeves* stories by P.G. Wodehouse; Musical Director, Michael O'Flaherty; Choreography, Sheila Carter; Sets, Roger Glossop; Costumes, Louise Belson; Lighting, Mick Hughes CAST: Nancy Anderson, Donna Lynne Champlin, Tom Ford, Merwin Goldsmith, Richard Kline, Ian Knauer, Kevin Ligon, Emily Loesser, Molly Renfroe, Randy Redd, John Scherer, Jonathan Stewart, Court Whisman

Diane Sobolewski Photos

John Scherer, Richard Kline in *By Jeeves*

189

Phylicia Rashad, Sean C. Squire in
Blues for an Alabama Sky

Davis Gaines, Marie Danvers, Angela Lockett, Kim Lindsay in
Company

Kate Goehring, Garret Dillahunt, Jennifer Harmon in
Glass Menagerie

HUNTINGTON THEATRE COMPANY

Boston, Massachusetts

Fifteenth Season

Producing Director, Peter Altman; Managing Director, Michael Maso; Press, Martin Blanco.

ARCADIA by Tom Stoppard; Director, Jacques Cartier; Sets, Karl Eigsti; Lighting, Roger Meeker; Costumes, Lindsay W. Davis CAST: Gretchen Cleevely, Connor Trinneer, Michael Bradshaw, Stephen Temperley, Christopher Wynkoop, Linda Gehringer, Anthony Newfield, Kandis Chappell, Annika Peterson, Terrence Caza, Willis Sparks, Liam Sullivan.

JOURNEY TO THE WEST; Adapted and Directed by Mary Zimmerman; Sets, Scott Bradley; Lighting, T.J. Gerckens; Costumes, Allison Reeds CAST: Jane C. Cho, Christopher Donahue, Kim Miyori, Doug Hara, Kelvin Han Yee, Lisa Tejero, Colman Domingo, Remi Sandri, Michael Ordona, Nelson Mashita, Emilie Talbot, Soren Oliver, Paul Oakley Stoval, Jennie Yee, Chyong-Hwa Chang, Valentin Gregor, William Schwarz.

TWILIGHT: LOS ANGELES, 1992; Conceived, Written and Performed by Anna Deavere Smith; Director, Sharon Ott; Set, Christopher Barreca; Lighting, Pat Collins; Costumes, Candace Donnelly

THE GLASS MENAGERIE by Tennessee Williams; Director, Charles Towers; Sets, Bill Clarke; Lighting, Nancy Schertler; Costumes, Mariann Verheyen CAST: Garret Dillahunt, Jennifer Harmon, Kate Goehring, Rick Holmes.

BLUES FOR AN ALABAMA SKY by Pearl Cleage; Director, Kenny Leon; Set, Marjorie Bradley Kellogg; Lighting, Ann G. Wrightson; Costumes, Susan E. Mickey CAST: Phylicia Rashad, Tyrone Mitchell Henderson, Sean C. Squire, Deidrie N. Henry, John Henry Redwood.

COMPANY; Music/Lyrics, Stephen Sondheim; Book, George Furth; Director, Larry Carpenter; Choreographer, Daniel Pelzig; Music Director, F. Wade Russo; Set, Loren Sherman; Lighting, Phil Monat; Costumes, Toni-Leslie James CAST: Davis Gaines, Andy Umberger, Susan Cella, John Schiappa, Teri Bibb, William Parry, Maureen Silliman, Dann Fink, Tia Speros, Walter Charles, Don Chastain, Karen Mason, Kim Lindsay, Angela Lockett, Marie Danvers.

T. Charles Erickson Photos

ILLINOIS THEATRE CENTER

Park Forest, Illinois

Twenty-first Season

Producing Director, Etel Billig; Associate Director, Jonathan R. Billig; Production Manager, James Corey; Administrative Associate, Alexandra Murdoch

TRAVELS WITH MY AUNT by Graham Greene; Adaptation, Giles Havergal; Director, David Perkovich CAST: Kent Klineman, John Dunleavy, Steven Anderson, Kevin Kennedy

THE PRISONER OF SECOND AVENUE by Neil Simon; Director, Etel Billig CAST: Frederic Stone, Iris Lieberman, Jerry Miller, Rebecca Borter, Etel Billig, Jan Mitchell

A TREE GROWS IN BROOKLYN; Music, Arthur Schwartz; Lyrics, Dorothy Fields; Book, Betty Smith, George Abbott; Director, Etel Billig CAST: Judy McLaughlin, Pete Thelen, Sara Baur, Phil Hollingsworth, Chritina Mild, Siobhan Sullivan, Carrie Corrigan, Kari Ball, David G. Peryam, Chris McNamara, Sam Nykaza-Jones, Al Becker, Bobby Schmidt

CAMPING WITH HENRY AND TOM by Mark St. Germain; Director, Gary Houston CAST: Garry Rayppy, Richard Henzel, Glenn Allen Pruett, Matt Janes

SPUNK by George C. Wolfe; Based on stories by Zora Neale Hurston; Music, Chic Street Man; Director, Ta-Tanisha Payne CAST: Bernadette L. Clarke, Laura Collins, Sam Sanders, Trent Harrison Smith, Joe Wright, Dexter Zollicoffer

CROSSING DELANCEY by Susan Sandler; Director, Judy McLaughlin CAST: Franette Liebow, Howard Friedland, Troy West, Etel Billig, Rebecca Borter

PLAYING THE PALACE by Bernard Rice; Director, Pete Thelen CAST: Shelley Crosby, Tracy Payne, Erin Annarella, Howard Hahn, Bernard Rice, Pete Thelen.

Top: Glenn Allen Pruett, Gary Rayppy, Richard Henzel in *Camping with Henry and Tom*
Center: Trent Harrison Smith, Bernadette L. Clarke, Sam Sanders in *Spunk*
Left: (back) Howard Hahn, Tracy Payne, Bernard Rice, Shelley Crosby, (front) Erin Annarella, Pete Thelen in *Playing the Palace*

LA JOLLA PLAYHOUSE

La Jolla, California

Fifteenth Season (since 1983 Revival); First Founded, 1947

Artistic Director, Michael Greif; Managing Director, Terrence Dwyer; Director-in-Residence, Des McAnuff; Press, Josh Ellis.

THE IMPORTANCE OF BEING EARNEST by Oscar Wilde; Director, Les Waters; Sets/Costumes, Annie Smart; Lighting, James F. Ingalls CAST: Peter Bartlett, Barnaby C. Carpenter, Veanne Cox, Christine Estabrook, Tom Fitzpatrick, Aimee Guillot, Paul H. Juhn, Jefferson Mays, Ursula Meyer.

THE SCHOOL FOR WIVES by Moliere; Translation/Adaptation, Paul Schmidt; Director, Neel Keeler; Sets, Mark Wendland; Lighting, James F. Ingalls; Costumes, Allison Reeds CAST: Michi Barall, Kevin Bernston, Mark Danisovszky, Louis Fanucchi, Katie Grant, Rodney Scott Hudson, Scott Hudson, Ira Marks, Tom McGowan, Jacques C. Smith.

RENT; Music/Book/Lyrics, Jonathan Larson; Director, Michael Greif; Choreographer, Marlies Yearby; Music Supervision, Tim Weil; Original Concept/Additional Lyrics, Billy Aronson; Set, Paul Clay; Lighting, Blake Burba; Costumes, Angela Wendt CAST: Carla Bianco, Kevyn Brackett, Sharon Brown, Hallie Bulleit, Wilson Cruz, Monique Daniels, Laura Dias, D'Monroe, Neil Patrick Harris, Leigh Hetherington, Sala Iwamatsu, Mark Leroy Jackson, Owen Johnston II, Christian Mena, Ron Christopher Patric, Kenna Ramsey, Julia Santana, Andy Senor, Curt Skinner, Paul Oakley Stovall, Brent Davin Vance.

THE MODEL APARTMENT by Donald Margulies; Director, Mark Rucker; Set, Christopher Acebo; Lighting, Blake Burba; Costumes, Katherine Roth CAST: George Coe, Akili Prince, Rosemary Prinz, Roberta Wallach.

HAVING OUR SAY by Emily Mann; Adapted from the book by Sarah L. Delany, A. Elizabeth Delany, Amy Hill Hearth; Set, Robert Brill; Lighting, Chris Parry; Costumes, V. Nadja Lancelot CAST: Micki Grant, Lizan Mitchell.

HARMONY; Music, Barry Manilow; Book/Lyrics, Bruce Sussman; Director, David Warren; Choreographer, Charles Moulton; Music Director, Joseph Thalken; Orchestrations, Ralph Burns; Set, Derek McLane; Lighting, Kenneth Posner; Costumes, Mark Wendland CAST: Danny Burstein, Mark Chmiel, James Clow, Trent DeLong, Thursday Farrar, Christiane Farr-Wersinger, Pascale Faye, Steven Goldstein, Sean Grant, Rebecca Luker, Lisa Mayer, Janet Metz, Jennifer Morris, Casey Nicholaw, Arte Phillips, Scott Robertson, Scott Robinson, Jessica Sheridan, Jodi Stevens, Tom Titone, Kiersten Van Horne, Thom Christopher Warren, Patrick Wilson, Kurt Ziskie.

John Johnson Photos

Neil Patrick Harris, Christian Mena in *Rent*

Steven Goldstein, Thom Christopher Warren, Mark Chmiel, Bruce Sussman, James Clow, Patrick Wilson, Danny Burstein, (front) Barry Manilow of *Harmony*

Veanne Cox, Jefferson Mays in *Importance of Being Earnest*

LONG WHARF THEATRE

New Haven, Connecticut

Thirty-second Season

Artistic Director, Arvin Brown; Interim Executive Director, Janice Muirhead; Press, Kimberly Sewright.

DEALER'S CHOICE by Patrick Marber; Director, David Esbjornson; Set, Hugh Landwehr; Lighting, Frances Aronson; Costumes, Elizabeth Hope Clancy CAST: Ritchie Coster, Reg Rogers, Dermot Crowley, Alec Phoenix, Mark H. Dold, Tom Spackman.

THE SHOW-OFF by George Kelly; Director, Arvin Brown; Set, Michael Yeargan; Lighting, Mark Stanley; Costumes, David Murin; Wigs, Paul Huntley CAST: Ann McDonough, Joyce Ebert, Julia Gibson, Joel Stedman, Rex Robbins, Stephen Barker Turner, Tim Choate, Tim Donoghue, Richard Spore.

THE ROAD TO MECCA by Athol Fugard; Director, John Tillinger; Set, James Noone; Lighting, Dennis Parichy; Costumes, Jess Goldstein CAST: Julie Harris, Linda Purl, Tom Aldredge.

THE OLD SETTLER by John Henry Redwood; Director, Walter Dalls; Set, Loren Sherman; Lighting, Frances Aronson; Costumes, David Murin; Wigs, Paul Huntley CAST: Brenda Pressley, Myra Lucretia Taylor, Tico Wells, Caroline Stefanie Clay.

THE JOY LUCK CLUB by Susan Kim, from the novel by Amy Tann; Director, Seret Scott; Set, Ming Cho Lee; Lighting, Mark Stanley; Costumes, Candice Donnelly CAST: Takayo Fischer, Wai Ching Ho, Mary Lum, June Kyoko Lu, Yunjin Kim, Karen Tsen Lee, Elaine Tse, Constance Boardman, Chao-Li Chi, Mel Duane Gionson, Ben Wang, Curt Hostetter, Andrew Pang, Dian Kobayashi, Jennifer Kato, Kati Kuroda, Duc Luu, Lisa Li, James Andreassi.

VOIR DIRE by Joe Sutton; Director, Gordon Edelstein; Set, Andrew Wood Boughton; Lighting, Allen Lee Hughes; Costumes, Paul Tazewell CAST: Vanessa Aspillaga, Steve Cell, Robin Weigert, Pamela Payton-Wright, Karen Kandel, Miranda Kent, Richard E. Bean, Joseph Jude Zito.

T. Charles Erickson Photos

Top: Julie Harris, Linda Purl, Tom Aldredge in *Road to Mecca*
Center: Wai Ching Ho, Lisa Li in *Joy Luck Club*
Right: Dermot Crowley, Ritchie Coster, Alec Phoenix in
Dealer's Choice

The Vanishing Twin Company

LOOKINGGLASS THEATRE COMPANY

Chicago, Illinois

Artistic Director, Laura Eason; Managing Director, David Catlin; Administrative Director, Hillary Metcalf; Press/Marketing, Mary Kate Barley Jenkins

THE VANISHING TWIN; Written/Directed by Bruce Norris; Music/Lyrics, Bruce Norris, Rick Sims, Laura Eason; Musical Director, Rick Sims; Sets, Dan Ostling; Lighting, Shannon McKinney; Costumes, Mara Blumenfeld CAST: David Catlin, Thomas J. Cox, Lawrence E. DiStasi, Christine Dunford, Laura Eason, Raymond Fox, David Kersnar, Todd Marino, Rick Sims, Heidi Stillman, Philip R. Smith, Andrew White

IN THE EYE OF THE BEHOLDER; Conceived/Directed by Laura Eason CAST: Eva Barr, David Kersnar, Kim Leigh Smith, Misty B. Springer, Tracy Walsh, Andrew White

28 PICTURES OF LIFE IN HIGH-TECH WORLD; Written/Directed by Laura Eason; Costumes, Mara Blumenfeld; Sets, Daniel Ostling; Sound, Mark Messing; Lighting, Joel Moritz CAST: Shirley Anderson, Jane C. Cho, Thomas J. Cox, Raymond Fox, Doug Hara, Paul Christopher Hobbs, Rich Hutchman, Heidi Stillman, Tracy Walsh

David Caitlin Photos

28 Pictures of Life... Company

194

MARRIOTT'S LINCOLNSHIRE THEATRE

Lincolnshire, Illinois

Executive Producer, Kary M. Walker; Artistic Director, Dyanne Earley; Associate Producer, Terry James; Musical Director, Terry James; Set Design, Thomas M. Ryan; Costume Design, Nancy Missimi; Lighting Designers, Diane Ferry Williams, Kenneth Moore; Press, Director, Mary Thimios

THE BEST LITTLE WHOREHOUSE IN TEXAS; Music/Lyrics, Carol Hall; Book, Larry L. King, Peter Masterson; Director/Choreography, Mark S. Hoebee CAST: Stephen P. Full, Kelli Cramer, Jennifer Gordon, Felicia P. Fields, Paula Scrofano, Angela Berra, Annie DePrima, Julie Ann Emery, Catherine Brown, Leisa Mather, Larry Yando, Scott Calcagno, Kevin Earley, Brian Herriott, Aaron Thielen, James Anthony, Don Forston, John Reeger, Catherine Lord, John Reegen, Don Forston, K.C. Lupp, Matthew Orlando, Paul Sullenger

HOW TO SUCCEED IN BUSINESS WITHOUT REALLY TRYING; Music/Lyrics, Frank Loesser; Book, Abe Burrows, Jack Weinstock, Willie Gilbert; Director, Dyanne Earley; Choreography, Marc Robin CAST: Sam Samuelson, Paul Harvey, Brian Robert Mani, David Studwell, Ray Frewen, Jonathan Weir, Don Forston, Kelley Anne Clark, Elizabeth Gelman, Paul Slade Smith, Leisa Mather, Brian Robert Mani, E. Faye Butler, Ronald Keaton, Angela Berra, Deborah E. Johnson, Rob Rahn, Julie Ann Emery

SINGIN' IN THE RAIN; Original Script/Adaptation, Betty Comden, Adolph Green; Songs, Nacio Herb Brown, Arthur Freed; Director, Mark S. Hoebee; Choreography, Marc Robin CAST: Kelli Cramer, Deidre Dolan, Sarah Green, Don Forston, Stephen P. Full, William Akey, Angela Berra, Michael Cline, Rob Rahn, Mary Beth Dolan, Aaron Thielen, Scott Calcagno, Paul Slade Smith, Ron J. Hutchins, Dan Collins, Stacey Flaster, Tammy Ann Mader, Linda Parsons, Buddy Reeder, Annette Thurman, Andrew Waters

THE WILL ROGERS FOLLIES; Music, Cy Coleman; Lyrics, Betty Comden, Adolph Green; Book, Peter Stone; Director, Mark S. Hoebee; Choreography, Marc Robin CAST: Jason Edwards, Catherine Lord, Ronald Keaton, Angela Berra, Michael Haws, Kevin Earley, Kent Lewis, K.C. Lupp, Aaron Thielen, Marci Caliendo, Ariane Dolan, Deidre Dolan, Kelly Etter, Sloan Just, Susan Kokot, Emily Kosloski, Jennifer Kemp Lupp, Tysh Nelson, Linda Parsons, Shane Partlow, Ron J. Hutchins, Simon Lewis, Tom Brackney's Madcap Mutts, Michael Fratantuno

KISMET; Music/Lyrics, Robert Wright and George Forrest based on Borodin; Book, Charles Lederer, Luther Davis; Director, Dominic Missimi; Choreography, Harrison McEldowney CAST: Timothy Nolen, Alene Robertson, Susan Moniz, Tony Capone, James FitzGerald, David Studwell, Tom Roland, Scott Alan, Tait Runnfeldt, Aaron Thielen, David Studwell, Ronald Keaton, Phillip Pickens, Kevin Earley, Sean Allan Krill, Stephanie Burton, Emily Kosloski, Jill Walmsley, Stephanie Burton, Matthew Orlando, Stacey Flaster, Jennifer Kemp Lupp, Kelli Cramer, Elizabeth Heath Fauntleroy

Tom Maday, Brian McCormick Photos

Sam Samuelson in *How to Succeed...*

Annie DePrima, Catherine Brown, Angela Berra, Felicia P. Fields, Paula Scrofano, Kelli Cramer, Leisa Mather, Julie Emery, Jennifer Gordon in *Best Little Whorehouse...*

Alene Robertson, Timothy Nolen in *Kismet*

Wayne David Parker, John Seibert, Henrietta Hermelin, David Ellenstein, Robert Grossman (in chair) in *Beau Jest*

John Seibert, Robert Grossman in *Woman in Black*

Luray Cooper, Lou Beatty Jr., Esau Pritchett in *I Am a Man*

MEADOW BROOK THEATRE

Rochester, Michigan

Thirty-first Season

Artistic Director, Geoffrey Sherman; Managing Director, Gregg Bloomfield; Associate Director, Phillip Locker; Press Director, Michael C. Vigilant.

BEAU JEST by James Sherman; Director, Geoffrey Sherman; Sets, Peter W. Hicks; Lighting, Reid G. Johnson; Costumes, Edith Leavis Bookstein CAST: David Ellenstein, Robert Grossman, Henrietta Hermelin, Wayne David Parker, John Seibert, Linnea Todd.

JUST A SECOND! by James Sherman; Director, Phillip Locker; Sets, Peter W. Hicks; Lighting, Reid G. Johnson; Costumes, Edith Leavis Bookstein CAST: David Ellenstein, Robert Grossman, Henrietta Hermelin, John Michael Manfredi, John Seibert, Linnea Todd.

A CHRISTMAS CAROL by Charles Dickens; Adapted by Mary Spalding; Director, Geoffrey Sherman; Sets, Peter W. Hicks; Lighting, Reid G. Johnson; Costumes, Barbara Jenks CAST: Geoffrey Beauchamp, Mary Benson, Corrine Carrier, Booth Colman, David Ellenstein, Paul Hopper, Thomas D. Mahard, John Michael Manfredi, Richard A. Schrot, Diana Van Fossen, Denise Michelle Young, Jodie Wagner Kuhn, Larry Schrot, Earl C. Bain, Renee Lee, Gregory Wilson, Michael Robert Brandon, Nina Kircher, Carey Crim, Eric Czarnik, Mike Kopera, Shannon Murphy, Alice Sherman, Elizabeth Hawley, Rebecca Hyke, Adam Carpenter, Nicholas Cornfield, Melody Peng, Maddie Ellison, Scott Goci, Jakob Locker, Zachary-John Manfred, Jessic Hall, Hannah Locker.

THE WOMAN IN BLACK; Adapted by Stephen Mallatratt; Based on a novel by Susan Hill; Director, Phillip Locker; Sets, Peter W. Hicks; Lighting, Reid G. Johnson; Costumes, Barbara Jenks CAST: Robert Grossman, John Seibert, Nancy Rominger.

I AM A MAN by OyamO; Director, Gary Anderson; Sets, Peter W. Hicks; Lighting, Reid G. Johnson; Costumes, Barbara Jenks CAST: Lou Beatty Jr., Charles Bevel, Luray Cooper, Robert Grossman, Clyde T. Harper, Paul Hopper, Michael Jay, Jennifer Kay Jones, Phillip Locker, Charlotte J. Nelson, Phillip Sekou Glass, Esau Pritchett.

ARCADIA by Tom Stoppard; Director, Geoffrey Sherman; Sets/Costumes, Peter W. Hicks; Lighting, Reid G. Johnson CAST: Dana Powers Acheson, Robin Chadwick, Carey Crim, Raul E. Esparza, Raymond Fox, Paul Hopper, Thomas D. Mahard, Mark Rademacher, Margo Skinner, Diana Van Fossen, John Seibert, Mike Kopera.

APPALACHIAN STRINGS by Randal Myler, Dan Wheetman; Director, Randal Myler; Musical Director, Dan Wheetman; Choreographer, Sandy Silva; Sets/Lighting, Paul Wonsek; Costumes, Barbara Jenks CAST: Molly Andrews, Bob Burrus, Melinda Deane, Tony Marcus, Adale O'Brien, Sandy Silva, L.J. Slavin, Dan Wheetman.

Rick Smith Photos

Peri Gilpin, Allison Mackie in *Midsummer Night's Dream*

Stephen Lee Anderson, Gayton Scott in *Threepenny Opera*

Becky Ann Baker, Paul Mullins in *Blithe Spirit*

NEW JERSEY SHAKESPEARE FESTIVAL

Madison, New Jersey

Artistic Director, Bonnie J. Monte; Managing Director, Michael Stotts; Artistic Associate, Joe Discher; Press/Marketing Director, Rick Engler.

PRODUCTIONS (1997)

A MIDSUMMER NIGHT'S DREAM by William Shakespeare; Director/Design, Bonnie J. Monte; Costumes, Murell Horton; Lighting, Michael Giannitti CAST: Tom Delling, Dominic Hoffman, Marion Adler, Jim Mohr, Thomas Beauchamp, Kathleen Connelly, Rebecca Goacher, Jared Zeus, Allison Mackie, Steve Wklson, Cameron Watson, Peri Gilpin, David Chandler, William Wierzejewski, Bryan Umiker, Clark S. Carmichael, Brian Taylor, Zander Massey, Sarah Murphy, Tricia Paoluccio, Onique Vukovic.

MUCH ADO ABOUT NOTHING by William Shakespeare; Director, Joe Discher; Sets, Chris Muller; Costumes, Jacqueline Firkins; Lighting, Bruce Auerbach CAST: Michael Daly, Meg DeFore, William Greville, Gregory Jackson, Ken Kliban, Laura Nicholas, James Michael Reilly, Susan Riley Stevens, Mark Elliot Wilson, Coleman Zeigen.

THE THREEPENNY OPERA; Book/Lyrics, Bertolt Brecht; Music, Kurt Weill; Director, Paul Mullins; Sets, P.K. Wish; Costumes, Amela Baksic; Lighting, Michael Giannitti CAST: Joshua Finkel, Stephen Lee Anderson, Gayton Scott, Ron Lee Savin, Clark S. Carmichael, Debbie Lee Jones, Joe Roseto, Kristie Dale Sanders, Jeff Applegate, Don Meehan, Michael Criscuolo, Bret Mosley, Kurt Ziskie, Kate Ward, Kathleen Connolly, Kim Barron, Danielle Duvall, Dee Billia, Kimberly Kay, Todd Ross.

THE LIFE OF KING HENRY V by William Shakespeare; Director, Scott Wentworth; Sets, Michael Cutler; Costumes, Murell Horton; Lighting, Mathew Williams CAST: Michael Allen, Lenny Bart, Torquil Campbell, Dru Dempsey, Crystal Gandrud, Marc Goodman, Peter Husovsky, Conan McCarty, William Meisle, Christopher Moore, Jack Moran, Tricia Paoluccio, Andy Paterson, Michael Rudko, Brian Taylor, Bryan Umiker, William Vogt, Matt Walker, Brian Weddington, Scott Whitehurst, Steve Wilson.

BLITHE SPIRIT by Noel Coward; Director, Dylan Baker; Sets/Costumes, Michael Vaughn Sims; Lighting, Michael Giannitti CAST: Alice Saltzman, Becky Ann Baker, Paul Mullins, Marcus Giamatti, Amy Hohn, Peggy Pope, Kathryn Meisle.

Gerry Goodstein Photos

OLD GLOBE THEATRE

San Diego, California

Sixty-second Season

Artistic Director, Jack O'Brien; Associate Artistic Director, Sheldon Epps; Executive Director, Craig Noel; Managing Director, Thomas Hall; Press, David Tucker II, Laura Lee Juliano

THE TAMING OF THE SHREW by William Shakespeare; Director, James Dunn; Sets, Ralph Funicello; Costumes, Andrew V. Yelusich; Lighting, Michael Gilliam   CAST: James Harper, Colleen Quinn, Henry Ruseell, Randy Moore, Daniel Mastrogiorgio, Don Sparks, James Joseph O'Neil, David Van Pelt, Mark Rubald, Mark Harelik, William Ontiveros, David Mann, Jack Banning, Scott Ferrara, Erika Rolfsrud, David Prentiss, Dan Sanky, Eric Almquist, Russell Edge, Paul Fitzgerald, John Worley, Crystal Allen, Melissa Friedman, Andee Mason, Lina Patel

Victor Garber, Joan McMurtrey in *Macbeth*

AMERICAN BUFFALO by David Mamet; Director, Stephen Metcalfe; Sets, Ralph Funicello; Costumes, Dione Lebhar; Lighting, Ashley York Kennedy   CAST: Dann Florek, Seth Green, Jonathan McMurtry

MACBETH by William Shakespeare; Director, Nicholas Martin; Sets, Ralph Funicello; Costumes, Robert Morgan; Lighting, Kenneth Posner   CAST: Richard Easton, Scott Ferrara, John Worley, Victor Garber, Ray Chambers, Jay Heiserman, Vaughn Armstrong, Henry J. Jordan, Paul Fitzgerald, David Prentiss, Russell Edge, Jim Wallert, Rey Magdaluyo, Joan McMurtrey, Erika Rolfsrud, Jonathan McMurtry, Eric Almquist, James Joseph O'Neil, David Mann, Katherine McGrath, Melissa Friedman, Lina Patel, Henry Russell, Christian Casper, Andrea Cirie, Michelle Cordero, Heather Raffo, Matt Shapiro, Matthew Troncone, Philip G. Turco

Jonathan McMurty, Seth Green and Dann Florek in
American Buffalo

PLAY ON; Conception/Direction, Sheldon Epps; Book, Cheryl L. West; Songs, Duke Ellington; Choreography, Mercedes Ellington; Musical Director, Leonard Oxley; Sets, James Leonard Joy; Costumes, Marianna Elliott; Lighting, Jeff Davis   CAST: Cheryl Freeman, Andre De Shields, Larry Marshall, Yvette Cason, Carl Anderson, Lawrence Hamilton, Tonya Pinkins, Crystal Allen, Wendee Lee Curtis, Frantz G. Hall, Bryan Haynes, Kimberly Hester, Derrick Demetrius Parker, Stacie Precia, Lisa Scialabba, William Wesley, Darius Keith Williams

SYLVIA by A.R. Gurney; Director, John Rando; Sets, Robin Sanford Roberts; Costumes, Christina Haatainen; Lighting, Ashley York Kennedy   CAST: William Anton, Jane Carr, Don Sparks, Kellie Waymire

PRIDE'S CROSSING by Tina Howe; Director, Jack O'Brien; Sets, Ralph Funicello; Costumes, Robert Morgan; Lighting, Michael Gilliam   CAST: Cherry Jones, Marceline Hugot, Jeffrey Hayenga, Robert Knepper, Willian Anton, Monique Fowler, Hilary Elizabeth Clarke, Nichole Danielle Givans

A MOON FOR THE MISBEGOTTEN by Eugene O'Neill; Director, John Rando; Sets/Costumes, Robert Morgan; Lighting, Ashley York Kennedy   CAST: Ron Choularton, Bruce Gooch, David Mann, Katherine McGrath, Michael McGuire

Cheryl Freeman (center) in *Play On*

Reg Rogers, Nina Landey in *Dracula*

DRACULA by Steven Dietz from the novel by Bram Stoker; Director, Mark Rucker; Sets, David Jenkins; Costumes, Katherine Beatrice Roth; Lighting, Michael Gilliam   CAST: Enrico Colantoni, Nina Landey, Julie Fain Lawrence, Michael Eric Strickland, Joshua Fardon, Richard Easton, Reg Rogers, David Prentiss, James Wallert, Henry Russell, Andrea Cirie, Michelle Cordero

TRAVELS WITH MY AUNT by Giles Havergal from the novel by Graham Greene; Director, Craig Noel; Sets, Kent Dorsey; Costumes, Jack Taggart; Lighting, Barth Ballard   CAST: Jefrey Alan Chandler, Brian Lohmann, William Roesch, James Saba

THE REAL THING by Tom Stoppard; Director, Sheldon Epps; Sets, James Leonard Joy; Costumes, Marianna Elliott; Lighting, Jeff Davis   CAST: John Bolger, Joey Collins, Christina Haas, Becky London, David Mann, Annie Meisels, Craig Wroe

BELOW THE BELT by Richard Dresser; Director, Andrew J. Traister; Costumes, Marianna Elliott; Sets/Lighting, Kent Dorsey   CAST: Robert Foxworth, Michael Louden, Alan Oppenheimer

Ken Howard Photos

OREGON SHAKESPEARE FESTIVAL

Ashland, Oregon

Artistic Director, Libby Appel; Executive Director, Paul Nicholson; Press, Deborah Elliott

(1996 Productions)

ROMEO AND JULIET by William Shakespeare; Director, Rene Buch; Sets, Richard L. Hay; Costumes, Susan Mickey; Lighting, Robert Peterson CAST: J.P. Phillips, Demetra Pittman, Mikael Salazar, Triney Sandoval, James J. Peck, Lorenzo Gonzalez, Dan Kremer, Michelle Blackmon, Vilma Silva, Tyrone Wilson, Susan Corzatte, David Kelly, Ted Deasy, Karl Backus, Jesse Petrick, Clayton Corzatte, John Resenhouse, Steve Cardamone, Shawn Galloway, Robert M. Owens, Andres Alcala, Davon Russell, Andres, Gina Daniels, Lorenzo Gonzalez, Nadine Griffith, Cindy Lu, Robert M. Owens

Mikael Salazar, Vilma Silva in *Romeo and Juliet*

CORIOLANUS by William Shakespeare; Director, Tony Taccone; Sets, William Bloodgood; Costumes, Deborah M. Dryden; Lighting, Robert Peterson CAST: Derrick Lee Weeden, Debra Lynne Wicks, Cindy Basco, D'Marion Joseph, Dennis Robertson, Dan Kremer, Shawn Galloway, Susan Corzatte, Richard Elmore, Richard Howard, David Kelly, Barry Kraft, Clayton Corzatte, Catherine E. Coulson, Johanna Jackson, Karl Backus, Jay Karnes, Triney Sandoval, Ray Porter, U. Jonathan Toppo, Kevin Kenerly, John Pribyl, Tyrone Wilson, Tony DeBruno, Phil Preston, Cindy Basco, Andrew Borba, August Gabriel, Carey Gibbar, Jay Karnes, Cindy Lu, Jesse Patrick, Phil Preston, Triney Sandoval, Paul Shikany, U. Jonathan Toppo

LOVE'S LOBOR'S LOST by William Shakespeare; Director, Pat Patton; Sets, Michael Ganio; Costumes, Shigeru Yaji; Lighting, Robert Peterson CAST: Jay Karnes, John Pribyl, Mikael Salazar, Dan Donohue, Douglas Markkanen, Christine Williams, Carey Lorenzo Gonzalez, Lise Bruneau, Robin Goodrin Nordli, Vilma Silva, Mhari Sandoval, Philip Davidson, Lorenzo Gonzalez, James J. Peck, Triney Sandoval, Carole Healey, Anthony DeFonte, Andrew Borba

ARCADIA by Tom Stoppard; Director, Stephen Hollis; Sets, Richard L. Hay; Costumes, David Crank; Lighting, Marcus Dilliard CAST: Christine Williams, Andrew Borba, Paul Vincent O'Connor, Dan Donohue, John Pribyl, Linda Alper, Anthony DeFonte, Carole Healey, Mhari Sandoval, Richard Howard, Jay Karnes, Adam M. Hogan

Derrick Lee Weeden (center) in *Coriolanus*

200

MOLIERE PLAYS PARIS by Moliere; Translated/Contrived by Nagle Jackson; Director, James Edmondson; Sets, Michael Ganio; Costumes, Deborah M. Dryden; Lighting, Robert Peterson CAST: Ray Porter, Sandy McCallum, Kirsten Giroux, Cindy Basco, Ted Deasy, Robert Vincent Frank, U. Jonathan Toppo, Derrick Lee Weeden, David Kelly, Jesse Petrick, Becky S. Jones, Cindy Lu, Steve Cardamone, Karl Backus

THE WINTER'S TALE by William Shakespeare; Director, Fontaine Syer; Sets, William Bloodgood; Costumes, Marie Ann Chiment; Lighting, Robert Peterson CAST: Michelle Blackmon, Mark Murphey, John Rensenhouse, Lise Bruneau, Travis Goodman, Sol Weisbard, Paul Vincent O'Connor, Anthony DeFonte, Tamu Gray, James J. Peck, Lorenzo Gonzalez, Ted Deasy, Steve Cardamone, Eileen DeSandre, Nadine Griffith, Mhari Sandoval, Christine Williams, James J. Peck, Dan Donohue, Robert M. Owens, J.P. Phillips, Michael J. Hume, Gina Daniels, Andres Alcala

AWAKE AND SING by Clifford Odets; Director, Debra Wicks; Sets, William Bloodgood; Costumes, Deborah M. Dryden; Lighting, Dawn Chiang CAST: Eileen DeSandre, Dennis Robertson, Cindy Basco, U. Jonathan Toppo, Sandy McCallum, Tony DeBruno, Michael Elich, Robert Vincent Frank, Phil Preston, Samantha

U. Jonathan Toppo, Sandy McCallum in *Awake and Sing*

THE DARKER FACE OF THE EARTH by Rita Dove; Director, Ricardo Khan; Sets, Richard L. Hay; Costumes, Karen Lin; Lighting, James Sale CAST: BW Gonzalez, Gina Daniles, Thomas Byrd, J.P. Phillips, Tamu Gray, Debra Lynne Wicks, Johanna Jackson, Nadine Griffith, Davon Russell, Ezra Knight, Elizabeth Norment, Mark Murphey, Dennis Robertson, Paul Vincent O'Connor, Tyrone Wilson, August Gabriel, Kevin Kenerly, Russ Appleyard, Craig Goodmond

STRINDBERG IN HOLLYWOOD by Drury Pifer; Director, Pat Patton; Sets, William Bloodgood; Costumes, Claudia Everett; Lighting, Marcus Dilliard CAST: Philip Davidson, Kirsten Giroux, Karole Foreman, Douglas Markkanen

A PAIR OF THREES: *Three Viewings* by Jeffrey Hatcher; Director, Fontaine Syer; *Three Hotels* by Jon Robin Baitz; Director, Michael J. Hume; Sets, Richard L. Hay; Costumes, Janice Benning; Lighting, Collier Woods Jr. CASTS: Michael J. Hume, Linda Alper, Catherine E. Coulson, Richard Elmore, Fontaine Syer

CABARET VERBOTEN; Created by Jeremy Lawrence; Director, Penny Metropulos; Sets, William Bloodgood; Costumes, Tom Broecker; Lighting, James Sale; Music Director, Darcy Danielson CAST: Michael Elich, Robin Goodrin Nordli, Demetra Pittman, Robert Vincent Frank, Darcy Danielson, Jim Malachi, David Wright

David Cooper, Dale M. Peterson, T. Charles Erickson, Chris Bennion Photos

Catherine E. Coulson, Michael J. Hume, Linda Alper in
Three Viewings

PLAYHOUSE ON THE SQUARE

Memphis, Tennessee

Executive Producer, Jackie Nichols; Artistic Director, Ken Zimmerman; Press, Natalie Jalenak.

REISDENT COMPANY: Michael Detroit, Kevin Jones, Jenny Odle, Jim Ostrander. GUEST ARTISTS: Harry Bryce, Leslie Churchill Ward, Mark Chambers, Sara Morsey, Jane Heller, John Butterfield, Jack Rogers, Patrick Alan Kearns; Shorey Walker, Scott Fergson (Directors); Frank Foster, Michae Brewer (Scenic Designers).

PRODUCTIONS: *Forever Plaid, Ain't Misbehavin', Steel Magnolias, Peter Pan, A Tuna Christmas, Laughter on the 23rd Floor, The Diary of Anne Frank, Three Tall Women, The Rocky Horror Show*; at Circuit Playhouse: *Broken Glass, Jeffrey, 10 November, The Lion the Witch & the Wardrobe, Zara Spook & Other Lures, The Ant and the Grasshopper, Voices of the Souht, Kindertransport, Sylvia, After Play*.

Jimmy Wagner Photos

Marjorie Fitzsimmons, Shannon Convery in
Zara Spook and Other Lures

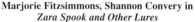

Cequita Monique, James Solomon Benn, Kimberly Crutcher, Marquez Rhyne, Barbara Clinton in
Ain't Misbehavin

REPERTORY THEATRE OF ST. LOUIS

St. Louis, Missouri

Artistic Director, Steven Wooolf; Managing Director, Mark D. Bernstein; Press, Judy Andrews.

THE MOST HAPPY FELLA; Book/Music/Lyrics by Frank Loesser, based on Sidney Howard's *They Knew What They Wanted*; Director, Victoria Bussert; Choreographer, Williamichael Badolato; Musical Director, Larry Pressgrove; Costumes, James Scott; Lighting, Peter E. Sargent; Sets, John Ezell CAST: Whit Reichert, Lovette George, Kirsti Carnahan, Stephanie Lynge, Tara Tyrrell, Julia Klein, Gina Carlette, Bill Bush, Eric Millegan, Monte Black, John Payonk, Alma Cuervo, Hunter Bell, Timothy Scott Bennett, Timothy Cole, Brian Sutherland, Tom Souhrada, Keith Weirich, Scott Brush, Michael Etziler.

THE HEIRESS by Ruth and Augustus Goetz; Director, John Going; Sets, James Wolk; Costumes, Elizabeth Covey; Lighting, James Sale CAST: Tarah Flanagan, Joneal Hoplin, Ruby Holbrook, Melissa King, Zoe Vonder Haar, Matthew Cody, Jami Lee Gertz, Stevie Ray Dallimore, Robin Moseley.

SONGPLAY: THE SONGS AND MUSIC OF KURT WEILL; Music, Kurt Weill; Conceived, Adapted and Directed by Jonathan Eaton; Musical Director, Scot Woolley; Choreographer, Daniel Pelzig; Sets, Paul Shortt; Costumes, David Kay Mickelsen; Lighting, James Sale. CAST: Michael Brian, Herb Downer, Kim Lindsay, Karen Murphy, Pedro Porro, Craig Priebe.

THE THREE MUSKETEERS; Adapted by Charles Morey; Director, Edward Stern; Sets, John Ezell; Costumes, Dorothy Marhsall Englis; Lighting, Phillip Monat CAST: Anderson Matthews, Charles Antalosky, Michael James Reed, Joe Palmieri, Timothy Gulan, Douglas Mumaw, James Gall, Nancy Bell, Mark Mineart, Gregory Simmons, Thomas Schall, Noble Shropshire, Brian A. Peters, Jackie Farrington, Anne Newhall, Greg Thornton, Jane Stoub, Joneal Hoplin, Jami Lee Gertz, Randy Lee Bailey, John Bellomo, Wayne Stemmler, Jacob Daniel Thomas.

Jonreal Joplin in *The Heiress*

Venida Evans, Emily Yancy in *Having Our Say*

Ashley West, Matthew Rauch in *Arcadia*

HAVING OUR SAY by Emily Mann; Adatped from the book by Sarah L. Delany, A. Elizabeth Delany, Amy Hill Hearth; Director, Loretta Greco; Sets, Robert Brill; Costumes, Clyde Ruffin; Lighting, Max De Volder CAST: Venida Evans, Emily Yancy.

THE WOMAN IN BLACK; Adapted by Stephen Mallatratt, from the book by Susan Hill; Director, Susan Gregg; Sets, Arthur Ridley; Costumes, J. Bruce Summers; Lighting, Peter Sargent CAST: Philip Lehl, Joe Palmieri, Susan E. Scott.

ARCADIA by Tom Stoppard; Director, Steven Woolf; Sets, Michael Ganio; Costumes, James Scott; Lighting, Mary Jo Dondlinger CAST: Ashley West, Matthew Rauch, Whit Reichert, Anderson Matthews, Joneal Hoplin, Glynis Bell, John Rensenhouse, Carol Schultz, Jessica Jaques, Jim Abele, Chris Hietikko, Ben Grimes.

THE GLASS MENAGERIE by Tennesse Williams; Director, Timothy Near; Sets, Carolyn Ross; Costumes, B. Modern; Lighting, Max De Volder CAST: Robin Moseley, Ian Kahn, Pilar Witherspoon, Michael Butler.

VOIR DIRE by Joe Sutton; Director, Jay E. Raphael; Sets, John Roselovich Jr.; Costumes, Dorothy Marshall Englis; Lighting, Mark Wilson CAST: Selenis Leyva, R. Ward Duffy, Melissa King, Susan Cella, Leah Maddrie, Nicole Marcks, Alex Miller, Jami Lee Gertz.

Judy Andrews Photos

Robin Moseley, Pilar Witherspoon in *Glass Menagerie*

SEATTLE REPERTORY THEATRE

Seattle, Washington

Artistic Director, Daniel Sullivan; Managing Director, Benjamin Moore; Associate Artistic Director, David Saint; Press Director, Jeff Fickes

UNCLE VANYA by Anton Chekhov; Adaptation, David Mamet; Director, Dan Sullivan; Sets, Thomas Lynch; Costumes, David Murin; Lighting, Peter Kaczorowski CAST: Jeanie Carson, Jacqueline Kim, Biff McGuire, Marjorie Nelson, Tony Pasqualini, Martha Plimpton, John Procaccino, Daniel Sullivan, James Sutorius

SYLVIA by A.R. Gurney; Director, David Saint; Sets, James Youmans; Costumes, David Murin; Lighting, Kenneth Posner   CAST: Barbara Dirickson, Jim Fyfe, Sally Smythe, R. Hamilton Wright

BALLAD OF YACHIYO by Philip Kan Gotanda; Director, Sharon Ott; Sets, Loy Arcenas; Costumes, Lydia Tanji; Lighting, Peter Maradudin CAST: Kim Evey, Gigi Jhong, Yunjin Kim, Dian Kobayashi, Emily Kuroda, Naoki Mimuro, Lane Nishkawa, Sab Shimono, Greg Watanabe, Annie Yee

NEAT; Written/Performed by Charlayne Woodard; Director, Tazewell Thompson; Set, Donald Eastman; Costumes, Jane Greenwood; Lighting, Brian Nason

AN AMERICAN DAUGHTER by Wendy Wasserstein; Director, David Saint; Sets, John Lee Beatty; Costumes, David Murin; Lighting, Pat Collins CAST: Mark Chamberlin, James Chestnutt, Barbara Dirickson, Luce Ennis, Peggy Gannon, James Garver, Demene E. Hall, Peter Lohnes, Henri Lubatti, Ryland Merkey, Mari Nelson, John Procaccino, Rex Robbins, Shona Tucker

THE CIDER HOUSE RULES by Peter Parnell; From the novel by John Irving; Conceived/Directed by Tom Hulce and Jane Jones; Sets, Christine Jones; Costumes, David Zinn; Lighting, Greg Sullivan CAST: Jillian Armenante, Tom Beyer, Sarah Brooke, Brienin Bryant, Rebecca Chace, James Chestnutt, Christopher Collet, Neal Huff, A. Bryan Humphrey, Reginald A. Jackson, Edd Key, Anthony Lee, Novella Nelson, Dougald Park, Myra Platt, Jim Ragland, Stephanie Shine, Todd Sible, Ron Simons, Jayne Taini, Lauren Tewes, David-Paul Wichert, Michael Winters

TRAVELS WITH MY AUNT by Graham Greene; Adaptation, Giles Havergal; Director, David Saint; Sets, Brad Stokes; Costumes, Deb Trout; Lighting, Joe Saint CAST: Margaret Hilton, Richmond Hoxie, Bill Kux, R. Hamilton Wright

TRUE WEST by Sam Shepard; Director, Kurt Beattie; Sets, Bill Forrester; Costumes, Rose Pederson; Lighting, Rick Paulsen CAST: Mike Regan, Eve Roberts, Tom Spiller, R. Hamilton Wright

Patrick Bennett Photos

Barbara Dirickson, R. Hamilton Wright, Jim Fyfe in *Sylvia*

John Procaccino, Barbara Dirickson in
An American Daughter

Cider House Rules **Company**

SHAKESPEARE & COMPANY

Lenox, Massachusetts

Twentieth Season

Artistic Director, Tina Packer; Managing Director, Christopher Sink; Press, Elizabeth Aspenlieder.

OFF THE MAP by Joan Ackermann; Director, Normi Noel; Costumes, Alison Ragland; Sets, Jim Youngerman CAST: Corinna May, Jonathan Croy, Rory Hammond, Dennis Krausnick, Ariel Bock, Jim Nutter.

KING HENRY THE FOURTH PART 1 by William Shakespeare; Director, Tina Packer, Kevin Coleman; Costumes/Sets, John Pennoyer; Lighting, Michael Giannitti CAST: Malcolm Ingram, Jason Asprey, David Wiles, Allyn Burrows, Jonathan Epstein, Leslie Toth, John Hadden, Hugh d'Autremont, Dan McCleary, Rob Pensalfini, Derrick Sanders, Josef Hansen, Ken Butler, Randy Petrides, Amanda Barron, Jocelyn Rachel, Tiger Coleman, Ann Podlozny, Nate Coleman, Stephen Cebik, Kristin Kuttner, Jane Nichols, Benjamin Smith, Walton Wilson, Craig Bacon, Christine Calfas, Erik Sherr, Shawn Elinoff, Brett Penney, David F. Vaillancourt Jr.

A MIDSUMMER NIGHT'S DREAM by William Shakespeare; Director, Tony Simotes; Costumes, Tracy Hinman; Sets, Jim Youngerman; Lighting, Steve Ball CAST: Hugh d'Autermont, Jen Bosworth, Justine Moore, Antonia Freeland, Marybeth Bentwood, Ted Hewlett, Krstin Kuttner, Leslie Toth, Max Vogler, Susan Keill, Stephen Cebik, Kay Arita, Dave Vaillancourt, Jonah Bay, Christine Calfas.

TWELFTH NIGHT by William Shakespeare; Directors, Dennis Krausnick, Virginia Ness Ray; Costumes, Tracy Hinman; Sets, Patricik Brennan CAST: David White, Shawn Elinoff, James Louis Levine, Jocelyn Rosenthal, Brett Penney, Amanda Barron, Derrick Sanders, Ken Butler, Benjamin Smith, Rebecca Holderness, Erik Sherr, Rob Pensalfini, Randy Petrides.

THE WINTER'S TALE by William Shakespeare; Director, Rocco Sisto; Costumes, Arthur Oliver; Sets, Diva Locks Burrows; Lighting, Steve Ball CAST: Malcolm Ingram, Jonathan Croy, John Hadden, Virginia Ness Ray, Tiger Coleman, Ariel Bock, Walton Wilson, Elizabeth Aspenlieder, Jason Asprey.

THE WHARTON ONE-ACTS: THE PRETEXT, adapted by Alison Ragland; THE VERDICT, adapted by Jim Nutter; Directors, Andrew Borthwick-Leslie, Jonathan Epstein; Costumes, Celestine Ranney-Howes; Sets, Patrick Brennan; Lighting, Harry Rosenblum, Steve Ball CAST: Robin Hynek, Diane Prusha, Robert Lohbauer, John Beale, Andrew Borthwick-Leslie, Karen Torbjornsen.

ETHAN FROME; Adapted from Edith Wharton by Dennis Krausnick; Director, Dennis Krausnick; Costumes, Govane Lohbauer; Sets, Jim Youngerman; Lighting, Steve Ball CAST: Josef Hansen, Kevin G. Coleman, Annette Miller, Elizabeth Aspenlieder.

BRIEF LIVES; Adapted from John Aubrey by Patrick Garland; Director, Andrew Borthwick-Leslie; Costumes, Arthur Oliver; Sets, Patrick Brennan; Lighting, Steve Ball, Harry Rosenblum CAST: Jonathan Epstein.

BETRAYAL by Harold Pinter; Director, Normi Noel; Costumes, Govane Lohbauer; Sets, Patrick Brenna; Lighting, Steve Ball CAST: Corinna May, Allyn Burrows, Dan McCleary, Marc Scipione.

Rick Bambery Photos

Allyn Burrows, Dan McCleary in *Henry IV, Part I*

Allyn Burrows, Corinna May in *Betrayal*

Kevin Coleman, Josef Hansen in *Ethan Frome*

SOUTH COAST REPERTORY

Costa Mesa, California

Thirty-third Season

Producing Artistic Director, David Emmes; Artistic Director, Martin Benson; Press, Cristofer Gross.

DIRECTORS: Martin Benson, David Chambers, David Emmes, James Lapine, John-David Keller, Lisa Peterson, Mark Rucker, Seret Scott, Octavio Solis, Evan Yionoulis

ACTORS: Hope Alexander-Willis, Philip Anglim, Rene Augesen, Tom Beckett, Simon Billig, Rona Binebaum, Ron Boussom, Michael Reilly Burke, Mark Capri, Lars Carlson, Kandis Chappell, Patricia Clarkson, Tsai Chin, Suzanne Cryer, Robert Curtis-Brown, Nike Doukas, Richard Doyle, Brian Drillinger, Stan Egi, John Ellington, Joshua Farerell, Michael Faulkner, Colby French, George Galvan, Debbie Grattan, Crissy Guerrero, Jeanie Hackett, Dorian Harewood, Nancy Harewood, John Christopher Jones, Ella Joyce, John-David Keller, Patrick, Kerr, Colette Kilroy, Susan Knight, Art Koustik, Hal Landon Jr., Benjamin Livingston, Jodi Long, Jane Macfie, Benito Martinez, Lynsey McLeod, Martha McFarland, Lynn Milgrim, Allan Miller, Marnie Nosiman, Patrick O'Connell, Liana Pai, Susan Patterson, Jeanne Paulsen, Larry Paulsen, Julia Pearlstein, Devon Raymond, Thom Rivera, Marco Rodriguez, Susannah Schulman, John Slattery, Julyana Soelistyo, Richard Soto, Michael Strickland, Jack Sydow, Hisa Takakuwa, Jon Tenney, Darryl Thierse, Don Took, Vetza Trussell, Deborah Van Valkenburgh, Teresa Velarde, Renee Victor, James Warwick, Karen Malina White, Paxton Whitehead, Mary Kay Wulf

PRODUCTIONS: *An Ideal Husband* by Oscar Wilde, *Six Degrees of Separation* by John Guare; *Golden Child* by David Henry Hwang, *The Triumph of Love* by Marivaux, *Death of a Salesman* by Arthur Miller, *How the Other Half Loves* by Alan Ayckbourn, *A Christmas Carol* by Charles Dickens, adapted by Jerry Patch; *Crumbs from the Table of Joy* by Lynn Nottage, *Collected Stories* by Donald Margulies, *Bafo* by Tom Strelich, *Three Days of Rain* by Richard Greenberg, *Old Times* by Harold Pinter, *La Posada Magica* by Octavio Solis

Michal Daniel Photo

Patricia Clarkson, John Slattery, Jon Tenney in *Three Days of Rain*

VIRGINIA STAGE COMPANY

Norfolk, Virginia

Artistic Director, Charlie Hensley; Managing Director, Steven Martin; Press, Laura E. Laing

THE MYSTERY OF IRMA VEP by Charles Ludlam; Director, Chris Clavelli; Sets, Dex Edwards; Costumes, Howard Tsvi Kaplan; Lighting, Joe Saint

SNAPSHOTS; Music/Lyrics, Stephen Schwartz; Conception, Michael Scheman and David Stern; Book, Mr. Stern; Additional Music/Lyrics, David Crane, Marta Kauffman, Seth Friedman, Charles Strouse; Director, Mr. Scheman; Musical Director, Andrew Lippa; Sets, James Youmans; Costumes, Howard Tsvi Kaplan; Lighting, Kenton Yeager

TERRA NOVA by Ted Tally; Director, Charlie Hensley; Sets, Chris Pickart; Costumes, Paticia Darden; Lighting, Kenton L. Yeager

TWELFTH NIGHT by William Shakespeare; Director, Charlie Hensley; Sets, Dex Edwards; Costumes, Constance Hoffman; Lighting, Kenton L. Yeager

ALWAYS...PATSY CLINE; Written/Directed by Ted Swindley; Sets, Chris Pickart; Costumes, Patty Darden; Lighting, Liz Lee

Helen Anrod Jones Photo

Snapshots Company

WILLIAMSTOWN THEATRE FESTIVAL

Williamstown, Massachusetts

Producer, Michael Ritchie

THE MILK TRAIN DOESN'T STOP HERE ANYMORE by Tennessee Williams; Director, David Schweizer; Sets, James Noone; Costumes, Laura Cunningham; Lighting, Rui Rita CAST: Olympia Dukakis, Anne Scurria, Garret Dillahunt, Mary Louise Wilson, Ned Van Zandt, Juan Hernandez, Theresa Lamm, Christopher Fitzgerald, Ronobir Lahiri, Pete Simpson

THE ROYAL FAMILY by George S. Kaufman and Edna Ferber; Director, Nicholas Martin; Sets, James Noone; Costumes, Michael Krass; Lighting, Rui Rita CAST: Kate Burton, John Hines, Josh Stamberg, Matt Schapiro, Sam Wright, Simon Jones, Andrea Martin, Hope Davis, Hank Stratton, Marian Seldes, Jerry Grayson, Blythe Danner, Victor Garber, William Dawes, Munson Hicks, Gregory Wallace, Kandis Chappell

THE RIDE DOWN MOUNT MORGAN by Arthur Miller; Director, Scott Elliott; Sets, Derek McLane; Costumes, Eric Becker; Lighting, Brian MacDevitt CAST: Adina Porter, F. Murray Abraham, Ben Hammer, Michael Learned, Amy Ryan, Patricia Clarkson, Larry Bryggman

THE LEARNED LADIES by Moliere; Translation, Richard Wilbur; Director, Jim Simpson; Sets, Narelle Sissons; Costumes, Claudia Brown; Lighting, Frances Aronson CAST: Kate Burton, Jill Tasker, Hank Stratton, Kandis Chappell, Munson Hicks, Richard Libertini, Becky Ann Baker, Miriam Margolyes, Gregory Wallace, Pete Simpson, William Dawes, Josh Stamberg, Liam Craig, Winslow Corbett, Mark Doskow, Robert Serrell, Elisabeth Waterston

FILUMENA by Eduardo de Filippo; Translation, Maria Tucci; Director, James Naughton; Sets, Hugh Landwehr; Costumes, David Murin; Lighting, Rui Rita CAST: Tony Amendola, Joe Grifasi, Maria Tucci, Mary Fogarty, Denise Faye, Greg Naughton, Lenny Venito, Juan Hernandez, Beata Fido, Christopher Fitzgerald, Eric Blossom, Suzi Takahashi, Josh Stamberg

Richard Feldman Photos

Patricia Clarkson, F. Murray Abraham, Michael Learned in *Ride Down Mt. Morgan*

Pete Simpson, Kate Burton, Kandis Chappell, Gregory Wallace, Miriam Margolyes in *Learned Ladies*

YALE REPERTORY THEATRE

New Haven, Connecticut

Artistic Director, Stan Wojewodski, Jr.; Managing Director, Victoria Nolan; Associate Artistic Director, Mark Bly; Press Director, Martha Bowden

FIRST LADY by Katharine Dayton, George S. Kaufman; Director, Stan Wojewodski, Jr.; Sets, John Coyne; Costumes, Meg Neville; Lighting, Stephen Strawbridge CAST: Pippa Pearthree, Herman A. Shemonsky, Kim Wimmer, Maureen Anderman, Sam Groom, Peg Murray, Karen Lee Pickett, Kimberly Ross, Annette Granucci, Susan Browning, Don Chastain, Russ Anderson, Cecilia Hart, George Ede, Ken Parker, John Randolph Jones, Ken Parker, Joe Reynolds.

TRIUMPH OF LOVE; Book, James Magruder; Music, Jeffrey Stock; Lyrics, Susan Birkenhead; Director, Michael Mayer; Choreographer, Doug Varone; Musical Director, Bradley Vieth; Sets, Heidi Landesman; Costumes, Catherine Zuber; Lighting, Brian MacDevitt CAST: Susan Egan, Denny Dillon, Christopher Sieber, Robert LuPone, Mary Beth Peil, Kenny Raskin, Daniel Marcus.

THE SKIN OF OUR TEETH by Thornton Wilder; Director, Liz Diamond; Sets, Walt Spangler; Costumes, Michael Oberle; Lighting, Jennifer Tipton CAST: Amy Cronise, Jackeline Duprey, Svetlana Efremova, Annette Granucci, Elizabeth Greer, John Hines, Clark Jackson, Tod Kent, Jill Marie Lawrence, Christopher Mattox, Obi Ndefo, Paul Niebanck, Evan Dexter Parke, Scott C. Reeves, Joe Reynolds, James Shankin, Brandy Zarle.

THE ADVENTURES OF AMY BROCK by Julie McKee; Director, Stan Wojewodski, Jr.; Sets, Scott Pask; Costumes, Suttirat Larlarb; Lighting, Les Dickert CAST: Enid Graham, Alec Phoenix, Blair Sams, Sandra Shipley, Audrie Neenan, Reno Roop, Frank Deal, Kristine Nielsen.

THUNDER KNOCKING ON THE DOOR by Keith Glover; Director, Reggie Montgomery; Music/Lyrics, Keb' Mo'; Musical Director, Steve Bargonetti; Sets, Charles McClennahan; Costumes, Jess Goldstein; Lighting, Donald Holder CAST: Cedric Turner, Ron Cephas Jones, Jerry Dixon, Kim Brockington, Sheyvonne Wright.

T. Charles Erickson, Martha Bowden Photos

Top: Susan Egan in *Triumph of Love*
Center: Blair Sams, Frank Deal, Enid Graham in
Adventures of Amy Bock
Right: Jerry Dixon, Cedric Turner, Sheyvonne Wright in
Thunder Knocking on the Door

NATIONAL TOURING COMPANY HIGHLIGHTS

DEATHTRAP

By Ira Levin; Director, John Tillinger; Sets, James Noone; Costumes, Jess Goldstein; Lighting, Ken Billington; Stage Manager, Thomas P. Carr; Presented by Magic Promotoions & Theatricals, Pace Theatrical Group, and Manny Kladitis

CAST: Elliott Gould, Mariette Hartley succeeded by Alexandra O'Karma and Cindy Williams, Douglas Wert, Marilyn Cooper, Doug Stender

Elliott Gould, Mariette Hartley, Douglas Wert in *Deathtrap*

THE DIARIES OF ADAM AND EVE

By Mark Twain; Adaptation/Direction, David Birney; Music, Jac Redford; Lighting, Robert Mumm; Stage Manager, Tracy Stickfaden; Presented by Grail Productions

CAST: David Birney, Harriet Hall

David Birney, Harriet Hall in *Diaries of Adam and Eve*

GREASE

For creative credits see BROADWAY- PAST SEASONS section; Director/Choreography, Jeff Calhoun; Musical Director, John Samorian; Presented by Barry & Fran Weissler and Jujamcyn Theatres

CASTS: Adrian Zmed, Rex Smith, Jon Secada, Joseph Barbara, Mackenzie Phillips, Sally Struthers, Brian Bradley, Kevin-Anthony, Christopher Carothers, Roy Chicas, Stephen Gnojewski, Jennifer Hughes, David Josefberg, Beth Lipari, Lori Lynch, Cory Middlebrook,, Stefani Rae, Stephanie Seeley, Kelli Bond Secerson, Shannon Bailey, Ashton Byrum, Thomas M. Conroy, Amy Dolan, Scot Fedderly, Christa Jackson, Joelle Letta, Greg LoBuono, Flynn Roberts, Mary Ruvolo, Thomas Scott, Loren Stolarsky, Michael Lee Wright, Dody Goodman, Mimi Hines, Anegela Pupello, Wendy Springer, Debbie Gibson, Sheena Easton, Jasmine Guy, Tracy Nelson, Scott Beck, Ric Ryder, Douglas Crawford, Steve Geyer, Jennifer Naimo, Megan Lawrence, Trisha M. Gorman, Sutton Foster, Lacey Hornkohl, Melissa Papp, Lesley Jennings, Leanna Polk, Lee Truesdale, Davy Jones, Mickey Dolenz, Don Most, Nick Santa Maria, Joe Piscopo, Brian Bradley, Peter Scolari

Carol Rosegg Photo

Adrian Zmed in *Grease*

Lee Roy Reams, Scott Bridges in *Hello Dolly!*

HELLO, DOLLY!

Music/Lyrics, Jerry Herman; Book, Michael Stewart; Director, Lee Roy Reams; For other creative credits see last season's Broadway engagement in Theatre World Vol.52

CAST INCLUDES: Carol Channing, Jeanne Lehman, Lee Roy Reams, Scott Bridges

Joan Marcus Photo

JOSEPH AND THE AMAZING TECHNICOLOR DREAMCOAT

Music, Andrew Lloyd Webber; Lyrics, Tim Rice; Director, Steven Pimlott; Design, Mark Thompson; Choreography, Anthony Van Laast; Lighting, Andrew Bridge; Musical Director, Kevin Finn; Presented by Livent (US) and The Really Usefull Theatre Company

CAST: Donny Osmond, Donna Kane, James Harms, Johnny Seaton, Miguel Lange, Erich McMillan-McCall, Julia Alicia Fowler, Patrick Wetzel, Coleen Braganza, Robin Lyon, Stephen R. Buntrock, Glenn Sneed, Stephen Campanella, Sal Scozzari, Chuck Saculla, Joey Gyondla, Alton Fitzgerald White, Jamie Dawn Gangi, Melanie Malicote, Jacquie Porter, Angela O'Donnell, Stacey Haughton, Susan Craig, Juliann Kuchocki, Gail Matheson, Risa Waldman

Catherine Ashmore Photo

Donny Osmond in *Joseph...and the Dreamcoat*

Faye Dunaway in *Master Class*

MASTER CLASS

By Terrence McNally; Director, Leonard Foglia; For other creative credits see BROADWAY-PAST SEASONS section; Press, Bill Evans

CAST; Faye Dunaway, Gary Green, Melinda Klump, Scott Davidson,. Suzan Hanson, Kevin Paul Anderson

Joan Marcus Photo

PHANTOM OF THE OPERA

Music, Andrew Lloyd Webber; Lyrics, Charles Hart, Richard Stilgoe; Book, Mr. Stilgoe, Lloyd Webber; Director, Harold Prince; Musical Directors, John David Scott, Mark McLaren; For other creative credits see BROADWAY-PAST SEASONS section

(I) Franc D'Ambrosio, Lisa Vroman, Christopher Carl, Richard Gould, Joseph Dellger, Geena Jeffries, Ravil Atlas, Connie Dykstra, Jennifer Gould, Cristin Mortenson, Madelyn Berdes, Kathryn Blake, Connie Marie Chambers, Robert Close, Marcie L. Conat, Marcia Cope-Hart, Cecilia Dangcil, Henrietta Davis-Blackmon, Ron Ealy, Mark Erickson, Michael Gerhart, Randall Gremillion, Jennifer Kulz, Michael M. Lackey, Martin Lewis, Deborah Milsom, John P. Minagro, Linda Montaner, Amy Moorhead, Nancy Dobbs Owen, Robert K. Rutt, David Scamardo, Lee Strawn, John Swenson, Michael F. Taylor, Traci Tornquist, Krista Wigle, Wendee Yung

(II) Rick Hilsabeck, Sandra Joseph, Lawrence Anderson, Ian Jon Bourg, T.J. Meyers, Kelly Ellenwood, Olga Talyn, Stefano Fucile, Kitty Skillman Hilsabeck, Kate Suber, Diane Anastasio, Roger Befeler, Steve Blair, Bill Carmichael, Valerie DeBartolo, Dorene Falcetta, Leslie Giammanco, Susan Gladstone, Stephen Gould, James R. Guthrie, Robert Hildreth, Robert Hovencamp, Rebecca Jefferson, Leslie Judge, Brad Keating, Jennifer Little, Antonio Lopez, David Loring, Paula LoVerne, Jayne Ackley Lynch, Mary Jo Mc Connell, Scott Mikita, Susan Owen, Richard L. Reardon, Karalyn Rutherford, Lawson Skala, Laura Streets, Susan Zaguire

Joan Marcus Photo

T.J. Meyers, Ian Jon Bourg in *Phantom of the Opera*

Paul Provenza, Rebecca Creskoff, Mark Nelson in *Picasso at the Lapin Agile*

PICASSO AT THE LAPIN AGILE

By Steve Martin; Director, Randall Arney; Set, Scott Bradley; Costumes, Patricia Zipprodt; Lighting, Kevin Rigdon; Stage Managers, Mark Cole, Alice Elliott Smith; Press, Peter Cromarty; Presented by Stephen Eich, Joan Stein, Richard Martini, Leavitt/Fox Theatricals/Mages

CASTS: Mark Nelson (Einstein), Paul Provenza (Picasso), Ian Barford, Ken Grantham, Kimberly King, James Kruk, Jim Mohr, Michael Oosterom, Susannah Schulman, Robert Ari, Bill Buell, Rebecca Creskoff, Peter Jacobson, Richard Kuss, Gabriel Macht, Rondi Reed

Marty Sohl Photo

RENT

Music/Lyrics/Book, Jonathan Larson; Director, Michael Greif; Musical Director, Jim Abbott; For other creative credits see BROADWAY-PAST SEASONS section; Presented by Jeffrey Seller, Kevin McCollum, Alan S. Gordon and New York Theatre Workshop; Tour opened in Boston's Shubert Theatre on November 18, 1996

CAST: Sean Keller, Manley Pope, Luther Creek, C.C. Brown, James Rich, Sylvia MacCalla, Stephan Alexander, Simone, Carrie Hamilton, Amy Spangler, Cristina Ablaza, Christian Anderson, Julie P. (Relova) Danao, D'Monroe, Ray Garcia, Lambert Moss, John Eric Parker, Queen Esther, Daniel J. Robbins, Schlee Williams

Joan Marcus/Carol Rosegg Photo

Luther Creek, C.C. Brown, Manley Pope in *Rent*

Julie Harris in *Sonya*

SONYA

By Leon Katz; Director, Bram Lewis; Sets, Campbell Baird; Costumes, Amela Baksic; Lighting, Dennis Parichy, Shawn K. Kaufman; Stage Manager, Anne Marie Paolucci; Presented by The Phoenix Theatre Company; Opened July 2, 1996 at SUNY/Purchase, New York

CAST: Julie Harris, Van Cockcroft, Philip Baker Hall, Jennifer Harmon, Miriam Healy-Louie, Timothy Jerome, Eileen McMahon, Daniel Marcus, Jud Meyers, Tony O'Donoghue, Christopher Ries, Reno Roop, Peter Smith, Carol Todes, Branislav Tomich, Jonathan Turner

Gerry Goodstein Photo

SUNSET BLVD.

Music, Andrew Lloyd Webber; Lyrics/Book, Don Black and Christopher Hampton; Director, Trevor Nunn; For other creative credits see BROAD-WAY-PAST SEASONS section; Press, Boneau~Bryan-Brown; Presented by The Really Useful Company; Tour opened at Denver Center for the Performing Arts on June 28, 1996

CAST: Linda Balgord (Norma), Ron Bohmer (Joe), Ed Dixon (Max), Lauren Kennedy (Betty), William Chapman, James Clow, John Antony, Philip Michael Baskerville, Sandy Binion, Carol Denise, David Dollase, Harvey Evans, Jennifer Frankel, Fiama Fricano, Mark Hardy, Leslie Trayer Harvery, Pamela Jordan, Randal Keith, Kenny Morris, Joan Leslie Simms, Timothy Smith, William Solo, Mark Edgar Stephens, Jillana Urbi

TORONTO CAST: Diahann Carroll (Norma), Rex Smith (Joe), Walter Charles (Max), Anita Louise Combe (Betty), John Braden, Christopher Shyer, Barbara Barsky, Timothy J. Alex, Christine Brooks, Marilyn Caskey, Betsy Chang, Paul Clausen, Michael Fawkes, Susan Gattoni, Sara Henry, Brian Hill, John Hoshko, Mary Illes, Peter Kevoian, George Kmeck, Lisa Mandel, Marianne McCord, Gordon Mclaren, Lindsey Mitchell, Martin Murphy, Avery Saltzman, Jennifer Stetor, Matthew Thibedeau, James Vezina

Joan Marcus Photos

Ron Bohmer, Linda Balgord

Linda Balgord, Ron Bohmer

214

1997 Theatre World Award Recipients
(Outstanding New Talent)

Terry Beaver of *Last Night of Ballyhoo*

Helen Carey of *London Assurance*

Kristin Chenoweth of *Steel Pier*

Jason Danieley of *Candide*

Linda Eder of *Jekyll & Hyde*

Daniel McDonald of *Steel Pier*

Mark Ruffalo of *This Is Our Youth*

Allison Janney of *Present Laughter*

216

Janet McTeer of *A Doll's House*

Antony Sher of *Stanley*

Alan Tudyk of *Bunny Bunny*

Fiona Shaw of *The Waste Land*

Alec Baldwin

Karen Kay Cody

JohnLeguizamo

1944-45: Betty Comden, Richard Davis, Richard Hart, Judy Holliday, Charles Lang, Bambi Linn, John Lund, Donald Murphy, Nancy Noland, Margaret Phillips, John Raitt
1945-46: Barbara Bel Geddes, Marlon Brando, Bill Callahan, Wendell Corey, Paul Douglas, Mary James, Burt Lancaster, Patricia Marshall, Beatrice Pearson
1946-47: Keith Andes, Marion Bell, Peter Cookson, Ann Crowley, Ellen Hanley, John Jordan, George Keane, Dorothea MacFarland, James Mitchell, Patricia Neal, David Wayne
1947-48: Valerie Bettis, Edward Bryce, Whitfield Connor, Mark Dawson, June Lockhart, Estelle Loring, Peggy Maley, Ralph Meeker, Meg Mundy, Douglass Watson, James Whitmore, Patrice Wymore
1948-49: Tod Andrews, Doe Avedon, Jean Carson, Carol Channing, Richard Derr, Julie Harris, Mary McCarty, Allyn Ann McLerie, Cameron Mitchell, Gene Nelson, Byron Palmer, Bob Scheerer
1949-50: Nancy Andrews, Phil Arthur, Barbara Brady, Lydia Clarke, Priscilla Gillette, Don Hanmer, Marcia Henderson, Charlton Heston, Rick Jason, Grace Kelly, Charles Nolte, Roger Price
1950-51: Barbara Ashley, Isabel Bigley, Martin Brooks, Richard Burton, Pat Crowley, James Daley, Cloris Leachman, Russell Nype, Jack Palance, William Smithers, Maureen Stapleton, Marcia Van Dyke, Eli Wallach
1951-52: Tony Bavaar, Patricia Benoit, Peter Conlow, Virginia de Luce, Ronny Graham, Audrey Hepburn, Diana Herbert, Conrad Janis, Dick Kallman, Charles Proctor, Eric Sinclair, Kim Stanley, Marian Winters, Helen Wood
1952-53: Edie Adams, Rosemary Harris, Eileen Heckart, Peter Kelley, John Kerr, Richard Kiley, Gloria Marlowe, Penelope Munday, Paul Newman, Sheree North, Geraldine Page, John Stewart, Ray Stricklyn, Gwen Verdon
1953-54: Orson Bean, Harry Belafonte, James Dean, Joan Diener, Ben Gazzara,

Carol Haney, Jonathan Lucas, Kay Medford, Scott Merrill, Elizabeth Montgomery, Leo Penn, Eva Marie Saint
1954-55: Julie Andrews, Jacqueline Brookes, Shirl Conway, Barbara Cook, David Daniels, Mary Fickett, Page Johnson, Loretta Leversee, Jack Lord, Dennis Patrick, Anthony Perkins, Christopher Plummer
1955-56: Diane Cilento, Dick Davalos, Anthony Franciosa, Andy Griffith, Laurence Harvey, David Hedison, Earle Hyman, Susan Johnson, John Michael King, Jayne Mansfield, Sara Marshall, Gaby Rodgers, Susan Strasberg, Fritz Weaver
1956-57: Peggy Cass, Sydney Chaplin, Sylvia Daneel, Bradford Dillman, Peter Donat, George Grizzard, Carol Lynley, Peter Palmer, Jason Robards, Cliff Robertson, Pippa Scott, Inga Swenson
1957-58: Anne Bancroft, Warren Berlinger, Colleen Dewhurst, Richard Easton, Tim Everett, Eddie Hodges, Joan Hovis, Carol Lawrence, Jacqueline McKeever, Wynne Miller, Robert Morse, George C. Scott
1958-59: Lou Antonio, Ina Balin, Richard Cross, Tammy Grimes, Larry Hagman, Dolores Hart, Roger Mollien, France Nuyen, Susan Oliver, Ben Piazza, Paul Roebling, William Shatner, Pat Suzuki, Rip Torn
1959-60: Warren Beatty, Eileen Brennan, Carol Burnett, Patty Duke, Jane Fonda, Anita Gillette, Elisa Loti, Donald Madden, George Maharis, John McMartin, Lauri Peters, Dick Van Dyke
1960-61: Joyce Bulifant, Dennis Cooney, Sandy Dennis, Nancy Dussault, Robert Goulet, Joan Hackett, June Harding, Ron Husmann, James MacArthur, Bruce Yarnell
1961-62: Elizabeth Ashley, Keith Baxter, Peter Fonda, Don Galloway, Sean Garrison, Barbara Harris, James Earl Jones, Janet Margolin, Karen Morrow, Robert Redford, John Stride, Brenda Vaccaro
1962-63: Alan Arkin, Stuart Damon, Melinda Dillon, Robert Drivas, Bob Gentry,

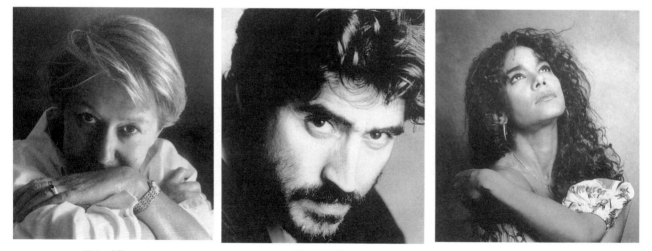

Helen Mirren

Alfred Molina

Daphne Rubin-Vega

218

Dorothy Loudon, Brandon Maggart, Julienne Marie, Liza Minnelli, Estelle Parsons, Diana Sands, Swen Swenson

1963-64: Alan Alda, Gloria Bleezarde, Imelda De Martin, Claude Giraud, Ketty Lester, Barbara Loden, Lawrence Pressman, Gilbert Price, Philip Proctor, John Tracy, Jennifer West

1964-65: Carolyn Coates, Joyce Jillson, Linda Lavin, Luba Lisa, Michael O'Sullivan, Joanna Pettet, Beah Richards, Jaime Sanchez, Victor Spinetti, Nicolas Surovy, Robert Walker, Clarence Williams III

1965-66: Zoe Caldwell, David Carradine, John Cullum, John Davidson, Faye Dunaway, Gloria Foster, Robert Hooks, Jerry Lanning, Richard Mulligan, April Shawhan, Sandra Smith, Leslie Ann Warren

1966-67: Bonnie Bedelia, Richard Benjamin, Dustin Hoffman, Terry Kiser, Reva Rose, Robert Salvio, Sheila Smith, Connie Stevens, Pamela Tiffin, Leslie Uggams, Jon Voight, Christopher Walken

1967-68: David Birney, Pamela Burrell, Jordan Christopher, Jack Crowder (Thalmus Rasulala), Sandy Duncan, Julie Gregg, Stephen Joyce, Bernadette Peters, Alice Playten, Michael Rupert, Brenda Smiley, Russ Thacker

1968-69: Jane Alexander, David Cryer, Blythe Danner, Ed Evanko, Ken Howard, Lauren Jones, Ron Leibman, Marian Mercer, Jill O'Hara, Ron O'Neal, Al Pacino, Marlene Warfield

1969-70: Susan Browning, Donny Burks, Catherine Burns, Len Cariou, Bonnie Franklin, David Holliday, Katharine Houghton, Melba Moore, David Rounds, Lewis J. Stadlen, Kristoffer Tabori, Fredricka Weber

1970-71: Clifton Davis, Michael Douglas, Julie Garfield, Martha Henry, James Naughton, Tricia O'Neil, Kipp Osborne, Roger Rathburn, Ayn Ruymen, Jennifer Salt, Joan Van Ark, Walter Willison

1971-72: Jonelle Allen, Maureen Anderman, William Atherton, Richard Backus, Adrienne Barbeau, Cara Duff-MacCormick, Robert Foxworth, Elaine Joyce, Jess Richards, Ben Vereen, Beatrice Winde, James Woods

1972-73: D'Jamin Bartlett, Patricia Elliott, James Farentino, Brian Farrell, Victor Garber, Kelly Garrett, Mari Gorman, Laurence Guittard, Trish Hawkins, Monte Markham, John Rubinstein, Jennifer Warren, Alexander H. Cohen (Special Award)

1973-74: Mark Baker, Maureen Brennan, Ralph Carter, Thom Christopher, John Driver, Conchata Ferrell, Ernestine Jackson, Michael Moriarty, Joe Morton, Ann Reinking, Janie Sell, Mary Woronov, Sammy Cahn (Special Award)

1974-75: Peter Burnell, Zan Charisse, Lola Falana, Peter Firth, Dorian Harewood, Joel Higgins, Marcia McClain, Linda Miller, Marti Rolph, John Sheridan, Scott Stevensen, Donna Theodore, Equity Library Theatre (Special Award)

1975-76: Danny Aiello, Christine Andreas, Dixie Carter, Tovah Feldshuh, Chip Garnett, Richard Kelton, Vivian Reed, Charles Repole, Virginia Seidel, Daniel Seltzer, John V. Shea, Meryl Streep, A Chorus Line (Special Award)

1976-77: Trazana Beverley, Michael Cristofer, Joe Fields, Joanna Gleason, Cecilia Hart, John Heard, Gloria Hodes, Juliette Koka, Andrea McArdle, Ken Page, Jonathan Pryce, Chick Vennera, Eva LeGallienne (Special Award)

1977-78: Vasili Bogazianos, Nell Carter, Carlin Glynn, Christopher Goutman, William Hurt, Judy Kaye, Florence Lacy, Armelia McQueen, Gordana Rashovich, Bo Rucker, Richard Seer, Colin Stinton, Joseph Papp (Special Award)

1978-79: Philip Anglim, Lucie Arnaz, Gregory Hines, Ken Jennings, Michael Jeter, Laurie Kennedy, Susan Kingsley, Christine Lahti, Edward James Olmos, Kathleen Quinlan, Sarah Rice, Max Wright, Marshall W. Mason (Special Award)

1979-80: Maxwell Caulfield, Leslie Denniston, Boyd Gaines, Richard Gere, Harry

Groener, Stephen James, Susan Kellermann, Dinah Manoff, Lonny Price, Marianne Tatum, Anne Twomey, Dianne Wiest, Mickey Rooney (Special Award)

1980-81: Brian Backer, Lisa Banes, Meg Bussert, Michael Allen Davis, Giancarlo Esposito, Daniel Gerroll, Phyllis Hyman, Cynthia Nixon, Amanda Plummer, Adam Redfield, Wanda Richert, Rex Smith, Elizabeth Taylor (Special Award)

1981-82: Karen Akers, Laurie Beechman, Danny Glover, David Alan Grier, Jennifer Holliday, Anthony Heald, Lizbeth Mackay, Peter MacNicol, Elizabeth McGovern, Ann Morrison, Michael O'Keefe, James Widdoes, Manhattan Theatre Club (Special Award)

1982-83: Karen Allen, Suzanne Bertish, Matthew Broderick, Kate Burton, Joanne Camp, Harvey Fierstein, Peter Gallagher, John Malkovich, Anne Pitoniak, James Russo, Brian Tarantina, Linda Thorson, Natalia Makarova (Special Award)

1983-84: Martine Allard, Joan Allen, Kathy Whitton Baker, Mark Capri, Laura Dean, Stephen Geoffreys, Todd Graff, Glenne Headly, J.J. Johnston, Bonnie Koloc, Calvin Levels, Robert Westenberg, Ron Moody (Special Award)

1984-85: Kevin Anderson, Richard Chaves, Patti Cohenour, Charles S. Dutton, Nancy Giles, Whoopi Goldberg, Leilani Jones, John Mahoney, Laurie Metcalf, Barry Miller, John Turturro, Amelia White, Lucille Lortel (Special Award)

1985-86: Suzy Amis, Alec Baldwin, Aled Davies, Faye Grant, Julie Hagerty, Ed Harris, Mark Jacoby, Donna Kane, Cleo Laine, Howard McGillin, Marisa Tomei, Joe Urla, Ensemble Studio Theatre (Special Award)

1986-87: Annette Bening, Timothy Daly, Lindsay Duncan, Frank Ferrante, Robert Lindsay, Amy Madigan, Michael Maguire, Demi Moore, Molly Ringwald, Frances Ruffelle, Courtney B. Vance, Colm Wilkinson, Robert DeNiro (Special Award)

1987-88: Yvonne Bryceland, Philip Casnoff, Danielle Ferland, Melissa Gilbert, Linda Hart, Linzi Hately, Brian Kerwin, Brian Mitchell, Mary Murfitt, Aidan Quinn, Eric Roberts, B.D. Wong, Special Awards: Tisa Chang, Martin E. Segal.

1988-89: Dylan Baker, Joan Cusack, Loren Dean, Peter Frechette, Sally Mayes, Sharon McNight, Jennie Moreau, Paul Provenza, Kyra Sedgwick, Howard Spiegel, Eric Stoltz, Joanne Whalley-Kilmer, Special Awards: Pauline Collins, Mikhail Baryshnikov

1989-90: Denise Burse, Erma Campbell, Megan Gallagher, Tommy Hollis, Robert Lambert, Kathleen Rowe McAllen, Michael McKean, Crista Moore, Mary-Louise Parker, Daniel von Bargen, Jason Workman, Special Awards: Stewart Granger, Kathleen Turner

1990-91: Jane Adams, Gillian Anderson, Adam Arkin, Brenda Blethyne, Marcus Chong, Paul Hipp, LaChanze, Kenny Neal, Kevin Ramsey, Francis Ruivivar, Lea Salonga, Chandra Wilson, Special Awards: Tracey Ullman, Ellen Stewart

1991-92: Talia Balsam, Lindsay Crouse, Griffin Dunne, Larry Fishburne, Mel Harris, Jonathan Kaplan, Jessica Lange, Laura Linney, Spiro Malas, Mark Rosenthal, Helen Shaver, Al White, Special Awards: *Dancing at Lughnasa* company, *Plays for Living.*

1992-93: Brent Carver, Michael Cerveris, Marcia Gay Harden, Stephanie Lawrence, Andrea Martin, Liam Neeson, Stephen Rea, Natasha Richardson, Martin Short, Dina Spybey, Stephen Spinella, Jennifer Tilly. Special Awards: John Leguizamo, Rosetta LeNoire.

1993-94: Marcus D'Amico, Jarrod Emick, Arabella Field, Adam Gillett, Sherry Glaser, Michael Hayden, Margaret Illman, Audra Ann McDonald, Burke Moses, Anna Deavere Smith, Jere Shea, Harriet Walter.

1994-95: Gretha Boston, Billy Crudup, Ralph Fiennes, Beverly D'Angelo, Calista Flockhart, Kevin Kilner, Anthony LaPaglia, Julie Johnson, Helen Mirren, Jude Law, Rufus Sewell, Vanessa Williams, Special Award: Brooke Shields

1995-96: Jordan Baker, Joohee Choi, Karen Kay Cody, Viola Davis, Kate Forbes, Michael McGrath, Alfred Molina, Timothy Olyphant, Adam Pascal, Lou Diamond Phillips, Daphne Rubin-Vega, Brett Tabisel, Special Award: *An Ideal Husband* Cast

1997 Special Theatre World Award: Cast of *Skylight*
Michael Gambon, Lia Williams, Christian Camargo (not pictured)

219

THEATRE WORLD AWARDS

PRESENTED IN THE ROUNDABOUT THEATRE ON THURSDAY MAY 29, 1997

Top: Chritsopher Plummer, Patricia Elliott, Ken Page, Mary Murfitt, Michael Cerveris, Carol Channing; Peter Filichia; Julie Harris, John Cullum, Leslie Ann Warren, Lou Diamond Phillips, Talia Balsam, Matthew Broderick
Below: Patricia Elliott; Robert Roznowski, Jordan Leeds, Melissa Weil, Jennifer Simard of "I Love You, You're Perfect, Now Change;" Carol Channing
3rd Row: Alan Tudyk, Carol Channing, Ken Page; John Cullum, Matthew Broderick, Leslie Ann Warren;
Bottom: Julie Harris, Patricia Elliot, Maia Walter; Linda Eder, Kristin Chenoweth; Terry Beaver

Top: Christian Camargo; Lisa Williams; Alan Tudyk; Fiona Shaw; Michael Gambon
Below: Lou Diamond Phillips; Daniel McDonald, Jere Shea, Joyce Van Patten, Talia Balsam; Marni Nixon, Shelia Smith
3rd Row: Joan Cullman; Gregory Mosher; Linda Eder; Christopher Plummer
Bottom: Kristen Chenoweth, Jason Danieley; Carol Channing, Julie Harris; Mark Ruffalo, Linda Eder, Daniel McDonald
Photos by *Carol Henderson, MichaelRiordan, Michael Viade, Peter Warrack, Jack Williams*

221

PULITZER PRIZE PRODUCTIONS

1918–Why Marry?, 1919–no award, 1920–Beyond the Horizon, 1921–Miss Lulu Bett, 1922–Anna Christie, 1923–Icebound, 1924–Hell-Bent fer Heaven, 1925–They Knew What They Wanted, 1926–Craig's Wife, 1927–In Abraham's Bosom, 1928–Strange Interlude, 1929–Street Scene, 1930–The Green Pastures, 1931–Alison's House, 1932–Of Thee I Sing, 1933–Both Your Houses, 1934–Men in White, 1935–The Old Maid, 1936–Idiot's Delight, 1937–You Can't Take It with You, 1938–Our Town, 1939–Abe Lincoln in Illinois, 1940–The Time of Your Life, 1941–There Shall Be No Night, 1942–no award, 1943–The Skin of Our Teeth, 1944–no award, 1945–Harvey, 1946–State of the Union, 1947–no award, 1948–A Streetcar Named Desire, 1949–Death of a Salesman, 1950–South Pacific, 1951–no award, 1952–The Shrike, 1953–Picnic, 1954–The Teahouse of the August Moon, 1955–Cat on a Hot Tin Roof, 1956–The Diary of Anne Frank, 1957–Long Day's Journey into Night, 1958–Look Homeward, Angel, 1959–J.B., 1960–Fiorello!, 1961–All the Way Home,

1962–How to Succeed in Business without Really Trying, 1963–no award, 1964–no award, 1965–The Subject Was Roses, 1966–no award, 1967–A Delicate Balance, 1968–no award, 1969–The Great White Hope, 1970–No Place to Be Somebody, 1971–The Effect of Gamma Rays on Man-in-the-Moon Marigolds, 1972–no award, 1973–That Championship Season, 1974–no award, 1975–Seascape, 1976–A Chorus Line, 1977–The Shadow Box, 1978–The Gin Game, 1979–Buried Child, 1980–Talley's Folly, 1981–Crimes of the Heart, 1982–A Soldier's Play, 1983–'night, Mother, 1984–Glengarry Glen Ross, 1985–Sunday in the Park with George, 1986–no award, 1987–Fences, 1988–Driving Miss Daisy, 1989–The Heidi Chronicles, 1990–The Piano Lesson, 1991–Lost in Yonkers, 1992–The Kentucky Cycle, 1993–Angels in America: Millenium Approaches, 1994–Three Tall Women, 1995–Young Man from Atlanta, 1996- Rent, 1997- no award.

NEW YORK DRAMA CRITICS CIRCLE AWARDS

1936–Winterset, 1937–High Tor, 1938–Of Mice and Men, Shadow and Substance, 1939–The White Steed, 1940–The Time of Your Life, 1941–Watch on the Rhine, The Corn Is Green, 1942–Blithe Spirit, 1943–The Patriots, 1944–Jacobowsky and the Colonel, 1945–The Glass Menagerie, 1946–Carousel, 1947–All My Sons, No Exit, Brigadoon, 1948–A Streetcar Named Desire, The Winslow Boy, 1949–Death of a Salesman, The Madwoman of Chaillot, South Pacific, 1950–The Member of the Wedding, The Cocktail Party, The Consul, 1951–Darkness at Noon, The Lady's Not for Burning, Guys and Dolls, 1952–I Am a Camera, Venus Observed, Pal Joey, 1953–Picnic, The Love of Four Colonels, Wonderful Town, 1954–Teahouse of the August Moon, Ondine, The Golden Apple, 1955–Cat on a Hot Tin Roof, Witness for the Prosecution, The Saint of Bleecker Street, 1956–The Diary of Anne Frank, Tiger at the Gates, My Fair Lady, 1957–Long Day's Journey into Night, The Waltz of the Toreadors, The Most Happy Fella, 1958–Look Homeward Angel, Look Back in Anger, The Music Man, 1959–A Raisin in the Sun, The Visit, La Plume de Ma Tante, 1960–Toys in the Attic, Five Finger Exercise, Fiorello!, 1961–All the Way Home, A Taste of Honey, Carnival, 1962–Night of the Iguana, A Man for All Seasons, How to Succeed in Business without Really Trying, 1963–Who's Afraid of Virginia Woolf?, 1964–Luther, Hello Dolly!, 1965–The Subject Was Roses, Fiddler on the Roof, 1966–The Persecution and Assassination of Marat as Performed by the Inmates of the Asylum of Charenton under the Direction of the Marquis de Sade, Man of La Mancha, 1967–The Homecoming, Cabaret, 1968–Rosencrantz and Guildenstern Are Dead, Your Own Thing, 1969–The Great White Hope, 1776, 1970–The Effect of Gamma Rays on Man-in-the-Moon Marigolds,

Borstal Boy, Company, 1971–Home, Follies, The House of Blue Leaves, 1972–That Championship Season, Two Gentlemen of Verona, 1973–The Hot l Baltimore, The Changing Room, A Little Night Music, 1974–The Contractor, Short Eyes, Candide, 1975–Equus, The Taking of Miss Janie, A Chorus Line, 1976–Travesties, Streamers, Pacific Overtures, 1977–Otherwise Engaged, American Buffalo, Annie, 1978–Da, Ain't Misbehavin', 1979–The Elephant Man, Sweeney Todd, 1980–Talley's Folley, Evita, Betrayal, 1981–Crimes of the Heart, A Lesson from Aloes, Special Citation to Lena Horne, The Pirates of Penzance, 1982–The Life and Adventures of Nicholas Nickleby, A Soldier's Play, (no musical), 1983–Brighton Beach Memoirs, Plenty, Little Shop of Horrors, 1984–The Real Thing, Glengarry Glen Ross, Sunday in the Park with George, 1985–Ma Rainey's Black Bottom, (no musical), 1986–A Lie of the Mind, Benefactors, (no musical), Special Citation to Lily Tomlin and Jane Wagner, 1987–Fences, Les Liaisons Dangereuses, Les Misérables, 1988–Joe Turner's Come and Gone, The Road to Mecca, Into the Woods, 1989–The Heidi Chronicles, Aristocrats, Largely New York (Special), (no musical), 1990–The Piano Lesson, City of Angels, Privates on Parade, 1991–Six Degrees of Separation, The Will Rogers Follies, Our Country's Good, Special Citation to Eileen Atkins, 1992–Two Trains Running, Dancing at Lughnasa, 1993–Angels in America: Millenium Approaches, Someone Who'll Watch Over Me, Kiss of the Spider Woman, 1994–Three Tall Women, Anna Deavere Smith (Special), 1995–Arcadia, Love! Valour! Compassion!, Special Award: Signature Theatre Company, 1996- Seven Guitars, Molly Sweeny, Rent, 1997-How I Learned to Drive, Skylight, Violet, Chicago (special)

AMERICAN THEATRE WING ANTOINETTE PERRY (TONY) AWARD PRODUCTIONS

1948–Mister Roberts, 1949–Death of a Salesman, Kiss Me, Kate, 1950–The Cocktail Party, South Pacific, 1951–The Rose Tattoo, Guys and Dolls, 1952–The Fourposter, The King and I, 1953–The Crucible, Wonderful Town, 1954–The Teahouse of the August Moon, Kismet, 1955–The Desperate Hours, The Pajama Game, 1956–The Diary of Anne Frank, Damn Yankees, 1957–Long Day's Journey into Night, My Fair Lady, 1958–Sunrise at Campobello, The Music Man, 1959–J.B., Redhead, 1960–The Miracle Worker, Fiorello! tied with The Sound of Music, 1961–Becket, Bye Bye Birdie, 1962–A Man for All Seasons, How to Succeed in Business without Really Trying, 1963–Who's Afraid of Virginia Woolf?, A Funny Thing Happened on the Way to the Forum, 1964–Luther, Hello Dolly!, 1965–The Subject Was Roses, Fiddler on the Roof, 1966–The Persecution and Assassination of Marat as Performed by the Inmates of the Asylum of Charenton under the Direction of the Marquis de Sade, Man of La Mancha, 1967–The Homecoming, Cabaret, 1968–Rosencrantz and Guildenstern Are Dead, Hallelujah Baby!, 1969–The Great White Hope, 1776, 1970–Borstal Boy, Applause, 1971–Sleuth, Company, 1972–Sticks and Bones, Two Gentlemen of Verona, 1973–That Championship Season, A Little Night Music, 1974–The River Niger, Raisin, 1975–Equus, The Wiz, 1976–Travesties, A Chorus Line, 1977–The Shadow Box, Annie,

1978–Da, Ain't Misbehavin', Dracula, 1979–The Elephant Man, Sweeney Todd, 1980–Children of a Lesser God, Evita, Morning's at Seven, 1981–Amadeus, 42nd Street, The Pirates of Penzance, 1982–The Life and Adventures of Nicholas Nickleby, Nine, Othello, 1983–Torch Song Trilogy, Cats, On Your Toes, 1984–The Real Thing, La Cage aux Folles, 1985–Biloxi Blues, Big River, Joe Egg, 1986–I'm Not Rappaport, The Mystery of Edwin Drood, Sweet Charity, 1987–Fences, Les Misérables, All My Sons, 1988–M. Butterfly, The Phantom of the Opera, 1989–The Heidi Chronicles, Jerome Robbins' Broadway, Our Town, Anything Goes, 1990–The Grapes of Wrath, City of Angels, Gypsy, 1991–Lost in Yonkers, The Will Rogers' Follies, Fiddler on the Roof, 1992–Dancing at Lughnasa, Crazy For You, Guys & Dolls, 1993–Angels in America: Millenium Approaches, Kiss of the Spider Woman, 1994–Angels in America: Perestroika, Passion, An Inspector Calls, Carousel, 1995–Love! Valour! Compassion! (play), Sunset Boulevard (musical), Show Boat (musical revival), The Heiress (play revival), 1996- Master Class (play), Rent (musical), A Delicate Balance (play revival), King and I (musical revival), 1997-Last Night of Ballyhoo (play), Titanic (musical), Doll's House (play revival), Chicago (musical Revival)

**Above: Terry Beaver, Cynthia Nixon,
Celia Weston, Carole Shelley in
Last Night of Ballyhoo (Carol Rosegg)**

**Left: Michael McElroy in *Violet*
(Joan Marcus)**

**Right: Mary-Louise Parker in
How I Learned to Drive (Carol Rosegg)**

**Below: Cast of *Titanic*
(Joan Marcus)**

Konrad Aderer

Marilyn Alex

Matthew Aibel

Crystall Allen

Keith Anderson

Christina Anbri

Biographical Data On This Season's Casts

ABELE, JIM. Born Nov. 14, 1960 in Syracuse, NY. Graduate Ithaca Col. Debut 1984 OB in *Shepardsets*, followed by *The Cabbagehead, Country Girl, Any Place But Here Jack, Godot Arrives, Edith Stein, Great Kahn, Gift of Spice People, View of the Dome.*

ABUBA, ERNEST. Born Aug. 25, 1947 in Honolulu, HI. Attended Southwestern Col. Bdwy debut 1976 in *Pacific Overtures*, followed by *Loose Ends, Zoya's Apartment, Shimada*, OB in *Sunrise, Monkey Music, Station J., Yellow Fever, Pacific Overtures, Empress of China, Man Who Turned Into a Stick, Shogun Macbeth, Three Sisters, Song of Shim Chung, It's Our Town Too, Mishima Montage, Detective Story, Chang Fragments, Freiheit Makes a Stand.*

ADAMS, J. B. Born Sept. 29, 1954 in Oklahoma City, OK. Graduate Okla. City U. Debut 1980 OB in *ELT's Plain and Fancy,* followed by *Annie Warbucks*, Bdwy 1997 in *Annie.*

ADAMS, JOSEPH. Born February 4, 1956 in Concord, Ca. Debut 1980 in ELT's *Romeo and Juliet,* followed by *Don Juan and the Non Don Juan, Perfect Crime,* Bdwy in *The Survivor* (1981).

ADAMS, MALCOLM. Born Feb.21, 1962 in Cork, Ireland. Graduate U of Ireland. Debut 1992 OB in *Lovechild* followed by *Public Enemy, Da.*

ADAMS, POLLY. Born in Nashville, TN. Graduate Stanford U., Columbia U. Bdwy debut 1976 in *Zalmen or the Madness of God*, OB in *Ordway Ames-gay, The Free Zone, Flyboy, Getting In.*

ADDISON, BERNARD K. Born Jan.16, 1993 in Columbia, SC. Graduate USC,UNC. Debut 1995 OB in *Oedipus at Colonus, Othello, Venice Preserv'd, Cymbeline.*

ADERER, KONRAD. Born July 7, 1968 in NYC. Graduate NYU. 1996 Debut OB in *Cymbeline* followed by *Venice Preserv'd.*

AIBEL, MATTHEW. Born Dec.5, 1967 in NYC. Graduate Yale. 1992 debut OB in *Columbus* followed by *Cymbeline*, Bdwy 1997 in *Candide.*

ALDREDGE, TOM. Born Feb. 28, 1928 in Dayton, OH. Attended Dayton U. Goodman Th. Bdwy debut 1959 in *Nervous Set,* followed by *UTBU, Slapstick Tragedy, Everything in the Garden, Indians, Engagement Baby, How the Other Half Loves, Sticks and Bones, Where's Charley?, Leaf People, Rex, Vieux Carre, St. Joan, Stages, On Golden Pond, The Little Foxes, Into the Woods, Two Shakespearean Actors, Inherit the Wind, Boys from Syracuse (Encores),* OB in *The Tempest, Between Two Thieves, Henry V, The Premise, Love's Labour's Lost, Troilus and Cressida, The Butter and Egg Man, Ergo, Boys in the Band, Twelfth Night, Colette, Hamlet, The Orphan, King Lear, The Iceman Cometh, Black Angel, Getting Along Famously, Fool for Love, Neon Psalms, Richard II, Last Yankee, Incommunicado*

ALEX, MARILYN. Born Oct.30, 1930 in Hollywood, CA. Attended RADA. Bdwy debut 1981 in *Deathtrap.* OB in *Invitation to a March, Not Now Darling, Fassbinder in the Frying Pan.*

ALEXANDER, JACE. Born April 7, 1964 in NYC. Attended NYU. Bdwy debut 1983 in *Caine Mutiny Court Martial followed by Six Degrees of Separation.* OB in *I'm Not Rappaport, Wasted, The Good Coach, Heart of a Dog, Price of Fame, Assassins, Flyovers.*

ALEXANDER, JAMES. Born June 15, 1941 in Albany, OR. Graduate MichSt. Bdwy debut 1968 in *House of Atreus* followed by *Arturo Ui,* OB in *Marouf, Falling Apart, Bried History of White Music.*

ALEXI-MALLE, ADAM. Born Sept.24, 1964 in Siena, Italy. Graduate U of WI,U of MD, Paris Conserv., Moscow St Cosv. 1996 debut OB in *Three Sisters, Misanthrope, Measure for Measure,* Bdwy 1997 in *Titanic.*

ALLEN, CRYSTAL. Born April 17. 1970 in Seattle, WA. Bdwy debut 1997 in *Play On.*

ALLINSON, MICHAEL. Bom in London, England. Attended RADA. Bdwy debut 1960 in *My Fair Lady,* followed by *Hostile Witness, Come Live With Me, Coco, Angel, Ideal Husband .*

AMBROSE, JOE. Born April 7, 1931 in Chicago, IL. Graduate Rutgers U. AADA, Columbia U. Debut 1986 OB in *Buried Child* followed by *Diary of a Scoundrel, The Crucible, Hotel Paradiso, Deep Dish,* Bdwy in *An Inspector Calls* (1994).

ANBRI, CHRISTIANA. Born Aug.11, 1990 in Philadelphia, PA. Bdwy debut 1997 in *Annie.*

ANCHETA, SUSAN. Born Jan.1 in Hololulu, HI. Graduate So Meth U. 1997 debut OB in *Shanghai Lil's,* Bdwy 1997 in *Miss Saigon.*

ANDERSON, KEITH. Born Apr.22, 1972 in Lincoln, IL. Attended Northwestern, Lincoln Col. Debut OB in *Fairy Tales .*

ANDERSON, KEVIN. Born Jan.13, 1960 in Illinois. Attended Goodman Sch. Debut 1985 OB in *Orphans* for which he received a Theatre World Award, followed by *Moonchildren, Brilliant Traces, Red Address,* Bdwy in *Orpheus Descending* (1989).

ANDRES, BARBARA. Born Feb. 11, 1939 in NYC. Graduate Catholic U. Bdwy debut 1969 in *Jimmy,* followed by *Boy Friend, Rodgers and Hart, Rex, On Golden Pond, Doonesbury, Kiss of the Spiderwoman,* OB in *Threepenny Opera, Landscape of the Body, Harold Arlen's Cabaret, Suzanna Andler, One-Act Festival, Company, Marathon '87, Arms and the Man, A Woman without a Name. First is Supper, Fore!, On My Knees.*

ANTHONY, TREVOR. Born Dec.4, 1967 in Pasadena, CA. Graduate Duke, Yale. 1995 debut OB in *Crash Course* followed by *Napoleonade, Gross Indecency.*

ANTHONY, VICTOR. Born July 2, 1970 in NYC. Graduate Wesleyan U. Debut 1997 OB in *Clean.*

APPEL, PETER. Born Oct.19, 1959 in NYC. Graduate BrandeisU. Debut 1987 OB in *Richard II* followed by *Henry IV Part I, Midsummer Night's Dream, Saved from Obscurity, Titus Andronicus, Taming of the Shrew, Good Times are Killing Me, Him, Orestes.*

ARCARO, ROBERT/BOB. Born Aug. 9, 1952 in Brooklyn, NY. Graduate Wesleyan U. Debut 1977 OB in *New York City Street Show,* followed by *Working Theatre Festival, Man with a Raincoat, Working One-Acts, Henry Lumpur, Special Interests, Measure for Measure, Our Lady of Perpetual Danger, Brotherly Love, I Am a Man, Brotherly Love, Nellie.*

ARI, ROBERT/BOB. Born July 1, 1949 in NYC. Graduate Camegie-Mellon U. Debut 1976 OB in *Boys from Syracuse* followed by *Gay Divorce, Devour the Snow, Carbondale Dreams, Show Me Where the Good TimesAre, CBS Live, Picasso at the Lapin Agile, Twelfth Night, Baby Anger, Names, June Moon.*

ARNAZ, LUCIE. Born July 17, 1951 in Los Angeles, CA. Bdwy debut 1979 in *They're Playing Our Song* for which she received a Theatre World Award, followed by *Lost in Yonkers ,* OB in *Grace and Gloria.*

ARNESON, KAREN. Born in Chicago, IL. Graduate UCLA. Debut 1996 in *Cybele: A Love Story* . OB also includes *Liberty Smith, What I Did Last Summer,The Sorcerer, When the Stars Begin to Fall, Saltwater Moon.*

ASHFORD, ROBERT. Born Nov. 19, 1959 in Orlando, FL. Attended Washington & Lee U. Bdwy debut 1987 in *Anything Goes*, followed by *Radio City Music Hall Christmas Spectacular, The Most Happy Fella* (1992), *My Favorite Year., Victor Victoria.*

ASHLEY, ELIZABETH. Born Aug.30, 1939 in Ocala, FL. Attended Neighborhood Playhouse. Bdwy debut 1959 in *Highest Tree* followed by *Take Her She's Mine* for which she received a Theatre World Award, *Barefoot in the Park, Ring Round the Bathtub, Cat on a Hot Tin Roof, Skin of Our Teeth, Legend, Caesar and Cleopatra, Hide and Seek, Agnes of God, Garden District,* OB in *Milk Train Doesn't Stop Here Anymore, When She Danced, Red Devil Battery Sign.*

ATKINSON, JAYNE. Born February 18, 1959 in Bournemouth, Engl. Graduate Northwestern U., Yale. Debut 1986 OB in *Bloody Poetry*, followed by *Terminal Bar, Return of Pinocchio, The Art of Success, The Way of the World, Appointment with a High Wire Lady, Why We Have a Body,* Bdwy in *All My Sons* (1987).

ATLEE, HOWARD. Born May 14, 1926 in Bucyrus, OH. Graduate Emerson Col. Debut 1990 OB in *Historical Productions*, followed by *The 15th Ward, The Hells of Dante, What a Royal Pain in the Farce, Rimers of Eldtrich, Dream Alliance, Vampyr Theatre, Captain!, Tiny Closets, In a Garden, Out of the South.*

BAGDEN, RONALD. Born Dec. 26, 1953 in Philadelphia, PA. Graduate Temple U., RADA. Debut 1977 OB in *Oedipus Rex*, followed by *Oh! What a Lovely War, Jack, Gonza the Lancer, Dead Mother, Home Show Pieces, Moose Mating, My Night with Reg,* Bdwy in *Amadeus* (1980).

BAGNERIS, VERNEL. Born July 31, 1949 in New Orleans, LA. Graduate Xavier U. Debut 1979 OB in *One Mo' Time*, followed by *Staggerlee, Further Mo', Jelly Roll Morton: A Me-Morial, Jelly Roll Morton: Hoo Dude, Jelly Roll, Slow Drag* all of which he wrote. Bdwy 1997 in *The Life.*

BAKER, ALLISON. Born Dec.14 in St.Louis, MO. Graduate Washington U. Off Bdwy in *Unbroken Chain, Clasical Variations, Night at the Movies, Cybele.*

BAKER, BECKY ANN. (formerly Gelke) Born Feb. 17, 1953 in Ft. Knox, KY. Graduate WkyU. Bdwy debut 1978 in *Best Little Whorehouse in Texas* followed by *Streetcar Named Desire* (1988), *Titanic,* OB in *Altitude Sickness, John Brown's Body, Chamber Music, To Whom It May Concern, Two Gentlemen of Verona, Bob's Guns, Buzzsaw Berkeley, Colorado Catechism, Jeremy Rudge, Laura Dennis, June Moon.*

BAKER, DARRIN. Born May 7, 1965 in Toronto, Can. Attended Center for Actors. Bdwy debut 1994 in *Sunset Blvd.*

BAKER, DAVID AARON. Born August 14, 1963 in Durham, NC. Graduate U. Tex., Juilliard. Bdwy debut 1993 in *White Liars/Black Comedy* followed by *Abe Lincoln in Illinois, Flowering Peach,Moliere Comedies, Once Upon a Mattress,* OB in *Richard III, 110 in the Shade* (NYCO), *Durang Durang, Oblivion Postpones, Blue Window.*

BALABAN, BOB. Born Aug.16, 1945 in Chicago, IL. Attended Colgate, NYU. Debut 1967 OB in *You're a Good Man Charlie Brown* followed by *Up Eden, White House Murder Case, Basic Training of Pavlo Hummel, The Children, Marie and Bruce, Three Sisters, Some Americans Abroad, Mistresses,* Bdwy in *Plaza Suite* (1968), *Some of My Best Friends, Inspector General, Speed-the-Plow.*

BARANSKI, CHRISTINE. Born May 2, 1952 in Buffalo, NY. Graduate Juilliard. Debut OB 1978 in *One Crack Out*, followed by *Says I Says He, Trouble with Europe, Coming Attractions, Operation Midnight Climax, Sally and Marsha, Midsummer Night's Dream, It's Only a Play, Marathon '86, Elliot Loves, Lips Together Teeth Apart, A Christmas Memory, Loman Family Picnic,* Bdwy in *Hide and Seek* (1980), *The Real Thing, Hurlyburly, House of Blue Leaves, Rumors, Nick & Nora, Promises Promises* (Encores).

BAREIKIS, ARIJA. Born July 21, 1966 in Bloomington, IN. Bdwy debut 1997 in *Last Night of Ballyhoo.*

BARRETT, BRENT. Born Feb.28, 1957 in Quinter, KS. Graduate Carnegie-Mellon U. Bdwy debut 1980 in *West Side Story* followed by *Dance a Little Closer, Grand Hotel, Candide* (1997), OB in *March of the Falsettos, Portrait of Jenny, Death of Von Richthofen, Sweethearts, What's a Nice Country Like You..., Time of the Cuckoo, Swan Song, Closer Than Ever.*

BART, ROGER. Born Sept.29, 1962 in Norwalk, CT. Graduate Rutgers U. 1984 debut OB in *Second Wind* followed by *Lessons, Up Against It, Henry IV Parts 1 and 2,* Bdwy in *Big River* (1987),*King David.*

BARTENIEFF, GEORGE. Born Jan. 24, 1933 in Berlin, Ger. Bdwy debut 1947 in *The Whole World Over,* followed by *Venus Is, All's Well That Ends Well, Quotations from Chairman Mao Tse-Tung, Death of Bessie Smith, Cop-Out, Room Service, Unlikely Heroes,* OB in *Walking in Waldheim, Memorandum, Increased Difficulty of Concentration, Trelawny of the Wells, Charley Chestnut Rides the IRT, Radio (Wisdom): Sophia Part I, Images of the Dead, Dead End Kids, The Blonde Leading the Blonde, The Dispossessed, Growing Up Gothic, Rosetti's Apologies, On the Lam, Samuel Beckett Trilogy, Quartet, Help Wanted, Matter of Life and Death, Heart That Eats Itself, Coney Island Kid, Cymbeline, Better People, Blue Heaven, He Saw His Reflection, Sabina, Beekeeper's Daughter.*

BARTON, MISCHA. Born Jan.24, 1986 in London. Debut 1995 OB in *Slavs!* followed by *Twelve Dreams, Where the Truth Lies, One Flea Spare.*

BATEN, BLYTHE. Born in NYC. Graduate Colorado Col. 1996 debut OB in *Plough and the Stars* , Other OB: *Any Open Window, Summercamp, Yeats: A Celebration, When a Diva Dreams.*

BATT, BRYAN. Bom March 1, 1963 in New Orleans, LA. Graduate Tulane U. Debut 1987 OB in *Too Many Girls*, followed by *Golden Apple, Jeffrey, Forbidden Bdwy , Forbidden Bdwy Strikes Back,* Bdwy in *Starlight Express* (1987), *Sunset Blvd.*

BEACH, DAVID. Born Feb. 20, 1964 in Dayton, OH. Attended Darmouth Col, LAMDA. Debut 1990 OB in *Big Fat and Ugly with a Moustache* followed by *Modigliani, Octoberfest, Pets, That's Life!, Message to Michael,* Bdwy in *Moon Over Buffalo* (1995), *Beauty and the Beast., Sweet Adeline* (Encores).

BEDFORD, BRIAN. Born Feb. 16, 1935 in Morley, England. Attended RADA. Bdwy debut 1960 in *Five Finger Exercise* followed by *Lord Pengo, The Private Ear, The Astrakhan Coat, Unknown Soldier and His Wife, Seven Descents of Myrtle, Jumpers, Cocktail Party, Hamlet, Private Lives, School for Wives, The Misanthrope, Two Shakespearean Actors, Timon of Athens, Moliere Comedies, London Assurance,* OB in *The Knack, The Lunatic the Lover and the Poet.*

BEN-ARI, NEAL. (Formerly Neal Klein) Born March 20, 1952 in Brooklyn, NY. Graduate UPA. Bdwy debut 1981 in *The First* followed by *Roza, Chess, Merchant of Venice, Joseph and the Amazing Technicolor Dreamcoat* (1993), *Victor Victoria,* , OB in *La Boheme, 1-2-3-4-5.*

BEAVER, TERRY. Born June 2, 1948 in W. Palm Beach, FL. Graduate Palm Beach Jr. Col., U of So. FL. Bdwy debut 1997 in *Last Night of Ballyhoo* for which he won a 1997 Theatre World Award.

BIENSKIE, STEPHEN. Born May 15 in NJ. Graduate MontclairU. OB in *Zombie Prom* (1996), *Koppelvision, There's a War Going On, Balm in Gilead, Last Session.*

BLAISDELL, GEOFFREY. Born Aug.16, 1958 in Danville, KY. Graduate San Fran St U. Bdwy debut 1993 in *Cyrano*, OB in *Petrified Prince* (1994).

BENEDICT, PAUL. Born Sept.17 in Silver City, NM. Graduate SuffolkU. Debut 1965 OB in *Live Like Pigs* followed by *Local Stigmatic, Play's the Thing, Cherry Orchard, It's Only a Play* Bdwy includes *Leda Had a Swan*(1968), *Bad Habits, Little Murders, White House Murder Case, Richard III, Hughie.*

BENJAMIN, P.J. Born September 2, 1951 in Chicago, IL. Attended Loyola U., Columbia U. Bdwy debut 1973 in *Pajama Game*, followed by *Pippin, Sarava, Charlie and Algernon, Sophisticated Ladies, Torch Song Trilogy, Wind in the Willows, Ain't Broadway Grand,* OB in *Memories of Riding with Joe Cool, Marathon Dancing, Carmelina.*

MIMI BENSINGER. Born May 5 in Pottsville, PA. NYC debut in 1961 *Electra* followed by *Say de Kooning, Two Orphans, Doll's House, Stonewall Jackson's House.*

BEREZIN, TANYA. Born Mar.25, 1941 in Philadelphia, PA. Attended Boston U. 1967 debut OB in *The Sandcastle* followed by *Three Sisters, Great Nebula in Orion, Him, Amazing Activity of Charlie Contrare, Battle of Angels, Mound Builders, Serenading Louie, My Life, Brontosaurus, Glorious Morning, Mary Stuart, Beaver Coat, Balm in Gilead, Caligula, Quiet in the Land, Sympathetic Magic,* Bdwy in *Fifth of July* (1981), *Angels Fall.*

BERN, MINA. Born May 5, 1920 in Poland. Bdwy debut 1967 in *Let's Sing Yiddish* followed by *Light Lively and Yiddish, Sing Israel Sing, Those Were the Days,* OB in *The Special, Old Lady's Guide to Survival, Maiden of Ludmir.*

BERRESSE, MICHAEL. Born August 15, 1964 in Holyoke, MA. Bdwy debut 1990 in *Fiddler on the Roof* followed by *Guys and Dolls, Damn Yankees, One Touch of Venus (Encores), Chicago.*

BEVAN, ALISON. Born November 20, 1959 in Cincinnati, OH. Attended NYU. Debut 1980 OB in *Trixie True Teen Detective* followed by *Brigadoon* (LC), *Little Lies, The Mayor Musicals*, Bdwy in *City of Angels, Steel Pier.*

BEVERLEY, TRAZANA. Born Aug. 9, 1945 in Baltimore, MD. Graduate NYU. Debut 1969 OB in *Rules for Running,* followed by *Les Femmes Noires, Geronimo, Antigone, The Brothers, God's Trombones, Marathon '91,Sleep Deprivation Chamber , God's Trombones,* Bdwy in *My Sister My Sister, For Colored Girls Who Have Considered Suicide* for which she received a Theatre World Award, *Death and the King's Horseman* (LC), *The Crucible.*

BIGLIN, TOM. Born Aug.24, 1967 in Woodhaven, NY. Graduate U of Penn. Debut 1996 OB in *Gender Wars* followed by *Measure for Measure, In a Garden .*

BILLECI, JOHN. Born April 19, 1957 in Brooklyn, NY. Graduate Loyola Marymount U. Debut 1993 OB in *3 by Wilder* followed by *As You Like It, SSS Glencairn, Twelfth Night, Goose and TomTom, Anatomy of Sound, Child's Christmas in Wales, Street Scene,* Bdwy 1993 in *Wilder Wilder Wilder.*

BILLMAN, SEKIYA. Born in Culver City, CA. Graduate UCLA. Bdwy debut 1996 in *Miss Saigon.*

BIRNEY, REED. Born Sept. 11, 1954 in Alexandria, VA. Attended Boston U. Bdwy debut 1977 in *Gemini,* OB in *Master and Margarita, Bella Figura, Winterplay, Flight of the Earls, Filthy Rich, Lady Moonsong, Mr. Monsoon, Common Pursuit, Zero Positive, Moving Targets, Spare Parts, Murder of Crows, 7 Blowjobs, Loose Knot, The Undertaker, An Imaginary Life, Family of Mann, Dark Ride, Minor Demons, Volunteer Man.*

BLACKHURST, KLEA (formerly Michelle Horman). Born Feb.6, 1963 in Salt Lake City, UT. Graduate U UT. Debut 1988 in OB in *Oil City Symphony* followed by *Sweet Deliverance, Radio Gals.*

BLANKFORT, JASE. Born April 16, 1987 in Suffern, NY. Bdwy debut 1997 in *Stanley.*

BLAZER, JUDITH. Born Oct. 22, 1956 in *Oh Boy!,* followed by *Roberta, A Little Night Music, Company, Babes in Arms, Hello Again, Jack's Holiday, Louisana Purchase* Bdwy in *Me and My Girl, A Change in the Heir, Titanic.*

BLOCK, LARRY. Born Oct. 30, 1942, in NYC. Graduate URI. Bdwy debut 1966 in *Hail Scrawdyke,* followed by *La Turista, Wonderful Town* (NYCO), OB in *Eh?, Fingernails Blue as Flowers, Comedy of Errors, Coming Attractions, Henry IV Part 2, Feuhrer Bunker, Manhattan Love Songs, Souvenirs, The Golem, Responsible Parties, Hit Parade, Largo Desolato, The Square Root of 3, Young Playwrights Festival, Hunting Cockroaches, Two Gentlemen of Verona, Yellow Dog Contract, Temptation, Festival of 1 Acts, Faithful Brethern of Pitt Street, Loman Family Picnic, One of the All-Time Greats, Pericles, Comedy of Errors, The Work Room, Don Juan in Chicago, Him, Devil Inside.*

BLOCH, SCOTTY. Born Jan. 28 in New Rochelle, NY. Attended AADA. Debut 1945 OB in *Craig's Wife* followed by *Lemon Sky, Battering Ram, Richard III, In Celebration, An Act of Kindness, The Price, Grace, Neon Psalms, Other People's Money, Walking The Dead, EST Marathon '92, The Stand-In, Unexpected Tenderness, Brutality of Fact, What I Meant Was,* Bdwy in *Children of a Lesser God* (1980).

BLOOM, TOM. Born Nov. 1, 1944 in Washington, D.C. Graduate Western MD Col., Emerson Col. Debut 1989 OB in *Widow's Blind Date,* followed by *A Cup of Coffee, Major Barbara, A Perfect Diamond, Lips Together Teeth Apart, Winter's Tale, The Guardsman,* Bdwy in *Racing Demon* (1995).

BLUM, JOEL. Born May 19, 1952 in San Francisco, CA. Attended Marin Col., NYU, Bdwy debut 1976 in *Debbie Reynolds on Broadway,* followed by *42nd Street, Stardust, Radio City Easter Show, Show Boat* (1994), *Steel Pier,* OB in *And the World Goes Round.*

BLUMENFELD, ROBERT. Born Feb.26, 1943 in NYC. Graduate Rutgers, ColumbiaU. Bdwy debut 1970 in *Othello,* OB in *Fall and Redemption of Man, Tempest, The Dybbuk, Count Dracula, Nature and Purpose of the Universe, House Music, The Keymaker, Epic Proportions, Tatterdemalion, Iolanthe, Temple, Friends in High Places, Rough Crossing, Petrified Prince, Gross Indecency.*

BOGARDUS, STEPHEN. Born Mar. 11, 1954 in Norfolk, VA. Graduate Princeton. Bdwy debut 1980 in *West Side Story* followed by *Les Miserables, Grapes of Wrath, Falsettos, Allegro (Encores), Love! Valour! Compassion!*(also OB), *Sweet Adeline, King David,* OB in *Genesis, March of the Falsettos, In Trousers, Feathertop, No Way to Treat a Lady, Falsettoland, Unbrellas of Cherbourg.*

BOGUE, ROBERT. Born Aug.27, 1964 in Minden, NE. Graduate Colorado Col. Debut 1991 OB in *Nothing to Dream About* followed by *Adding Machine, Waiting for Lefty, The Undertakers, Hotel Universe, Boys in the Band,* Bdwy in *Three Sisters* (1997).

BOJARSKI, STANLEY. Born June 1, 1950 in Fonda, NY. Graduate Marist Col. Debut 1984 OB in *Red Hot and Blue* followed by *The Pretender, When Pigs Fly.*

BOLOGNA, JOSEPH. Born Dec.30, 1936 in Brooklyn, NY. Attended Brown U. Bdwy debut 1968 in *Lovers and Other Strangers* followed by *It Had to Be You,* OB in *Bermuda Ave. Triangle.*

BOLTON, JOHN (KEENE). Born December 29, 1963 in Rochester, NY. Graduate St. John Fisher Col. Debut 1991 OB in *Cinderella.,* Bdwy in *Damn Yankees* (1994), *How to Succeed..., Titanic.*

BOOTHBY, VICTORIA. Born in Chicago, IL. Graduate Barnard Col. Debut 1971 OB in *Jungle of the Cities* followed by *Man's a Man, Coarse Acting Show, Beethoven/Karl, False Confessions, Professor George, Mother Bickerdyke and Me,* Bdwy in *Beethoven's Tenth* (1984), *Stepping Out, Roza, Stanley.*

BOVE, ELIZABETH. Bom Sept. 30 in Melbourne, Australia. Graduate U. Tex. Debut 1986 OB in *Witness for the Prosecution,* followed by *House of Bernarda Alba, Country Girl, The Maids, Round & Peakheads, The Dream Cure, House of the Dog, Shadow Box, Kiss the Blarney Stone, Moon for the Misbegotten, No Exit, Madwoman of Chaillot, Box Office Poison, Fautus A Ritual, Volunteer Man.*

DOVE, MARK. Born Jan.9, 1960 in Pittsburgh, PA. Bdwy debut in *West Side Story* (1980) followed by *Woman of the Year, Chorus Line, Kiss of the Spider Woman, The Life.*

BOYD, CAMERON. Born Sept. 6, 1984 in Carmel, NY. Bdwy debut 1992 in *Four Baboons Adoring the Sun* followed by *Abe Lincoln in Illinois,* OB in *Missing Persons, Nine Armenians.*

BOYD, PATRICK M. Born March 5, 1965 in Welch, WVA. Graduate W.VA.U. Bdwy debut 1994 in *Grease* followed by *Wizard of Oz (MSG).*

BRADLEY, BRAD. Born Dec.9, 1971 in San Diego, CA. Graduate USC. Bdwy debut 1995 in *Christmas Carol, Steel Pier,* OB in *Cocoanuts.*

BRAND, GIBBY. Born May 20, 1946 in NYC. Graduate Ithaca Col. Debut 1977 OB in *The Castaways* followed by *Music Man, Real Life Funnies,* Bdwy in *Little Me* (1981), *Passion, Beauty and the Beast..*

BREEN, (J.) PATRICK. Born Oct. 26, 1960 in Brooklyn, NY. NYU graduate. Debut 1982 OB in *Epiphanyu,* followed by *Little Murders, Blood Sports, Class I Acts, Baba Goya, Chelsea Walls, Naked Rights, Substance of Fire, Saturday Morning Cartoons, A Fair Country, Night and Her Stars, View of the Dome,* Bdwy in *Brighton Beach Memoirs* (1983), *Sweet Adeline* (Encores).

BRENNAN, MAUREEN. Born Oct.11, 1952 in Washington, DC. Attended U Conn. Bdwy debut 1974 in *Candide* for which she received a Theatre World Award, followed by *Going Up, Knickerbocker Holiday, Little Johnny Jones, Stardust,* OB in *Shakespeare's Cabaret, Cat and the Fiddle, Nuts and Bolts: Tightened, Hart & Hammerstein Centennial.*

BRENNAN, TOM. Born April 16, 1926 in Cleveland, OH. Graduate Oberlin, Western Reserve U. 1958 debut in *Synge Trilogy* followed by *Between Two Theives, East, All in Love, Under Milk Wood, Evening with James Purdy, Golden Six, Pullman Car Hiawatha, Are You Now or Have You Ever, Diary of Anne Frank, Milk of Paradise, Transcendental Love, Beaver Coat, The Overcoat, Summer, Asian Shade, Inheritors, Paradise Lost, Madwoman of Chaillot, Time of Your Life, Dead Man's Apartment,* Bdwy in *Play Memory, Our Town, The Miser.*

BRIAN, MICHAEL. Born Nov.14, 1958 in Utica, NY. Attended Boston Consv. Debut 1979 OB in *Kennedy's Children* followed by *Street Scene, Death of von Ricthofen as Witnessed from Earth, Lenny and the Heartbreakers, Gifts of the Magi, Human Comedy, Next Please!, Love in Two Countries,* Bdwy in *Baby* (1984), *Big River, Sweeney Todd, Guys and Dolls, The Life.*

BRIGHTMAN, JULIAN. Bom March 5 1964 in Philadelphia, Pa. Graduate U. PA. Debut 1987 OB in *1984,* followed by *Critic, Leaves of Grass, Songbox,* Bdwy in *Peter Pan* (1990/1991), *Hello Dolly* (1995).

BROADHURST, KENT. Born Feb.4, 1940 in St. Louis, MO. Graduate U NE. Debut 1968 OB on *Fouth Wall* followed by *Design for Living, Marching Song, Heartbreak House, Dark of the Moon, Hunchback of Notre Dame, Cold Sweat, April Snow, Early One Evening at The Rainbow Bar and Grill,* Bdwy in *Caine Mutiny Court-Martial (1983), Doll's House.*

BRODY, JONATHAN. Born June 16, 1963 in Englewood, NJ. Debut 1982 OB in *Shulamith,* followed by *The Desk Set, Eating Raoul, Theda Bara and the Frontier Rabbi, Miami Stories,* Bdwy in *Me and My Girl* (1986), *Sally Marr and Her Escorts, Titanic.*

BROGGER, IVAR. Born Jan. 10 in St. Paul, MN. Graduate U. Minn. Debut 1979 OB in *In The Jungle of Cities*, followed by *Collected Works of Billy the Kid, Magic Time, Cloud 9, Richard III, Clarence, Madwoman of Chaillot, Seascapes with Sharks and Dancer, Second Man, Twelfth Night, Almost Perfect, Up 'N' Under, Progress, Juno, Madwoman of Chaillot, The Beauty Part, Heartbreak House,* Bdwy in *Macbeth* (1981), *Pygmalion* (1987), *Saint Joan, Blood Brothers.*

BROMKA, ELAINE. Born Jan. 6 in Rochester, NY. Graduate Smith Col. Debut 1975 OB in *The Dybbuk*, followed by *Naked, Museum, The Son, Inadmissible Evidence, The Double Game, Cloud 9, Light Up the Sky, What I Meant Was,* Bdwy in *Macbeth* (1982), *Rose Tattoo* (1995).

BROWN, ANN. Born Dec. 1, 1960 in Westwood, NJ. Graduate Trinity Col. Debut 1987 OB in *Pacific Overtures* followed by *Side by Side by Sondheim, Stages, Golden Apple, 20 Fingers 20 Toes, Salute to Tom Jones and Harvey Schmidt,* Bdwy in *Once Upon a Mattress* (1996).

BROWN, GRAHAM. Born Oct. 24 in NYC. Graduate Howard U. OB in *Widowers Houses* (1959), *The Emperor's Clothes, Time of Storm, Major Barbara, Land Beyond the River, The Blacks, Firebugs, God Is a (Guess Who?), Evening of 1Acts, Man Better Man, Behold Cometh the Vanderkellans, Ride a Black Horse, The Great MacDaddy, Eden, Nevis Mountain Dew, Season Unravel, The Devil's Tear, Sons and Father of Sons, Abercrombie Apacolypse, Ceremonies in Dark Old Men, Eyes of the American, Richard 11, Taming of the Shrew, Winter's Tale, Black Eagles, Henry V, Two Gentlemen of Verona,* Bdwy in *Weekend* (1968) *Man in the Glass Booth, River Niger, Pericles, Black Picture Show, Kings, Lifetimes, Burners' Frolic, Jonquil, Talented Tenth.*

BROWN, P.J. Born Nov.5, 1956 in Staten Island, NYC. Graduate Boston Col. Debut 1990 OB in *Othello* followed by *America Dreaming,Waiting for Lefty, Soldier's Play,* Bdwy in *Grapes of Wrath* (1990).

BROWN, ROBIN LESLIE. Born Jan. 18, in Canandaigua, NY. Graduate LIU. Debut 1980 OB in *Mother of Us All*, followed by *Yours Truly, Two Gentlemen of Verona, Taming of the Shrew, The Mollusc, The Contrast, Pericles, Andromache, Macbeth, Electra, She Stoops to Conquer, Berneice, Hedda Gabler, Midsummer Night's Dream, Three Sisters, Major Barbara, Fine Art of Finesse, Two by Schnitzler, As You Like It, Ghosts, Chekhov Very Funny, Beaux Strategem, God of Vengeance, Good Natured Man, Twelfth Night, Little Eyolf, Ventian Twins, King Lear, Doll's House, Antigone, Venice Preserv'd.*

BROWNSTONE, DIANA. Born Nov. 15, in NYC. Graduate High School Perf. Arts, School of Am Ballet. Debut 1992 OB in *Galina Lives,* Bdwy in *Joseph and the Amazng Technicolor Dreamcoat* (1993), *Candide* (1997).

BRUMMEL, DAVID. Born Nov. 1, 1942 in Brooklyn, NY. Bdwy debut 1973 in *The Pajama Game*, followed by *Music Is, Oklahoma!,* OB in *Cole Porter, The Fantasticks, Prom Queens Unchained, Camilla, Carmelina.*

BRYDON, W. B. Born Sept. 20, 1933 in Newcastle, Eng. Debut 1962 OB in *The Long the Short and the Tall*, followed by *Live Like Pigs, Sgt. Musgrave's Dance, The Kitchen, Come Slowly Eden, Unknown Soldier and His Wife, Moon for the Misbegotten, The Orphan, Possession, Total Abandon, Madwoman of Challot, The Circle, Romeo and Juliet, Philadelphia Here I Come, Making History, Spinoza, Mme. MacAdam Traveling Theatre, Last Sortie, Juno and the Paycock, Invisible Man, Henry VIII,* Bdwy in *The Lincoln Mask, Ulysses in Nighttown, The Father.*

BRYGGMAN, LARRY. Born Dec. 21, 1938 in Concord, GA. Attended CCSF, Am. Th. Wing. Debut 1962 OB in *A Pair of Pairs*, followed by *Live Like Pigs, Stop You're Killing Me, Mod Donna, Waiting for Godot, Ballymurphy, Marco Polo Sings a Solo, Brownsville Raid, Two Small Bodies, Museum, Winter Dancers, Resurrection of Lady Lester, Royal Bob, Modern Ladies of Guanabacoa, Rum and Coke, Bodies Rest and Motion, Blood Sports, Class 1 Acts, Spoils of War, Coriolanus, Macbeth, Henry IV Parts 1 and 2, The White Rose, Nothing Sacred, As You Like It, New England* Bdwy in *Ulysses in Nighttown* (1974), *Checking Out, Basic Training of Pavlo Hummel, Richard III, Prelude to a Kiss* (also OB), *Picnic.*

BUCKLEY, CANDY. Born March 10 in Albuquerque, MN. Graduate TCU, UTx, Trinity. Debut 1994 OB in *Petrified Prince, Funnyhouse of a Negro, View of the Dome.*

BUELL, BILL. Born Sept. 21, 1952 in Paipai, Taiwan. Attended Portland State U. Debut 1972 OB in *Crazy Now*, followed by *Declassee, Lorenzaccio, Promenade, The Common Pursuit, Coyote Ugly, Alias Jimmy Valentine, Kiss Me Quick, Bad Habits, Groundhog, On the Bum, Picasso at the Lapin Agile,* Bdwy in *Once a Catholic* (1979), *The First, Welcome to the Club, The Miser, Taking Steps, Titanic.*

BULOS, YUSEF. Born Sept. 14, 1940 in Jerusalem. Attended American U., AADA. Debut 1965 OB with *American Savoyards* in rep, followed by *Saints, Trouble with Europe, Penultimate Problem of Sherlock Holmes, In the Jungle of Cities, Hermani, Bertrano, Duck Variations, Insignificance, Panache, Arms and the Man, The Promise, Crowbar, Hannah 1939, Strange Feet, Hyacinth Macaw, Henry V, Golden Boy, Timon of Athens,* Bdwy in *Indians* (1970), *Capt. Brassbound's Conversion.*

BURK, TERENCE. Born Aug. 11, 1947 in Lebanon, IL. Graduate S. IL. U. Bdwy debut 1976 in *Equus,* OB in *Religion, The Future, Sacred and Profane Love, Crime and Punishment.*

BURRELL, FRED. Born Sept. 18, 1936. Graduate UNC, RADA. Bdwy debut 1964 in *Never Too Late*, followed by *Illya Darling, Cactus Flower, On Golden Pond, Inherit the Wind* OB in *The Memorandum, Throckmorton, Texas, Voices in the Head, Chili Queen, The Queen's Knight, In Pursuit of the Song of Hydrogen, Unchanging Love, More Fun Than Bowling, Woman without a Name, Sorrows of Fredrick, Voice of the Prairie, Spain, Democracy and Esther, Last Sortie, Rough/Play, Life is a Dream, Taming of the Shrew, Twelfth Night, Modest Proposal, Oedipus at Colonus, A Hamlet, 3 in the Back 2 in the Head, True Crimes, Rhinoceros.*

BURSTEIN, DANNY. Born June 16, 1964 in NYC. Graduate U. Cal/San Diego. Moscow Art Theatre. Debut 1991 OB in *The Rothschilds, Weird Romance, Merrily We Roll Along, All in the Timing, I Love You You're Perfect Now Change,* Bdwy in *A Little Hotel on the Side* (1992), *The Sea Gull, Saint Joan, Three Men on a Horse, Flowering Peach, Company, DuBarry Was a Lady (Encores), Boys from Syracuse (Encores).*

BURTON, ARNIE. Born Sept. 22, 1958 in Emmett, ID. Graduate U. Ariz. Bdwy debut 1983 in *Amadeus*, OB in *Measure for Measure, Major Barbara, Schnitzler One Acts, Tartuffe, As You Like It, Ghosts, Othello, Moon for the Misbegotten, Twelfth Night, Little Eyolf, Mollusc, Venetain Twins, Beaux Stratagem, King Lear, Winter's Tale, When Ladies Battle, Barber of Seville, Mere Mortals, Cymbeline.*

BURTON, KATE. Born Sept. 10, 1957 in Geneva, Switz. Graduate Brown U., Yale. Bdwy debut 1982 in *Present Laughter* followed by *Alice in Wonderland, Doonesbury, Wild Honey, Some Americans Abroad, Jake's Women,Company, An American Daughter,* OB in *Winners* for which she received a 1983 Theatre World Award, *Romeo and Juliet, The Accrington Pals, Playboy of the Western World, Measure for Measure, London Suite.*

BUSCH, CHARLES. Born Aug. 23, 1954 in Hartsdale, NY. Graduate Northwestern U. Debut OB 1985 in *Vampire Lesbians of Sodom*, followed by *Times Square Angel, Psycho Beach Party, Lady in Question, Red Scare on Sunset, Charles Busch Revue, You Should Be So Lucky, Flipping My Wig,* all of which he wrote, and *Swingtime Canteen* (co-writer).

BUTLER, KERRY. Born in Brooklyn, NY. Graduate Ithaca. Bdwy debut 1993 in *Blood Brothers* followed by *Beauty and the Beast.*

BUTTRAM, JAN. Born June 19, 1946 in Clarksville, TX. Graduate N.TxStU. Debut 1974 OB in *Fashion* by *Startup, Camp Meeting, German Games, Short Subjects on Tall Topics,* Bdwy in *Best Little Whorehouse.*(1978).

BYERS, RALPH. Born Jan.10, 1950 in Washington, DC. Graduate Wm & Mary Col., CatholicU. Debut 1975 OB in *Hamlet* folowed by *Julius Caesar, Rebel Women, No End of Blame, Henry IV Part I, Petrified Prince,* Bdwy in *Herzl* (1976),*Goodbye Fidel, Big River, Sunday in the Park with George, Promises Promises (Encores).*

CAHN, LARRY. Born Dec. 19, 1955 in Nassau, NY. Graduate Northwestern U. Bdwy debut 1980 in *Music Man* followed by *Anything Goes, Guys and Dolls,* OB in *Susan B!, Jim Thorpe All American, Play to Win, Portable Pioneer.*

CALABRESE, MARIA. Born Dec. 7, 1967 in Secone, PA. Bdwy debut 1991 in *Will Rogers Follies, My Favorite Year, How to Succeed* (1995), *Once Upon a Mattress.*

CAMP, JOANNE. Born April 4, 1951 in Atlanta, GA. Graduate Fl. Atlantic U., Geo. Wash. U. Debut 1981 OB in *The Dry Martini*, followed by *Geniuses* for which she received a Theatre World Award, *June Moon, Painting Churches, Merchant of Venice, Lady from the Sea, The Contrast, Coastal Disturbances, The Rivals, Andromache, Electra, Uncle Vanya, She Stoops to Conquer, Hedda Gabler, Heidi Chronicles, Importance of Being Earnest, Medea, Three Sisters, Midsummer Night's Dream, School for Wives, Measure for Measure, Dance of Death, Two Schnitzler One-Acts, Tartuffe, Lips Together Teeth Apart, As You Like It, Moon for the Misbegotten, Phaedra, Little Eyolf, Beaux Strategem, King Lear, Life Is a Dream, Winter's Tale, When Ladies Battle, The Guardsman,* Bdwy in *Heidi Chronicles* (1989), *Sisters Rosensweig.*

CAMPBELL, AMELIA. Born Aug. 4, 1965 in Montreal, Can. Graduate Syracuse U. Debut 1988 OB in *Fun,* followed by *Member of the Wedding, Tunnel of Love, Five Women Wearing the Same Dress, Wild Dogs, Intensive Care, Wasp and Other Plays, Dolores,* Bdwy in *Our Country's Good* (1991), *Small Family Business, Translations.*

CANNON, ALICE. Born June 25 in Rochester, NY. Graduate Cornell U. Debut 1962 OB in *The Fantasticks* followed by *Silent Night Lonely Night, By Bernstein, Man with a Load of Mischief, All in Love, Sufragette, Northern Boulevard, Mr. Pim Passes By,* Bdwy in *Fiddler on the Roof* (1965), *Johnny Johnson, Education of Hyman Kaplan, Company.*

CANTONE, MARIO. Born Dec.9, 1959 in Boston, MA. Graduate Emerson Col. Bdwy debut 1995 in *Love! Valour! Compassion!* followed by *Tempest., Boys from Syracuse (Encores).*

CAPPIELLO, CHRISTOPHER. Born Sept.4, 1964 in the Bronx, NY. Graduate Brown U. Debut 1988 OB in *Macbeth* followed by *Hedda Gabler, The Philanderer, St. Vitus' Dance, Doll House, Man and Superman, Mock Trail.*

CARDONA, ANNETTE. Born March 5, 1948 in Los Angeles, CA. 1996 debut OB in *Red Devil Battery Sign.*

CAREY, HELEN. Born Jan.13, 1944 in Boston, MA. Graduate Marquette U. Bdwy debut 1997 in *London Assurance* for which she received a 1997 Theatre World Award.

CARNDUFF, HEATHER. Born April 2, 1970 in Walnut Creek, CA. Graduate Chico St U, Brandeis U. Debut 1996 OB in *Rhinoceros* followed by *Begot.*

CARTER, CAITLIN. Born February 1 in San Francisco, CA. Graduate Rice U., NC School of Arts. Bdwy debut 1993 in *Ain't Broadway Grand* followed by *Chicago, Victor Victoria, Chicago.*

CARTER, DIXIE. Born May 25, 1939 in McLemoresville, TN. Graduate Memphis St.U. Debut 1963 OB in *Winter's Tale* followed by *Carousel, Merry Widow* and *King and I* (LC), *Sextet, Jesse and the Bandit Queen* for which she received a Theatre World Award, *Fathers and Sons, A Couple of White Chicks, Taken in Marriage, Buried Inside Extra,* Bdwy 1976 in *Pal Joey* followed by *Master Class.*

CARTER, MYRA. Born October 27, 1930 in Chicago, IL. Attended Glasgow U. Bdwy debut 1957 in *Major Barbara* followed by *Maybe Tuesday, Present Laughter, Sweet Adeline,* OB in *Trials of Oz, Abingdon Square, Three Tall Women.*

CARTER, NELL. Born Sept.13 in Birmingham, AL. Bdwy debut 1971 in *Soon* followed by *Jesus Christ Superstar, Dude, Don't Bother Me I Can't Cope, Ain't Misbehaving* (1978/1988) for which she received a Theatre World Award, *Annie* (1997), OB in *Iphigenia in Taurus, Bury the Dead, Fire in the Mindhouse, Dirtiest Show in Town, Black Broadway, Rhadsody in Gershwin.*

CARUSO, JOE. Born Feb.14, 1955 in Long Branch, NJ. Graduate Montclair St U. 1991 debut OB in *Damon Runyon's Tales of Broadway* followed by *Curse of the Starving Class.*

CAULFIELD, MAXWELL. Born Nov.23, 1959 in Glasgow, Scot. Debut 1979 OB in *Class Enemy* for which he received a Theatre World Award, followed by *Crimes and Dreams, Entertaining Mr. Sloan, Inheritors, Paradise Lost, Salonika, My Night with Reg,* Bdwy 1995 in *Inspector Calls.*

CEREVIS, MICHAEL. Bdwy debut 1993 in *Tommy* followed by *Titanic.* OB in *Total Eclipse, Abingdon Square, The Games.*

CHAIKIN, SHAMI. Born April 21, 1938 in NYC. Debut 1966 OB in *American Hurrah* followed by *Serpent, Terminal (1969/1996), Mutation Show, Viet Rock, Mystery Play, Electra, The Dybbuk, Endgame, Bag Lady, The Haggadah, Antigone, Loving Reno, Early Warnings, Uncle Vanya, Mr. Unoverse, 5 Women in a Chapel.*

CHALFANT, KATHLEEN. Born Jan. 14, 1945 in San Francisco, CA. Graduate Stanford U. Bdwy debut 1975 in *Dance with Me* followed by *M. Butterfly, Angels in America, Racing Demon,* OB in *Jules Feiffer's Hold Me, Killings on the Last Line, The Boor, Blood Relations, Signs of Life, Sister Mary Ignatius Explains it All, Actor's Nightmare, Faith Healer, All the Nice People, Hard Times, Investigation of the Murder in El Salvador, 3 Poets, The Crucible, The Party, Iphigenia and Other Daughters, Cowboy Pictures, Twelve Dreams, Henry V, Endgame, When It Comes Early, Nine Armenians.*

CHAMPION, KELLY. Born February 14, 1952 in Syracuse, NY. Graduate Northwestem U. Debut 1982 OB in *Wives,* followed by *Worm in the Heart., Alone at the Beach.*

CHANNING, STOCKARD. Born Feb. 13, 1944 in NYC. Attended Radcliffe Col. Debut 1970 OB in *Adaptation/Next* followed by *Lady and the Clarinet, Golden Age, Woman in Mind, Hapgood,* Bdwy in *Two Gentlemen of Verona, They're Playing Our Song, The Rink, Joe Egg, House of Blue Leaves, Six Degrees of Separation* (also OB), *Four Baboons Adoring the Sun, Normal Heart benefit, Little Foxes.*

CHEN, TINA. Born Nov.2 in Chung King, China. Graduate BrownU. Debut 1972 OB in *Maid's Tragedy* followed by *Family Devotions, Midsummer Night's Dream, Empress of China, Year of the Dragon, Tropical Tree, Madame de Sade, Arthur and Leila, Chang Fragments, Innocence of Ghosts,* Bdwy in *King and I, Love Suicide at Schofield Barracks.*

CHENOWITH, KRISTIN. Born July 24, 1968 in Tulsa, OK. Graduate OK City U. OB in *Dames at Sea, The Fantasticks, Scapin.* Bdwy debut 1997 in *Steel Pier* for which she received a 1997 Theatre World Award.

CHERNOV, HOPE. Born June 13 in Philadelphia, PA. Graduate Temple U, U CA/Irvine. Debut 1996 OB in *Barber of Seville* followed by *Venice Preserv'd, As Bees in Honey Drown.*

CHIANESE, DOMINIC. Born Feb.24, 1932 in NYC. Graduate Brooklyn Col. Debut 1952 OB in *American Savoyards* followed by *Winterset, Jacques Brel is Alive, Ballad for a Firing Squad, City Scene, End of the War, Passione, Midsummer Night's Dream, Recruting Officer, Wild Duck, Oedipus the King, Hunting Scenes, Operation, Midnight Climax, Rosario and the Gypsies, Bella Figura, House Arrest, The Return, Major Crimes,* Bdwy in *Oliver!, Scratch, Water Engine, Richard III, Requiem for a Heavyweight, Rose Tattoo.*

CHIBAS, MARISSA. Born June 13, 1961 in NYC. Graudate SUNY/Purchase. Debut 1983 OB in *Asian Shade* followed by *Sudden Death, Total Eclipse, Another Antigone, Fresh Horses, Fortune's Fools, Overtime, Major Crimes, South,* Bdwy in *Brighton Beach Memiors* (1984), *Abe Lincoln in Illinois.*

CHRIS, MARILYN. Bom May 19, 1939 in NYC. Bdwy debut 1966 in *The Office,* followed by *Birthday Party, 7 Descents of Myrtle, Lenny,* OB in *Nobody Hears a Broken Drum Fame, Juda Applause, Junebug Graduates Tonight, Man is Man, In the Jungle of Cities, Good Soldier Schweik, The Tempest, Ride a Black Horse, Screens, Kaddish, Lady from the Sea, Bread, Leaving Home, Curtains, Elephants, The Upper Depths, Man Enough, Loose Connections, Yard Sale, God of Vengeance, Lobster Reef, Young Girl and the Monsoon.*

CHRISTIAN, WILLIAM. Bom Sept. 30, 1955 in Washington, DC. Graduate CatholicU, AmericanU. OB in *She Stoops to Conquer, A Sleep of Prisoners, American Voices, Member of the Wedding, Them That's Got, Winter's Tale, Major Crimes, Boys in the Band.*

CHRISTOPHER, DONALD. Born May 16, 1939 in Terre Haute, In. Graduate Ind. State U. Debut 1992 OB in *First the Supper* followed by *Rose and Crown, On My Knees.*

CHRISTOPHER, THOM. Born October 5, 1940 in Jackson Heights, NY. Attended Ithaca Col., Neighborhood Playhouse. Debut 1972 OB in *One Flew Over the Cuckoo's Nest* followed by *Tamara, Investigation of the Murder in El Salvador, Sublime Lives, Triumph of Love, The Changeling,* Bdwy in *Emperor Henry IV* (1973), *Noel Coward in Two Keys* for which he received a Theatre World Award, *Caesar and Cleopatra.*

CIOPPA. LAWRENCE. Born Dec.29, 1933 in Albany, NY. Graduate Syracuse U, St. Johns. 1962 debut OB in *Song of Bernadette* followed by *Captain of Koepenick, Don Carlos, Putting Them to Pasture, Hot l Baltimore.*

CLARK, VICTORIA. Born Oct.10 in Dallas, TX. Graduate Yale. Bdwy debut 1992 in *Guys and Dolls* followed by *Grand Night for Singing, How to Succeed..., Titanic.* OB in *Marathon Dancing.*

CLARKE, RICHARD. Bom Jan. 31, 1933 in England. Graduate U. Reading. With LCRep in St. Joan *(1968), Tiger at the Gates, Cyrano de Bergerac,* Bdwy in *Conduct Unbecoming, Elephant Man, Breaking the Code, Devils Disciple, M. Butterfly, Six Degrees of Separation, Two Shakespearean Actors, Arcadia, Racing Demon, Taking Sides,* OB in *Old Glory, Trials of Oz, Looking Glass, Trelawney of the Wells, Fair Country.*

CLAYTON, LAWRENCE. Born Oct. 10, 1956 in Mocksville, NC. Attended NC Central U. Debut 1980 in *Tambourines to Glory,* followed by *Skyline, Across the Universe, Two by Two, Romance in Hard Times, Juba, Tapestry,* Bdwy in *Dreamgirls* (1984), *High Rollers, Once Upon a Mattress.*

Trevor Anthony

Susan Ancheta

Victor Anthony

Karen Arneson

Jase Blankfort

Arija Bareikis

Joseph Bologna

Blythe Baten

John Bolton

Mimi Bensinger

Gibby Brand

Alison Bevan

Danny Burstein

Kate Burton

Christopher
Cappiello

Annette Cardona

Joe Caruso

Kathleen Chalfant

Joey Collins

Hope Chernov

Bradford Cover

Victoria Clark

Keith Cromwell

Emy Coligado

Dermot Crowley

Kelly Curtis

Craig Dudley

Janis Dardaris

George Dudley

Lisa Datz

229

COHEN, LYNN. Born August 10 in Kansas City, Mo. Graduate Northwestern U. Debut 1979 OB in *Don Juan Comes Back From the Wars* followed by *Getting Out, The Arbor, Cat and the Canary, Suddenly Last Summer, Bella Figura, The Smash, Chinese Viewing Pavillion, Isn't It Romatic, Total Eclipse, Angelo's Wedding, Hamlet, Love Diatribe, A Couple with a Cat, XXX Love Acts, Model Apt., The Devils,* Bdwy in *Orpheus Descending* (1989).

COHEN, SAMUEL D. Bom March 10, 1963 in Memphis, TN. Graduate Penn State. Debut 1989 OB in *The Witch* followed by *Lover's Labour's Lost, Yiddle with a Fiddle, Portable Pioneer.*

COHENOUR, PATTI. Born Oct. 17, 1952 in Albuquerque, NM. Attended U. NM. Bdwy debut 1982 in *A Doll's Life,* followed by *Pirates of Penzance, Big River, Mystery of Edwin Drood, Phantom of the Opera, Sweet Adeline (Encores),* OB in *La Boheme* for which she received a Theatre World Award.

COKAS, NICK. Born April 11, 1965 in San Francisco, CA. Graduate UCLA. Bdwy debut 1993 in *Blood Brothers* followed by *Once Upon a Mattress.*

COLEMAN, ROSALYN. Born July 20, 1965 in Ann Arbor, MI. Graduate Harvard U., Yale Drama. Bdwy debut 1990 in *Piano Lesson* followed by *Mule Bone, Seven Guitars,* OB in *Destiny of Me* (1992), *Major Crimes.*

COLIGADO, EMY. Born June 5, 1971 in Geneva, OH. Bdwy debut 1995 in *Miss Saigon,* OB in *Shanghai Lil's* (1997).

COLLET, CHRISTOPHER. Born March 13, 1968 in NYC. Attended Strasberg Inst. Bdwy debut 1983 in *Torch Song Trilogy* followed by *Spoils of War* (also OB), OB in *Coming of Age in Soho, Executive Council, Unfinished Stories, An Imaginary Life, Gravity of Means.*

COLLINS, JOEY. Born Feb.14, 1969 in Gainesville, GA. Graduate U of NC (Wilmington), Alabama Shakespeare Fest. 1997 debut OB in *Venice Preserv'd.*

COLODNER, JOEL. Born May 1, 1946 in Brooklyn, NY. Graduate Cornell, SMU. Bdwu debut 1973 in *Three Sisters* followed by *Beggar's Opera, Measure for Measure,* OB in *Do I Hear a Waltz?, Memory of Two Mondays, They Knew What They Wanted, Daisy, Dona Rosita, How I Learned to Drive.*

COLTON, CHEVI. Born Dec. 21 in NYC. Attended Hunter Col. OB in *Time of Storm, Insect Comedy, Adding Machine, O Marry Me, Penny Change, Mad Show, Jacques Brel Is Alive.., Bits and Pieces, Spelling Bee, Uncle Money, Miami, Come Blow Your Horn, Almost Perfect, Susnset Gang, Milk and Honey, On Deaf Ears,* Bdwy in *Over Here, Cabaret, Grand Tour, Torch Song Trilogy, Roza.*

CONROY, FRANCES. Born in 1953 in Monroe, GA. Attended Dickinson Col., Juilliard, Neighborhood Playhouse. Debut 1978 OB with the Acting Co. in *Mother Courage, King Lear, The Other Half* followed by *All's Well That Ends Well, Othello, Sorrows of Stephen, Girls Girls Girls, Zastrozzi, Painting Churches, Uncle Vanya, Romance Language, To Gillian on Her 37th Birthday, Man and Superman, Zero Positive, Bright Room Called Day, Lips Together Teeth Apart, Booth, Last Yankee, Three Tall Women, Arts and Leisure,* Bdwy in *Lady from Dubuque* (1980), *Our Town, Secret Rapture* (also OB), *Some Americans Abroad* (also OB), *Two Shakespearian Actors, In the Summer House, Broken Glass, The Rehearsal, Little Foxes.*

COOK, LINDA. Born Juen 8 in Lubbock, TX. Attended Auburn U. Debut 1974 OB in *The Wager* followed by *Hole in the Wall, Shadow of a Gunman, Be My Father, Ghosts of the Loyal Oaks, Different People Different Rooms, Saigon Rose, Romantic Arrangements, No Time Flat, Dearly Deaprted, All That Glitters, Next Door Down.*

COOPER, CHUCK. Born Nov. 8, 1954 in Cleveland, OH. Graduate Ohio U. Debut 1982 OB in *Colored People's Time* followed by *Riff Raff Revue, Primary English Class, Break/Agnes/Eulogy/Lucky, Avenue X,* Bdwy in *Amen Corner* (1983), *Someone Who'll Watch Over Me, Getting Away with Murder, The Life.*

CORDDRY, ROBERT. Born Feb.4, 1971 in Weymouth, MA. Graduate U.Mass Amherst. Debut 1994 OB in *Manchurian Candidate* followed by *What Doesn't Kill Us.*

CORMIER, TONY. Born November 2, 1951 in Camp Roberts, CA. Attended Pierce Col., Wash.StU. Debut 1984 in *Kennedy at Colonus* followed by *Pericles, Something Cloudy Something Clear, Three Sisters, Love's Labour's Lost, Angel in the House, Measure for Measure, Titus Andronicus, Hamlet., Spirit of Man, Absent Friends.*

COUNCIL, RICHARD E. Born Oct. 1, 1947 in Tampa, FL. Graduate U. Fl. Debut 1973 OB in *Merchant of Venice* followed by *Ghost Dance, Look We've Come Through, Arms and the Man, Isadora Duncan Sleeps with the Russian Navy, Arthur, The Winter Dancer, The Prevalence of Mrs. Seal, Jane Avril, Young Playwrights Festival, Sleeping Dogs, The Good Coach, Subfertile, Nine Armenians,* Bdwy in *Royal Family* (1975), *Philadelphia Story, I'm Not Rappaport, Conversations with My Father, Pal Joey, Uncle Vanya, Little Foxes.*

COUNTRYMAN, MICHAEL. Born Sept. 15, 1955 in St. Paul, MN. Graduate Trinity Col., AADA. Debut 1983 OB in *Changing Palettes,* followed by *June Moon, Terra Nova, Out!, Claptrap, The Common Pursuit, Woman in Mind, Making Movies, The Tempest, Tales of the Lost Formicans, Marathon '91, The Stick Wife, Lips Together Teeth Apart, All in the Timing, The Ashfire, Where the Truth Lies, Nine Armenians,* Bdwy in *A Few Good Men* (1990), *Face Value, Holiday.*

COURTENAY, TOM. Born Feb.25, 1937 in Hull, Eng. Graduate RADA. Bdwy debut 1977 in *Otherwise Engaged* followed by *The Dresser, Uncle Vanya,* OB in *Moscow Station.*

COVER, BRADFORD. Born Jan.26, 1967 in NYC. Graduate DenisonU, UWis. Debut 1994 OB in *King Lear* followed by *Beaux Strategem, Venetian Twins, Oedipus at Colonus, Mrs. Warren's Profession, Winter's Tale, Life Is a Dream, When Ladies Battle, Antigone, Misalliance.*

COX, RICHARD. Born May 6, 1948 in NYC. Graduate Yale. Debut 1970 OB in *Saved* followed by *Fugs, Moonchildren, Alice in Concert, Richard II, Fishing, What a Man Weighs, Family of Mann, Scar,* Bdwy in *Sign in Sidney Brustein's Window, Platinum, Blood Brothers, Apple Doesn't Fall.*

COX, VEANNE. Born Jan.19, 1963 in Virginia. Bdwy debut in *Smile* (1986) followed by *Company,* OB in *Nat'l Lampoon's Class of '86, Flora the Red Menace, Showing Off, Food Chain, Question of Mercy, Waiting Room.*

CREST, ROBERT. Born July 21, 1938 in Pecos, TX. Attended Trinity U, Pasadena Playhouse. Debut 1969 OB in *The Fantasticks* followed by *Servant of Two Masters, Andorra, Under Milk Wood, Don't Make a Scene*

CROFT, PADDY. Born in Worthing, England. Attended Avondale Col. Debut 1961 OB in *The Hostage* followed by *Billy Liar, Live Like Pigs, Hogan's Goat, Long Day's Journey into Night, Shadow of a Gunman, Pygmalion, Plough and the Stars, Kill, Starting Monday, Philadephia Here I Come!, Grandchild of Kings, Fragments, Same Old Moon, Nightingale and Not the Lark, Da,* Bdwy in *Killing of Sister George, Prime of Miss Jean Brodie, Crown Matrimonial, Major Barbara.*

CROMWELL, KEITH A. Born July 5, 1963 in Tripoli, Lybia, No.Africa. Graduate James MadisonU. Debut 1993 OB in *Whoop-Dee-Doo* followed by *When Pigs Fly.*

CROWLEY, DERMOT. Born March 19, 1947 in Cork, Ireland. Graduate UCC. 1997 debut OB in *Dealer's Choice.*

CROWTHER, JOHN. Born March 28, 1939 in NYC. Attended Princeton. Bdwy debut 1962 in *Something about a Soldier* followed by *Seidman and Son, Where's Daddy.* OB in *Einstein: A Stage Portrait.*

CRUDUP, BILLY. Born July 8, 1968 in Manhasset, NY. Graduate UNC,NYU. Debut 1994 OB in *America Dreaming,* Bdwy 1995 in *Arcadia* for which he received a Theatre World Award, followed by *Bus Stop, Three Sisters.*

CRUTCHFIELD, BUDDY. Born June 4, 1957 in Dallas, TX. Graduate SMU. Debut 1979 in *Radio City Christmas Spectacular* followed by OB in *HMS Pinafore, Pirates of Penzance, Tent Show, Church is Born, Senior Discretion, Widow Clair, Six Wives, Doctor! Doctor!,* Bdwy in *The Most Happy Fella* (1992).

CRYER, JON. Born April 16, 1965 in NYC. Attended RADA. Bdwy debut 1983 in *Torch Song Trilogy* followed by *Brighton Beach Memoirs,* OB in *900 Oneonta.*

CUCCIOLI, ROBERT/BOB. Born May 3, 1958 in Hempstead, NY. Graduate St. John's U. Debut 1982 OB in *HMS Pinafore* followed by *Senor Discretion,Gigi, The Rothschilds, And the World Goes Round,* Bdwy in *Les Miserables, Jekyll & Hyde.*

CUERVO, ALMA. Born Aug. 13, 1951 in Tampa, Fl. Graduate TulaneU. Debut 1977 in *Uncommon Women and Others* followed by *Foot in the Door, Put Them All Together, Isn't It Romatic?, Miss Julie, Quilters, Sneaker Factor, Songs on a Shipwrecked Sofa, Uncle Vanya, Grandma Plays, The Nest, Secret Rapture, Christine Alberta's Father, Music from Down the Hall, Donahue Sisters, 3 in the Back 2 in the Head,* Bdwy in *Once in a Lifetime, Bedroom Farce, Censored Scenes from King Kong, Is There Life After High School?, Ghetto, Secret Rapture, Titanic.*

CULLUM, JOHN. Bom Mar. 2, 1930 in Knoxville, TN. Graduate U.Tenn. Bdwy debut 1960 in *Camelot*, followed by *Infidel Caesar, The Rehearsal, Hamlet, On a Clear Day You Can See Forever* for which he received a Theatre World Award, *Man of La Mancha, 1776, Vivat! Vivat Regina!, Shenandoah (1975/1989), Kings, Trip Back Down, On the 20th Century, Deathtrap, Doubles, You Never Can Tell, Boys in Autumn, Aspecu of Love, Show Boat*, OB in *3 Hand Reel, The Elizabethans, Carousel, In the Voodoo Parlor of Marie Leveau, King and I, Whistler, All My Sons*.

CUMPSTY, MICHAEL. Born in England. Graudate UNC. Bdwy debut 1989 in *Artist Descending a Staircase* followed by *La Bete, Timon of Athens, Translations, Heiress, Racing Demon*, OB in *Art of Success, Man and Superman, Hamlet, Cymbeline, Winter's Tale, King John, Romeo and Juliet, All's Well That Ends Well., Timon of Athens*.

CUNNINGHAM, JOHN. Born June 22, 1932 in Auburn, NY. Graduate Yale, Dartmouth U. OB in *Love Me a Little, Pimpernel, The Fantasticks, Love and Let Love, The Bone Room, Dancing in the Dark, Father's Day, Snapshot, Head Over Heels, Quartermaine's Terms, Wednesday, On Approval, Miami, Perfect Party, Birds of Paradise, Naked Truth, Cheever Evening, Camping with Henry and Tom, Sylvia, Heartbreak House*, Bdwy in *Hot Spot* (1963), *Zorba, Company, 1776, Rose, The Devil's Disciple, Six Degrees of Separation* (also OB), *Anna Karenina, The Sisters Rosensweig, Allegro(Encores), Titanic*.

CUNNINGHAM, T. SCOTT. Born December 15 in Los Angeles, CA. Graduate NC School of Arts. Debut 1992 OB in *Pterodactyls* followed by *Takes on Women, Stand-In, Don Juan in Chicago, Wally's Ghost, New England, Fit to Be Ties, As Bees in Honey Drown*, Bdwy in *Love! Valour! Compassion! (1995), Tartuffe: Born Again*.

CURTIS, KEENE. Born Feb. 15, 1925 in Salt Lake City UT. Graduate U. Utah. Bdwy debut 1949 in *Shop at Sly Corner*, with APA in *School for Scandal, The Tavern, Anatole, Scapin, Right You Are, Importance of Being Earnest, Twelfth Night, King Lear, Seagull, Lower Depths, Man and Superman, Judith, War and Peace, You Can't Take It with You, Pantaglieze, Cherry Orchard, Misanthrope, Cocktail Party, Cock-a-Doodle Dandy, and Hamlet, A Patriot for Me, The Rothschilds, Night Watch, Via Galactica, Annie, Division Street, La Cage aux Folles,White Liars/Black Comedy*, OB in *Colette, Ride Across Lake Consequence, Cocktail Hour*.

CURTIS, KELLY. Born June 17 in Santa Monica, CA. Graduate Skidmore Col. 1984 debut OB in *Andorra* followed by *Iowa Boys, Summer at Pilares, The Last Manhattan, Antigone, Two Tents, Major Crimes*.

CWIKOWSKI, BILL. Bom Aug. 4, 1945 in Newark, NJ. Graduate Smith and Monmouth Col. Debut 1972 OB in *Charlie the Chicken* followed by *Summer Brave, Desperate Hours, Mandrogola, Two by Noonan, Soft Touch, Innocent Pleasures, 3 from the Marathon, Two Part Harmony; Bathroom Plays, Little Victories, Dolphin Position, Cabal of Hypocrites, Split Second, Rose Cottages, Good Coach, Marathon '88, Tunnel of Love, Dead Man's Apartment, De Donde?, Scarlett Letter, Getting In*.

CYR, MYRIAM. Born in New Brunswick, Can. Attended Conserv. d'Art Dramatique de Montreal, Ecole Nat'l de Strasbourg, LAMDA. 1995 debut OB in *Floating Rhoda and the Glue Man* followed by *Green Bird*.

DAILY, DANIEL. Bom July 25, 1955 in Chicago, IL. Graduate Notre Dame, U. Wash. Debut 1988 OB in *Boy 's Breath* followed by *A Ronde, Iron Bars, Chekhov Very Funny, Macbeth, As You Like It, Free Zone, Scarlet Letter, Two Nikita, The Adoption, Tenth Man, Helmut Sees America*.

DAFOE, WILLEM (WILLIAM). Born July 22, 1955. Has performed with OB's Wooster Group since 1977. OB in *Hairy Ape*.

DAKIN, LINNEA. Born Mar.21, 1972 in Kansas, City, Kan. Graduate U of Hartford. Bdwy debut in *State Fair* (1996), OB in *Cedar Creek* .

DALE, JIM. Born Aug.15, 1935 in Rothwell, Eng. Debut 1974 OB in *Taming of the Shrew* (Young Vic) followed by *Privates on Parade, Tavels with My Aunt*, Bdwy in *Scapino* (also OB), *Barnum, Joe Egg, Me and My Girl, Candide (1997)*.

DANIELEY, JASON. Born July 13, 1971 in St. Louis, MO. Attended So. IL U.1994 debut OB in *Hit the Lights* followed by *Floyd Collins, Trojan Women: A Love Story*, Bdwy in *Allegro(Encores/1994), Candide*(1997) for which he received a 1997 Theatre World Award.

DANSON, RANDY. Born April 30, 1950 in Plainfield NJ. Graduate Carnegie-Mellon U. Debut 1978 OB in *Gimme Shelter* followed by *Big and Little, Winter Dancers, Time Steps, Casualties, Red and Blue, Resurrection of Lady Lester, Jazz Poets at the Grotto, Plenty, Macbeth, Blue Window, Cave Life, Romeo and Juliet, One-Act Festival, Mad Forest, Triumph of Love, The Treatment, Phaedra, Arts & Leisure, The Devils, The Erinyes*.

d'ARCY JAMES, BRIAN. Born 1968 in Saginaw, MI. Graduate Northwestern U. Bdwy in *Carousel, Blood Brothers, Titanic*, OB in *Public Enemy, Floyd Collins, Violet*.

DARDARIS, JANIS. Born Jan.7, 1960 in Philadelphia, PA. Attended Boston U (Lenox), Bucks County Col. 1992 debut OB in *Breaking Legs* followed by *Matt the Killer, Finding Doris Anne, Those Left Behind*.

DARLOW, CYNTHIA. Born June 13, 1949 in Detroit, MI. Attended NCSch of Arts, Penn State U. Debut 1974 OB in *This Property Is Condemned* followed by *Portrait of a Madonna, Clytemnestra, Unexpurgated Memoirs of Bernard Morgandigler, Actor's Nightmare, Sister MaryIgnatius Explains.., Fables for Friends, That's It Folks!, Baby with the Bath Water, Dandy Dick, Naked Truth, Cover of Life, Death Deying Acts*, Bdwy in *Grease* (1976), *Rumors, Prelude to a Kiss* (also OB), *Sex and Longing*.

DATZ, LISA. Born April 24, 1973 in Evanston, IL. Graduate U of MI. Bdwy debut in *Titanic* (1997).

DAVIES, JOSEPH C. Born June 29, 1928 in Charlton, IA. Attended MichStCol., WayneU. Debut 1961 OB in *7 at Dawn* followed by *Jo, Long Voyage Home, Time of the Key, Good Soldier Schweik, Why Hanna's Skirt Won't Stay Down, Ghandi, Coney Island Kid, The Cause, It's Toast*, Bdwy in *Skin of Our Teeth* (1975).

DAVIS, BRUCE ANTHONY. Born March 4, 1959 in Dayton, OH. Attended Juilliard. Bdwy debut 1979 in *Dancin'* followed by *Big Deal, Chorus Line, High Rollers, Damn Yankees, Chicago*, OB in *Carnival*.

DAVIS, KATIE. Born April 14, 1965 in Tulsa, OK. Graduate U of OK. OB in *Time of Your Life, Trust, Zero Hour, Fault Line, Women of Manhattan*.

DAVIS, MARY BOND. Born June 3, 1958 in Los Angeles, CA. Attended Cal. State U./Northridge, LACC. Debut 1985 in *Trousers* followed by *Hysterical Blindness, Scapin*, Bdwy in *Mail* (1988), *Jelly's Last Jam*.

DAVIS, VIOLA. Born Aug.11, 1965 in St. Matthews, So.Carolina. Graduate, Rhode Island Col., Juilliard. Debut 1992 OB in *As You Like It* followed by *House of Lear, God's Heart*, Bdwy in *Seven Guitars* (1996) for which she received a Theatre World Award.

DAVISON, BRUCE. Born June 28, 1946 in Philadelphia, PA. Graduate Penn St, NYU. 1969 debut OB in *A Home Away From* followed by *Richard III, Tiger at the Gates, Cry of Players, King Lear, How I Learned to Drive*, Bdwy in *Elephant Man, Glass Menagerie*.

DAVYS, EDMUND C. Born Jan. 21, 1947 in Nashua, NH. Graduate Oberlin Col. Debut 1977 OB in *Othello*, Bdwy in *Crucifer of Blood* (1979), *Shadowlands, A Small Family Business, The Show-off, St. Joan, Three Men on a Horse, Ideal Husband*.

DEAK, TIM. Born March 15, 1968 in Ravennam, OH. Graduate Otterbein Col. Debut 1974 OB in *Kentucky Cycle* followed by *Dark of the Moon, Childe Byron, Cater Waiter*.

DEAL, FRANK. Born October 7, 1958 in Birmingham, AL. Attended Duke U. Debut 1982 OB in *American Princess* followed by *Richard III, Ruffian on the Stair, Midsummer Night's Dream, We Shall Not All Sleep, Legend of Sleepy Hollow, Three Sisters, Triangle Project, One Neck, Window Man, Othello, Junk Bonds, Dark Ride, Second-Hand Smoke, Gross Indecency*.

DEEP, MICHAEL. Born June 12, 1954 in Macon, GA. Graduate MercerU. Debut 1979 OB in *Ragged Trousered Philanthropists* followed by *Engaged, Bring Mother Down, Short Subjects on Tall Topics, Tooth of Crime (Second Dance)*.

DEIGNAN, DEANNA. Born Oct.12, 1950 in Lake Geneva, WI. Graduate MI St U, Goodman Sch. 1984 debut OB in *Enter a Free Man* followed by *Love's Labour's Lost, Returner*.

DEL POZO, EMILIO. Bom Aug. 6, 1948 in Havana, Cuba. Attended AMDA. Debut 1983 OB in *Union City Thanksgiving* followed by *El Grande de Coca Cola, Senorita from Tacna, Twelfth Night, Wonderful Ice Cream Suit, In Miami as It Is in Heaven*, Bdwy in *Salome (1992), Summer and Smoke*.

DENMAN, JEFFREY. Born Oct.7, 1970 in Buffalo, NY. Graduate UBuffalo. Bdwy debut 1995 in *How to Succeed...*followed by *Dream*.

DeSHIELDS, ANDRE. Bom Jan. 12, 1946 in Baltimore, MD. Graduate U. Wis. Bdwy debut 1973 in *Warp* followed by *Rachel Lily Rosenbloom, The Wiz, Ain't Misbehavin' (1978/1988), Haarlem Nocturne, Just So, Stardust, Play On*, OB in *2008-1/2 Jazzbo Brown, Soldier's Tale, Little Prince, Haarlem Nocturne, Sovereign State of Boogedy Boogedy, Kiss Me When It's Over, Saint Tous, Ascension Day, Casino Paradise, The Wiz, Angel Levine, Ghost Cafe......*

DeVRIES, JON. Born March 26, 1947 in NYC. Graduate Bennington Col. Pasadena Playhouse. Debut 1977 OB in *Cherry Orchard* followed by *Agameinnon, Ballad of Soapy Smith, Titus Andronicus, Dreamer Examines his Pillow, Sight Unseen, Patient A, Scarlet Letter, One Flea Spare, Red Address,* Bdwy in I*nspector General, Devour the Snow, Major Barbara, Execution of Justice.*

DiBENEDETTO, JOHN. Born Oct.9, 1955 in Brooklyn, NYC. Attended Hunter Col., HB Studio. Debut 1979 OB in *Prisoners of Quai Dong* followed by *Greatest of All Time, Apple Crest, Tales of Another City, Out at Sea, Heartdrops, Good Woman of Setzuan, Squeeze, Drunken Boat, Venus Dances Nightly, Not a Single Blade of Grass, Flashpoint, Sea Gull, Bruno's Donuts, Happy Birthday America, Full Circle, Across Arkansas, Jurlyburly, Wedding, Candide, Unrecognizable Characters, Secret Sits in the Middle, Wolf at the Door, Ruby and Pearl, Once Upon a Time in the Bronx.*

DOLINER, ROY. Born June 27, 1954 in Boston, MA. Attended Tufts U. Debut 1977 OB in *Don't Cry Child Your Father's an American* followed by *Zwi Kanar Show, Big Bad Burlesque, Lysistrata, Rats, Casanova, Midsummer Night's Dream.*

DOMAN, JOHN. Born Jan.9, 1945 in Philadelphia, PA. Debut 1990 OB in *Fool for Love* followed by *True West, Lady Swims Today, Sea Gull, Robbers.*

DONNELLY, DONAL. Born July 6, 1931 in Bradford, Eng. Bdwy debut in *Philadelphia, Here I Come! (1966)* followed by *Day in the Death of Joe Egg, Sheuth, The Faith Healer, The Elephant Man, Execution of Justice, Sherlock's Last Case, Chetto, Dancing at Lughnasa, Translations,* OB in *My Astonishing Self (solo), The Chalk Garden, Big Maggie.*

DONOHOE, ROB. Born Dec.25, 1950 in Bossier City, LA. Graduate E.NewMxU., AmThArts. Debut 1987 OB in *Long Boat* followed by *Last Resort, Leave It to Jane* Bdwy in *Christmas Carol* (1995), *1776* .

DOVA, NINA. Born jan.15, 1926 in London, Eng. Attended Neighborhood Playhouse. Debut 1954 OB in *I Feel Wonderful* followed by *Delicate Balance, Naked, Carmelina,* Bdwy in *Zorba, The Rothschilds, Saturday Sunday Monday, Strider* (also OB).

DRAKE, DAVID. Born June 27, 1963 in Baltimore, Md. Attended Essex Col., Peabody Consv. Debut 1984 OB in *Street Theatre* followed by *Pretty Boy, Vampire Lesbians of Sodom, The Life, Night Larry Kramer Kissed Me, Pageant, Normal Heart (benefit), Language of Their Own, Boys in the Band.*

DuART, LOUISE. Born Oct.30, 1950 in Quincy, MA. Attended L.A. City Coll. Bdwy debut 1994 in *Catskills on Broadway,* OB in *Me and Jezebel* (1995), *Dreamstuff.*

DUDLEY, CRAIG. Born Jan. 22, 1945 in Sheepshead Bay, NY. Graduate AADA, Am.Th.Wing. Debut 1970 OB in *Macbeth* followed by *Zou, I Have Always Believed in Ghosts, Othello, War and Peace, Dial "M" for Murder, Misalliance, Crown of Kings, Trelawny of The Wells, Ursula's Permanent.*

DUDLEY, GEORGE. Born April 6, 1958 in Santa Monica. CA. Graduate Humboldt State U. Bdwy debut 1990 in *Grand Hotel* followed by *Victor Victoria.*

DUNDAS, JENNIFER. Born Jan. 14, 1971 in Boston, MA. Bdwy debut 1981 in *Grownups* followed by *Arcadia, Little Foxes,* OB in *Before the Dawn, I Love You I Love You Not, Autobiography of Aiken Fiction, Good as New.*

DUNLOP, TOM. Born Jan.14, 1961 in Waterbury, CT. Graduate BrownU, Juilliard. Debut 1989 OB in *Macbeth* followed by *Midsummer Night's Dream, King John, Misalliance.*

DURAN, SHERRITA. Born March 18, 1970 in Fresno, CA. Graduate USC. Bdwy debut in *Showboat* (1996) followed by *Candide* (1997).

DURNING, CHARLES. Born Feb.28, 1923 in Highland Falls, NY. Attended Columbia, NYU. Bdwy in *Poor Bitros, Drat the Cat, Pousse Cafe, Happy Time, Indians, That Championship Season, Knock Knock, Cat on a Hot Tin Roof (1990), Inherit the Wind, Gin Game,* OB in *Two by Saroyan, Child Buyer, Album of Gunter Grass, Huui Huui, Invitation to a Beheading, Lemon Sky, Henry VI, Happiness Cage, Hamlet, In the BoomBoom Room, Au Pair Man.*

DVORSKY, GEORGE. Born May 11, 1959 in Greensburg, PA. Attended Carnegie-Mellon. Bdwy debut 1981 in *The Best Little Whorehouse in Texas* followed by *Marilyn: An American Fable, Brigadoon. Cinderella, Passion, Gentlemen Prefer Blondes* (1995), OB in *Dames at Sea* (1985), *Leading Men Don't Dance.*

DYBAS, JAMES. Born Feb.7, 1944 in Chicago, IL. Bdwy debut in *Do I Hear a Waltz* (1965) followed by *George M, Via Galactica, Pacific Overtures, Sunset Blvd.*

DYS, DEANNA. Born April 23, 1966 in Dearborn, MI. Bdwy debut 1988 in *Legs Diamond* followed by *Meet Me in St. Louis, Crazy for You, Candide* (1997).

EBERSOLE, CHRISTINE. Born Feb.21, 1953 in Park Forest, IL. Attended AADA. Bdwy debut in *Angel Street* (1976) followed by *I Love My Wife, On the 20th Century, Oklahoma, Camelot, Harrigan and Hart, Getting Away with Murder,* OB in *Green Pond, Three Sisters, Geniuses, Good as New.*

ECK, SCOTT. Born April 2, 1957 in Ellenville, NY. Attended Hofstra U. Debut 1980 OB in *The Lover* followed by *Lady's Not for Burning,* Bdwy in *Inspector Calls* (1995).

EDER, LINDA. Born 1961 in Tucson, AZ. Bdwy debut 1997 in *Jekyll & Hyde* for which she received a 1997 Theatre World Award.

EDMEAD, WENDY. Born July 6, 1956 in New York City. Graduate NYCU. Bdwy debut 1974 in *The Wiz,* followed by *Stop the World..., America, Dancin', Encore, Cats,* OB 1995 in *Petrified Prince, Brief History of White Music.*

EDWARDS, BURT. Born Jan.11, 1928 in Richmond, VA. Graduate UVA. Debut 1949 OB in *Fifth Horseman of the Apocalypse* followed by *Cenci, Camel Has His Nose Under the Tent, Cocktail Hour, Rhinoceros,* Bdwy in *King and I (1985).*

EDWARDS, DAVID. Born Dec.13, 1957 in NYC. Graduate NYU. Bdwy debut 1972 in *The Rothschilds* followed by *Best Little Whorehouse in Texas, 42nd St., Chorus Line,* OB in *Wish You Were Here, Bruitsite, One More Time, Zion, Company, The Disputation, What's a Nice Country Like You Doing...*

EGAN, JOHN TRACY. Born July 10, 1962 in NYC. Graduate SUNY/Purchase, Attended Westchester Comm Col. Debut 1990 OB in *Whatnot* followed by *When Pigs Fly.* Bdwy in *Jekyll & Hyde* (1997).

EISENBERG, NED. Born Jan. 13, 1957 in NYC. Attended Acl. Inst. of Arts. Debut 1980 OB in *Time of the Cuckoo* followed by *Our Lord of Lynchville, Dream of a Blacklisted Actor, Second Avenue, Moving Targets, Claus, Titus Adronicus, Saturday Morning Cartoons, Antigone in NY, Green Bird, Red Address,* Bdwy in *Pal Joey (Encores, 1995).*

ELDER, DAVID. Born July 7, 1966 in Houston, TX. Attended U. Houston. Bdwy debut 1992 in *Guys and Dolls* followed by *Beauty and the Beast, Once Upon a Mattress, Titanic.*

ELKINS, ELIZABETH. Born July 24, 1967 in Ft. Lauderdale, FL. Debut 1991 OB in *Blue Window* followed by *Lion in the Streets, Never the Same Rhyme Twice, Night of Knave.*

EMERSON, MICHAEL. Born 1955 in Cedar Rapids, IA. Graduate Drake U, U AL. Debut 1997 OB in *Gross Indecency.*

EMERSON, SUSAN. Born in Charleston, WV. Graduate W VA U. Debut 1985 OB in *Bells are Ringing* followed by *Nunsense II, Portable Pioneer & Prarie Show,* Bdwy in *Boys from Syracuse (Encores, 1997).*

EMERY, LISA. Born Jan. 29 in Pittsburgh, PA. Graduate Hollins Col. Debut 1981 OB in *In Connecticut* followed by *Talley & Son, Dalton's Back, Growaups!, The Matchmaker, Marvin's Room, Watbanaland, Monogomist, Curtains,* Bdwy in *Passion (1983), Burn This, Rumors, Present Laughter.*

EMOND, LINDA. Born May 22, 1959 in New Brunswick, NJ. Graduate U of WA. Debut 1996 OB in *Nine Armenians,* Bdwy in *1776* (1997).

ENDERS, CAMILLA. Born Sept.6, 1967 in Boston, MA. Graduate Oberlin Col. U of London. Debut 1995 in *Sylvia* followed by *Ivanov.*

ENGLISH, DONNA. Born January 13, 1962 in Norman, Ok. Graduate Northwestern U. Bdwy debut 1987 in *Broadway,* OB in *Company, Last Musical Comedy, Kiss Me Quick, Ruthless!, Fordidden Bdwy Strikes Back.*

EPSTEIN, ALVIN. Born May 14, 1925 in NYC. Attended Queens Col. Bdwy includes *Marcel Marceau, King Lear, Waiting for Godot, From A to Z, No Strings, Passion of Josef D, Postmark Zero, Kurt Weill Cabaret,* OB in *Purple Dust, Pictures in a Hallway, Clerambard, Endgame (1958/1984), Whores Wares and Tin Pan Alley, Place without Doors, Crossing Niagara, Beckett Plays, Waltz of the Torreadors, 6 Characters in Search of an Author, When the World was Green.*

ERRICO, MELISSA. Born March 23, 1970 in NYC. Graduate Yale U. BADA. Bdwy debut in *Anna Karenina* (1992) followed by *My Fair Lady*(1994), *Call Me Madam (Encores), One Touch of Venus (Encores),* OB in *After Crystal Night, Spring Awakening, Importance of Being Earnest.*

ESTERMAN, LAURA. Born April 12 in NYC. Attended Radcliffe Col., LAMDA. Debut 1969 OB in *Time of Your Life* followed by *Pig Pen, Carpenters, Ghosts, Macbeth, Sea Gull, Rubbers, Yankees 3 Detroit 0, Golden Boy, Out of Our Father's House, The Master and Margarita, Chinchilla, Dusa, Fish Stas and Vi, Midsummer Night's Dream, Recruiting Officer, Oedipus the King, Two Fish in the Sky, Mary Barnes, Tamara, Marvin's Room, Edith Stein, Curtains, Yiddish Trojan Women, Good as New,* Bdwy in *Waltz of the Toreadors, The Show-off.*

ESTEY, SUELLEN. Born Nov. 21 in Mason City, IA. Graduate Stephens Col., Northwestern U. Debut 1970 OB in *Some Other Time* followed by *June Moon, Buy Bonds Buster, Smile Smile Smile, Carousel, Lullaby of Broadway, I Can't Keep Running, Guys in the Truck, Stop the World..., Bittersuite—One More Time, Passionate Extremes, Sweeney Todd, Love in Two Countries, After the Ball, Oh Captain,* Bdwy in *The Selling of the President* (1972), *Barnum, Sweethearts in Concert, Sweeney Todd* (1989), *State Fair.*

EVANS, VENIDA. Born Sept.2, 1947 in Ypsilanti, MI. Attended Fisk U. Debut 1981 OB in *Tarbuckle* followed by *Ladies, Dinah Washington Is Dead, Ground People, East Texas, 900 Oneonta,* Bdwy in *Amen Corner* (1983).

EWIN, PAULA. Born Dec.6, 1955 in Warwick, Rhode Island. Attended King's College/Wilkes-Barre, PA, Graduate Rhode Island College. Debut 1991 OB in *Necktie Breakfast* followed by *As You Like It, Lion in the Streets, Baptists, Night of Nave, Never the Same Rhyme Twice, Pig.*

EWING, GEOFFREY C. Born Aug. 10, 1951 in Minneapolis, MN. Graduate U. Minn. Bdwy debut 1983 in *Guys in the Truck,* followed OB by *Cork, The Leader/The Bald Soprano, Freefall, Ali, Soldier's Play.*

FABER, RON. Born Feb. 16, 1933 in Milwaukee, WI. Graduate Marquette U. OB Debut 1959 in *An Enemy of the People* followed by *Exception and the Rule, America Hurrah, They Put Handcuffs on Flowers, Dr. Selavy's Magic Theatre, Troilus and Cressida, Beauty Part, Woyzeck, St. Joan of the Stockyards, Jungle of Cities, Scenes from Everyday Life, Mary Stuart, 3 by Pirandello, Times and Appetites of Toulouse-Lautrec, Hamlet, Johnstown Vendicator, Don Juan of Seville, Between the Acts, Baba Goya, Moving Targets, Arturo Ui, Words Divine, Dracula, 3 By Beckett, Stonewall Jackson's House, Sixth Commandment,* Bdwy in *Medea* (1973), *First Monday in October.*

FABRAY, NANETTE. Born Oct.27, 1922 in San Diego, CA. Attended Max Reinhardt Sch. Bdwy debut 1940 in *Meet the People* followed by *Let's Face It, By Jupiter, Jackpot, My Dear Public, Bloomer Girl, High Button Shoes, Love Life, Arms and the Girl, Make a Wish, Mr. President, No Hard Feelings,* OB in *Bermuda Ave Triangle* .

FALK, WILLY. Born July 21 in New York City. Harvard, LAMDA graduate. Debut 1982 OB in *Robber Bridegroom* followed by *Pactfic Overtures, House in the Woods, Elizabeth and Essex, Nightmare Alley, Last Sweet Days,* Bdwy in *Marilyn: An American Fable, Starlight Express, Les Miserables, Miss Saigon.*

FARLEY, LEO G. Born Oct.30, 1950 in Flushing, NY. Graduate Queensboro Comm Col. Debut 1986 OB in *Rimmers of Eldrich* followed by *Convulsions, Necktie Breakfast, Under Control, Visiting Oliver, Killer Joe, Pig, Night of Nave.*

FAVIER, LOUISE. Born March 25, 1964 in Auckland, NZ. Graduate U. College Cork. Debut 1992 OB in *All Must Be Admitted,* followed by *Grandchild of Kings, Plough and the Stars.*

FAVRE, KENNETH. Born Mar.15, 1956 in NYC. Graduate Hunter Col. Debut 1989 OB in *Working Her Way Down* followed by *Sundance, Morning Song, Tartuffe, Judgement Day, Macbeth, Rosencrantz and Guildenstern are Dead, Sea Plays, Anatomy of Sound, As You Like It. Twelfth Night, Street Scene.*

FAUVELL, TIM. Born Aug.2, 1961 in Queens, NYC. Attended Hunter Col. Debut 1978 OB in *Sojourner Truth* followed by *King of the Schnorrers,* Bdwy in *Grease* (1979) followed by *Joseph and the..Dreamcoat, Sondheim Celebration at Carnegie Hall, State Fair, 1776.*

FAY, RICHARD. Born Dec.26, 1952 in Ravenna, OH. Graduate AADA. Debut 1973 OB in *Waiting for Lefty* followed by *Seagull, Break a Leg, Dr. Jekyll and Mr. Hyde, Loose Ends, As You Like It, Midsummer Night's Dream, Hot l Baltimore, Tartuffe, Evening with Dorothy Parker, Faith Healer.*

FAYE, PASCALE. Born Jan. 6, 1964 in Paris, France. Bdwy debut in *Grand Hotel*(1991) followed by *Guys and Dolls, Victor Victoria, Once Upon a Mattress* (1996).

FEAGAN, LESLIE. Born Jan. 9, 1951 in Hinckley, OH. Graduate Ohio U. Debut 1978 OB in *Can-Can,* followed by *Merton of the Movies, Promises Promises, Mowgli, Yiddle with a Fiddle,* Bdwy in *Anything Goes* (1987), *Guys and Dolls.*

FELDSHUH, TOVAH. Born Dec. 28, 1953 in New York City. Graduate Sarah Lawrence Col., U. Minn. Bdwy debut 1973 in *Cyrano* followed by *Dreyfus in Rehearsal, Rodgers and Hart, Yentl* for which she received a Theatre World Award, *Sarava, Lend Me a Tenor,* OB in *Yentl the Yeshiva Boy, Straws in the Wind, Three Sisters, She Stoops to Conquer, Springtime for Henry, The Time of Your Life, Children of the Sun, The Last of the Red Hot Lovers, Mistress of the Inn, A Fierce Attachment, Custody, Six Wives, Hello Muddah Hello Faddah, Best of the West, Awake and Sing, Tovah: Out of Her Mind, Tovah in Concert, Names.*

FERLAND, DANIELLE. Born Jan. 31, 1971 in Derby, CT. OB Debut 1983 in *Sunday in the Park with George* followed by *Paradise, Young Playwrights Festival, Camp Paradox, Uncommon Women and Others, In Circles,* Bdwy in *Sunday in the Park with George* (1984), *Into the Woods* for which she received a Theatre World Award, *A Little Night Music* (NYCO/LC), *Crucible, A Little Hotel on the Side.*

FERRANTE, FRANK. Born April 26, 1963 in Los Angeles, CA. Graduate USC. Debut 1986 OB in *Groucho: A Life in Revue* for which he received a Theatre World Award, followed by *Cocoanuts.*

FIEDLER, JOHN. Bom Feb. 3, 1925 in Plateville, WI. Attended Neighborhood Playhouse. OB in *Sea Gull, Sing Me No Lullaby, Terrible Swift Sword, Rasberry Picker; Frog Prince, Raisin in the Sun, Marathon '88, Human Nature, Importance of Being Earnest,* Bdwy in *One Eye Closed* (1954), *Howie, Raisin in the Sun, Harold, The Odd Couple, Our Town, The Crucible, A Little Hotel on the Side.*

FIELD, CRYSTAL. Born Dec. 10, 1942 in NYC. Attended Juilliard, Hunter Col., Debut 1960 OB in *A Country Scandal* followed by *A Matter of Life and Death, Heart That Eats Itself, Ruzzante Returns from the Wars, Evening of British Music Hall, Ride That Never Was, House Arrest, Us, Beverly's Yard Sale, Bruno's Donuts, Coney Island Kid, Till The Eagle Hollars, Rivalry of Dolls, Pineapple Face, It is It is Not, Little Book of Prof. Enigma, Half Off, It's Toast.*

FIGLIOLI, DAVID. Born March 2,1968 in Detroit, MI. Graduate Wayne St U. Debut 1997 OB in *Dreamstuff.*

FINCH, SUSAN. Born Aug.30, 1959 in Germantown, PA. Attended Juilliard. Debut 1986 OB in *Orchards* followed by *Fair Fight, Sisters Dance, On Deaf Ears.*

FINE, ROSEMARY. Bom Dec. 9, 1961 in Limerick, Ireland. Graduate Trinity Col./Dublin. Bdwy debut 1988 in *Juno and the Paycock.* OB in *Grandchild of Kings* (1992), *Mme. Macadam, Plough and the Stars.*

FINKEL, FYVUSH. Born Oct. 9, 1922 in Brooklyn, NY. Bdwy debut 1970 in Fiddler on the Roof (also 1981) followed by Cafe Crown (1989), OB in Gorky, Little Shop of Horrors, Cafe Crown, Dividends, Finkel's Follies, From 2nd Ave. to Broadway.

FITZPATICK, ALLEN. Born Jan. 31, 1955 in Boston, MA. Graduate U. Va. Debut 1977 OB in *Come Back Little Sheba* followed by *Wonderful Town, Rothschilds, Group One Acts, Jack's Holiday, Mata Hari, Carmelina,* Bdwy in *Gentlemen Prefer Blondes*(1995), *Boys from Syracuse (Encores).*

FLAGG, TOM. Born March 30 in Canton, OH. Attended Kent State U., AADA. Debut 1975 OB in *The Fantasticks,* followed by *Give Me Liberty, Subject Was Roses, Lola, Red Hot and Blue, Episode 26, Dazy, Dr. Dietrick's Process,Carmelina,* Bdwy in *Legend* (1976), *Shenandoah, Players, The Will Rogers Follies, Best Little Whorehouse Goes Public, How to Succeed...*

FLANAGAN, PAULINE. Born June 29, 1925 in Sligo, Ire. Debut 1958 OB in *Ulysses in Nighttown* followed by *Pictures in the Hallway, Later, Antigone, The Crucible, Plough and the Stars, Summer, Close of Play, In Celebration, Without Apologies, Yeats, A Celebration, Philadelphia Here I Come!, Grandchild of Kings, Shadow of a Gunman, Juno and the Paycock, Plough and the Stars,* Bdwy in *God and Kate Murphy, The Living Room, The Innocents, The Father, Medea, Steaming, Corpse, Philadelphia Here I Come (1994)*

FLOCKHART, CALISTA. Born Nov.11 in Stockton, IL. Graduate RutgersU. Debut 1989 OB in *Beside Herself* followed by *Bovver Boys, Mad Forest, Wrong Turn at Lungfish, Sophistry, All for One, The Loop, The Imposter,* Bdwy in *Glass Menagerie* (1994) for which she received a Theatre World Award, *Three Sisters.*

FLYNN, THOMAS. Born Dec.16, 1946 in Albany, NY. Graduate Union Col., Neighborhood Playhouse. Debut 1970 OB in *House of Blue Leaves,* Bdwy in *Jiuan Darien* (1996).

FOOTE, HALLIE. *Born 1955 in NYC. OB in Night Seasons, Roads to Home, Widow Claire, Courtship, 1918, On Valentine's Day, Talking Pictures, Laura Dennis, Young Man from Atlanta, 900 Oneonta.*

Richard Fay

Louise DuArt

David Figlioli

Sherrita Durán

Sean Fredricks

Denna Dys

Todd Gearhart

Susan Emerson

James Georgiades

Nanette Fabray

Steven Goldstein

Mandy Fox

Kevin Gray

Tanya Gingerich

Donald Grody

Kate Jennings Grant

Albert Hall

Carol Halstead

Dominic Hawksley

Mary Gleere Haran

James Heatherly

Sophie Hayden

Tyrone Henderson

Julie Harris

Phillip Hoffman

Marilu Henner

Charlie Hofheimer

Bette Henritze

Stephen Hope

Dana Ivey

FORBES, KATE. Born Oct.10, 1963 in Athens, GA. Graduate Sarah Lawrence Col., NYU. Debut 1994 OB in *Doll's House* followed by *Othello, The Entertainer,* Bdwy in *School for Scandal* (1995) for which she received a Theatre World Award, *Inherit the Wind.*

FORMAN, KEN. Born Sept. 22, 1961 in Boston, MA. Attended NYU. Debut 1985 OB in *Measure for Measure* followed by *Rosencrantz and Guildenstern Are Dead, Macbeth, I Stand Before You Naked, Romeo and Juliet, 3 by Wilder, As You Like It, SS Glencairn, Goose and Tom Tom, Twelfth Night, Anatomy of Sound, Ends of the Earth, Child's Christmas in Wales, Street Scene,* Bdwy in *Wilder Wilder Wilder* (1983).

FOSTER, HERBERT. Born May 14, 1936 in Winnipeg, Can. Bdwy in *Ways and Means, Touch of the Poet, Imaginary Invalid, Tonight at 8:30, Henry V, Noises Off, Me and My Girl, Lettice and Lovage, Timon of Athens, Government Inspector, Sacrilege, Getting Away with Murder* OB in *Afternoon Tea, Papers, Mary Stuart, Playboy of the Western World, Good Woman of Setzuan, Scenes from American Life, Twelfth Night, All's Well That Ends Well, Richard II, Gifts of the Magi, Heliotrope Bouquet, Troilus and Cressida, Sympathetic Magic, Henry VIII, Timon of Athens.*

FOWLER, BETH. Born Nov. 1, 1940 in New Jersey. Graduate Caldwell Col. Bdwy debut 1970 in *Gantry* followed by *Little Night Music, Over Here, 1600 Pennsylvania Avenue, Peter Pan, Baby, Teddy and Alice, Sweeney Todd* (1989), *Beauty and the Beast,* OB in *Preppies, The Blessing, Sweeney Todd.*

FOX, MANDY. Born Aug.24, 1971 in Columbus, OH. Graduate Otterbein Col., Yale Drama. Bdwy debut 1997 in *Last Night of Ballyhoo.*

FRANKLIN, NANCY. Born in NYC. Debut 1959 OB in *Buffalo Skinner* followed by *Power of Darkness, Oh Dad Poor Dad..., Theatre of Peretz, 7 Days of Mourning, Here Be Dragons, Beach Children, Safe Place, Innocent Pleasures, Loves of Cass McGuire, After the Fall, Bloodletters, Briar Patch, Lost Drums, Ivanov,* Bdwy in *Never Live Over a Pretzel Factory* (1964), *Happily Never After, The White House, Charlie and Algernon.*

FRANZ, ELIZABETH. Born June 18, 1941 in Akron, OH. Attended AADA. Debut 1965 in *In White America* followed by *One Night Stands of a Noisey Passenger, Real Inspector Hound, Augusta, Yesterday Is Over, Actor's Nightmare, Sister Mary Ignatius Explains It All, Time of Your Life, Children of the Sun, Minutes from the Blue Route,* Bdwy in *Rosencrantz and Guildenstern Are Dead, Cherry Orchard, Brighton Beach Memoirs, Octette Bridge Club, Broadway Bound, Cemetery Club, Getting Married, Uncle Vanya..*

FRASER, ALISON. Born July 8, 1955 in Natick, MA. Attended Carnegie-Mellon, Boston Consv. Debut 1979 OB in *In Trousers* followed by *March of the Falsettos, Beehive, Four One- Act Musicals, Tales of Tinseltown, Next Please!, Up Against It, Dirtiest Show in Town, Quarrel of Sparrows, The Gig, Cock-a-Doodle Dandy, Swingtime Canteen, Oh That Wily Snake, America's Sweetheart, Green Heart,* Bdwy in *Mystery of Edwin Drood* (1986), *Romance Romance, Secret Garden, Tartuffe: Born Again.*

FRASER, BRYANT. Born Feb.10, 1955 in Newark, NJ. Attended Fordham U. Bdwy debut 1962 in *Oliver* followed by *Poor Bitos, Child's Play, The Yearling, Our Town* (1969), OB in *Vestigial Parts, Love's labour's Lost, Richard III.*

FREDRICKS, SEAN. Born April 18, 1985 in NYC. Debut 1997 OB in *All My Sons.*

FREEMAN, TONY. Born March 5, 1959 in Murray, KY. Graduate UNC, Miami U. Debut 1989 OB in *Dogg's Hamlet* followed by *Gullible's Travels, Young Abe Lincoln, Believe Me, Measure for Measure, Godspell, Wednesdays, Velvet Pumpernickel, Alone at the Beach*

FRENCH, ARTHUR. Born in New York City and attended Brooklyn Col. Debut 1962 OB in *Raisin' Hell in the Sun* followed by *Ballad of Bimshire, Day of Absence, Happy Ending, Brotherhood, Perry's Mission, Rosalee Pritchett, Moonlight Arms, Dark Tower, Brownsville Raid, Nevis Mountain Dew, Julius Caesar, Friends, Court of Miracles, The Beautiful LaSalles, Blues for a Gospel Queen, Black Girl, Driving Miss Daisy, The Spring Thing, George Washington Slept Here, Ascension Day, Boxing Day Parade, A Tempest, Hills of Massabielle, Treatment, As You Like It, Swamp Dwellers, Tower of Burden, Henry VI, Black Girl, Last Street Play, Out of the South,* Bdwy in *Ain't Supposed to Die a Natural Death, The Iceman Cometh, All God's Chillun Got Wings, Resurrection of Lady Lester, You Can't Take It with You, Design for Living, Ma Rainey's Black Bottom, Mule Bone, Playboy of the West Indies.*

FRIERSON, EDDIE. Born Nov.22, 1959 in Akron, OH. Graduate UCLA. Debut 1996 OB in *Matty.*

FRUGE, ROMAIN. Born March 4, 1959 in Los Angeles, CA. Graduate Allentown Col. Bdwy debut 1986 in *Big River* followed by *Tommy,* OB in *Shabbatai* (1995), *Last Sweet Days, Sam Shepard One-Acts.*

GALINDO, EILEEN. Bom Dec. 5, 1956 in the Bronx, NY. Attended U. Miani. Debut 1989 OB in *Chinese Charade* followed by *Ariano, In Miamias It Is In Heaven, Waiting Women.*

GAMBON, MICHAEL. Born Oct.14, 1940 in Dublin, Ire. Bdwy debut 1996 in *Skylight.*

GARITO, KEN. Bom Dec. 27, 1968 in Brooklyn, NY. Graduate Brooklyn Col. Debut 1991 OB in *Tony 'n' Tina's Wedding* followed by *Peacetime, Map of the City, Watbanaland, On House.*

GARRICK, BARBARA. Born Feb. 3, 1962 in NYC. Debut 1986 OB in *Today I Am a Fountain Pen* followed by *Midsummer Night's Dream, Rosencrantz and Guildenstern Are Dead,* Bdwy in *Eastern Standard* (1988,also OB), *Small Family Business, Stanley.*

GARRISON, DAVID. Born June 30, 1952 in Long Branch, NJ. Graduate BostonU. Debut 1976 OB in *Joseph and the Amazing Technicolor Dreamcoat* followed by *Living at Home, Geniuses, It's Only a Play, Make Someone Happy, Family of Mann, I Do I Do* (1996), Bdwy in *History of the American Film* (1978), *Day in Hollywood/A Night in the Ukraine, Pirates of Penzance, Snoopy, Torch Song Trilogy, One Touch of Venus (Encores), Titanic.*

GAYSUNIS, CHERYL. Born Jan. 8, in Westminster, CA. Graduate Otterbein Col. Bdwy debut 1991 in *La Bete* followed by *Moliere Comedies, Ideal Husband,* OB in *Finding the Sun* (1994), *An Enraged Reading, Fragments.*

GEARHART, TODD. Born May 6, 1969 in Dayton, OH. Graduate U of Cin. Debut 1997 OB in *Young Girl and the Monsoon.*

GEIER, PAUL. Born Aug.7, 1944 in NYC. Graduate Pratt Inst. Debut 1980 OB in *Family Business* followed by *Women in Shoes, Johnstown Vindicator, No Time Flat, Marathon '90, Sleep Deprivation Chamber, Major Crimes,* Bdwy in *Lunch Hour* (1981).

GELB, JODY. Born March 11 in Cincinnatti, OH. Graduate Boston U. Debut 1983 OB in *Wild Life* followed by *36 Dramatic Situations, Love Suicides, Baal, Past Lives, Marathon '89,* Bdwy in *Titanic* (1997).

GELLER, MARC. Born July 5, 1959 in Rhode Island. Debut 1981 OB in *Butterflies are Free* followed by *As Is, Marat/Sade, Equus, Cloud 9, Orphans, Bomber Jackets, Faustus, Box Office Poison, Unidentified Human Remains, Exit the King.*

GENELLE, JOANNE. Born Nov.21, 1956 in Brooklyn, NY. Attended Queens Col. Debut 1982 OB in *Get Happy* followed by *Larry Loeber Show, Sing Me Sunshine, Secret of Life,* Bdwy in *Dance a Little Closer* (1983).

GEORGIADES, JAMES. Born May 11, 1959 in Jersey City, NJ. Graduate Rutgers U. Debut 1989 OB in *Tony 'n' Tina's Wedding* followed by *I've Got Ink, Baseball in Zanzibar, Cater Waiter.*

GERBER, CHARLES. Born April 2, 1949 in Chicago, IL. Attended Wright Col., Juilliard. Bdwy debut 1981 in *Oh! Calcutta!,* followed by *Hamlet,* OB in *Midsummer Night's Dream, One-Act Festival, Richard II, Drowning of Manhattan, Going On.*

GERROLL, DANIEL. Born Oct. 16, 1951 in London, England. Attended Central School of Speech. Debut 1980 OB in *Slab Boys* followed by *Knuckle/Translations* for which he received a Theatre World Award, *The Caretaker, Scences from La Vie De Boheme, The Knack, Terra Nova, Dr. Faustus, Second Man, Cheapside, Bloody Poetry, Common Pursuit, Woman in Mind, Poet's Corner, Film Society, Emerald City, Arms and the Man, One Shoe Off, The Holy Terror, Three Birds Alighting on a Field, Loose Knit, Psychopathia Sexualis, Importance of Being Earnest,* Bdwy in *Plenty, The Homecoming* (1991).

GIAMATTI, MARCUS. Born Oct.31, 1961 in New Haven, CT. Graduate Bowdoin Col. Debut 1989 OB in *Measure for Measure* followed by *Italian American Reconciliation, All This and Moonlight, Durang Durang, Brutality of Fact, Blues are Running,* Bdwy in *Young Man from Atlanta* (1997).

GIBSON, JULIA. Born June 8, 1962 in Norman, OK. Graduate U. Iowa, NYU. Debut 1987 OB in *Midsummer Night's Dream* followed by *Love's Labor's Lost, Crucible, Man Who Fell in Love with His Wife, Learned Ladies, Machinal, Candide., Dracula, Arabian Nights, View of the Dome, Henry VIII, Da.*

GILLAN, TONY. Born Aug. 15, 1963 in NYC. Attended Queens Col., California Inst. Debut 1990 OB in *Rosetta Street* followed by *Oblivion Postponed,* Bdwy in *Conversations with My Father* (1992), *Taking Sides.*

GINGERICH, TANYA. Born March 14, 1972 in Tarrytown, NY. Graduate Yale, Oxford. Debut 1996 OB in *Pericles* followed by *Sam Shepard One-Acts (Action).*

GIONSON, MEL (DUANE). Bom Feb. 23, 1954 in Honolulu, HI. Graduate U. HI. Debut 1979 OB in *Richard II* followed by *Sunrise, Monkey Music, Behind Enemy Lines, Station J, Teahouse, Midsummer Night's Dream, Empress of China, Chip Shot, Manoa Valley, Ghashiram, Shogun, Macbeth, Life of the Land, Noiresque, Three Sisters, Lucky Come Hawaii, Henry IV Parts I & 2, Working l -Acts '91, School for Wives, How He Lied to Her Husband, Village Wooing, King Lear, Innocence of Ghosts.*

GLEZOS, IRENE. Born June 15, in Washington, DC. Graduate Catholic U. Debut OB in *Modigliani* followed by *Last Good Moment of Lily Baker, Antigone, Rose Tattoo, Top Girls, Lie of the Mind, Barbed Wire, Workplay.*

GLOVER, BETH. Born July 25 in Hattiesburg, MS. Graduate U So. MS, AADA. Debut 1993 OB in *Primetime Prophet* followed by *Bodyshop, Heartbreak.*

GOETZ, PETER MICHAEL. Born Dec. 10, 1941 in Buffalo, NY. Graduate SUNY/Fredonia, So. IL U. Debut 1980 OB in *Jail Diary of Albie Sacks* followed by *Before the Dawn,* Bdwy in *Ned and Jack* (1981), *Beyond Therapy, Queen and the Rebels, Brighton Beach Memoirs, Government Inspector, Sex and Longing.*

GOLD, MICHAEL E. Born Aug. 2, 1955 in Denver, CO. Graduate Loretto Heights Col. Debut 1990 OB in *Give My Regards to Broadway* followed by *Annie Warbucks,* Bdwy in *Annie* (1997).

GOLDSTEIN, STEVEN. Born Oct. 22, 1963 in New York City. Graduate NYU. Debut 1987 OB in *Boy's Life* followed by *Oh Hell, Three Sisters, Marathon '91, Angel of Death, Five Very Live, Casino Paradise, Orpheus in Love, Nothing Sacred, Jolly, Marathon Dancing, Shaker Heights, The Lights, El Greco, Luck Pluck Virtue,* Bdwy in *Our Town* (1988), *Sweet Adeline (Encores).*

GOODSPEED, DON. Bom Apr. 1, 1958 in Truro, NS, Can. Bdwy debut 1983 in *Pirates of Penzance* followed by *Into the Woods, Aspects of Love,* OB in *Diamonds, Charley's Tale, Green Heart.*

GORDON-CLARK, SUSAN. Born Dec. 31, 1947 in Jackson, MS. Graduate Purdue U. Debut 1984 OB in *The Nunsense Story* followed by *Chip Shot, Nunsense, Perfect for You.*

GORMAN, MARK. Born Sept.1, 1967 in Roanoke, VA. Graduate Radford U. Debut 1996 OB in *Sleep Deprivation Chamber, Big Trees, Month of Sundaes, Bipolar Expeditions.*

GORNEY, KAREN LYNN. Bom Jan. 28, 1945 in Los Angeles, CA. Graduate Carnegie Tech, Bradeis U. Debut 1972 OB in *Dylan* followed by *Life on the Third Rail, Academy Street, Unconditional Communication, Something to Eat, Curved Ladder, Love Museum, King John, Hamlet, Richard III.*

GRAAE, JASON. Born May 15, 1958 in Chicago, IL. Graduate Cincinnati Consv. Debut 1981 OB in *Godspell* followed by *Snoopy, Heaven on Earth, Promenade, Feathertop, Tales of Tinseltown, Living Color, Just So, Olympus on My Mind, Sitting Pretty in Concert, Babes in Arms, Cat and the Fiddle, Forever Plaid, Funny Thing Happened on the Way to the Forum, 50 Million Frenchmen, Rodgers and Hart Revue, Hello Muddah Hello Faddah, All in the Timing, I Married an Angel, Hart & Hammerstein Centennial,* Bdwy in *Falsettos* (1993), *Grand Night for Singing* (also OB).

GRACE, GINGER. Born in Beaumont, TX. Graduate U. Tex, Penn State U. Debut 1981 OB in *Peer Gynt* followed by *Wild Oats, Ghost Sonata, Cherry Orchard, Faust, Hamlet, The Oresteia, Mourning Becomes Electra, Beaux Defeated, To Moscow.*

GRANT, DAVID MARSHALL. Born June 21, 1955 in New Haven, CT. Attended Conn. Col., Yale U. Debut 1978 OB in *Sganarelle* followed by *Table Settings, The Tempest, Making Movies, Naked Rights,* Bdwy in *Bent* (1979), *The Survivor, Angels in America, Three Sisters.*

GRANT, KATE JENNINGS. Born March 23, 1970 in Elizabeth, NJ. Graduate U of PA, Juilliard. Bdwy debut 1997 in *American Daughter.*

GRANT, SCHUYLER. Born Apr.29, 1970 in San Jose, CA. Attended YaleU. Debut 1987 OB in *Hooded Eye* followed by *Mortal Friends, Banner, Only Angels, Importance of Being Earnest..*

GRANT, SEAN. Born July 13, 1966 in Brooklyn, NY. Attended NC School of Arts. Bdwy debut in *Starlight Express* (1987) followed by *Prince of Central Park, Goodbye Girl, DuBarry Was a Lady (Encores), Boys from Syracuse (Encores),* OB in *Bring in the Morning.*

GRANVILLE, CYNTHIA. Born April 28, 1960 in Brooklyn, NY. Graduate U of Tenn. Debut 1983 OB in *Sound of Music* followed by *After Breakfast, Automatic Telling, Boys in the Backroom, Blackberry Frost, Found in the Garden, Cucumbers.*

GRAVITTE, DEBBIE SHAPIRO. Born Sept. 29, 1954 in Los Angeles, CA. Graduate LACC. Bdwy debut in *They're Playing Our Song* (1979) followed by *Perfectly Frank, Blues in the Night, Zorba, Jerome Robbins' Broadway, Ain't Broadway Grand, Les Miserables, Boys from Syracuse (Encores),* OB in *They Say It's Wonderful, New Moon in Concert, Louisianna Purchase, Carmelina.*

GRAY, KEVIN. Born Feb. 25, 1958 in Westport, CT. Graduate Duke U. Debut 1982 OB in *Lola* followed by *Pacific Overtures, Family Snapshots, Baker's Wife, The Knife, Magdalena in Concert,* Bdwy in *Phantom of the Opera* (1989), *King and I.*

GRAYBILL, KATHRYN. Born Sept.11 in Enid, OK. Graduate SMU. Debut 1977 OB in *Jabberwock* followed by *Boarders, Beau Defeated, Wolf of the Door, Cedar Creek.*

GREEN, DAVID. Born June 16, 1942 in Cleveland, OH. Attended Kan. State U. Bdwy debut 1980 in *Annie* followed by *Evita, Teddy and Alice, Pajama Game* (LC), *Flowering Peach,* OB in *Once on a Summer's Day, Miami, On the 20th Century, What About Luv?, Tom and Viv, Rhinoceros.*

GREENSPAN, DAVID. Born 1956 In Los Angeles, CA. OB in *Phaedra, Education of Skinny Spyz, Boys in the Band, Moose Mating, Second Hand Smoke.*

GRENIER, ZACH. Born Feb. 12, 1954 in Englewood, NJ. Graduate U MI, Boston U. Debut 1982 OB in *Baal* followed by *Tomorrowland, Water Music, Morocco, The Cure, Birth of the Poet, Talk Radio, Marathon '90, Lilith, Arturo Ui, The Creditors, Fiery Furnace, Three Birds Alighting on a Field, Question of Mercy, Rhinoceros,* Bdwy in *Mastergate* (1989).

GREY, JOEL. Born Apr.11, 1932 in Cleveland, OH. Attended Cleveland Playhouse. Bdwy debut 1951 in *Borscht Capades* followed by *Come Blow Your Horn, Stop the World I Want to Get Off, Half a Sixpence, Cabaret (1966/1987), George M!, Goodtime Charley, Grand Tour, Chicago (1996),* OB in *Littlest Revue, Harry Noon and Night, Marco Polo Sings a Solo, Normal Heart, Greenwich Village Follies.*

GRIER, DAVID ALAN. Born June 30, 1955 in Detroit, MI. Graduate UMi., YaleU. Bdwy debut in *The First* (1981) for which he received a Theatre World Award, followed by *Dreamgirls, One Touch of Venus (Encores), Funny Thing Happened on the Way to the Forum,* OB in *Soldier's Play, Richard III, Merry Wives of Windsor.*

GRIFFITH, KRISTIN. Born Sept. 7, 1953 in Odessa, TX. Graduate Juilliard. Bdwy debut 1976 in *Texas Trilogy,* OB in *Rib Cage, Character Lines, 3 Friends, 2 Rooms, A Month in the Country, Fables for Friends, Trading Post, Marching in Georgia, American Garage, Midsummer Night's Dream, Marathon '87, Bunker Reveries, On the Bench, EST Marathon '92 and '93, Holy Terror, Black, Bonds of Affection, Crocodiles in the Potomac, Potato Creek Chair of Death.*

GRODY, DONALD. Born Dec.18, 1927 in NYC. Debut 1951 OB in *Othello* followed by *Measure for Measure, Saint Joan,* Bdwy in *Wonderful Town* (1954), *Ankles Away, The Vamp, Bells are Ringing, Happy Hunting, Jekyll & Hyde.*

GROVE, JESSICA. Born 1982 in Columbus, OH. Bdwy debut 1997 in *Wizard of Oz* (MSG).

GUNCLER, SAM. Born Oct.17, 1955 in Bethlehem, PA. Graduate Lehigh U. Debut 1983 OB in *Her Honor the Mayor* followed by *The Racket, Sail Away, Winning.*

GUNN, ANNA. Born Aug.11, 1968 in Cleveland, OH. Graduate Northwestern U. Bdwy debut 1996 in *The Rehearsal.*

HADARY, JONATHAN. Born Oct. 11, 1948 in Chicago, IL. Attended Tufts U. Debut 1974 OB in *White Nights* followed by *El Grande de Coca Cola, Songs from Pins and Needles, God Bless You Mr. Rosewater, Pushing 30, Scrambled Feet, Coming Attractions, Tom Foolery, Charley Bacon and Family, Road Show, 1-2-3-4-5, Wenceslas Square, Assassins, Lips Together Teeth Apart, Weird Romance, Destiny of Me, Robbers,* Bdwy in *Gemini* (1977 also OB), *Torch Song Trilogy, As Is, Gypsy, Guys and Dolls.*

HAFNER, JULIE J. Born June 4, 1952 in Dover, OH. Graduate Kent State U. Debut 1976 OB in *The Club* followed by *Nunsense, Green Heart,* Bdwy in *Nine.*

HAINES, MERVYN JR. Born Aug.20, 1933 in Newark, NJ. Attended AADA. With NYSF in *All's Well That Ends Well, Measure for Measure, Richard III, Henry VI,* with LCRep in *King Lear, Cry of Players, Henry* (1969), *Hamlet, King John,* OB in *Cymbeline, Richard III.*

HALL, ALBERT. Born Nov.10, 1937 in Boothton, AL. Graduate Columbia. Debut 1971 OB in *Basic Training of Pavlo Hummel* followed by *Duplex, Wedding Band, Are You Now or Have Ever Been, As You Like It, Miss Julie, Black Picture Show, Yankees 3 Detroit 0, Soldier's Play,* Bdwy in *Ain't Supposed to Die a Natural Death, We Interrupt This Program.*

HALSTEAD, CAROL. Born Sept.12 in Hempstead, NY. Graduate FlStU., ACT. Debut 1992 OB in *The Mask* followed by *Bats, Margo's Party, Cucumbers.*

HALSTON, JULIE. Born December 7, 1954 in New York. Graduate Hofstra U. Debut OB 1985 in *Times Square Angel* followed by *Vampire Lesbians of Sodom, Sleeping Beauty or Coma, The Dubliners, Lady in Question, Money Talks, Red Scare on Sunset, I 'll be the Judge of That, Lifetime of Comedy, Honeymoon Is Over, You Should Be So Lucky, This Is Not Going to Be Pretty.* Bdwy in *Boys from Syracuse (Encores).*

HAMILTON, JOSH. Born in NYC. Attended BrownU. OB in *Women and Wallace, Korea, As Sure As You Live, Four Corners, Eden Cinema, A Joke, Sons and Fathers, Wild Dogs, Suburbia, Wonderful Time, This Is Our Youth, As Bees in Honey Drown.*

HAMILTON, LAWRENCE. Born Sept.14, 1954 in Ashdown, AR. Graduate Henderson St U. Debut 1981 OB in *Purlie* followed by *Blues in the Night, The River,* Bdwy in *Sophisticated Ladies* (1982), *Porgy and Bess, The Wiz, Uptown It's Hot, Play On!*

HAMLIN, HARRY. Bom Oct. 30, 1951 in Pasadena, CA. Yale graduate. Bdwy debut 1984 in *Awake and Sing* followed by *Normal Heart* (benefit reading), *Summer and Smoke.*

HAMMER, BEN. Bom Dec. 8, 1925 in Brooklyn, NY. Graduate Brooklyn Col. Bdwy debut 1955 in *Creat Sebastians* followed by *Diary of Anne Frank, Tenth Man, Mother Courage, The Deputy, Royal Hunt of the Sun, Colda, Broadway Bound, Three Sisters,* OB in *The Crucible. Murderous Angels, Richard III, Slavs!*

HAMMER, MARK. Born April 28, 1937 in San Jose, CA. Graduate Stanford U., Catholic U. Debut 1966 OB in *Jouney of the Fifth Horse* followed by *Witness for the Prosecution, Cymbeline, Richard III, Taming of the Shrew, As You Like It, Henry VI, Twelve Dreams, Henry VIII, Problem Child, Criminal Genius,* Bdwy in *Much Ado about Nothing* (1972).

HAMMERLY, RICK. Born Aug.25, 1964 in Wincester, VA. Graduate U of VA. Debut 1996 OB in *Message to Michael.*

HARAN, MARY-CLEERE. Born May 13, 1952 in *San* Francisco, Ca. Attended San Francisco St U. Bdwy debut in *1940's Radio Hour* (1979), OB in *Hollywood Opera, What a Swell Party!, Hart & Hammerstein Centennial.*

HARDING, JAN LESLIE. Born in 1956 in Cambridge, MA. Graduate Boston U. Debut 1980 OB in *Album* followed by *Sunday Picnic, Buddies, The Lunch Girls, Marathon '86, Traps, Father Was a Peculiar Man, Murder of Crows, David's Red-Haired Death, Strange Feet, Impassioned Embraces, Storm Patterns, Bondage, My Head was a Sledgehammer, Bremen Freedom, Shades of Grey, I' ve Got the Shakes, Swoop, Cats and Dogs, Hell's Kitchen Sink, Henry VI.*

HARMAN, PAUL. Born July 29, 1952 in Mieola, NY. Graduate TuftsU. Bdwy debut 1980 in *It's So Nice to Be Civilized* followed by *Les Miserables, Chess, Candide,* OB in *City Suite, Sheik of Avenue B, Decline of the Middle West.*

HARRINGTON, DELPHI. Born Aug.26 in Chicago, IL. Graduate NorthwesternU. Debut 1960 OB in *Country Scandal* followed by *Moon for the Misbegotten, Baker's Dozen, The Zykovs, Character Lines, Richie, American Garage, After the Fall, Rosencrantz and Guildenstern are Dead, Good Grief, Hay Fever, Madwoman of Chaillot, Too Clever by Half, Beauty Part, Heartbreak House,* Bdwy in *Thieves (1974), Everything in the Garden, Romeo and Juliet, Chapter Two, Sea Gull.*

HARRIS, ED. Born Nov.28, 1950 in Tenafly, NJ. Attended ColumbiaU., U OK., Debut 1983 OB in *Fool for Love* followed by *Simpatico,* Bdwy in *Precious Sons* for which he received a Theatre World Award, *Taking Sides.*

HARRIS, JULIE. Born Dec. 2, 1925 in Grosse Pointe, MI. Yale graduate. Bdwy debut 1945 in *It's a Gift* followed by *Henry V, Oedipus, Playboy of the Western World, Alice in Wonderland, Macbeth, Sundown Beach* for which she received a Theatre World Award, *Young and the Fair, Magnolia Alley, Montserrat, Member of the Wedding, I Am a Camera, Mlle. Colombe, The Lark, Country Wife, Warm Peninsula, Little Moon of Alban, A Shot in the Dark, Marathon '33, Ready When You Are C. B., Hamlet (CP), Skyscraper, 40 Carats, And Miss Reardon Drinks a Little, Voices, Last of Mrs. Lincoln, Au Pair Man, In Praise of Love, Belle of Amherst, Mixed Couples, Break a Leg, Lucifer's Child, A Christmas Carol, Glass Menagrie, Gin Game,* OB in *Fiery Furnace.*

HARRIS, SAM. Born June 4, 1961 in Cushing, OK. Attended UCLA. Bdwy debut 1994 in *Grease* followed by *The Life.*

HARRISON, GREGORY. Born May 31, 1950 on Catalina Island, CA. Graduate Actors Stdio. Bdwy debut 1997 in *Steel Pier.*

HART, MELISSA (JOAN). Born April 18, 1976 in Smithtown, NY. Debut 1989 OB in *Beside Herself* followed by *Imaging Brad, Radio Gals,* Bdwy in *The Crucible* (1991).

HAWKE, ETHAN. Born November 6, 1970 in Austin, TX. Debut 1991 OB in *Casanova* followed by *A Joke, Sophistry, Sons and Fathers, Hesh, Great Unwashed, Killer's Head,* Bdwy in *The Sea Gull* (1992).

HAWKINS, HOLLY. Born Aug. 22, 1959 in Shreveport, La. Attended Tulane U. LAMDA, NC School of Arts. Debut 1988 OB in *Man and Superman* followed by *R`aherford & Son, Absent Friends.*

HAWKSLEY, DOMINIC. Born Aug.11, 1961 in Kansas City, MO. Graduate Drama Centre (London). Bdwy debut 1996 in *Ideal Husband.*

HAYDEN, MICHAEL. Born Feb. 28 1963 in St. Paul, MN. Graduated Juilliard. Debut 1991 OB in *The Matchmaker* followed by *Hello Again, Off-Key, Nebraska, All My Sons,* Bdwy debut 1994 in *Carousel* for which he received a Theatre World Award.

HAYDEN, SOPHIE. Born Feb. 23 in Miami, FL. Graduate Northwestern U. Bdwy debut 1979 in *Whoopee!* followed by *Barnum, Comedy of Errors, Most Happy Fella* (1992), *The Show-Off, Nine Armenians,* OB in *She Loves Me, Jessie's Land, Passover, Lies My Father Told Me, Torpedo Bra, Fun, How the Other Half Loves.*

HAYNES, BRYAN S. Born June 20, 1967 in The Bronx, NYC. Graduate YaleU. Bdwy debut 1995 in *Gentlemen Prefer Blondes* followed by *Play On!*

HAYNES, ROBIN. Born July 20, 1953 in Lincoln, NE. Graduate U. WA. Debut 1976 OB in *A Touch of the Poet* followed by *She Loves Me, Romeo and Juliet, Twelfth Night, Billy Bishop Goes to War, Max and Maxie, Oh Captain, Minor Demons,* Bdwy in *Best Little Whorehouse in Texas* (1978), *Blood Brothers.*

HEARD, CORDIS. Born July 27, 1944 in Washington, DC. Graduate Chatham Col. Bdwy debut 1973 in *Warp* followed by *Elephant Man, Macbeth,* OB in *Vanities, City Junket, Details without a Map, Inside Out, Jasper in Grammercy Park.*

HEATHERLY, JAMES. Born Aug. 10, 1965 in Jefferson City, TN. Graduate W Texas St U. Debut 1991 OB in *Prom Queens Unchained* followed by *Most Men Are, When Pigs Fly.*

HEBERT, RICH. Born Dec.14, 1956 in Quincy, MA. Graduate BostonU. Debut 1978 OB in *Rimers of Eldritch* followed by *110 in the Shade, Dazy, Easy Money, Ballad of SamGrey,* Bdwy in *Rock 'n' Roll: First 5000 Years*(1982), *Cats, Les Miserables, Sunset Blvd., The Life.*

HECHT, JESSICA. Born 1965 in Bloomfiled, CT. Graduate NYU. Bdwy 1997 in *Last Night of Ballyhoo.*

HEDWALL, DEBORAH. Born in 1952 in Washington State. OB includes *Blind Date, Intimacy, Amulets against the Dragon Forces, Savage in Limbo, Ertremities, Sight Unseen, Wreck on the 5:25, Iphigenia and Other Daughters, Why We Have a Body, Curse of the Starving Class,* Bdwy in *Heidi Chronicles (1989).*

HELLER, ADAM. Born June 8, 1960 in Englewood, NJ. Graduate NYU. Debut 1984 OB in *Kuni-Leml* followed by *The Special, Half a World Away, Encore!, Mererily We Roll Along,* Bdwy in *Les Miserables* (1989), *Victor Victoria.*

HENDERSON, TYRONE MITCHELL. Born June 22, 1963 in Geneva, NY. Graduate AADA. Atended Hobart, SUNY (Stony Brook). OB in *Medea* followed by *America Play, Stonewall, The Tempest, Cater Waiter.*

HENNER, MARILU. Born April 6, 1952 in Chicago, IL. Bdwy in *Over Here* (1974), *Chicago* (1997).

HENRITZE, BETTE. Born May 23 in Betsy Layne, KY. Graduate TN. OB in *Lion in Love, Abe Lincoln in Illinois, Othello, Baal, A Long Christmas Dinner, Queens of France, Rimers of Eldritch, Displaced Person, Acquisition, Crime of Passion, Happiness Cage, Henry VI, Richard III, Older People, Lotta, Catsplay. A Month in the Country. The Golem, Daughters, Steel Magnolias, All's Well That Ends Well, Henry VIII,* Bdwy in *Jenny Kissed Me (1948), Pictures in the Hallway, Giants Sons of Giants, Ballad of the Sad Cafe, The White House, Dr. Cook's Garden, Here's Where I Belong, Much Ado about Nothing, Over Here, Angel Street, Man and Superman, Macbeth (1981), Present Laughter, Octette Bridge Club, Orpheus Descending, Lettice and Lovage, On Borrowed Time, Hedda Gabler, Uncle Vanya, Inherit the Wind.*

HENSLEY, DALE. Bom April 9, 1954 in Nevada, MO. Graduate Southwest MO. State U. Debut 1980 OB in *Annie Get Your Gun,* Bdwy in *Anything Goes* (1987), *Guys and Dolls* (1992), *Sunset Blvd.*

HERNANDEZ, PHILIP. Born Dec. 12, 1959 in Queens, NYC. Graduate SUNY. Debut 1987 OB in *Gingerbread Lady* followed by *Ad Hock, Troilus and Cressida, King John,* Bdwy in *Kiss of the Spider Woman* (1993).

HERRICK, PETER. Born Sept.7, 1970 in Minneapolis, MN. Debut 1995 OB in *Glory Girls* followed by *Velocity of Light, Paris Then, Short Subjects on Tall Topics.*

HERRMANN, EDWARD. Born July 21, 1943 in Washington, DC. Graduate Bucknell U., LAMDA. Debut 1970 OB in *Basic Training of Pavlo Hummel* followed by *Midsummer Night's Dream, Tom and Viv, Not about Heroes ,Julius Caesar, Life Sentences, Psychopathia Sexualis,* Bdwy in *Moonchildren* (1971), *Mrs. Warren's Profession, Philadelphia Story, Plenty.*

HIBBARD, DAVID. Born June 21, 1965. Graduate OhioStU. Debut 1989 OB in *Leave It to Jane* followed by *Chess, Forbidden Bdwy Strikes Back,* Bdwy in *Cats, Once Upon a Mattress* (1996).

HIBBERT, EDWARD. Born Sept. 9, 1955 in NYC. Attended Hurstpierpoint Col., RADA. Bdwy debut 1982 in *Alice in Wonderland* followed by *Me and My Girl, Lady in the Dark (Encores),* OB in *Candide in Concert, Dandy Dick, Privates on Parade, Lady Bracknell's Confinement, Candide, Jeffrey, My Night with Reg, Gross Indecency.*

HIDALGO, ALLEN. Born Dec.15, 1967 in NYC. Attended Bard Col., NYU. Debut 1992 OB in *Eating Raoul,* Bdwy in *Candide* (1997).

HILL, ERIN. Born February 13, 1968 in Louisville, Ky. Graduate Syracuse U. Debut 1991 OB in *Return to the Forbidden Planet* followed by *Rent, True Crimes,* Bdwy in *Titanic* (1997).

HILLAN, PATRICK. Born Dec.18, 1962 in Ely, Cambridgeshire, Eng. Graduate Webber Douglas Acad. Debut 1992 OB in *Heartsongs* followed by *Rat in the Skull, Night Must Fall, Screwdrivers and Sunday Brunch, Rosencrantz and Guildenstern Are Dead, Faith Healer.*

HINGSTON, SEAN MARTIN. Born Dec.16, 1965 in Melbourne, Australia. Bdwy debut 1994 in *Crazy for You.* followed by *Boys from Syracuse (Encores), Promises Promises (Encores).*

HIRSCH, JUDD. Born March 15, 1935 in NYC. Attended AADA. Bdwy debut 1966 in *Barefoot in the Park* followed by *Chapter Two, Talley's Folly, I'm Not Rappaport (also OB),Conversations with My Father, A Thousand Clowns,* OB in *On the Necessity of Being Polygamous, Scuba Duba, Mystery Play, The Hot l Baltimore, Prodigal, Knock Knock, Life and/or Death, Talley's Folly, Sea Gull, Below the Belt.*

HOCH, DANNY. Born 1971 in Queens, NY. OB in *Some People* followed by *Flatted Fifth..*

HOCK, ROBERT. Born May 20, 1931 in Phoenixville, PA. Yale Graduate. Debut 1982 OB in *Caucasian Chalk Circle* followed by *Adding Machine, Romeo and Juliet, Edward II, Creditors, Two Orphans,Macbeth, Kitty Hawk, Heathen Valley, Comedy of Errors, Phaedra, Good Natur'd Man, Oedipus the King, Game of Love and Chance, Twelfth Night, Mrs. Warren's Profession, Oedipus at Colonus, King Lear, Beaux Stratagem, Life Is a Dream, Doll's House,Antigone, he Chairs, Venice Preserv'd, Misalliance,* Bdwy in *Some Americans Abroad* (1990).

HOFFMAN, PHILIP. Born May 12, 1954 in Chicago, IL. Graduate U. Ill. Bdwy debut 1981 in *Moony Shapiro Songbook,* followed by *Is There Life After High School?, Baby, Into the Woods, Falsettos,* OB in *The Fabulous 50's, Isn't It Romantic, 1-2-3-4-5, Rags, All in the Timing, The Treatment, Merrily We Roll Along, Yiddle with a Fiddle.*

HOFHEIMER, CHARLIE. Born Apr.17, 1981 in Detroit, MI. Bdwy debut 1995 in *On the Waterfront,* OB in *Minor Demons.*

HOHN, AMY. Born in Royal Oak, MI. Graduate Syracuse U. Debut 1994 OB in *The Stand-in,* followed by *Hide Your Love Away, June Moon.*

HOLBROOK, RUBY. Born Aug. 28, 1930 in St. Johns, Nfld. Attended Denison U. Debut 1963 OB in *Abe Lincoln in Illinois* followed by *Hamlet, James Joyce's Dubliners, Measure for Measure, The Farm, Do You Still Believe the Rumor?, Killing of Sister George, An Enemy of the People, Amulets Against the Dragon Forces, The Rose Quartet, The Workroom, The Guardsman,* Bdwy in *Da* (1979), *5th of July, Musical Comedy Murders of 1940.*

HOLLIS, TOMMY. Born March 27, 1954 in Jacksonville, TX. Attended Lon Morris Col., U. Houston. Debut 1985 OB in *Diamonds* followed by *Secrets of the Lava Lamp, Paradise, Africanus Instructus, Colored Museum, Yip & Gershwin,* Bdwy in *Piano Lesson* (1990) for which he received a Theatre World Award, *Seven Guitars.*

HOLMES, DENIS. Born June 7, 1921 in Coventry, Eng. Graduate LAMDA. Bdwy debut in *Troilus and Cressida* (1955) followed by *Homecoming, Merchant of Venice, Moliere Comedies, Hamlet, Ideal Husband,* OB in *Dandy Dick*(1987).

HOLMES, SCOTT. Born May 30, 1952 in West Grove, PA. Graduate Catawba Col. Bdwy debut 1979 in *Grease* followed by *Evita, The Rink, Jerome Kern Goes to Hollywood, Best Little Whorehouse Goes Public,* OB in *Diamonds, Leading Men Don't Dance.*

HOPE, STEPHEN. Born Jan.23, 1957 in Savannah, GA. Attended ULouisville, Cin. Consv. Debut 1980 OB in *Anyone Can Whistle* followed by *Manhattan Showboat, Rabboni, Dames at Sea, Fairy Tales,* Bdwy in *Joseph and the..Dreamcoat* (1982).

HORGAN, CON. Born in Cork City, Ire. OB in twenty *Five, In the Shadow of the Glen, Riders to the Sea, Plough and the Stars, Translations.*

HORNE, CHERYL. Born Nov.15 in Stamford, CT. Graduate SMU. Debut 1975 OB in *The Fantasticks* followed by *Indomitable Huntresses, Andorra, Lady Windermere's Fan, Let's Get a Divorce, Mourning Becomes Electra, Uncle Vanya, Live Witness, Craig's Wife, Edward II, Great God Brown.*

HOSHKO, JOHN. Born July 28, 1959 in Bethesda, MD. Graduate USC. Bdwy debut 1989 in *Prince of Central Park* followed by *Gentlemen Prefer Blondes, Sunset Blvd,* OB in *Two by Two.*

HOWER, NANCY. Born May 11 in Wyckoff, NJ. Graduate Rollins Col., Juilliard. Debut 1991 OB in *Othello* followed by *As You Like It, The Years,Why We Have a Body, Anthony and Cleopattra,* Bdwy in *Government Inspector*(1994).

HUFFMAN, FELICITY. Born Dec.9, 1962 in Westchesyter, NY. Graduate NYU, AADA, RADA. Debut 1988 OB in *Boys' Life* followed by *Been Taken, Grotesque Lovesongs, Three Sisters, Shaker Heights, Jolly, Cryptogram, Stories of Women in Love, Dangerous Corner, Joy of Going Somewhere Definite,* Bdwy in *Speed-the-Plow (1988).*

HUGHES, LAURA. Born Jan. 28. 1959 in NYC. Graduate Neighborhood Playhouse. Debut 1980 OB in *The Diviners* followed by *A Tale Told, Time Framed, Fables for Friends, Talley and Son, Kate's Diary, Playboy of the Western World, Missing/Kissing.*

HUNTER, KIM. Born Nov.12, 1922 in Detroit, MI. Attended Actors Studio. Bdwy debut in *Streetcar Named Desire* (1947) followed by *Darkness at Noon, The Chase, Children's Hour, Tender Trap, Write Me a Murder, Weekend, Penny Wars, The Women, To Grandmother's House We Go, Ideal Husband,* OB in *Come Slowly Eden, All is Bright, Cherry Orchard, When We Dead Awaken, Territorial Rites, Faulkner's Bicycle, Man and Superman, Murder of Crows, Eye of the Beholder, The Visit, Driving Miss Daisy.*

HURLBUT, BRUCE. Born May 7, 1953 in Great Falls, MT. Graduate Yale Sch Drama. OB in *Lizzie Borden Family Vaudeville Show, Ephrom, Daisy and and Jack the Ripper, Scapin.*

HURST, MELISSA. Born June 8, 1955 in Cleveland, OH. Graduate NYU. Debut 1980 OB in *Dark Ride* followed by *Walk on Lake Erie, The Houseguests, Reunion, American Camera, Enter the Greek, Basic Black and Pearls, Grover Bob Loves You, One Neck, Half Off.*

IERARDI, ROBERT. Born Nov.4, 1961 in Southington, CT. Debut 1987 OB in *The Trial* followed by *Hamlet, Three Sisters, The Rehearsal, Importance of Being Earnest, Rockland County No Vaudeville, Play, Peanut.*

ILLES, MARY. Born Jan. 20, 1962 in Dayton, OH. Graduate OH St U. Debut 1992 OB in *Chess,* Bdwy in *She Loves Me* (1992), *Steel Pier.*

ILO, ANGELIQUE. Born Aug.23, 1957 in Japan. Attended Pierce Col. Bdwy debut 1979 in *Chorus Line* followed by *Crazy for You, Steel Pier.*

IRVING, AMY. Born Sept. 10, 1953 in Palo Alto, CA. Attended LAMDA. Debut 1970 OB in *And Chocolate on Her Chin* followed by *Road to Mecca,* Bdwy in *Amadeus* (1983), *Heartbreak House, Broken Glass, Three Sisters.*

IRWIN, BILL. Born April 11, 1950 in Santa Monica, CA. Attended UCLA, Clown Col. Debut 1982 OB in *Regard of Flight* followed by *The Courtroom, Waiting for Godot, Scapin,* Bdwy in *5-6-7-8 Dance* (1983), *Accidental Death of an Anarchist, Regard of Flight, Largely New York, Fool Moon, Tempest.*

ISOLA, KEVIN. Born Jan.27, 1970 in Ft. Irwin, CA. Graduate DukeU., NYU. Debut 1995 in *Wasp and Other Plays* followed by *Venus, Winter Is the Coldest Season.*

IVEY, DANA. Born Aug. 12 in Atlanta, GA. Graduate Rollins Col., LAMDA. Bdwy debut in *Macbeth* (LC-1981) followed by *Present Laughter, Heartbreak House, Sunday in the Park with George, Pack of Lies, Marriage of Figaro, Indiscretions, Last Night of Ballyhoo, Sex and Longing,* OB in *Call from the East, Vivien, Candida, Major Barbara, Quartermaine's Terms, Baby with the Bath Water, Driving Miss Daisy, Wenceslas Square, Love Letters, Hamlet, Subject Was Roses, Beggars in the House of Plenty, Kindertransport.*

Con Horgan

Nancy Johnston

Bruce Hurlbut

Katherine Kellner

Keevin Isola

Jane Krakowski

Arte Johnson

Jill Larson

Richard Kline

Denise Lor

Joseph Kolinski

Patti LuPone

Chad Larget

Maruerite
MacIntyre

Paul Lieber

Stephanie
McClaine

Terry Londree

Robin Miles

Seth Malicw

Christine Morsère

Michael Malone

Cynthia Nixon

Donald McCann

Park Overall

Michael John
McGann

Sarah Jessica
Parker

Matt McGrath

Christine Pedi

Christopher
Morelock

Jennifer Piech

239

JACOBSON, PETER. Born Mar.24, 1965 in Chicago, IL. Graduate BrownU, Juilliard. Debut 1992 OB in *Comedy of Errors* followed by *Hot Keys, Two Noble Kingsmen, Love's Labours Lost, Four Dogs and a Bone, Compleat Wrks of Wllm Shkspr, The Workroom, Picasso at the Lapin Agile, Rhinoceros, June Moon, Waiting for Lefty.*

JAMES, KRICKER. Born May 17, 1939 in Cleveland, OH. Graduate Denison U. Debut 1966 OB in *Winterset*, followed by *Out of Control, Rainbows for Sale, The Firebugs, Darkness at Noon, The Hunting Man, Sacraments, Trifles, Batting Practice, Uncle Vanya, Mourning Becomes Electra, Shelter, Edward II, To Moscow.*

JANKO, IBI. Born Feb. 18, 1966 in Carmel, CA. Graduate Yale U. Debut 1993 OB in *Somewhere I Have Never Travelled* followed by *Vinegar Tom, Waiting, Your Mom's a Man, Cinoman and Rebeck, Kidnapped, Street Scene.*

JANNEY, ALLISON. Born Nov.20, 1960 in Dayton, OH. Graduate Kenyon Col., Neighborhood Playhouse, RADA. Debut 1994 OB in *Fat Men in Skirts* followed by *New England, Blue Window*, Bdwy 1996 in *Present Laughter* for which she received a 1997 Theatre World Award.

JENKINS, KEN. Born 1940 in Kentucky. Bdwy debut 1986 in *Big River* followed by *Summer and Smoke*, OB in *Feast Here Tonight.*

JENNINGS, KEN Born Oct. 10, 1947 in Jersey City, NJ. Graduate St. Peter's .Col. Bdwy debut 1975 in *All God's Chillun Got Wings* followed by *Sweeney Todd* for which he received a 1979 Theatre World Award, *Present Laughter, Grand Hotel, Christmas Carol, London Assurance*, OB in *Once on a Summer's Day, Mayor, Rabboni, Gifts of the Magi, Carmilla, Sharon, Mayor, Amphigory, Shabbatai.*

JOHNSON, ARTE. Born March 20, 1931 in Chicago, IL. Attended U of IL. Debut 1955 OB in *Showstring Revue*, Bdwy in *Candide* (1997).

JOHNSON, DANNY. Bom in Lafayette, IN. Graduate Goodman/DePaul U.Bdwy debut 1993 in *Song of Jacob Zulu*, OB in *Soldier's Play.*

JOHNSON, DAVID CALE. Born Dec.28, 1947 in El Paso, TX. Attended AmConsvTh. Bdwy debut in *Shenandoah* (1975) followed by *My Fair Lady* (1981), *Doll's Life, Human Comedy*, OB in *True Crimes, Mock Trial.*

JOHNSON, JEREMY. Bom Oct. 2, 1933 in New Bedford, MA. Graduate CCNY, Columbia U. Debut 1975 OB in *Moby Dick* followed by *Anna Christie, Harrison Texas, Romeo and Juliet, Much Ado about Nothing, Merchant of Venice, Winter's Tale, Bob's Butch Bar, Beirut.*

JOHNSON, JULIE. Born Nov.16 in Whitewright, TX. Graduate Austin Col. Debut 1994 OB in *Das Barbecu* for which she received a 1995 Theatre World Award, followed by *The Rink*, Bdwy in *Candide* (1997).

JOHNSON, MEL, JR. Born Apr.16, 1949 in NYC. Graduate HofstraU. Debut 1972 OB in *Hamlet* followed by *Love! Love! Love!, Shakespeare's Cabaret, Peanut Man, The Lottery, Spell #7, Do Lord Remember Me, Venus, My on the 20th Century, Eubie, The Rink, Big Deal, Boys from Syracuse (Encores).*

JOHNSON, PAGE. Born Aug. 25, 1930 in Welch, WV. Graduate Ithaca Col. Bdwy 1951 in *Romeo and Juliet* followed by *Electra, Oedipus, Camino Real, In April Once* for which he received a Theatre World Award, *Red Roses for Me, The Lovers, Equus, You Can't Take it with You, Brush Arbor Revival*, OB in *The Enchanted Guitar, 4 in 1, Journey of the Fifth Horse*, APA's *School for Scandal, The Tavern*, and *The Seagull, Odd Couple, Boys in the Band, Medea, Deathtrap, Best Little Whorehouse in Texas, Fool for Love, East Texas.*

JOHNSTON, NANCY. Born Jan. 15, 1949 in Statesville, NC. Graduate Carson Newman Col., UNC/Greensboro. Debut 1987 OB in *Olympus on My Mind* followed by *Nunsense, Living Color, White Lies, You Can Be a New Yorker Too, Splendora, Doctor Doctor*, Bdwy in *Secret Garden, Allegro(Encores).*

JOLLEY, NICK. Born Feb.17, 1948 in Hindsboro, IL. Graduate So. IL U. Bdwy debut 1979 in *Oklahoma*, OB in *Brooklyn Bridge, Up in Central Park, Nightmare Alley.*

JONES, JAY AUBREY. Born March 30, 1954 in Atlantic City, NJ. Graduate Syracuse U. Debut 1981 OB in *Sea Dream* followed by *Divine Hysteria, Inacent Black and the Brothers, La Belle Helene, Oh Captain*, Bdwy in *Cats* (1986), *How to Succeed..*

JONES, WALKER. Born Aug. 27, 1956 in Pensacola, Fl. Graduate Boston U. Yale U. Debut 1989 OB in *Wonderful Town* followed by *Scapin, Byzantium, Inacent Black and the Brothers, Merchant of Venice, Henry VI.*

JOY,ROBERT. Born Aug. l7, 1951 inMontreal,Can. Graduate Oxford U. Debut 1978 OB in *Diary of Anne Frank* followed by *Fables for Friends, Lydie Breeze Sister Mary Ignatius Explains It All, Actor's Nightmare, What I Did Last Summer, Death of von Ricthofen, Lenny and the Heartbreakers, Found a Peanut, Field Day, Life and Limb, Hyde in Hollywood, Taming of the Shrew, Man in His Underwear, Goodnight Desdemona, No One will Be Immune, June Moon,* Bdwy in *Hay Fever (1985), The Nerd, Shimada.*

JOYCE, ELLA. Born June 12, 1954 in Rural Township, IL. Attended E.MI U. Debut 1989 OB in *Don't Get God Started* followed by *Crumbs from the Table of Joy, Last Street Play.*

JUDD, REBECCA. Born in Fresno, CA. Graduate U. NV. Debut 1988 OB in *Dutchman* followed by *Lost in the Stars, Golden Apple, Carmelina*, Bdwy in *Sweeney Todd* (1989), *Secret Garden.*

KANDEL, PAUL. Born Feb. 15, 1951 in Queens, NY. Graduate Harpur Col. Debut 1977 OB in *Nightclub Cantata* followed by *Two Grown Men, Scrambled Feet, Taming of the Shrew, Lucky Stiff, 20 Fingers 20 Toes, Earth and Sky, One Flea Spare*, Bdwy in *The Visit* (1992).

KATZMAN, BRUCE. Born Dec. 19, 1951 in NYC. Graduate Ithaca Col. Yale U. Debut 1990 OB in *Richard III* followed by *Othello, Sylvia, Death in a Landslide*, Bdwy in *The Crucible* (1991), *A Little Hotel on the Side.*

KEITH, LAWRENCE/LARRY. Born March 4, 1931 in Brooklyn, NY. Graduate Brooklyn Col., IndU. Bdwy debut 1960 in *My Fair Lady* followed by *High Spirits, I Had a Ball, Best Laid Plans, Mother Lover, Titanic*, OB in *The Homecoming, Conflict of Interest, Brownsville Raid, M. Amilcar, Rise of David Levinsky, Miami, Song for a Saturday, Rose Quartet, I Am a Man, Androcles and the Lion, Madwoman of Chaillot, Too Clever by Half, After-Play, Heartbreak House.*

KELL, MICHAEL. Born Jan.18, 1944 in Jersey City, NJ. Attended HB Studio. Debut 1972 OB in *One Flew Over the Cuckoo's Nest* followed by *Boom Boom Room, Golden Boy, Streamers, Awake and Sing, Mr. Shandy, Sunday Runners, Question of Mercy*, Bdwy in *Loose Ends* (1979).

KELLNER, CATHERINE. Born Oct. 2, 1970 in NYC. Graduate Vassar Col., NYU. Debut 1994 OB in *Escape from Happiness* followed by *Troilus and Cressida, Minutes from the Blue Route.*

KELLY, MICHAEL. Born May 22, 1969 in Philadelphia, PA. Graduate Coastal Carolina Col. OB in *Miss Julie, 4-H Club, Major Crimes.*

KEPROS, NICHOLAS. Born Nov. 8, 1932 in Salt Lake City, UT. Graduate U. UT, RADA. Debut 1958 OB in *Golden Six* followed by *Wars and Roses, Julius Caesar, Hamlet, Henry IV, She Stoops to Conquer, Peer Gynt, Octaroon, Endicott and the Red Cross, Judas Applause, Irish Hebrew Lesson, Judgment in Havana, The Millionairess, Androcles and the Lion, The Redempter, Othello, Times and Appetites of Toulouse-Lautrec, Two Fridays, Rameau's Nephew, Good Grief, Overtime, Measure for Measure* Bdwy in *Saint Joan* (1968/1993), *Amadeus, Execution of Justice, Timon of Athens, Government Inspector, The Rehearsal.*

KERR, PATRICK. Born Jan. 23, 1956 in Wilmington, Del. Graduate Temple U. Debut 1980 OB in *Jerry* followed by *Romeo and Juliet,Warrior Ant, Midsummer Night's Dream, Jeffrey, The Devils.*

KERWIN, BRIAN. Born Oct. 25, 1949 in Chicago, IL. Graduate USC. Debut 1988 OB in *Emily* for which he received a Theatre World Award, followed by *Lips Together Teeth Apart, One Shoe Off, Raised in Captivity*, Bdwy in *Little Foxes* (1997).

KIRBY, BRUNO. Born Apr.28,1949 in NYC. Bdwy debut 1991 in *Lost in Yonkers*, OB in *In-Betweens, Bunny Bunny.*

KIRK, JUSTIN. Born May 28, 1969 in Salem, OR. Debut 1990 OB in *The Applicant* followed by *Shardston, Loose Ends, Thanksgiving, Lovequest Live, Old Wicked Songs*, Bdwy in *Any Given Day* (1993), *Love!Valour!Compassion!(also OB).*

KLIBAN, KEN. Bom July 26, 1943 in Norwalk, CT. Graduate U. Miami, NYU. Bdwy debut 1967 in *War and Peace* followed by *As Is, Stanley*, OB in *War and Peace, Puppy Dog Tails, Istanbul, Persians, Home, Elizabeth the Queen, Judith, Man and Superman, Boom Boom Room, Ulysses, Mr. Pim Passes By.*

KLINE, RICHARD. Born April 29, 1944 in NYC. Graduate Queens Col., Northwestern. U. Debut 1971 OB in *Mary Stuart* followed by *Narrow Road to the Deep North, Twelfth Night, The Crucible, We Bombed in New Haven, Troilus and Cressida, Boychik*, Bdwy in *City of Angels.*

KNAPP, SARAH. Born Jan. 20, 1959 in Kansas City, MO. Graduate AADA. Debut 1986 OB in *Gifts of the Magi* followed by *No Frills Revue, Nunsense. Manhattan Class One-Acts, Opal, In Circles.*

KNIGHT, EZRA. Born July 7, 1962 in Atlanta, GA. Debut 1995 OB in *Othello* followed by *King Lear, You Say What I Mean.*

KNIGHT, SHIRLEY. Born July 5, 1936 in Goessel, KS. Attended Phillips U, Wichita U. Bdwy debut 1964 in *Three Sisters* followed by *We Have Always Lived in a Castle, Watering Place, Kennedy's Children, Young Man from Atlanta*, OB in *Journey to the Day, Rooms, Happy End, Landscape of the Body, Lovely Sunday for Creve Coeur, Losing Time, Come Back Little Sheba, Woman Heroes, The Depot.*

KOENIG, JACK. Born May 14, 1959 in Rockville Centre, NY. Graduate ColumbiaU. Debut 1991 OB in *Grand Finale* followed by *Misalliance, Cymbeline, American Plan, Mad Forest, Not about Heroes, Trip to the Beach, Misalliance, Cymbeline.*

KOLINSKI, JOSEPH. Born June 26, 1953 in Detroit, MI. Attended U. Detroit. Bdwy debut 1980 in *Brigadoon* followed by *Dance a Little Closer, The Human Comedy* (also OB), *Three Musketeers, Les Miserables, Christmas Carol, Titanic,* OB in *HiJinks!, Picking up the Pieces.*

KOREY, ALIX. (formerly Alexandra) Born May 14 in Brooklyn, NY. Graduate Columbia U. Debut 1976 OB in *Fiorello!,* followed by *Annie Get Your Gun, Jerry's Girls, Rosalie in Concert, America Kicks Up Its Heels, Gallery, Feathertop, Bittersuite, Romance in Hard Times, Songs You Might Have Missed, Forbidden Broadway 10th Anniversary, Camp Paradox, Cinderella* (LC), *Best of the West, Jack's Holiday, No Way to Treat a Lady,* Bdwy in *Hello Dolly* (1978), *Show Boat* (1983), *Ain't Broadway Grand.*

KOTLER, JILL. Born Oct.3, 1952 in Chicago, IL. Graduate USC. OB in *The Piaglies, Goatman, Willie, Play with an Ending, Sh-Boom, Etiquette, Heart That Eats Itself, Hail to the Chief, Short Subjects on Tall Topics, Infant Society, Perfect of You.*

KRAKOWSKI, JANE. Born Sept. 11, 1968 in New Jersey. Debut 1984 OB in *American Passion* followed by *Miami, A Little Night Music,* Bdwy in *Starlight Express* (1987), *Grand Hotel, Face Value, Company* (1995),*One Touch of Venus(Encores), Tartuffe: Born Again, Once Upon a Mattress (1996).*

KUBALA, MICHAEL. Bom Feb. 4, 1958 in Reading, PA. Attended NYU. Bdwy debut 1978 in *A Broadway Musical* followed by *Dancin', Woman of the Year, Marilyn, Jerome Robbins' Broadway, Crazy for You, Chicago (1996),* OB in *Double Feature (1981).*

KUDISCH, MARC. Born Sept.22, 1966 in Hackensack, NJ. Attended FlAtlanticU. Debut 1990 OB in *Tamara* followed by *Quiet on the Set, Beauty Part,* Bdwy in *Joseph and the..Dreamcoat*(1994), *Beauty and the Beast, Chicago(Encores).*

KUHN, JUDY. Born May 20, 1958 in NYC. Graduate Oberlin Col. Debut 1985 OB in *Pearls* followed by *Rodgers & Hart Revue,* Bdwy in *Mystery of Edwin Drood* (1985-also OB), *Rags, Les Miserables, Chess, Two Shakespearean Actors, She Loves Me, King David.*

LACHOW, STAN. Born Dec. 20, 1931 in Brooklyn, NY. Graduate Roger Williams Col. Debut 1977 OB in *Come Back, Little Sheba* followed by *Diary of Anne Frank, Time of the Cuckoo, Angelus, The Middleman, Charley Bacon and Family, Crossing the Bar, Today I Am a Fountain Pen, Substance of Fire, Vilna's Got a Golem,* Bdwy in *On Golden Pond (1979), Sisters Rosensweig.*

LACY, TOM. Born Aug. 30, 1933 in NYC. Debut 1965 OB in *Fourth Pig* followed by *The Fantasticks, Shoemakers Holiday, Love and Let Love, The Millionairess, Crimes of Passion, Real Inspector Hound, Enemies, Flying Blind, Abel & Bela/Archtruc, Kingdom of Earth,* Bdwy in *Last of the Red Hot Lovers* (1971), *Two Shakesperean Actors, Timon of Athens, Government Inspector, Holiday.*

LAGE, JORDAN. Born Feb. 17, 1963 in Palo Alto, CA. Graduate NYU. Debut 1988 OB in *Boy's Life* followed by *Three Sisters,Virgin Molly, Distant Fires, Macbeth, Yes But So What?, Blue Hour, Been Taken, The Woods, Five Very Live, Hot Keys, As Sure as You Live, The Arrangement, The Lights, Shaker Heights, Missing Persons, Blaming Mom, Night and Her Stars, Dangerous Corner, Edmond, Joy of Going Somewhere Definite, Heart of Man,* Bdwy in *Our Town* (1989).

LAMB, MARY ANN. Born July 4, 1959 in Seattle, WA. Attended Neighborhood Playhouse. Bdwy debut in *Song and Dance* (1985) followed by *Starlight Express, Jerome Robbins' Broadway, Goodbye Girl, Fiorello! (Encores), Out of This World(Encores), Pal Joey(Encores), A Funny Thing...(1996), Chicago, Promises Promises (Encores).*

LAMBERT, MIKEL SARAH. Born in Spokane, WA. Graduate Radcliffe, RADA. After much work in England, debut 1996 OB in *900 Oneonta.*

LAMEDMAN, DEBBIE. Born Sept.19, 1960 in Bethpage, NY. Graduate CA St (Northridge), Brandeis U. Debut 1996 OB in *Rhinoceros.*

LANDAU, VIVIEN.(formerly Tisa Barone). Born Jan.31 in NYC. Graduate CCNY. Debut 1958 OB in *Clerambard* followed by *Once in a Lifetime, Golden Six, Death Takes a Holiday, Invitation to a March, Two by Chaim Potok, Taming of the Shrew, Richard III.*

LANDEY, CLAYTON. Born March 24, 1951 in the Bronx, NYC. Graduate U of Houston. Debut 1973 OB in *Morning's Light ,Obituary of Dreams* followed by *Night Before Thinking, Measure for Measure, Names.*

LANG, MARK EDWARD. Born May 2 in NYC. Graduate Vassar Col. Debut 1986 OB in *In Their Own Words* followed by *Initiation Rites, Milestones, Midsummer Night's Dream, Julius Caesar, The Tempest, Radical Roots, Mary Stuart, Dark of the Moon, Jim the Lionhearted, Some Things You Need to Know.*

LANGE, ANNE. Born June 24, 1953 in Pipestone, MN. Attended Carnegie-Mellon U. Debut 1979 OB in *Rats Nest* followed by *Hunting Scenes from Lower Bavaria, Crossfire, Linda Her and the Fairy Garden, Little Footsteps, Hotel Play, 10th Young Playwrights Festival, Jeffrey, Family of Mann, 12 Dreams, All My Sons,* Bdwy in *The Survivor* (1981), *Heidi Chronicles, Holiday.*

LANGELLA, FRANK. Born Jan. 1, 1940 in Bayonne, NJ. Graduate Syracuse U. Debut 1963 OB in *The Immoralist* followed by *The Old Glory, Good Day, White Devil Yerma, Iphigenia in Aulis, A Cry of Players, Prince of Homburg, After the Fall, The Tempest, Booth,* Bdwy in *Seascape* (1975), *Dracula, Amadeus, Passion, Design for Living, Hurlyburly, Sherlock's Last Case, Present Laughter.*

LARGET, CHAD. Born Feb.12, 1970 in Madison, WI. Graduate IN U, U of WI. Bdwy debut in *Candide* (1997).

LARMER, ADAM SOHAM. Born Sept.6, 1973 in Anchorage, AK. Graduate U.CA (Berkeley). Debut 1996 in *Henry V* followed by *Timon of Athens.*

LARSON, JILL. Born Oct. 7, 1947 in Minneapolis, MN. Graduate Hunter Col. Debut 1980 OB in *These Men* followed by *Peep, Serious Business, It's Only a Play, Red Rover, Enter a Free Man, Scooncat, Dearly Departed, ..the Lost Dreams.., Hysterical Blindness,* Bdwy in *Romantic Comedy* (1980), *Death and the King's Horseman* (LC).

LAVIN, LINDA. Born Oct. 15, 1939 in Portland, ME. Graduate Wm. & Mary Col. Bdwy debut 1962 in *A Family Affair* followed by *Riot Act, The Game Is Up, Hotel Passionata, It's a Bird It's Superman!, On a Clear Day You Can See Forever, Something Different, Cop-Out, Last of the Red Hot Lovers, Story Theatre, The Enemy Is Dead, Broadway Bound, Gypsy (1990), Sisters Rosensweig,* OB in *Wet Paint (1965) for which she received a Theatre World Award, Death Defying Acts, Cakewalk.*

LAWRENCE, MAL Z. Born Sept. 2, 1937 in NYC. Attended CCNY. Bdwy debut 1991 in *Catskills on Broadway* followed by *Candide* (1997), OB in *Petrified Prince.*

LAWRENCE, TASHA. Born Jan. 31, 1967 in Alberta, Can. Graduate UGuelph. 1992 OB in *Loose Ends* followed by *Cowboy in His Underwear, Ten Blocks on the Camino Real, 3 by Wilder, Who Will Carry the Word?, Anatomy of Sound, Goose and Tom Tom, Killing of Sister George, Problem Child, Risk Everything, Street Scene,* Bdwy in *Wilder Wilder Wilder* (1993).

LAWSON, RANDY. Born June 18 in Strawberry Plains, TN. Graduate U TN. Debut 1990 OB in *Theme and Variations* followed by *Voice of the Prairie, Better Days, New York Actor, The Rehearsal, Skyscraper, Nebraska, Native Speech, All Day Sucker, Scaring the Fish, Those Left Behind, Honky-Tonk Highway, Defying Gravity.*

LEASK, KATHERINE. Born Sept.2, 1957 in Munich, Ger. Graduate SMU. Debut 1988 OB in *Man Who Climbed the Pecan Trees* followed by *Cahoots, Melville Boys, Amphitryon, The Imposter, Stonewall Jackson's House.*

LECESNE, JAMES. Born Nov.24, 1954 in NJ. Debut 1982 OB in *One-Man Band* followed by *Cloud 9, Word of Mouth, Extraordinary Measures, Boys in the Band.*

LEE, DARREN. Bom June 8, 1972 in Long Beach, CA. Bdwy debut in *Shogun*(1990), followed by *Miss Saigon, Victor Victoria, Boys from Syracuse(Encores),* OB in *Petrified Prince*(1994),*Chang Fragments.*

LEEDS, JORDAN. Born Nov. 29, 1961 in Queens, NYC. Graduate SUNY/Binghamton. Bdwy debut in *Les Miserables* (1987) followed by *Sunset Blvd.,* OB in *Beau Jest, Angel Levine, I Love You You're Perfect Now Change.*

LeFEVRE, ADAM. Bom Aug. 11, 1950 in Albany, NY. Graduate Williams Col., U. Iowa. Debut 1981 OB in *Turnbuckle* followed by *Badgers, Goose and Tomtom, In the Country, Submariners, Boys Next Door, Doctor's Dilemma,* Bdwy in *Devil's Discipk (1988), Our Country's Good, Summer and Smoke.*

LEIGHTON, JOHN. Bom Dec. 30 on Staten Island. NY. Anended NYU, Columbia U. Debut 1954 OB in *Splendid Error* followed by *Juno and the Paycock, Christmas Carol, Quare Fellow, Brothers Karamazov, Montserrat, Othello, Merchant of Venice, Enter a Free Man, Bone Ring, Romeo and Juliet, Plough in the Stars, Da,* Bdwy in *Of the Fields Lately (1980).*

LEONARDO, LOUIE. Debut 1995 OB in *Bomber Jackets* followed by *Carmen's Community, Portrait of the Artist as Filipino.*

LeSTRANGE, PHILIP. Bom May 9, 1942 in the Bronx, NY. Graduate Catholic U., Fordham U. Debut 1970 OB in *Getting Married* followed by *Erogenous Zones, Quilling of Prue, Front Page, Six Degrees of Separation*, Bdwy in *A Small Family Business* (1992), *Guys and Dolls, Rose Tattoo, Last Night of Ballyhoo.*

LEUNG, KEN. Born Jan.21, 1970 in NYC. Graduate NYU. Debut 1994 OB in *Ghost in the Machine* followed by *Admissions, Flipzoids, Language of Their Own, Hot Keys, Portrait of the Artist as Filipino.*

LEWIS, JENNIFER. Born Jan.25, 1957 in St. Louis, MO. Graduate Webster Col. Bdwy debut 1979 in *Eubie* followed by *Comin' Uptown, Promises Promises (Encores)*, OB in *Sister Aimee, El Bravo.*

LEWIS, MARCIA. Born Aug. 18, 1938 in Melrose, MA. Attended UCinn. OB in *Impudent Wolf, Who's Who Baby, God Bless Coney, Let Yourself Go, Romance Language, When She Danced, Big City Rhythms, Greenwillow, Big City Rhythm*, Bdwy in *Time of Your Life, Hello Dolly!, Annie, Rags, Roza, Orpheus Descending, Gypsy* (1991), *Grease, Chicago.*

LEYDENFROST, ALEX. Born Sept. 14, 1965 in Nyack, NY. Graduate Franklin & Marshall Col., New Actors Workshop. Debut 1990 OB in *Measure for Measure* followed by *TartufJe, As You Like It, Valley of the Dolls.*

LIBERATORE, LOU. Bom Aug. 4, 1959 in Jersey City, NJ. Graduate Fordham U. Debut 1982 OB in *Great Grandson of Jeddiah Kohler* followed by *Threads, Black Angel, Richard II, Thymus Vulgaris, Unidentified Human Remains, One of the All-Time Greats, Sight Unseen, Waiting Room*, Bdwy in *As Is* (1985-also OB), *Burn This* (also OB).

LIEBER, PAUL. Born June 4, 1951 in NYC. Graduate CCNY. Debut 1970 OB in *Cherry* followed by *Consoling Virgin, Suburban Tremens, Lullabye, The Comeback, Beautiful, Names*, Bdwy in *And Miss Reardon Drinks a Little (1971), Lenny.*

LIGON, KEVIN. Born May 17, 1961 in Dallas, Tx. Graduate SMU. Debut 1988 OB in *The Chosen* followed by *Forbidden Broadway*, Bdwy in *Secret Garden* (1991), *Boys from Syracuse (Encores).*

LINES, (MARION) SYBIL. Born Feb. 10th in London , Eng. Attended Central School. Debut 1976 OB in *The Philanderer* followed by *Claw, Penultimate Problem of Sherlock Holmes, The Wit to Woo, The Team, Quartermaine's Terms, Rockabye, Crimes of Vautrain, I Count the Hours*, Bdwy in *London Assurance* (1974), *Bedroom Farce, Aren't We All, Lettice and Lovage, White Liars/Black Comedy.*

LITZSINGER, SARAH E. Born Oct.22, 1971 in Indianapolis, IN. Bdwy debut 1983 in *Marilyn* followed by *Oliver*, OB in *Nightmare Alley.*

LOAR, ROSEMARY. Born in NYC. Attended U Oh, U OR. Bdwy debut in *You Can't Take It with You* (1984) followed by *Chess, Cats, Sunset Blvd.*, OB in *Encore, Sally in concert, Chess, Rhinoceros.*

LOEFFELHOLZ, JEFF. Born Jan.26, 1961 in Norman, OK. Graduate U of OK. Debut 1989 OB in *Dangerous Duets*, Bdwy in *Chicago* (1996).

LOH, SANDRA TSING. Born Feb.11, 1962 in Los Angeles, CA. Graduate Cal Tech. Debut 1996 OB in *Aliens in America.*

LONDEREE, TERRY. Born June 9, 1947 in Lynchburg, VA. Graduate William & Mary. Debut 1989 OB in *Cheri* followed by *Of Mice and Men, Perfect Crime.*

LONG, JODI. Bom in New York City. Graduate SUNY/Purchase. Bdwy debut in *Nowhere to Go But Up* (1962) followed by *Loose Ends, Bacchae, Getting Away with Murder*, OB in *Fathers and Sons, Family Devotions, Rohwer, Tooth of the Crime, Dream of Kitamura, Midsummer Night's Dream, Madame de Sade, Thc Wash, Golden Child.*

LOOMIS, ROD. Born Apr.21, 1942 in St. Albans, VT. Graduate BostonU. BrandeisU. Debut 1972 OB in *Two if by Sea* followed by *You Never Know, Uncle Vanya*, Bdwy in *Sunset Blvd.*

LOR, DENISE. Bom May 3, 1929 in Los Angeles, CA. Debut 1968 OB in *To Be or Not to Be* followed by *Alias Jimmy Valentine, Ruthless*, Bdwy in *42nd St., Dream.*

LOUDON, DOROTHY. Born Sept. 17, 1933 in Boston, MA. Attended Emerson Col., Syracuse U. Debut 1961 OB in *World of Jules Feiffer* followed by *The Matchmaker*, Bdwy in *Nowhere to Go but Up* (1962) for which she received a Theatre World Award, *Noel Coward's Sweet Potato, Fig Leaves Are Falling, Three Men on a Horse, The Women, Annie, Ballroom, West Side Waltz, Noises Off, Jerry's Girls, Comedy Tonight, Sweet Adeline (Encores).*

LOVETT, MARCUS. Born in 1965 in Glen-Ellen, IL. Graduate Carnegie-Mellon U. Bdwy 1987 in *Les Miserables* followed by *Aspects of Love, Phantom of the Opera, Carousel, King David*, OB in *And the World Goes Round.*

LUKER, REBECCA. Born 1961 in Birmingham, AL. Graduate UMontevello. Bdwy debut in *Phantom of the Opera* followed by *Secret Garden, X(NYCO), Show Boat, Boys from Syracuse (Encores)*, OB in *Jubilee, Music in the Air, No No Nanette, Trouble in Tahiti, Gay Divorce.*

LuPONE, PATTI. Born Apr.21, 1949 in Northport, NY. Graduate Julliard. Debut 1972 OB in *School for Scandal* followed by *Women Beware Women, Next Time I'll Sing to You, Beggars Opera, Scapin, Robber Bridegroom, Edward II, The Woods, Edmond, America Kicks Up Its Heals, Cradle Will Rock*, Bdwy in *Water Engine(1978), Working, Evita, Oliver!, Accidental Death of an Anarchist, Anything Goes, Pal Joey(Encores), Patti LuPone on Broadway, Master Class.*

MA, JASON. Born in Palo Alto, CA. Graduate UCLA. Bdwy debut 1989 in *Chu Chem* followed by *Prince of Central Park, Shogun, Miss Saigon*, OB in *Wilderness* (1994), *Anthony and Cleopatra.*

MacDONALD,DAVID ANDREW. Born June 1, 1961 in Washington, DC. Graduate Col Col., Juilliard. Bdwy debut 1991 in *Two Shakespearean Actors*, OB in *Strike of '92, History of President JFK, Night and Her Stars, Green Heart.*

MacINTYRE, MARGUERITE. Born in Detroit, MI. Graduate USC, RADA. Debut 1988 OB in *Some Summer Night* followed by *Weird Romance, Awakening of Spring, Annie Warbucks, Mata Hari, No Way to Treat a Lady*, Bdwy in *City of Angels* (1991).

MACKENZIE, JAMIE. Born Aug. 30, 1959 in Saginaw, MI. Attended Dartmouth Col. Bdwy debut in *My Fair Lady* (1993), OB in *Disappearing Act.*

MACKLIN, ALBERT. Born Nov. 18, 1958 in Los Angeles, CA. Graduate StanfordU. Debut 1982 OB in *Poor Little Lambs* followed by *Ten Little Indians, Anteroom, Finding Donis Anne, Library of Congress, Howling in the Night, Fortinbras, The Houseguests, Dog Opera, Jeffrey, Hide Your Love Away, Wally's Ghost, June Moon*, Bdwy in *Doonesbury(1983), Floating Light Bulb, I Hate Hamlet.*

MacMILLAN, ANN. Born Apr.7, 1942 in Scotland. Attended RADA. Debut 1970 OB in *Merry Wives of Windsor* followed by *Winslow Boy, Learned Ladies, The Housekeeper, Ivanov.*

MacVITTIE, BRUCE. Born Oct. 14, 1956 in Providence, RI. Graduate BostonU. Bdwy debut in *American Buffalo* (1983), OB in *California Dog Fight, Worker's Life, Cleveland and Halfway Back, Marathon '87, One of the Guys, Young Playwrights '90, Darker Purpose, Body of Water, Darp Ride, Golden Boy, Dark Rapture, Sam Shepard One-Acts.*

MAKKENA, WENDY. Bom in New York City. Attended Juilliard; danced with NYC Ballet. OB debut 1982 in *Divine Fire* followed by *Wedding Presence, The Rivals, Taming of the Shrew, Loman Family Picnic, Birthday Party, Mountain Language, Prin, American Plan, The Shawl, Hysterical Blindness*, Bdwy in *Pygmalion (1987). Lend Me a Tenor.*

MALKIN, SETH. Born June 17, 1961 in Youngstown, OH. Graduate Curtis Inst of Music, Cleveland Inst of Music. Bdwy debut 1995 in *Christmas Carol (MSG)* followed by *Candide* (1997), OB in *By Jupiter, Petrouchka.*

MALONE, MICHAEL. Born April 3, 1968 in Nashville, TN. Graduate Harvard, Amer Rep Inst.. Debut 1993 OB in *Orestes* followed by *Anything Cole, Stonewall: Night Variations, Message to Michael.*

MANN, TERRENCE. Born in 1951 in Kentucky. Graduate N.C. Sch. Of Arts. Bdwy debut in *Barnum(1980)* followed by *Cats, Rags, Les Miserables, Jerome Robbins' Broadway, Beauty and the Beast, Christmas Carol, Getting Away with Murder, Promises Promises (Encores)*, OB in *Night at the Fights, Queen's Diamond, Assassins.*

MARCHAND, NANCY. Born June 19, 1928 in Buffalo, NY. Graduate Carnegie Tech. U. Debut 1951 in *Taming of the Shrew* followed by *Merchant of Venice, Much Ado about Nothing, Three Bags Full, After the Rain, The Alchemist, Yerma, Cyrano, Mary Stuart, Enemies, Plough and the Stars, 40 Carats, And Miss Reardon Drinks a Little, Veronica's Room, Awake and Sing, Morning's at 7, Octette Bridge Club, After the Fall, Cinderella (NYCO.LC), White Liars/Black Comedy, Sweet Adeline (Encores)*, OB in *The Balcony, Children, Awake and Sing, Cocktail Hour, Love Letters, Taken in Marriage, Sister Mary Ignatius..., End of the Day, A Darker Purpose, Importance of Being Earnest.*

MARCUS DANIEL. Bom May 26, 1955 in Redwood City, CA. Graduate Boston U. Bdwy debut 1981 in *Pirates of Penzance*, OB in *La Boheme, Kuni Leml, Flash of Lightning, Pajama Game, Gunmetal Blues, Merchant of Venice, Carmelina.*

MARDIROSIAN, TOM. Born Dec. 14, 1947 in Buffalo, NY. Graduate U. Buffalo. Debut 1976 OB in *Gemini* followed by *Grand Magic, Losing Time, Passione, Success and Succession, Groud Zero Club, Cliffhanger, Cap and Bells, Normal Heart, Measure for Measure, Largo Desolato, Good Coach, Subfertile, Oh Captain,* Bdwy in *Happy End* (1977), *Magic Show, My Favorite Year.*

MARINO, JOHN. Born Oct.29, 1943 in Staten Island, NYC. Graduate Manhattan Col. Debut 1991 OB in *Paths of Escape* followed by *Sacrifice to Eros, Claims, Man in Sensible Brown Shoes, Summer at Casa Magni, Courtesan and the Eunuch, The Philanderer, Over the River & Through the Woods, Adding Machine, Packwood Papers.*

MARKELL, JODIE. Born Apr. 13, 1959 in Memphis, TN. Attended Northwestern U. Debut 1984 OB in *Balm in Gilead* followed by *Carring School Children, UBU, Sleeping Dogs, Machinal, Italian American Reconciliation, Moe's Lucky 7, La Ronde, House of Yes, Saturday Mourning Cartoons, Flyovers, Easter.*

MARKS, JACK R. Born Feb. 28, 1935 in Brooklyn, NY. Debut 1975 OB in *Hamlet* followed by *Midsummer Night's Dream, Getting Out, Basic Training of Pavlo Hummel, We Bombed in New Haven, Angel Street, Birthday Party, Tarzan and Boy, Goose and Tom Tom, The Carpenters, Appear and Show Cause, Uncle Vanya, Acts of Faith, Curse of the Starving Class,* Bdwy in *The Queen and the Rebels, Ma Rainey's Black Bottom.*

MARKS, KENNETH. Born Feb. 17, 1954 in Harwick, PA. Graduate UPenn., LehighU. Debut 1978 OB in *Clara Bow Loves Gary Cooper* followed by *Canadian Cothic, Time and the Conways, Savoury Meringue, Thrombo, Fun, 1-2-3-4-5, Manhattan Class I Acts, Bright Room Called Day, Pix, Sabina, Easter,* Bdwy in *Dancing at Lughnasa* (1992).

MARSHALL, AMELIA. Born Apr. 2, 1958 in Albany, GA. Graduate U. TX. Debut 1982 OB in *Applause* followed by *Group One Acts, Minor Demons,* Bdwy in *Harrigan 'n' Hart* (1985), *Big Deal.*

MARSHALL, LARRY. Born Apr. 3, 1944 in Spartanburg, SC. Attended Fordham U. New Eng. Consv. Bdwy debut in *Hair* followed by *Two Gentlemen of Verona, Midsummer Night's Dream, Rockabye Hamlet, Porgy and Bess, A Broadway Musical, Comin' Uptown, Oh Brother!, Big Deal, 3 Penny Opera, Play On!,* OB in *Spell #7, Jus' Like Livin', The Haggadah, Lullabye and Coodnight, Aladin, In the House of the Blues, The Life.*

MARSHALL, WILLIAM. Born Aug.19, 1924 in Gary, IN. Attended NYU, Amer Th Wing. Bdwy debut 1944 in *Carmen Jones* followed by *Peter Pan, Lost in the Stars, Green Pastures, Othello,* OB in *Javelin, Driving Miss Daisy.*

MARTIN, ANDREA. Born Jan. 15, 1947 in Portland, ME. Graduate Stephens Col., Emerson Col., Sorbonne/Paris. Debut 1980 OB in *Sorrows of Stephen* followed by *Hardsell, She Loves Me, Merry Wives of Windsor,* Bdwy in *My Favorite Year* (1992) for which she received a Theatre World Award, *Out of This World(Encores), Candide* (1997).

MARTIN, SEVANNE. Born Oct.9, 1969 in Cambridge, MA. Graduate Brown U, U of CA (San Diego). Debut 1996 OB in *Nine Armenians.*

MARVEL, ELIZABETH. Born 1970 in Fullerton, CA. Graduate Juilliard. Debut 1995 OB in *Silence Cunning Exile* followed by *Henry V, Arts and Leisure, King Lear,* Bdwy in *Taking Sides* (1996).

MASSEY, DANIEL. Born Oct.10, 1933 in London, Eng. Attended Eaton and Kings Col. Bdwy debut 1957 in *Small War on Murray Hill* followed by *She Loves Me, Gigi, Taking Sides.*

MASTRONE, FRANK. Born Nov. 1, 1960 in Bridgeport, CT. Graduate CentralStU. Bdwy debut in *Phantom of the Opera* (1988) followed by *Big, Jekyll & Hyde.*

MATSON, JILL. Born in Torrance, CA. Bdwy debut in *Crazy for You* (1993) followed by *Big, Promises Promises (Encores).*

MAU, LES J.N. Born Jan.8, 1954 in Honolulu, HI. Graduate U of HI. Debut 1983 OB in *Teahouse* followed by *Empress of China, Eat a Bowl of Tea, Lucky Come Hawaii, Wilderness, Pacific Overtures, New Living Newspaper, Geniuses, Friends, Dog and His Master, The Gaol Gate/Purgatory.*

MAUGANS, WAYNE. Bom Sept. 26, 1964 in Harrisburg, PA. Graduate NYU. Debut 1990 OB in *Lusting after Pipino's Wife* followed by *Ancient Boys, Take It to Bed, Chicago.*

MAXWELL, JAN. Born Nov. 20, 1956 in Fargo, ND. Graduate MoorheadStU. Bdwy debut 1990 in *City of Angels* followed by *Dancing at Lughnasa, Doll's House,* OB in *Everybody Everybody, Hot Feet, Light Years to Chicago, Ladies of the Fortnight, Two Gentlemen of Verona, Marriage Fool, Oedipus Private Eye, Inside Out, The Professional.*

MAXWELL, ROBERTA. Born in Canada. Debut 1968 OB in *Two Gentlemen of Verona* followed by *A Whistle in the Dark, Slag, Plough and the Stars, Merchant of Venice, Ashes, Mary Stuart, Lydie Breeze, Before the Dawn, Real Estate,* Bdwy in *Prime of Miss Jean Brodie, Henry V, House of Atreus, Resistible Rise of Arturo Ui, Othello, Hay Fever, There's One in Every Marriage, Equus, The Merchant, Our Town, Summer and Smoke.*

MAYER, JERRY. Born May 12, 1941 in NYC. Debut 1968 OB in *Alice in Wonderland* followed by *L'Ete, Marouf, Trelawny of the Wells, King of the Schnorrers, Mother Courage, You Know Al, Goose and Tom-Tom, The Rivals, For Sale, Two Gentlemen of Verona, Julius Caesar, Couple with a Cat, Silence Cunning Exile, Henry VI, Greater Good, Waiting for Lefty, Timon of Athens,* Bdwy in *Much Ado about Nothing* (1972), *Play Memory.*

MAYO, DON. Born Oct. 4, 1960 in Chicago, IL. Graduate Loyola U. Debut 1988 OB in *Much Ado about Nothing,* followed by *Christina Alberta's Father,* Bdwy in *Wizard of Oz (MSG).*

McCANN, CHRISTOPHER. Born Sept. 29, 1952 in New York City. Graduate NYU. Debut 1975 OB in *The Measures Taken* followed by *Ghosts, Woyzeck, St. Joan of the Stockyards, Buried Child, Dwelling in Milk, Tongues, 3 Acts of Recognition, Don Juan, Michi's Blood, Five of Us, Richard III, The Golem, Kafka Father and Son, Flatbush Faithful, Black Market, King Lear, Virgin Molly, Mad Forest, Ladies of Fisher Cove, The Lights, Grey Zone, The Changeling, The Devils.*

McCANN, DONAL. Born May 7, 1943 in Dublin, Ire. Graduate Terenore Col. Bdwy in *Juno and the Paycock, Wonderful Tennessee,* OB in *Steward of Christendom.*(1997).

McCARTHY, ANDREW. Born Nov.29, 1962 in NYC. Attended NYU. Debut 1985 OB in *Mariens Kammer* and *Life Under Water* followed by *Bodies, Rest and Motion, Neptune's Hips, Psychopathia Sexualis,* Bdwy in *Boys of Winter* (1985).

McCARTHY, JEFF. Born Oct.16, 1954 in Los Angeles, CA. Graduate Amer Consv. Bdwy debut 1982 in *Pirates of Penzance* followed by *Zorba(1983), Beauty and the Beast,* OB in *Gifts of the Maji, On the 20th Century, Sisters Rosensweig, Sympathetic Magic.*

McCAULEY, JUDITH. Born Dec.14 in Marietta, OH. Graduate Cincinnati Conserv. Debut 1964 OB in *Jo* followed by *Oklahoma (LC),* Bdwy in *Applause, Seesaw, Wizard of Oz (MSG).*

McCLAINE, STEPHANIE. Born Nov.16, 1959 in Yuba City, CA. Attended Chico St U, Sacramento St U. Yuba Col. Debut 1997 OB in *Fairy Tales.*

McCORMICK, MICHAEL. Born July 24, 1951 in Gary, IN. Graduate Northwestern U. Bdwy debut 1964 in *Oliver!* followed by *Kiss of the Spider Woman,* OB in *Coming Attractions, Tomfoolery, Regard of Flight, Charlotte's Secret, Half A World Away, In a Pig's Valise, Arturo Ui, Scapin, Mafia on Prozac.*

McCRADY, TUCKER. Born Sept. 24, 1965 in Sewanee, TN. Graduate HarvardU, Juilliard. Bdwy debut in *Camelot* (1993) followed by OB in *Sherlock Holmes and the Speckled Band, Ballad of Little Joe, Rosencrantz and Guildenstern are Dead.*

McDERMOTT, SEAN. Bom Oct. 23, 1961 in Denver, CO. Attended Loretto Heights. Debut 1986 on Bdwy in *Starlight Express* followed by *Miss Saigon, Falsettos,* OB in *New Yorkers, Boys in the Band.*

McDONALD, DANIEL. Born July 30 in Scranton, PA. 1994 debut OB in *First Night* followed by *Chesterfield,* Bdwy 1997 in *Steel Pier* for which he won a 1997 Theatre World Award.

McDONIEL, NANCY. Born Feb.6, 1950 in Henderson, NV. Graduate SWMo.StU., WayneStU. OB includes *Grandma Sylvia's Funeral* (1995), *Bob Funk, Blackberry Frost, Touch My Face, Pie Supper, Blackout, Cucumbers, Touch My Face.*

McDONNELL, MARY. Born April 28, 1952 in Wilkes Barre, PA. Graduate SUNY/Fredonia. Debut 1978 OB in *Buried Child* followed by *Letters Home, Still Life, Death of a Miner, Black Angel, Weekend Near Madison, All Night Long, Savage in Limbo, Three Ways Home,* Bdwy in *Execution of Justice*(1986), *Heidi Chronicles, Summer and Smoke.*

McGANN, JOHN MICHAEL. Born Feb. 2, 1952 in Cleveland, OH. Debut 1975 OB in *Three Musketeers* followed by *Panama Hattie,Winter's Tale, Johnny-on-a-Spot, Barbarians, Midsummer Night's Dream, Wild Duck, Jungle of Cities, The Tempest Hamlet, Hunchback of Notre Dame,* Bdwy in *Annie*(1997).

McGIVER, BORIS. Born Jan. 23, 1962 in Cobleskill, NY. Graduate Ithaca Col., SUNY/Cobleskill, NYU. Debut 1994 OB in *Richard II* followed by *Hapgood, Troilus and Cressida, Timon of Athens, Henry VI, Anthony and Cleopatra, The Devils.*

Javi Mulero

Rita Pietropinto

Emmett Murphy

Tonya Pinkins

Geoffrey Nauffts

Jacquelyn Piro

Robert Neill

Paula Pizzi

Timothy Olyphant

Amanda Posner

John Ortiz

Janan Raoulf

John Ottavino

Eileen Rivera

Joe Palmieri

Angela Roberts

Daniel Pollack

Darcie Roberts

Kevin Ramsey

Heather Robinson

Sean Allen Rector

Stephanie Rota

Robert Ronzowski

Sophia Salguero

Peter Sarsgard

Camilia Sanes

David Schramm

Mary Setrakian

William Selby

Mandy Siegrfied

244

McGRATH, MATT. Born June 11, 1969 in NYC. Attended FordhamU. Bdwy debut in *Working* (1978) followed by *Streetcar Named Desire*, OB in *Dalton's Back* (1989), *Amulets Against the Dragon Forces, Life During Wartime, The Old Boy, Nothing Sacred, The Dadshuttle, Fat Men in Skirts, A Fair Country, Minutes from the Blue Route.*

McGRATH, MICHAEL. Born Sept.25, 1957 in Worcester, MA. Debut 1988 OB in *Forbidden Bdwy* followed by *Cocoanuts, Forbidden Hollywood, Louisiana Purchase,* Bdwy in *My Favorite Year* (1992), *Goodbye Girl, DuBarry Was a Lady (Encores), Swinging on a Star* for which he received a 1996 Theatre World Award, *Boys from Syracuse(Encores).*

McGUIRE, BIFF. Born Oct.25, 1926 in New Haven, CT. Attended Mass. State Col. Bdwy in *Make Mine Manhattan, South Pacific, Dance Me a Song, Time of Your Life, View From the Bridge, Greatest Man Alive, The Egghead, Triple Play, Happy Town, Beg Borrow or Steal, Finian's Rainbow, Beggar on Horseback, Father's Day, Trial of the Catonsville 9, Streetcar Named Desire, Conversations with My Father, Young Man from Atlanta,* OB in *Present Tense, Marathon '91.*

McLACHLAN, RODERICK. Born Sept. 9, 1960 in Detroit, MI. Graduate Northwestern U. Bdwy debut in *Death and the King's Horseman* (LC-1987) followed by *Our Town, Real Inspector Hound, Saint Joan, Timon in Athens, Government Inspector, Holiday,* OB in *Madame Bovary, Julius Caesar, Oh Hell!, Hauptmann, Make Up Your Mind, Edmond, Clean, Home Therapy Kit.*

McROBBIE, PETER. Born Jan. 31, 1943 in Hawick, Scotland. Graduate Yale U. Debut 1976 OB in *The Wobblies* followed by *Devil's Disciple, Cinders, The Ballad of Soapy Smith, Rosmersholm, American Bagpipes, Richard III, Timon of Athens,* Bdwy in *Whose Life Is It Anyway?* (1979), *Macbeth* (1981), *Mystery of Edwin Drood, Master Builder* (1992), *Saint Joan.*

McVETY, DREW. Born April 16, 1965 in Port Huron, MI. Graduate NYU. Debut OB 1988 in *Heidi Chronicles* followed by *Substance of Fire,* Bdwy 1989 in *Heidi Chronicles, Titanic.*

MEIDEIROS, MICHAEL. Born Sept.15, 1949 in San Francisco, CA. Attended U of HI. Debut 1977 OB in *Museum* followed by *Stray Vessels, A New World, Split, Nip & the Bite, The Dwarfs, Jasper in Gramercy Park, Dammit Shakespeare, Violet..*

MEDINA, AIXA M. ROSARIO. Born July 5, 1965 in Rio Piedras, PR. Graduate UPR. Bdwy debut in *Victor Victoria* (1995) followed by *Once Upon a Mattress* (1996).

MEINDL, ANTHONY/TONY. Born Jan.14, 1970 in LaPorte, IN. Graduate CA St U, U of London. Debut 1995 OB in *Titus Andronicus* followed by *Like a Brother, Party, Cybele, Message to Michael.*

MEISLE, KATHRYN. Born June 7 in Appleton,WI. Graduate Smith Col., UNC/Chapel Hill. Debut 1988 OB in *Dandy Dick* followed by *Cahoots, Othello, As You Like It* (CP), *Brutality of Fact,* Bdwy in *Racing Demon* (1995), *The Rehearsal, London Assurance.*

MENDILLO, STEPHEN. Born Oct. 9, 1942 in New Haven, CT. Graduate Colo. Col., Yale U. Debut 1973 OB in *Nourish the Beast* followed by *Gorky, Time Steps, The Marriage, Loot, Subject to Fits, Wedding Band, As You Like It, Fool for Love, Twelfth Night, Grotesque Lovesongs, Nowhere, Portrait of My Bikini, Country Girl, Last Yankee, Ivanov, Black Ink, Red Devil Battery Sign, Minutes from the Blue Route, Ivanov,* Bdwy in *National Health* (1974), *Ah! Wilderness, View from the Bridge, Wild Honey, Orpheus Descending, Guys and Dolls.*

MERKERSON, S. EPATHA. Born Nov. 28, 1952 in Saginaw, MI. Graduate Wayne State U. Debut 1979 OB in *Spell #7* followed by *Home, Puppetplay, Tintypes, Every Goodbye Ain't Gone, Hospice, The Harvesting, Moms, Lady Day at Emerson's Bar and Grifl, 10th Young Playwrights Festival, Fear Itself,* Bdwy in *Tintypes* (1982), *Piano Lesson.*

MERKIN, LEWIS. Born Dec.18, 1955 in Philadelphia, PA. Attended CA St U. Bdwy debut 1980 in *Children of a Lesser God,* OB in *Child's Christmas in Wales, On House, A Not So Quiet Nocturne.*

MERRITT, GEORGE. Born July 10, 1942 in Raleigh, NC. Graduate CatholicU. Bdwy debut in *Porgy and Bess*(1976) followed by *Ain't Misbehavin'* (1983), *Big River, Jekyll & Hyde,* OB in *Step into My World, Midsummer Night's Dream, Petrified Prince.*

MERRITT, THERESA. Born Sept. 24, 1922 in Newport News, VA. Bdwy includes *Carmen Jones, Golden Boy, Tambou'-ines to Glory, Trumpets of the Lord, Don't Play Us Cheap, Division Street, The Wiz, Ma Rainey's Black Bottom, Mule Bone,* OB in *The Crucible, F. Jasmine Adams, Trouble in Mind, Henry VI Part 1, God's Tromhones.*

MEYERS, T. J. Born July 18, 1953 in Pittsburgh, PA. Graduate Mesa Col., Knox U. Bdwy debut 1984 in *Sunday in the Park with George* followed by *Big River, Prince of Central Park, Metamorphosis, Passion,* OB in *Richard II*(1994), *Luck Pluck and Virtue.*

MICHAELS, DEVON. Born Oct.22, 1973 in NYC. Bdwy debut 1986 in *Rags,* OB in *Passover, The Knife, King John, 1-2-3-4-5, Cymbeline, Great God Brown.*

MIGLIORE, BILL. Born July 23, 1970 in Massachusetts. Debut 1990 OB in *Dreamer Examines His Pillow* followed by *Edward II.*

MILES, ROBIN. Born March 5, 1964 in Red Bank, NJ. Graduate Yale, Yale Drama. Debut 1988 OB in *Singing Joy* followed by *Chang Fragments, J.P. Morgan Saves the Nation, In Circles.*

MILLER, ANDREW. Born May 25 in Racine, WI. Attended U of IL, Royal Nat'l Th Studio. Debut 1995 OB in *Blue Man Group:Tubes* followed by *A Hamlet, Macbeth, Hunting Humans, In Betweens.*

MILLER, BETTY. Born Mar.27, 1925 in Boston, MA. Attended UCLA. OB in *Summer and Smoke, Cradle Song, La Ronde, Plays for Bleeker St., Desire Under the Elms, The Balcony, Power and the Glory, Beaux Stratagem, Gandhi, Girl on the Via Flammia, Hamlet, Summer, Before the Dawn, Curtains,* Bdwy in *You Can't Take it with You, Right You Are, Wild Duck, Cherry Orchard, Touch of the Poet, Eminent Domain, Queen and the Rebels, Richard III.*

MINNELLI, LIZA. Born March 12, 1946 in Los Angeles, CA. Attended U Paris, HB Studio. Debut 1963 OB in *Best Foot Forward* for which she received a Theatre World Award followed by *Are You Now or Have You Ever Been,* Bdwy in *Flora the Red Menace* (1965), *Liza at the Winter Garden, Chicago, The Act, The Rink, Stepping Out at Radio City, Victor Victoria.*

MINOT, ANNA. Born in Boston, MA. Attended Vassar Col. Bdwy debut in *The Strings My Lord Are False* (1942) followed by *Russian People, The Visitor, Iceman Cometh, Enemy of the People, Love of Four Colonels, Trip to Bountiful, Tunnel of Love, Ivanov,* OB in *Sands of the Niger, Gettin Out, Vieux Carre, State of the Union, Her Great Match, Rivals, Hedda Gabler, All's Well That Ends Well, Tarfuffe, Good Natur'd Man, Little Eyolf, Beaux Stratagem, Doll's House, The Guardsman.*

MISTRETTA, SAL. Born Jan.9, 1945 in Brooklyn, NYC. Graduate Ithaca Col. Bdwy debut in *Something's Afoot*(1976) followed by *On the 20th Century, Evita, King and I, Sunset Blvd.,* OB in *Charley's Tale, Education of Hyman Kaplan, Sunset Blvd.*

MITCHELL, GREGORY. Born Dec. 9, 1951 in Brooklyn, NY. Graduate Juilliard, Principle with Eliot Feld Ballet before Bdwy debut in *Merlin*(1983) followed by *Song and Dance, Phantom of the Opera, Dangerous Games, Aspects of Love, Man of La Mancha* (1992), *Kiss of the Spider Woman, Chronicle of a Death Foretold, Steel Pier,* OB in *Kicks*(1961),*One More Song One More Dance, Young Strangers, Tango Apasionado.*

MITCHELL, JOHN CAMERON. Born April 21, 1963 in El Paso, TX. Attended Northwestern U. Bdwy debut 1985 in *Big River* followed by *Six Degrees of Separation*(also OB), *Secret Garden,* OB in *Destiny of Me, No to Nine, It's Our Town Too, Hello Again, Little Monsters, Missing Persons, Hedwig and the Angry Inch.*

MOGENTALE, DAVID. Born Dec. 28, 1959 in Pittsburgh, PA. Graduate Auburn U. Debut 1987 OB in *Signal Season of Dummy Hoy* followed by *Holy Note, Killers, Battery, Necktie Breakfast, Under Control, 1 Act Festival, Charmer, Killer Joe., Breast Men, The Killer and the Comic, Night of Nave, Pick Up Ax.*

MOLASKEY, JESSICA. Born in Waterbury, CT. Bdwy debut in *Oklahoma* (1980), *Chess, Cats, Les Miserables, Crazy for You, Tommy, Dream,* OB in *Weird Romance* (1991), *Songs for a New World.*

MONK, DEBRA. Born Feb. 27, 1949 in Middletown, OH. Graduate Frostburg State Col., Southern Methodist U. Bdwy debut in *Pump Boys and Dinettes*(1982) followed by *Prelude to a Kiss, Redwood Curtain, Picnic, Company, Steel Pier,* OB in *Young Playwrights Festival, A Narrow Bed, Oil City Symphony, Assassins, Man in His Underwear, Innocents Crusade, Three Hotels, Death Defying Acts.*

MONK, ISABELL. Born Oct.4, 1952 in Washington, D.C. Graduate Towson St U, Yale. Debut 1981 OB in *The Tempest* followed by *Gospel at Colonus, Elecktra, Ladies, Spring Thing, Gospel at Colonus,* Bdwy in *Execution of Justice.*

MOONEY, JOHN C. Born Dec.18, 1949 in Teaneck, NJ. Graduate Villa Nova U. Debut 1997 OB in *Names.*

MOORE, CHARLOTTE. Born July 7, 1939 in Herrin, IL. Attended Smith Col. Bdwy debut 1972 in *Great God Brown* followed by *Don Juan, The Visit, Chemin de Fer, Holiday, Love for Love, Member of the Wedding, Morning's at 7, Meet Me in St. Louis,* OB in *Out of Our Father's House, Lovely Sunday for Creve Coeur, Summer, Beside the Seaside, Perfect Party, Au Pair Man, Perfect Ganesh, Only Angels, Venice Preserv'd.*

MORALES, MARK. Born Nov.9, 1954 in NYC. Attended Trenton St U, SUNY/Purchase. Debut 1978 OB in *Coolest Cat in Town* followed by *Transposed Heads,* Bdwy in *West Side Story*(1980), *Cats, Sunset Blvd.*

MORAN, DAN. Born July 31, 1953 in Corcoran, CA. Graduate NYU. Debut 1977 OB in *Homebodies* followed by *True West, Pericles, Merchant of Venice, The Vampires, Sincerely Forever, The Illusion, Class 1-Acts, Dark Rapture, Criminal Genius,* Bdwy in *Month in the Country*(1995).

MORAN, MARTIN. Born Dec. 29, 1959 in Denver, CO. Attended StanfordU., Am Consv Th. Debut 1983 OB in *Spring Awakening* followed by *Once on a Summer's Day, 1-2~3~4~5, Jacques Brel Is Alive* (1992), *Bed and Sofa, Floyd Collins, Fallen Angles,* Bdwy in *Oliver!* (1984), *Big River, How to Succeed..*(1995), *Titanic.*

MORELOCK, CHRISTOPHER. Born Nov.6, 1973 in Morristown, TN. Graduate Carson Newman Col. Debut 1996 OB in *Rock Around the Clock.*

MORFOGEN, GEORGE. Born March 30, 1933 in New York City. Graduate Brown U., Yale. Debut 1957 OB in *Trial of D. Karamazov* followed by *Christmas Oratorio, Othello, Good Soldier Schweik, Cave Dwellers, Once in a Lifetime, Total Eclipse, Ice Age, Prince of Homburg, Biography: A Game, Mrs. Warren's Profession, Principia Scriptoriae, Tamara, Maggie and Misha, Country Girl, Othello, As You Like It* (CP), *Uncle Bob, Henry V, Hope Zone, The Disputation,* Bdwy in *Fun Couple* (1962), *Kingdoms, Arms and the Man, An Inspector Calls.*

MORRA, GENE A. Born July 16, 1935 in Rochester, NY. Graduate CCNY. Debut 1972 OB in *Prime of Miss Jean Brodie* followed by *Men in White, Songs from the Piano Bar, Unemployment Line, Blessed Event, Good and Faithful Servant, Heating and Cooling.*

MOSERE, CHRISTINE. Born May 11 in Germany. Attended Carnegie-Mellon, Towson St. Debut 1992 OB in *Package Deal* followed by *Senses, Prettiest Girl, Can't Buy Me Love, Women in Prison, Silver Cord, Quare Music.*

MOZER, ELIZABETH. Born Nov.17, 1960 in Jamaica, NY. Graduate SUNY/Brockport. Debut 1986 OB in *Funny Girl,* Bdwy in *Dangerous Games* (1989), *Victor Victoria.*

MUENZ, RICHARD. Bom in 1948 in Hartford, CT. Attended Eastem Baptist Col. Bdwy debut 1976 in *1600 Pennsylvania Avenue* followed by *Most Happy Fella, Camelot, Rosalie in Concert, Chess, Pajama Game* (LC), *Nick and Nora, 110 in the Shade* (LC), *Wonderful Town*(LC), OB in *Leading Men Don't Dance.*

MULERO, JAVI. Born in San Juan, Puerto Rico. Graduate U of Notre Dame. Debut 1997 OB in *Cloud Tectonics.*

MURPHY, EMMETT. Born May 6, 1970 in Grat Falls, MT. Graduate U of Nevada (Reno). Debut 1997 OB in *On the Road to Victory* followed by *Take It Easy.*

MURRAY, BRIAN. Born Oct. 9, 1939 in Johannesburg, SA. Debut 1964 OB in *The Knack* followed by *King Lear, Ashes, Jail Diary of Albie Sachs, Winter's Tale, Barbarians, The Purging, Midsummer Night's Dream, Recruiting Officer, Arcata Promise, Candide in Concert, Much Ado about Nothing, Hamlet, Merry Wives of Windsor, Travels with My Aunt, Entertaing Mr. Sloane, Molly Sweeney, The Entertainer, Da,* Bdwy in *All in Good Time* (1965), *Rosencrantz and Guildenstern Are Dead, Sleuth, Da, Noises Off, Small Family Business, Black Comedy, Racing Demon, Little Foxes.*

NAIMO, JENNIFER. Born Oct. 2, 1962 in Oaklawn, IL. Graduate NYU. Debut 1985 OB in *Jack and Jill* followed by *Bachelor's Wife, Malcolm and Silverstar, Elizabeth and Essex, And the Beat Goes On, Our Lady of the Tortilla, To Whom It May Concern, Amphigory, Bunny Bunny,* Bdwy in *Les Miserables.*

NAKAMURA, MIDORI. Born in Missoula, MT. Graduate YaleU., UChicago. Debut 1991 OB in *Piece of My Heart* followed by *King Lear, Madame de Sade, Prometheus Bound, Kokoro, Richard III.*

NASTASI, FRANK. Born Jan. 7, 1923 in Detroit, MI. Graduate Wayne U.. NYU. Bdwy debut in *Lorenzo* (1963) followed by *Avanti,* OB in *Bonds of Interest, One Day More, Nathan the Wise, Chief Things, Cindy, Escurial, Shrinking Bride, Macbird, Cakes with the Wine, Metropolitan Madness, Rockaway Boulevard, Scenes from La Vie de Boheme, Agamemnon, Happy Sunset Inc.!, 3 Last Plays of O'Neill, Taking Steam, Lulu, Body! Body!, Legend of Sharon Shashanova, Enrico IV, Stealing Fire, Mourning Becomes Electra, Beautiful People, Great God Brown.*

NAUFFTS, GOEFFREY. Bom Feb.3, 1961 in Arlington, MA. Graduate NYU. Debut 1987 OB in *Moonchildren* followed by *Stories from Home, Another Time Anothet Place, The Alarm, Jerusalem Oratorio, The Survivor, Spring Awakening, Summer Winds, Saturday Mourning Cartoons, Flyovers, June Moon,* Bdwy in *A Few Good Men* (1989).

NAUGHTON, GREG. Born June 1, 1968 in New Haven, CT. Graduate Middlebury Col., LAMDA. Debut 1994 OB in *Dogg's Hamlet Cahoot's Macbeth* followed by *Jack's Holiday, Golden Boy, Scenes From an Execution, Waiting for Lefty, Two Gentleman of Verona.*

NAUGHTON, JAMES. Born Dec. 6, 1945 in Middletown, CT. Graduate Brown U., Yale. Debut 1971 OB in *Long Day's Journey into Night* for which he received a Theatre World Award, followed by *Drinks before Dinner, Losing Time,* Bdwy in I *Love My Wife, Whose Life Is It Anyway?, City of Angels, Four Baboons Adoring the Sun, Chicago* (1996).

NEASE, BYRON. Born Oct.22, 1953 in Los Angeles, CA. Attended CA St U/Northridge. Debut 1979 OB in *Annie Get Your Gun* followed by *Lola, Bittersuite, Leading Men Don't Dance,* Bdwy in *Mame* (1983).

NEILL, ROBERT. Born Jan.15, 1969 in Williamsburg, VA. Graduate Grinnell, Attended LAMDA. Debut 1995 OB in *Too Much Light Makes the Baby Go Blind,* Bdwy 1997 in *London Assurance.*

NELSON, MARK. Born September 26, 1955 in Hackensack, NJ. Graduate Princeton U. Debut 1977 OB in *The Dybbuk* followed by *Green Fields, The Keymaker, Common Pursuit, Cabaret Verboten, Flaubert's Latest, Picasso at the Lapin Agile, As Bees in Honey Drown,* Bdwy in *Amadeus* (1981), *Brighton Beach Memoirs, Biloxi Blues, Broadway Bound, Rumors, A Few Good Men.*

NEUMANN, FREDERICK. Born May 17, 1926 in Detroit, MI. Attended U of UT, U of Paris. Debut 1972 OB in *B. Beaver Animation* followed by *Red Devil Battery Sign, The Changeling,* Bdwy in *Richard III* (1980), *Iceman Cometh* (1985).

NEUSTADT, TED. Born May 28, 1954 in Baltimore, MD. Graduate NYU, Fordham U. Debut 1990 OB in *Money Talks* followed by *Jackie, Fore!, EST Marathon 93, All in the Timing, Potato Creek, Chair of Death.*

NEVARD, ANGELA. Born March 19, 1963 in Montreal, Can. Graduate Skidmore Col. Debut 1988 OB in *Faith Hope and Charity* followed by *3 by Wilder, Macbeth, The Balcony, Harm's Way, Judgment Day, Tartuffe, Morning Song, Who Will Carry the Word, Sea Plays, Twelfth Night, Camino Real, As You Like It, Goose and TomTom, Child's Christmas in Wales, Ends of the Earth, Street Scene,* Bdwy in *Wilder Wilder Wilder* (1993).

NICHOLAW, CASEY. Born Oct. 6, 1992. Attended UCLA. Debut 1986 OB in *Pajama Game* followed by *Petrifeid Prince,* Bdwy in *Crazy for You* (1992), *Best Little Whorehouse Goes Public, Victor Victoria, Steel Pier.*

NIXON, CYNTHIA. Born April 9, 1966 in New York City. Debut 1980 in *The Philadelphia Story* (LC) for which she received a Theatre World Award followed by *The Real Thing, Hurlyburly, Heidi Chronicles, Angels in America, Indiscretions,* OB in *Lydie Breeze, Hurlyburly, Sally's Gone She Left Her Name, Lemon Sky, Cleveland and Half-Way Back, Alterations, Young Playwrights, Moonchildren, Romeo and Juliet, The Cherry Orchard, The Balcony Scene, Servy-n-Bernice 4Ever, On the Bum, The Illusion, Scarlet Letter, Kingdom of Earth, As Bees in Honey Drown, June Moon.*

O'BRIEN, ERIN J. Born Oct. 15 in Shakopee, MN. Graduate U MN, NYU. Debut 1992 OB in *Juno* followed by *As You Like It., Rhinocerous.*

O'KARMA, ALEXANDRA. Born Mar.28, 1948 in Cincinnati, OH. Graduate Swarthmore Col. Debut 1976 OB in *Month in the Country* followed by *Warbeck, Flea in Her Ear, Knitters in the Sun, The Beethoven, Clownmaker, Minor Demons.*

O'KEEFE, MICHAEL. Born April 24, 1955 in Larchmont, NY. Attended NYU. Debut 1974 OB in *The Kilideer* followed by*Christmas on Mars, Short Eyes, Uncle Vanya, Young Girl and the Monsson,* Bdwy in *5th of July, Mass Appeal* for which he received a 1982 Theatre World Award.

O'KELLY, AIDEEN. Bom in Dalkey, Ireland. Member Dublin's Abbey Theatre. Bdwy debut in *A Life* (1980) followed by *Othello,* OB in *Killing of Sister George, Man Enough, Resistance, Remembrance, Somewhere I Have Never Traveled, Same Old Moon, Da.*

O'LEARY, JOHN. Born May 5, 1926 in Newton, MA. Graduate Northwestern U. Bdwy debut in *General Seeger*(1962), OB in *Picture of Dorian Gray, Rimers of Eldritch, Big Broadcast, Car, Workplay.*

O'LEARY, THOMAS JAMES. Bom June 21, 1956 in Windsor Locks, CT. Graduate U. Conn. Bdwy debut 1991 in *Miss Saigon* followed by *Phantom of the Opera.*

OLYPHANT, TIMOTHY. Born May 20 in Honolulu, HI. Attended USC. OB includes *Jimmy and Evelyn, Joe's Not Home, The Monogamist* for which he received a 1996 Theatre World Award, *Santaland Diaries.*

O'MALLEY, KERRY. Born Sept. 5, 1969, in Nashua, NH. Graduate, Duke U., Harvard U. Bdwy debut 1993 in *Cyrano* followed by *Translations, Promises Promises(Encores), How I Learned to Drive.*

O'MARA, MOLLIE. Born Sept. 5, 1960 in Pittsburgh, PA. Attended Catholic U. Debut 1989 OB in *Rodents and Radios* followed by *Crowbar, Famine Plays, Homo Sapien Shuffle, Vast Wreck, Gut Girls, Apocrypha, Budd, King of Rats.*

O'REILLY, CIARAN. Born March 13, 1959 in Ireland. Attended Carmelite Col., Juilliard. Debut 1978 OB in *Playboy of the Western World* followed by *Summer, Freedom of the City,Fannie, Interrogation of Ambrose Fogarty, King Lear, Shadow of a Gunman, Mary Month of May, I Do Not Live Like Thee Dr. Fell, Plough and the Stars, Yeats: A Celebration, Philadelphia Here I Come, Making History, Mme. MacAdam Traveling Theater, Au Pair Man, Same Old Moon, Whistle in the Dark, Da, Only Angels.*

ORESKES, DANIEL. Born in NYC. Graduate U. PA., LAMDA. Debut 1990 OB in *Henry IV* followed by *Othello, 'Tis Pity She's a Whore, Richard II, Henry VI, Troilus and Cressida, Quills, Missing/Kissing, The Devils,* Bdwy in *Crazy He Calls Me* (1992).

ORMAN, ROSCOE. Bom June 11, 1944 in NYC. Debut 1962 OB in *If We Grew Up* followed by *Electronic Nigger, The Great McDaddy, The Sirens, Every Night When the Sun Goes Down, Last Street Play, Julius Caesar, Coriolanus, The 16th Round, 20 Years Friends, Talented Tenth, Confessions of Stepin Fetchit, Do Lord Remember Me,* Bdwy in *Fences* (1988).

ORTIZ, JOHN. Born Nov.21, 1969 in Brooklyn, NY. Attended SUNY/Albany. Debut 1990 OB in *De Donde* followed by *The Persians, Merchant of Venice, Cloud Tectonics.*

OSCAR, BRAD. Born Sept. 22, 1964 in Washington, DC. Graduate Boston U. Bdwy debut 1990 in *Aspects of Love* followed by *Jekyll & Hyde,* OB in *Forbidden Broadway 1993.*

O'SULLIVAN, ANNE. Bom Feb. 6, 1952 in Limerick City, Ire. Debut 1977 OB in *Kid Champion* followed by *Hello Out There, Fly Away Home, The Drunkard, Dennis, Three Sisters. Another Paradise, Living Quarters, Welcome to the Noon, Dreamer Examines His Pillow, Mama Drama, Free Fall, Magic Act, Plough and the Stars, Marathon '88, Bobo's Guns, Marathon '90, Festival of 1 Acts, Marathon '91, Murder of Crows, Cats and Dogs, Mere Mortals and Others.*

OTTAVINO, JOHN. Born July 26 in NYC. OB in *Dandy Dick, White People, Open Boat, Long Ago and Far Away,* Bdwy in *Doll's House* (1997).

OVERALL, PARK. Born March 15, 1957 in Nashville, TN. Graduate Tusculum Col. Bdwy debut in *Biloxi Blues* (1986), OB in *Skin of Our Teeth, Wild Blue, Only You, Loose Ends, Marathon'88, Psychopathia Sexualis.*

OVERBEY, KELLIE. Born Nov. 21, 1964 in Cincinnati, OH. Graduate Northwestern U. Debut 1988 OB in *Debutante Ball* followed by *Second Coming, Face Divided, Melville Boys,* Bdwy in *Buried Child* (1996), *Present Laughter.*

OWENS, GEOFFREY. Born Mar.18, 1961 in Brooklyn, NYC. Graduate YaleU. Debut 1985 OB in *Man Who Killed the Buddah* followed by *Midsummer Night's Dream, RichardII, Luck Pluck and Virtue, Macbeth, As You Like It, Othello, Rhinoceros, Timon of Athens.*

PACE, STARLA. Born Nov.20, 1967 in Lubbock, TX. Graduate Texas Tech U. Bdwy debut in *Candide* (1997).

PACINO, AL. Born April 25, 1940 in NYC. Attended Actors Studio. Bdwy debut 1960 in *Does a Tiger Wear a Necktie?* for which he received a Theatre World Award. followed by *Basic Training of Pavlo Hummel, Richard 111, American Buffalo, Salome, Chinese Coffee, Hughie,* OB in *Why Is a Crooked Letter ?, Peace Creeps, Indian Wants the Bronx, Local Stigmatic, Camino Real, Jungle of Cities, American Buffalo, Julius Caesar.*

PAEPER, ERIC. Bom September 20, 1965 in NYC. Graduate SUNY/Purchase. Debut 1992 OB in *Pageant* followed by *Night Larry Kramer Kissed Me, Message to Michael.*

PAGE, KEN. Born Jan.20, 1954 in St.Louis, MO. Attended Fontbonne Col. Bdwy debut in *Guys and Dolls*(1976) for which he received a Theatre World Award, followed by *Ain't Misbehavin'* (1978/1988), *Cats, Out of This World(Encores), Wizard of Oz(MSG),* OB in *Louis, Can't Help Singing.*

PALMIERI, JOSEPH. Born Aug.1, 1939 in Brooklyn, NY. Attended Catholic U. OB in *Cyrano de Bergerac, Butter and Egg Man, Boys in the Band, Beggar's Opera, The Family, Crazy Locomotive, Umbrella of Cherbourg, Amidst the Gladiolas, The Disputation,* Bdwy in *Lysistrada, Candide, Zoya's Apartment.*

PALZERE, EMMA. Born June 15, 1962 in Manchester, CT. Graduate Emerson Col. Debut 1991 OB in *Born in the R.S.A.* followed by *Montage, Rimers of Eldritch, Live from the Milky Way, Working Women.*

PANARO, HUGH. Born Feb. 19, 1964 in Philadelphia, PA. Graduate Temple U. Debut 1985 OB in *What's a Nice Country Like You Doing in a State Like This* followed by *I Have Found Home, Juba, Splendora,* Bdwy in *Phantom of the Opera* (1990), *Red Shoes, Show Boat, Sweet Adeline(Encores).*

PANKOW, JOHN. Born 1955 in St. Louis, MO. Attended St. Nichols Sch. of Arts. Debut 1980 OB in *Merton of the Movies* followed by *Slab Boys, Forty Deuce, Hunting Scenes from Lower Bovaria, Cloud 9, Jaz,z Poets at the Crotto, Henry V, North Shore Fish, Two Gentlemen of Verona, Italian American Reconciliation Aristocrats, Ice Cream with Hot Fudge, EST Marathon '92, Tempest(CP), Baby Anger,* Bdwy in *Amadeus* (1981), *The Iceman Cometh, Serious Money.*

PARISEAU, KEVIN. Born Jan.23, 1963 in Providence, RI. Graduate Brown U. Debut 1996 OB in *I Love You You're Perfect Now Change.*

PARK, MICHAEL. Born July 20, 1968 in Canandaigua, NY. Graduate Nazareth Col. of Rochester. Debut 1994 OB in *Hello Again* followed by *Violet,* Bdwy in *Smokey Joe's Cafe*(1995).

PARK, STEPHANIE. Born Aug.11, 1967 in Framingham, MA. Graduate Carnegie-Mellon. Debut OB in *Song of Singapore,* Bdwy in *Getting Away with Murder* (1996), *Titanic.*

PARKER, MARY-LOUISE. Born Aug. 2, 1964 in Ft. Jackson, SC. Graduate NC Sch of Arts. Debut 1989 OB in *Art of Success* followed by *Babylon Gardens, EST Marathon '92, Four Dogs and a Bone, How I Learned to Drive,* Bdwy in *Prelude to a Kiss* (1990-also OB) for which she received a 1990 Theatre World Award, *Bus Stop.*

PARKER, SARAH JESSICA. Bom March 25, 1965 in Nelsonville, OH. Bdwy debut in *Annie* (1978) followed by *How to Succeed...* (1996), *Once Upon a Mattress* (1996), OB in *The Innocents, One-Act Festival, To Gillian on Her 37th Birthday, Broadway Scandals of 1928, Heidi Chronicles, Substance of Fire, Sylvia.*

PARSONS, ESTELLE. Bom Nov. 20, 1927 in Lynn, MA. Attended Boston U., Actors Studio. Bdwy debut 1956 in *Happy Hunting* followed by *Whoop Up, Beg Borrow or Steal, Mother Courage, Ready When You Are C.B., Malcolm, Seven Descents of Myrtle, And Miss Reardon Drinks a Little, Norman Conquests, Ladies at the Alamo, Miss Marguerida's Way, Pirates of Penzance, Shadow Box*(1994), OB in *DemiDozen, Pieces of Eight, Threepenny Opera, Automobile Graveyard, Mrs. Dally Has a Lover* (1963) for which she received a Theatre World Award, *Next Time I'll Sing to You, Come to the Palace of Sin, In the Summer House, Monopoly, The East Wind, Galileo, Peer Gynt, Mahagonny, People Are Living There, Barbary Shore, Oh Glorious Tintinnabulation, Mert and Paul, Elizabeth and Essex, Dialogue for Lovers, New Moon* (in concert), *Orgasmo Adulto Escapes from the Zoo, Unguided Missile, Baba Goya, Extended Forecast, Deja Revue, Grace and Gloria.*

PEDI, CHRISTINE. Born Oct.24 in Yonkers, NY. Graduate FordhamU. Debut 1993 OB in *Forbidden Bdwy* followed by *Fordidden Bdwy Strikes Back.*

PEERCE, HARRY. Born Feb.21, 1952 in Detroit, MI. Graduate UMi., Goodman Sch. Debut 1982 OB in *Little Murders* followed by *Anatol, Songs of Paradise, Double Identity, Spirit of Man.*

PELLEGRINO, SUSAN. Born June 3, 1950 in Baltimore, MD. Attended CCSan Francisco, CalStU. Debut 1982 OB in *Wisteria Trees* followed by *Steel on Steel, Master Builder, Equal Wrights, Come as You Are, Painting Churches, Marvin's Room, Glory Girls, Minor Demons,* Bdwy in *Kentucky Cycle* (1994), *Present Laughter.*

PELTY, ADAM. Born July 31, 1967 in Chicago, IL. Graduate Purdue U. Bdwy debut 1993 in *Cyrano: The Musical* followed by *Steel Pier.*

PENDLETON, AUSTIN. Born March 27, 1940 in Warren, OH. Debut 1962 OB in *Oh Dad Poor Dad...* followed by *Last Sweet Days of Isaac, Three Sisters, Say Goodnight Gracie, Office Murders, Up from Paradise, The Overcoat, Two Character Play, Master Class, Educating Rita, Uncle Vanya, Serious Company, Philotetes, Hamlet, Richard III, What about Luv?, Sorrows of Frederick, The Show-Off, Jeremy Rudge, Sophistry, The Imposter, Keats, Othello,* Bdwy in *Fiddler on the Roof* (1964), *Hail Scrawdyke, Little Foxes, American Millionaire, The Runner Stumbles, Doubles.*

PEPE, NEIL. Bom June 23, 1963 in Bloomington, IN. Graduate Kenyon Col. Debut 1988 OB in *Boys' Life* followed by *Three Sisters, Virgin Molly, Return to Sender, Five Very Live, Down the Shore, The Lights, Trafficking in Broken Hearts, Edmond, Joy of Going Somewhere Definite.*

PEREZ, LUIS. Born July 28, 1959 in Atlanta, GA. With Joffrey Ballet before Bdwy debut in *Brigadoon* (LC-1986) followed by *Phantom of the Opera, Jerome Robbins' Broadway, Dangerous Games, Grand Hotel, Man of La Mancha* (1992), *Ain't Broadway Grand, Chronicle of a Death Foretold, Chicago*(1996), OB in *Wonderful Ice Cream Suit, Tango Apasionada.*

PEREZ, MIGUEL. Born September 7, 1957 in San Jose, CA. Attended Natl. Shakespeare Consv. Debut 1986 OB in *Women Beware Women*, followed by *Don Juan of Seville, Cymbeline, Mountain Language, Birthday Party, Hamlet, Henry IV Parts 1 & 2, Arturo Ui, Merry Wives of Windsor, Henry VIII*, Bdwy in *Tempest* (1995)

PERRECA, MICHAEL. Born Jan.13, 1961 in Long Island, NY. Graduate Seton Hall U. Debut 1997 OB in *Jest a Second.*

PESCE, VINCE. Born Dec. 3, 1966 in Brooklyn NY. Bdwy debut in *Guys and Dolls* (1993), *Victor Victoria, Promises Promises (Encores)*, OB in *Hunchback of Notre Dame.*

PETERS, MARK. Born Nov. 20, 1952 in Council Bluffs, IA. Yale Graduate. Debut 1977 OB in *Crazy Locomotive* followed by *Legend of Sleepy Hollow, Kismet, Awakening of Spring, Appelemando's Dreams, Most Men Are, Merry Muildoons, Marriage of Bette & Boo.*

PEVSNER, DAVID. Born Dec. 31, 1958 in Skokie, IL. Graduate CarnegieMellonU. Debut 1985 OB in *A Flash of Lightning* followed by *Rags, Rag on a Stick and a Star, Party, When Pigs Fly,* Bdwy in *Fiddler on the Roof* (1990).

PHILLIPS, ANGIE. Born in Denison, TX. Graduate NYU. Debut 1991 OB in *Bright Room Called Day* followed by *Way of the World, Suppliant Women, The Treatment, Midsummer Night's Dream, Golden Boy, Dark Ride, Many and Lo, 15 Minute Hamlet, The Skriker, Henry VI, All My Sons.*

PHILLIPS, ARTE. Born Feb. 13, 1959 in Astoria, Queens, NYC. Attended Baruch Col. Bdwy debut in *Grand Hotel*(1990) followed by *Victor Victoria, Once Upon a Mattress*(1996).

PHILLIPS, GARRISON. Born Oct. 8, 1929 in Tallahasee, Fl. Graduate U. W.Va. Debut 1956 OB in *Eastward in Eden* followed by *Romeo and Juliet, Time of the Cuckoo, Triptych, After the Fall, Two Gentlemen of Verona, Ambrosio, Sorrows of Frederick, La Ronde, Playing with Fire (After Frankenstein), Rough/Play, Godot Arrives, Nellie,* Bdwy in *Clothes for a Summer Hotel* (1980).

PHILLIPS, LACY DARRYL. Born Feb.24, 1963 in NYC. Attended Lehman Col. Debut 1981 OB in *Raisin* followed by *Late Great Ladies,* Bdwy in *Anything Goes*(1987), *Play On!*

PIECH, JENNIFER (LYNN). Born Jan.25, 1967 in Camden, NJ. Graduate College of William & Mary. Debut 1995 OB in *Lust.* followed by *Playboy of the Western World,* Bdwy in *Titanic*(1997).

PIETROPINTO, ANGELA. Born Feb.4 in NYC. Graduate NYU. OB in *Henry IV, Alice in Wonderland, Endgame, Sea Gull, Jinx Bridge, The Mandrake, Marie and Bruce, Green Card Blues, 3 by Pirandello, Broken Pitcher, Cymbeline, Romeo and Juliet, Midsummer Night's Dream, Twelve Dreams, The Rivals, Cap and Bells, Thrombo, Lies My Father Told Me, Sorrows of Stephen, Between the Wars, Hotel Play, Rain Some Fish No Elephants, Young Playwrights 90, Tunnel of Love, Thanksgiving Day, Vilna's Got a Golem,* Bdwy in *The Suicide* (1980), *Eastern Standard.*

PIETROPINTO, RITA. Born June 26, 1971. Graduate Columbia U. Debut 1995 OB in *Three Classics* followed by *Julius Caesar, Green Bird, Love the Greatest Enchantment,* Bdwy in *London Assurance.*

PIKSER, ROBERTA. Born in Chicago, IL. Graduate U Chicago. Debut 1986 OB in *War Party* followed by *The Exterminator.*

PINE, LARRY. Born March 3, 1945 in Tucson, AZ. Graduate NYU. Debut 1967 OB in *Cyrano* followed by *Alice in Wonderland, Mandrake, Aunt Dan and Lemon, Taming of the Shrew, Better Days, Dolphin Project, Treasure Island, Preservation Society, The Disputation,* Bdwy in *End of the World* (1984), *Angels in America, Bus*

PINKINS, TONYA. Born May 30, 1962 in Chicago Il. Attended Carnegie-Mellon U. Bdwy debut in *Merrily We Roll Along* (1981) followed by *Jelly's Last Jam, Chronicle of a Death Foretold, Play On!,* OB in *Five Points, Winter's Tale, An Ounce of Prevention, Just Say No, Mexican Hayride, Young Playwrights '90, Approximating Mother, Merry Wives of Windsor.*

PIRE, FELIX A. Born May 27, 1971 in Tampa, FL. Graduate So. Meth U. Debut 1996 OB in *Men on the Verge of a His-Panic Breakdown.*

PIRO, JACQUELYN. Born Jan. 8, 1965 in Boston MA. Graduate Boston U. Debut 1987 OB in *Company* followed by Bdwy in *Les Miserables* (1990), *Sweet Adeline(Encores).*

PITTU, DAVID. Born April 4, 1967 in Fairfield, CT. Graduate NYU. Debut 1987 OB in *Film is Evil: Radio is Good* followed by *Five Very Live, White Cotton Sheets, Nothing Sacred, Stand-In, The Lights, Three Postcards, Dangerous Corner, Sympathetic Magic,* Bdwy in *Tenth Man*(1989).

PIZZI, PAULA. Born Oct.9, 1963 in Buenos Aires, Argentina. Attended Universidad Catolica. Debut 1997 OB in *Another Part of the House* followed by *Clean.*

POE, RICHARD. Born Jan. 25, 1946 in Portola, CA. Graduate USanFran., U. Cal/Davis Debut 1971 OB in *Hamlet* followed by *Seasons Greetings, Twelfth Night, Naked Rights, Approximating Mother, Jeffrey, View of the Dome,* Bdwy in *Broadway* (1987), *M. Butterfly, Our Country's Good, Moon Over Buffalo.*

POLIS, JOEL. Born Oct. 3, 1951 in Philadelphia, PA. Graduate USC, Yale. Debut 1976 OB in *Marco Polo* followed by *Family Business, Just Like the Night, Claptrap, Baby Dance, Names.*

POLLACK, DANIEL. Born July 25, 1927 in NYC. Graduate CCNY, Adelphi, NYU. Debut 1949 OB in *An American Tragedy* followed by *Goodnight Grandpa, Victory Bonds, Imaginary Invalid, Six Candles, Those Left Behind,* Bdwy in *The Price*(1979).

PORTER, ADINA. Born Feb.18, 1963 in NYC. Attended SUNY/Purchase. Debut 1988 OB in *Debutante Ball* followed by *Inside Out, Tiny Mommie, Footsteps in the Rain, Jersey City, The Mysteries?, Aven U' Boys, Silence Cunning Exile, Girl Gone, Dancing on Moonlight, Saturday Mourning Cartoons, Venus, Marking.*

POSNER, AMANDA. Born May 8, 1982 in Long Beach, CA. Debut 1997 OB in *King John* followed by *Violet.*

PRESTON, CARRIE. Born 1967 in Macon, GA. Graduate Juilliard, UofEvansville, IN. Bdwy debut in *Tempest* (1995), OB in *In No Man's Land, Anthony and Cleopatra.*

PRINCE, FAITH. Born Aug. 5, 1957 in Augusta, GA. Graduate UCinn. Debut 1981 OB in *Scrambled Feet* followed by *Olympus on My Mind, Groucho, Living Color, Bad Habits, Falsettoland, 3 of Hearts,* Bdwy in *Jerome Robbins' Broadway* (1989), *Nick & Nora, Guys and Dolls* (1992), *Fiorello(Encores), What's Wrong with This Picture, DuBarry Was a Lady (Encores), King and I.*

PRITCHETT, JAMES. Born Oct.27 in Lenoir, NC. Graduate UNC, UChicago, AADA. Debut 1955 OB in *Ideal Husband* followed by *Report to the Stockholders, Electra, Home of the Brave, New Girl in Town, Embers, The Killer, Death of Bessie Smith, Round with a Ring, An Evening's Frost, Phaedre, The Inheritors, Night Seasons, Young Man from Atlanta,* Bdwy in *Two for the Seesaw*(1959), *Sail Away, Lord Pengo, Summer and Smoke.*

QUINN, PATRICK. Born Feb. 12, 1950 in Philadelphia, PA. Graduate TempleU. Bdwy debut in *Fiddler on the Roof* (1976) followed by *Day in Hollywood/Night in the Ukraine, Oh, Coward!, Lend Me a Tenor, Damn Yankees, Beauty and the Beast, Boys from Syracuse(Encores),* OB in *It's Better with a Bank, By Strouse, Forbidden Broadway, Best of Forbidden Broadway, Raft of Medusa, Forbidden Broadway's 10th Anniversary, A Helluva Town, After the Ball.*

RAINES, RON. Born Dec.2, 1949 in Texas City, TX. Graduate OK City U, Juilliard. Bdwy debut in *Showboat*(1983) followed by *Teddy and Alice,* OB in *Olympus On My Mind, Little Night Music, Hart & Hammerstein Plus One.*

RAITER, FRANK. Born Jan. 17, 1932 in Cloquet, MN. Yale graduate. Bdwy debut in *Cranks* (1958) followed by *Dark at the Top of the Stairs, J.B., Camelot, Salome, Sacrilege,* OB in *Soft Core Pornographer, Winter's Tale, Twelfth Night, Tower of Evil, Endangered Species, Bright Room Called Day, Learned Ladies, 'Tis Pity She's A Whore, Othello, Comedy of Errors, Orestes, Marathon Dancing, Sudden Devotion, The Devils.*

RAMSEY, KEVIN. Born Sept. 24, 1959 in New Orleans, LA. Graduate NYU. Bdwy debut in *Black and Blue* (1989) followed by *Oh Kay!* for which he received a Theatre World Award, *5 Guys Named Moe, The Life,* OB in *Liberation Suite, Sweet Dreams, Prison Made Tuxedos, Staggerlee, Juba.*

RANDALL, TONY. Born Feb. 26, 1920 in Tulsa, OK. Attended Northwestern, Columbia, Neighborhood Playhouse. Bdwy debut in *Antony and Cleopatra* (1947) followed by *To Tell You the Truth, Caesar and Cleopatra, Oh Men! Oh Women!, Inherit the Wind, Oh! Captain!, UTBU, M. Butterfly, A Little Hotel on the Side, 3 Men on a Horse, Government Inspector, School for Scandal, Inherit the Wind, Christmas Carol (MSG), Sweet Adeline(Encores).*

RANDELL, PATRICIA. Born Mar.18 in Worcester, MA. Graduate BostonU. Debut 1995 OB in *Durang Durang* followed by *Waiter Waiter, The Shattering, Goddess Cure.*

RAOUF, JANAN. Born Dec.22, 1974 in Indianapolis, IN. Graduate Carnegie Mellon U. Debut 1996 OB in *Anne Frank and Me*.

RAPHAEL, GERRIANNE. Born Feb. 23, 1935 in NYC. Attended New School, Columbia U. Bdwy debut 1941 in *Solitaire* followed by *Ghost in the House, Violet, Goodbye My Fancy, Seventh Heaven, Li'l Abner, Saratoga, Man of La Mancha, King of Hearts,* OB in *Threepenny Opera, The Boy Friend, Ernest in Love, Say When, the Prime of Miss Jean Brodie, The Butler Did It, The Ninth Step, An Evening with Sid Caesar, Dorian Gray*.

RAPP, ANTHONY. Born Oct.26, 1971 in Joliet, IL. Bdwy debut in *Little Prince and the Aviator* (1981) followed by *Precious Sons, Six Degrees of Separation* (also OB), *Rent* (also OB), OB in *Youth Is Wasted, Destiny of Me, Family Animal, Reproducing Georgia, Prosthetics and the Twenty-Five Thousand Dollar Pyramid, Making of Edward III, Sophistry, Traficking in Broken Hearts, Raised in Captivity*.

RASCHE, DAVID. Bom Aug. 7, 1944 in St. Louis, MO. Graduate Elmhurst Col., U. Chicago. Debut 1976 OB in *John* followed by *Snow White, Isadora Duncan Sleeps with the Russian Navy, End of the War, A Sermon, Routed, Geniuses, Dolphin Position, To Gillian on Her 37th Birthday, Custom of the Country, Country Girl, Marathon '91, No One Will Be Immune, Edmond,* Bdwy in *Shadow Box* (1977), *Loose Ends, Lunch Hour, Speed-the-Plow, Mastergate, Christmas Carol*.

RASHOVICH, GORDANA. Bom Sept. 18 in Chicago, Il. Graduate Roosevelt U, RADA. Debut 1977 OB in *Fefu and Her Friends* for which she received a Theatre World Award, followed by *Selma, Couple of the Year, Mick Sonata, Class One-Acts, Morocco, A Shayna Maidel, The Misanthrope, EST Marathon '93, Springtime,* Bdwy in *Conversations with My Father* (1992).

RECTOR, SEAN ALLEN. Born Aug.20 in NYC. Attended U of Albany. Debut 1996 OB in *North 17th St.* followed by *Boy X Man, Scapin*.

REDGRAVE, VANESSA. Born Jan.30, 1937 in London, Eng. Attended Central School of Speech and Drama. Bdwy debut in *Lady from the Sea* (1976) followed by *Orpheus Descending* (1989), OB in *Vita and Virginia, Anthony and Cleopatra*.

REED, VIVIAN. Born June 6, 1947 in Pittsburgh, PA. Attended Juilliard. Bdwy debut 1971 in *That's Entertainment* followed by *Don't Bother Me I Can't Cope, Brown Sugar* for which she received a Theatre World Award, *It's So Nice to Be Civilized, High Rollers,* OB in *The End of the Day, Queenie Pie, 20th Century R&B*.

REES, ROGER. Born May 5, 1944 in Wales. Graduate Glade School of Fine Art. Bdwy debut 1975 in *London Assurance* followed by *Nicholas Nickleby* (1981), *Red Shoes* (previews only), *Indiscretions, The Rehearsal,* OB in *End of the Day* (1992).

REGAN, MOLLY. Born Oct. 8 in Maakato, MN. Graduate Northwestern U. Debut 1979 OB in *Say Goodnight Gracie* followed by *Personals, Etiquette, Booth, Two Gentlemen of Verona,* Bdwy in *Stepping Out* (1987), *The Crucible* (1991).

REINKING, ANN. Born Nov.10, 1949 in Seattle WA. Attended Joffrey Sch, HB Studio. Bdwy debut in *Cabaret* (1969) followed by *Coco, Pippin, Over Here* for which she received a Theatre World Award, *Goodtime Charley, Chorus Line, Chicago* (1975/1996), *Dancin', Sweet Charity* (1986), OB in *One More Song One More Dance, Music Moves Me*.

REMMES, DAN. Born Aug.19, 1966 in Stoughton, MA. Graduate AADA. Debut 1989 OB in *I Love Lucy Who?* followed by *Pvt. Wars, What Doesn't Kill Us, Waiting Women*.

RENDERER, SCOTT. Bom in Palo Alto, CA. Graduate Whitman Col. Bdwy debut 1983 in *Teaneck Tanzi,* OB in *And Things That Go Bump in the Night, Crossfire, Just Like the Lions, Dreamer Examines His Pillow, Nasty Little Secrets, Unidentified Human Remains, Hairy Ape*.

REYNOLDS, RUSTY. Born Sept. 13, 1968 in Summit, NJ. Attended U IA, Manhattan Sch Music. Debut 1993 OB in *Carnival* followed by *Littlest Clown, On the Road to Victory*.

RICHARDSON, LEE. Bom Sept.11, 1926 in Chicago, IL. Graduate Goodman Th. Debut 1952 OB in *Summer and Smoke* followed by *St. Joan, Volpone, American Dream, Bartleby, Plays for Bleecker Street, Merchant of Venice, King Lear, Thieves Carnival, Waltz of the Toreadors, Talented Tenth, Ivanov,* Bdwy in *Legend of Lizzie* (1959), *Lord Pengo, House of Atreus, Find Your Way Home, Othello, Jockey Club Stakes, Devii's Disciple, Getting Married*.

RIDEOUT, LEENYA. Born Mar.22, 1969 in Missoula, MT. Graduate U of CO. Debut 1996 OB in *Cowgirls* followed by *Portable Pioneer Show*.

RIPLEY, ALICE. Bom Dec. 14, 1963 in San Leandro, CA. Graduate Kent St U. Bdwy debut in *Tommy* (1993) followed by *Sunset Blvd, King David*.

RIVERA, EILEEN. Born March 3, 1970 in Queens, NYC. Graduate Boston U. Debut 1995 OB in *Cambodia Agonistes*.

ROBERTS, ANGELA. Born Oct.25, 1961 in Pasadena, TX. Graduate Rice U, So. Methodist U. Debut 1990 OB in *Love's Labours Lost* followed by *Twelfth Night, Extras, Spirit of Man*.

ROBERTS, DARCIE. Born Dec.12, 1973 in Pomona, CA. Bdwy in *Crazy for You* (1993) followed by *Dream*.

ROBINSON, HAL. Born in Bedford, IN. Graduate IN U. Debut 1972 OB in *Memphis Store Bought Teeth* followed by *From Berlin to Broadway, Fantasticks, Promenade, Baker's Wife, Yours Anne, Personals, And a Nightingale Sang, Old Wicked Songs, Only Angels,* Bdwy in *On Your Toes* (1983), *Broadway, Grand Hotel, Nick & Nora*.

ROBINSON, HEATHER. Born Jan.27, 1970 in NJ. Graduate Hofstra U. Debut 1993 OB in *Arrivals* followed by *Barn, Winter's Tale, 343 Days, Gifts, Dead Guys, Rain, Mock Trial*.

ROCHA, KALI. Born Dec.5, 1971 in Memphis, TN. Graduate Carnegie-MellonU. Bdwy debut in *In the Summer House* (1993) followed by *Inspector Calls,* OB in *The Devils*.

RODGERS, ELISABETH S. Born Jan.8, 1964 in Houston, TX. Graduate PrincetonU. OB 1989 in *Loving Dutch* followed by *Guilty Innocence, White Water, Richard Foreman Trilogy, Gender Wars, Faith Healer*.

RODRIGUEZ, RAYMOND. Born Dec.6, 1961 in Puerto Rico. Attended Cerritos Col., Orange County Col. Bdwy debut in *Kiss of the Spider Woman* (1993), *Promises Promises*.

ROGERS, GIL. Born Feb.4, 1934 in Lexington, KY. Attended Harvard U. OB in *Ivory Branch, Vanity of Nothing, Warrior's Husband, Hell Bent for Heaven, Gods of Lighting, Pictures in a Hallway, Rose, Memory Bank, A Recent Killing, Birth, Come Back Little Sheba, Life of Galileo, Remembrance, Mortally Fine, Frankie, History of President JFK Part I, On Deaf Ears,* Bdwy in *Great White Hope, Best Little Whorehouse in Texas, Corn is Green* (1983).

ROSENBAUM, DAVID. Born in NYC. Debut 1968 OB in *America Hurrah!* followed by *Cave Dwellers, Evenings with Chekhov, Out of the Death Cart, After Miriam, Indian Wants the Bronx, Allergy, Family Business, Beagleman and Brackett, Last Sortie, Awake and Sing, Spirit of Man,* Bdwy in *Oh! Calcutta!, Ghetto*.

ROSEN-STONE, MEKENZIE. Born Jan.12, 1988 in Baltimore, MD. Bdwy debut in *Annie* (1997).

ROSS, STEVE. Born Dec.8, 1938 in New Rochelle, NY. Attended Georgetown U, Catholic U. Debut 1991 OB in *I Won't Dance,* Bdwy in *Present Laughter* (1996).

ROTH, STEPHANIE. Born in 1963 in Boston, MA. Juilliard graduate. Bdwy debut 1987 in *Les Liaisons Dangereuses* followed by *Artist Descending a Staircase,* OB in *Cherry Orchard, Measure for Measure, A Body of Water, Uncommon Women and Others, Crumbs from the Table of Joy, A Backward Glance, Two Gentlemen of Verona*.

ROZNOWSKI, ROBERT. Born July 16, 1963 in Baltimore, MD. Graduate Point Park Col., OhioStU. Debut 1992 OB in *Lightin' Out* followed by *Young Abe Lincoln, Identical Twins from Baltimore, Hysterical Blindness, I Love You You're Perfect Now Change*.

RUDD, PAUL. Born April 6, 1969 in Passaic, NJ. Graduate U KS, AADA/West. Debut 1993 in *Bloody Poetry,* Bdwy debut in *Last Night of Ballyhoo* (1996).

RUFFALO, MARK. Born Nov.22, 1967 in Kenosha, WI. Graduate Stella Adler Conserv. Debut 1996 OB in *This Is Our Youth* for which he won a 1997 Theatre World Award.

RUSSELL, CATHERINE. Born Aug.6, 1955 in New Canaan, CT. Graduate Cornel U. Debut 1980 OB in *City Sugar* followed by *Miss Schulman's Quartet, Resounding Tinkle, Right to Life, Collective Choices, Lunch Girls, Home of the Range, Perfect Crime*.

RYAN, AMY. Born May 3, 1968 in NYC. Debut 1988 OB in *A Shayna Maidel* followed by *Rimers of Eldritch, Eleemosynary, Marking, Hysterical Blindness,* Bdwy in *Sisters Rosensweig* (1993).

RYAN, STEVEN. Born June 19, 1947 in New York City. Graduate Boston U, U MN. Debut 1978 OB in *Winning Isn't Everything* followed by *The Beethoven, September in the Rain, Romance Language, Love's Labour's Last, Love and Anger, Approximating Mother, Merry Wives of Windsor, Unexpected Tenderness, Minor Demons,* Bdwy in *I'm Not Rappaport* (1986), *Guys and Dolls* (1992), *On the Waterfront*.

RYAN, THOMAS JAY. Born Aug.1, 1962 in Pittsburgh, PA. Graduate Carnegie-Mellon. Debut 1992 OB in *Samuel's Major Problem* followed by *Egypt, My Head was a Sledgehammer, Robert Zucco, Dracula, Venus, South*.

RYLANCE, MARK. Born Jan. 18, 1960 in Ashford, Kent, England. Graduate RADA. Debut 1993 OB in *Henry V* followed by *As You Like It, Two Gentlemen of Verona.*

RYNN, MARGIE. Born in Princeton, NJ. Graduate U CA/Berkeley, ULA. Debut 1988 OB in *Autobahn* followed by *Bed Experiment, Suite Sixteen, Les Miserables, Paradise Is Closing Down.*

SAITO, JAMES. Born March 6, 1955 in Los Angeles, CA. Graduate UCLA. Debut 1988 OB in *Rashomon* followed by *Day Standing on Its Head, Ripples in the Pond, Wilderness, Friends, Waiting Room.*

SALAMANDYK, TIM. Born Feb.25, 1967 in Minneapolis, MN.Graduate Illinois WesleyanU. Debut 1996 OB in *Food Chain* followed by *Green Heart.*

SALATA, GREGORY. Born July 21, 1949 in NYC. Graduate Queens Col. Bdwy debut in *Dance with Me* (1975) followed by *Equus, Bent*, OB in *Piaf: A Remembrance, Sacraments, Measure for Measure, Subject of Childhood, Jacques and His Master, Androcles and the Lion, Madwoman of Chaillot, Beauty Part, Heartbreak House.*

SALGUERO, SOPHIA. Born July 5, 1972 in Ann Arbor, MI. Graduate Carnegie Mellon U. Debut 1995 OB in *I Was Looking at the Ceiling* followed by *Green Bird*, Bdwy 1996 in *Juan Darien.*

SAMUEL, PETER. Bom Aug. 15, 1958 in Pana, IL. Graduate E.IL U. Bdwy debut in *The First*(1981) followed by *Joseph and the ...Dreamcoat, Three Musketeers, Rags, Les Miserables, Secret Garden,* OB in *Human Comedy, 3 Guys Naked from the Waist Down, Road to Hollywood, Elizabeth and Essex, Little Eyolf, King David.*

SANES, CAMILIA. Born June 23, 1965 in St. Croix, VA. Debut 1997 OB in *Cloud Tectonics* followed by *187, Unmerciful Good Fortune, Two Gentlemen of Verona.*

SANTIAGO, SAUNDRA. Born April 14, 1957 in NYC. Graduate U. Miami, SMU. Bdwy debut in *View from the Bridge* (1983) followed by *Chronicle of a Death Foretold,* OB in *Road to Nirvana, Spike Heels, Hello Again, Young Girl and the Monsson.*

SANTIAGO, SOCORRO. Born July 12, 1957 in NYC. Attend Juilliard. Debut 1977 OB in *Crack* followed by *Poets from the Inside, Unfinished Women, Family Portrait, Domino, The Promise, Death and the Maiden, Phaedra, Sparrow,* Bdwy in *The Basement* (1980).

SARSGAARD, PETER. Born Mar.7, 1971 in Scott A.F.B., IL. Graduate WA U. Debut 1995 OB in *Laura Dennis* followed by *Kingdom of Earth.*

SCHERER, JOHN. Born May 16, 1961 in Buffalo, NY. Graduate Carnegie-Mellon U. Debut 1983 OB in *Preppies* followed by *Jass, Downriver, Ladies and Gentlemen Jerome Kern, Olympus on My Mind, Music Makes Me,* Bdwy in *Sunset Blvd.*(1996).

SCHOEFFLER, PAUL. Born Nov. 21, 1958 in Montreal, Can. Graduate U.CA/Berkley, Carnegie-Mellon, U Brussels. Debut 1988 OB in *Much Ado about Nothing* followed by *Cherry Orchard, Carnival, Doll's Life, No Way to Treat a Lady,* Bdwy in *Cyrano the Musical* (1993).

SCHRAMM, DAVID. Born Aug.14, 1946 in Louisville, KY. Attended Western KyU. Juilliard. Debut 1972 OB in *School for Scandal* followed by *Lower Depths, Women Beware Women, Mother Courage, King Lear, Duck Variations, Cradle Will Rock, Twelfth Night, Palace of Amateurs,* Bdwy in *Three Sisters, Next Time I'll Sing to You, Edward II, Measure for Measure, Robber Bridegroom, Bedroom Farce, Goodbye Fidel, The Misanthrope, Tartuffe: Born Again, London Assurance.*

SCHULTZ, ARMAND. Bom May 17, 1959 in Rochester, NY. Graduate NiagaraU., Catholic U. Debut OB 1988 in *Coriolanus* followed by *Crystal Clear, Titus Andronicus, Tower of Evil, Richard III, Sight Unseen, King Lear, Where the Truth Lies, Seeking the Genesis, Major Crimes.*

SCHULTZ, CAROL. Born Feb. 12 in Chicago, IL. Graduate Case Western Reserve U, U IL. Debut 1982 OB in *Peer Gynt* followed by *Cherry Orchard, King Lear, Ghost Sonata, Doll's House, Antigone, Misalliance, Cymberline,* Bdwy in *Abe Lincoln in Illinois* (1993).

SCHWARTZ, GARY. Born Nov. 20, 1964 in Englewood, NJ. Attended Hofstra U., Debut 1987 OB in *The Chosen* followed by *What's a Nice Country Like You Doing in a State Like This?, Bent,* Bdwy in *Fiddler on the Roof* (1990), *Kiss of the Spider Woman.*

SEALE, DOUGLAS. Born Oct.28, 1913 in London, Eng. Graduate Washington Col., RADA. Bdwy debut 1974 in *Emperor Henry IV* followed by *Frankenstein, The Dresser, Noises Off, Madwoman of Chaillot.,* OB in *The Entertainer.*

SEAMON, EDWARD. Born Apr. 15, 1937 in San Diego, CA. Attended San Diego St Col. Debut 1971 OB in *Life and Times of J. Walter Smintheus* followed by *The Contractor, The Family, Fishing, Feedlot, Cabin 12, Rear Column, Devour the Snow, Buried Child, Friends, Extenuating Circumstances, Confluence, Richard II, Great Grandson of Jedediah Kohler, Marvelous Gray, Time Framed, Master Builder, Fall Hookup, Fool for Love, The Harvesting, Country for Old Men, Love's Labour's Lost, Caligula, Mound Builders, Quiet in the Land, Talley & Son, Tomorrow's Monday, Ghosts, Or Mice and Men, Beside Herself, You Can't Think of Everything, Tales of the Last Formicans, Love Diatribe, Empty Hearts, Sandbox, Winter's Tale, Cymbeline, Barber of Seville, Venice Preserv'd,* Bdwy in *The Trip Back Down* (1977), *Devour the Snow, American Clock.*

SEDGWICK, KYRA. Born Aug.19, 1965 in NYC. Attended USC. Debut 1981 OB in *Time Was* followed by *Dakota's Belly Wyoming, Not Waving,* Bdwy in *Ah Wilderness* (1989) for which she received a Theatre World Award.

SELBY, WILLIAM. Born Nov.22, 1961 in Melrose, MA. Graduate Emerson Col. Debut 1987 OB in *Apple Tree* followed by *Juba, Forbidden Bdwy, Forbidden Hollywood, Forbidden Bdwy Strikes Back.*

SELDES, MARIAN. Born Aug. 23, 1928 in NYC. Attended Neighborhood Playhouse. Bdwy debut in *Media* (1947) followed by *Crime and Punishment, That Lady, Town Beyond Tragedy, Ondine, On High Ground, Come of Age, Chalk Garden, Milk Train Doesn't Stop Here Anymore, The Wall, Gift of Time, Delicate Balance, Before You Go, Father's Day, Equus, The Merchant, Deathtrap, Boys from Syracuse(Encores),* OB in *Different, Ginger Man, Mercy Street, Isadora Duncan Sleeps with the Russion Navy, Painting Churches, Gertrude Stein and Companion, Richard II, The Milk Train Doesn't Stop..., Bright Room Called Day, Another Time, Three Tall Women.*

SETRAKIAN, ED. Born Oct. 1, 1928 in Jenkinstown, WVA. Graduate Concord Col., NYU. Debut 1966 OB *I Dreams in the Night* followed by *Othello, Coriolanus, Macbeth, Hamlet, Baal, Old Glory, Futz, Hey Rube, Seduced, Shout across the River, American Days, Sheepskin, Inserts, Crossing the Bar, Boys Next Door, The Mensch, Adoring the Madonna, Tack Room, Water and Wine, Nine Armenians,* Bdwy in *Days in the Trees* (1976) *St. Joan, Best Little Whorehouse in Texas.*

SETRAKIAN, MARY. Born in San Francisco, CA. Graduate StanfordU., New England Consv. Debut 1990 OB in *Hannah 1939* followed by *Colette Collage, New York Romance, Dorian Gray,* Bdwy in *Hello Dolly* (1995).

SEVERS, WILLIAM. Born Jan. 8, 1932 in Britton, OK. Attended Pasadena Playhouse, Columbia Col. Bdwy debut in *Cut of the Axe* (1960) followed by *On Borrowed Time* (1991), OB in *Moon Is Blue, Lulu, Big Maggie, Mixed Doubles, The Rivals, Beaver Coat, Twister, Midnight Mass, Gas Station, Firebugs, Fellow Travelers, Iowa Boys, Carpool, Winning.*

SHALLO, KAREN. Born Sept.26, 1946 in Philadelphia, PA. Graduate PA St U. Debut 1973 OB in *Children of Darkness* followed by *Moliere in Spite of Himself, We Won't Pay!, The Overcoat, Angelus, Question Marks and Periods, Anne Frank and Me,* Bdwy in *Passione*(1980).

SHANNON, SARAH (SOLIE). Born May 23, 1966 in LaCrosse, WI. Graduate U WI. Bdwy debut 1992 in *Cats* followed by *Beauty and the Beast, Steel Pier.*

SHAW, FIONA. Born July 10, 1955 in Cork, Ire. Attended RADA. Debut 1996 OB in *The Waste Land* for which she received a 1997 Theatre World Award.

SHELTON, SLOANE. Born Mar. 17, 1934 in Asheville, NC. Attended Bates Col., RADA. Bdwy Debut 1967 in *Imaginary Invalid* followed by *Touch of the Poet, Tonight at 8:30, I Never Sang for My Father, Sticks and Bones, Runner Stumbles, Shadow Box, Passione, Open Admission, Orpheus Descending,* OB in *Androcles and the Lion, The Maids, Basic Training of Pavlo Hummel, Play and Other Plays, Julius Caesar, Chieftans, Passione, Chinese Viewing Pavilion, Blood Relations, Great Divide, Highest Standard of Living, Flower Palace, April Snow, Nightingale, Dearly Departed, Other People's Money, Dog Opera, Importance of Being Earnest, Not Waving.*

SHEPARD, DUANE. Born Sept.15, 1951 in Detroit, MI. Debut 1986 OB in *Brother Malcolm X* (also 1997).

SHER, ANTONY. After much work in London, Bdwy debut 1997 in *Stanley* for which he received a 1997 Theatre World Award.

SHIPLEY, SANDRA. Born Feb.1 in Rainham, Kent, Eng. Attended New Col. of Speech and Drama, LondonU. Debut 1988 OB in *Six Characters in Search of an Author* followed by *Big Time, Kindertransport, Venus, Backward Glance,* Bdwy in *Indiscretions* (1995).

SHORT, MARTIN. Born March 26, 1950 in Hamilton, Ont. Canada. Graduate McMaster U. Bdwy debut 1993 in *Goodbye Girl* for which he received a Theatre World Award, followed by *Promises Promises (Encores).*

Duane Shepard

J. Smith-Cameron

Richard B. Schull

Mara Stephens

Ted Sperling

Jodi Stevens

Heath C.A. Stanwhyck

Renee Taylor

Tom Treadwell

Michele Tibbits

James Urbaniak

Marisa Tomei

Paul Urcioli

Rachel Ulanet

James Victor

Sharon Washington

Ben Walden

Margaret Whiting

James Weatherstone

Dianne Wiest

Michael West

Jacqueline Williams

Dwight Wigfall

Valerie Wright

Timothy Leigh Williams

Deborah Yates

Ray Wills

Bellamy Young

Daniel Ziskie

Leigh Zimmerman

251

SHULL, RICHARD B. Born Feb. 24, 1929 in Evanston, Il. Graduate St U IA. Debut 1953 OB in *Coriolanus* followed by *Purple Dust, Journey to the Day, American Hamburger League, Frimbo, Fade the Game, Desire under the Elms, Marriage of Betty and Boo, One of the All-Time Greats, Sausage Eaters, The Gig,* Bdwy in *Black-eyed Susan* (1954), *Wake Up Darling, Red Roses for Me, I Knock at the Door, Pictures in the Hallway, Have I Got a Girl for You, Minnie's Boys, Goodtime Charley, Fools, Oh Brother!, Front Page, Ain't Broadway Grand, Victor Victoria.*

SIEBER, CHRISTOPHER. Born Feb.18, 1969 in St. Paul, MN. Attended AMDA. Bdwy debut in *Christmas Carol (MSG /1994)* followed by *Pal Joey (Encores),* OB in *Boys in the Band*(1996).

SIEGFRIED, MANDY. Born June 19 in Pittsburgh, PA. Debut 1996 OB in *Anne Frank and Me* followed by *Over the Edge.*

SISTO, ROCCO. Born Feb. 8, 1953 in Bari, Italy. Graduate UIl., NYU. Debut 1982 OB in *Hamlet* followed by *Country Doctor, Times and Appetites of Toulouse-Lautrec, Merchant of Venice, What Did He See, Winter's Tale, The Tempest, Dream of a Common Language, Tis Pity She's a Whore, Mad Forest, Careless Love, All's Well That Ends Well, The Illusion, Merry Wives of Windsor, Quills, Overtime, Demonology,* Bdwy in *Month in the Country* (1995).

SKINNER, EMILY. Born June 29, 1970 in Richmond, VA. Graduate Carnegie-MellonU. Bdwy debut 1994 in *Christmas Carol* followed by *Jekyll & Hyde,* OB in *Watbanaland.*

SLEZAK, VICTOR. Born July 7, 1957 in Youngstown, OH. Debut 1979 OB in *Electra Myth* followed by *Hasty Heart, Ghosts, Alice and Fred, Window Claire, Miracle Worker, Talk Radio, Marathon '88, One Act Festival, Briar Patch, Appointment with a High Wire Lady, Sam 1 Am, White Rose, Born Guilty, Naked Truth, Ivanov, Mafia on Prozac,* Bdwy in *Any Given Day* (1993), *Garden District.*

SLOAN, JOHN. Born April 26, 1973 in San Francisco, CA. Graduate Skidmore Col. Debut 1996 OB in *Anne Frank and Me.*

SMITH, DANA. Born Nov.30, 1953 in NYC. Graduate SyracuseU, YaleU. Debut 1983 OB in *Richard III* followed by *Nora, Miami Stories, On Deaf Ears.*

SMITH, JENNIFER. Born Mar.9, 1956 in Lubbock, TX. Graduate TX Tech U. Debut 1981 OB in *Seesaw* followed by *Suffragette, Henry the 8th and the Grand Old Opry, No Frills Revue, Whatnot, 1-2-3-4-5, You Die at Recess, White Lies,* Bdwy in *La Cage aux Folles*(1983), *Change in the Heir, Secret Garden, Once Upon a Mattress*(1996).

SMITH-CAMERON, J. Born Sept. 7 in Louisville, KY. Attended FL St U. Debut 1982 OB in *Crimes of the Heart* (1982) followed by *Wild Honey, Lend Me a Tenor, Our Country's Good, Real Inspector Hound, 15 Minute Hamlet,* OB in *Asian Shade, The Knack, Second Prize: Two Weeks in Leningrad, Great Divide, Voice of the Turtle, Women of Manhattan, Alice and Fred, Mi Vida Loca, Little Egypt, On the Bum, Traps/Owners, Desdemona, Naked Truth, Don Juan in Chicago, Blue Window, As Bees in Honey Drown.*

SOPHIEA, CYNTHIA. Born Oct.26, 1954 in Flint, MI. Bdwy debut in *My Fair Lady* (1981) followed by *She Loves Me, Victor Petravia,* OB in *Lysistrata, Sufragette, Golden Apple, Winter's Tale, Petrified Prince.*

SPAISMAN, ZYPORA. Born Jan. 2, 1920 in Lublin, Poland. Debut 1955 OB in *Lonesome Ship* followed by *My Father's Court, Thousand and One Nights, Eleventh Inheritor, Enchanting Melody, Fifth Commandment, Bronx Express, Melody Lingers On, Yoshke Musikant, Stempenya, Generation of Green Fields, Ship, Play for the Devil, Broome Street America, Flowering Peach, Riverside Drive, Big Winner, Land of Dreams, Father's Inheritance, At the Crossroads, Stempenyu, Mirele Efros, Double Identity, Maiden of Ludmir.*

SPARKS, HAYLEY. Born April 27, 1971 in Salzburg, Austria. Attended NYU. Debut 1992 OB in *Diminished Capacity* followed by *Miracle Worker, Savage in Limbo, Liverpool Fantasy,* Bdwy in *Summer and Smoke* (1996).

SPENCER, REBECCA. Born April 29, 1960 in Levittown, PA. Graduate Ithaca Col. Debut 1986 OB in *Desert Song,* Bdwy in *Call Me Madam (Encores/1995), Jekyll & Hyde.*

SPERLING, TED. Born Feb.23, 1962 in NYC. Graduate Yale. Worked as musical director on and off-Bdwy before acting debut in Bdwy's *Titanic*(1997).

SPINELLA, STEPHEN. Born Oct. 11, 1956 in Naples, Italy. Graduate NYU. Debut 1982 OB in *Age of Assassins* followed by *Dance for Me Rosetta, Bremen Coffee, Taming of the Shrew, L'Illusion, Burrhead, Love!Valour!Compassion!, Troilus and Cressida, Question of Mercy,* Bdwy in *Angles in America* (1993) for which he received a Theatre World Award.

STANWHYCK, HEATH C.A. Born March 4, 1949 in England. Debut 1997 OB in *Mrs. Cage.*

STAPLETON, JEAN. Born Jan. 19 1923 in NYC. Attended Hunter Col. AmThWing. Bdwy debut 1953 in *In the Summer House* followed by *Damn Yankees, Bells Are Ringing, Juno, Rhinoceros, Funny Girl, Arsenic and Old Lace,* OB in *Mountain Language/Birthday Party, Learned Ladies, Roads to Home, Night Seasons, The Entertainer.*

STATTEL, ROBERT. Born Nov. 20, 1937 in Floral Park, NY. Graduate Manhattan Col. Debut 1958 in *Heloise* followed by *When I Was a Child, Man and Superman, The Storm, Don Carlos, Taming of the Shrew, Titus Andronicus, Henry IV, Peer Gynt, Hamlet, Danton's Death, Country Wife, Caucasian Chalk Circle, King Lear, Iphigenia in Aulis, Ergo, The Persians, Blue Boys, Minister's Black Veil, Four Friends, Two Character Play, Merchant of Venice, Cuchulain, Oedipus Cycle, Guilles de Rais, Woyzeck, Feuhrer Bunker, Learned Ladies, Domestic Issues, Great Days, The Tempest, Brand, Man for All Seasons, Bunker Reveries, Enrico IV, Selling Off, Titus Andronicus, Misalliance,* Bdwy in *Zoya's Apartment* (1990), *Black Comedy, Philadelphia Here I Come.*

STEHLIN, JACK. Born June 21, 1936 in Allentown, PA. Graduate Julliard. Debut 1984 OB in *Henry V* followed by *Gravity Shoes, Julius Caesar, Romeo and Juliet, Phaedra Britannica, Don Juan of Seville, Uncle Vanya, Henry IV Part 1, Life on Earth, Danton's Death, Casanova, Washington Square Moves, Richard II, Macbeth, Timon of Athens.*

STEIN-GRAINGER, STEVEN. Born Oct.17, 1958 in Chicago, IL. Graduate N.IllU, AmConsvMusic. Bdwy debut 1994 in *Sunset Blvd.*

STEINHARDT, LEE. Born Sept.4, 1959 in Philadelphia, PA. Graduate Brooklyn Col., NYU, ACT. Debut 1986 OB in *Beautiful Truth* followed by *Twelfth Night, Stranger on the Road to Jericho, M Club, Tell Veronica, The Hollow, Most Important American Playwright Since Tennessee Williams.*

STEPHENS, MARA. Born Sept.22, 1969 in NYC. Graduate U of VT. Debut 1995 OB in *Coming Through* followed by *Wally's Ghost, Children Of,* Bdwy in *Titanic*(1997).

STEPHENSON, DON. Born Sept. 10, 1964 in Chattanooga, TN. Graduate U TN. Debut 1986 OB in *Southern Lights* followed by *Hypothetic, The Tavern, Young Rube, Charles Dickens Christmas, Follies, Wonderful Town*(LC/NYCO), Bdwy in *Titanic*(1997).

STERN, CHERYL. Born July 1, 1956 in Buffalo, NY. Graduate NorthwesternU. Debut 1984 OB in *Daydreams* followed by *White Lies, Pets, That's Life!, I Love You You're Perfect Now Change.*

STEVENS, JODI. Born Apr.24 in Summit, NJ. Graduate PA St. Debut OB in *My Name Is Pablo Picasso* followed by *27 Wagons Full of Cotton, Antigone, Meet Him, Bodyshop, Cardenio, Gender Wars,* Bdwy in *Jekyll & Hyde*(1997).

STILLER, JERRY. Born June 8, 1931 in NYC. Graduate USyracuse. Debut 1953 OB in *Coriolanus* followed by *Power and the Glory, Golden Apple, Measure for Measure, Taming of the Shrew, Carefree Tree, Diary of a Scoundrel, Romeo and Juliet, As You Like It, Two Gentlemen of Verona, Passione, Prairie/Shawl, Much Ado about Nothing, After-Play,* Bdwy in *The Ritz* (1975), *Unexpected Guests, Passione, Hurlyburly* (also OB), *3 Men on a Horse, What's Wrong with This Picture?, Three Sisters.*

STILLMAN, ROBERT. Born Dec. 2, 1954 in NYC. Graduate Princeton U. Debut 1981 OB in *The Haggadah* followed by *Street Scene, Lola, No Frills Revue, Six Wives, Last Session,* Bdwy in *Grand Hotel* (1989).

STOLTZ, ERIC. Born Sept.30, 1961 in Whittier, CA. Attended USC. Debut 1987 OB in *Widow Claire* followed by *American Plan, Down the Road, Importance of Being Earnest,* Bdwy in *Our Town,* for which he received a 1989 Theatre World Award, *Two Shakespearean Actors, Three Sisters.*

STONE, DANTON. Born in Queens, NYC. Debut 1976 OB in *Mrs. Murray's Farm* followed by *In This Fallen City, Say Goodnight Gracie, Angels Fall, Balm in Gilead, Fortune's Fools, Mere Mortals and Others,* Bdwy in *5th of July*(1980).

STOVALL, COUNT. Born Jan.15, 1946 in Los Angeles, CA. Graduate U CA. Debut 1973 OB in *He's Got a Jones* followed by *In White America, Rashomon, Sidnee Poet Heroical, A Photo, Julius Caesar, Coriolanus, Spell #7, Jail Diary of Albie Sachs, To Make a Poet Black, Transcendental Blues, Edward II, Children of the Sun, Shades of Brown, American Dreams, Pantomime, Stovall, Telltale Heart, Fear Itself, Scapin,* Bdwy in *Inacent Black*(1981), *Philadelphia Story.*

STRAM, HENRY. Born Sept. 10, 1954 in Lafayette, IN. Attended Juilliard. Debut 1978 OB in *King Lear* followed by *Shout and Twist, Cradle Will Rock, Prison-made Tuxedos, Cinderella/Cendrillon, Making of Americans, Black Sea Follies, Eddie Goes to Poetry City, Bright Room Called Day, Mind King, On the Open Road, My Head was a Sledge Hammer, Christina Alberta's Father, All's Well that Ends Well, Jack's Holiday, Dancing on Her Knees, Troilus and Cressida, Henry V, Grey Zone, Timon of Athens*, Bdwy in *Titanic*(1997).

SULLIVAN, KIM. Born July 21, 1952 in Philadelphia, PA. Graduate NYU. Debut 1972 OB in *Black Terror* followed by *Legend of the West, Deadwood Dick, Big Apple Messenger, Dreams Deferred, Raisin in the Sun, The Tempest, Ground People, Celebration, In My Father's House*.

SUMMERHAYS, JANE. Born Oct. 11 in Salt Lake City UT. Graduate U UT Catholic U. Debut 1980 OB in *Paris Lights* followed by *On Approval, One Act Festival, Taking Steps, Noel and Gertie*, Bdwy in *Sugar Babies* (1980), *Chorus Line, Me and My Girl, Lend Me A Tenor, Dream*.

SUTTON, DOLORES. Born in NYC. Graduate NYU. Bdwy debut 1962 in *Rhinoceros* followed by *General Seeger, My Fair Lady* (1993), OB in *Man with the Golden Arm, Machinal, Career, Brecht on Brecht, To Be Young Gifted and Black, Web and the Rock, My Prince My King, Our Own Family, What's Wrong with this Picture?, Drop in the Bucket*.

SWANSEN, LARRY. Born Nov. 10, 1930 in Roosevelt, OK. Graduate U OK. Bdwy debut 1966 in *Those That Play the Clowns* followed by *Great White Hope, King and I*, OB in *Dr. Faustus Lights the Lights, Thistle in My Bed, Darker Flower, Vincent, MacBird, Unknown Soldier and His Wife, Sound of Music, Conditioning of Charlie One, Ice Age, Prince of Homburg, Who's There?, Heart of a Dog, Grandma Pray for Me, Frankenstein, Knights of the Round Table, Returner*.

SWARTZ, DANNY. Born July 5, 1964 in Dowagiac, MI. Graduate Fresno St U, NYU. Debut 1993 OB in *Game of Love and Chance* followed by *Twelfth Night, As You Like It*.

SWIFT, FRANCIE. Born March 27, 1969 in Amarillo, TX. Graduate SUNY/Purchase. Debut 1993 OB in *Listening* followed by *Hyacinth Macaw, Marking*.

TAYLOR, ANDY. Born Oct. 3 in Eugene, OR. Graduate Oberlin Col., U MT. Debut 1990 OB in *Romeo and Juliet* followed by *Rodgers and Hart, On The Open Road, Juno, Painting it Red, Christina Alberta's Father, Golden Boy*, Bdwy in *One Touch of Venus* (Encores-1996), *Moon Over Buffalo, Titanic*.

TAYLOR, DREW. Born March 9, 1955 in Milwaukee, WI. Attended AADA. Debut 1985 OB in *She Loves Me* followed by *Kiss Me Kate, You Can Be a New Yorker Too*, Bdwy in *The Secret Garden* (1991), *Annie*(1997).

TAYLOR, LILI. Born Feb.20, 1967 in Glencoe, IL. Attended DePaul U. OB in *Increase, What Did He See, Aven U Boys* , Bdwy in *Three Sisters*(1997).

TAYLOR, RENEE. Born March 19, 1935 in NYC. Attended AADA. Bdwy debut in *Luv*(1964) followed by *Agatha Sue I Love You, Lovers and Other Strangers, The Rehearsal, It Had to Be You*, OB in *Third Ear, Three Sisters, Machinal, One of the All Time Greats, Bermuda Ave. Triangle*.

TAYLOR, SCOTT. Born June 29, 1962 in Milan, TN. Attended MS St U. Bdwy in *Wind in the Willows* (1985) followed by *Cats, Crazy for You, Victor Victoria, Steel Pier*.

TEETER, LARA. Born 1955 in Tulsa, OK. Graduate OK City U. Bdwy debut in *Best Little Whorehouse in Texas* followed by *Pirates of Penzance, 7 Brides for 7 Brothers, On Your Yoes, Wizard of Oz* (MSG), OB in *Jack and Jill*.

TESCHENDORF, DAVID (CHARLES). Born May 31, 1953 in Oakland, CA. Attended U So.Carolina., New School. Debut 1989 OB in *Ulysses In Nightown* followed by *Apollo of Bellac, The Tempest, Hamlet, Bound East for Cardiff, Message for the Broken Hearted*.

THOMAS, RAY ANTHONY Born Dec. 19, 1956 in Kentwood, LA. Graduate U. TX/El Paso. Debut 1981 OB in *Escape to Freedom* followed by *Sun Gets Blue, Blues for Mr. Charlie, Hunchback of Notre Dame, Ground People, The Weather Outside, One Act Festival, Caucasian Chalk Circle, Virgin Molly, Black Eagles, Distant Fires, Shaker Heights, The Lights, Dancing on Moonlight, Volunteer Man, The Devils*.

THOMPSON, EVAN. Born Sep. 3, 1931 in NYC. Graduate U CA. Bdwy debut 1969 in *Jimmy* followed by *1776, City of Angels*, OB in *Mahogonny, Treasure Island, Knitters in the Sun, HalfLife, Fasnacht Dau, Importance of Being Earnest, Under the Gaslight, Henry V, The Fantasticks, Walk the Dog Willie, Macbeth, 1984, Leave It to Me, Earth and Sky, No Conductor, Nightmare Alley*.

THORNE, RAYMOND. Born Nov. 27, 1934 in Lackawanna, NY. Graduate U CT. Debut 1966 OB in *Man with a Load of Mischief* followed by *Rose, Dames at Sea, Love Course, Blue Boys, Jack and Jill, Annie Warbucks, New Yorkers*, Bdwy in *Annie* (1977/1997), *Teddy and Alice*.

THORNTON, ANGELA. Born in Leeds, Eng. Attended Webber-Douglas Sch. Bdwy debut in *Little Glass Clock* (1956) followed by *Nude with Violin, Present Laughter, Hostile Witness, Pygmalion* (1987), *Racing Demon, An Ideal Husband*, OB in *Mousetrap, Big Broadcast, Mary Barnes, What the Butler Saw*.

THRELFALL, DAVID. Born Oct.12, 1953 in Manchester, Eng. Graduate Polytechnic Sch Theatre. Bdwy debut in *Nicholas Nickleby* (1981) followed by *The Rehearsal*.

TIBBITTS, MICHELE. Born Feb.21, 1970 in Albany, NY. Attended AMDA. Debut 1993 OB in *Amy Fisher The Musical*, Bdwy in *Hello Dolly* (1995).

TIRRELL, BARBARA. Born Nov.24, 1953 in Nahant, MA. Graduate Temple U, Webber-Douglas Acad. Debut 1977 OB in *Six Characters in Search of an Author* followed by *Cyrano, Romeo and Juliet, Louis Quinse, Day Out of Time, King Lear, Oedipus Texas, Father West*, Bdwy in *Annie*(1997).

TITONE, THOMAS. Born March 24, 1959 in Secaucus, NJ. Attended N Car Sch of Arts. With Amer Ballet Th. before Bdwy debut in *Most Happy Fella* (1992) followed by *My Favorite Year, Once Upon a Mattress*(1996), OB in *Hunchback of Notre Dame*.

TOMEI, MARISA. Born Dec. 4, 1964 in Brooklyn, NY. Attended BostonU, NYU. Debut 1986 OB in *Daughters* for which she received a Theatre World Award, followed by *Class 1 Acts, Evening Star, What the Butler Saw, Marathon '88, Sharon and Billy, Chelsea Walls, Summer Winds, Comedy of Errors, Fat Men in Skirts, Slavs!, Dark Rapture, Demonology, Waiting for Lefty*.

TOREN, SUZANNE. Born March 15, 1947 in NYC. Graduate CCNY, U WI. Bdwy debut in *Goodbye Fidel*(1980), OB in *Who'll Save the Plowboy?, Further Inquiry, French Toast, The Disputation*.

TORN, RIP. Born Feb. 6, 1931 in Temple, TX. Graduate UTX. Bdwy debut 1956 in *Cat on a Hot Tin Roof* followed by *Sweet Bird of Youth* for which he received a Theatre World Award, *Daughter of Silence, Strange Interlude, Blues for Mr. Charlie, Country Girl, Glass Menagerie*(1975), *Anna Christie* (1992), *Young Man from Atlanta*, OB in *Chaparral, The Cuban Thing, The Kitchen, Deer Park, Dream of a Blacklisted Actor, Dance of Death Macbeth, Barbary Shore, The Creditors, Seduced, Man and the Fly, Terrible Jim Fitch, Village Wooing*.

TRACY, LISA. Born July 20, 1945 in Lexington, VA. Graduate Oberlin Col. Debut 1970 OB in *Dark of the Moon* followed by *Red Lights and Dragons*.

TRACY, STAN. Born Dec.2, 1950 in Oceanside, CA. Graduate San Diego St. Debut 1976 OB in *Love's Labour's Lost* followed by *King of the Castle, Yesterday Continued, Henhouse, Playboy of the Western World*.

TRAMMELL, SAM. Born May 15 in Louisiana. Graduate Brown U. Debut 1997 OB in *Wir Spielen Seechach* followed by *Dealers Choice, My Night with Reg*.

TREADWELL, TOM. Born May 7, 1955 in Seattle, WA. Debut 1982 OB in *Silver on Silver* followed by *Elephant Piece, Camilla, Madame Bovary: The Musical, Wizard of Oz, Mata Hari*, Bdwy in *Annie*(1997).

TROTT, KAREN. Born March 13, 1954 in Lawrence, MA. Graduate U VT. Debut 1979 OB in *Strider* followed by *3 Postcards, Green Heart*, Bdwy in *Strider*(1979), *Barnum, Arsenic and Old Lace*.

TRUJILLO, ROBERT. Born Feb. 8, 1938 in San Rafael, CA. Graduate U Toronto. Bdwy debut 1989 in *Jerome Robbins' Broadway*, followed by *Guys and Dolls, Promises Promises(Encores)*.

TSOUTSOUVAS, SAM. Born Aug. 20, 1948 in Santa Barbara, CA. Attended U. Cal., Juilliard. Debut 1969 OB in *Peer Gynt* followed by *Twelfth Night, Timon of Athens, Cymbeline, School for Scandal, The Hostage, Women Beware Women, Lower Depths, Emigre, Hello Dali, Merchant of Venice, The Leader, Bald Soprano, Taming of the Shrew, Gus & Al, Tamara, Man Who Shot Lincoln, Puppetmaster of Lodz, Richard III, Snowing at Delphi, Richard II, Phaedra, Timon of Athens, Antony and Cleopatra*, Bdwy in *Three Sisters, Measure for Measure, Beggar's Opera, Scapin, Dracula, Our Country's Good, The Misanthrope*.

TUCCI, MARIA. Born June 19, 1941 in Florence, Italy. Attended Actors Studio. Bdwy debut 1963 in *Milk Train Doesn't Stop Here Anymore* followed by *Rose Tattoo, Little Foxes, Cuban Thing, Great White Hope, School for Wives, Lesson from Aloes, Kingdoms, Requiem for a Heavyweight, Night of the Iguana, Marking, Collected Stories,* OB in *Corruption in the Palace of Justice, Five Evenings, Trojan Women, White Devil, Horseman Pass By, Yerma, Shepherd of Avenue B., The Gathering, Man for All Seasons, Love Letters, Substance of Fire, A Fair Country.*

TUDYK, ALAN. Born March 17, 1971 in El Paso, TX.Graduate Lon Morris Col, Juilliard. Debut 1997 OB in *Bunny Bunny* for which he received a 1997 Theatre World Award.

TULL, PATRICK. Born July 28, 1941 in Sussex, England. Attended LAMDA. Bdwy debut in *Astrakhan Coat* (1967) followed *The Crucible, Master Builder, Getting Married, Little Hotel on the Side,* OB in *Ten Little Indians, The Tamer Tamed, Brand, Frankenstein, What the Butler Saw, She Stoops to Conquer, Art of Success, Ivanov, Last Manhattan.*

TULLY, EDWARD. Born June 2, 1965 in NYC. Attended NYU. Debut 1992 OB in *Una Pooka* followed by *Twelfth Nigh, Driving By Numbers, Admissions, Ourselves Alone.*

TURK, BRUCE. Born Dec. 27, 1962 in California. Graduate Northwestern U. Debut 1994 OB in *Titus Andronicus* followed by *Green Bird,* Bdwy in *Juan Darien*(1996).

TURNER, GLENN. Born Sept. 21, 1957 in Atlanta, GA. Bdwy debut 1984 in *My One and Only* followed by *Chorus Line, Grand Hotel, 5 Guys Named Moe,* OB in *Brief History of White Music.*

ULANET, RACHEL. Born Aug.28, 1970 in Long Branch, NJ. Graduate Columbia U, Attended Barnard Col. Debut 1996 OB in *Anne Frank and Me.*

URBANIAK, JAMES. Born Sept.17, 1963 in Bayonne, NJ. Debut 1988 OB in *Giants of the Mountain* followed by *The Universe, Imaginary Invalid, South.*

URCIOLI, PAUL. Born Jan.27, 1964 in Rutherford, NJ. Graduate NYU. OB in *Saved, Rosemary for Remembrance, Troilus and Cressida, Vomit and Roses, Trafficking in Broken Hearts, Paper Man, Wolverine Dream, Jest a Second.*

VAN TREUREN, MARTIN. Born Dec.6, 1952 in Hawthorne, NJ. Graduate Montclair St. Col. Debut 1978 OB in *Oklanhoma!* followed by *The Miser,* Bdwy in *Allegro* (Encores/1994), *Christmas Carol(MSG), Jekyll & Hyde.*

VAUGHAN, MELANIE. Born Sept. 18 in Yazoo City, MS. Graduate LA St U. Bdwy debut 1976 in *Rex* followed by *Sunday in the Park with George, On the 20th Century, Music Is, Starlight Express, Most Happy Fella* (1992), OB in *Canterbury Tales, Big City Rhythm.*

VEREEN, BEN. Born Oct. 10, 1946 in Miami, FL. Debut 1965 OB in *Prodigal Son,* Bdwy in *Sweet Charity, Golden Boy, Hair, Jesus Christ Superstar* for which he received a Theatre World Award, *Pippin, Grind, Jelly's Last Jam, Christmas Carol (MSG).*

VICTOR, JAMES. Born July 27, 1939 in Santiago, Dominican Republic. Debut 1958 OB in *El Casorio* followed by *Red Devil Battery Sign.*

VIDNOVIC, MARTIN. Born Jann 4, 1948 in Falls Church, VA. Graduate Cinn. Consv. Of Music. Debut 1972 OB in *The Fantasticks* followed by *Lies and Legends,* Bdwy in *Home Sweet Homer* (1976), *King and I* (1977), *Oklahoma* (1979), *Brigadoon* (1980), *Baby, Some Enchanted Evening*(also OB), *Guys and Dolls* (1994), *King David.*

VIRTA, RAY. Born June 18, 1958 in L'Anse, MI. Debut 1982 OB in *Twelfth Night* followed by *Country Wife, The Dubliners, Pericles, Tartuffe, Taming of the Shrew, No One Dances, Jacques and His Master, Progress, Snowing at Delphi, Eye of the Beholder, King Lear, Macbeth,* Bdwy in *School for Scandal.*

VON BARGEN, DANIEL. Born June 5, 1950 in Cincinnati, OH. Graduate Purdue U. Debut 1981 OB in *Missing Persons* followed by *Macbeth, Beggars in the House of Plenty, Angel of Death, The Treatment, The Erinyes,* Bdwy in *Mastergate* (1989) for which he received a Theatre World Award.

WAGNER, CHUCK. Born June 20, 1958 in Nashville, TN. Graduate USC. Bdwy debut 1985 in *Three Musketeers* followed by *Into the Woods, Les Miserables, Beauty and the Beast.*

WALBYE, KAY. Born Ft. Collins, CO. Attended KS St U. Debut 1984 OB in *Once on a Summer's Day* followed by *Majestic Kid,* Bdwy in *Run for Your Wife*(1989), *Secret Garden, Rose Tattoo, Titanic.*

WALDEN, BEN. Born Aug.10, 1969 in London, Eng. After work in London, debut 1997 OB in *Two Gentleman of Verona.*

WALDROP, MARK. Born July 30, 1954 in Washington, DC. Graduate CinConsv. Debut 1977 OB in *Movie Buff* followed by *Hey Love, 3 of Hearts,* Bdwy in *Hello Dolly!* (1978), *Grand Tour, Evita, La Cage aux Folles.*

WALKER, SYBYL. Born April 30 in Chicago, IL. Graduate SMU. Debut 1991 OB in *From the Mississippi Delta, Henry VIII,* Bdwy in *The Tempest.*

WALLNAU, CARN N. Born July 8, 1953 in NYC. Graduate Dickenson Col., Rutgers U. Debut 1984 OB in *Custom of the Country* followed by *Dance with Me, Sixth Commandment.*

WALTER, WENDY. Born Nov. 13, 1961 in Dallas, TX. Attended U KS. Bdwy debut 1994 in *Sunset Blvd.*

WARD, ELIZABETH. Born Nov.16, 1962 in Denver, CO. Graduate U Pacific, U CA. Bdwy debut 1990 in *City of Angels* , OB in *Green Heart.*

WARD, LAUREN. Born June 19, 1970 in Lincoln, NE. Graduate NC Sch of Arts. Bdwy debut 1994 in *Carousel,* OB in *Jack's Holiday,Violet.*

WARFIELD, DONALD. Born Aug. 25 in Rhinelander, WI. Graduate Brown U., Yale U. Debut 1968 OB in *People vs Ranchman* followed by *War Games, Saved, Love Your Crooked Neighbor, Mystery Play, Children's Mass, G.R. Point, Romeo and Juliet, Othello,* Bdwy in *Watercolor.*

WARREN, LESLEY ANN. Born Aug.16, 1946 in NYC. Bdwy debut 1963 in *110 in the Shade* followed by *Drat! The Cat!* for which she received a Theatre World Award, *Dream.*

WARREN-GIBSON, DAVID. Born Dec.31 in Detroit, MI. Attended U of Houston, U of St. Thomas. Bdwy debut 1978 in *Dancin'* followed by *Chorus Line, Dreamgirls, Sweet Charity, Chicago*(1996).

WARWICK, JAMES. Born Nov.17, 1947 in London, Eng. Attended Central Sch, London. After work in London Theatre, made Bdwy debut 1996 in *Ideal Husband.*

WASHINGTON, SHARON. Born Sept.12, 1959 in NYC. Graduate Dartmouth Col., YaleU. Debut 1988 OB in *Coriolanus* followed by *Cymbeline, Richard III, The Balcony, Caucasian Chalk Circle, Before It Hit Home, Radical Mystique, Fear Itself, Seeking the Genesis.*

WASSON, SUSANNE. Born Sept.19 in Searcy, AR. Attended TX Womens U. Debut 1972 OB in *Whitsuntide* followed by *Cracks, Late Snow, Lady Strass.*

WEATHERSTONE, JAMES. Born March 20, 1959 in Decatur, IL. Attended Nat'l Th Inst. Bdwy debut 1993 in *Red Shoes,* OB in *She Stoops to Conquer, Onward Victoria, Doctor! Doctor!*

WEAVER, SIGOURNEY (SUSAN). Born Oct.8, 1949 in NYC. Attended Yale, Stanford U. Debut 1976 OB in *Titanic* followed by *Das Lusitania Songspiel, Merchant of Venice, Beyond Therapy,* Bdwy in *Hurlyburly*(1984), *Sex and Longing.*

WEBER, JAKE. Born March 12, 1963 in London, Eng. Graduate Middlebury Col., Juilliard Debut 1988 OB in *Road* followed by *Twelfth Night, Maids of Honor, Richard III, Big Funk, Othello, Mad Forest, As You Like it* (CP) *Othello, Radical Mystique, Missing/Kissing,* Bdwy in *Small Family Business* (1992).

WEEMS, ANDREW. Born July 18, 1961 in Seoul, S. Korea. Graduate Brown U, U CA. Debut 1993 OB in *A Quarrel of Sparrows* followed by *Marathon Dancing, Mud Angel, Midsummer Night's Dream, Dolphin Position, Green Bird,* Bdwy in *London Assurance.*

WEILL, MELISSA. Born May 9, 1959 in Chicago, IL. Graduate U IL, Yale. OB in *Festival of 1 Acts*(1988) followed by *I Love You You're Perfect Now Change.*

WEISS, JEFF. Born in 1940 in Allentown, PA. Debut 1986 OB in *Hamlet* followed by *Front Page, Casanova, Hot Keys, Henry V, The Wallenberg Mission,* Bdwy in *Macbeth,* (1988), *Our Town, Mastergate, Face Value, Real Inspector Hound/15 Minute Hamlet, Carousel* (1994), *Present Laughter.*

WEISS, GORDON JOSEPH. Born June 16, 1949 in Bismarck, ND. Attended Moorhead College. Bdwy debut 1974 in *Jumpers* followed by *Goodtime Charley, King of Hearts, Raggedy Ann, Ghetto, Jelly's Last Jam, The Life,* OB in *Walk on the Wild Side* (1988), *Ragtime Blues, Andorra, Tourists of the Mindfield, God in Bed, The Undertakers, Sausage Eaters.*

WEISSER, NORBERT. Born July 9, 1946 in Germany. Bdwy debut 1996 in *Taking Sides.*

WELCH (TEJADA), RAQUEL . Born Sept.5, 1940 in Chicago, IL. Attended San Diego St Col. Bdwy debut 1981 in *Woman of the Year* followed by *Victor Victoria.*

WELDON, CHARLES. Born June 1, 1940 in Wetumka, OK. Bdwy debut 1969 in *Big Time Buck White* followed by *River Niger*, OB in *Ride a Black Horse, Long Time Coming, Jamimma, In The Deepest Part of Sleep, Brownsville Raid, The Great MacDaddy, The Offering, Colored People's Time, Raisin in the Sun, Lifetimes, Jonquil, Burner's Frolic, Little Tommy Parker Celebrated Minstrel Show, In My Father's House.*

WELLER, FREDERICK. Born April 18, 1966 in New Orleans, LA. Graduate U NC/Chapel Hill, Juilliard. Bdwy debut 1991 in *Six Degrees of Separartion* followed by *The Rehearsal, Little Foxes.*

WENCKER, LEIGH-ANNE. Born June 16 in St. Louis, MO. Graduate Webster U. Bdwy debut 1993 in *Crazy for You* followed by *Steel Pier.*

WEST, JENNIFER. Born Sept. 22, 1939 in Ft. Smith, AK. Attended CCLA. Debut OB in *Dutchman* for which she received a Theatre World Award, followed by *After the Fall* (LCRep), *Diamond Orchid, Malcolm, Harold,* and *Sondra* (OB), *Hemingway Hero, Tiger at the Gates* (LCRep), Bdwy in *Sunset Blvd.*

WEST, MICHAEL. Born July 4, 1960 in Atlanta, GA. Graduate Boston U, GA St U. Debut 1993 OB in *Whoop Dee Doo* followed by *Live from the Betty Ford Center, Forbidden Hollywood, When Pigs Fly.*

WESTENBERG, ROBERT. Born Oct. 26, 1953 in Miami Beach, FL. Graduate U CA/Fresco. Debut 1981 OB in *Henry IV Part I* followed by *Hamlet, Death of von Richthofen, 3 Birds Alighting on a Field, Violet,* Bdwy in *Zorba* (1983), for which he received a Theatre World Award, *Sunday in the Park with George, Into the Woods, Les Miserables, Secret Garden, Abe Lincoln in Illinois, Christmas Carol, Company.*

WESTON, CELIA. Born in South Carolina. Attended Salem Col., NC Sch of Arts. Bdwy debut 1979 in *Loose Ends* followed by *Garden District, Summer and Smoke, Last Night of Ballyhoo,* OB in *Bargains, Laura Dennis.*

WESTON, DOUGLAS. Born Jan. 13, 1960 in London, England. Graduate Princeton U, RADA. Debut 1991 OB in *Whitestones* followed by *Working Title, Sleeping Hippo,* Bdwy in *Blood Brothers* (1993).

WHITE, LILLIAS D. Born July 21, 1951 in Brooklyn, NYC. Graduate NYCC. Debut 1975 OB in *Solidad Tetrad* followed by *Romance in Hard Times, Back to Bacharach,* Bdwy in *Barnum*(1981), *Dreamgirls, Rock n' Roll: The First 5000 Years, Once on This Island, Carrie, How to Succeed..*(1995), *The Life*(also OB).

WHITEHURST, SCOTT. Born Dec. 24, 1962 in Indianapolis, IN. Graduate ColumbiaU., RutgersU. Debut 1991 OB in *Black Eagles* followed by *Gunplay, Incommunicado, Waiting for Lefty.*

WHITING, MARGARET. Born July 22, 1924 in Detroit, MI. OB in *Taking My Turn,* Bdwy debut 1997 in *Dream.*

WHITTHORNE, PAUL. Born Feb. 17, 1970 in Tucson, AZ. Graduate Juilliard. Bdwy debut 1995 in *The Tempest,* OB in *Orestes: I Murdered My Mother* (1996), *Getting In.*

WHITTON, MARGARET. (formerly Peggy). Born Nov. 30 in Philadelphia, PA. Debut 1973 OB in *Baba Goya* followed by *Arthur, Nourish the Beast, Another Language, Chinchilla, Othello, Art of Dining, One Tiger to a Hill, Henry IV Parts 1 and 2, Don Juan, My Uncle Sam, Aunt Dan and Lemon, Ice Cream and Hot Fudge, Merry Wives of Windsor, Silence Cunning Exile, Three Viewings,New England, Major Crimes,* Bdwy in *Steaming* (1982), *The Apple Doesn't Fall.*

WIEST, DIANNE. Born March 28, 1948 in Kansas City, MO. Attended U MD. Debut 1976 OB in *Ashes* followed by *Leave it to Beaver is Dead, The Art of Dining,* for which she received a 1980 Theatre World Award, *Bonjour La Bonjour, Three Sisters, Serenading Louie, Other Places, Hunting Cockroaches, After the Fall, Square One, Don Juan in Hell, The Shawl, One Flea Spare,* Bdwy in *Frankenstein* (1981), *Othello, Beyond Therapy, In the Summer House.*

WILKOF, LEE. Born June 25, 1951 in Canton, OH. Graduate U. Cinn. Debut 1977 OB in *Present Tense* followed by *Little Shop of Horrors, Holding Patterns, Angry Housewives, Assassins, Born Guilty, Treasure Island, Golden Boy, Names, Waiting for Lefty,* Bdwy in *Sweet Charity* (1986), *Front Page, She Loves Me.*

WILKS, ELAYNE. Born Sept. 25, 1933 in Bronx, NY. Graduate Adelphi U, NYU. Debut OB 1995 in *Babyluv* followed by *Theory of Relatives.*

WILLIAMS, JACQUELINE. Born In Evanston, IL. Graduate Goodman Sch/DePaul U. Debut 1989 OB in *Mill Fire* followed by *Talented Tenth, From the Mississippi Delta,* Bdwy in *Young Man from Atlanta*(1997).

WILLIAMS, LIA. Born 1964 in Northern Eng. Attended London Studio Center. Bdwy debut 1996 in *Skylight.*

WILLIAMS, TIMOTHY LEIGH. Born Aug.16 in Houston, TX. Attended U TX. Debut 1996 OB in *Strangers in the Land of Canaan* followed by *Red Devil Battery Sign, Hysterical Blindness.*

WILLIAMSON, GLEN. Born Sept. 10 1959 in Greeley, CO. Graduate UCA/Santa Cruz, Juilliard. Debut 1992 OB in *Boy Who Saw True, Red Lights and Dragons, The Godsend.*

WILLIAMSON, RUTH. Born Jan. 25, 1954 in Baltimore, MD. Graduate U MD. Bdwy debut 1981 in *Annie* followed by *Smile, Guys and Dolls, DuBarry was a Lady(Encores),* OB in *Preppies, Bodo, A Helluva Town, Green Heart.*

WILLISON, WALTER. Born June 24, 1947 in Monterey Park, CA. Bdwy debut 1970 in *Norman Is That You?* followed by *Two by Two,* for which he received a Theatre World Award, *Wild and Wonderful, Celebration of Richard Rodgers, Pippin, Tribute to Joshua Logan, Tribute to George Abbott, Grand Hotel, A Christmas Carol (MSG),* OB in *South Pacific in Concert, They Say It's Wonderful, Broadway Scandals of 1928* and *Options,* both of which he wrote, *Aldersgate '88.*

WILLS, RAY. Born Sept. 14, 1960 in Santa Monica, CA. Graduate Wichita St U, Brandeis U. Debut 1988 OB in *Side by Side by Sondheim* followed by *Kiss Me Quick Before the Lava Reaches the Village, Grand Tour, The Cardigans, The Rothschilds, Hello Muddah Hello Faddah, Little Me, A Backers Audition, All in the Timing, Young Playwrights Festival/Guy World,* Bdwy in *Anna Karenina* (1993), *Big.*

WINDE, BEATRICE. Born Jan.6 in Chicago, IL. Debut 1966 OB in *In White America* followed by *June Bug Graduates Tonight, Strike Heaven on the Face, Divine Comedy, Crazy Horse, My Mother My Father and Me, Steal Away, The Actress, Richard II, 1-2-3-4-5, Le Bourgeois Gentilhomme, American Plan, Night Seasons,* Bdwy 1971 in *Ain't Supposed to Die a Natural Death* for which she received a Theatre World Award, followed by *Young Man from Atlanta*(also OB).

WISE, WILLIAM. Born May 11 in Chicago, IL. Attended Bradley U, Northwestern U. Debut 1970 OB in *Adaptation/Next* followed by *Him, Hot L Baltimore, Just the Immediate Family, 36, For the Use of the Hall, Orphans, Working Theatre Festival, Copperhead, Early One Evening at the Rainhow Bar & Grill, Special Interests, Theme and Variations, Marathon '91, Drop in the Bucket, Hysterical Blindness.*

WOJDA, JOHN. Born Feb. 19, 1957 in Detroit, MI. Attended U MI. Bdwy debut 1982 in *Macbeth* followed by *Merchant of Venice, Two Shakespearean Actors, Present Laughter,* OB in *Natural Disasters, Merchant of Venice, Coming of Mr. Pine, Henry IV Parts 1 & 2, Crackdancing, Black, Henry VI, Ecstacy.*

WOODARD, CHARLAYNE. Born Dec. 29, in Albany, NY. Graduate Goodman Th School, SUNY. Debut 1975 OB in *Don't Bother Me I Can't Cope* followed by *Dementos, Under Fire, A..My Name is Alice, Twelfth Night, Hang On to the Good Times, Paradise, Caucasian Chalk Circle, Pretty Fire, Neat,* Bdwy in *Hair* (1977), *Ain't Misbehavin'* (1978/1988).

WOODMAN, BRANCH. Born Aug.31, 1964 in Upland, CA. Attended Chaffee Col., CalStU/Fullerton. Debut 1989 OB in *Out of This World* followed by *Disappearing Act,* Bdwy 1994 in *Crazy for You.*

WOODS, CAROL. Born Nov. 13, 1943 in Jamaica, NY. Graduate Ithaca Col. Debut 1980 OB in *One Mo' Time* followed by *Blues in the Night, Dreamstuff,* Bdwy in *Grind* (1985), *Big River, Stepping Out, The Crucible, A Little Hotel on the Side, Goodbye Girl, One Touch of Venus(Encores).*

WORKMAN, JASON. Born Oct. 9, 1962 in Omaha, Neb. Attended U KY, Goodman. Bdwy debut 1989 in *Meet Me in St. Louis* for which he received a Theatre World Award, followed by *Damn Yankees*(1994), OB in *Haunted Host, Safe Sex, Music in the Air, Bed & Sofa, 3 of Hearts.*

WORTH, IRENE. Born June 23, 1916 in Nebraska. Graduate UCLA. Bdwy debut 1943 in *The Two Mrs. Carrolls* followed by *Cocktail Party, Mary Stuart, Toys in the Attic, King Lear, Tiny Alice, Sweet Bird of Youth, Cherry Orchard, Lady from Dubuque, John Gabriel Borkman,* OB in *Happy Days, Letters of Love and Affection, Chalk Garden, Golden Age, Coriolanus, Edith Wharton, Gypsy and the Yellow Canary.*

WRIGHT, VALERIE. Born in Las Vegas, NV. Graduate USC. Bdwy debut 1984 in *Cats* followed by *Song and Dance, Sally Marr & Her Escorts, Damn* Yankees(1994), *Steel Pier,* OB in *Showing Off, And the World Goes Round.*

WYLIE, JOHN. Born Dec. 14, 1925 in Peacock, TX. Graduate No. TX St U.Debut 1987 OB in *Lucky Spot* followed by *Life is a Dream, Winter's Tale, Venetian Turn, Cymbeline, Venice Preserv'd, Barber of Seville,* Bdwy in *Born Yesterday* (1989), *Grand Hotel.*

YATES, DEBORAH. Born June 5, 1970 in Dallas, TX. Graduate So. Methodist U. Bdwy debut 1997 in *Dream.*

YOUNG, BELLAMY. Born Feb.19 in Asheville, NC. Graduate Yale, British Amer Drama Acad. Debut 1994 OB in *Merrily We Roll Along,* Bdwy 1997 in *The Life.*

YULIN, HARRIS. Born Nov. 5, 1937 in California. Attended USC. Debut 1963 OB in *Next Time I'll Sing to You* followed by *Midsummer Night's Dream, Troubled Waters, Richard III, King John, The Cannibals, Lesson from Aloes, Hedda Gabler, Barnum's Last Life, Hamlet, Mrs. Warren's Profession, Don Juan in Hell, Arts and Leisure, When It Comes Early,* Bdwy in *Watch on the Rhine* (1980), *The Visit.*

ZACHARIAS, EMILY. Born July 27, 1953 in Memphis, TN. Graduate Northwestern U. Debut 1980 OB in *March of the Falsettos* followed by *America Kicks Up It's Heels, Crazy He calls Me, Olympus on My Mind, Dirty Work, 3 Pieces for a Warehouse,* Bdwy in *Perfectly Frank*(1980), *Chu Chem*(also OB), *Jekyll & Hyde.*

ZARISH, JANET. Born April 21, 1954 in Chicago, Il. Graduate Juilliard. Debut 1981 OB in *The Villager* followed by *Playing with Fire, Royal Bob, An Enemy of the People, Midsummer Night's Dream, Festival of l-Acts, Other People's Money, Human Nature, Selling Off, EST Marathon '93, Potato Creek Chair of Death, Misalliance.*

ZIEMBA, KAREN. Born Nov. 12, 1957 in St. Joseph, MO. Graduate U Akron. Debut 1981 OB in *Seesaw* followed by *I Married an Angel, Sing for Your Supper, 50 Million Frenchmen, And the World Goes Round, 110 in the Shade* (NYCO/LC), *A Grand Night for Singing, I Do! I Do!, Oh Captain,* Bdwy in *Crazy for You* (1994), *Allegro (Encores), Crazy for You,Steel Pier.*

ZIMMERMAN, LEIGH. Born Mar. 28, 1969 in Stoughton, WI. Attended Fordham U. Bdwy debut 1991 in *Will Rogers Follies* followed by *Crazy for You, Chicago*(1996).

ZISKIE, DANIEL. Born in Detroit MI. Debut 1970 OB in *Second City* followed by *Sea Gull, Ballymurohy, The Rivals, Listen to the Lions, Halloween, Bandit, Mamet Plays, At Home, The Castaways, Marathon '93, Bed and Breakfast, Flyboy, Patronage,* Bdwy in *Mornings at 7, Breakfast with Les and Bess, I'm Not Rappaport.*

ZUSY, JEANNIE. Born in Washington, DC. Graduate SMU. Debut 1993 OB in *Top Girls* followed by *Lie of the Mind.*

Wesley Addy

John Beal

Claudette Colbert

Howard E. Crabtree

Virginia Downing

Herb Edelman

OBITUARIES
(June 1, 1996-May 31, 1997)

WESLEY ADDY, 83, Nebraska-born actor, died Dec.31, 1996 in Danbury, CT. Bdwy debut 1935 in *Panic* followed by *How Beautiful with Shoes, Hamlet, Richard II, Henry IV, Summer Night, Romeo and Juliet, Twelfth Night, Antigone, Candida* (1946), *Another Part of the Forest, Galileo, Leading Lady, The Traitor, The Enchanted, King Lear, Strong are Lonely, First Gentleman, South Pacific, Stitch in Time*, OB included *Month in the Country, Ghosts, John Brown's Body, Curtains* and *With Love and Laughter*. He frequently acted with wife Celeste Holm, who survives him, including *Invitation to a March* and a 1970 production of *Candida*.

ANABELLA (SUZANNE GEORGETTE CHARPENTIER), 86, French-born actress, died Sept.18, 1996 in Neuilly-sur-Seine, France of a heart attack. Known for French and American films, her Bdwy roles included *Jacobowsky and the Colnel* and *No Exit*. Survived by a daughter.

NORMA ANDREWS, 66, dancer, died June 29, 1996 in Tarzana, CA of an aneurysm. She performed on Bdwy in *As the Girls Go, Pal Joey, Make a Wish* and *Gentlemen Prefer Blondes*. Survived by her husband, mother, six children and grandchildren.

LA VERN BAKER (DELORES WILLIAMS), 67, Chicago-born singer, died March 9, 1997. Best known as a blues/rock singer, she appeared in Bdwy's *Black and Blue*.

MAE BARNES (EDITH MAY STITH), 89, NY-born jazz singer, died Dec.13, 1996 in Boston of cancer. She made her Bdwy debut in 1924 in the revue *Runnin' Wild* followed by *Lucky Sambo, Hot Rhythm, Rang Tang, Shuffle Along* (revival), *Ziegfeld Follies* (1950 edition-closed in Boston) and *By the Beautiful Sea* (1954). She was a mainstay of the Bon Soir nightclub. No immediate survivors.

JANE BAXTER (FEODORA FORDE), 87, German-born actress, died Sept.13, 1996 in South London. On the London stage at age 15 in the 1925 musical *Love's Prisoner*, she made her Bdwy debut in the 1947 *Importance of Being Earnest*. Survived by two daughters and a son.

BEAL, JOHN (JAMES ALEXANDER BLIEDUNG), 87, Missouri-born actor, died April 26, 1997 in Santa Cruz, CA. A versatile actor who worked in film and television, his many stage credits included Broadway roles in *Wild Waves, Another Language, She Loves Me Not, Russet Mantle, Soliloquy, Miss Swan Expects, Liverty Jones, The Voice of the Turtle, Lend an Ear, Teahouse of the August Moon, Calculated Risk, Billy, Our Town, The Crucible, The Master Builder, A Little Hotel on the Side, The Sea Gull, Three Men on a Horse*, and off-Bdwy roles in *Wilder's Triple Bull, To Be Young Gifted and Black, Candyapple, Long Day's Journey into Night, Rivers Return*.

ROBERT BENDORFF, 44, Honolulu-born composer/musical director, died Oct.10, 1996 of AIDS. He was musical director of *Ethel Merman's Broadway* and wrote music and lyrics for *Totie, Over My Dead Body, Strike* and *Great Expectations*. Survived by parents and a brother.

TED BESSELL, 61, actor-producer-director best known for his role on the television series "That Girl," died of an aortic aneurysm in Los Angeles on Oct. 6, 1996. He was seen on Broadway in *Same Time Next Year*. Survived by his wife, two daughters, his mother, and a brother.

STEVE S. BILLIG, 66, NYC-born artistic director/actor, died Aug.30, 1996 in Park Forest, IL, the victim of a homicide. As an actor he performed in many Chicago area productions before founding the Illinois Theater Center in 1976 with his wife Ethel Billig. There he performed in or directed over 125 productions. Survived by his wife, parents and two sons.

CHARLES BOWDEN, 83, Mass.-born producer/actor, died Dec.22, 1996 in NYC. He produced 1961's *Night of the Iguana, Slapstick Tragedy, All in One, 27 Wagons Full of Cotton, Caligula*, and Lily Tomlin & Jane Wagner's *Search for Signs of Intelligent Life in the Universe*. As an actor he appeared in *Ten Million Ghosts* (1936) and toured with Lunt and Fontanne. Survived by his wife, actress Paula Lawrence.

IRVING CAESAR, 101, NYC-born lyricist, died Dec.17, 1996 in NYC. He collaborated with many great Bdwy songwriters including George Gershwin, Vincent Youmans and George M. Cohan. His Bdwy shows included *Greenwich Village Follies* (1924), several editions of *George White's Scandals* and *No No Nanette* (1925/revived 1971) which gave the world "Tea for Two" and "I Want to Be Happy". He wrote lyrics to George Gershwin's music for the hit song "Swanee" which Al Jolson incorporated into the musical *Sinbad*. Survived by his wife.

PEGGY CLARK (MARGARET BRONSON CLARK), 80, noted lighting designer, died June 19, 1996 in Lexington, GA after a series of strokes. Starting in 1941, she designed more than 60 Bdwy shows including many George Abbott productions. Some highlights were *Brigadoon, Auntie Mame, Bye Bye Birdie, Paint Your Wagon, Pal Joey, Wonderful Town, Threepenny Opera* and Judith Anderson's *Medea*. Survived by a brother.

CLAUDETTE COLBERT (CLAUDETTE LILY CHAUCHOIN), 92, Paris-born actress, died July 30, 1996 in Barbados after a stroke. A major movie star of the 1930s and 1940s, she won an Academy Award for the film *It Happened One Night*. 1923 Bdwy debut in *Wild Westcotts* followed by *Ghost Train, A Kiss in a Taxi, The Barker, The Mulberry Bush, La Gringa, Tin Pan Alley, Dynamo, See Naples and Die, Janus, The Marriage-Go-Round, Jake Julia and Uncle Joe, The Irregular Verb to Love, The Kingfisher* and *A Talent for Murder*. Her last Bdwy role was in the 1985 *Aren't We All?*.

BARBARA CORNETT (ALLEN/WOODELL), 86, Illinois-born actress, died Jan.16, 1997 in Ojai, CA. The first wife of pianist Oscar Levant, her stage debut in *Ziegfeld Follies of 1931* was followed by Bdwy's *American Way* (1939) and other tours and regional productions. Survived by a brother and sister.

CHANDLER COWLES, 79, Connecticut-born actor/producer, died Feb.1, 1997 in NYC of a heart attack. Aboard the USS California during the Dec.7, 1941 Pearl Harbor attack, he made Bdwy debut 1946 in *Call Me Mister*. Bdwy included *Cradle Will Rock* and *Small Wonder* before becoming a producer. Survived by his wife, two sons and grandchildren.

| Larry Gates | Ralston Hill | Gene Nelson | William Prince | Don Porter |

HOWARD CRABTREE, 41, Missouri-born costume designer/author/performer, died June 28, 1996 in Bucks County, PA of AIDS. He was co-creator of the Off-Bdwy shows *Howard and Drew Meet the Invisible Man* (1987),*Whatnot* (1990), *Whoop-Dee-Doo!* (1993) and *When Pigs Fly* (1996), the last two which gained attention for his humourous costumes. As a performer, he toured with Barbara Eden in *Woman of the Year* and was a dresser for many Bdwy shows. Survived by his companion, parents and two brothers.

JACK DANON (BERGAL), 64, St.Louis-born actor, died Aug.12, 1996 in Burbank, CA of lung cancer/emphysema. Bdwy included *Two Thieves, Inherit the Wind* and *Take Me Along*. He worked in many national tours. Survived by his wife, actress Beth Peters, two daughters, a son, five sisters, two brothers, and grandchildren.

VIRGINIA DOWNING, 92, Washington-born actress, died Nov.21, 1996 in NYC of a heart attack. Her Bdwy work started with 1937's *Father Malachy's Miracle* followed by *Forward the Heart, Cradle Will Rock, Gift of Time, We Have Always Lived in a Castle* and *Arsenic and Old Lace*. Off-Bdwy included *Juno and the Paycock, Man with the Golden Arm, Palm Tree in a Rose Garden, Play with a Tiger, The Weives, The Idiot, Medea, Mrs. Warren's Profession, Mercy Street, Thunder Rock, Pygmalion, First Week in Bogota, Rimers of Eldritch, Les Blancs, Shadow of a Gunman, All the Way Home, Winter's tale, Billy Liar, Shadow and Substance, Silent Catastrophe, Ernest in Love, Night Games, Frog in His Throat, All that Fall* and *Richard III* (1990). Survived by her husband, actor John Leighton.

DAVID DOYLE, 67, Omaha-born character actor, best known for his roles on the television series "Charlie's Angels," died of a heart attack on Feb. 27, 1997 in Los Angeles. His New York stage credits include *Bonds of Interest, Beg Borrow or Steal* (which he also directed), *Under the Sycamore Tree, Camino Real, Something About a Soldier, The Beauty Part, Here's Love, I Was Dancing, Sergeant Musgrave's Dance, Elizabeth the Queen*, and *South Pacific* (revival). He is survived by his wife, a daughter, and two grandchildren.

PAUL DRAPER, Italian-born American tap dancer died of emphysema at his home in Woodstock, NY, on Sept. 20, 1996. In addition to his many untitled concert and recital appearances at various theatres he was seen on the New York stage in *Thumbs Up!, Priorities of 1942,* and *All in One*. He was married to ballerina Heidi Vosseler who died in 1992. He is survived by three daughters and two grandchildren.

JOANNE DRU, 73, W.Virginia-born actress, died Sept.10, 1996 in Beverly Hills, CA of respiratory failure. Best known as a screen actress, she started in the 1940 Bdwy musical *Hold Onto Your Hats*. Survived by two brothers (including actor/host Peter Marshall), a daughter, son and grandchildren.

DORTHA DUCKWORTH, 91, Kansas-born actress, died Nov.14, 1996 in Camp Hill, PA. She made her 1926 Bdwy debut in *Goodbye Again* followed by many shows including *Strange Bedfellows, Oliver* and *Pippin*.

HERB EDELMAN, 62, Brooklyn-born actor, died July 21, 1996 in Los Angeles of emphysema. After 1961 stage debut in a touring *Threepenny Opera* he appeared in *Bajour, Barefoot in the Park* and many tours. Survived by two daughters, his companion, father, sister and brother.

LONNE ELDER 3rd, 69, playwright/actor, died June 11, 1996 in Woodland Hills, CA after a chronic illness. His 1967 play *Ceremonies in Dark Old Men* distinguished the first season of the Negro Ensemble Company. Other plays included 1988's *Splendid Mummer*. As an actor he appeared in the original 1959 *Raisin in the Sun* and *Day of Absence*. Survived by his former wife, a daughter and two sons.

BRENDA FORBES, 87, London-born actress, died Sept.11, 1996 in NYC of cancer. Stage debut 1927 with the Old Vic was followed by 1931 Bdwy debut in *Barretts of Wimpole Street*. She often worked with Katharine Cornell, Alfred Lunt and Lynn Fontanne. Bdwy included *Candida, Lucree, Flowers of the Forest, Pride and Prejudice, Storm over Patsy, Heartbreak House, Ring Around the Moon, One for the Money, Two for the Show, Three to Make Ready, Yesterday's Magic, Suds in Your Eyes, Quadrille, Reluctant Debutante, Loves of Cass McGuire, Darling of the Day, Constant Wife, My Fair Lady* (1976) and 1985's *Aren't We All?* Off-Bdwy included *Busybody* and *Pygmalion*. Survived by ten nieces and nephews.

MICHAEL FOX, 75, Yonkers, NY-born actor, died June 1, 1996 in Los Angeles of pneumonia. He appeared in the 1947 Bdwy play *Story of Mary Surratt* and often worked in tv and film. Survived by his wife, daughter and son.

LARRY GATES, 81, St. Paul-born actor, died Dec.12, 1996 in Sharon, CT. Bdwy included 1939 debut in *Speak of the Devil* followed by *Twelfth Night, Bell Book and Candle, Taming of the Shrew, Love of Four Colonels, Teahouse of the August Moon, Case of Libel, Sing Me No Lullaby, Carefree Tree, Poor Murderer* and *First Monday in October*. Off-Bdwy included *Carving a Statue* and *Hamlet*.

PERCY GRANGER, 51, NY-born playwright, died March 10, 1997 in NYC of cardiac arrest. His plays included *Complete Workd of Studs Edsel, Eminent Domain, Vixen, The Dolphin Position, Scheherazade* and many one-act plays for Ensemble Studio and other theatres. Survived by his wife and two sons.

ALVALETA GUESS,36 or 41, Missouri-born actress/singer, died Sept.2, 1996 in NYC of cancer. She was on Bdwy last season in *Swinging on a Star* and her Off-Bdwy credits included *Avenue X* and *Nunsense*. Survived by her mother.

RALSTON HILL, 69, Cleveland-born actor who played Charles Thomson in the original 1969 Broadway production of *1776,* died of natural causes while in rehearsal for *Gigi* at New Jersey's Paper Mill Playhouse. His other New York stage credits include *The Changeling, Streets of New York, Valmouth,* and *Carousel*. Survived by his sister.

BERNARD B. JACOBS, 80, president of the Shubert Organization for twenty four years, died in Roslyn, Long Island, New York, on Aug. 27, 1996 of complications after heart surgery. His organization helped produce dozens of notable Broadway shows including *A Chorus Line, Cats, The Life and Times of Nicholas Nickleby, Glengarry Glen Ross, Gin Game, Amadeus, Jerome Robbins' Broadway, Ain't Misbehavin, Dreamgirls,* and *The Heidi Chronicles*. Lights were dimmed in memory of him in every Broadway Theatre. Survived by his wife, a daughter, a son, a sister, and three grandchildren.

| Beryl Reid | Howard Rollins | Jo Van Fleet | Janet Hayes Walker | Jesse White |

BERNARD JOHNSON, 60, Detroit-born dancer/costume designer, died Jan.22, 1997 in NYC of pneumonia. On Bdwy he danced in *On a Clear Day* (1965) and *Hallelujah Baby!* Costume design included *Bubbling Brown Sugar, Eubie!, Waltz of the Stork, Guys and Dolls* and *Raisin.* Survived by his companion, a son and two sisters.

WALTER F. KERR, 83, theatre reviewer, director and writer, eied on Oct. 9, 1996 in Dobbs Ferry, NY. He served as a critic for the *New York Herald Tribune* from 1951 to 1966 when he joined the *Times* where he remained until his retirement in 1983. He co-wrote the musicals *Count Me In, Sing Out Sweet Land, Touch and Go,* and *Goldilocks,* the last with his wife, Jean Kerr. He also directed her play *King of Hearts* in 1954. In 1990 he had a Broadway theatre named in his honor. He is survived by his wife, five sons, a daughter, and nine grandchildren.

BURTON LANE (BURTON LEVY), 84, New York City-born composer for the shows *Finian's Rainbow* and *On a Clear Day You Can See Forever,* died of a stroke at his Manhattan home on Jan. 5, 1997. He also wrote songs for *Carmelina,* and the Broadway revues *Three's a Crowd, The Third Little Show,* and *Hold on to Your Hats.* He is survived by his wife, a daughter, a three stepdaughters.

PETER LEEDS, 79, actor-comedian died of cancer on Nov. 12, 1996. A frequent television actor he also appeared on Broadway in such productions as *My Heart is in the Highlands* and *Sugar Babies.* He is survived by his wife and a granddaughter.

MARK LENARD, 68, Chicago-born actor died of multiple myeloma on Nov. 22, 1996 in Manhattan. He appeared on the New York stage in *The Hasty Heart, Exiles, Square Root of Wonderful, A Country Scandal, Measure for Measure, Gideon,* and *Little Eyolf.* On television he was best known for playing Spock's father in "Star Trek." He is survived by his wife, and two daughters.

SHELDON LEONARD (SHELDON LEONARD BERSHAD), 89, New York City-born actor and television producer-director, died on Jan. 1, 1997 at his home in Beverly Hills, CA. He was seen on Broadway in such plays as *Fly Away Home* and *Kiss the Boys Goodbye* prior to his movie career. On television he won Emmy Awards for his work on *The Danny Thomas Show* and *My World and Welcome to It.* He is survived by his wife, a son, a daughter, and four grandchildren.

FRANK MARCUS, 68, British playwright best known for *The Killing of Sister George,* which came to New York in 1966, died of a pulmonary embolism on Aug. 5, 1996. Survived by his son and two daughters.

GERALD MARKS, 96, Michigan-born songwriter, died Jan.27, 1997 in NYC. A popular songwriter, he contributed to Bdwy shows including *Ziegfeld Follies.*

PAMELA MASON (PAMELA OSTRER), 80, British actress and talk-show host, died on June 29, 1996 at her home in Beverly Hills, CA. With her then-husband James Mason, she appeared on Broadway in 1947 in *Bathsheba,* under the name Pamela Kellino (using the name of her previous husband). She is survived by her two children with Mason.

SANFORD MEISNER, 91, notable Brooklyn-born acting teacher, died Feb.2, 1997 in Sherman Oaks, CA. His Bdwy acting debut was 1924 in *They Knew What They Wanted* . An original memeber of the Group Theatre (1931), he was director of NYC's Neighborhood Playhouse for most of the period 1935-90. He also worked as an actor and director in stage and tv.Survived by his companion, an adopted son, a brother, nephew and nieces.

JEAN MUIR, 85, New York City-born actress, died of natural causes in Mesa, AZ, on July 23, 1996. Her Broadway credits include *Saint Wench, Tenting Tonight,* and *Semi-Detached.* She is survived by two sons and a daughter.

GENE NELSON (EUGENE BERG), 76, Seattle-born dancer/actor, died Sept.16, 1996 in Calabas, CA of cancer. Bdwy debut in *This is the Army* (1942) followed by *Lend an Ear* (Theatre World Award) *Follies, Music! Music!* and *Good News.* He performed in many film musicals including playing "Will Parker" in the *Oklahoma* film. Survived by two sons and grandchildren.

RICHARD NELSON, 57, lighting designer who received a Tony Award for his work on *Sunday in the Park With George,* died of a brain tumor on Nov. 6, 1996 in Manhattan. His other credits include *Morning's at Seven, The Tap Dance Kid,* and *Into the Woods.* He is survived by his wife, a son, two sisters, a brother, and two grandchildren.

DON PORTER, 84, Oklahoma-born actor, best known for playing on the series "Private Secretary" and "Gidget," died on Feb. 11, 1997 in Los Angeles, CA. His Broadway theatre credits include *Any Wednesday, The Front Page,* and *Plaza Suite.* He is survived by his wife, actress Peggy Converse; his daughter; and a son.

WILLIAM PRINCE, 83, New York-born character actor died on Oct. 8, 1996 in Tarrytown, NY. Following his 1937 debut on Broadway in *The Eternal Road,* he was seen in *Richard II, Hamlet, Ah Wilderness, Guest in the House, Across the Board on Tomorrow Morning, The Eve of St. Mark, John Loves Mary, Forward the Heart, As You Lik It, I Am a Camera, The Affair of Honor, Third Best Sport, Highest Tree, Venus at Large, Strange Interlude, Ballad of the Sad Cafe, The Little Foxes, Man with Three Arms, Heartbreak House,* and Off-Broadway in *Stephen D., Mercy Street, The Caretaker,* and *Tausk.* He is survived by his wife, a sister, two daughters, two sons, and three grandchildren.

ALEXANDER RACOLIN, 88, NYC-born producer, died June 6, 1996 in NYC. A loyal friend of Off-Bdwy's smaller theatres, he produced over 200 plays in New York and London in conjunction with theatrical partner Annette Moskowitz. Survived by two daughters, a son and grandchildren.

GUY RAYMOND, 85, dancer, comedian and character actor, died on Jan. 26, 1997 in Santa Monica. Among his New York theatre credits were *Hook' n Ladder* and *Pipe Dream.*

BERYL REID, 76, British actress, who won a Tony Award in 1967 for her performance in *The Killing of Sister George,* died in England of pneumonia on Oct. 13, 1996. She repeated the role in the 1968 film version. No reported survivors.

HOWARD ROLLINS, 46, Baltimore-born stage, screen and television actor died of cancer on Dec. 8, 1996 in NYC. He appeared on Broadway in *We Interrupt This Program* and Off-Broadway in *G.R. Point, The Mighty Gents, Medal of Honor Rag,* and *Fathers and Sons.* He received an Oscar nomination for the film *Ragtime* and starred in the television series "In the Heat of the Night." Survived by his mother and sister.

WINSTON ROSS, 84, NYC-born actor/singer, died Nov.26, 1996 near Montrose, PA. His Bdwy appearances included *Idiot's Delight, Billy Budd, Julius Caesar* and *Twelfth Night.* Survived by his wife, son, daughter and grandchildren.

JOE SENECA, early 80's, Cleveland-born actor, died Aug.15, 1996 on Roosevelt Island, NYC after an asthma attack. Starting as a singer, he moved into songwriting and switched to acting in the early 1970s. Bdwy debut in the 1974 *Of Mice and Men* was followed by the 1981 *Little Foxes* and Off-Bdwy's *Rhinestone.* His final Bdwy role was in *Ma Rainey's Black Bottom* (1984). Survived by his wife, Betty.

RICHARD X. SLATERY, 72, NYC-born actor, died Jan.27, 1997 in Woodland Hills, CA of a stroke. A street cop who turned to acting, his Off-Bdwy included *Streetcar Named Desire, Iceman Cometh* and *Born Yesterday.* Bdwy included *A Cook for Mr. General* (1961) and *Dark at the Top of the Stairs.* Survived by his wife, eight children and grandchildren.

STEVE TESICH, 53, Yugoslavian-born playwright, died July 1, 1996 in Novia Scotia of a heart attack. Plays included *The Carpenters* (1970), *Baba Goya, Division Street, Speed of Darkness, Square One, On the Open Road* and *Arts and Leisure.* He also worked on the 1978 musical *King of Hearts* and won an Oscar for the 1979 film *Breaking Away.* Survived by his wife and daughter.

MAURICE VALENCY, 93, NY-born playwright, died Sept.28, 1996 in NYC. His award-winning adaptations of European plays *Madwoman of Chaillot, Ondine* (both adaptations of Jean Giradoux works), and *The Visit* (adapted from Friedrich Duerrenmatt) remain the accepted versions. Other adaptations included *The Enchanted, The Virtuous Island, Apollo of Bellac* . Original plays included *Savonarola, Electra* and *The Thracian Horses.* He also taught and wrote extensively on theatre. Survived by his wife.

JO VAN FLEET, 81, Oakland, CA-born actress, died June 10, 1996 in Queens, NY. Her Bdwy debut in*Winter's Tale* (1946) was followed by roles on and Off-Bdwy including*The World Over, The Closing Door, King Lear, Flight into Egypt, Camino Real, Trip to Bountiful* (Tony Award), *Look Homeward Angel, Rosemary/The AlligatorsOh Dad Poor Dad...* and followed Maureen Stapleton in the 1965 *Glass Menagerie.* Her films include an Academy Award-winning role in *East of Eden.* Durvived by a son and granddaughter.

JANET HAYES WALKER, 71, Shanghai-born performer/producer, died Feb.20, 1997 in NYC of cancer. Bdwy appearances included *Damn Yankees, Plain and Fancy, Music Man, Camelot* and *Anyone Can Whistle.* As producing director of Off-Bdwy's York Theatre Company from 1969 to her death, she presented countless musicals. Survived by her husband, two children, a brother and sister, and grandchildren.

JESSE WHITE (WEIDENFELD), 79, Buffalo, NY-born actor, died Jan.9, 1997 in Los Angeles. Bdwy included both the original 1944 *Harvey* and the 1970 revival. Survived by his wife, two daughters, two brothers and grandchildren.

VINCE WILLIAMS, 39, Louisiana-born actor/composer, died Jan.6, 1997 in Englewood, NJ of cancer. Appearances included Bdwy's *Fences* and as actor and composer, the NYSF productions *Romeo and Juliet* and *As You Like It.*

BILL ZUCKERT, 76, stage, theatre and television actor died of pneumonia on Jan. 23, 1997 in Woodland Hills, CA. Among his New York stage credits are *Sixth Finger in a Five Finger Glove, A Shadow of My Enemy,* and *The Gang's All Here.* Surivors include his wife, actress Gladys Holland and three children.

INDEX

262

264

274

276

281